St. Stephen's Episcopal Church
1344 Nipomo Street
San Luis Obispo, CA 93401

THE BOOK OF CONCORD

The Confessions of the Evangelical Lutheran Church

The
Book of Concord

The Confessions of the Evangelical Lutheran Church

Translated and edited by

THEODORE G. TAPPERT

in collaboration with

Jaroslav Pelikan   Robert H. Fischer
Arthur C. Piepkorn

FORTRESS PRESS   PHILADELPHIA

COPYRIGHT © 1959 BY FORTRESS PRESS

All rights reserved. No part of this publication may be reproduced, stored in a retrieval system, or transmitted in any form or by any means, electronic, mechanical, photocopying, recording, or otherwise, without the prior permission of the copyright owner.

Library of Congress Catalog Card Number 59-11369

ISBN 0-8006-0825-9

Printed in the United States of America   1-825

01   00   99   98   97   25   26   27   28   29   30   31   32   33   34

FOREWORD

The publication of a new translation of the Book of Concord has been made desirable, if not necessary, by a number of considerations. In the first place, in so far as every translation is an interpretation, the tremendous advances must be taken into account which have been made during the last generation in our understanding of the literary and historical backgrounds of the documents included in this book. In the second place, allowance must be made for the literary tastes of modern readers for whom the English style of earlier generations seems heavy, cumbersome, and sometimes almost unintelligible. In the third place, the needs of those who may use the volume must be considered by furnishing them with quick and easy reference, in both the introductions to the several documents and the footnotes, to persons, events, literary citations, and other tools essential to understanding and study.

Serious students of the Lutheran Confessions will continue to consult the original Latin and German texts on which the present translations are based. These are available in the critically superior and typographically incomparable second, revised edition of *Die Bekenntnisschriften der evangelisch-lutherischen Kirche* (Göttingen: Vandenhoeck & Ruprecht, 1952), edited by Hans Lietzmann, Heinrich Bornkamm, Hans Volz, and Ernst Wolf. The translators gratefully acknowledge their indebtedness to and reliance on this edition and commend it to the use of others.

Several English translations of individual documents, notably the Augsburg Confession, have been available since the sixteenth century. Three major English editions of the entire Book of Concord have been published before the present edition. The first was by David Henkel and others and appeared in 1851 (published by Solomon Henkel & Brothers in New Market, Va., with an improved edition in 1854). The second was by Henry E. Jacobs and others and appeared in 1882 (published by G. W. Frederick in Philadelphia, with a revised "People's Edition" in 1911). The third was by F. Bente and others and appeared in 1921 (published by the Concordia Publishing House, St. Louis, in three languages, and then also in English alone). In 1940 John C. Mattes undertook to make a revised translation but died (in 1948) before the work was completed. It is of course inevitable that the present translators should have been influenced by the work of those who preceded them (sometimes helped by felicitous renderings, sometimes hampered by renderings which have become domesticated), but a comparison will reveal the extent to which the present translations are dependent on the original texts rather than on earlier translations.

Attention should be called to some special features of this edition. The earlier practice of inserting variants in the text (in square brackets) has not been followed because of its disturbance to the reader. Translations of the several documents are made from the original, whether Latin or German, and only such variants in the alternative language as seem especially significant are indicated in the footnotes. Only in the case of the Augsburg Confession, for reasons given in the Introduction to that document, are full translations of both Latin and German texts given. All cross-references in the footnotes are to articles (or chapters) and sections—the sections, indicated in the right margins of the text, having originally been inserted in the Latin text alone. For most quotations from the Bible, the Revised Standard Version has been used as on the whole closest to the rendering in the text, but where the context requires it other versions or literal translations have been used. A few commonly accepted abbreviations have been employed in the footnotes: *WA* for the Weimar edition of Luther's works, *EA* for the Erlangen edition of Luther's works, *C.R.* for the *Corpus Reformatorum* containing works of Reformers other than Luther. Because the primary concern has been the presentation of English translations which are as faithful as possible to the original texts, no bibliographies of secondary literature, whether expository or apologetic, have been included.

Some editions of the Book of Concord have included such additional documents as Luther's Order of Baptism (1523), Luther's Marriage Booklet (1529), the Catalog of Testimonies (1580), and the Christian Visitation Articles (1592). These are here omitted because they are not among the historic standards of faith commonly acknowledged in the Lutheran Church.

The Apology of the Augsburg Confession was translated for this edition by Jaroslav Pelikan; the Large Catechism by Robert H. Fischer; the Formula of Concord by Arthur C. Piepkorn; and the remaining pieces by the undersigned, who also assumed general editorial supervision of the entire work and is responsible for such outward uniformity as may have been achieved.

THEODORE G. TAPPERT

CONTENTS

CONCORDIA

Christian, Reiterated, and Unanimous Confession
of the Doctrine and Faith of the undersigned
Electors, Princes, and Estates
who Embrace the Augsburg Confession
and of their Theologians,
Together with an Appended Declaration,
Firmly Founded on the Word of God as the Only Norm,
of Several Articles about which Disputation and Strife Arose
after the blessed Death of Martin Luther,
Prepared for Publication by the Unanimous Agreement and Order
of the aforementioned Electors, Princes, and Estates
for the Instruction and Admonition
of their Lands, Churches, Schools, and Descendants

1580

PREFACE[1]

To each and every reader, according to the requirements of his station and dignity, under whose eyes this document comes, we, the electors, princes, and estates in the Holy Empire of the German Nation who are named below, tender our due service, friendship, gracious greeting, and favorably inclined will, as well as our most respectful, humble, and willing service, and hereby declare:

In these last times of this transitory world almighty God in his immeasurable love, grace, and mercy toward mankind has permitted the pure, unalloyed, and unadulterated light of his holy Gospel and of the Word that alone brings salvation to appear to our beloved fatherland, the German nation, and to light its way out of papistic superstition and darkness. Thereupon a short confession was compiled out of the divine, prophetic, and apostolic Scriptures. It was submitted in the German and Latin languages by our pious and Christian predecessors to the then Emperor Charles V, of most praiseworthy memory, at the Diet of Augsburg in the year 1530, presented in the presence of all the estates of the empire, and published and proclaimed in all of Christendom throughout the wide world.

Subsequently many churches and schools committed themselves to this confession as the contemporary symbol of their faith in the chief articles in controversy over against both the papacy and all sorts of factions. They referred and appealed to it without either controversy or doubt in a Christian and unanimous interpretation thereof. They have held fast and loyally to the doctrine that is contained in it, that is based solidly on the divine Scriptures, and that is also briefly summarized in the approved ancient symbols, recognizing the doctrine as the ancient consensus which the universal and orthodox church of Christ has believed, fought for against many heresies and errors, and repeatedly affirmed.

It is a matter of common knowledge, patent and unconcealed, what very perilous events and troublesome disturbances took place in our beloved German fatherland shortly after the Christian death of that enlightened and pious person, Dr. Martin Luther, and how in this anguished situation and amid the disruption of well-ordered government the foe of mankind bestirred himself to scatter his seed of false

[1] This preface underwent extensive revisions between the fall of 1578 and the spring of 1580, when it was put into its final form by James Andreae and Martin Chemnitz. As the contents reveal, it was a preface at once for the Formula of Concord (1577) and for the entire Book of Concord (1580).

doctrine and discord and to bring about destructive and scandalous division in churches and schools so that he might thereby adulterate the pure doctrine of God's Word, sever the bond of Christian charity and agreement, and in this way hold back and perceptibly impede the course of the holy Gospel. Everybody also knows how the adversaries of divine truth took occasion to discredit us and our schools and churches so as to palliate their own errors, to divert poor, erring consciences from an understanding of pure evangelical doctrine, and to make them more compliant in submitting to the papal yoke as well as in embracing other errors that militate against God's Word.

We should have preferred, and we besought and petitioned the Almighty, that our churches and schools might have been preserved in the teaching of God's Word and in agreeable Christian concord and that they might have been well managed and carried on in a Christian fashion and in harmony with God's Word, as they were while Dr. Luther was alive. Nevertheless, just as, while the holy apostles were still alive,[2] it happened that false teachers insinuated perverted teachings into the churches in which the apostles themselves had planted the pure, unadulterated Word of God, so such false teachers were also inflicted on our churches because of our own and the ungrateful world's impenitence and sin.

Mindful of the office which God has committed to us and which we bear, we have not ceased to apply our diligence to the end that the false and misleading doctrines which have been introduced into our lands and territories and which are insinuating themselves increasingly into them might be checked and that our subjects might be preserved from straying from the right course of divine truth which they had once acknowledged and confessed.

With this in mind and to this end our praiseworthy predecessors, and also some of us, decided (on the basis of a memorandum[3] agreed to at Frankfurt-on-the-Main on the occasion of a meeting of the electors in the year 1558) that we should assemble in a general convention and should discuss in a thorough and friendly way various matters which our adversaries had been interpreting to the very great disadvantage of ourselves and of our churches and schools.[4]

[2] Cf. II Tim. 4:3, 4; I John 4:1; II Pet. 2:1.

[3] Originally the printed draft read "Christian memorandum." Andreae struck out "Christian," primarily because the Lower Saxons objected to it. Through what he described as an oversight the word was included in some of the drafts sent out for subscription. Various substitutes were proposed, among them "well-intended" and "princely."

[4] The meeting of electors took place in February and March, 1558, in connection with the election of Emperor Ferdinand I. On March 18 they adopted the so-called Frankfurt Book (Latin: the Frankfurt Formula of Peace), based on a theological opinion prepared by Melanchthon (cf. *C.R.*, IX, 365-378) which included discussions of justification, good works, the Lord's Supper, and adiaphora, the method to be followed in settling other

At a later date our sainted predecessors and some of us gathered at Naumburg, in Thuringia.[5] We took up the repeatedly mentioned Augsburg Confession, which had been submitted to Emperor Charles V in the great imperial assembly at Augsburg in the year 1530, and again unanimously subscribed this Christian confession, based as it is on the witness of the unalterable truth of the divine Word, in order thereby to warn and, as far as we might, to secure our posterity in the future against doctrine that is impure, false, and contrary to the Word of God. This we did that we might testify and declare to our most gracious lord, His Roman Imperial Majesty, and to everyone else that it was in no way our disposition and intention to adopt, to defend, or to spread a different or a new doctrine. Rather, with divine assistance, it was our intention to remain and abide loyally by the truth once recognized and confessed at Augsburg in the year 1530, in the confidence and hope that thereby the adversaries of pure evangelical doctrine would be constrained to desist from their fabricated slanders and defamation of us and that other good-hearted people would have been reminded and stimulated by this our reiterated and repeated confession the more seriously to investigate the truth of the divine Word that alone gives salvation, to commit themselves to it, and for the salvation of their

controverted issues, and an agreement on censorship of the press. It was designed to serve as a basis for uniting the Evangelical estates in lieu of a still somewhat doubtful general synod of the churches involved. Not only the intransigent Flacians of Jena but also many much more moderate Lutherans denounced the deliberate ambiguity and latitudinarianism of this document.

⁵ The prospective reopening of the Council of Trent induced Elector August of Saxony, encouraged by Duke Christopher of Württemberg and Duke John Frederick of Saxony, to summon Elector Frederick III of the Palatinate, Landgrave Philip of Hesse, and Palsgrave Wolfgang of Zweibrücken to an assembly of Evangelical estates which met in Naumburg from January 20 to February 1, 1561. Frederick and August urged acceptance of the 1540 variata edition of the Augsburg Confession (an edition "altered" by Philip Melanchthon) on the ground that it precluded transubstantiation; the former described the variata edition as "a good and Christian explanation of the original confession." The others ranged themselves on the side of the 1530 edition, and Chytraeus even attempted to have the Smalcald Articles officially adopted. A compromise settled on the German text of the Augsburg Confession contained in the Wittenberg quarto edition of 1530-1531 and—at Frederick's insistence—the Latin text of the 1531 quarto edition, plus a preface (addressed to the emperor and drafted by the two electors) and a disavowal of transubstantiation. The preface committed the signatories both to the 1530 edition of the Augsburg Confession and to the variata edition of 1540 (by the latter, they affirmed, the 1530 edition "is repeated somewhat more sumptuously and exhaustively and is explained and expanded on the basis of Holy Scripture"), as well as to the Apology. The two electors, Duke Christopher, Landgrave Philip, Margrave Charles of Baden, and (through their councilors-of-state) Margraves John and George Frederick of Brandenburg, Palsgrave Wolfgang, and the rulers of Pomerania, Anhalt, and Henneberg signed it. Dukes Ulrich of Württemberg and John Frederick of Saxony, followed by Lower Saxony, the maritime cities, and some others, refused to sign.

souls and their eternal welfare to abide by it and persist in it in a Christian way without any further disputation and dissension.

In spite of all this we found, not without distress on our part, that little account was taken by our adversaries of this explanation and repetition of our previous Christian confession and that neither we nor our churches were delivered thereby from the calumnies that had been circulated. On the contrary, this well-intended action of ours was again understood and interpreted in such a way by adherents of erroneous opinions which are opposed to us and to our Christian religion as if we were so uncertain of our faith and of the confession of our religion and had altered it so much and so often that neither we nor our theologians knew which version was the true and originally submitted Augsburg Confession. By this unfounded allegation many pious hearts were frightened away and deterred from our churches, schools, doctrine, faith, and confession. In addition, we sustained the further disadvantage that, under the name of the frequently mentioned Augsburg Confession, the contrary doctrine about the holy sacrament of the body and the blood of Christ and other erroneous opinions were now and again introduced into our churches and schools.

When a number of pious, irenic, and learned theologians[6] noted these developments, they saw clearly that there was no better way to counteract the mendacious calumnies and the religious controversies that were expanding with each passing day than, on the basis of God's Word, carefully and accurately to explain and decide the differences that had arisen with reference to all the articles in controversy, to expose and to reject false doctrine, and clearly to confess the divine truth. In this way the mouths of the adversaries might be stopped by solid reasoning, and a correct explanation and direction might be provided for simple and pious hearts, so that they might know what attitude to take toward these differences and how by God's grace they might be preserved from false doctrine in the future.

At first the said theologians clearly and correctly described to one another, in extensive writings based on God's Word, how the aforementioned offensive differences might be settled and brought to a conclusion without violation of divine truth, and in this way the pretext and basis for slander that the adversaries were looking for could be abolished and taken away. Finally they took to hand the controverted articles, examined, evaluated, and explained them in the fear of God, and produced a document in which they set forth how the differences that had occurred were to be decided in a Christian way.

When information about this Christian undertaking reached some of us, we not only were gratified by it but we also regarded ourselves

[6] Notably James Andreae, of Tübingen, and Martin Chemnitz, of Brunswick.

bound to promote it with Christian earnestness and zeal in view of the office that we bear and that God has committed to us.

Accordingly we, the elector of Saxony, etc., with the counsel and cooperation of some of our fellow believers among the electors and princes, convoked a number of prominent, trustworthy, experienced, and learned theologians at Torgau in the year 1576 for the promotion of concord among Christian teachers. In a Christian fashion they discussed with one another the articles in controversy and also the just cited written agreement composed with reference thereto. Finally, after invoking almighty God to his praise and glory and after mature reflection and careful diligence, they brought together in good order, by the singular grace of the Holy Spirit, everything that pertains to and is necessary for this end and put it down in one book.[7] Afterward it was sent to a considerable number of electors, princes, and estates adhering to the Augsburg Confession with the request that they and their chief theologians peruse it with particular earnestness and Christian zeal, consider it in all its aspects, have their opinions and criticisms reduced to writing, and communicate to us without reserve their considered judgment concerning every part of it.

When the requested judgments had been received they were found to contain all kinds of Christian, necessary, and useful memoranda on the way in which the Christian doctrine set forth in the explanation that had been sent out might be fortified with the Word of God against all sorts of perilous misunderstanding, so that no adulterated doctrine might in the future be hidden thereunder and that a pure declaration of the truth might be transmitted to our posterity as well. The Formula of Christian Concord, in the form that follows hereafter, was completed with the help of such memoranda.

Although not all of us have to date been able to undertake such a plan because special circumstances interfered, as they did in the case of some other estates not of our number,[8] some of us have had this document read article by article to each and every theologian, minister, and schoolmaster in our lands and territories and have had them reminded and exhorted to consider diligently and earnestly the doctrine contained in it.

When they had found that the explanation of the dissensions which

---

[7] Invited to this assembly, which sat at Hartenberg Castle from April 9 to June 7, 1576, and which produced the so-called Torgau Book (which James Andreae condensed at once into the Epitome of the Formula of Concord), were Andreae (chairman), Martin Chemnitz, David Chytraeus, Andrew Musculus, Nicholas Selnecker, Christopher Cornerus, Caspar Heyderich, Paul Crell, Maximilian Moerlin, Wolfgang Harder, Daniel Graeser, Nicholas Jagenteufel, John Cornicaelius, John Schuetz, Martin Mirus, George Listenius, and Peter Glaser.

[8] This clause was added at the insistence of the electors of Saxony and Brandenburg to leave the way open for uncommitted estates to adopt the Formula of Concord.

had arisen was agreeable and conformable first of all to the Word of God and then to the Augsburg Confession as well, the persons to whom it had been presented, as indicated above, gladly and with heartfelt thanks to almighty God testified that of their own volition and with due consideration they accepted, approved, and subscribed this Book of Concord as the correct[9] Christian interpretation of the Augsburg Confession and publicly attested this with their hearts, lips, and hands. Therefore this Christian agreement is called and also is the unanimous and concordant confession not only of a few of our theologians but generally of each and every minister and schoolmaster in our lands and territories.

The above-mentioned and well-intended agreements reached by our praiseworthy predecessors and by ourselves at Frankfurt-on-the-Main and at Naumburg failed to accomplish the desired end of Christian concord, and some even tried to appeal to them for the confirmation of their erroneous doctrine although it never entered our minds and hearts to want to introduce, palliate, or confirm any new, false, or erroneous doctrine or in the least point to depart from the Augsburg Confession as submitted in the year 1530. Those of us who were present at the above-mentioned discussions at Naumburg reserved to ourselves the right and served notice that we would furnish further specifications concerning our confession if it should ever be attacked by any one or if at any time it might become necessary to do so. In accordance therewith we have reached Christian unanimity and agreement among ourselves in this Book of Concord and repetition of our Christian faith and confession as a final explanation of our conviction.

Furthermore, lest anybody allow himself to be led astray by the unwarranted calumny of our adversaries that we ourselves do not know which is the genuine Augsburg Confession, and in order that our contemporaries as well as our beloved posterity may be clearly and thoroughly informed and possess final certainty as to which Christian confession it is that we and the churches and schools of our lands have hitherto at all times adhered and appealed to, we have in what follows purposed to commit ourselves exclusively and only, in accordance with the pure, infallible, and unalterable Word of God, to that[1] Augsburg Confession which was submitted to Emperor Charles V at the great imperial assembly in Augsburg in the year 1530, which has

---

[9] In response to objections to the word "correct," the electors of Saxony and Brandenburg stressed that the Formula was not intended to be a norm for the Augsburg Confession.

[1] A draft of the early part of 1576 added after "that" the words "first and unaltered," and they occur in the Torgau Book. In view of the determined opposition to the words in many quarters, they were finally dropped, lest they be interpreted as a rejection either of the variata edition of 1540 or of the Naumburg Agreement of 1561, to the embarrassment of those signers of the Formula who themselves or whose predecessors had signed the Naumburg Agreement.

been available in the archives of those sainted forebears of ours who themselves submitted it to Emperor Charles V at the said imperial diet, which was afterward collated very diligently by well-certified persons with the actual original that was submitted to the emperor and that remained in the custody of the Holy Empire,[2] and of which both the German and the Latin copies were afterward found to be identical in sense. For that reason, likewise, we have ordered the incorporation of the Augsburg Confession that was then submitted into our declaration and Book of Concord that follows hereunder, so that everyone may see that we were not minded to permit any doctrine in our lands, churches, and schools other than in the form in which it was once confessed at Augsburg in the year 1530 by the electors,[3] princes, and estates referred to above. By the help of God's grace we, too, intend to persist in this confession until our blessed end and to appear before the judgment seat of our Lord Jesus Christ with joyful and fearless hearts and consciences. We also hope that from now on our adversaries will spare us and our churches and their ministers the onerous burden of their pretense that we are uncertain of our faith and for that reason allegedly make a new confession almost every year or every month.

As far as the second edition of the Augsburg Confession, referred to in the Naumburg discussions,[4] is concerned, it is apparent to us and to everyone and is concealed from no one that some have attempted to hide their error concerning the Holy Supper as well as other adulterated teaching under the words of this same second edition and in their open writings and in public print have tried to palm them off on simple folk in spite of the fact that this erroneous doctrine is expressly rejected in the confession submitted at Augsburg and that a very different doctrine by far can be proved therefrom. We have therefore desired hereby to attest and affirm publicly that, then as now, it never was our purpose and intention to palliate, to extenuate, or to confirm as concordant with Evangelical doctrine any false and adulterated teaching that might be concealed therein, inasmuch as we never understood or accepted the second edition in any other sense than that of the first Augsburg Confession as it was submitted.[5] Nor do we want to have rejected or condemned any other profitable writings of Master Philip Melanchthon or of [John] Brenz, Urban Rhegius, [John Bugenhagen] of Pomerania,

---

[2] The copy of the Archives at Mayence with which the Lutheran estates collated their own archival copies was actually not the original. See the Introduction to the Augsburg Confession, below.

[3] Use of the plural is here a formula, since actually only one elector, John of Saxony, signed the Augsburg Confession.

[4] The variata (or altered) edition of 1540, notably Article X.

[5] Duke Julius III, the faculty of the University of Helmstedt, and Tilemann Heshusius clamored for the striking of this entire section on the ground that it endorsed the variata and the Naumburg Agreement.

and others in so far as they are in agreement with the norm incorporated in the [Formula of] Concord.[6]

Furthermore, even though a number of theologians, like Luther himself, were drawn by adversaries (although against the will of the former) from a consideration of the Holy Supper into a discussion of the personal union of the two natures in Christ, our theologians clearly assert in the Formula of Concord itself and in the norm comprehended therein that according to our and the Formula's constant intention Christians are to be directed in the treatment of the Lord's Supper to this and only this one basis and foundation, namely, the words of institution of Christ's testament. He is almighty and veracious, and hence he is able to accomplish what he has ordained and promised in his Word. When they remain unattacked on this basis, theologians are not to argue from some other basis, but with ingenuous faith they are to stay with the plain words of Christ.[7] This is the surest and most edifying way as far as the common layman is concerned, for he cannot comprehend this discussion. But when the adversaries assail this our ingenuous faith and interpretation of the words of the testament of Christ and decry and condemn them as impiety, as if our ingenuous interpretation and faith contradicted the articles of our Christian Creed (especially those pertaining to the incarnation of God's Son, his ascension, and his session at the right hand of God's almighty power and majesty)[8] and hence must be false and incorrect, we should indicate and demonstrate by a correct explanation of the articles of our Christian Creed that our ingenuous understanding of the words of Christ as described above does not contradict these articles.

Turning to the kind and manner of speech employed with reference to the majesty of the human nature in the person of Christ, in that it is seated at the right hand of God and is exalted,[9] our theologians declare in clear and candid words (so that all misunderstanding and scandal on this account will be removed inasmuch as the word "abstract" has not been used univocally by teachers in the schools and

---

[6] The Lower Saxon cities, the Pomeranians, and the Brunswick-Wolfenbüttel theologians wanted an endorsement of the "profitable" works of Melanchthon, but they were equally insistent that the criterion of conformity with the Formula of Concord and "Luther's writings" be expressed "either in the preface or at the end or somewhere else in this Formula."

[7] Some of the opponents of the Formula of Concord objected that Article VII introduced the omnipresence of our Lord's human nature as a "secondary basis" for the sacramental union. The theologians of Electoral Saxony and Electoral Brandenburg insisted in turn that the Formula based its doctrine of the Lord's Supper wholly on the words of institution and that only the Sacramentarian misinterpretation of the words of institution constrained the authors of the Formula to bring the person of Christ into the discussion.

[8] The words "especially . . . majesty" were added at Duke Julius' urging.

[9] The printed draft added at this point: "when it is said in this connection that the human nature of Christ is almighty, all-knowing, present everywhere, etc."

the churches): This divine majesty is not ascribed to the human nature of Christ outside the personal union, or in such a way that even in the personal union[1] it is alleged to have this majesty intrinsically, essentially, formally, habitually, and subjectively[2] (to use scholastic terminology), as if somewhere or sometimes it were being taught that the divine and human natures, together with their respective properties, are mixed together and the human nature according to its essence and properties is equalized with the divine nature and is thus negated. On the contrary, as the teachers of the ancient church put it, it takes place on account of the personal union,[3] which is an inscrutable mystery.

With reference to the condemnations, censures, and rejections of false and adulterated doctrine, especially in the article concerning the Lord's Supper,[4] these have to be set forth expressly and distinctly in this explanation and thorough settlement of the controverted articles in order that everybody may know that he must guard himself against them. There are also many other reasons why condemnations cannot by any means be avoided. However, it is not our purpose and intention to mean thereby those persons[5] who err ingenuously and who do not blaspheme the truth of the divine Word, and far less do we mean entire churches inside or outside the Holy Empire of the German Nation.[6] On the contrary, we mean specifically to condemn only false and seductive doctrines and their stiff-necked proponents and blasphemers. These we do not by any means intend to tolerate in our lands, churches, and schools inasmuch as such teachings are contrary to the expressed Word of God and cannot coexist with it. Besides, pious people should be warned against them. But we have no doubt at all that one can find many pious, innocent people even in those churches which have up to now admittedly not come to agreement with us. These people go their way in the simplicity of their hearts, do not understand the issues, and take no pleasure in blasphemies against

[1] These five words were added by Andreae and Chemnitz in the final revision.

[2] Latin: *essentialiter, formaliter, habitualiter, subiective.* Tilemann Heshusius wanted all Latin terms ("the sordid, obscure, unnecessary, and obsolete vocables of scholastic theologians, which not one parish rector out of a hundred understands") replaced by "good, intelligible German words." Dukes Julius and Christopher also called for emendation.

[3] See below, Formula of Concord, Solid Declaration, VIII, 73.

[4] See below, Formula of Concord, Solid Declaration, VII, 112-127.

[5] The faculty of the University of Helmstedt had objected that error and the errorist were inseparable. Heshusius went so far as to say that charity toward those who had been misled was untimely. The retention of these words therefore is significantly the result of careful deliberation.

[6] This phrase was designed to accommodate particularly the Pomeranian theologians who pointed out that one must take cognizance of the fact that "the queen in England [Elizabeth I] and the king in Navarre [later Henry IV, king of France] had prayed and petitioned with active diligence, in their own name and that of their coreligionists in France, Spain, England, the Low Countries, and Switzerland, not to condemn them and their adherents" until they had been heard at a general synod in Germany.

the Holy Supper as it is celebrated in our churches according to Christ's institution and as we concordantly teach about it on the basis of the words of his testament. It is furthermore to be hoped that when they are rightly instructed in this doctrine, they will, through the guidance of the Holy Spirit, turn to the infallible truth of the divine Word and unite with us and our churches and schools. Consequently the responsibility devolves upon the theologians and ministers duly to remind even those who err ingenuously and ignorantly of the danger to their souls and to warn them against it, lest one blind person let himself be misled by another.[7] For this reason we desire to testify before the face of almighty God and the whole of Christendom that it is in no way our disposition and purpose to give occasion by this Christian agreement for any molestation and persecution of poor, oppressed Christians. For just as Christian charity causes us to have special sympathy with them, so we entertain a corresponding loathing for and a cordial disapproval of the raging of their persecutors. We want absolutely no share of the responsibility for this bloodshed. Payment for it will without doubt be required of the persecutors on the great day of the Lord before the solemn and severe throne of God's judgment, and there they will have to give a hard accounting.

As indicated above, our disposition and intention has always been directed toward the goal that no other doctrine be treated and taught in our lands, territories, schools, and churches than that alone which is based on the Holy Scriptures of God and is embodied in the Augsburg Confession and its Apology, correctly understood, and that no doctrine be permitted entrance which is contrary to these. To this end the present agreement was proposed, purposed, and undertaken, and we desire once more to have witnessed publicly before God and all mankind that with the repeatedly mentioned present explanation[8] of the controverted articles we have made no new or different confession from the one that was previously submitted at Augsburg in the year 1530 to Emperor Charles V, of Christian memory. On the contrary, we have directed our churches and schools first of all to the Holy Scriptures and the Creeds, and then to the aforementioned Augsburg Confession. We desire particularly that the young men who are being trained for service in the church and for the holy ministry be faithfully and diligently instructed therein, so that the pure teaching and confession of the faith may be preserved and perpetuated among our posterity through the help and assistance of the Holy Spirit until the glorious advent of our only Redeemer and Saviour Jesus Christ.

Since this is the way things are, and since we are certain of our Christian confession and faith on the basis of the divine, prophetic, and

---

[7] Andreae added this sentence in the margin of the printed draft as a last-minute revision to satisfy Duke Julius.
[8] I.e., the Formula of Concord.

apostolic Scriptures and have been adequately assured of this in our hearts and Christian consciences through the grace of the Holy Spirit, the most acute and urgent necessity demands that in the presence of so many intrusive errors, aggravated scandals, dissensions, and long-standing schisms a Christian explanation and reconciliation of all of the disputes which have arisen should come into being. Such an explanation must be thoroughly grounded in God's Word so that pure doctrine can be recognized and distinguished from adulterated doctrine and so that the way may not be left free and open to restless, contentious individuals, who do not want to be bound to any certain formula of pure doctrine, to start scandalous controversies at will and to introduce and defend monstrous errors, the only possible consequence of which is that finally correct doctrine will be entirely obscured and lost and nothing beyond uncertain opinions and dubious, disputable imaginations and views will be transmitted to subsequent generations. We are accordingly mindful of the obligation that we have by divine precept, on account of the office we bear, over against the temporal and eternal welfare of our own selves and of the subjects that belong to us, to do and to continue to do everything that is useful and profitable to the increase and expansion of God's praise and glory, to the propagation of that Word of his that alone brings salvation, to the tranquillity and peace of Christian schools and churches, and to the needed consolation and instruction of poor, misguided consciences. It is further apparent to us that many good-hearted Christian persons, of high station and low, are sighing anxiously for this salutary work of Christian concord and have a particular longing for it. Therefore, just as from the very beginning of this Christian agreement of ours it was never our disposition or intention—as it is not now—to keep this salutary and most necessary effort toward concord hidden and concealed in darkness, away from everyone's eyes, or to put the light of divine truth under a basket or a table, we ought not suspend or postpone its printing and publication any longer. We do not have the slightest doubt that all pious people who have an upright love for divine truth and for Christian, God-pleasing concord will, together with us, take Christian pleasure in this salutary, most necessary, and Christian effort and will allow nothing to stand in the way of this cause and the promotion of God's glory and the common welfare, both eternal and temporal.

In conclusion, we repeat once again that we are not minded to manufacture anything new by this work of agreement or to depart in any way at all, either in content or in formulation, from the divine truth that our pious forebears and we have acknowledged and confessed in the past, for our agreement is based on the prophetic and apostolic Scriptures and is comprehended in the three Creeds as well as in the Augsburg Confession, submitted in the year 1530 to Emperor Charles V, of kindest memory, in the Apology that followed it, and in the

Smalcald Articles and the Large and Small Catechisms of that highly enlightened man, Dr. Luther. On the contrary, we are minded by the grace of the Holy Spirit to abide and remain unanimously in this confession of faith and to regulate all religious controversies and their explanations according to it. In addition, we have resolved and purpose to live in genuine peace and concord with our fellow-members, the electors and estates in the Holy Roman Empire, and also with other Christian potentates, according to the content of the ordinances of the Holy Empire and of the special treaties into which we have entered with them, and to demonstrate toward everyone, according to his station, all affection, service, and friendship.

We likewise purpose to cooperate with one another in the future in the implementation of this effort at concord in our lands, according to our own and each community's circumstances, through diligent visitation of churches and schools, the supervision of printers,[9] and other salutary means. If the current controversies about our Christian religion should continue or new ones arise, we shall see to it that they are settled and composed in timely fashion before they become dangerously widespread in order that all kinds of scandal might be obviated.

In testimony whereof we have with one mind and heart subscribed our names hereto and ordered our privy seals impressed hereon.

LOUIS, count palatine on the Rhine, elector

AUGUST, duke of Saxony, elector

JOHN GEORGE, margrave of Brandenburg, elector

JOACHIM FREDERICK, margrave of Brandenburg, administrator of the archdiocese of Magdeburg

JOHN, bishop of Meissen

EBERHARD, bishop of Lübeck, administrator of the diocese of Verden

PHILIP LOUIS, palsgrave [of Pfalz-Neuburg]

Duke FREDERICK WILLIAM [of Saxe-Altenburg] and ⎰ through their
Duke JOHN [of Saxe-Weimar] ⎱ guardian

Duke JOHN CASIMIR [of Saxe-Coburg] and ⎰ through their guardians
Duke JOHN ERNEST [of Saxe-Eisenach] ⎱

GEORGE FREDERICK, margrave of Brandenburg [-Ansbach-Bayreuth]

JULIUS, duke of Brunswick [-Wolfenbüttel] and Lüneburg

OTTO, duke of Brunswick and Lüneburg [-Harburg]

HENRY THE YOUNGER, duke of Brunswick [-Wolfenbüttel] and Lüneburg

WILLIAM THE YOUNGER, duke of Brunswick and Lüneburg [-Hanover]

WOLF, duke of Brunswick [-Grubenhagen] and Lüneburg

* The Brunswick theologians in particular laid great stress on censorship.

ULRICH, duke of Mecklenburg [-Güstrow]

Duke JOHN and

Duke SIGISMUND AUGUST of Mecklenburg [in Ivernack]

LOUIS, duke of Württemberg

} through their guardians

Margrave ERNEST [of Baden-Durlach] and

Margrave JAMES of Baden [-Hachberg]

} through their guardians

GEORGE ERNEST, count and lord of Henneberg [-Schleusingen]

FREDERICK, count of Württemberg and Montbéliard

JOHN GÜNTHER, count of Schwarzburg [-Sondershausen]

WILLIAM, count of Schwarzburg [-Frankenhausen]

ALBERT, count of Schwarzburg [-Rudolstadt]

EMICH, count of Leiningen

PHILIP, count of Hanau [-Lichtenburg]

GODFREY, count of Oettingen

GEORGE, count and lord of Castell [-Rüdenhausen]

HENRY, count and lord of Castell [-Remlingen]

JOHN HOYER, count of Mansfeld [-Artern]

BRUNO, count of Mansfeld [-Bronstedt]

HOYER CHRISTOPHER, count of Mansfeld [-Eisleben]

PETER ERNEST THE YOUNGER, count of Mansfeld [-Eisleben]

CHRISTOPHER, count of Mansfeld

OTTO, count of Hoya [-Nienburg] and Burghausen

JOHN, count of Oldenburg and Delmenhorst

ALBERT GEORGE, count of Stolberg

WOLF ERNEST, count of Stolberg

LOUIS, count of Gleichen [-Blankenhain]

CHARLES, count of Gleichen [-Blankenhain]

ERNEST, count of Regenstein

BODO, count of Regenstein

LOUIS, count of Löwenstein

HENRY, baron of Limpurg [-Schmiedelfeld], Semperfrei

GEORGE, baron of Schönburg [-Waldenburg]

WOLF, baron of Schönburg [-Penig-Remissa]

ANARCK FREDERICK, baron of Wildenfels

Mayor and Council of the City of Lübeck

Mayor and Council of the City of Landau

Mayor and Council of the City of Münster-in-St. Georgental

The Council of the City of Goslar

Mayor and Council of the City of Ulm

Mayor and Council of the City of Esslingen

The Council of the City of Reutlingen

Mayor and Council of the City of Nördlingen

Mayor and Council of Rothenburg-on-the-Tauber

Mayor and Council of the City of Schwäbisch-Hall

Mayor and Council of the City of Heilbronn
Mayor and Council of the City of Memmingen
Mayor and Council of the City of Lindau
Mayor and Council of the City of Schweinfurt
The Council of the City of Donawerda
Chamberlain and Council of the City of Regensburg
Mayor and Council of the City of Wimpfen
Mayor and Council of the City of Giengen
Mayor and Council of Bopfingen
Mayor and Council of the City of Aalen
Mayor and Council of the City of Kaufbeuren
Mayor and Council of the City of Isna
Mayor and Council of the City of Kempten
The Council of the City of Hamburg
The Council of the City of Göttingen
The Council of the City of Brunswick
Mayor and Council of the City of Lüneburg
Mayor and Council of the City of Leutkirch
The whole administration of the City of Hildesheim
Mayor and Council of the City of Hameln
Mayor and Council of the City of Hanover
The Council of Mühlhausen
The Council of Erfurt
The Council of the City of Einbeck
The Council of the City of Northeim

I

THE THREE CHIEF SYMBOLS

or

Creeds of the Christian Faith
which are Commonly Used in the Church

INTRODUCTION

One or more of the three ancient Creeds (styled "the three catholic or ecumenical symbols" in the Latin text of the Book of Concord) is quoted or mentioned in each of the Lutheran Confessions. Often they are cited to claim the identity of Lutheran teaching with the teaching of the ancient church and thus to counter the charge of doctrinal innovation. It was only natural therefore that when the Book of Concord was published in 1580, these symbols of the ancient church should be incorporated at the very beginning. It was also natural that they should be reproduced in the form in which they were currently used in the West.

The text of the Apostles' Creed as we now have it dates from the eighth century. However, it is a revision of the so-called Old Roman Creed, which had currency in the West by the third century. Behind the Old Roman Creed, in turn, were various creedal formulations which betray their relationship to root forms encountered in the New Testament itself. While the Apostles' Creed as we now have it does not come from the apostles, its roots are apostolic.

A greater variety of creedal formulations appeared in the East than in the West. When the Council of Nicaea (A.D. 325) rejected the teaching of Arius, it expressed its position by adopting one of the current Eastern symbols and inserting into it some anti-Arian phrases. At the Council of Constantinople (381) some minor changes were made in this Nicene Creed, as we still call it, and it was reaffirmed at the Council of Chalcedon (451). In the ninth century the filioque ("and the Son," in the third article) was first inserted in the West, and it became a bone of contention between East and West especially in the eleventh century.

The Athanasian Creed is of uncertain origin. What is quite certain is that it was not written by Athanasius, the great theologian of the fourth century. It is supposed by some that it was prepared in his time, although it seems more likely that it dates from the fifth or sixth centuries and is of Western provenance.

I. THE APOSTLES' CREED[1]

I believe in God, the Father almighty, maker of heaven and earth:
And in Jesus Christ, his only Son, our Lord: who was conceived by the Holy Spirit, born of the virgin Mary, suffered under Pontius Pilate, was crucified, dead, and buried: he descended into hell, the third day he rose from the dead, he ascended into heaven, and is seated on the right hand of God, the Father almighty, whence he shall come to judge the living and the dead.

I believe in the Holy Spirit, the holy Christian[2] church, the communion of saints, the forgiveness of sins, the resurrection of the body, and the life everlasting. Amen.

II. THE NICENE CREED[3]

I believe in one God, the Father almighty, maker of heaven and earth and of all things visible and invisible.

And in one Lord Jesus Christ, the only-begotten Son of God, begotten of the Father before all ages, God of God, Light of Light, very God of very God, begotten not made, being of one substance with the Father, through whom all things were made: who for us men and for our salvation came down from heaven, was incarnate by the Holy Spirit of the virgin Mary, and was made man: who for us, too, was crucified under Pontius Pilate, suffered, and was buried: the third day he rose according to the Scriptures, ascended into heaven, and is seated on the right hand of the Father: he shall come again with

[1] German heading: The first creed or symbol is the commonly received Apostles' Creed, which sets forth the rudiments of the Christian faith and reads as follows.
[2] Latin: catholic. It had been customary since the fifteenth century to translate *catholica* with *christlich*.
[3] German heading: The second creed, or symbol of Nicaea.

glory to judge the living and the dead, and his kingdom shall have no end.

And in the Holy Spirit, the lord and giver of life, who proceeds from the Father and the Son: who together with the Father and the Son is worshiped and glorified: who spoke by the prophets.

And I believe one holy, Christian,[4] and apostolic church.

I acknowledge one Baptism for the remission of sins, and I look for the resurrection of the dead and the life of the age to come. Amen.

III. THE ATHANASIAN CREED[5]

Whoever wishes to be saved must, above all else, hold the true   1
Christian[4] faith. Whoever does not keep it whole and undefiled   2
will without doubt perish for eternity.

This is the true Christian faith, that we worship one God in   3
three persons and three persons in one God

without confusing the persons or dividing the divine substance.   4

For the Father is one person, the Son is another, and the Holy   5
Spirit is still another,

but there is one Godhead of the Father and of the Son and of   6
the Holy Spirit, equal in glory and coequal in majesty.

What the Father is, that is the Son and that is the Holy Spirit: 7

the Father is uncreated, the Son is uncreated, the Holy Spirit is   8
uncreated;

the Father is unlimited, the Son is unlimited, the Holy Spirit is   9
unlimited;

the Father is eternal, the Son is eternal, the Holy Spirit is   10
eternal;

and yet they are not three eternals but one eternal,   11

just as there are not three who are uncreated and who are   12
unlimited, but there is one who is uncreated and unlimited.

Likewise the Father is almighty, the Son is almighty, the Holy   13
Spirit is almighty,

and yet there are not three who are almighty but there is one   14
who is almighty.

So the Father is God, the Son is God, the Holy Spirit is God,   15
and yet they are not three Gods but one God.   16

---

[4] Latin, here and in parallel cases below: catholic.
[5] German heading: The third creed or symbol is named after St. Athanasius, who composed it against the heretics called Arians, and it reads as follows.

So the Father is Lord, the Son is Lord, the Holy Spirit is Lord, 17
and yet they are not three Lords but one Lord. 18

For just as we are compelled by Christian truth to acknowledge 19
each person by himself to be God and Lord,

so we are forbidden by the Christian religion to say that there are
three Gods or three Lords.

The Father was neither made nor created nor begotten by 20
anybody.

The Son was not made or created, but was begotten by the 21
Father.

The Holy Spirit was not made or created or begotten, but 22
proceeds from the Father and the Son.

Accordingly there is one Father and not three Fathers, one Son 23
and not three Sons, one Holy Spirit and not three Holy Spirits.

And among these three persons none is before or after another, 24
none is greater or less than another,

but all three persons are coequal and coeternal, and accord- 25
ingly, as has been stated above, three persons are to be worshiped in
one Godhead and one God is to be worshiped in three persons.

Whoever wishes to be saved must think thus about the Trinity. 26

It is also necessary for eternal salvation that one faithfully 27
believe that our Lord Jesus Christ became man,

for this is the right faith, that we believe and confess that our 28
Lord Jesus Christ, the Son of God, is at once God and man:

he is God, begotten before the ages of the substance of the 29
Father, and he is man, born in the world of the substance of his mother,

perfect God and perfect man, with reasonable soul and human 30
flesh,

equal to the Father with respect to his Godhead and inferior 31
to the Father with respect to his manhood.

Although he is God and man, he is not two Christs but one 32
Christ:

one, that is to say, not by changing the Godhead into flesh but 33
by taking on the humanity into God,

one, indeed, not by confusion of substance but by unity in one 34
person.

For just as the reasonable soul and the flesh are one man, so 35
God and man are one Christ,

who suffered for our salvation, descended into hell, rose from 36
the dead,

ascended into heaven, is seated on the right hand of the Father, 37
whence he shall come to judge the living and the dead.

At his coming all men shall rise with their bodies and give an 38
account of their own deeds.

Those who have done good will enter eternal life, and those   39
who have done evil will go into everlasting fire.

This is the true Christian faith. Unless a man believe this firmly   40
and faithfully, he cannot be saved.

II

THE AUGSBURG CONFESSION

A Confession of Faith Presented in Augsburg
by certain Princes and Cities to His
Imperial Majesty Charles V
in the Year 1530

Psalm 119:46

"I will also speak of thy testimonies before kings,
and shall not be put to shame."

INTRODUCTION

*Under date of Jan. 21, 1530, Emperor Charles V summoned an
imperial diet to meet the following April in Augsburg, Germany. He
desired a united front in his military operations against the Turks,
and this seemed to demand that an end be made of the religious disunity which had been introduced at home as a result of the Reformation. Accordingly he invited the princes and representatives of free
cities in the empire to discuss the religious differences at the forth-
coming diet in the hope of overcoming them and restoring unity. In
keeping with this invitation the elector of Saxony asked his theologians
in Wittenberg to prepare an account of the beliefs and practices in
the churches of his land. Since a statement of doctrines, known as
the Schwabach Articles, had already been prepared in the summer
of 1529, all that seemed to be needed now was an additional statement
concerning the changes in practice which had been made in the churches
of Saxony. Such a statement was therefore prepared by the Wittenberg theologians, and since it was approved at a meeting in Torgau at
the end of March, 1530, it is commonly referred to as the Torgau
Articles.*

*Together with other documents, the Schwabach and the Torgau
Articles were taken to Augsburg. There it was decided to make a
common Lutheran statement, rather than merely a Saxon statement,
of the account which was to be submitted to the emperor. Circum-*

23

stances also demanded that it be made clear in the statement that Lutherans were not casually to be lumped together with all the other opponents of Rome, and other considerations suggested the desirability of emphasizing the agreements with Rome rather than the differences from Rome. All these factors played a part in determining the character of the document which was now prepared under the hands of Philip Melanchthon. The Schwabach Articles became the principal basis for the first part and the Torgau Articles became the principal basis for the second part of what came to be the Augsburg Confession. Luther, who was not present in Augsburg, was consulted through correspondence, but revisions and emendations were made to the very eve of the formal presentation to the emperor on June 25, 1530. Signed by seven princes and the representatives of two free cities, the confession immediately achieved peculiar importance as a public declaration of faith.

In accordance with the emperor's instructions, texts of the confession were prepared and presented in both German and Latin. The actual reading before the diet was from the German text, which may therefore be regarded as more official. Unfortunately neither the German nor the Latin text is extant in the exact forms in which these were submitted. However, more than fifty copies dating from the year 1530 have been found, including drafts which represent various stages in the preparation before June 25 as well as copies with a variety of new changes in wording made after June 25. These versions have been the object of extended critical study on the part of many scholars, and a German and a Latin text have been reconstructed which can claim to be close to, even if not identical with, the documents presented to the emperor. There are differences between the two texts, and therefore both are here reproduced in translation, the German at the top of the page and the Latin below it.

PREFACE

Most serene, most mighty, invincible Emperor, most gracious Lord:

A short time ago Your Imperial Majesty graciously summoned a diet of the empire to convene here in Augsburg. In the summons Your Majesty indicated an earnest desire to deliberate concerning matters pertaining to the Turk, that traditional foe of ours and of the Christian religion, and how with continuing help he might effectively be resisted. The desire was also expressed for deliberation on what 2 might be done about the dissension concerning our holy faith and the Christian religion, and to this end it was proposed to employ all diligence amicably and charitably to hear, understand, and weigh the judgments, opinions, and beliefs of the several parties among us, to unite the same in agreement on one Christian truth, to put 3 aside whatever may not have been rightly interpreted or treated by either side,[1] to have all of us embrace and adhere to a single, true 4 religion and live together in unity and in one fellowship and church, even as we are all enlisted under one Christ.[2] Inasmuch as we, 5 the undersigned elector and princes and our associates, have been summoned for these purposes, together with other electors, princes, and estates,[3] we have complied with the command and can say without boasting that we were among the first to arrive.[4]

In connection with the matter pertaining to the faith and in 6 conformity with the imperial summons, Your Imperial Majesty also graciously and earnestly requested[5] that each of the electors, princes, and estates should commit to writing and present, in German and Latin, his judgments, opinions, and beliefs with reference to the said errors, dissensions, and abuses. Accordingly, after due delibera- 7 tion and counsel, it was decided last Wednesday that, in keeping with Your Majesty's wish, we should present our case in German and Latin today (Friday).[6] Wherefore, in dutiful obedience to Your Imperial 8 Majesty, we offer and present a confession of our pastors' and preachers' teaching and of our own faith, setting forth how and in what manner, on the basis of the Holy Scriptures, these things are preached, taught, communicated, and embraced in our lands, principalities, dominions, cities, and territories.

If the other electors, princes, and estates also submit a similar 9 written statement of their judgments and opinions, in Latin and German, we are prepared, in obedience to Your Imperial Majesty, 10 our most gracious lord, to discuss with them and their associates, in so far as this can honorably be done, such practical and equitable ways as may restore unity. Thus the matters at issue between us may be presented in writing on both sides, they may be discussed amicably and charitably, our differences may be reconciled, and we may be united in one, true religion, even as we are all under one Christ 11 and should confess and contend for Christ. All of this is in accord

---

[1] Latin: in the writings of either party.

[2] The actual language of the imperial summons is here reproduced.

[3] The diets, or parliamentary assemblies of the empire, were made up of the seven princes who were called "electors," of the other princes, and of representatives of the free cities.

[4] Elector John of Saxony and Landgrave Philip of Hesse arrived in Augsburg ahead of the emperor.

[5] At the formal opening of the diet on June 20, 1530.

[6] At the last minute the presentation was postponed from Friday (June 24) to Saturday (June 25).

with Your Imperial Majesty's aforementioned summons. That it may be done according to divine truth we invoke almighty God in deepest humility and implore him to bestow his grace to this end. Amen.

If, however, our lords, friends, and associates who represent |2 the electors, princes, and estates of the other party do not comply with the procedure intended by Your Imperial Majesty's summons, if no amicable and charitable negotiations take place between us, and if no results are attained, nevertheless we on our part shall |3 not omit doing anything, in so far as God and conscience allow, that may serve the cause of Christian unity. Of this Your Imperial |4 Majesty, our aforementioned friends (the electors, princes, and estates), and every lover of the Christian religion who is concerned about these questions will be graciously and sufficiently assured from what follows in the confession which we and our associates submit.

In the past[7] Your Imperial Majesty graciously gave assurance |5 to the electors, princes, and estates of the empire, especially in a public instruction at the diet in Spires in 1526, that for reasons |6 there stated Your Imperial Majesty was not disposed to render decisions in matters pertaining to our holy faith but would diligently urge it upon the pope to call a council. Again, by means of a written |7 instruction at the last diet in Spires a year ago, the electors, princes, |8 and estates of the empire were, among other things, informed and notified by Your Imperial Majesty's viceroy (His Royal Majesty of Hungary and Bohemia, etc.) and by Your Imperial Majesty's orator and appointed commissioners, that Your Imperial Majesty's viceroy, administrators, and councilors of the imperial government (together with the absent electors, princes, and representatives of the estates) who were assembled at the diet convened in Ratisbon[8] had considered the proposal concerning a general council and acknowledged that |9 it would be profitable to have such a council called. Since the relations between Your Imperial Majesty and the pope were improving and were progressing toward a good, Christian understanding,[9] Your Imperial Majesty was sure that the pope would not refuse to call a general council, and so Your Imperial Majesty graciously offered 20 to promote and bring about the calling of such a general council by the pope, along with Your Imperial Majesty, at the earliest opportunity and to allow no hindrance to be put in the way.

If the outcome should be such as we mentioned above,[1] we 2| offer in full obedience, even beyond what is required, to participate

[7] Latin adds: not only once, but many times.
[8] The diet of 1527 in Ratisbon was poorly attended and adjourned without accomplishing much.
[9] The peace of Barcelona (1529) was followed by an alliance (1529) and the coronation of the emperor in February, 1530.
[1] Latin: If the outcome should be such that these differences between us and the other party should not be amicably settled.

in such a general, free, and Christian council as the electors, princes, and estates have with the highest and best motives requested in all the diets of the empire which have been held during Your Imperial Majesty's reign. We have at various times made our protestations 22 and appeals concerning these most weighty matters, and have done so in legal form and procedure. To these we declare our con- 23 tinuing adherence, and we shall not be turned aside from our position by these or any following negotiations (unless the matters in dissension are finally heard, amicably weighed, charitably settled, and brought to Christian concord in accordance with Your Imperial Majesty's summons) as we herewith publicly witness and assert. This is 24 our confession and that of our associates, and it is specifically stated, article by article, in what follows.

ARTICLES OF FAITH AND DOCTRINE

I. [GOD]²

We unanimously hold and teach, in accordance with the decree 1 of the Council of Nicaea,³ that there is one divine essence, which 2 is called and which is truly God, and that there are three persons in this one divine essence, equal in power and alike eternal: God the Father, God the Son, God the Holy Spirit. All three are one 3 divine essence, eternal, without division, without end, of infinite power,

---

CHIEF ARTICLES OF FAITH

I. [GOD]

Our churches teach with great unanimity that the decree of the 1 Council of Nicaea concerning the unity of the divine essence and concerning the three persons is true and should be believed without any doubting. That is to say, there is one divine essence, which 2 is called and which is God, eternal, incorporeal, indivisible, of infinite power, wisdom, and goodness, the maker and preserver of all things, visible and invisible. Yet there are three persons, of the same 3

---

² The titles of some articles, here enclosed in square brackets, were inserted in and after 1533.
³ The Nicene Creed.

wisdom, and goodness, one creator and preserver of all things visible
and invisible. The word "person" is to be understood as the Fathers   4
employed the term in this connection, not as a part or a property of
another but as that which exists of itself.[4]

Therefore all the heresies which are contrary to this article are   5
rejected. Among these are the heresy of the Manichaeans,[5] who assert
that there are two gods, one good and one evil; also that of the Valentinians,[6] Arians,[7] Eunomians,[8] Mohammedans,[9] and others like
them; also that of the Samosatenes,[1] old and new, who hold that   6
there is only one person and sophistically assert that the other two,
the Word and the Holy Spirit, are not necessarily distinct persons but
that the Word signifies a physical word or voice and that the Holy
Spirit is a movement induced in creatures.

---

essence and power, who are also coeternal: the Father, the Son, and
the Holy Spirit. And the term "person" is used, as the ancient   4
Fathers employed it in this connection, to signify not a part or a
quality in another but that which subsists of itself.

Our churches condemn all heresies which have sprung up against   5
this article, such as that of the Manichaeans, who posited two prin-
ciples, one good and the other evil, and also those of the Valentinians,
Arians, Eunomians, Mohammedans, and all others like these. They   6
also condemn the Samosatenes, old and new, who contend that there
is only one person and craftily and impiously argue that the Word
and the Holy Spirit are not distinct persons since "Word" signifies a
spoken word and "Spirit" signifies a movement which is produced
in things.

[4] The terms *hypostasis* in Greek or *persona* in Latin were used in the
ancient church to repudiate Modalism, which regarded the Father, Son, and
Holy Spirit as three modes or manifestations of the one God.

[5] A religion based on Persian dualism combined with Christian and other
elements, founded in the third century by Mani and named after him. The
Albigensians of the late Middle Ages held similar notions.

[6] Gnostics of the second century who took their name from Valentinus.

[7] Followers of Arius who were condemned at the Council of Nicaea in
325 and who held that the Son was created and was of different "substance"
from the Father.

[8] Followers of Eunomius, an extreme Arian of the late fourth century.

[9] The Reformers frequently referred to Mohammedanism as an anti-
Trinitarian heresy.

[1] Followers of Paul of Samosata, who taught in the third century that
Jesus was a man specially endowed by the Spirit. The "new Samosatenes"
were anti-Trinitarian spiritualists of the sixteenth century like John Cam-
panus and Hans Denck.

II. [ORIGINAL SIN]

It is also taught among us that since the fall of Adam all men   1
who are born according to the course of nature are conceived and
born in sin. That is, all men are full of evil lust and inclinations from
their mothers' wombs and are unable by nature to have true fear of
God and true faith in God. Moreover, this inborn sickness and   2
hereditary sin[2] is truly sin and condemns to the eternal wrath of God
all those who are not born again through Baptism and the Holy Spirit.

Rejected in this connection are the Pelagians[3] and others who   3
deny that original sin is sin, for they hold that natural man is made
righteous by his own powers, thus disparaging the sufferings and merit
of Christ.

III. [THE SON OF GOD]

It is also taught among us that God the Son became man, born   1
of the virgin Mary, and that the two natures, divine and human,   2
are so inseparably united in one person that there is one Christ, true
God and true man, who was truly born, suffered, was crucified, died,

---

II. [ORIGINAL SIN]

Our churches also teach that since the fall of Adam all men   1
who are propagated according to nature are born in sin. That is to
say, they are without fear of God, are without trust in God, and are
concupiscent. And this disease or vice of origin is truly sin, which   2
even now damns and brings eternal death on those who are not born
again through Baptism and the Holy Spirit.

Our churches condemn the Pelagians and others who deny   3
that the vice of origin is sin and who obscure the glory of Christ's
merit and benefits by contending that man can be justified before God
by his own strength and reason.

III. [THE SON OF GOD]

Our churches also teach that the Word—that is, the Son of God   1
—took on man's nature in the womb of the blessed virgin Mary.
So there are two natures, divine and human, inseparably conjoined   2
in the unity of his person, one Christ, true God and true man, who

[2] The traditional term *Erbsünde* is employed.

[3] Followers of Pelagius, who at the beginning of the fifth century taught
that man is not sinful by nature and can be saved by an act of his own will
aided by God's grace. The Reformers charged Ulrich Zwingli and the
scholastic theologians with teaching Pelagianism.

and was buried in order to be a sacrifice not only for original sin   3
but also for all other sins and to propitiate God's wrath. The   4
same Christ also descended into hell, truly rose from the dead on
the third day, ascended into heaven, and sits on the right hand of
God, that he may eternally rule and have dominion over all creatures,
that through the Holy Spirit he may sanctify, purify, strengthen, and
comfort all who believe in him, that he may bestow on them life   5
and every grace and blessing, and that he may protect and defend
them against the devil and against sin. The same Lord Christ will   6
return openly to judge the living and the dead, as stated in the Apostles'
Creed.

IV. [JUSTIFICATION]

It is also taught among us that we cannot obtain forgiveness   1
of sin and righteousness before God by our own merits, works, or
satisfactions, but that we receive forgiveness of sin and become righteous before God by grace, for Christ's sake, through faith, when   2
we believe that Christ suffered for us and that for his sake our sin is
forgiven and righteousness and eternal life are given to us. For   3
God will regard and reckon this faith as righteousness, as Paul says
in Romans 3:21-26 and 4:5.

---

was born of the virgin Mary, truly suffered, was crucified, dead, and
buried, that he might reconcile the Father to us and be a sacrifice   3
not only for original guilt but also for all actual sins of men. He   4
also descended into hell, and on the third day truly rose again. Afterward he ascended into heaven to sit on the right hand of the Father,
forever reign and have dominion over all creatures, and sanctify those
who believe in him by sending the Holy Spirit into their hearts   5
to rule, comfort, and quicken them and defend them against the devil
and the power of sin. The same Christ will openly come again   6
to judge the living and the dead, etc., according to the Apostles' Creed.

IV. [JUSTIFICATION]

Our churches also teach that men cannot be justified before God   1
by their own strength, merits, or works but are freely justified for
Christ's sake through faith when they believe that they are received   2
into favor and that their sins are forgiven on account of Christ, who
by his death made satisfaction for our sins. This faith God imputes   3
for righteousness in his sight (Rom. 3, 4).

V. [THE OFFICE OF THE MINISTRY][4]

To obtain such faith God instituted the office of the ministry, 1
that is, provided the Gospel and the sacraments. Through these, 2
as through means, he gives the Holy Spirit, who works faith, when
and where he pleases, in those who hear the Gospel. And the 3
Gospel teaches that we have a gracious God, not by our own merits
but by the merit of Christ, when we believe this.

Condemned are the Anabaptists and others[5] who teach that the 4
Holy Spirit comes to us through our own preparations, thoughts,
and works without the external word of the Gospel.

VI. [THE NEW OBEDIENCE]

It is also taught among us that such faith should produce good 1
fruits and good works and that we must do all such good works as
God has commanded,[6] but we should do them for God's sake and

---

V. [THE MINISTRY OF THE CHURCH]

In order that we may obtain this faith, the ministry of teaching 1
the Gospel and administering the sacraments was instituted. For 2
through the Word and the sacraments, as through instruments, the
Holy Spirit is given, and the Holy Spirit produces faith, where and
when it pleases God, in those who hear the Gospel. That is to say, 3
it is not on account of our own merits but on account of Christ that
God justifies those who believe that they are received into favor for
Christ's sake. Gal. 3:14, "That we might receive the promise of the
Spirit through faith."

Our churches condemn the Anabaptists and others who think 4
that the Holy Spirit comes to men without the external Word, through
their own preparations and works.

VI. [THE NEW OBEDIENCE]

Our churches also teach that this faith is bound to bring forth 1
good fruits and that it is necessary to do the good works commanded
by God. We must do so because it is God's will and not because we

---

    [4] This title would be misleading if it were not observed (as the text of the
article makes clear) that the Reformers thought of "the office of the ministry" in other than clerical terms.

    [5] For example, Sebastian Franck and Caspar Schwenkfeld taught in the
sixteenth century that the Spirit comes to men without means.

    [6] In contrast to unnecessary works which are not commanded by God,
mentioned below in Art. XX, 3, and XXVI, 2.

not place our trust in them as if thereby to merit favor before God.
For we receive forgiveness of sin and righteousness through faith   2
in Christ, as Christ himself says, "So you also, when you have done
all that is commanded you, say, 'We are unworthy servants' " (Luke
17:10). The Fathers also teach thus, for Ambrose says, "It is or-   3
dained of God that whoever believes in Christ shall be saved, and
he shall have forgiveness of sins, not through works but through faith
alone, without merit." [7]

VII. [THE CHURCH]

It is also taught among us that one holy Christian church will   1
be and remain forever. This is the assembly of all believers among
whom the Gospel is preached in its purity and the holy sacraments
are administered according to the Gospel. For it is sufficient for   2
the true unity of the Christian church that the Gospel be preached
in conformity with a pure understanding of it and that the sacraments
be administered in accordance with the divine Word. It is not   3
necessary for the true unity of the Christian church that ceremonies,
instituted by men, should be observed uniformly in all places. It   4
is as Paul says in Eph. 4:4, 5, "There is one body and one Spirit,
just as you were called to the one hope that belongs to your call, one
Lord, one faith, one baptism."

---

rely on such works to merit justification before God, for forgive-   2
ness of sins and justification are apprehended by faith, as Christ himself also testifies, "When you have done all these things, say, 'We are
unprofitable servants' " (Luke 17:10). The same is also taught   3
by the Fathers of the ancient church, for Ambrose says, "It is ordained
of God that whoever believes in Christ shall be saved, not through
works but through faith alone, and he shall receive forgiveness of
sins by grace."

VII. [THE CHURCH]

Our churches also teach that one holy church is to continue   1
forever. The church is the assembly of saints in which the Gospel is
taught purely and the sacraments are administered rightly. For   2
the true unity of the church it is enough to agree concerning the teaching of the Gospel and the administration of the sacraments. It is   3
not necessary that human traditions or rites and ceremonies, instituted
by men, should be alike everywhere. It is as Paul says, "One faith,   4
one baptism, one God and Father of all," etc. (Eph. 4:5, 6).

[7] Ambrosiaster, *The First Epistle to the Corinthians*, 1:4.

VIII. [What the Church Is]

Again, although the Christian church, properly speaking, is 1
nothing else than the assembly of all believers and saints, yet because
in this life many false Christians, hypocrites, and even open sinners
remain among the godly, the sacraments are efficacious even if the
priests who administer them are wicked men, for as Christ himself
indicated, "The Pharisees sit on Moses' seat" (Matt. 23:2).

Accordingly the Donatists[8] and all others who hold contrary 3
views are condemned.

IX. Baptism

It is taught among us that Baptism is necessary and that grace 1
is offered through it. Children, too, should be baptized, for in 2
Baptism they are committed to God and become acceptable to him.

On this account the Anabaptists who teach that infant Baptism 3
is not right are rejected.

VIII. [What is the Church?]

Properly speaking, the church is the assembly of saints and true 1
believers. However, since in this life many hypocrites and evil persons are mingled with believers, it is allowable to use the sacraments
even when they are administered by evil men, according to the saying
of Christ, "The scribes and Pharisees sit on Moses' seat," etc. (Matt.
23:2). Both the sacraments and the Word are effectual by reason 2
of the institution and commandment of Christ even if they are administered by evil men.

Our churches condemn the Donatists and others like them who 3
have denied that the ministry of evil men may be used in the church
and who have thought the ministry of evil men to be unprofitable and
without effect.

IX. Baptism

Our churches teach that Baptism is necessary for salvation, 1
that the grace of God is offered through Baptism, and that chil- 2
dren should be baptized, for being offered to God through Baptism
they are received into his grace.

Our churches condemn the Anabaptists who reject the Baptism 3
of children and declare that children are saved without Baptism.

* Rigorists of the fourth century who denied the validity of the ministry
of those who apostatized under persecution.

X. THE HOLY SUPPER OF OUR LORD

It is taught among us that the true body and blood of Christ 1
are really present in the Supper of our Lord under 'the form of bread
and wine and are there distributed and received. The contrary 2
doctrine is therefore rejected.

XI. CONFESSION

It is taught among us that private absolution should be retained 1
and not allowed to fall into disuse. However, in confession it is not
necessary to enumerate all trespasses and sins,[9] for this is im- 2
possible. Ps. 19:12, "Who can discern his errors?"

XII. REPENTANCE

It is taught among us that those who sin after Baptism receive 1
forgiveness of sin whenever they come to repentance, and absolu- 2
tion should not be denied them by the church. Properly speaking, 3
true repentance is nothing else than to have contrition and sorrow,
or terror, on account of sin, and yet at the same time to believe 5
the Gospel and absolution (namely, that sin has been forgiven and

---

X. LORD'S SUPPER

Our churches teach that the body and blood of Christ are truly 1
present and are distributed to those who eat in the Supper of the
Lord. They disapprove of those who teach otherwise. 2

XI. CONFESSION

Our churches teach that private absolution should be retained in 1
the churches. However, in confession an enumeration of all sins
is not necessary, for this is not possible according to the Psalm, 2
"Who can discern his errors?" (Ps. 19:12).

XII. REPENTANCE

Our churches teach that those who have fallen after Baptism 1
can receive forgiveness of sins whenever they are converted, and 2
that the church ought to impart absolution to those who return to
repentance. Properly speaking, repentance consists of these two 3
parts: one is contrition, that is, terror smiting the conscience 4
with a knowledge of sin, and the other is faith, which is born of 5
the Gospel, or of absolution, believes that sins are forgiven for Christ's

* Required by the Fourth Lateran Council (1215), cap. 21.

grace has been obtained through Christ), and this faith will comfort
the heart and again set it at rest.[1] Amendment of life and the   6
forsaking of sin should then follow, for these must be the fruits of
repentance, as John says, "Bear fruit that befits repentance" (Matt. 3:8).

Rejected here are those who teach that persons who have once   7
become godly cannot fall again.[2]

Condemned on the other hand are the Novatians[3] who denied   9
absolution to such as had sinned after Baptism.

Rejected also are those who teach that forgiveness of sin is not   10
obtained through faith but through the satisfactions made by man.

XIII. The Use of the Sacraments

It is taught among us that the sacraments were instituted not   1
only to be signs by which people might be identified outwardly as
Christians, but that they are signs and testimonies of God's will toward
us for the purpose of awakening and strengthening our faith.

---

sake, comforts the conscience, and delivers it from terror. Then   6
good works, which are the fruits of repentance, are bound to follow.

Our churches condemn the Anabaptists who deny that those   7
who have once been justified can lose the Holy Spirit, and also   8
those who contend that some may attain such perfection in this life
that they cannot sin. Also condemned are the Novatians who   9
were unwilling to absolve those who had fallen after Baptism although
they returned to repentance. Rejected also are those who do not   10
teach that remission of sins comes through faith but command us to
merit grace through satisfactions of our own.

XIII. The Use of the Sacraments

Our churches teach that the sacraments were instituted not   1
merely to be marks of profession among men but especially to be
signs and testimonies of the will of God toward us, intended to awaken
and confirm faith in those who use them. Consequently the sac-   2
raments should be so used that faith, which believes the promises
that are set forth and offered, is added.

[1] The Latin text sharpens the distinction from the Roman sacrament of
penance (contrition, confession, absolution, and satisfaction).

[2] Such was the teaching, for example, of Hans Denck.

[3] Rigorists in Rome during the third century who denied restoration, even
after repentance, to those who were guilty of grave sins.

For this reason they require faith, and they are rightly used when 2
they are received in faith and for the purpose of strengthening faith.

XIV. ORDER IN THE CHURCH

It is taught among us that nobody should publicly teach or preach
or administer the sacraments in the church without a regular call.

XV. CHURCH USAGES

With regard to church usages that have been established by men,   I
it is taught among us that those usages are to be observed which may
be observed without sin and which contribute to peace and good order
in the church, among them being certain holy days, festivals,[4] and
the like. Yet we accompany these observances with instruction 2
so that consciences may not be burdened by the notion that such
things are necessary for salvation. Moreover it is taught that all 3
ordinances and traditions instituted by men for the purpose of pro-
pitiating God and earning grace are contrary to the Gospel and the

---

[Our churches therefore condemn those who teach that the sac- 3
raments justify by the outward act[5] and who do not teach that faith,
which believes that sins are forgiven, is required in the use of the
sacraments.][6]

XIV. ECCLESIASTICAL ORDER

Our churches teach that nobody should preach publicly in the
church or administer the sacraments unless he is regularly called.

XV. ECCLESIASTICAL RITES

Our churches teach that those rites should be observed which   I
can be observed without sin and which contribute to peace and good
order in the church. Such are certain holy days, festivals, and the like.

Nevertheless, men are admonished not to burden consciences 2
with such things, as if observances of this kind were necessary for
salvation. They are also admonished that human traditions which 3
are instituted to propitiate God, merit grace, and make satisfaction

---

[4] Among the Lutherans at this time numerous saints' days were abolished
and most of the apostles' days were transferred to the succeeding Sundays,
but many of the festivals of the church year were retained.

[5] *Ex opere operato,* a formula customary since the thirteenth century.
See below, Apology, IV, 63, and note.

[6] Text in square brackets added later in the so-called *editio princeps.*

teaching about faith in Christ. Accordingly monastic vows and 4
other traditions concerning distinctions of foods, days, etc.,[7] by which
it is intended to earn grace and make satisfaction for sin, are useless
and contrary to the Gospel.

XVI. Civil Government

It is taught among us that all government in the world and all 1
established rule and laws were instituted and ordained by God for
the sake of good order, and that Christians may without sin 2
occupy civil offices or serve as princes and judges, render decisions
and pass sentence according to imperial and other existing laws,
punish evildoers with the sword, engage in just wars, serve as soldiers,
buy and sell, take required oaths, possess property, be married, etc.

Condemned here are the Anabaptists who teach that none of the 3
things indicated above is Christian.[8]

Also condemned are those who teach that Christian perfection 4
requires the forsaking of house and home, wife and child, and the
renunciation of such activities as are mentioned above.[9] Actually,
true perfection consists alone of proper fear of God and real faith in

---

for sins are opposed to the Gospel and the teaching about faith.
Wherefore vows and traditions about foods and days, etc., in- 4
stituted to merit grace and make satisfaction for sins, are useless and
contrary to the Gospel.

XVI. Civil Affairs

Our churches teach that lawful civil ordinances are good works 1
of God and that it is right for Christians to hold civil office, to sit 2
as judges, to decide matters by the imperial and other existing laws,
to award just punishments, to engage in just wars, to serve as soldiers,
to make legal contracts, to hold property, to swear oaths when required
by magistrates, to marry, to be given in marriage.

Our churches condemn the Anabaptists who forbid Christians to 3
engage in these civil functions. They also condemn those who place 4

[7] Such fast days of the Roman Church as Fridays, ember days, days in
Lent, etc.

[8] The Anabaptists actually differed from one another in their attitudes
toward the state, marriage, and economic life, but some took the negative
position here indicated.

[9] The notion of Christian perfection here referred to was embodied in
monasticism (called the "state of perfection") and was embraced by some
Anabaptists. See also Art. XXVII, below.

God, for the Gospel does not teach an outward and temporal but an inward and eternal mode of existence and righteousness of the heart. The Gospel does not overthrow civil authority, the state,   5 and marriage but requires that all these be kept as true orders of God[1] and that everyone, each according to his own calling, manifest Christian love and genuine good works in his station of life. Accordingly   6 Christians are obliged to be subject to civil authority and obey its commands and laws in all that can be done without sin. But   7 when commands of the civil authority cannot be obeyed without sin, we must obey God rather than men (Acts 5:29).

XVII. [THE RETURN OF CHRIST TO JUDGMENT]

It is also taught among us that our Lord Jesus Christ will return   1 on the last day for judgment and will raise up all the dead, to   2 give eternal life and everlasting joy to believers and the elect but to   3 condemn ungodly men and the devil to hell and eternal punishment.

Rejected, therefore, are the Anabaptists who teach that the devil   4 and condemned men will not suffer eternal pain and torment.[2]

Rejected, too, are certain Jewish opinions which are even now   5

---

the perfection of the Gospel not in the fear of God and in faith but in forsaking civil duties. The Gospel teaches an eternal righteousness of the heart, but it does not destroy the state or the family. On the   5 contrary, it especially requires their preservation as ordinances of God and the exercise of love in these ordinances. Therefore Chris-   6 tians are necessarily bound to obey their magistrates and laws except when commanded to sin, for then they ought to obey God   7 rather than men (Acts 5:29).

XVII. [THE RETURN OF CHRIST FOR JUDGMENT]

Our churches also teach that at the consummation of the world   1 Christ will appear for judgment and will raise up all the dead. To the godly and elect he will give eternal life and endless joy,   2 but ungodly men and devils he will condemn to be tormented   3 without end.

Our churches condemn the Anabaptists who think that there   4 will be an end to the punishments of condemned men and devils. They also condemn others who are now spreading Jewish opinions   5 to the effect that before the resurrection of the dead the godly will

---

[1] *Wahrhaftige Gottesordnung.*

[2] Taught, for example, by Hans Denck and Melchior Rinck.

making an appearance and which teach that, before the resurrection of the dead, saints and godly men will possess a worldly kingdom and annihilate all the godless.[3]

XVIII. FREEDOM OF THE WILL

It is also taught among us that man possesses some measure of 1 freedom of the will which enables him to live an outwardly honorable life and to make choices among the things that reason comprehends. But without the grace, help, and activity of the Holy Spirit man is 2 not capable of making himself acceptable to God, of fearing God and believing in God with his whole heart, or of expelling inborn evil lusts from his heart. This is accomplished by the Holy Spirit, who 3 is given through the Word of God, for Paul says in I Cor. 2:14, "Natural man does not receive the gifts of the Spirit of God."

In order that it may be evident that this teaching is no novelty, 4 the clear words of Augustine on free will are here quoted from the third book of his *Hypognosticon*:[4] "We concede that all men have a free will, for all have a natural, innate understanding and reason. However, this does not enable them to act in matters pertaining to God (such as loving God with their whole heart or fearing him), for

---

take possession of the kingdom of the world, the ungodly being suppressed everywhere.

XVIII. FREE WILL

Our churches teach that man's will has some liberty for the 1 attainment of civil righteousness and for the choice of things subject to reason. However, it does not have the power, without the Holy 2 Spirit, to attain the righteousness of God—that is, spiritual righteousness—because natural man does not perceive the gifts of the Spirit of God (I Cor. 2:14); but this righteousness is wrought in 3 the heart when the Holy Spirit is received through the Word. In 4 Book III of his *Hypognosticon* Augustine said these things in so many words: "We concede that all men have a free will which enables them to make judgments according to reason. However, this does not enable them, without God, to begin or (much less) to accomplish anything in those things which pertain to God, for it is only in acts of this life that they have freedom to choose good or evil. By 5

---

[3] Incited by Hans Hut and some Jews in Worms, Melchior Rinck predicted that the millennium would be ushered in during Easter, 1530.

[4] *Hypomnesticon contra Pelagianos et Coelestinianos*, III, 4, 5, ascribed to Augustine in older collections of his works.

it is only in the outward acts of this life that they have freedom to choose good or evil. By good I mean what they are capable of by 5 nature: whether or not to labor in the fields, whether or not to eat or drink or visit a friend, whether to dress or undress, whether to build a house, take a wife, engage in a trade, or do whatever else may be good and profitable. None of these is or exists without 6 God, but all things are from him and through him. On the other 7 hand, by his own choice man can also undertake evil, as when he wills to kneel before an idol, commit murder, etc." [5]

XIX. THE CAUSE OF SIN

It is taught among us that although almighty God has created and still preserves nature, yet sin is caused in all wicked men and despisers

---

'good' I mean the acts which spring from the good in nature, that is, to will to labor in the field, will to eat and drink, will to have a friend, will to clothe oneself, will to build a house, will to marry, will to keep cattle, will to learn various useful arts, or will to do whatever good pertains to this life. None of these exists without the 6 providence of God; indeed, it is from and through him that all these things come into being and are. On the other hand, by 'evil' I 7 mean such things as to will to worship an idol, will to commit murder," etc.

[Our churches condemn the Pelagians and others who teach 8 that without the Holy Spirit, by the power of nature alone, we are able to love God above all things, and can also keep the commandments of God in so far as the substance of the acts is concerned. Although nature is able in some measure to perform the out- 9 ward works (for it can keep the hands from theft and murder), yet it cannot produce the inward affections, such as fear of God, trust in God, patience, etc.][6]

XIX. THE CAUSE OF SIN

Our churches teach that although God creates and preserves nature, the cause of sin is the will of the wicked, that is, of the devil and

[5] Early variants add at this point: Rejected here are those who teach that we can keep the commandments of God without grace and the Holy Spirit. For although we are by nature capable of performing the outward act enjoined in a commandment, we are not capable of performing in our hearts what the commandments supremely require, namely, truly to fear, love, and trust God, etc.

[6] Text in square brackets added later in the so-called *editio princeps.*

of God by the perverted will. This is the will of the devil and of all ungodly men; as soon as God withdraws his support, the will turns away from God to evil. It is as Christ says in John 8:44, "When the devil lies, he speaks according to his own nature."

XX. FAITH AND GOOD WORKS

Our teachers have been falsely accused of forbidding good i works. Their writings on the Ten Commandments, and other 2 writings as well, show that they have given good and profitable accounts and instructions concerning true Christian estates and works. About these little was taught in former times, when for the 3 most part sermons were concerned with childish and useless works like rosaries, the cult of saints, monasticism, pilgrimages, appointed fasts, holy days, brotherhoods,[7] etc. Our opponents no longer praise these 4 useless works so highly as they once did, and they have also 5 learned to speak now of faith, about which they did not preach at all in former times. They do not teach now that we become right- 6 eous before God by our works alone, but they add faith in Christ

---

ungodly men. If not aided by God, the will of the wicked turns away from God, as Christ says in John 8:44, "When the devil lies, he speaks according to his own nature."

XX. FAITH AND GOOD WORKS

Our teachers are falsely accused of forbidding good works. 1 Their publications on the Ten Commandments and others of like 2 import bear witness that they have taught to good purpose about all stations and duties of life, indicating what manners of life and what kinds of work are pleasing to God in the several callings. Con- 3 cerning such things preachers used to teach little. Instead, they urged childish and needless works, such as particular holy days, prescribed fasts, brotherhoods, pilgrimages, services in honor of saints, rosaries, monasticism, and the like. Since our adversaries have been ad- 4 monished about these things, they are now unlearning them and do not preach about such unprofitable works as much as formerly. They are even beginning to mention faith, about which there used 5 to be marvelous silence. They teach that we are justified not by 6 works only, but conjoining faith with works they say that we are justified by faith and works. This teaching is more tolerable than 7

[7] Societies of laymen for devotional exercises and good works.

and say that faith and works make us righteous before God. This   7
teaching may offer a little more comfort than the teaching that we are
to rely solely on our works.

Since the teaching about faith, which is the chief article in the   8
Christian life, has been neglected so long (as all must admit) while
nothing but works was preached everywhere, our people have been
instructed as follows:

We begin by teaching that our works cannot reconcile us with   9
God or obtain grace for us, for this happens only through faith, that
is, when we believe that our sins are forgiven for Christ's sake, who
alone is the mediator who reconciles the Father. Whoever im-   10
agines that he can accomplish this by works, or that he can merit
grace, despises Christ and seeks his own way to God, contrary to
the Gospel.

This teaching about faith is plainly and clearly treated by Paul   11
in many passages, especially in Eph. 2:8, 9, "For by grace you have
been saved through faith; and this is not your own doing, it is the
gift of God—not because of works, lest any man should boast," etc.

That no new interpretation is here introduced can be demon-   12

---

the former one, and it can afford more consolation than their old
teaching.

Inasmuch, then, as the teaching about faith, which ought to be   8
the chief teaching in the church, has so long been neglected (for everybody must grant that there has been profound silence concerning the
righteousness of faith in sermons while only the teaching about works
has been treated in the church), our teachers have instructed our
churches concerning faith as follows:

We begin by teaching that our works cannot reconcile God or   9
merit forgiveness of sins and grace but that we obtain forgiveness
and grace only by faith when we believe that we are received into
favor for Christ's sake, who alone has been ordained to be the mediator
and propitiation through whom the Father is reconciled. Con-   10
sequently whoever trusts that he merits grace by works despises the
merit and grace of Christ and seeks a way to God without Christ,
by human strength, although Christ has said of himself, "I am the
way, and the truth, and the life" (John 14:6).

This teaching concerning faith is everywhere treated in Paul, as   11
in Eph. 2:8, "For by grace you have been saved through faith; and this
is not because of works," etc.

Lest anyone should captiously object that we have invented   12

strated from Augustine, who discusses this question thoroughly   13
and teaches the same thing, namely, that we obtain grace and are
justified before God through faith in Christ and not through works.
His whole book, *De spiritu et litera*,[8] proves this.

Although this teaching is held in great contempt among untried   15
people, yet it is a matter of experience that weak and terrified consciences find it most comforting and salutary. The conscience cannot
come to rest and peace through works, but only through faith, that is,
when it is assured and knows that for Christ's sake it has a gracious
God, as Paul says in Rom. 5:1, "Since we are justified by faith,   16
we have peace with God."

In former times this comfort was not heard in preaching, but   19
poor consciences were driven to rely on their own efforts, and all
sorts of works were undertaken. Some were driven by their con-   20

---

a new interpretation of Paul, this whole matter is supported by testimonies of the Fathers. In many volumes Augustine defends grace   13
and the righteousness of faith against the merits of works.
Ambrose teaches similarly in *De vocatione gentium* and else-   14
where, for in his *De vocatione gentium* he says: "Redemption by the
blood of Christ would become of little value and the preeminence
of human works would not be superseded by the mercy of God if
justification, which is accomplished by grace, were due to antecedent
merits, for then it would be a reward for works rather than a free
gift." [9]

Although this teaching is despised by inexperienced men, God-   15
fearing and anxious consciences find by experience that it offers the
greatest consolation because the consciences of men cannot be pacified
by any work but only by faith when they are sure that for Christ's
sake they have a gracious God. It is as Paul teaches in Rom. 5:1,   16
"Since we are justified by faith, we have peace with God." This   17
whole teaching is to be referred to that conflict of the terrified conscience, nor can it be understood apart from that conflict. Ac-   18
cordingly inexperienced and profane men, who dream that Christian
righteousness is nothing else than civil or philosophical righteousness,
have bad judgment concerning this teaching.

Consciences used to be plagued by the doctrine of works when   19
consolation from the Gospel was not heard. Some persons were   20

---

[8] *The Spirit and the Letter*, XIX, 34.
[9] Pseudo-Ambrose, *The Calling of the Gentiles*, I, 17.

science into monasteries in the hope that there they might merit grace through monastic life. Others devised other works for the 2l purpose of earning grace and making satisfaction for sins. Many 22 of them discovered that they did not obtain peace by such means. It was therefore necessary to preach this doctrine about faith in Christ and diligently to apply it in order that men may know that the grace of God is appropriated without merits, through faith alone.

Instruction is also given among us to show that the faith here 23 spoken of is not that possessed by the devil and the ungodly,[1] who also believe the history of Christ's suffering and his resurrection from the dead, but we mean such true faith as believes that we receive grace and forgiveness of sin through Christ.

Whoever knows that in Christ he has a gracious God, truly 24 knows God, calls upon him, and is not, like the heathen, without God. For the devil and the ungodly do not believe this article 25 concerning the forgiveness of sin, and so they are at enmity with God, cannot call upon him, and have no hope of receiving good from him. Therefore, as has just been indicated, the Scriptures speak of faith but do not mean by it such knowledge as the devil and ungodly men possess. Heb. 11:1 teaches about faith in such a way as to make

---

by their consciences driven into the desert, into monasteries, in the hope that there they might merit grace by monastic life. Others 2l invented works of another kind to merit grace and make satisfaction for sins. Hence there was very great need to treat of and to restore 22 this teaching concerning faith in Christ in order that anxious consciences should not be deprived of consolation but know that grace and forgiveness of sins are apprehended by faith in Christ.

Men are also admonished that here the term "faith" does not 23 signify merely knowledge of the history (such as is in the ungodly and the devil), but it signifies faith which believes not only the history but also the effect of the history, namely, this article of the forgiveness of sins—that is, that we have grace, righteousness, and forgiveness of sins through Christ.

Whoever knows that he has a Father reconciled to him through 24 Christ truly knows God, knows that God cares for him, and calls upon God. He is not without God, as are the heathen, for devils 25 and ungodly men are not able to believe this article of the forgiveness of sins; hence they hate God as an enemy, do not call upon him, and

[1] Cf. James 2:19.

it clear that faith is not merely a knowledge of historical events but is a confidence in God and in the fulfillment of his promises. Au- 26 gustine[2] also reminds us that we should understand the word "faith" in the Scriptures to mean confidence in God, assurance that God is gracious to us, and not merely such a knowledge of historical events as the devil also possesses.

It is also taught among us that good works should and must 27 be done, not that we are to rely on them to earn grace but that we may do God's will and glorify him. It is always faith alone that 28 apprehends grace and forgiveness of sin. When through faith 29 the Holy Spirit is given, the heart is moved to do good works. Before that, when it is without the Holy Spirit, the heart is too 31 weak. Moreover, it is in the power of the devil, who drives poor 32 human beings into many sins. We see this in the philosophers 33 who undertook to lead honorable and blameless lives; they failed to accomplish this, and instead fell into many great and open sins. This is what happens when a man is without true faith and the 34 Holy Spirit and governs himself by his own human strength alone.

---

expect no good from him. Augustine, too, admonishes his readers 26 in this way concerning the word "faith" when he teaches that in the Scriptures the word "faith" is to be understood not as knowledge, such as is in the ungodly, but as confidence which consoles and lifts up terrified hearts.

Our teachers teach in addition that it is necessary to do good 27 works, not that we should trust to merit grace by them but because it is the will of God. It is only by faith that forgiveness of sins 28 and grace are apprehended, and because through faith the Holy 29 Spirit is received, hearts are so renewed and endowed with new affections as to be able to bring forth good works. Ambrose says, "Faith 30 is the mother of the good will and the right deed." [3] For without 31 the Holy Spirit man's powers are full of ungodly affections and are too weak to do works which are good in God's sight. Besides, they 32 are in the power of the devil, who impels men to various sins, impious opinions, and manifest crimes. This we may see in the phi- 33 losophers, who, although they tried to live honest lives, were not able to do so but were defiled by many manifest crimes. Such is the 34 feebleness of man when he governs himself by human strength alone without faith and without the Holy Spirit.

---

[2] *Homilies on the Epistle of John to the Parthians,* X, 2.
[3] Pseudo-Ambrose, *The Calling of the Gentiles,* I, 25.

Consequently this teaching concerning faith is not to be accused   35
of forbidding good works but is rather to be praised for teaching that
good works are to be done and for offering help as to how they may
be done. For without faith and without Christ human nature and   36
human strength are much too weak to do good works, call upon   37
God, have patience in suffering, love one's neighbor, diligently engage
in callings which are commanded, render obedience, avoid evil lusts,
etc. Such great and genuine works cannot be done without the   38
help of Christ, as he himself says in John 15:5, "Apart from me   39
you can do nothing."

XXI. The Cult of Saints

It is also taught among us that saints should be kept in remem-   1
brance so that our faith may be strengthened when we see what grace
they received and how they were sustained by faith. Moreover, their
good works are to be an example for us, each of us in his own calling.
So His Imperial Majesty may in salutary and godly fashion imitate
the example of David in making war on the Turk, for both are in-
cumbents of a royal office which demands the defense and protection
of their subjects.

Hence it may readily be seen that this teaching is not to be   35
charged with forbidding good works. On the contrary, it should rather
be commended for showing how we are enabled to do good works.
For without faith human nature cannot possibly do the works of   36
the First or Second Commandments. Without faith it does not call   37
upon God, expect anything of God, or bear the cross, but it seeks
and trusts in man's help. Accordingly, when there is no faith   38
and trust in God, all manner of lusts and human devices rule in the
heart. Wherefore Christ said, "Apart from me you can do nothing"   39
(John 15:5), and the church sings,   40

> "Where Thou art not, man hath naught,
> Nothing good in deed or thought,
> Nothing free from taint of ill." [4]

XXI. The Cult of Saints

Our churches teach that the remembrance of saints may be   1
commended to us so that we imitate their faith and good works according to our calling. Thus the emperor may follow the example of
David in waging war to drive the Turk out of his country, for like

[4] From the hymn, *Veni, sancte spiritus;* translation of Edward Caswall.

However, it cannot be proved from the Scriptures that we are 2
to invoke saints or seek help from them. "For there is one mediator
between God and men, Christ Jesus" (I Tim. 2:5), who is the only
saviour, the only highpriest, advocate, and intercessor before God
(Rom. 8:34). He alone has promised to hear our prayers. More- 3
over, according to the Scriptures, the highest form of divine service
is sincerely to seek and call upon this same Jesus Christ in every time
of need. "If anyone sins, we have an advocate with the Father, 4
Jesus Christ the righteous" (I John 2:1).

This is just about a summary of the doctrines that are preached 1
and taught in our churches for proper Christian instruction, the consolation of consciences, and the amendment of believers. Certainly
we should not wish to put our own souls and consciences in grave
peril before God by misusing his name or Word, nor should we wish
to bequeath to our children and posterity any other teaching than
that which agrees with the pure Word of God and Christian truth.
Since this teaching is grounded clearly on the Holy Scriptures and
is not contrary or opposed to that of the universal Christian church,
or even of the Roman church (in so far as the latter's teaching is
reflected in the writings of the Fathers),[5] we think that our opponents
cannot disagree with us in the articles set forth above. Therefore,

---

David the emperor is a king. However, the Scriptures do not 2
teach us to pray to the saints or seek their help, for the only mediator,
propitiation, highpriest, and intercessor whom the Scriptures set before
us is Christ. He is to be prayed to, and he has promised to hear 3
our prayers. Such worship Christ especially approves, namely, that
in all afflictions he be called upon. "If anyone sins, we have an 4
advocate with the Father," etc. (I John 2:1).

This is about the sum of our teaching. As can be seen, there 1
is nothing here that departs from the Scriptures or the catholic church
or the church of Rome, in so far as the ancient church is known to
us from its writers. Since this is so, those who insist that our teachers
are to be regarded as heretics judge too harshly. The whole dissen- 2
sion is concerned with a certain few abuses which have crept into
the churches without proper authority. Even if there were some difference in these, the bishops should have been so lenient as to bear

[5] Fathers of the ancient church in the West.

those who presume to reject, avoid, and separate from our churches as if our teaching were heretical, act in an unkind and hasty fashion, contrary to all Christian unity and love, and do so without any solid basis of divine command or Scripture. The dispute and dissension 2 are concerned chiefly with various traditions and abuses. Since, then, there is nothing unfounded or defective in the principal articles and since this our confession is seen to be godly and Christian, the bishops should in all fairness act more leniently, even if there were some defect among us in regard to traditions, although we hope to offer firm grounds and reasons why we have changed certain traditions and abuses.

ARTICLES ABOUT MATTERS IN DISPUTE, IN WHICH AN ACCOUNT IS GIVEN OF THE ABUSES WHICH HAVE BEEN CORRECTED

From the above it is manifest that nothing is taught in our churches concerning articles of faith that is contrary to the Holy Scriptures or what is common to the Christian church. However, inasmuch as some

---

with us on account of the confession which we have now drawn up, for even the canons are not so severe as to demand that rites should be the same everywhere, nor have the rites of all the churches ever 3 been the same. Among us the ancient rites are for the most part 4 diligently observed, for it is false and malicious to charge that all ceremonies and all old ordinances are abolished in our churches. But it has been a common complaint that certain abuses were con- 5 nected with ordinary rites. Because these could not be approved with a good conscience, they have to some extent been corrected.

ARTICLES IN WHICH AN ACCOUNT IS GIVEN OF THE ABUSES WHICH HAVE BEEN CORRECTED

Inasmuch as our churches dissent from the church catholic in 1 no article of faith but only omit some few abuses which are new and have been adopted by the fault of the times although contrary to the

abuses have been corrected (some of the abuses having crept in over the years and others of them having been introduced with violence), we are obliged by our circumstances to give an account of them and to indicate our reasons for permitting changes in these cases in order that Your Imperial Majesty may perceive that we have not acted in an unchristian and frivolous manner but have been compelled by God's command (which is rightly to be regarded as above all custom) to allow such changes.

XXII. Both Kinds in the Sacrament

Among us both kinds are given to laymen in the sacrament. The   1 reason is that there is a clear command and order of Christ, "Drink of it, all of you" (Matt. 26:27). Concerning the chalice Christ   2 here commands with clear words that all should drink of it.

In order that no one might question these words and interpret   3 them as if they apply only to priests, Paul shows in I Cor. 11:20ff.

---

intent of the canons, we pray that Your Imperial Majesty will graciously hear both what has been changed and what our reasons for such changes are in order that the people may not be compelled to observe these abuses against their conscience.

Your Imperial Majesty should not believe those who disseminate   2 astonishing slanders among the people in order to inflame the hatred of men against us. By thus exciting the minds of good men, they   3 first gave occasion to this controversy, and now they are trying by the same method to increase the discord. Your Imperial Majesty   4 will undoubtedly discover that the forms of teaching and of ceremonies observed among us are not so intolerable as those ungodly and malicious men represent. The truth cannot be gathered from common   5 rumors or the accusations of our enemies. However, it can readily   6 be judged that nothing contributes so much to the maintenance of dignity in public worship and the cultivation of reverence and devotion among the people as the proper observance of ceremonies in the churches.

XXII. Both Kinds

In the sacrament of the Lord's Supper both kinds are given to   1 laymen because this usage has the command of the Lord in Matt. 26:27, "Drink of it, all of you." Christ has here manifestly commanded with reference to the cup that all should drink of it.   2

Lest anybody should captiously object that this refers only to   3 priests, Paul in I Cor. 11:20ff. cites an example from which it appears

that the whole assembly of the congregation in Corinth received both
kinds. This usage continued in the church for a long time, as can   4
be demonstrated from history and from writings of the Fathers.[6]
In several places Cyprian mentions that the cup was given to   5
laymen in his time.[7] St. Jerome also states that the priests who   6
administered the sacrament distributed the blood of Christ to the
people.[8] Pope Gelasius himself ordered that the sacrament was not   7
to be divided.[9] Not a single canon can be found which requires   8
the reception of only one kind. Nobody knows when or through
whom this custom of receiving only one kind was introduced, although
Cardinal Cusanus mentions when the use was approved.[1] It is   10
evident that such a custom, introduced contrary to God's command
and also contrary to the ancient canons, is unjust. Accordingly   11
it is not proper to burden the consciences of those who desire to
observe the sacrament according to Christ's institution or to compel
them to act contrary to the arrangement of our Lord Christ.

---

that a whole congregation used both kinds. This usage continued   4
in the church for a long time. It is not known when or by whom it
was changed, although Cardinal Cusanus mentions when the change
was approved. Cyprian in several places testifies that the blood   5
was given to the people. The same is testified by Jerome, who said,   6
"The priests administer the Eucharist and distribute the blood of
Christ to the people." In fact, Pope Gelasius commanded that the   7
sacrament should not be divided. It is only a custom of quite recent 8
times that holds otherwise. But it is evident that a custom intro-   9
duced contrary to the commands of God is not to be approved, as
the canons testify (Dist. 3, chap. "Veritate" and the following chapters). This custom has been adopted not only in defiance of the   10
Scriptures but also in contradiction to ancient canons and the example
of the church. Consequently, if any people preferred to use both   11
kinds in the sacrament, they should not have been compelled, with
offense to their consciences, to do otherwise. Because the division 12

[6] In the West the cup was generally given to the laity until the thirteenth
century.

[7] Cyprian, Epistle 57

[8] Jerome, *Commentary on Zephaniah*, 3.

[9] Gratian, *Decretum*, Part III, *De consecratione*, dist. 2, chap. 12.

[1] Nicholas of Cusa (1401-1464), Epistle III to the Bohemians, refers the
authorization for the withdrawal of the cup to the Fourth Lateran Council,
1215.

Because the division of the sacrament is contrary to the institution   12
of Christ, the customary carrying about of the sacrament in processions is also omitted by us.[2]

XXIII. THE MARRIAGE OF PRIESTS

Among all people, both of high and of low degree, there has   1
been loud complaint throughout the world concerning the flagrant
immorality and the dissolute life of priests who were not able to
remain continent and who went so far as to engage in abominable
vices. In order to avoid such unbecoming offense, adultery, and   3
other lechery, some of our priests have entered the married state.
They have given as their reason that they have been impelled and
moved to take this step by the great distress of their consciences,
especially since the Scriptures clearly assert that the estate of marriage was instituted by the Lord God to avoid immorality, for Paul   4
says, "Because of the temptation to immorality, each man should
have his own wife" (I Cor. 7:2), and again, "It is better to marry
than to be aflame with passion" (I Cor. 7:9). Moreover, when   5
Christ said in Matt. 19:11, "Not all men can receive this precept,"

---

of the sacrament does not agree with the institution of Christ, the
processions which were hitherto held are also omitted among us.

XXIII. THE MARRIAGE OF PRIESTS

There has been common complaint concerning priests who have   1
not been continent. On this account Pope Pius is reported to have   2
said that there were some reasons why priests were forbidden to marry
but that there are now far weightier reasons why this right should
be restored. Platina writes to this effect.[3] Since priests among us   3
desired to avoid such open scandals, they took wives and taught that
it was lawful for them to contract matrimony. In the first place,   4
this was done because Paul says, "Because of the temptation to immorality each man should have his own wife" (I Cor. 7:2), and again,
"It is better to marry than to be aflame with passion" (I Cor. 7:9).
In the second place, Christ said, "Not all men can receive this pre-   5
cept" (Matt. 19:11), by which he declared that all men are not suited

---

[2] Reference is to the observance of the Corpus Christi festival on the
Thursday following Trinity Sunday. The Evangelical princes refused to
participate in the Corpus Christi procession in Augsburg on June 16, 1530.
Even "carrying the sacrament across the street" was later forbidden.

[3] See note 7 which follows.

he indicated that few people have the gift of living in celibacy, and he certainly knew man's nature. God created man as male and female according to Gen. 1:27. Experience has made it all too manifest 6 whether or not it lies in human power and ability to improve or change the creation of God, the supreme Majesty, by means of human resolutions or vows without a special gift or grace of God. What good has resulted? What honest and chaste manner of life, what Christian, upright, and honorable sort of conduct has resulted in many cases? It is well known what terrible torment and frightful disturbance of conscience many have experienced on their death-beds on this account, and many have themselves acknowledged this. Since God's Word and command cannot be altered by any 8 human vows or laws, our priests and other clergy have taken 9 wives to themselves for these and other reasons and causes.

It can be demonstrated from history and from the writings of 10 the Fathers that it was customary for priests and deacons to marry in the Christian church of former times. Paul therefore said in 11 I Tim. 3:2, "A bishop must be above reproach, married only once." It was only four hundred years ago that the priests in Germany 12 were compelled by force to take the vows of celibacy.[4] At that time there was such serious and strong resistance that an archbishop of Mayence[5] who had published the new papal decree was almost killed

---

for celibacy because God created man for procreation (Gen. 1:28). Moreover, it is not in man's power to alter his creation without 6 a singular gift and work of God. Therefore those who are not 7 suited for celibacy ought to marry, for no law of man and no vow 8 can nullify a commandment of God and an institution of God. For these reasons our priests teach that it is lawful for them 9 to have wives.

It is also evident that in the ancient church priests were married 10 men. Paul said that a married man should be chosen to be bishop 11 (I Tim. 3:2), and not until four hundred years ago were priests 12 in Germany compelled by force to live in celibacy. In fact, they offered such resistance that the archbishop of Mayence, when about to publish the Roman pontiff's edict on this matter, was almost killed

[4] Although the requirement of celibacy was frequently asserted and practiced in earlier centuries, it was not until the end of the eleventh century that it was generally enforced by Pope Gregory VII. At that time most of the priests in Germany were still married.

[5] Siegfried of Mayence at synods in Erfurt and Mayence in 1075.

during an uprising of the entire body of priests. The decree concerning celibacy was at once enforced so hastily and indecently that the
pope at the time not only forbade future marriages of priests but also
broke up the marriages which were of long standing. This was of   13
course not only contrary to all divine, natural, and civil law, but
was also utterly opposed and contrary to the canons which the popes
had themselves made and to the decisions of the most renowned
councils.[6]

Many devout and intelligent people in high station have expressed
similar opinions and the misgiving that such enforced celibacy and
such prohibition of marriage (which God himself instituted and left
free to man) never produced any good but rather gave occasion
for many great and evil vices and much scandal. As his biography
shows, even one of the popes, Pius II, often said and allowed himself
to be quoted as saying that while there may well have been some
reasons for prohibiting the marriage of clergymen, there were now
more important, better, and weightier reasons for permitting them
to be married.[7] There is no doubt that Pope Pius, as a prudent and
intelligent man, made this statement because of grave misgivings.

In loyalty to Your Imperial Majesty we therefore feel confident   14
that, as a most renowned Christian emperor, Your Majesty will graciously take into account the fact that, in these last times of which
the Scriptures prophesy, the world is growing worse and men are
becoming weaker and more infirm.

Therefore it is most necessary, profitable, and Christian to recognize this fact in order that the prohibition of marriage may not cause

---

by the enraged priests in an uprising. In such a harsh manner   13
was the edict carried out that not only were future marriages prohibited but existing marriages were also dissolved, although this was
contrary to all laws, divine and human, and contrary even to the
canons, both those made by the popes and those made by the most
celebrated councils.

Inasmuch as the world is growing old and man's nature is be-   14
coming weaker, it is also well to take precautions against the introduction into Germany of more vices.

[6] Gratian, *Decretum*, I, dist. 82, chap. 2-5; also dist. 84, chap. 4. The
Council of Nicaea refused to require celibacy; see Evagrius, *Ecclesiastical
History*, I, 11.
[7] In his history of the popes (1479) the Italian humanist Bartolomeo
Platina reported Pope Pius II (1458-64) as saying this.

worse and more disgraceful lewdness and vice to prevail in German lands. No one is able to alter or arrange such matters in a better or wiser way than God himself, who instituted marriage to aid 15 human infirmity and prevent unchastity.

The old canons also state that it is sometimes necessary to 16 relax severity and rigor for the sake of human weakness and to prevent and avoid greater offense.[8]

In this case relaxation would certainly be both Christian and very necessary. How would the marriage of priests and the clergy, and especially of the pastors and others who are to minister to the church, be of disadvantage to the Christian church as a whole? If this hard 17 prohibition of marriage is to continue longer, there may be a shortage of priests and pastors in the future.

As we have observed, the assertion that priests and clergymen 18 may marry is based on God's Word and command. Besides, history demonstrates both that priests were married and that the vow of celibacy has been the cause of so much frightful and unchristian offense, so much adultery, and such terrible, shocking immorality and abominable vice that even some honest men among the cathedral clergy and some of the courtiers in Rome have often acknowledged this and have complained that such vices among the clergy would, on account of their abomination and prevalence, arouse the wrath of God. It is therefore deplorable that Christian marriage has not only been forbidden but has in many places been swiftly punished, as if it were a great crime, in spite of the fact that in the Holy Scrip- 19 tures God commanded that marriage be held in honor. Marriage 20

Besides, God instituted marriage to be a remedy against human 15 infirmity. The canons themselves state that in later times the old 16 rigor should be relaxed now and then on account of man's weakness, and it is devoutly to be desired that this be done in the case of sacerdotal marriage. And it seems that the churches will soon be 17 lacking in pastors if marriage continues to be forbidden.

Although the commandment of God is in force, although the 18 custom of the church is well known, and although impure celibacy causes many scandals, adulteries, and other crimes which deserve the punishments of just magistrates, yet it is a marvelous thing that nowhere is greater cruelty exercised than in opposition to the marriage of priests. God has commanded that marriage be held in 19

[8] Gratian, *Decretum*, Part I, dist. 34, chap. 7; Part II, chap. 1, q.7, c.5.

has also been highly praised in the imperial laws and in all states in which there have been laws and justice. Only in our time does 21 one begin to persecute innocent people simply because they are married—and especially priests, who above all others should be spared —although this is done contrary not only to divine law but also to canon law. In I Tim. 4:1, 3 the apostle Paul calls the teaching 22 that forbids marriage a doctrine of the devil. Christ himself 23 asserts that the devil is a murderer from the beginning (John 8:44). These two statements fit together well, for it must be a doctrine of the devil to forbid marriage and then to be so bold as to maintain such a teaching with the shedding of blood.

However, just as no human law can alter or abolish a command 24 of God, neither can any vow alter a command of God. St. Cyprian 25 therefore offered the counsel that women who were unable to keep their vows of chastity should marry. He wrote in his eleventh letter, "If they are unwilling or unable to keep their chastity, it is better for them to marry than to fall into the fire through their lusts, and they should see to it that they do not give their brothers and sisters occasion for offense." [9]

In addition, all the canons show great leniency and fairness 26 toward those who have made vows in their youth[1]—and most of the

---

honor. The laws of all well-ordered states, even among the 20 heathen, have adorned marriage with the greatest praise. But now 21 men, and even priests, are cruelly put to death, contrary to the intent of the canons, for no other cause than marriage. To prohibit 22 marriage is called a doctrine of demons by Paul in I Tim. 4:3. This can be readily understood now that the prohibition of marriage is maintained by means of such penalties. 23

Just as no human law can nullify a command of God, so no vow 24 can do so. Accordingly Cyprian advised that women who did not 25 keep the chastity which they had promised should marry. His words in the first book of his letters, Epistle XI, are these: "If they are unwilling or unable to persevere, it is better for them to marry than to fall into the fire through their lusts; at least they should give no offense to their brothers and sisters."

The canons show some consideration toward those who have 26

---

[9] Cyprian, *Epistles*, 62, 2. The text refers to the numbering of Cyprian's letters adopted by Erasmus.

[1] Gratian, *Decretum*, Part II, chap. 20, q.1, c.5, 7, 9, 10, 14, 15.

priests and monks entered into their estates ignorantly when they were young.

XXIV. THE MASS

We are unjustly accused of having abolished the Mass.[2] With- | 9 out boasting, it is manifest that the Mass is observed among us with greater devotion and more earnestness than among our opponents. Moreover, the people are instructed often and with great diligence 7 concerning the holy sacrament, why it was instituted, and how it is to be used (namely, as a comfort for terrified consciences) in order that the people may be drawn to the Communion and Mass. The people are also given instruction about other false teachings concerning the sacrament. Meanwhile no conspicuous changes have 2 been made in the public ceremonies of the Mass, except that in certain places German hymns are sung in addition to the Latin responses for the instruction and exercise of the people. After all, the chief 3 purpose of all ceremonies is to teach the people what they need to know about Christ.

---

made vows before attaining a proper age, and as a rule vows used to be so made in former times.

XXIV. THE MASS

Our churches are falsely accused of abolishing the Mass. Actu- | ally, the Mass is retained among us and is celebrated with the greatest reverence. Almost all the customary ceremonies are also retained, 2 except that German hymns are interspersed here and there among the parts sung in Latin. These are added for the instruction of the people, for ceremonies are needed especially in order that the 3 unlearned may be taught. Paul prescribed that in church a language 4 should be used which is understood by the people.[3] The people 5 are accustomed to receive the sacrament together, in so far as they are fit to do so. This likewise increases the reverence and devotion 6 of public worship, for none are admitted unless they are first heard and examined. The people are also admonished concerning the 7 value and use of the sacrament and the great consolation it offers to anxious consciences, that they may learn to believe in God and ask for and expect whatever is good from God. Such worship pleases 8

[2] E.g., by John Eck, *404 Theses*, Nos. 269-278. This article makes it clear, of course, that retention of the Mass does not mean retention of abuses.
[3] I Cor. 14:2, 9.

Before our time, however, the Mass came to be misused in   10
many ways, as is well known, by turning it into a sort of fair, by
buying and selling it, and by observing it in almost all churches for a
monetary consideration. Such abuses were often condemned by learned
and devout men even before our time.[4] Then when our preachers   12
preached about these things and the priests were reminded of the
terrible responsibility which should properly concern every Christian
(namely, that whoever uses the sacrament unworthily is guilty of the
body and blood of Christ),[5] such mercenary Masses and private   13
Masses,[6] which had hitherto been held under compulsion for the sake
of revenues and stipends, were discontinued in our churches.

God, and such use of the sacrament nourishes devotion to God.
Accordingly it does not appear that the Mass is observed with   9
more devotion among our adversaries than among us.

However, it is evident that for a long time there has been   10
open and very grievous complaint by all good men that Masses were
being shamefully profaned and applied to purposes of gain. It is   11
also well known how widely this abuse extends in all the churches,
by what manner of men Masses are celebrated only for revenues
or stipends, and how many celebrate Masses contrary to the canons. But Paul severely threatened those who dealt unworthily   12
with the Eucharist when he said, "Whoever eats the bread or drinks
the cup of the Lord in an unworthy manner will be guilty of profaning the body and blood of the Lord." Accordingly when our   13
priests were admonished concerning this sin, private Masses were
discontinued among us inasmuch as hardly any private Masses were
held except for the sake of gain.

The bishops were not ignorant of these abuses. If they had   14
corrected them in time, there would now have been less dissension.
By their own negligence they let many corruptions creep into   15
the church. Now when it is too late they are beginning to com-   16
plain about the troubles of the church, although the disturbance was
brought about by nothing else than those abuses which had become
so manifest that they could no longer be borne. Great dissensions   17
have arisen concerning the Mass, concerning the sacrament. Per-   18

---

[4] By men like Nicholas of Cusa, John Tauler, John Gerson, and Gabriel
Biel.

[5] I Cor. 11:27.

[6] Masses said for the special intentions of individuals, often called Votive
Masses.

At the same time the abominable error was condemned accord- 21
ing to which it was taught that our Lord Christ had by his death made
satisfaction only for original sin, and had instituted the Mass as a
sacrifice for other sins. This transformed the Mass into a sacrifice 22
for the living and the dead, a sacrifice by means of which sin was
taken away and God was reconciled. Thereupon followed a de- 23
bate as to whether one Mass held for many people merited as much
as a special Mass held for an individual. Out of this grew the countless multiplication of Masses, by the performance of which men
expected to get everything they needed from God. Meanwhile faith
in Christ and true service of God were forgotten.

Demanded without doubt by the necessity of such circum- 24
stances, instruction was given so that our people might know how the
sacrament is to be used rightly. They were taught, first of all, 26
that the Scriptures show in many places that there is no sacrifice for
original sin, or for any other sin, except the one death of Christ.

---

haps the world is being punished for such long continued profanations
of the Mass as have been tolerated in the church for many centuries
by the very men who were able to correct them and were under
obligation to do so. For in the Decalogue it is written, "The 19
Lord will not hold him guiltless who takes his name in vain." [7]
Since the beginning of the world nothing of divine institution 20
seems ever to have been so abused for the sake of gain as the Mass.

To all this was added an opinion which infinitely increased 21
private Masses, namely, that Christ had by his passion made satisfaction for original sin and had instituted the Mass in which an oblation
should be made for daily sins, mortal and venial. From this has 22
come the common opinion that the Mass is a work which by its
performance[8] takes away the sins of the living and the dead. Thus 23
was introduced a debate on whether one Mass said for many people
is worth as much as special Masses said for individuals, and this
produced that infinite proliferation of Masses to which reference has
been made.

Concerning these opinions our teachers have warned that they 24
depart from the Holy Scriptures and diminish the glory of Christ's
passion, for the passion of Christ was an oblation and satisfaction 25
not only for original guilt but also for other sins. So it is written 26

[7] Ex. 20:7.
[8] *Ex opere operato.*

For it is written in the Epistle to the Hebrews that Christ 27 offered himself once and by this offering made satisfaction for all sin.[9] It is an unprecedented novelty in church doctrine that Christ's 25 death should have made satisfaction only for original sin and not for other sins as well. Accordingly it is to be hoped that everyone will understand that this error is not unjustly condemned.

In the second place, St. Paul taught that we obtain grace before 28 God through faith and not through works. Manifestly contrary 29 to this teaching is the misuse of the Mass by those who think that grace is obtained through the performance of this work, for it is well known that the Mass is used to remove sin and obtain grace and all sorts of benefits from God, not only for the priest himself but also for the whole world and for others, both living and dead.

In the third place, the holy sacrament was not instituted to 30 make provision for a sacrifice for sin—for the sacrifice has already taken place—but to awaken our faith and comfort our consciences when we perceive that through the sacrament grace and forgiveness of sin are promised us by Christ. Accordingly the sacrament requires faith, and without faith it is used in vain.

---

in the Epistle to the Hebrews, "We have been sanctified through the offering of the body of Jesus Christ once for all," and again, 27 "By a single offering he has perfected for all time those who are sanctified."

The Scriptures also teach that we are justified before God 28 through faith in Christ.[1] Now, if the Mass takes away the sins 29 of the living and the dead by a performance of the outward act,[2] justification comes from the work of the Mass and not from faith. But the Scriptures do not allow this.

Christ commands us to do this in remembrance of him.[3] There- 30 fore the Mass was instituted that faith on the part of those who use the sacrament should remember what benefits are received through Christ and should cheer and comfort anxious consciences. For 31 to remember Christ is to remember his benefits and realize that they are truly offered to us; and it is not enough to remember the 32 history, for the Jews and the ungodly can also remember this.

[9] Heb. 9:28; 10:10, 14.
[1] Early variants add: when we believe that our sins are forgiven for Christ's sake.
[2] *Ex opere operato.*
[3] I Cor. 11:25.

Inasmuch, then, as the Mass is not a sacrifice to remove the   34
sins of others, whether living or dead, but should be a Communion
in which the priest and others receive the sacrament for themselves,
it is observed among us in the following manner: On holy days, and
at other times when communicants are present, Mass is held and
those who desire it are communicated. Thus the Mass is pre-   35
served among us in its proper use, the use which was formerly
observed in the church and which can be proved by St. Paul's statement in I Cor. 11:20ff. and by many statements of the Fathers.
For Chrysostom reports how the priest stood every day, inviting   36
some to Communion and forbidding others to approach.[4] The   37
ancient canons also indicate that one man officiated and communicated
the other priests and deacons, for the words of the Nicene canon   38
read, "After the priests the deacons shall receive the sacrament in
order from the bishop or priest." [5]

Since, therefore, no novelty has been introduced which did not   40

Consequently the Mass is to be used to this end, that the sacra-   33
ment is administered to those who have need of consolation. So
Ambrose said, "Because I always sin, I ought always take the
medicine." [6]

Inasmuch as the Mass is such a giving of the sacrament, one   34
common Mass is observed among us on every holy day, and on other
days, if any desire the sacrament, it is also administered to those who
ask for it. Nor is this custom new in the church, for before the   35
time of Gregory the ancients do not mention private Masses but
speak often of the common Mass. Chrysostom says that the   36
priest stands daily at the altar, inviting some to Communion and
keeping others away. And it appears from the ancient canons   37
that some one person or other celebrated Mass and the rest of the
presbyters and deacons received the body of the Lord from him,
for the words of the Nicene canon read, "In order, after the   38
presbyters, let the deacons receive Holy Communion from the bishop
or from a presbyter." Paul also commands concerning Com-   39
munion that one wait for another in order that there may be a
common participation.[7]

Since, therefore, the Mass among us is supported by the ex-   40

[4] Chrysostom, Homily 3 in *Epistle to the Ephesians*, chap. 1.
[5] Canon 18 of the Council of Nicaea.
[6] Free citation from Pseudo-Ambrose, *The Sacraments*, V, 4, 25.
[7] I Cor. 11:33.

exist in the church from ancient times, and since no conspicuous change has been made in the public ceremonies of the Mass except that other unnecessary Masses which were held in addition to the parochial Mass, probably through abuse, have been discontinued, this manner of holding Mass ought not in fairness be condemned as heretical or unchristian. In times past, even in large churches 41 where there were many people, Mass was not held on every day that the people assembled, for according to the Tripartite History, Book 9, on Wednesday and Friday the Scriptures were read and expounded in Alexandria, and all these services were held without Mass.[8]

XXV. CONFESSION

Confession has not been abolished by the preachers on our side. 1 The custom has been retained among us of not administering the sacrament to those who have not previously been examined and absolved. At the same time the people are carefully instructed 2 concerning the consolation of the Word of absolution so that they may esteem absolution as a great and precious thing. It is not the 3 voice or word of the man who speaks it, but it is the Word of God,

---

ample of the church as seen from the Scriptures and the Fathers, we are confident that it cannot be disapproved, especially since the customary public ceremonies are for the most part retained. Only the number of Masses is different, and on account of the great and manifest abuses it would certainly be of advantage to reduce the number. In former times, even in churches most frequented, 41 Mass was not held every day; as the Tripartite History testifies in Book 9, "Again, in Alexandria, the Scriptures are read and the doctors expound them on Wednesday and Friday, and all things are done except for the solemn remembrance of the sacrifice."

XXV. CONFESSION

Confession has not been abolished in our churches, for it is 1 not customary to administer the body of Christ except to those who have previously been examined and absolved. The people are 2 very diligently taught concerning faith in connection with absolution, a matter about which there has been profound silence before this time. Our people are taught to esteem absolution highly because it is 3

[8] The *Tripartite Ecclesiastical History* by the Roman monk Cassiodorus (480-570) was the principal book of church history used in the late Middle Ages, and it quotes here from Socrates, *Ecclesiastical History*, V, 22.

who forgives sin, for it is spoken in God's stead and by God's command. We teach with great diligence about this command and 4 power of keys and how comforting and necessary it is for terrified consciences. We also teach that God requires us to believe this absolution as much as if we heard God's voice from heaven, that we should joyfully comfort ourselves with absolution, and that we should know that through such faith we obtain forgiveness of sins. In 5 former times the preachers who taught much about confession never mentioned a word concerning these necessary matters but only tormented consciences with long enumerations of sins, with satisfactions, with indulgences, with pilgrimages and the like. Many of our op- 6 ponents themselves acknowledge that we have written about and treated of true Christian repentance in a more fitting fashion than had been done for a long time.

Concerning confession we teach that no one should be com- 7 pelled to recount sins in detail, for this is impossible. As the 8 psalmist says, "Who can discern his errors?" [9] Jeremiah also says, "The heart is desperately corrupt; who can understand it?" [1] Our wretched human nature is so deeply submerged in sins that it is unable to perceive or know them all, and if we were to be absolved 9 only from those which we can enumerate we would be helped but

---

the voice of God and is pronounced by God's command. The 4 power of keys is praised, and people are reminded of the great consolation it brings to terrified consciences, are told that God requires faith to believe such absolution as God's own voice heard from heaven, and are assured that such faith truly obtains and receives the forgiveness of sins. In former times satisfactions were immoderately 5 extolled, but nothing was said about faith. Accordingly no fault is to be found with our churches on this point, for even our adver- 6 saries are forced to concede to us that our teachers have shed light on the doctrine of repentance and have treated it with great care.

Concerning confession they teach that an enumeration of sins 7 is not necessary and that consciences should not be burdened with a scrupulous enumeration of all sins because it is impossible to recount all of them. So the Psalm testifies, "Who can discern his errors?" Jeremiah also says, "The heart of man is corrupt and inscrutable." 8 But if no sins were forgiven except those which are recounted, 9

---

* Ps. 19:12.
[1] Jer. 17:9.

little. On this account there is no need to compel people to give a detailed account of their sins. That this was also the view of | 0 the Fathers can be seen in Dist. I, *De poenitentia,* where these | | words of Chrysostom are quoted: "I do not say that you should expose yourself in public or should accuse yourself before others, but obey the prophet who says, 'Show your way to the Lord.' [2] Therefore confess to the Lord God, the true judge, in your prayer, telling him of your sins not with your tongue but in your conscience." [3] Here it can be clearly seen that Chrysostom does not require a detailed enumeration of sins. The marginal note in *De poenitentia,* | 2 Dist. 5,[4] also teaches that such confession is not commanded by the Scriptures but was instituted by the church. Yet the preachers | 3 on our side diligently teach that confession is to be retained for the sake of absolution (which is its chief and most important part), for the consolation of terrified consciences, and also for other reasons.

XXVI. The Distinction of Foods

In former times men taught, preached, and wrote that distinc- | tions among foods and similar traditions which had been instituted

---

our consciences would never find peace, for many sins can neither be perceived nor remembered. The ancient writers also testify | 0 that such an enumeration is not necessary, for Chrysostom is | | quoted in the canons as saying, "I do not say that you should expose yourself in public or should accuse yourself before others, but I wish you to obey the prophet who says, 'Show your way to the Lord.' Therefore, confess your sins to God, the true judge, in your prayer. Tell him of your sins not with your tongue but with the memory of your conscience." The marginal note in *De poenitentia,* Dist. 5, | 2 in the chapter "Consideret," admits that such confession is of human right. Nevertheless, confession is retained among us on account | 3 of the great benefit of absolution and because it is otherwise useful to consciences.

XXVI. The Distinction of Foods

It has been the common opinion not only of the people but | also of those who teach in the churches that distinctions among foods

---

[2] Ps. 37:5 (Vulgate rendering).
[3] Gratian, *Decretum,* Part II, chap. 33, q.3, *De poenitentia,* dist. I, c. 87:4. The quotation is from Chrysostom, Homily 31, in *Epistle to the Hebrews.*
[4] Gloss to Gratian, *Decretum, De poenitentia,* 5:1.

by men serve to earn grace and make satisfaction for sin.[5] For 2 this reason new fasts, new ceremonies, new orders, and the like were invented daily, and were ardently and urgently promoted, as if these were a necessary service of God by means of which grace would be earned if they were observed and a great sin committed if they were omitted. Many harmful errors in the church have resulted from 3 this.

In the first place, the grace of Christ and the teaching concern- 4 ing faith are thereby obscured, and yet the Gospel earnestly urges them upon us and strongly insists that we regard the merit of Christ as something great and precious and know that faith in Christ is to be esteemed far above all works. On this account St. Paul con- 5 tended mightily against the law of Moses and against human tradition so that we should learn that we do not become good in God's sight by our works but that it is only through faith in Christ that we obtain grace for Christ's sake. This teaching has been almost 6 completely extinguished by those who have taught that grace is to be earned by prescribed fasts, distinctions among foods, vestments, etc.

---

and similar human traditions are works which are profitable to merit grace and make satisfactions for sins. That the world thought so 2 is evident from the fact that new ceremonies, new orders, new holy days, and new fasts were daily instituted, and the learned men in the churches exacted these works as a service necessary to merit grace and sorely terrified the consciences of those who omitted any of them. From this opinion concerning traditions much harm has resulted 3 in the church.

In the first place, it has obscured the doctrine concerning grace 4 and the righteousness of faith, which is the chief part of the Gospel and ought above all else to be in the church, and to be prominent in it, so that the merit of Christ may be well known and that faith which believes that sins are forgiven for Christ's sake may be exalted far above works and above all other acts of worship. Paul there- 5 fore lays the greatest weight on this article and puts aside the law and human traditions in order to show that the righteousness of a Christian is something other than works of this sort; it is faith which believes that for Christ's sake we are received into grace. This 6 teaching of Paul has been almost wholly smothered by traditions which have produced the opinion that it is necessary to merit grace and

[5] E.g., Thomas Aquinas, *Summa theologica*, II, 2. q.147, a, 1, c.

In the second place, such traditions have also obscured the 8 commands of God, for these traditions were exalted far above God's commands. This also was regarded as Christian life: whoever 9 observed festivals in this way, prayed in this way, fasted in this way, and dressed in this way was said to live a spiritual and Christian life. On the other hand, other necessary good works were considered 10 secular and unspiritual: the works which everybody is obliged to do according to his calling—for example, that a husband should labor to support his wife and children and bring them up in the fear of God, that a wife should bear children and care for them, that a prince and magistrates should govern land and people, etc. Such works, 11 commanded by God, were to be regarded as secular and imperfect, while traditions were to be given the glamorous title of alone being holy and perfect works. Accordingly there was no end or limit to the making of such traditions.

In the third place, such traditions have turned out to be a 12 grievous burden to consciences, for it was not possible to keep all the traditions, and yet the people were of the opinion that they were

---

righteousness by distinctions among foods and similar acts of worship. In treating of repentance no mention was made of faith; only 7 works of satisfaction were proposed, and the whole of repentance was thought to consist of these.

In the second place, these precepts obscured the commands of 8 God, for traditions were exalted far above the commands of God. Christianity was thought to consist wholly in the observance of certain holy days, rites, fasts, and vestments. Such observances claimed 9 for themselves the glamorous title of comprising the spiritual life and the perfect life. Meanwhile the commands of God pertaining to 10 callings were without honor—for example, that a father should bring up his children, that a mother should bear children, that a prince should govern his country. These were regarded as secular and imperfect works, far inferior to those glittering observances. This error 11 greatly tormented the consciences of devout people who grieved that they were bound to an imperfect kind of life—in marriage, in the magistracy, or in other civil occupations—and admired the monks and others like them, falsely imagining that the observances of such men were more pleasing to God.

In the third place, traditions brought great dangers to con- 12 sciences, for it was impossible to keep all traditions, and yet men judged these observances to be necessary acts of worship. Gerson 13

a necessary service of God. Gerson writes that many fell into   13
despair on this account, and some even committed suicide, because
they had not heard anything of the consolation of the grace of
Christ. We can see in the writings of the summists[6] and can-   14
onists[7] how consciences have been confused, for they undertook to
collate the traditions and sought mitigations to relieve consciences,
but they were so occupied with such efforts that they neglected all   15
wholesome Christian teachings about more important things, such
as faith, consolation in severe trials, and the like. Many devout   16
and learned people before our time have also complained that such
traditions caused so much strife in the church that godly people were
thereby hindered from coming to a right knowledge of Christ. Gerson
and others have complained bitterly about this.[8] In fact, Augustine   17
was also displeased that consciences were burdened with so many
traditions, and he taught in this connection that they were not to
be considered necessary observances.[9]

Our teachers have not taught concerning these matters out of   18

---

writes that many fell into despair, and some even took their own lives,
because they felt that they could not keep the traditions and, meanwhile, they had never heard the consolation of grace and of the righteousness of faith. We see that the summists and theologians   14
gathered the traditions together and sought mitigations to relieve
consciences; yet they did not altogether succeed in releasing them but
rather entangled consciences even more. Schools and sermons   15
were so preoccupied with gathering traditions that they have had no
time to treat the Scriptures and seek for the more profitable teachings
concerning faith, the cross, hope, the importance of civil affairs, and
the consolation of sorely tried consciences. Hence Gerson and   16
certain other theologians greatly lamented that they were so hindered
by these bickerings about traditions that they were unable to devote
their attention to a better kind of teaching. Augustine also forbids   17
the burdening of consciences with such observances and prudently
admonishes Januarius that he should know that they are to be as
things indifferent, for these are his words.

Our teachers, therefore, must not be looked upon as having   18

[6] Authors of such collections of cases of conscience in the Middle Ages
as Sylvester Prierias' *Summa summarum*.

[7] Experts in canon law.

[8] John Gerson, *The Spiritual Life*, lectio 2

[9] Augustine, Epistle 54 to Januarius, 2:2.

malice or contempt of spiritual authority, but dire need has 19
compelled them to give instruction about the aforementioned errors
which have arisen from a wrong estimation of tradition. The 20
Gospel demands that the teaching about faith should and must be
emphasized in the church, but this teaching cannot be understood if
it is supposed that grace is earned through self-chosen works.

It is therefore taught that grace cannot be earned, God cannot 21
be reconciled, and sin cannot be atoned for by observing the said
human traditions. Accordingly they should not be made into a
necessary service of God. Reasons for this shall be cited from 22
the Scriptures. In Matt. 15:1-20 Christ defends the apostles for not
observing the customary traditions, and he adds, "In vain do they
worship me, teaching as doctrines the precepts of men" (Matt.
15:9). Since he calls them vain service, they must not be neces- 23
sary. Thereupon Christ says, "Not what goes into the mouth defiles
a man." [1] Paul also says in Rom. 14:17, "The kingdom of God 24
does not mean food and drink," and in Col. 2:16 he says, "Let 25
no one pass judgment on you in questions of food and drink or with

---

taken up this matter rashly or out of hatred for the bishops, as some
wrongly suspect. There was great need to warn the churches of 19
these errors which had arisen from misunderstanding of traditions.
For the Gospel compels us to insist in the church on the teaching 20
concerning grace and the righteousness of faith, and this cannot be
understood if men suppose that they merit grace by observances of
their own choice.

Accordingly our teachers have taught that we cannot merit 21
grace or make satisfaction for sins by the observance of human traditions. Hence observances of this kind are not to be thought of as
necessary acts of worship. Our teachers add testimonies from 22
the Scriptures. In Matt. 15:1-20 Christ defends the apostles for
not observing the customary tradition, a tradition which was seen
to be legalistic and to have a relationship with the purifications of
the law, and he says, "In vain do they worship me with the precepts
of men." So he does not require an unprofitable act of worship. 23
Shortly afterward Christ says, "Not what goes into the mouth defiles
a man." It is also written in Rom. 14:17, "The kingdom of God 24
is not food and drink," and in Col. 2:16, "Let no one pass judg- 25
ment on you in questions of food and drink or with regard to a

[1] Matt. 15:11.

regard to a festival," etc. In Acts 15:10, 11 Peter says, "Why do   27
you make trial of God by putting a yoke upon the neck of the disciples which neither our fathers nor we have been able to bear? But
we believe that we shall be saved through the grace of the Lord Jesus,
just as they will." Here Peter forbids the burdening of con-   28
sciences with additional outward ceremonies, whether of Moses or
of another. In I Tim. 4:1, 3 such prohibitions as forbid food or   29
marriage are called a doctrine of the devil, for it is diametrically
opposed to the Gospel to institute or practice such works for the
purpose of earning forgiveness of sin or with the notion that nobody
is a Christian unless he performs such services.

Although our teachers are, like Jovinian,[2] accused of forbid-   30
ding mortification and discipline, their writings reveal something
quite different. They have always taught concerning the holy   31
cross that Christians are obliged to suffer, and this is true and   32
real rather than invented mortification.

---

festival or a sabbath." [3] In Acts 15:10, 11 Peter says, "Why do   27
you make trial of God by putting a yoke upon the neck of the
disciples which neither our fathers nor we have been able to bear?
But we believe that we shall be saved through the grace of the Lord
Jesus, just as they will." Here Peter forbids the burdening of   28
consciences with numerous rites, whether of Moses or of others.
And in I Tim. 4:1, 3 Paul calls the prohibition of foods a doctrine   29
of demons, for it is in conflict with the Gospel to institute or practice
such works for the purpose of meriting grace through them or with
the notion that Christian righteousness cannot exist without such acts
of worship.

Here our adversaries charge that our teachers, like Jovinian,   30
forbid discipline and mortification of the flesh. But something different
may be perceived in the writings of our teachers, for they have   31
always taught concerning the cross that Christians are obliged to suffer
afflictions. To be harassed by various afflictions and to be cru-   32
cified with Christ is true and real, rather than invented, mortification.

---

  [2] The Reformers were here misled by Jerome's slanderous misrepresentation of Jovinian, Roman ascetic of the fourth century who contended against
the monastic teaching about merits and the stages of ethical perfection but
not against "mortification and discipline."

  [3] The so-called *editio princeps* here inserts: "If with Christ you died   26
to the elemental spirits of the universe, why do you live as if you still belonged to the world? Why do you submit to regulations, 'Do not handle,
Do not taste, Do not touch'?" (Col. 2:20, 21).

They also teach that everybody is under obligation to conduct 33 himself, with reference to such bodily exercise as fasting and other discipline, so that he does not give occasion to sin, but not as if he earned grace by such works. Such bodily exercise should not be 34 limited to certain specified days but should be practiced continually. Christ speaks of this in Luke 21:34, "Take heed to your- 35 selves lest your hearts be weighed down with dissipation," and 36 again, "This kind of demon cannot be driven out by anything but fasting and prayer." [4] Paul said that he pommeled his body and 37 subdued it,[5] and by this he indicated that it is not the purpose of 38 mortification to merit grace but to keep the body in such a condition that one can perform the duties required by one's calling. Thus 39 fasting in itself is not rejected, but what is rejected is making a necessary service of fasts on prescribed days and with specified foods, for this confuses consciences.

We on our part also retain many ceremonies and traditions 40 (such as the liturgy of the Mass and various canticles, festivals, and the like) which serve to preserve order in the church. At the same 41

Besides, they teach that every Christian ought so to control 33 and curb himself with bodily discipline, or bodily exercises and labors, that neither plenty nor idleness may tempt him to sin, but not in order to merit forgiveness of sins or satisfaction for sins by means of such exercises. Such bodily discipline ought to be encouraged 34 at all times, and not merely on a few prescribed days. So Christ 35 commands, "Take heed to yourselves lest your hearts be weighed down with dissipation," and again, "This kind of demon cannot 36 be driven out by anything but fasting and prayer." Paul also said, 37 "I pommel my body and subdue it." By this he clearly shows that 38 he pommeled his body not to merit forgiveness of sins by that discipline but to keep his body in subjection and fit for spiritual things and for discharging his duty according to his calling. Condemned 39 therefore is not fasting in itself, but traditions which with peril to conscience prescribe certain days and certain foods as if works of this sort were necessary acts of worship.

Many traditions are nevertheless kept among us (such as the 40 order of lessons in the Mass, holy days, etc.) which are profitable for maintaining good order in the church. At the same time men are 41

[4] Mark 9:29.
[5] I Cor. 9:27.

time, however, the people are instructed that such outward forms
of service do not make us righteous before God and that they are
to be observed without burdening consciences, which is to say that
it is not a sin to omit them if this is done without causing scandal.
The ancient Fathers maintained such liberty with respect to out-   42
ward ceremonies, for in the East they kept Easter at a time dif-   43
ferent from that in Rome.[6] When some regarded this difference as
divisive of the church, they were admonished by others that it was not
necessary to maintain uniformity in such customs. Irenaeus said,   44
"Disagreement in fasting does not destroy unity in faith,"[7] and
there is a statement in Dist. 12 that such disagreement in human
ordinances is not in conflict with the unity of Christendom.[8]
Moreover, the Tripartite History, Book 9, gathers many examples   45
of dissimilar church usages and adds the profitable Christian observation, "It was not the intention of the apostles to institute holy days
but to teach faith and love."[9]

XXVII. MONASTIC VOWS

In discussing monastic vows it is necessary to begin by consider-   1

---

warned that such observances do not justify before God and that no
sin is committed if they are omitted without scandal. Such liberty   42
in human rites was not unknown to the Fathers, for Easter was   43
kept in the East at a time different from that in Rome, and when on
account of this difference the Romans accused the East of schism,
they were admonished by others that such customs need not be alike
everywhere. Irenaeus says, "Disagreement about fasting does not   44
destroy unity in faith," and Pope Gregory indicates in Dist. 12 that
such diversity does not violate the unity of the church. In the   45
Tripartite History, Book 9, many examples of dissimilar rites are
gathered, and this statement is made: "It was not the intention of the
apostles to enact binding laws with respect to holy days but to preach
piety toward God and good conversation among men."

XXVII. MONASTIC VOWS

What is taught among us concerning monastic vows will be   1

---

[6] In Asia Minor Easter was observed on the Jewish Passover while in the
West, as in Palestine and Egypt, it was observed on the Sunday following.
[7] In Eusebius, *Ecclesiastical History*, V. 24, 13.
[8] Gratian, *Decretum*, Part I, dist. 12, chap. 10.
[9] Cassiodorus, *Tripartite Ecclesiastical History*, IX, 38, quoting from
Socrates, *Ecclesiastical History*, V, 22.

ing what opinions have hitherto been held concerning them, what kind of life was lived in the monasteries, and how many of the daily observances in them were contrary not only to the Word of God but also to papal canons. In the days of St. Augustine monastic life   2 was voluntary. Later, when true discipline and doctrine had become corrupted, monastic vows were invented, and the attempt was made to restore discipline by means of these vows as if in a well-conceived prison.[1]

In addition to monastic vows many other requirements were im-   3 posed, and such fetters and burdens were laid on many before   4 they had attained an appropriate age.[2]

Many persons also entered monastic life ignorantly, for   5 although they were not too young, they had not sufficiently appreciated or understood their strength. All of those who were thus   6 ensnared and entangled were pressed and compelled to remain, in spite of the fact that even the papal canons might have set many of them free.[3] The practice was stricter in women's convents than   7 in those of men, though it would have been seemly to show more consideration to women as the weaker sex. Such severity and   8

---

better understood if it is recalled what the condition of monasteries was and how many things were done in these monasteries every day that were contrary to the canons. In Augustine's time they were   2 voluntary associations. Afterward, when discipline fell into decay, vows were added for the purpose of restoring discipline, as in a carefully planned prison. Many other observances were gradually   3 added in addition to vows. These fetters were laid on many,   4 contrary to the canons, before they had attained a lawful age. Many entered this kind of life through ignorance, for although   5 they were not wanting in years, they were unable to judge their own strength. Those who were thus ensnared were compelled to   6 remain, though some could have been freed by appealing to the canons. This was the case in convents of women more than in those of   7 men, although more consideration should have been given to the weaker sex. Such rigor displeased many good men before our   8

[1] Until the Benedictine Rule gained ascendancy in the West, about the eighth century, there was a variety of monastic rules. Withdrawal from monastic life was originally allowable.

[2] The dedication of children to monastic life by their parents was common in the Middle Ages and allowed by canon law.

[3] See above, Art. XXIII, 26.

rigor displeased many devout people in the past, for they must have
seen that both boys and girls were thrust into monasteries to provide
for their maintenance. They must also have seen what evils came
from this arrangement, what scandals and burdened consciences
resulted. Many people complained that in such a momentous   9
matter the canons were not strictly adhered to. Besides, monastic   10
vows gained such a reputation, as is well known, that many monks
with even a little understanding were displeased.

It was claimed that monastic vows were equal to Baptism, and   11
that by monastic life one could earn forgiveness of sin and justification before God.[4] What is more, they added that monastic life   12
not only earned righteousness and godliness, but also that by means
of this life both the precepts and the counsels included in the Gospel
were kept,[5] and so monastic vows were praised more highly than   13
Baptism. They also claimed that more merit could be obtained by
monastic life than by all other states of life instituted by God—whether

---

time when they saw that girls and boys were thrust into monasteries
for their maintenance and saw what unfortunately resulted from this
arrangement, what scandals were created, what snares were placed on
consciences. They regretted that in such a momentous matter the   9
authority of the canons was utterly ignored and despised. To   10
these evils was added the fact that vows had such a reputation that
it was clearly displeasing to those monks in former times who had a
little more understanding.

They said that vows were equal to Baptism, and they taught   11
that they merited forgiveness of sins and justification before God by
this kind of life. What is more, they added that monastic life   12
merited not only righteousness before God but even more, for it was
an observance not only of the precepts but also of the counsels of
the Gospel. Thus they made men believe that the monastic pro-   13
fession was far better than Baptism, and that monastic life was more
meritorious than the life of magistrates, pastors, and the like who,

---

[4] The comparison of monastic profession and Baptism was common in the
Middle Ages. E.g., Thomas Aquinas, *Summa theologica*, II, 2, q.189, a.3
ad 3.

[5] Medieval theologians, following a development which can be traced back
to Tertullian, distinguished between "precepts of the Gospel," which must
be observed for salvation, and "counsels of the Gospel," which are not
obligatory but enable one to attain salvation "better and more quickly."
See, e.g., Bonaventure, *Breviloquium*, V, 9; Thomas Aquinas, *Summa theologica*, II, 1, q.108, a.4.

the office of pastor and preacher, of ruler, prince, lord, or the like,
all of whom serve in their appointed calling according to God's Word
and command without invented spirituality. None of these things 14
can be denied, for they are found in their own books.

Furthermore, those who were thus ensnared and inveigled into 15
a monastery learned little about Christ. Formerly the monasteries
had conducted schools of Holy Scripture and other branches of
learning which are profitable to the Christian church, so that pastors
and bishops were taken from monasteries. But now the picture is
changed. In former times people gathered and adopted monastic 16
life for the purpose of learning the Scriptures, but now it is claimed
that monastic life is of such a nature that thereby God's grace and
righteousness before God are earned. In fact, it is called a state of
perfection[6] and is regarded as far superior to the other estates instituted by God. All this is mentioned, without misrepresenta- 17
tion, in order that one may better grasp and understand what our
teachers teach and preach.

For one thing, it is taught among us with regard to those who 18
desire to marry that all those who are not suited for celibacy have
the power, right, and authority to marry, for vows cannot nullify
God's order and command. God's command in I Cor. 7:2 reads, 19

---

without man-made observances, serve their calling in accordance with
God's commands. None of these things can be denied, for they 14
appear in their own books.

What happened after such people had entered monasteries? 15
Formerly there had been schools of the Holy Scriptures and other
branches of learning which were profitable to the church, and pastors
and bishops were taken from them. Now everything is different, and
it is needless to rehearse what is well known. Formerly people 16
came together in monasteries to learn. Now they pretend that this kind
of life was instituted to merit grace and righteousness. In fact, they
assert that it is a state of perfection, and they put it far above all other
kinds of life instituted by God. We have rehearsed these things 17
without odious exaggeration in order that our teaching on this topic
may better be understood.

In the first place, we teach concerning those who contract matri- 18
mony that it is lawful for all who are not suited for celibacy to marry,
for vows can not nullify the command and institution of God. This 19

---

[6] E.g., Thomas Aquinas, *Summa theologica*, II, 2, q. 186, a, 1, c.

"Because of the temptation to immorality, each man should have his own wife and each woman her own husband." It is not 20 alone God's command that urges, drives, and compels us to do this, but God's creation and order also direct all to marriage who are not endowed with the gift of virginity by a special act of God. This appears from God's own words in Gen. 2:18, "It is not good that the man should be alone; I will make him a helper fit for him."

What objection may be raised to this? No matter how much 22 one extols the vow and the obligation, no matter how highly one exalts them, it is still impossible to abrogate God's command. Learned men say that a vow made contrary to papal canons is not 23 binding.[7] How much less must be their obligation, lawfulness, and power when they are contrary to God's command!

If there were no reasons which allowed annulment of the obli- 24 gation of a vow, the popes could not have dispensed and released men from such obligation, for no man has the right to cancel an obligation which is derived from divine law. Consequently the 25 popes were well aware that some amelioration ought to be exercised in connection with this obligation and have often given dispensa-

---

is the command of God, "Because of fornication let every man have his own wife." Nor is it the command only, but God's creation 20 and institution also compel those to marry who are not excepted by a singular work of God. This is according to the text in Gen. 2:18, "It is not good that the man should be alone." Therefore those 21 who obey this command and institution of God do not sin.

What objection can be raised to this? Exaggerate the obligation 22 of a vow as much as one pleases, it cannot be brought about that a vow abrogates the command of God. The canons state that every 23 vow is subject to the right of a superior. How much less are those vows valid which are made contrary to God's commands!

If the obligation of vows could not be changed for any reason 24 at all, the Roman pontiffs would not have granted dispensations, for it is not lawful for a man to annul an obligation which is plainly derived from divine law. But the Roman pontiffs have prudently 25 judged that leniency should be observed in connection with this obligation. Therefore, we read that they often granted dispensation from

[7] Gratian, *Decretum,* Part II, chap. 20, q.4, c.2, states that a vow made by a monk without the consent of his abbot is without effect.

tions, as in the case of the king of Aragon[8] and many others. 26
If dispensations were granted for the maintenance of temporal interests, how much more should dispensations be granted for necessities
of men's souls!

Why, then, do our opponents insist so strongly that vows must 27
be kept without first ascertaining whether a vow is of the proper sort?
For a vow must involve what is possible and voluntary and must be
uncoerced.[9] Yet it is commonly known to what an extent per- 28
petual chastity lies within human power and ability, and there 29
are few, whether men or women, who have taken monastic vows
of themselves, willingly, and after due consideration. Before they
came to a right understanding they were persuaded to take monastic
vows, and sometimes they have been compelled and forced to do
so. Accordingly it is not right to argue so rashly and insistently 30
about the obligation of vows inasmuch as it is generally conceded
that it belongs to the very nature and character of a vow that it should
be voluntary and should be assumed only after due consideration
and counsel.

Several canons and papal regulations annul vows that are made 31
under the age of fifteen years.[1] They hold that before this age one

---

vows. Well known is the case of the king of Aragon, who was 26
recalled from a monastery, and there is no want of examples in
our time.

In the second place, why do our adversaries exaggerate the obli- 27
gation or effect of a vow while they remain silent concerning the
nature of a vow, which ought to be voluntary and chosen freely and
deliberately? Yet it is not unknown to what an extent perpetual 28
chastity lies in man's power. How few there are who have taken 29
the vow spontaneously and deliberately! Before they are able to judge,
boys and girls are persuaded, and sometimes even compelled, to take
the vow. Accordingly it is not fair to argue so insistently about 30
the obligation inasmuch as it is conceded by all that it is contrary to
the nature of a vow to make a promise which is not spontaneous and
deliberate.

Many canons annul vows made before the age of fifteen on 31
the ground that before that age a person does not seem to have suffi-

---

[8] Ramiro, II, a monk, was released from his vows after the death of his
childless brother so that he might assume the throne.

[9] Cf. Thomas Aquinas, *Summa theologica*, II, 2, q.88, a.1, 8.

[1] Gratian, *Decretum*, Part II, chap. 20, q.1, c.10.

does not possess sufficient understanding to determine or arrange the
order of one's whole future life. Another canon concedes still   32
more years to human frailty, for it prohibits the taking of monastic
vows before the eighteenth year.[2] On the basis of this provision   33
most monastics have excuse and reason for leaving their monasteries
inasmuch as a majority of them entered the cloister in their child-
hood, before attaining such age.

Finally, although the breaking of monastic vows might be   34
censured, it would not follow that the marriage of those who broke
them should be dissolved. For St. Augustine says in his *Nuptiarum,*   35
Question 27, Chapter I, that such a marriage should not be dissolved,[3]
and St. Augustine is no inconsiderable authority in the Christian
church, even though some have subsequently differed from him.

Although God's command concerning marriage frees and re-   36
leases many from monastic vows, our teachers offer still more reasons
why monastic vows are null and void. For all service of God that is
chosen and instituted by men to obtain righteousness and God's grace
without the command and authority of God is opposed to God and
the holy Gospel and contrary to God's command. So Christ himself
says in Matt. 15:9, "In vain do they worship me, teaching as doc-

---

cient judgment to make a decision involving the rest of his life.
Another canon, making a greater concession to human weakness,   32
adds a few years and forbids making a vow before the eighteenth year.
Whether we follow one canon or the other, most monastics have   33
an excuse for leaving the monastery because a majority of them took
vows before they reached such an age.

Finally, although the violation of vows might be rebuked, yet   34
it seems not to follow of necessity that the marriages of persons who
violated them ought to be dissolved. For Augustine denies that   35
they should be dissolved in *Nuptiarum,* Question 27, Chapter I, and
his authority is not inconsiderable, although others have subsequently
differed from him.

Although it appears that God's command concerning marriage   36
frees many from their vows, our teachers offer still another reason
to show that vows are void. Every service of God that is instituted
and chosen by men to merit justification and grace without the command of God is wicked, for Christ says, "In vain do they worship me

---

[2] *Ibid.,* chap. 5.
[3] Augustine, *De bono viduitatis,* chap. 9.

trines the precepts of men." St. Paul also teaches everywhere that 37
one is not to seek for righteousness in the precepts and services invented by men but that righteousness and godliness in God's sight
come from faith and trust when we believe that God receives us into
his favor for the sake of Christ, his only Son.

It is quite evident that the monks have taught and preached 38
that their invented spiritual life makes satisfaction for sin and obtains God's grace and righteousness.[4] What is this but to diminish
the glory and honor of the grace of Christ and deny the righteousness
of faith? It follows from this that the customary vows were an 39
improper and false service of God. Therefore they are not binding,
for an ungodly vow, made contrary to God's command, is null 40
and void. Even the canons teach that an oath should not be an
obligation to sin.[5]

St. Paul says in Gal. 5:4, "You are severed from Christ, you 41
who would be justified by the law; you have fallen away from
grace." In the same way, those who would be justified by vows 42
are severed from Christ and have fallen away from God's grace,
for they rob Christ, who alone justifies, of his honor and bestow 43
this honor on their vows and monastic life.

---

with the precepts of men." Paul also teaches everywhere that 37
righteousness is not to be sought for in observances and services devised
by men but that it comes through faith to those who believe that they
are received by God into favor for Christ's sake.

It is evident that the monks have taught that their invented 38
observances make satisfaction for sins and merit grace and justification.
What is this but to detract from the glory of Christ and obscure and
deny the righteousness of faith? It follows, therefore, that the 39
vows thus customarily taken were wicked services and on this account
were void, for a wicked vow, taken contrary to the commands of 40
God, is invalid. As the canon says, no vow ought to bind men to
iniquity.

Paul says, "You are severed from Christ, you who would be 41
justified by the law; you have fallen away from grace." Therefore 42
those who would be justified by vows are severed from Christ and
fall away from grace, for those who ascribe justification to their 43
vows ascribe to their own works what properly belongs to the glory
of Christ.

[4] Cf. Thomas Aquinas, as cited above under Art. XXVII, 11.
[5] Gratian, *Decretum*, II, chap. 22, q.4, c.22.

One cannot deny that the monks have taught and preached that   44
they were justified and earned forgiveness of sins by their vows and
their monastic life and observances. In fact, they have invented a
still more indecent and absurd claim, namely, that they could apply
their good works to others. If one were inclined to count up all   45
these claims for the purpose of casting them into their teeth, how
many items could be assembled which the monks themselves are now
ashamed of and wish had never occurred! Besides all this, they   46
persuaded the people that the invented spiritual estate of the orders
was Christian perfection.[6] Certainly this is exaltation of works   47
as a means of attaining justification. Now, it is no small offense   48
in the Christian church that the people should be presented with
such a service of God, invented by men without the command of
God, and should be taught that such a service would make men good
and righteous before God. For righteousness of faith, which should
be emphasized above all else in the Christian church, is obscured
when man's eyes are dazzled with this curious angelic spirituality and
sham of poverty, humility, and chastity.

Besides, the commands of God and true and proper service   49
of God are obscured when people are told that monks alone are in a
state of perfection. For this is Christian perfection: that we fear

---

It cannot be denied that the monks taught that they were   44
justified and merited forgiveness of sins by their vows and observances.
In fact, they invented greater absurdities when they claimed that they
could transfer their works to others. If out of hatred anybody   45
should be inclined to enlarge on these claims, how many things could
be collected of which even the monks are now ashamed! Besides   46
all this, they persuaded men that their invented observances were a
state of Christian perfection. Is not this attributing justification   47
to works? It is no light offense in the church to recommend to   48
the people a certain service invented by men without the command
of God and to teach that such service justifies men. For righteousness
of faith, which ought especially to be taught in the church, is obscured
when the eyes of men are blinded by these remarkable angelic observances and this pretense of poverty, humility, and chastity.

Furthermore, the commands of God and true service of God   49
are obscured when men hear that only monks are in a state of perfection. For this is Christian perfection: honestly to fear God and at

[6] See above, Art. XXVII, 16.

God honestly with our whole hearts, and yet have sincere confidence, faith, and trust that for Christ's sake we have a gracious, merciful God; that we may and should ask and pray God for those things of which we have need, and confidently expect help from him in every affliction connected with our particular calling and station in life; and that meanwhile we do good works for others and diligently attend to our calling. True perfection and right service of God consist   50 of these things and not of mendicancy or wearing a black or gray cowl, etc. However, the common people, hearing the state of   51 celibacy praised above all measure, draw many harmful conclusions from such false exaltation of monastic life, for it follows that   52 their consciences are troubled because they are married. When the   53 common man hears that only mendicants are perfect, he is uncertain whether he can keep his possessions and engage in business without sin. When the people hear that it is only a counsel[7] not to take   54 revenge, it is natural that some should conclude that it is not sinful to take revenge outside of the exercise of their office. Still others   55 think that it is not right at all for Christians, even in the government, to avenge wrong.

---

the same time to have great faith and to trust that for Christ's sake we have a gracious God; to ask of God, and assuredly to expect from him, help in all things which are to be borne in connection with our callings; meanwhile to be diligent in the performance of good works for others and to attend to our calling. True perfection and   50 true service of God consist of these things and not of celibacy, mendicancy, or humble attire. The people draw many pernicious con-   51 clusions from such false commendations of monastic life. They   52 hear celibacy praised above measure, and therefore they engage in their married life with a troubled conscience. They hear that only   53 mendicants are perfect, and therefore they have a troubled conscience when they keep their possessions or engage in business. They   54 hear that it is an evangelical counsel not to take revenge, and therefore some are not afraid to take vengeance in their private life since they are told that this is prohibited by a counsel and not by a precept. Others err still more, for they judge that all magistracy and all   55 civil offices are unworthy of Christians and in conflict with the evangelical counsel.

[7] A so-called "evangelical counsel." See above, Art. XXVII, 12, and note.

Many instances are also recorded of men who forsook wife   56
and child, and also their civil office, to take shelter in a monastery.
This, they said, is fleeing from the world and seeking a life   57
more pleasing to God than the other. They were unable to understand that one is to serve God by observing the commands God has
given and not by keeping the commands invented by men. That   58
is a good and perfect state of life which has God's command to support it; on the other hand, that is a dangerous state of life which does
not have God's command behind it. About such matters it was   59
necessary to give the people proper instruction.

In former times Gerson censured the error of the monks con-   60
cerning perfection and indicated that it was an innovation of his time
to speak of monastic life as a state of perfection.[8]

Thus there are many godless opinions and errors associated   61
with monastic vows: that they justify and render men righteous before
God, that they constitute Christian perfection, that they are the means
of fulfilling both evangelical counsels and precepts, and that they
furnish the works of supererogation[9] which we are not obligated to
render to God. Inasmuch as all these things are false, useless,   62
and invented, monastic vows are null and void.

Cases can be read of men who, forsaking marriage and the   56
administration of the state, withdrew into a monastery. They   57
called this "fleeing from the world" and "seeking a holy kind of life."
They did not perceive that God is to be served by observing the
commands he has given and not by keeping the commands invented
by men. A good and perfect kind of life is one which has God's   58
command in its favor. Concerning such things it was necessary   59
to admonish men.

Before our times Gerson rebuked the error of the monks con-   60
cerning perfection and testified that it was a novelty in his day to say
that monastic life is a state of perfection.

So there are many impious opinions which are associated with   61
vows: that they justify, that they constitute Christian perfection, that
the monks observe both the counsels and the precepts, and that monks
do works of supererogation. All these things, since they are false   62
and useless, make vows null and void.

[8] Among many other places, see John Gerson, *Evangelical Counsels,* in
Opera, II, 680.
[9] Works in addition to those which every Christian is obligated to perform.
See above, Art. XXVII, 12.

XXVIII. THE POWER OF BISHOPS

Many and various things have been written in former times   1
about the power of bishops, and some have improperly confused the
power of bishops with the temporal sword. Out of this careless   2
confusion many serious wars, tumults, and uprisings have resulted
because the bishops, under pretext of the power given them by Christ,
have not only introduced new forms of worship and burdened consciences with reserved cases[1] and violent use of the ban, but have also
presumed to set up and depose kings and emperors according to their
pleasure. Such outrage has long since been condemned by learned   3
and devout people in Christendom. On this account our teachers   4
have been compelled, for the sake of comforting consciences, to
point out the difference between spiritual and temporal power, sword,
and authority, and they have taught that because of God's command
both authorities and powers are to be honored and esteemed with
all reverence as the two highest gifts of God on earth.

Our teachers assert that according to the Gospel the power of   5
keys or the power of bishops is a power and command of God to
preach the Gospel, to forgive and retain sins, and to administer and
distribute the sacraments. For Christ sent out the apostles with   6

XXVIII. ECCLESIASTICAL POWER

In former times there has been great controversy about the power   1
of bishops, and some have improperly confused the power of the
church with the power of the sword. From this confusion great   2
wars and tumults have resulted, while the pontiffs, relying on the
power of keys, not only have instituted new forms of worship and
burdened consciences with reservation of cases and violent excommunications but also have undertaken to transfer kingdoms of this
world and take away the imperial power. These wrongs have   3
long since been rebuked in the church by devout and learned men.
Accordingly our teachers have been compelled, for the sake of   4
instructing consciences, to show the difference between the power of
the church and the power of the sword, and they have taught that on
account of God's command both are to be held in reverence and honor
as the chief gifts of God on earth.

Our teachers hold that according to the Gospel the power of   5
keys or the power of bishops is a power or command of God to preach
the Gospel, to remit and retain sins, and to administer the sacra-

---

[1] Cases in which absolution was reserved for bishops or the pope.

this command, "As the Father has sent me, even so I send you. Receive the Holy Spirit. If you forgive the sins of any, they are forgiven; if you retain the sins of any, they are retained" (John 20:21-23).

This power of keys or of bishops is used and exercised only by 8 teaching and preaching the Word of God and by administering the sacraments (to many persons or to individuals, depending on one's calling). In this way are imparted not bodily but eternal things and gifts, namely, eternal righteousness, the Holy Spirit, and eternal life. These gifts cannot be obtained except through the office of preach- 9 ing and of administering the holy sacraments, for St. Paul says, "The gospel is the power of God for salvation to everyone who has faith." [2] Inasmuch as the power of the church or of bishops 10 bestows eternal gifts and is used and exercised only through the office of preaching, it does not interfere at all with government or temporal authority. Temporal authority is concerned with matters alto- 11 gether different from the Gospel. Temporal power does not protect the soul, but with the sword and physical penalties it protects body and goods from the power of others.

---

ments. For Christ sent out the apostles with this command. "As 6 the Father has sent me, even so I send you. Receive the Holy Spirit. If you forgive the sins of any, they are forgiven; if you retain the sins of any, they are retained." According to Mark 16:15 he also 7 said, "Go and preach the gospel to the whole creation."

This power is exercised only by teaching or preaching the 8 Gospel and by administering the sacraments either to many or to individuals, depending on one's calling. For it is not bodily things that are thus given, but rather such eternal things as eternal righteousness, the Holy Spirit, and eternal life. These things cannot 9 come about except through the ministry of Word and sacraments, for Paul says, "The gospel is the power of God for salvation to everyone who has faith," and Ps. 119:50 states, "Thy Word gives me life." Inasmuch as the power of the church bestows eternal things 10 and is exercised only through the ministry of the Word, it interferes with civil government as little as the art of singing interferes with civil government. For civil government is concerned with other 11 things than the Gospel. The state protects not souls but bodies and goods from manifest harm, and constrains men with the sword and physical penalties, while the Gospel protects souls from heresies, the devil, and eternal death.

[2] Rom. 1:16.

Therefore, the two authorities, the spiritual and the temporal,   12
are not to be mingled or confused, for the spiritual power has its
commission to preach the Gospel and administer the sacraments.
Hence it should not invade the function of the other, should not   13
set up and depose kings, should not annul temporal laws or undermine obedience to government, should not make or prescribe to the
temporal power laws concerning worldly matters. Christ himself   14
said, "My kingship is not of this world," [3] and again, "Who made   15
me a judge or divider over you?" [4] Paul also wrote in Phil.   16
3:20, "Our commonwealth is in heaven," and in II Cor. 10:4, 5,   17
"The weapons of our warfare are not worldly but have divine power
to destroy strongholds and every proud obstacle to the knowledge of
God."

Thus our teachers distinguish the two authorities and the func-   18
tions of the two powers, directing that both be held in honor as the
highest gifts of God on earth.

In cases where bishops possess temporal authority and the   19
sword, they possess it not as bishops by divine right, but by human,
imperial right, bestowed by Roman emperors and kings for the tem-

---

Therefore, ecclesiastical and civil power are not to be confused.   12
The power of the church has its own commission to preach the Gospel
and administer the sacraments. Let it not invade the other's func-   13
tion, nor transfer the kingdoms of the world, nor abrogate the laws
of civil rulers, nor abolish lawful obedience, nor interfere with judgments concerning any civil ordinances or contracts, nor prescribe to
civil rulers laws about the forms of government that should be established. Christ says, "My kingdom is not of this world," and   14   15
again, "Who made me a judge or divider over you?" Paul   16
also wrote in Phil. 3:20, "Our commonwealth is in heaven," and   17
in II Cor. 10:4, 5, "The weapons of our warfare are not worldly but
have divine power to destroy arguments," etc.

In this way our teachers distinguish the functions of the two   18
powers, and they command that both be held in honor and acknowledged as gifts and blessings of God.

If bishops have any power of the sword, they have this not as   19
bishops under a commission of the Gospel, but by human right
granted by kings and emperors for the civil administration of their

* John 18:36.
* Luke 12:14.

poral administration of their lands. Such authority has nothing at
all to do with the office of the Gospel.

According to divine right, therefore, it is the office of the bishop   21
to preach the Gospel, forgive sins, judge doctrine and condemn doctrine that is contrary to the Gospel, and exclude from the Christian
community the ungodly whose wicked conduct is manifest. All this
is to be done not by human power but by God's Word alone. On   22
this account parish ministers and churches are bound to be obedient to the bishops according to the saying of Christ in Luke 10:16,
"He who hears you hears me." On the other hand, if they teach,   23
introduce, or institute anything contrary to the Gospel, we have God's
command not to be obedient in such cases, for Christ says in Matt.
7:15, "Beware of false prophets." St. Paul also writes in Gal. 1:8,   24
"Even if we, or an angel from heaven, should preach to you a gospel
contrary to that which we preached to you, let him be accursed,"
and in II Cor. 13:8, "We cannot do anything against the truth, but   25
only for the truth." Again Paul refers to "the authority which   26
the Lord has given me for building up and not for tearing down." [5]

---

lands. This, however, is a function other than the ministry of the
Gospel.

When one inquires about the jurisdiction of bishops, therefore,   20
civil authority must be distinguished from ecclesiastical jurisdiction. Hence according to the Gospel (or, as they say, by divine   21
right) no jurisdiction belongs to the bishops as bishops (that is, to those
to whom has been committed the ministry of Word and sacraments)
except to forgive sins, to reject doctrine which is contrary to the
Gospel, and to exclude from the fellowship of the church ungodly
persons whose wickedness is known, doing all this without human
power, simply by the Word. Churches are therefore bound by   22
divine law to be obedient to the bishops according to the text, "He
who hears you hears me."

However, when bishops teach or ordain anything contrary to   23
the Gospel, churches have a command of God that forbids obedience: "Beware of false prophets" (Matt. 7:15), "If an angel from   24
heaven should preach any other Gospel, let him be accursed" (Gal.
1:8), "We cannot do anything against the truth, but only for the   25
truth" (II Cor. 13:8), and also, "Given to me is the authority for   26
building up and not for tearing down." The canons require the   27

---

[5] II Cor. 13:10.

Canon law requires the same in Part II, Question 7, in the chap- 27
ters "Sacerdotes" and "Oves." [6]

St. Augustine also writes in his reply to the letters of Petilian 28
that one should not obey even regularly elected bishops if they err or if
they teach or command something contrary to the divine Holy
Scriptures.[7]

Whatever other power and jurisdiction bishops may have in 29
various matters (for example, in matrimonial cases and in tithes),[8]
they have these by virtue of human right. However, when bishops
are negligent in the performance of such duties, the princes are
obliged, whether they like to or not, to administer justice to their
subjects for the sake of peace and to prevent discord and great disorder in their lands.

Besides, there is dispute as to whether bishops have the power 30
to introduce ceremonies in the church or establish regulations concerning foods, holy days, and the different orders of the clergy.
Those who attribute such power to bishops cite Christ's saying 31
in John 16:12, 13, "I have yet many things to say to you, but you
cannot bear them now. When the Spirit of truth comes, he will guide
you into all the truth." [9] They also cite the example in Acts 32

---

same thing (II, question 7, in chapters "Sacerdotes" and "Oves").
Augustine also says in reply to the letters of Petilian that not 28
even catholic bishops are to be obeyed if they should happen to err
or hold anything contrary to the canonical Scriptures of God.

If they have any other power or jurisdiction to decide legal 29
cases (for example, pertaining to matrimony, tithes, etc.), bishops
have this by human right. When the bishops are negligent in the
performance of their duties, princes are bound, even against their
will, to administer justice to their subjects for the sake of maintaining
public peace.

Besides, it is disputed whether bishops or pastors have the right 30
to introduce ceremonies in the church and make laws concerning
foods, holy days, grades or orders of ministers, etc. Those who 31
attribute this right to bishops cite as evidence the passage, "I have yet
many things to say to you, but you cannot bear them now. When

[6] Gratian, *Decretum*, Part II, q.7, c.8, 13.
[7] Augustine, *The Unity of the Church*, 11, 28.
[8] The payment to the church of one-tenth of the gross income from all
lands and industries was required since the early Middle Ages.
[9] This passage was cited by John Eck in his *Handbook of Commonplaces
against Luther and Other Enemies of the Church* (1525), Nos. 1, 15.

15:20, 29, where the eating of blood and what is strangled was forbidden. Besides, they appeal to the fact that the Sabbath was   33
changed to Sunday—contrary, as they say, to the Ten Commandments.
No case is appealed to and urged so insistently as the change of the
Sabbath, for thereby they wish to maintain that the power of the
church is indeed great because the church has dispensed from and
altered part of the Ten Commandments.[1]

Concerning this question our teachers assert that bishops do not   34
have power to institute or establish anything contrary to the Gospel,
as has been indicated above and as is taught by canon law throughout
the whole of the ninth Distinction.[2] It is patently contrary to   35
God's command and Word to make laws out of opinions or to require
that they be observed in order to make satisfaction for sins and obtain
grace, for the glory of Christ's merit is blasphemed when we   36
presume to earn grace by such ordinances. It is also apparent that   37
because of this notion human ordinances have multiplied beyond
calculation while the teaching concerning faith and righteousness of
faith has almost been suppressed. Almost every day new holy days

---

the Spirit of truth comes, he will guide you into all the truth."
They also cite the example of the apostles who commanded men   32
to abstain from blood and from what is strangled. Besides, they   33
cite the change from the Sabbath to the Lord's Day—contrary to the
Decalogue, it appears. No case is made more of than this change of
the Sabbath. Great, they say, is the power of the church, for it dispensed from one of the Ten Commandments!

Concerning this question our teachers assert, as has been   34
pointed out above, that bishops do not have power to institute anything contrary to the Gospel. The canons concede this throughout
the whole of Dist. 9. Besides, it is against Scripture to require the   35
observance of traditions for the purpose of making satisfaction for
sins or meriting justification, for the glory of Christ's merit is   36
dishonored when we suppose that we are justified by such observances. It is also evident that as a result of this notion traditions   37
have multiplied in the church almost beyond calculation, while the
teaching concerning faith and the righteousness of faith has been
suppressed, for from time to time more holy days were appointed,
more fasts prescribed, and new ceremonies and new orders instituted

---

[1] Cf. Thomas Aquinas, *Summa theologica*, II, q.122, a.4 ad 4.
[2] Gratian, *Decretum*, I, dist. 9, c.8ff.

and new fasts have been prescribed, new ceremonies and new venerations of saints have been instituted in order that by such works grace and everything good might be earned from God.

Again, those who institute human ordinances also act contrary   39
to God's command when they attach sin to foods, days, and similar things and burden Christendom with the bondage of the law, as if in order to earn God's grace there had to be a service of God among Christians like the Levitical[3] service, and as if God had commanded the apostles and bishops to institute it, as some have written. It   40
is quite believable that some bishops were misled by the example of the law of Moses. The result was that countless regulations   41
came into being—for example, that it is a mortal sin to do manual work on holy days (even when it does not give offense to others), that it is a mortal sin to omit the seven hours,[4] that some foods defile the conscience, that fasting is a work by which God is reconciled, that in a reserved case sin is not forgiven unless forgiveness is secured from the person for whom the case is reserved, in spite of the fact that canon law says nothing of the reservation of guilt but speaks only about the reservation of ecclesiastical penalties.[5]

---

because the authors of these things thought that they would merit grace by these works. So the penitential canons formerly in-   38
creased, and we can still see some traces of these in the satisfactions.

Again, the authors of traditions act contrary to the command   39
of God when they attach sin to foods, days, and similar things and burden the church with the bondage of the law, as if in order to merit justification there had to be a service among Christians similar to the Levitical, and as if God had commissioned the apostles and bishops to institute it. For thus some have written, and the pontiffs seem   40
in some measure to have been misled by the example of the law of Moses. This is the origin of such burdens as this, that it is a mortal   41
sin to do manual work on holy days, even when it gives no offense to others, that certain foods defile the conscience, that fasting which is privative and not natural is a work that appeases God, that it is a mortal sin to omit the canonical hours, that in a reserved case a sin cannot be forgiven except by the authority of the person who reserved the case, although the canons themselves speak only of reserving ecclesiastical penalties and not of reserving guilt.

[3] I.e., Jewish.
[4] The canonical hours, or seven daily hours of prayer, prescribed for monastics and others.
[5] See note under Art. XXVIII, 2.

Where did the bishops get the right and power to impose such 42
requirements on Christendom to ensnare men's consciences? In Acts
15:10 St. Peter forbids putting a yoke on the neck of the disciples.
And St. Paul said in II Cor. 10:8 that authority was given for building
up and not for tearing down. Why, then, do they multiply sins with
such requirements?

Yet there are clear passages of divine Scripture which forbid 43
the establishment of such regulations for the purpose of earning God's
grace or as if they were necessary for salvation. Thus St. Paul 44
says in Col. 2:16, "Let no one pass judgment on you in questions of
food and drink or with regard to a festival or a new moon or a sabbath. These are only a shadow of what is to come; but the substance
belongs to Christ." Again in Col. 2:20-23, "If with Christ you 45
died to the regulations of the world, why do you live as if you still
belonged to the world? Why do you submit to regulations, 'Do not
handle, Do not taste, Do not touch' (referring to things which all
perish as they are used), according to human precepts and doctrines?
These have an appearance of wisdom." In Tit. 1:14 St. Paul also 46
forbids giving heed to Jewish myths or to commands of men who
reject the truth.

Christ himself says concerning those who urge human ordi- 47
nances on people, "Let them alone; they are blind guides" (Matt.

Where did the bishops get the right to impose such traditions 42
on the churches and thus ensnare consciences when Peter forbids
putting a yoke on the disciples and Paul says that authority was given
for building up and not for tearing down? Why do they multiply
sin with such traditions?

Yet there are clear testimonies which prohibit the making of 43
traditions for the purpose of appeasing God or as if they were necessary for salvation. In Col. 2 Paul says, "Let no one pass judgment 44
on you in questions of food and drink or with regard to a festival or
a new moon or a sabbath." Again, "If with Christ you died to the 45
elemental spirits of the universe, why do you live as if you still belonged to the world? Why do you submit to regulations, 'Do not
handle, Do not taste, Do not touch' (referring to things which all
perish as they are used), according to human precepts and doctrines?
These have an appearance of wisdom." In Tit. 1 Paul also says, 46
"Not giving heed to Jewish myths or to commands of men who reject
the truth."

In Matt. 15 Christ says concerning those who require tradi- 47

15:14). He rejects such service of God and says, "Every plant   48
which my heavenly Father has not planted will be rooted up" (Matt.
15:13).

If, then, bishops have the power to burden the churches with   49
countless requirements and thus ensnare consciences, why does the
divine Scripture so frequently forbid the making and keeping of human
regulations? Why does it call them doctrines of the devil?[6] Is it
possible that the Holy Spirit warned against them for nothing?

Inasmuch as such regulations as have been instituted as neces- 50
sary to propitiate God and merit grace are contrary to the Gospel,
it is not at all proper for the bishops to require such services of
God. It is necessary to preserve the teaching of Christian liberty 51
in Christendom, namely, that bondage to the law is not necessary
for justification, as St. Paul writes in Gal. 5:1, "For freedom   52
Christ has set us free; stand fast, therefore, and do not submit again
to a yoke of slavery." For the chief article of the Gospel must be
maintained, namely, that we obtain the grace of God through faith
in Christ without our merits; we do not merit it by services of God
instituted by men.

What are we to say, then, about Sunday and other similar   53

---

tions, "Let them alone; they are blind and leaders of the blind."
He rebukes such services and says, "Every plant which my heav-   48
enly Father has not planted will be rooted up."

If bishops have the right to burden consciences with such   49
traditions, why does Scripture so often prohibit the making of traditions? Why does it call them doctrines of demons? Was it in vain
that the Holy Spirit warned against these?

Inasmuch as ordinances which have been instituted as neces- 50
sary or instituted with the intention of meriting justification are in
conflict with the Gospel, it follows that it is not lawful for bishops
to institute such services or require them as necessary. It is neces- 51
sary to preserve the doctrine of Christian liberty in the churches,
namely, that bondage to the law is not necessary for justification,
as it is written in the Epistle to the Galatians, "Do not submit   52
again to a yoke of slavery." It is necessary to preserve the chief article
of the Gospel, namely, that we obtain grace through faith in Christ and
not through certain observances or acts of worship instituted by men.

What, then, are we to think about Sunday and about similar   53

[6] Cf. I Tim. 4:1.

church ordinances and ceremonies? To this our teachers reply[7] that bishops or pastors may make regulations so that everything in the churches is done in good order, but not as a means of obtaining God's grace or making satisfaction for sins, nor in order to bind men's consciences by considering these things necessary services of God and counting it a sin to omit their observance even when this is done without offense. So St. Paul directed in I Cor. 11:5 that women   54 should cover their heads in the assemb y. He also directed that in the assembly preachers should not all speak at once, but one after another, in order.[8]

It is proper for the Christian assembly to keep such ordinances   55 for the sake of love and peace, to be obedient to the bishops and parish ministers in such matters, and to observe the regulations in such a way that one does not give offense to another and so that there may be no disorder or unbecoming conduct in the church. How-   56 ever, consciences should not be burdened by contending that such things are necessary for salvation or that it is a sin to omit them, even when no offense is given to others, just as no one would say that a woman commits a sin if without offense to others she goes out with uncovered head.

---

rites in our churches? To this our teachers reply that it is lawful for bishops or pastors to make regulations so that things in the church may be done in good order, but not that by means of these we make satisfaction for sins, nor that consciences are bound so as to regard these as necessary services. So Paul ordained that women should   54 cover their heads in the assembly and that interpreters in the church should be heard one after another.

It is proper that the churches comply with such ordinances for   55 the sake of love and tranquility and that they keep them, in so far as one does not offend another, so that everything in the churches may be done in order and without confusion. However, con-   56 sciences should not be burdened by suggesting that they are necessary for salvation or by judging that those who omit them without offense to others commit a sin, any more than one would say that a woman sins by going out in public with her head uncovered, provided no offense is given.

[7] A reply was called for since John Eck had just attacked the Evangelicals for erroneous views of the Lord's Day. See Eck, *404 Theses*, Nos. 177-179.
[8] I Cor. 14:30.

Of like character is the observance of Sunday, Easter, Pente-   57
cost, and similar holy days and usages. Those who consider the   58
appointment of Sunday in place of the Sabbath as a necessary institution are very much mistaken, for the Holy Scriptures have   59
abrogated the Sabbath and teach that after the revelation of the
Gospel all ceremonies of the old law may be omitted. Never-   60
theless, because it was necessary to appoint a certain day so that the
people might know when they ought to assemble, the Christian church
appointed Sunday for this purpose, and it was the more inclined and
pleased to do this in order that the people might have an example
of Christian liberty and might know that the keeping neither of the
Sabbath nor of any other day is necessary.

There are many faulty discussions[9] of the transformation of   61
the law, of the ceremonies of the New Testament, and of the change
of the Sabbath, all of which have arisen from the false and erroneous
opinion that in Christendom one must have services of God like the
Levitical or Jewish services and that Christ commanded the apostles
and bishops to devise new ceremonies which would be necessary for
salvation. Such errors were introduced into Christendom when   62

Of the same sort is the observance of Sunday, Easter, Pente-   57
cost, and similar festivals and rites. Those who hold that the   58
observance of the Lord's Day in place of the Sabbath was instituted
by the church's authority as a necessary thing are mistaken. The   59
Scriptures, not the church, abrogated the Sabbath, for after the
revelation of the Gospel all ceremonies of the Mosaic law can be
omitted. Nevertheless, because it was necessary to appoint a cer-   60
tain day so that the people may know when they ought to assemble,
it appears that the church designated the Lord's Day for this purpose,
and it seems that the church was the more pleased to do this for the
additional reason that men would have an example of Christian liberty
and would know that the keeping neither of the Sabbath nor of any
other day is necessary.

There are monstrous discussions concerning the mutation of   61
the law, concerning ceremonies of the new law, concerning the change
of the Sabbath, all of which have arisen from the false notion that
there must be a service in the church like the Levitical service and
that Christ commissioned the apostles and bishops to devise new
ceremonies which would be necessary for salvation. These errors   62

* E.g., Thomas Aquinas, *Summa theologica,* II, 1, q.103.

the righteousness of faith was no longer taught and preached with
clarity and purity. Some argue that although Sunday must not be   63
kept as of divine obligation, it must nevertheless be kept as almost of
divine obligation, and they prescribe the kind and amount of work
that may be done on the day of rest. What are such discussions   64
but snares of conscience? For although they undertake to lighten
and mitigate human regulations,[1] yet there can be no moderation or
mitigation as long as the opinion remains and prevails that their
observance is necessary. And this opinion will remain as long as
there is no understanding of the righteousness of faith and Christian
liberty.

The apostles directed that one should abstain from blood   65
and from what is strangled. Who observes this prohibition now?
Those who do not observe it commit no sin, for the apostles did not
wish to burden consciences with such bondage but forbade such
eating for a time to avoid offense. One must pay attention to the   66
chief article of Christian doctrine, and this is not abrogated by the
decree.[2]

Scarcely any of the ancient canons are observed according to   67
the letter, and many of the regulations fall into disuse from day to

---

crept into the church when the righteousness of faith was not taught
with sufficient clarity. Some argue that the observance of the   63
Lord's Day is not *indeed* of divine obligation but is *as it were* of
divine obligation, and they prescribe the extent to which one is allowed
to work on holy days. What are discussions of this kind but snares   64
of conscience? Although they try to mitigate the traditions, moderation can never be achieved as long as the opinion remains that their
observance is necessary. And this opinion must remain where there
is no understanding of the righteousness of faith and Christian liberty.

The apostles commanded that one should abstain from blood,   65
etc. Who observes this prohibition now? Those who do not observe
it commit no sin, for the apostles did not wish to burden consciences
with such bondage but forbade such eating for a time to avoid
offense. In connection with the decree one must consider what   66
the perpetual aim of the Gospel is.

Scarcely any of the canons are observed according to the letter,   67
and many of them become obsolete from day to day even among

---

[1] Cf. above, Art. XXVI, 14.
[2] The so-called apostolic decree in Acts 15:23-29.

day even among those who observe such ordinances most jealously. It is impossible to give counsel or help to consciences unless this 68 mitigation is practiced, that one recognizes that such rules are not to be deemed necessary and that disregard of them does not injure consciences.

The bishops might easily retain the obedience of men if they 69 did not insist on the observance of regulations which cannot be kept without sin. Now, however, they administer the sacrament in one 70 kind and prohibit administration in both kinds. Again, they forbid clergymen to marry and admit no one to the ministry unless he first swears an oath that he will not preach this doctrine, although there is no doubt that it is in accord with the holy Gospel. Our churches 71 do not ask that the bishops should restore peace and unity at the expense of their honor and dignity (though it is incumbent on the bishops to do this, too, in case of need), but they ask only that 72 the bishops relax certain unreasonable burdens which did not exist in the church in former times and which were introduced contrary to the custom of the universal Christian church. Perhaps there 73 was some reason for introducing them, but they are not adapted to our times. Nor can it be denied that some regulations were 74 adopted from want of understanding. Accordingly the bishops ought to be so gracious as to temper these regulations inasmuch as such

---

those who favor traditions. It is not possible to counsel consciences 68 unless this mitigation is practiced, that one recognizes that canons are kept without holding them to be necessary and that no harm is done to consciences even if the usage of men changes in such matters.

The bishops might easily retain the lawful obedience of men 69 if they did not insist on the observance of traditions which cannot be kept with a good conscience. But now they demand celibacy 70 and will admit no one to the ministry unless he swears that he will not teach the pure doctrine of the Gospel. Our churches do not 71 ask that the bishops restore concord at the expense of their honor (which, however, good pastors ought to do), but ask only that 72 they relax unjust burdens which are new and were introduced contrary to the custom of the church catholic. Perhaps there were 73 acceptable reasons for these ordinances when they were introduced, but they are not adapted to later times. It is also apparent that 74 some were adopted out of misunderstanding. It would therefore befit the clemency of the bishops to mitigate these regulations now, for such change does not impair the unity of the church inasmuch as

changes do not destroy the unity of Christian churches. For many
regulations devised by men have with the passing of time fallen into
disuse and are not obligatory, as papal law itself testifies.[3] If, how-   75
ever, this is impossible and they cannot be persuaded to mitigate or
abrogate human regulations which are not to be observed without
sin, we are bound to follow the apostolic rule which commands us
to obey God rather than men.[4]

St. Peter forbids the bishops to exercise lordship as if they had   76
power to coerce the churches according to their will.[5] It is not   77
our intention to find ways of reducing the bishops' power, but we
desire and pray that they may not coerce our consciences to sin.   78
If they are unwilling to do this and ignore our petition, let them
consider how they will answer for it in God's sight, inasmuch as by
their obstinacy they offer occasion for division and schism, which
they should in truth help to prevent.

[CONCLUSION]

These are the chief articles that are regarded as controversial.   1
Although we could have mentioned many more abuses and wrongs,

---

many human traditions have been changed with the passing of time,
as the canons themselves show. However, if it is impossible to   75
obtain a relaxation of observances which cannot be kept without sin,
we are bound to follow the apostolic injunction which commands us
to obey God rather than men.

Peter forbids the bishops to be domineering and to coerce the   76
churches. It is not our intention that the bishops give up their   77
power to govern, but we ask for this one thing, that they allow the
Gospel to be taught purely and that they relax some few observances
which cannot be kept without sin. If they do not do this, they   78
must see to it how they will answer for it before God that by their
obstinacy they offer occasion for schism.

[CONCLUSION]

We have now reviewed the chief articles that are regarded as   1
controversial. Although more abuses could be mentioned, to avoid

---

[3] E.g., the penitential canons of the ancient church were supplanted in the
early Middle Ages when the sacrament of penance developed.
[4] Acts 5:29.
[5] I Pet. 5:2.

to avoid prolixity and undue length we have indicated only the principal ones. The others can readily be weighed in the light of these. In the past there have been grave complaints about indulgences, 2 pilgrimages, and misuse of the ban. Parish ministers also had endless quarrels with monks about the hearing of confessions, about burials, about sermons on special occasions, and about countless other matters. All these things we have discreetly passed over 3 for the common good in order that the chief points at issue may better be perceived.

It must not be thought that anything has been said or introduced 4 out of hatred or for the purpose of injuring anybody, but we 5 have related only matters which we have considered it necessary to adduce and mention in order that it may be made very clear that we have introduced nothing, either in doctrine or in ceremonies, that is contrary to Holy Scripture or the universal Christian church. For it is manifest and evident (to speak without boasting) that we have diligently and with God's help prevented any new and godless teaching from creeping into our churches and gaining the upper hand in them.

In keeping with the summons,[6] we have desired to present the 6 above articles as a declaration of our confession and the teaching of

---

undue length we have discussed only the principal ones. There 2 have been grave complaints about indulgences, pilgrimages, and misuse of excommunication. Parishes have been troubled in many ways by indulgence sellers. There have been endless quarrels between parish ministers and monks about parochial rights, confessions, burials, and countless other things. We have passed over matters of this sort 3 so that the chief points at issue, being briefly set forth, may more readily be understood.

Nothing has here been said or related for the purpose of injur- 4 ing anybody. Only those things have been recounted which it 5 seemed necessary to say in order that it may be understood that nothing has been received among us, in doctrine or in ceremonies, that is contrary to Scripture or to the church catholic. For it is manifest that we have guarded diligently against the introduction into our churches of any new and ungodly doctrines.

In keeping with the edict of Your Imperial Majesty, we have 6 desired to present the above articles in order that our confession may

---

⁸ See above, Preface, 1.

our preachers. If anyone should consider that it is lacking in   7
some respect, we are ready to present further information on the
basis of the divine Holy Scripture.

Your Imperial Majesty's most obedient servants:

> JOHN, duke of Saxony, elector
> GEORGE, margrave of Brandenburg
> ERNEST, duke of Lüneburg
> PHILIP, landgrave of Hesse
> JOHN FREDERICK, duke of Saxony
> FRANCIS, duke of Lüneburg
> WOLFGANG, prince of Anhalt
> Mayor and council of Nuremberg
> Mayor and council of Reutlingen

---

be exhibited in them and that a summary of the doctrine taught
among us may be discerned. If anything is found to be lacking in   7
this confession, we are ready, God willing, to present ampler information according to the Scriptures.

Your Imperial Majesty's faithful subjects:

> JOHN, duke of Saxony, elector
> GEORGE, margrave of Brandenburg
> ERNEST, with his own hand
> PHILIP, landgrave of Hesse, subscribes
> JOHN FREDERICK, duke of Saxony
> FRANCIS, duke of Lüneburg
> WOLFGANG, prince of Anhalt
> Senate and magistrate of Nuremberg
> Senate of Reutlingen

III

APOLOGY

OF THE AUGSBURG CONFESSION

INTRODUCTION

Emperor Charles V's summons to the diet which was to meet in Augsburg in 1530 requested that a statement of faith be presented not only by the princes and representatives of free cities who called themselves Evangelical but also by those who remained loyal to Rome (see above, Introduction, Augsburg Confession). Instead, two days after the Augsburg Confession had been read in the diet, the Roman party decided to prepare an answer to and refutation of the Lutheran document. This task was committed to a commission of theologians headed by the papal legate. After a first draft proved unsatisfactory, a shorter, abler, and more irenic statement was prepared, and this was the "Roman Confutation" which on August 3 was publicly read to the diet in the same hall in which the Augsburg Confession had previously been read. The emperor promptly demanded that the Evangelicals acknowledge that their position had been refuted, and until they did so he refused to let them have a copy of the Confutation.

Despite this handicap, the adherents of the Augsburg Confession decided to prepare a reply to the Roman Confutation on the basis of notes hastily taken during the public reading. The preparation was entrusted especially to Philip Melanchthon. Work on the reply was delayed by Melanchthon's participation during August in a series of conferences with Roman theologians intended to reconcile differences between the two parties. However, the first draft of the Apology of the Augsburg Confession was ready for submission on September 22. The document was refused by the emperor.

On his journey back to Wittenberg Melanchthon began to revise and expand the Apology, and he continued to work on it for months, aided at last by receipt of a copy of the Confutation, presumably from Nuremberg. In its enlarged form the Apology was published at the end of April or beginning of May, 1531. At first regarded as a private publication of Melanchthon, it became an official confession of faith when it was signed, along with the Augsburg Confession, in Smalcald in 1537 (see below, Introduction, Smalcald Articles). It is important as a contemporary commentary on the Augsburg Confession by the principal author of that Confession.

The translation which follows is made from the Latin original. Variants in the German version, a very free translation which has been called a "pious paraphrase," are not included.

PREFACE

Greetings from Philip Melanchthon to the reader.

After a public reading of our princes' Confession, a number of 1
theologians and monks prepared a Confutation of it. His Imperial Majesty had this read before the assembly of the princes, and he ordered our princes to accept this Confutation.

To see what our opponents condemned and to refute their 2
arguments, our party requested a copy of the Confutation; for we had heard that it condemned many articles that we could not conscientiously surrender. Since religion and consciences are involved, we assumed that the opponents would produce the document without hesitation. But we could have obtained it only on terms so risky that we could not accept them.

During the negotiations that followed, it was clear that our side 3
was willing to put up with anything, however unpleasant, that did not violate our consciences. But our opponents stubbornly insisted 4
that we sanction certain manifest abuses and errors. When we could not, His Imperial Majesty again ordered our princes to accept the Confutation. This they refused to do. In a religious issue, how could they accept a document they had not even seen—and one that was supposed to condemn several articles where they could not give in to the opponents' point of view with a clear conscience?

They commanded me and several others to prepare an apology 5
of our Confession, answering the opponents' objections and explaining to His Imperial Majesty why we could not accept the Confutation. For during the reading some of us had taken notes on the main 6
points of its argumentation. They finally offered the apology to 7
His Imperial Majesty, to show him that very weighty reasons prevented us from approving the Confutation, but his Imperial Majesty did not receive it. Later there appeared a decree in which our opponents 8
brag that they have refuted our Confession from the Scriptures.

And now, dear reader, you have our Apology. It will show you 9
what our opponents have judged, as we have reported this faithfully;

far from having disproved our contentions from the Scriptures, they
have condemned several articles in opposition to the clear Scripture
of the Holy Spirit.
Originally we undertook the Apology in consultation with 10
others, but as it was going through the press I added some things.
Therefore I am giving my name, so no one can complain that the
book has appeared anonymously. In these controversies I have 11
always made it a point to stick as closely as possible to traditional
doctrinal formulas in order to foster the attainment of harmony. I am
doing much the same thing here, even though I could lead our
contemporaries still further from the opponents' position. But our 12
opponents show by their actions that they are after neither truth nor
harmony, but our blood.
Now, I have written as moderately as I could. If any expression 13
seems too strong, let me explain that my quarrel is with the theologians
and monks who wrote the Confutation, not with the emperor or the
princes, whom I hold in due esteem. But recently, when I saw the 14
Confutation, I realized it was written so cleverly and slanderously that
in some places it could deceive even the cautious reader. I have 15
not taken up all their sophistries, for this would be an endless task.
Rather I have assembled the main arguments, to testify to all nations
that we hold to the Gospel of Christ correctly and faithfully. We 16
take no pleasure in discord, nor are we indifferent to our danger; its
extent is evident from the bitter hatred inflaming our opponents. But
we cannot surrender truth that is so clear and necessary for the
church.
We believe, therefore, that we must endure difficulties and dangers
for the glory of Christ and the good of the church. We trust that God
approves our faithfulness, and we hope that posterity will judge us
more equitably. For we have undoubtedly brought into view 17
many articles of Christian doctrine that the church sorely needs. We
need not describe here how they lay hidden under all sorts of dangerous
opinions in the writings of the monks, canonists, and scholastic
theologians.
Many good men have testified publicly and thanked God for 18
this great blessing, that on many points our Confession's teaching is
better than that which appears everywhere in our opponents' writings.
And so we shall commend our cause to Christ, who will one day 19
judge these controversies. We beseech him to regard his afflicted and
scattered churches and to restore them to a godly and abiding harmony

APOLOGY OF THE CONFESSION

[ARTICLE I. GOD]

Our opponents approve Article I of our Confession.[1] This |
asserts our faith and teaching that there is one undivided divine
essence, and that there are nevertheless three distinct and coeternal
persons of the same divine essence, Father, Son, and Holy Spirit.
We have always taught and defended this doctrine and we believe 2
that the Holy Scriptures testify to it firmly, surely, and irrefutably.
We steadfastly maintain that those who believe otherwise do not
belong to the church of Christ but are idolaters and blasphemers.

[ARTICLE II. ORIGINAL SIN]

The opponents approve Article II, "Original Sin," but they |
criticize our definition of original sin.[2] Here at the very outset His
Imperial Majesty will see that the authors of the Confutation are
lacking not only in judgment but also in honesty. While we wanted
simply to describe what original sin includes, they viciously misinterpret
and distort a statement that has nothing wrong in it. They say that
being without the fear of God and faith is actual guilt, and therefore
they deny that it is original guilt.

These quibbles have obviously come from the schools, and not 2
from the emperor's council. This sophistry is easy to refute. But to
show all good men that our teaching on this point is not absurd, we
ask them first to look at the German text of the Confession. This will
exonerate us of the charge of innovation, for it says: "It is also taught
that since the fall of Adam all men who are born according to the
course of nature are conceived and born in sin. That is, all men are
full of evil lusts and inclinations from their mothers' wombs and are
unable by nature to have true fear of God or true faith in God." [3]

---

[1] Roman Confutation: "When in the first article they [the Lutheran
princes] confess the unity of the divine essence in three persons according
to the decree of the Council of Nicaea, their Confession must be accepted
since it agrees in all respects with the rule of faith and the Roman
Church . . ." (Pt. I, Art. I). The Latin text for this quotation from the
Roman Confutation and for those which follow below is in *C.R.*, XXVII,
82-183.

[2] Roman Confutation: "But the assertion in the article that original sin
means that men are born without the fear of God and without trust in God
is to be entirely rejected because it is manifest to every Christian that to
be without fear of God and without trust in God is the actual guilt of an
adult rather than the offense of a recently born infant who does not as yet
possess the full use of reason. . . . Moreover, the statement is also rejected
whereby they [the Lutheran princes] call the fault of origin 'concupiscence,'
if they mean by this that concupiscence is a sin which remains sin in a child
even after Baptism . . ." (Pt. I, Art. II).

[3] Above, Augsburg Confession, II, 1.

This passage testifies that in those who are born according to the 3
flesh we deny the existence not only of actual fear and trust in God
but also of the possibility and gift to produce it. We say that anyone
born in this way has concupiscence and cannot produce true fear and
trust in God. What is wrong with this? This explanation should be
enough for any unprejudiced man. In this sense the Latin definition
denies that human nature has the gift and capacity to produce the
fear and trust of God, and it denies that adults actually produce it.
When we use the term "concupiscence," we do not mean only its acts
or fruits, but the continual inclination of nature.

Later on we shall show at length that our definition agrees with 4
the traditional one. First we must show why we used these words
here. Our scholastic opponents admit that concupiscence is the so-
called "material element" of original sin.[4] Hence it belongs in the
definition, especially now when so many philosophize about it
irreligiously.

There are some[5] who claim that original sin is not some vice or 5
corruption in human nature, but only the subjection to mortality that
Adam's descendants bear because of his guilt, without any evil of their
own. They go on to say that one is not condemned to eternal death
because of original sin but, like a child born of a slave, is in this
condition because of one's mother and not by one's own fault. To 6
show our disagreement with this evil doctrine, we made mention of
concupiscence; with the best of intentions we named it and explained
it as a disease since human nature is born full of corruption and
faults.

We have mentioned not only concupiscence but also the absence 7
of the fear of God and of faith. We have done this because the
scholastics misunderstand the patristic definition of original sin and
therefore minimize original sin. They argue that the inclination to evil
is a quality of the body; in their awkward way they ask whether it
came through contact with the apple or through the serpent's breath,
and whether medicine can cure it.[6] By such questions they miss the
main issue. Thus when they talk about original sin, they do not 8
mention the more serious faults of human nature, namely, ignoring
God, despising him, lacking fear and trust in him, hating his judgment
and fleeing it, being angry at him, despairing of his grace, trusting in
temporal things, etc. These evils, which are most contrary to the law
of God, the scholastics do not even mention. They even attribute to
human nature unimpaired power to love God above all things and to

---

[4] Cf. Thomas Aquinas, *Summa theologica*, II, 1, q.82, a.3c.
[5] See above, note 3 under Augsburg Confession, II.
[6] E.g., Gabriel Biel.

obey his commandments "according to the substance of the act."[7]
And they do not see the contradiction.

To be able to love God above all things by one's own power   9
and to obey his commandments, what else is this but to have original
righteousness? If human nature has such powers that by itself   10
it can love God above all things, as the scholastics confidently assert,
then what can original sin be? What need is there for the grace of
Christ if we can become righteous by our own righteousness? What
need is there for the Holy Spirit if human powers by themselves can
love God above all things and obey his commandments? Who   11
cannot see the foolishness of our opponents' position? They acknowledge the minor faults in human nature and ignore the major ones.
But it is of these that the Scripture everywhere warns us and of these
that the prophets constantly complain, namely, carnal security, contempt of God, hate of God, and similar faults that we are born
with. The scholastics mingled Christian doctrine with philosophical   12
views about the perfection of nature and attributed more than was
proper to free will and to "elicited acts." They taught that men are
justified before God by philosophical or civic righteousness, which we
agree is subject to reason and somewhat in our power. But thereby
they failed to see the inner uncleanness of human nature. This   13
cannot be adjudged except from the Word of God, which the
scholastics do not often employ in their discussions.

This was why in our definition of original sin we also mentioned   14
concupiscence and denied to man's natural powers the fear and trust
of God. We wanted to show that original sin also involves such faults
as ignorance of God, contempt of God, lack of the fear of God and
of trust in him, inability to love him. These are the chief flaws in
human nature, transgressing as they do the first table of the Decalogue.

We have said nothing new. Properly understood, the old   15
definition says exactly the same thing, "Original sin is the lack of
original righteousness." [8] But what is righteousness? Here the
scholastics quibble about philosophical questions and do not explain
what original righteousness is. In the Scriptures righteousness   16
contains not merely the second table of the Decalogue, but also the
first, commanding fear of God, faith and love toward him. So   17
original righteousness was intended to involve not only a balanced
physical constitution, but these gifts as well: a surer knowledge of
God, fear of God, trust in God, or at least the inclination and power
to do these things. This the Scripture shows when it says that   18
man was created in the image of God and after his likeness (Gen. 1:27).
What else is this than that a wisdom and righteousness was implanted

[7] E.g., Duns Scotus, Gabriel Biel.
[8] Anselm of Canterbury, etc.

in man that would grasp God and reflect him, that is, that man
received gifts like the knowledge of God, fear of God, and trust in
God? So Irenaeus interprets the likeness of God.[9] And after   19
saying a great deal about it, Ambrose says, "That soul is not in the
image of God in which God is not always present."[1] In Eph. 5:9   20
and Col. 3:10 Paul shows that the image of God is the knowledge
of God, righteousness, and truth. Peter Lombard is not afraid to   21
say that original righteousness is the very likeness of God which he
put into man.[2] We cite the opinions of the ancients, with which   22
Augustine's interpretation of the image agrees.[3]

Thus when the ancient definition says that sin is lack of   23
righteousness, it not only denies the obedience of man's lower powers,
but also denies that he has knowledge of God, trust in God, fear and
love of God, or surely the power to produce these things. Even the
scholastic theologians teach that these things cannot be produced
without certain gifts and help of grace. To make ourselves clear, we
are naming these gifts knowledge of God, fear of God, and trust in
God. From this it is evident that the ancient definition says just what
we do when we deny to natural man not only fear and trust of God
but also the gifts and power to produce them.

This is precisely the intention of Augustine's definition that   24
original sin is concupiscence.[4] It means that when righteousness is
lost, concupiscence follows. Since nature in its weakness cannot fear
and love God or believe in him, it seeks and loves carnal things;
either it despises the judgment of God in its security, or it hates him
in its terror. Thus Augustine includes both the defect and the vicious
disposition that follows. Concupiscence is not merely a corrup-   25
tion of the physical constitution, but the evil inclination of
man's higher capacities to carnal things. They do not know what they
are talking about when they simultaneously attribute to man a concupiscence that has not been quenched by the Holy Spirit and a love
for God above all things. In our definition of original sin, there-   26
fore, we have correctly expressed both elements: lack of ability to
trust, fear, or love God; and concupiscence, which pursues carnal
ends contrary to the Word of God (that is, not only the desires of the
body but also carnal wisdom and righteousness in which it trusts
while it despises God).

Not the ancient theologians alone, but even the more recent   27
ones—at least the more sensible among them—teach that original sin

---

[9] Irenaeus, *Against Heresies*, V, 11, 2.
[1] Ambrose, *Hexaemeron*, VI, 8, 45.
[2] Peter Lombard, *Sentences*, II, dist. 16, c.4.
[3] Augustine, *The Trinity*, XII, 7, 12, 14.
[4] Augustine, *Marriage and Concupiscence*, I, 24, 27.

is truly composed of the defects that I have listed, as well as of concupiscence. Thus Thomas says: "Original sin denotes the privation of original justice, and besides this, the inordinate disposition of the parts of the soul. Consequently it is not a pure privation, but also a corrupt habit." [5] Bonaventure writes: "When the question 28 is asked what original sin is, it is correct to answer that it is immoderate lust. It is also correct to answer that it is the lack of proper righteousness. And each of these answers includes the other." [6] Hugo 29 teaches the same thing when he says that original sin is ignorance in the mind and lust in the flesh.[7] He means that at birth we bring along an ignorance of God, unbelief, distrust, contempt, and hate of God. He includes these things in the term "ignorance." These 30 opinions agree with the Scriptures. For Paul sometimes mentions the deficiency, as in I Cor. 2:14, "The unspiritual man does not receive the gifts of the Spirit of God." Elsewhere (Rom. 7:5) he mentions lust at work in our members and bringing forth evil fruit. We 31 could quote many passages on both parts of our definition, but on so clear an issue there is no need of evidence. The wise reader will easily be able to see that when the fear of God and faith are lacking, this is not merely actual guilt but an abiding deficiency in an unrenewed human nature.

So we teach nothing about original sin that is contrary to the 32 Scripture or the church catholic, but we have cleansed and brought to light important teachings of the Scriptures and the Fathers that had been obscured by the sophistic arguments of modern theologians. Modern theologians have evidently not paid attention to what the Fathers meant to say about the deficiency. Recognition of 33 original sin is a necessity, nor can we know the magnitude of the grace of Christ unless we acknowledge our faults. All the righteousness of man is mere hypocrisy before God unless we acknowledge that of itself the heart is lacking in love, fear, and trust in God. Thus the prophet says, "After I was instructed, I smote upon 34 my thigh" (Jer. 31:19). And again (Ps. 116:11), "I said in my consternation, men are all liars," that is, they do not have the right view of God.

Here our opponents lash out at Luther because he wrote that 35 original sin remains after Baptism, and they add that this doctrine was properly condemned by Leo X.[8] His Imperial Majesty will

[5] Thomas Aquinas, *Summa theologica*, II, 1, q.82, a.1 ad 1.
[6] Bonaventure, *Commentary on the Sentences*, lib. II, dist. 30, q.un. art. 2c.
[7] Hugo of St. Victor, *The Sacraments*, I, 7, c.28.
[8] Roman Confutation: "The apostolic see has already condemned two articles of Martin Luther about sins remaining in a child after Baptism . . ." (Pt. I, Art. II). Cf. the papal bull *Exsurge Domine* of June, 1520.

recognize an obvious slander here. Our opponents know what Luther meant by this statement that original sin remains after Baptism. He has always written that Baptism removes the guilt of original sin, even though concupiscence remains—or, as they call it, the "material element" of sin. Concerning this material element, he has also said that the Holy Spirit, given in Baptism, begins to mortify lust and to create new impulses in man.[9] Augustine speaks the same way 36 when he says, "Sin is forgiven in Baptism, not that it no longer is, but it is not imputed."[1] Here he openly attests that sin is—that is, remains—even though it is not imputed. This view pleased later generations so much that they included it in the decretals.[2] Against Julian, Augustine says: "That law which is in the members is forgiven by spiritual regeneration, but it remains in the mortal flesh. It is forgiven because its guilt is absolved by the sacrament that regenerates the faithful. But it remains because there continue to work those desires against which the faithful struggle."[3] Our opponents know 37 that this is what Luther believes and teaches; and since they cannot refute the principle, they twist his words in order by this device to crush an innocent man.

But they maintain that concupiscence is a penalty and not a sin, 38 while Luther contends that it is a sin. We have said earlier that Augustine defines original sin as concupiscence. Let them argue with Augustine if this position displeases them! Besides, Paul says 39 (Rom. 7:7), "I should not have known lust if the law had not said, 'You shall not lust.'" And again, "I see in my members another law at war with the law of my mind and making me captive to the law of sin which dwells in my members" (Rom. 7:23). No 40 quibbling can overthrow these proofs. For they clearly call lust sin, by nature worthy of death if it is not forgiven, though it is not imputed to those who are in Christ. This is undoubtedly what 41 the Fathers believe. In a lengthy discussion Augustine refutes the opinion that human lust is not a fault but is a neutral thing, like the color of the skin or ill health.[4]

If our opponents claim that the inclination to evil is a neu- 42 tral thing, not only will many passages of the Scripture contradict them, but the whole church. Even though complete unanimity may be impossible, no one has dared to say that such attitudes as these are a neutral thing—doubt about God's wrath, his grace, and his Word; anger at his judgments; indignation because he does not

---

[9] E.g., *WA*, 6:534ff.
[1] Augustine, *Marriage and Concupiscence*, 1, 25.
[2] Probably Gratian, *Decretum*, III, *De consecratione*, d.4, c.2.
[3] Augustine, *Against Julian*, II, 3.
[4] E.g., *ibid.*, IV, 9ff.

deliver us from trouble right away; fretting because bad people are more fortunate than good people; yielding to anger, desire, ambition, wealth, etc. Pious men have confessed to these things, as the 43 Psalms and the prophets show. Here the scholastics have taken over from philosophy the totally foreign idea that because of our emotions we are neither good nor bad, neither to be praised nor condemned.[5] Or they say that nothing is sin unless it is voluntary.[6] The philosophers said this about the civil courts, not about the judgment of God. It is no wiser to say that nature is not evil. In its place we do not object to this statement, but it is not right to twist it in order to minimize original sin. Yet these ideas appear in the scholastics, who improperly mingle philosophical and civil ethics with the Gospel. As often 44 happens, these ideas did not remain purely academic, but moved out among the people. These notions prevailed, feeding a trust in human powers and obscuring the knowledge of the grace of Christ. So when Luther wanted to show the magnitude of original 45 sin and of human weakness, he taught that the remnants of original sin in man are not in their nature neutral, but they need the grace of Christ to be forgiven and the Holy Spirit to be mortified.

Although the scholastics minimize both sin and its penalty 46 when they teach that man can obey the commandments of God by his own powers, Genesis describes another penalty for original sin. There human nature is subjected not only to death and other physical ills, but also to the rule of the devil. For there this fearful sentence is pronounced, "I will put enmity between you and the woman, and between your seed and her seed" (Gen. 3:15). The deficiency 47 and concupiscence are sin as well as penalty; death, other physical ills, and the tyranny of the devil are, in the precise sense, penalties. Human nature is enslaved and held prisoner by the devil, who deludes it with wicked opinions and errors and incites it to all kinds of sins. Just as the devil cannot be conquered without Christ's help, so 48 we cannot buy our way out of the slavery by ourselves. World 49 history itself shows the great power of the devil's rule. Blasphemy and wicked doctrines fill the world, and by these bonds the devil has enthralled those who are wise and righteous in the eyes of the world. In others, even grosser vices appear. Christ was given to 50 us to bear both sin and penalty and to destroy the rule of the devil, sin, and death; so we cannot know his blessings unless we recognize our evil. Therefore our preachers have stressed this in their teaching. They have not introduced any innovations, but have set forth the Holy Scripture and the teachings of the holy Fathers.

This, we believe, will satisfy His Imperial Majesty about the 51

---

[5] Thomas Aquinas, *Summa theologica*, II, 1, q.24, a.1.
[6] *Ibid.*, II, 1, q.71, a.5c.; q.74, a.1c.

childish and trivial quibbling with which our opponents have slandered our article. We know that our doctrine is correct and in agreement with Christ's church catholic. If our opponents reopen the controversy, we shall not lack men to reply in defense of the truth, for in this case our opponents frequently do not know what they are talking about. They often contradict themselves and fail to explain logically and correctly either the formal element of original sin or the so-called deficiency. For our part, we have been reluctant to enter upon their arguments at great length. We have thought it worthwhile rather to list, in the usual familiar phrases, the opinions of the holy Fathers, which we also follow.

[Article III. Christ]

The opponents approve[7] our third article, in which we confess | that there are two natures in Christ, namely, that the Word assumed the human nature into the unity of his person; that this same Christ suffered and died to reconcile the Father to us; and that he was raised to rule, justify, and sanctify the believers, etc., according to the Apostles' and Nicene Creeds.

[Article IV. Justification]

In the fourth, fifth, and sixth articles, and later in the twentieth, | they condemn us for teaching that men do not receive the forgiveness of sins because of their own merits, but freely for Christ's sake, by faith in him. They condemn us both for denying that men receive the forgiveness of sins because of their merits, and for affirming that men receive the forgiveness of sins by faith and by faith in Christ are justified.[8]

In this controversy the main doctrine of Christianity is involved; 2 when it is properly understood, it illumines and magnifies the honor of Christ and brings to pious consciences the abundant consolation that they need. We therefore ask His Imperial Majesty kindly to hear us out on this important issue. For since they understand neither 3 the forgiveness of sins nor faith nor grace nor righteousness, our opponents confuse this doctrine miserably, they obscure the glory and the blessings of Christ, and they rob pious consciences of the consolation offered them in Christ. To substantiate our Con- 4

---

[7] Roman Confutation, Pt. I, Art. III.

[8] Roman Confutation: "It is entirely contrary to Holy Scripture to deny that our works are meritorious. . . . Nevertheless, all Catholics confess that of themselves our works have no merit but that God's grace makes them worthy of eternal life" (Pt. I, Art. IV). "Their [the Lutheran princes'] ascription of justification to faith alone is diametrically opposed to the truth of the Gospel, by which works are not excluded. . . . Their frequent ascription of justification to faith is not admitted since it pertains to grace and love . . ." (Pt. I, Art. VI).

fession and to refute the objections of our opponents, we shall have to say a few things by way of preface so that the sources of both kinds of doctrine, the opponents' and our own, might be recognized. All Scripture should be divided into these two chief doctrines, 5 the law and the promises. In some places it presents the law. In others it presents the promise of Christ; this it does either when it promises that the Messiah will come and promises forgiveness of sins, justification, and eternal life for his sake, or when, in the New Testament, the Christ who came promises forgiveness of sins, justification, and eternal life. By "law" in this discussion we mean the com- 6 mandments of the Decalogue, wherever they appear in the Scriptures. For the present we are saying nothing about the ceremonial and civil laws of Moses.

Of these two doctrines our opponents select the law and by it 7 they seek forgiveness of sins and justification. For to some extent human reason naturally understands the law since it has the same judgment naturally written in the mind. But the Decalogue does 8 not only require external works that reason can somehow perform. It also requires other works far beyond the reach of reason, like true fear of God, true love of God, true prayer to God, true conviction that God hears prayer, and the expectation of God's help in death and all afflictions. Finally, it requires obedience to God in death and all afflictions, lest we try to flee these things or turn away when God imposes them.

Here the scholastics have followed the philosophers. Thus 9 they teach only the righteousness of reason—that is, civil works— and maintain that without the Holy Spirit reason can love God above all things. As long as a man's mind is at rest and he does not feel God's wrath or judgment, he can imagine that he wants to love God and that he wants to do good for God's sake. In this way the scholastics teach men to merit the forgiveness of sins by doing what is within them, that is, if reason in its sorrow over sin elicits an act of love to God or does good for God's sake.[9] Because this view 10 naturally flatters men, it has produced and increased many types of worship in the church, like monastic vows and the abuses of the Mass; someone has always been making up this or that form of worship or devotion with this view in mind. To support and increase trust 11 in such works, the scholastics have declared that by necessity—the necessity of unchanging order, not of compulsion—God grants grace to those who do this.[1]

In this point of view there are many vicious errors that would 12 take a long time to enumerate. But let the intelligent reader just con-

[9] E.g., Gabriel Biel.
[1] So Bonaventure.

sider this. If this is Christian righteousness, what difference is there
between philosophy and the teaching of Christ? If we merit the forgiveness of sins by these elicited acts of ours, of what use is Christ?
If we can be justified by reason and its works, what need is there of
Christ or of regeneration? On the basis of these opinions, things   13
have come to such a pass that many people ridicule us for teaching
that men ought to seek some righteousness beyond the philosophical. We have heard of some who, in their sermons, laid aside the   14
Gospel and expounded the ethics of Aristotle. If the opponents' ideas
are correct, this was perfectly proper, for Aristotle wrote so well on
natural ethics that nothing further needs to be added. We see   15
that there are books in existence which compare certain teachings of
Christ with the teachings of Socrates, Zeno, and others, as though
Christ had come to give some sort of laws by which we could merit
the forgiveness of sins rather than receiving it freely for his merits.
So if we accept this teaching of the opponents that we merit for-   16
giveness of sins and justification by the works of reason, there will be
no difference between philosophical or Pharisaic righteousness and
Christian righteousness.

In order not to by-pass Christ altogether, our opponents require   17
a knowledge of the history about Christ and claim that he merited
for us a certain disposition or, as they call it, "initial grace," which
they understand as a disposition inclining us to love God more easily.
It is clear, however, what they ascribe to this disposition, for they
imagine that the acts of the will before the disposition and those after
it are of the same type. They imagine that the will can love God, but
that this disposition stimulates it to do so more freely. They bid us
merit this first disposition by our preceding merits. Then they bid us
merit an increase of this disposition and eternal life by the works of
the law. Thus they bury Christ; men should not use him as   18
mediator and believe that for his sake they freely receive the forgiveness of sins and reconciliation, but should dream that they merit
the forgiveness of sins and are accounted righteous by their own
keeping of the law before God. This in spite of the fact that the law
is never satisfied, that reason performs only certain external works and
meanwhile neither fears God nor truly believes that he cares. Though
they talk about this disposition, yet without the righteousness of faith
man can neither have nor understand the love of God.

When they make up a distinction between merit of congruity   19
and merit of condignity,[2] they are only playing in order to avoid the

---

[2] What a sinful man does for himself, in so far as he is able, was defined
as merit of fitness or congruity (*meritum congrui*). What a just man,
enabled by divine grace, does for himself or others was defined as merit of
worthiness or condignity (*meritum condigni*).

impression that they are outright Pelagians. For if God necessarily gives grace for the merit of congruity, it is no longer merit of congruity but merit of condignity. They do not know what they are talking about. They imagine that after that disposition of love a man can earn the merit of condignity, but they would have him doubt whether the disposition is truly present. How is one to know whether one has the merit of congruity or the merit of condignity? But this whole 20 business is the invention of idle men who do not know how the forgiveness of sins takes place, or how the judgment of God and the terrors of conscience drive out our trust in works. Smug hypocrites always believe that they have the merit of condignity, whether or not the disposition is there, because men naturally trust their own righteousness. But terrified consciences waver and doubt and then seek to pile up other works to find peace. They never suppose that they have the merit of condignity, and so they run headlong into despair, unless they hear, beyond the teaching of the law, the Gospel of the free forgiveness of sins and the righteousness of faith.

Thus our opponents teach nothing but the righteousness of 21 reason or of law, at which they look as the Jews did at the veiled face of Moses.[3] In smug hypocrites, who think that they are keeping the law, they arouse presumption, a vain trust in works and a contempt for the grace of Christ. Timid consciences, on the other hand, they drive to despair because in their doubt they can never experience what faith is and how effective it is. And at last they despair utterly.

We for our part maintain that God requires the righteousness 22 of reason. Because of God's command, honorable works commanded in the Decalogue should be performed, according to Gal. 3:24, "The law is a custodian," and I Tim. 1:9, "The law is laid down for the lawless." For God wants this civil discipline to restrain the unspiritual, and to preserve it he has given laws, learning, teaching, governments, and penalties. To some extent, reason can produce this righteous- 23 ness by its own strength, though it is often overwhelmed by its natural weakness and by the devil, who drives it to open crimes. We freely 24 give this righteousness of reason its due credit; for our corrupt nature has no greater good than this, as Aristotle correctly says, "Neither the evening star nor the morning star is more beautiful than righteousness."[4] God even honors it with material rewards. Nevertheless, it ought not be praised at the expense of Christ.

For it is false that by our works we merit the forgiveness of 25 sins.

It is false, too, that men are accounted righteous before God 26 because of the righteousness of reason.

[3] Cf. Ex. 34:30-35; II Cor. 3:13.
[4] *Nicomachean Ethics*, V, 3, II.

It is false, too, that by its own strength reason can love God 27
above all things and keep his law, truly fear him, truly believe that
he hears prayer, willingly obey him in death and in his other visitations,
and not covet. But reason can produce civil works.

It is false, too, and a reproach to Christ, that men who keep 28
the commandments of God outside a state of grace do not sin.

We have proof for this position of ours not only in the 29
Scriptures, but also in the Fathers. Against the Pelagians, Augustine
maintains at length that grace is not given because of our merits. In
Nature and Grace he says: "If natural capacity, with the help of free
will, is in itself sufficient both for discovering how one ought to live,
and also for leading a holy life, then 'Christ died to no purpose'
(Gal. 2:21), and therefore also 'the stumbling-block of the cross has
been removed' (Gal. 5:11). Why then may I not myself exclaim, 30
too—yes, I will exclaim and chide them with a Christian's sorrow—
'You are severed from Christ, you who would be justified by the law;
you have fallen away from grace' (Gal. 5:4); for 'being ignorant of
the righteousness that comes from God, and seeking to establish your
own, you did not submit to God's righteousness' (Rom. 10:3). For
even as Christ is 'the end of the law,' so likewise he is the Saviour of
man's corrupted nature, for righteousness to 'every one who has faith'
(Rom. 10:4)." [5]

John 8:36 says, "If the Son makes you free, you will be free 31
indeed." Therefore reason cannot free us from our sins or merit for
us the forgiveness of sins. And in John 3:5 it is written, "Unless one
is born of water and the Spirit, one cannot enter the kingdom of God."
But if we must be born again through the Holy Spirit, then the
righteousness of reason does not justify us before God, it does not
keep the law. And Rom. 3:23 says, "All fall short of the glory 32
of God," that is, they lack the wisdom and righteousness of God which
acknowledge and glorify him. And Rom. 8:7, 8, "The mind that is
set on the flesh is hostile to God; it does not submit to God's law, indeed
it cannot; and those who are in the flesh cannot please God."
These words are so clear that they do not need an acute under- 33
standing but only attentive listening—to use the words that Augustine
uses in discussing this matter.[6]

If the mind that is set on the flesh is hostile to God, then the flesh
sins even when it performs outward civil works. If it cannot submit
to God's law, it is certainly sinning even when it produces deeds that
are excellent and praiseworthy in human eyes. Our opponents 34
concentrate on the commandments of the second table, which contain
the civil righteousness that reason understands. Content with this, they

---

[5] Augustine, *Nature and Grace*, 40, 47.
[6] Augustine, *Grace and Free Will*, 8, 19.

think they satisfy the law of God. Meanwhile they do not see the first table, which commands us to love God, to be sure that God is wrathful at our sin, to fear him truly, and to be sure that he hears us. But without the Holy Spirit, the human heart either despises the judgment of God in its smugness, or in the midst of punishment it flees and hates his judgment. So it does not obey the first table. It is 35 inherent in man to despise God and to doubt his Word with its threats and promises. Therefore men really sin even when they do virtuous things without the Holy Spirit; for they do them with a wicked heart, and (Rom. 14:23) "whatever does not proceed from faith is sin." Such people despise God when they do these things, as Epicurus did not believe that God cared for him or regarded or heard him.[7] This contempt for God corrupts works that seem virtuous, for God judges the heart.

Finally, it was very foolish of our opponents to write that men 36 who are under eternal wrath merit the forgiveness of sins by an elicited act of love, since it is impossible to love God unless faith has first accepted the forgiveness of sins. A heart that really feels God's wrath cannot love him unless it sees that he is reconciled. While he terrifies us and seems to be casting us into eternal death, human nature cannot bring itself to love a wrathful, judging, punishing God. It 37 is easy enough for idle men to make up these dreams that a man guilty of mortal sin can love God above all things, since they themselves do not feel the wrath or judgment of God. But in the agony of conscience and in conflict, the conscience experiences how vain these philosophical speculations are. Paul says (Rom. 4:15), 38 "The law brings wrath." He does not say that by the law men merit the forgiveness of sins. For the law always accuses and terrifies consciences. It does not justify, because a conscience terrified by the law flees before God's judgment. It is an error, therefore, for men to trust that by the law and by their works they merit the forgiveness of sins. We have said enough about the righteousness of law 39 or of reason which our opponents teach. Later on, in the exposition of our doctrine of the righteousness of faith, the subject itself will compel us to cite further evidence; this will also help refute those errors of our opponents that we have been considering.

Therefore men cannot keep the law by their own strength, and 40 they are all under sin and subject to eternal wrath and death. On this account the law cannot free us from sin or justify us, but the promise of the forgiveness of sins and justification was given because of Christ. He was given for us to make satisfaction for the sins of the world and has been appointed as the mediator and the propitiator. This 41

[7] Cicero, *Laws*, I, 7, 21, 22.

promise is not conditional upon our merits but offers the forgiveness of sins and justification freely. As Paul says (Rom. 11:6), "If it is by works, it is no longer on the basis of grace." Elsewhere he says, "Now, the righteousness of God has been manifested apart from law" (Rom. 3:21), that is, the forgiveness of sins is offered freely. Reconciliation does not depend upon our merits. If the forgiveness of 42 sins depended upon our merits and if reconciliation were by the law, it would be useless. For since we do not keep the law, it would follow that we would never obtain the promise of reconciliation. So Paul reasons in Rom. 4:14, "If it is the adherents of the law who are to be the heirs, faith is null and the promise is void." For if the promise were conditional upon our merits and the law, which we never keep, it would follow that the promise is useless.

Since we obtain justification through a free promise, however, 43 it follows that we cannot justify ourselves. Otherwise, why would a promise be necessary? The Gospel is, strictly speaking, the promise of forgiveness of sins and justification because of Christ. Since we can accept this promise only by faith, the Gospel proclaims the righteousness of faith in Christ, which the law does not teach. And this is not the righteousness of the law. For the law requires our own 44 works and our own perfection. But to us, oppressed by sin and death, the promise freely offers reconciliation for Christ's sake, which we do not accept by works but by faith alone. This faith brings to God a trust not in our own merits, but only in the promise of mercy in Christ. Therefore, when a man believes that his sins are forgiven 45 because of Christ and that God is reconciled and favorably disposed to him because of Christ, this personal faith obtains the forgiveness of sins and justifies us. In penitence and the terrors of conscience it consoles and encourages our hearts. Thus it regenerates us and brings us the Holy Spirit, so that we can finally obey God's law, love him, truly fear him, be sure that he hears us, and obey him in all afflictions. It mortifies our lust. By freely accepting the forgive- 46 ness of sins, faith sets against God's wrath not our merits of love, but Christ the mediator and propitiator. This faith is the true knowledge of Christ, it uses his blessings, it regenerates our hearts, it precedes our keeping of the law. About this faith there is not a 47 syllable in the teaching of our opponents. Therefore we condemn our opponents for teaching the righteousness of the law instead of the righteousness of the Gospel, which proclaims the righteousness of faith in Christ.

WHAT IS JUSTIFYING FAITH?

Our opponents imagine that faith is only historical knowledge 48 and teach that it can exist with mortal sin. And so they say nothing about faith by which, as Paul says so often, men are justified, because those who are accounted righteous before God do not live in mortal sin. The faith that justifies, however, is no mere historical knowledge, but the firm acceptance of God's offer promising forgiveness of sins and justification. To avoid the impression that it is merely knowledge, we add that to have faith means to want and to accept the promised offer of forgiveness of sins and justification.

It is easy to determine the difference between this faith and the 49 righteousness of the law. Faith is that worship which receives God's offered blessings; the righteousness of the law is that worship which offers God our own merits. It is by faith that God wants to be worshiped, namely, that we receive from him what he promises and offers.

Paul clearly shows that faith does not simply mean historical 50 knowledge but is a firm acceptance of the promise (Rom. 4:16): "That is why it depends on faith, in order that the promise may be guaranteed." For he says that only faith can accept the promise. He therefore correlates and connects promise and faith. It will be 51 easy to determine what faith is if we pay attention to the article of the Creed on the forgiveness of sins. So it is not enough to believe that Christ was born, suffered, and was raised unless we add this article, the purpose of the history, "the forgiveness of sins." The rest must be integrated with this article, namely, that for Christ's sake and not because of our own merits the forgiveness of sins is bestowed upon us. For why did Christ have to be offered for our sins if our 52 merits make satisfaction for them?

In speaking of justifying faith, therefore, we must remember 53 that these three elements always belong together: the promise itself, the fact that the promise is free, and the merits of Christ as the price and propitiation. The promise is accepted by faith; the fact that it is free excludes our merits and shows that the blessing is offered only by mercy; the merits of Christ are the price because there must be a certain propitiation for our sins. Scripture contains many pleas 54 for mercy, and the holy Fathers often say that we are saved by mercy. And so at every mention of mercy we must remember 55 that this requires faith, which accepts the promise of mercy. Similarly, at every mention of faith we are also thinking of its object, the promised mercy. For faith does not justify or save because it 56 is a good work in itself, but only because it accepts the promised mercy.

This service and worship is especially praised throughout the 57 prophets and the Psalms. Even though the law does not teach the free forgiveness of sins, the patriarchs knew the promise of the Christ, that for his sake God intended to forgive sins. As they understood that the Christ would be the price for our sins, they knew that our works could not pay so high a price. Therefore they received free mercy and the ʃorgiveness of sins by faith, just as the saints in the

New Testament. The frequent references to mercy and faith in   58
the Psalms and the prophets belong here; for example, "If thou, O
Lord, shouldst mark iniquities, Lord, who shall stand?" (Ps. 130:3).
Here the psalmist confesses his sins, but he does not lay claim to any
merit of his own. He adds, "There is forgiveness with thee" (v. 4).
Here he comforts himself with his trust in God's mercy. He quotes the
promise: "My soul waits for his word, my soul hopes in the Lord,"
that is, because thou has promised the forgiveness of sins I am sustained by thy promise. Therefore the patriarchs, too, were justi-   59
fied not by the law but by the promise and faith. It is strange that
our opponents make so little of faith when they see it praised everywhere as the foremost kind of worship, as in Ps. 50:15: "Call upon
me in the day of trouble; I will deliver you, and you shall glorify
me." This is how God wants to be known and worshiped, that we   60
accept his blessings and receive them because of his mercy rather
than because of our own merits. This is the greatest consolation in
all afflictions, and our opponents take it away when they despise and
disparage faith and teach men to deal with God only by works and
merits.

FAITH IN CHRIST JUSTIFIES

First of all, lest anyone think that we are speaking of an idle   61
˙storical knowledge, we must tell how faith comes into being. Later
we shall show that it justifies and what this means, and we shall
answer our opponents' objections.

In the last chapter of Luke (24:47) Christ commands that   62
penitence and forgiveness of sins should be preached in his name.
The Gospel declares that all men are under sin and are worthy of
eternal wrath and death. For Christ's sake it offers forgiveness of
sins and justification, which are received by faith. By its accusations,
the preaching of penitence terrifies our consciences with real and
serious fears. For these, our hearts must again receive consolation.
This happens if they believe Christ's promise that for his sake we
have the forgiveness of sins. Amid such fears this faith brings peace
of mind, consoles us, receives the forgiveness of sins, justifies and
quickens us. For this consolation is a new and spiritual life. This   63
is plain and clear, the faithful can grasp it, and it has the testimony
of the church. Nowhere can our opponents say how the Holy Spirit
is given. They imagine that the sacraments bestow the Holy Spirit
ex opere operato without the proper attitude in the recipient,[8] as
though the gift of the Holy Spirit were a minor matter.

---

[8] Since the thirteenth century *ex opere operato* ("by the mere performance," or "by the outward act") was a formula customarily applied to the
sacraments, which were said to be efficacious if the recipient did not inter-
pose an obstacle and if he had what the Augsburg Confession and the
Apology call "historical faith," i.e. assent rather than trust.

But we are talking about a faith that is not an idle thought, but 64 frees us from death, brings forth a new life in our hearts, and is a work of the Holy Spirit. Therefore this cannot exist with mortal sin, but whenever it appears it brings forth good fruits, as we shall point out later. What can we say more simply and clearly about the 65 conversion of the wicked or the manner of regeneration? From such a great crowd of writers, let them produce one commentary on the *Sentences*[9] that tells how regeneration takes place. When they 66 talk about the disposition of love, they pretend that one merits it by works. Like the present-day Anabaptists, they deny that it is received through the Word.[1] But one cannot deal with God or grasp him 67 except through the Word. Therefore justification takes place through the Word, as Paul says (Rom. 1:16), "The Gospel is the power of God for salvation to every one who has faith," and (Rom. 10:17), "Faith comes from what is heard." From this we can prove that faith justifies. For if justification takes place only through the Word, and the Word is received only by faith, then it follows that faith justifies. But we have other more telling arguments. By what we 68 have said so far we have sought to show the manner of regeneration and the nature of the faith we have been discussing.

Now we shall show that faith justifies. In the first place, we 69 would remind our readers that if we must hold to the proposition, "Christ is the mediator," then we must defend the proposition, "Faith justifies." For how will Christ be the mediator if we do not use him as mediator in our justification and believe that for his sake we are accounted righteous? But to believe means to trust in Christ's merits, that because of him God wants to be reconciled to us. In the 70 same way, if we must defend the proposition, "The promise of Christ is necessary over and above the law," then we must defend the proposition, "Faith justifies." For the law does not teach the free forgiveness of sins. Again, we cannot keep the law unless we first receive the Holy Spirit. Therefore we must maintain that the promise of Christ is necessary. But this can be accepted only by faith. Therefore anyone who denies that faith justifies teaches only the law and does away with Christ and the Gospel.

When we say that faith justifies, some may think this refers 71 to the beginning, as though faith were the start of justification or a preparation for justification. Then it would be not faith, but the works that follow, by which we would become acceptable unto God. They imagine faith is praised so highly because it is this kind 72

---

[9] Peter Lombard's *Sentences,* the object of many commentaries at the close of the Middle Ages.

[1] Cf. above, Augsburg Confession, V, 4.

of beginning.[2] For beginnings are very important; or, as the common saying goes, "the beginning is half of everything." [3] Thus one can say that grammar produces the teachers of all the arts since it prepares for them, even though it is his own art that makes everyone an artist. Regarding faith we maintain not this, but rather that because of Christ by faith itself we are truly accounted righteous or acceptable before God. And "to be justified" means to make unrighteous men righteous or to regenerate them, as well as to be pronounced or accounted righteous. For Scripture speaks both ways. Therefore we want to show first that faith alone makes a righteous man out of an unrighteous one, that is, that it receives the forgiveness of sins.

The particle "alone" offends some people, even though Paul 73 says (Rom. 3:28), "We hold that a man is justified by faith apart from works of law," and again (Eph. 2:8, 9), "It is the gift of God, not because of works, lest any man should boast," and again (Rom. 3:24), "They are justified by his grace as a gift." If they dislike the exclusive particle "alone," let them remove the other exclusive terms from Paul, too, like "freely," "not of works," "it is a gift," etc., for these terms are also exclusive. We exclude the claim of merit, not the Word or the sacraments, as our opponents slanderously claim. We said earlier that faith is conceived by the Word, and we give the highest praise to the ministry of the Word. Love and good works 74 must also follow faith. So they are not excluded as though they did not follow, but trust in the merit of love or works is excluded from justification. This we shall clearly show.

WE OBTAIN THE FORGIVENESS OF SINS ONLY BY FAITH IN CHRIST

Even our opponents will grant, we suppose, that the forgive- 75 ness of sins is supremely necessary in justification. For we are all under sin. Therefore we argue this way:

First, forgiveness of sins is the same as justification according 76 to Ps. 32:1, "Blessed is he whose transgression is forgiven." We 77 obtain the forgiveness of sins only by faith in Christ, not through love, or because of love or works, though love does follow faith. There- 78 fore we are justified by faith alone, justification being understood as making an unrighteous man righteous or effecting his regeneration.

It is easy to state the minor premise if we know how the for- 79 giveness of sins takes place. Our idle opponents quibble as to whether the forgiveness of sins and the infusion of grace are the same thing, yet on this question they had nothing to say. In the forgiveness of sins, the terrors of sin and of eternal death must be conquered in

---

[2] Cf. Council of Trent, Sess. VI, 8.
[3] Plato.

our hearts, as Paul says in I Cor. 15:56, 57: "The sting of death is sin, and the power of sin is law. But thanks be to God, who gives us the victory through our Lord Jesus Christ." That is, sin terrifies consciences; this happens through the law, which shows God's wrath against sin. But we conquer through Christ. How? By faith, when we comfort ourselves by firm trust in the mercy promised because of Christ.

We prove the minor premise as follows. Since Christ is set   80 forth to be the propitiator, through whom the Father is reconciled to us, we cannot appease God's wrath by setting forth our own works. For it is only by faith that Christ is accepted as the mediator. By faith alone, therefore, we obtain the forgiveness of sins when we comfort our hearts with trust in the mercy promised for Christ's sake. Thus   81 Paul says in Rom. 5:2, "Through him we have obtained access" to the Father, and he adds, "through faith." In this way we are reconciled to the Father and receive the forgiveness of sins when we are comforted by trust in the mercy promised for Christ's sake. Our opponents suppose that Christ is the mediator and propitiator because he merited for us the disposition of love. And so they would not have us make use of him now as our mediator. Instead, as though Christ were completely buried, they imagine that we have access through our own works, by which we merit this disposition, and then, through this love, have access to God. Does this not bury Christ completely and do away with the whole teaching of faith? Paul, on the other hand, teaches that we have access (that is, reconciliation) through Christ. And to show how this happens, he adds that through faith we have access. By faith, therefore, for Christ's sake we receive the forgiveness of sins. We cannot set our love or our works against the wrath of God.

Second, it is certain that sins are forgiven because of Christ,   82 the propitiator, according to Rom. 3:25, "Whom God put forward as an expiation," and Paul adds, "to be received by faith." So this propitiator benefits us when by faith we receive the mercy promised in him and set it against the wrath and judgment of God. There is a similar statement in Heb. 4:14-16, "Since then we have a great high priest, . . . let us then with confidence draw near." By bidding us draw near to God with trust not in our merits but in Christ, the high priest, this statement requires faith.

Third, in Acts 10:43, Peter says, "To him all the prophets bear   83 witness that every one who believes in him receives forgiveness of sins through his name." How could he say it any more plainly? We receive the forgiveness of sins, he says, through his name, that is, for his sake: therefore, not for the sake of our merits, our contrition, attrition, love, worship, or works. And he adds, "when we believe in him." Thus he requires faith. We cannot take hold of the name of Christ except by faith. In addition, he cites the consensus of all the prophets, which is really citing the authority of the church. But we shall discuss this passage later on in considering penitence.[4]

Fourth, the forgiveness of sins is a thing promised for Christ's 84 sake. Therefore it can be accepted only by faith, since a promise can be accepted only on faith. In Rom. 4:16 Paul says, "That is why it depends on faith, in order that the promise may rest on grace and be guaranteed," as though he were to say, "If it depended on our merits, the promise would be uncertain and useless inasmuch as we could never determine whether we had merited enough." Experienced consciences can readily understand this. Therefore Paul says (Gal. 3:22), "God consigned all things to sin, that what was promised to faith in Jesus Christ might be given to those who believe." Here he denies us any merit, for he says that all are guilty and consigned to sin. Then he adds that the promise of the forgiveness of sins and justification is a gift, and further that the promise can be accepted by faith. Based upon the nature of a promise, this is Paul's chief argument, which he often repeats (Rom. 4:16; Gal. 3:18). Nothing one can devise or imagine will refute Paul's argument. So pious men should not let themselves be diverted from this 85 declaration, that we receive the forgiveness of sins for Christ's sake only by faith; here they have a certain and firm consolation against the terrors of sin, against eternal death, and against all the gates of hell (Matt. 16:18).

Faith alone justifies because we receive the forgiveness of sins 86 and the Holy Spirit by faith alone. The reconciled are accounted righteous and children of God not on account of their own purity but by mercy on account of Christ, if they grasp this mercy by faith. Thus the Scriptures testify that we are accounted righteous by faith. We shall therefore add clear testimonies stating that faith is the very righteousness by which we are accounted righteous before God. This is not because it is a work worthy in itself, but because it receives God's promise that for Christ's sake he wishes to be propitious to believers in Christ and because it believes that "God made Christ our wisdom, our righteousness and sanctification and redemption" (I Cor. 1:30).

In the Epistle to the Romans, especially, Paul deals with this 87 subject and states that when we believe that God is reconciled to us for Christ's sake we are justified freely by faith. In chap. 3 he advances this conclusion, embodying the basic issue of the whole discussion: "We hold that man is justified by faith apart from works of law"

<hr />

[4] Below. Art. XII. 66ff.

(Rom. 3:28). This our opponents interpret as referring to Levitical ceremonies, but Paul is talking about the whole law, not only about ceremonies. For later on he quotes the Decalogue, "You shall not covet" (Rom. 7:7). If moral works merited the forgiveness of sins and justification, there would be no need for Christ and the promise, and everything that Paul says about the promise would be overthrown. Then he would have been wrong in writing to the Ephesians (2:8) that we are saved freely by "the gift of God, not because of works." Paul also mentions Abraham and David, who had God's command regarding circumcision (Rom. 4:1-6). If any works justified, therefore, surely these works, having a command, would have to justify. But Paul is talking about the whole law, as Augustine correctly maintains in his lengthy discussion on *The Spirit and the Letter,* where he says toward the end, "Having therefore considered and discussed these matters according to the ability that the Lord saw fit to grant us, we conclude that a man is not justified by the precepts of a good life, but through faith in Jesus Christ." [5]

And lest we suppose that Paul made the statement "Faith 88 justifies" inadvertently, he reinforces and confirms it with a long discussion in Rom. 4 and repeats it later in all his epistles. In 89 Rom. 4:4, 5 he says, "To one who works, his wages are not reckoned as a gift but as his due. And to one who does not work but trusts in him who justifies the ungodly, his faith is reckoned as righteousness." Here he clearly says that faith itself is accounted for righteousness. It is faith, therefore, that God declares to be righteousness; he adds that it is accounted freely and denies that it could be accounted freely if it were a reward for works. Therefore he excludes even the merit of works according to the moral law; for if by these we earned justification before God, faith would not be accounted for righteousness without works. And afterwards (Rom. 4:9) Paul says, "We 90 say that faith was reckoned to Abraham as righteousness." In 91 Rom. 5:1 he says, "Since we are justified by faith, we have peace with God," that is, our consciences are tranquil and joyful before God, and in Rom. 10:10, "Man believes with his heart and so 92 is justified," where he declares that faith is the righteousness of the heart. Gal. 2:16, "We have believed in Christ Jesus, in order to 93 be justified by faith in Christ, and not by works of the law." Eph. 2:8, "For by grace you have been saved through faith; and this is not your own doing, it is the gift of God—not because of works, lest any man should boast."

John 1:12, 13, "To all who believed in his name, he gave 94 power to become children of God; who were born, not of blood nor of the will of the flesh nor of the will of man, but of God."

[5] Augustine, *The Spirit and the Letter.* 13, 22.

John 3:14, 15, "As Moses lifted up the serpent in the wilderness, 95
so must the Son of man be lifted up, that whoever believes in him
may have eternal life." Likewise John 3:17, 18, "God sent the Son 96
into the world, not to condemn the world, but that the world might
be saved through him. He who believes in him is not condemned."
Acts 13:38, 39, "Let it be known to you therefore, brethren, 97
that through this man forgiveness of sins is proclaimed to you, and by
him every one that believes is justified from everything from which
you could not be justified by the law of Moses." What could describe
the work of Christ and justification more clearly? The law, he says,
does not justify. Christ was given for us to believe that we are justified
because of him. He explicitly denies justification to the law. Therefore we are accounted righteous for Christ's sake when we believe that
God is reconciled to us because of him. Acts 4:11, 12, "This is 98
the stone which was rejected by you builders, but which has become
the head of the corner. And there is salvation in no one else, for
there is no other name under heaven given among men by which we
must be saved." But only faith takes hold of the name of Christ.
Therefore we are saved by trust in the name of Christ, not in our
works. For "name" here means that which is cited as the cause of
salvation. To cite the name of Christ is to trust in the name of Christ
as the cause or price on account of which we are saved. Acts 99
15:9, "He cleansed their hearts by faith." Therefore the faith of
which the apostles speak is not idle knowledge, but a thing that
receives the Holy Spirit and justifies us.

Hab. 2:4, "The righteous shall live by his faith." Here the 100
writer says first that men are righteous by the faith which believes
that God is propitious; and he adds that this same faith quickens
because it brings forth peace, joy, and eternal life in the heart.

Isa. 53:11, "By his knowledge he shall justify many." But 101
what is the knowledge of Christ except to know Christ's blessings,
the promises which by the Gospel he has spread throughout the
world? And to know these blessings is rightly and truly to believe
in Christ, to believe that God will certainly accomplish what he has
promised for Christ's sake.

But the Scripture is full of such testimonies. In some places 102
it teaches the law; in others it teaches the promises of Christ, of the
forgiveness of sins, and of our gracious acceptance for Christ's sake.

There are similar statements here and there in the holy Fathers. 103
In a letter to a certain Irenaeus, Ambrose says: "But the world was
subjected to him through the law; for by the commandment of the law
all are accused and by the works of the law none is justified, that is,
by the law sin is recognized but its guilt is not relieved. The law
would seem to be harmful since it has made all men sinners, but

when the Lord Jesus came he forgave all men the sin that none could escape and by shedding his blood canceled the bond that stood against us (Col. 2:14). This is what Paul says, 'Law came in, to increase the trespass; but where sin increased, grace abounded all the more' (Rom. 5:20) through Jesus. For after the whole world was subjected, he took away the sin of the whole world, as John testified when he said (John 1:29), 'Behold the Lamb of God, who takes away the sin of the world!' So let no one glory in his works since no one is justified by his deeds. But he who is righteous has it as a gift because he was justified after being washed. It is faith therefore that frees men through the blood of Christ; for 'blessed is he whose transgression is forgiven, whose sin is covered' (Ps. 32:1)." These are the words 104 of Ambrose, which clearly support our position; he denies justification to works and ascribes it to faith, which liberates us through the blood of Christ. If you pile up all the commentators on the *Sentences* 105 with all their magnificent titles—for some are called "angelic," others "subtle," and others "irrefutable" [6]—read them and reread them, they contribute less to an understanding of Paul than this one sentence from Ambrose.

Augustine writes many things in the same vein against the 106 Pelagians. In *The Spirit and the Letter* he says: "The righteousness of law is set forth in the statement that he who keeps the law will live in it, so that by recognizing his weakness one may attain to it, keep it, and live in it. He reconciles the justifier by faith, not by his own strength nor by the letter of that same law, for this is impossible. Only in a justified man is there a good work by the performance of which he can live. Justification is obtained by faith." Here he clearly says that the justifier is reconciled by faith and that justification is obtained by faith. A little later Augustine says: "By the law we fear God, by faith we hope in God. But to those who fear punishment grace is hidden; laboring under this fear, the soul by faith flees to the mercy of God, that he may give what he commands." [7] Here he teaches that our hearts are terrified by the law but receive consolation by faith, and that before we try to keep the law we should receive mercy by faith. A little later we shall quote several other statements.

It is surely amazing that our opponents are unmoved by the 107 many passages in the Scriptures that clearly attribute justification to faith and specifically deny it to works. Do they suppose that this 108 is repeated so often for no reason? Do they suppose that these words fell from the Holy Spirit unawares? But they have thought up 109

---

[6] Thomas Aquinas was called the "angelic doctor," Duns Scotus the "subtle doctor," and Alexander of Hales the "irrefutable doctor."

[7] Augustine, *The Spirit and the Letter*, 29, 51.

a piece of sophistry to evade them. They should be interpreted, so they say, as referring to "faith fashioned by love," that is, they do not attribute justification to faith except on account of love.[8] Indeed, they do not attribute justification to faith at all, but only to love, because they imagine that faith can exist with mortal sin. Where does | |0 this end but with the abolition of the promise and a return to the law? If faith receives the forgiveness of sins on account of love, the forgiveness of sins will always be unsure, for we never love as much as we should. In fact, we do not love at all unless our hearts are sure that the forgiveness of sins has been granted to us. If our opponents require us to trust in our own love for the forgiveness of sins and justification, they completely abolish the Gospel of the free forgiveness of sins. For men can neither render nor understand this love unless they believe that the forgiveness of sins is received freely.

We say, too, that love should follow faith, as Paul also says, | | | "In Christ Jesus neither circumcision nor uncircumcision is of any avail, but faith working through love" (Gal. 5:6). We are not | |2 to think from this that we receive the forgiveness of sins by trust in this love or on account of this love, just as little as we receive the forgiveness of sins on account of the other works that follow it. For the forgiveness of sins is received by faith alone—and we mean faith in the true sense of the word—since the promise can be received only by faith. But faith in the true sense, as the Scriptures use | |3 the word, is that which accepts the promise. And because it | |4 receives the forgiveness of sins and reconciles us to God, we must be accounted righteous by this faith for Christ's sake before we love and keep the law, although love must necessarily follow. This | |5 faith is no idle knowledge, nor can it exist with mortal sin; but it is a work of the Holy Spirit that frees us from death, comforting and quickening terrified minds. And since this faith alone receives | |6 the forgiveness of sins, renders us acceptable to God, and brings the Holy Spirit, it should be called "grace that makes us acceptable to God" rather than love, which is the effect resulting from it.

What we have shown thus far, on the basis of the Scriptures | |7 and arguments derived from the Scriptures, was to make clear that by faith alone we receive the forgiveness of sins for Christ's sake, and by faith alone are justified, that is, out of unrighteous we are made righteous and regenerated men. One can easily see how neces- | |8 sary it is to understand this faith, for through it alone we recognize Christ's work and receive his blessings and it alone provides a sure and firm consolation for devout minds. And there must needs | |9 be a proclamation in the church from which the faithful may receive the sure hope of salvation. Our opponents give men bad advice when

[8] Thomas Aquinas, *Summa theologica*, II, 1, q.113, a.4 ad 1.

they bid them doubt whether they have received the forgiveness of
sins. For in the hour of death, what will sustain those who have
heard nothing about this faith and who believe that they should doubt
about receiving the forgiveness of sins? Furthermore, the Gospel |20
(that is, the promise that sins are forgiven freely for Christ's sake)
must be retained in the church. Whoever fails to teach about this
faith we are discussing completely destroys the Gospel. The |2|
scholastics do not say a word about this faith. In following them
and rejecting this faith, our opponents fail to see that thereby they
destroy the entire promise of the free forgiveness of sins and of the
righteousness of Christ.

LOVE AND THE KEEPING OF THE LAW[9]

Here our opponents urge against us the texts, "If you would |22
enter life, keep the commandments" (Matt. 19:17), "The doers of
the law will be justified" (Rom. 2:13), and many similar passages
regarding the law and works. Before answering these, we must say
what we believe about love and the keeping of the law.

It is written in the prophet (Jer. 31:33), "I will put my law |23
upon their hearts." In Rom. 3:31 Paul says that faith does not overthrow but upholds the law. Christ says (Matt. 19:17), "If you would
enter life, keep the commandments." And again, "If I have not love,
I am nothing" (I Cor. 13:2). These and similar passages |24
assert that we should begin to keep the law ever more and more. We
are not speaking of ceremonies, but of the Decalogue, the law that
deals with the thoughts of the heart. Since faith brings the Holy |25
Spirit and produces a new life in our hearts, it must also produce
spiritual impulses in our hearts. What these impulses are, the prophet
shows when he says (Jer. 31:33), "I will put my law upon their
hearts." After we have been justified and regenerated by faith, therefore, we begin to fear and love God, to pray and expect help from
him, to thank and praise him, and to submit to him in our afflictions.
Then we also begin to love our neighbor because our hearts have
spiritual and holy impulses.

This cannot happen until, being justified and regenerated, we |26
receive the Holy Spirit. First, it is impossible to keep the law without
Christ; it is impossible to keep the law without the Holy Spirit.

---

[9] In some editions of the Book of Concord the remainder of Article II
appears as Article III, with new section numbers beginning at this point.
Secondary works on the confessions will therefore sometimes contain
references like "III, 23," which would correspond to "II, 144" in the
original arrangement of the Apology to which this edition returns. The
heading "Love and the Keeping of the Law" indicates not a new article,
but a new subdivision of the same article, following the subdivision headed
"We Obtain the Forgiveness of Sins Only by Faith in Christ" (Art. IV, 75).

But the Spirit is received by faith, according to Paul's word 127 (Gal. 3:14), "That we might receive the promise of the Spirit through faith." Then, too, how can the human heart love God while 128 it knows that in his terrible wrath he is overwhelming us with temporal and eternal calamities? The law always accuses us, it always shows that God is wrathful. We cannot love God until we have grasped 129 his mercy by faith. Only then does he become an object that can be loved.

Although it is somewhat possible to do civil works, that is, the 130 outward works of the law, without Christ and the Holy Spirit, still the impulses of the heart toward God, belonging to the essence of the divine law, are impossible without the Holy Spirit; this is evident from what we have already said. But our opponents are fine 131 theologians! They look at the second table and political works; about the first table they care nothing, as though it were irrelevant, or at best they require only outward acts of worship. They utterly overlook that eternal law, far beyond the senses and understanding of all creatures: "You shall love the Lord your God with all your heart" (Deut. 6:5).

But Christ was given so that for his sake we might receive 132 the gift of the forgiveness of sins and the Holy Spirit, to bring forth in us eternal righteousness and a new and eternal life. Therefore we cannot correctly keep the law unless by faith we have received the Holy Spirit. Paul says that faith does not overthrow but upholds the law (Rom. 3:31) because the law can be kept only when the Holy Spirit is given. In II Cor. 3:15-17 he states that the veil that 133 covered the face of Moses cannot be removed except by faith, which receives the Holy Spirit. For this is what he says: "Yes, to this day whenever Moses is read a veil lies over their minds; but when a man turns to the Lord the veil is removed. Now, the Lord is the Spirit, and where the Spirit of the Lord is, there is freedom." By the 134 "veil" Paul means human opinion about the entire law, both the moral and the ceremonial; that is, hypocrites think that outward and civil works satisfy the law of God and that sacrifice and ritual justify before God *ex opere operato*. But this veil is removed from us, 135 and this error taken away, when God shows us our uncleanness and the greatness of our sin. Only then do we see how far we are from keeping the law. Then we recognize how our flesh in its smugness and indifference does not fear God or truly believe in his providential care, but supposes that men are born and die by chance. Then we experience our failure to believe that God forgives and hears us. But when we are consoled by faith through hearing the Gospel of the forgiveness of sins, we receive the Holy Spirit, so that we can think rightly about God, fear him, and believe in him. From this it is clear that without Christ and without the Holy Spirit we cannot keep the law.

Therefore we also hold that the keeping of the law should 136 begin in us and increase more and more. But we mean to include both elements, namely, the inward spiritual impulses and the outward good works. Our opponents slanderously claim that we do not require good works, whereas we not only require them but show how they can be done. The results show that hypocrites who try 137 to keep the law by their own strength cannot achieve what they set out to do. For human nature is far too weak to be able by its 138 own strength to resist the devil, who holds enthralled all who have not been freed by faith. Nothing less than Christ's power is 139 needed for our conflict with the devil. We know that for Christ's sake we have a gracious God and his promise. And therefore we pray that the Holy Spirit may govern and defend us, so that we may not be deceived and err, nor be driven to do anything against God's will. So the Psalm teaches (Ps. 68:18), "He led captivity captive and gave gifts to men." For Christ conquered the devil and gave us his promise and the Holy Spirit, so that with the help of God we, too, might conquer. And I John 3:8 says, "The reason the Son of God appeared was to destroy the works of the devil."

We teach, furthermore, not only how the law can be kept, 140 but also that God is pleased when we keep it—not because we live up to it but because we are in Christ, as we shall show a little later. So it is clear that we require good works. In fact, we add that 141 it is impossible to separate faith from love for God, be it ever so small. For through Christ we come to the Father; and having received the forgiveness of sins, we become sure that we have a gracious God who cares about us, we call upon him, give thanks to him, fear and love him. So John teaches in his first epistle (4:19): "We love," he says, "because he first loved us," that is, because he gave his Son for us and forgave us our sins. So he indicates that faith precedes while love follows. The faith of which we are 142 speaking, moreover, has its existence in penitence; that is, it is conceived in the terrors of a conscience that feels God's wrath against our sins and looks for forgiveness of sins and deliverance from sin. This faith ought to grow and be strengthened in these terrors and in other afflictions. And so it cannot exist in those who live accord- 143 ing to the flesh, who take pleasure in their lusts and obey them. Therefore Paul says (Rom. 8:1), "There is therefore now no condemnation for those who are in Christ Jesus, who do not walk according to the flesh, but according to the Spirit." And in Rom. 8:12, 13 he says, "We are debtors, not to the flesh, to live according to the flesh—for if you live according to the flesh you will die, but

if by the Spirit you put to death the deeds of the body, you will
live." Receiving the forgiveness of sins for a heart terrified and   144
fleeing from sin, therefore, such a faith does not remain in those
who obey their lusts, nor does it exist together with mortal sin.

Selecting love, which is only one of these effects of faith, our   145
opponents teach that love justifies. From this it is clear that they
teach only the law. They do not teach that we must first receive the
forgiveness of sins by faith, nor that on account of Christ, the mediator,
we have a gracious God. They think this is on account of our love,
though they do not and cannot say what the nature of this love
is. They claim to keep the law, though this glory properly   146
belongs to Christ. In opposition to the judgment of God they set
a trust in their own works, for they say they earn grace and eternal
life by merit. Such a trust is simply wicked and vain. In this life
we cannot satisfy the law, because our unspiritual nature continually
brings forth evil desires, though the Spirit in us resists them.

But someone may ask: Since we also grant that love is the   147
work of the Holy Spirit and since it is righteousness because it is
the keeping of the law, why do we deny that it justifies? To this we
must answer, first of all, that we do not receive the forgiveness of
sins through love or on account of love, but on account of Christ
by faith alone. Faith alone, looking to the promise and believing   148
with full assurance that God forgives because Christ did not die in
vain, conquers the terrors of sin and death. If somebody doubts   149
that his sins are forgiven, he insults Christ because he thinks that his
sin is greater and stronger than the death and promise of Christ,
though Paul says that grace abounded more than sin (Rom. 5:20),
that mercy is more powerful than sin. If somebody believes   150
that he obtains the forgiveness of sins because he loves, he insults
Christ and in God's judgment he will discover that this trust in his
own righteousness was wicked and empty. Therefore it must be faith
that reconciles and justifies. We do not receive the forgiveness   151
of sins by other virtues of the law or on account of them (whether
patience, chastity, or obedience to the government, etc.), even though
these virtues must follow. Just as little do we receive the forgiveness
of sins on account of love, though it, too, must follow.

There is a familiar figure of speech, called synecdoche, by   152
which we sometimes combine cause and effect in the same phrase.
Christ says in Luke 7:47, "Her sins, which are many, are forgiven,
because she loved much." But he interprets his own words when
he adds: "Your faith has saved you" (v. 50). Now Christ did not
want to say that by her works of love the woman had merited the
forgiveness of sins. Therefore he clearly says, "Your faith has   153
saved you." But faith is that which grasps God's free mercy because

of God's Word. If anybody denies that this is faith, he utterly mis-
understands the nature of faith. And the account here shows |54
what he calls "love." The woman came, believing that she should
seek the forgiveness of sins from Christ. This is the highest way of
worshiping Christ. Nothing greater could she ascribe to him. By
looking for the forgiveness of sins from him, she truly acknowledged
him as the Messiah. Truly to believe means to think of Christ in
this way, and in this way to worship and take hold of him. Moreover,
Christ used the word "love" not toward the woman but against the
Pharisee, because Christ contrasted the whole act of reverence of
the Pharisee with that of the woman. He chides the Pharisee for not
acknowledging him as the Messiah, though he did show him the
outward courtesies due a guest and a great and holy man. He points
to the woman and praises her reverence, her anointing and crying,
all of which were a sign and confession of faith that she was looking
for the forgiveness of sins from Christ. It was not without reason
that this truly powerful example moved Christ to chide the Pharisee,
this wise and honest but unbelieving man. He charges him with
irreverence and reproves him with the example of the woman. What
a disgrace that an uneducated woman should believe God, while a
doctor of the law does not believe or accept the Messiah or seek from
him the forgiveness of sins and salvation!

In this way, therefore, he praises her entire act of worship, |55
as the Scriptures often do when they include many things in one
phrase. Later we shall take up similar passages, like Luke 11:41,
"Give alms; and behold, everything is clean." He demands not only
alms, but also the righteousness of faith. In the same way he says
here, "Her sins, which are many, are forgiven, because she loved
much," that is, because she truly worshiped me with faith and with
the acts and signs of faith. He includes the whole act of worship;
but meanwhile he teaches that it is faith that properly accepts the
forgiveness of sins, though love, confession, and other good fruits
ought to follow. He does not mean that these fruits are the price or
propitiation which earns the forgiveness of sins that reconciles us
to God.

We are debating about an important issue, the honor of |56
Christ and the source of sure and firm consolation for pious minds
—whether we should put our trust in Christ or in our own works.
If we put it in our works, we rob Christ of his honor as mediator |57
and propitiator. And in the judgment of God we shall learn that
this trust was vain and our consciences will then plunge into despair.
For if the forgiveness of sins and reconciliation do not come freely
for Christ's sake, but for the sake of our love, nobody will have the
forgiveness of sins unless he keeps the whole law, because the law

does not justify so long as it can accuse us. Justification is 158 reconciliation for Christ's sake. Therefore it is clear that we are justified by faith, for it is sure that we receive the forgiveness of sins by faith alone.

Now let us reply to the objection of the opponents referred 159 to above. They are right when they say that love is the keeping of the law, and obedience to the law certainly is righteousness. But they are mistaken when they think that we are justified by the law. We are not justified by the law; but we receive the forgiveness of sins and reconciliation by faith for Christ's sake, not for the sake of love or the keeping of the law. From this it necessarily follows that we are justified by faith in Christ.

When this keeping of the law and obedience to the law is 160 perfect, it is indeed righteousness; but in us it is weak and impure. Therefore it does not please God for its own sake, and it is not acceptable for its own sake. From what we have said it is clear 161 that justification does not mean merely the beginning of our renewal, but the reconciliation by which we are later accepted. Nevertheless, it is more clearly evident now that this incipient keeping of the law does not justify, because it is accepted only on account of faith. We must not trust that we are accounted righteous before God by our own perfection and keeping of the law, but only because of Christ.

This is so because, first of all, Christ does not stop being the 162 mediator after our renewal. It is an error to suppose that he merely merited "initial grace" and that afterward we please God and merit eternal life by our keeping of the' law. Christ remains the 163 mediator. We must always be sure that for his sake we have a gracious God in spite of our unworthiness. Paul clearly teaches this when he says (I Cor. 4:4), "I am not aware of anything against me, but I am not thereby justified." But he believes that he is accounted righteous by faith for Christ's sake, according to the statement (Ps. 32:1; Rom. 4:7), "Blessed is he whose transgression is forgiven." This forgiveness is always received by faith. Thus also the imputation of the righteousness of the Gospel is through the promise. Therefore it is always received by faith; we must always hold that we are accounted righteous by faith for the sake of Christ. If those who are regenerated are supposed later to believe that 164 they will be accepted because they have kept the law, how can our conscience be sure that it pleases God, since we never satisfy the law? Therefore we must always go back to the promise. This 165 must sustain us in our weakness, and we must firmly believe that we are accounted righteous on account of Christ, "who is at the right hand of God, who indeed intercedes for us" (Rom. 8:34). If anyone thinks that he is righteous and acceptable because of his own keeping of the law rather than because of Christ's promise, he insults this high priest. It is hard to understand how a man can do away with Christ, the propitiator and mediator, and then imagine that he is righteous before God.

Again, what need is there for a long argument? All the Scrip- 166 tures and the church proclaim that the law cannot be satisfied. The incipient keeping of the law does not please God for its own sake, but for the sake of faith in Christ. Without this, the law always 167 accuses us. For who loves or fears God enough? Who endures patiently enough the afflictions that God sends? Who does not often wonder whether history is governed by God's counsels or by chance? Who does not often doubt whether God hears him? Who does not often complain because the wicked have better luck than the devout, because the wicked persecute the devout? Who lives up to the requirements of his calling? Who loves his neighbor as himself? Who is not tempted by lust? Therefore Paul says (Rom. 7:19), 168 "I do not do the good I want, but the evil I do not want is what I do." Again (Rom. 7:25), "I of myself serve the law of God with my mind, but with my flesh I serve the law of sin." Here he openly says that he serves the law of sin. And David says (Ps. 143:2), "Enter not into judgment with thy servant; for no man living is righteous before thee." Even this servant of God prays God to avert his judgment. Again (Ps. 32:2), "Blessed is the man to whom the Lord imputes no iniquity." Therefore in our present weakness there is always sin that could be imputed to us; about this he says a little later, "Therefore let every one who is godly offer prayer to thee" (Ps. 32:6). Here he shows that even the godly must pray for the forgiveness of sins.

More than blind are those who do not believe that evil desires 169 in the flesh are sins, about which Paul says (Gal. 5:17), "The desires of the flesh are against the Spirit, and the desires of the Spirit are against the flesh." The flesh distrusts God and trusts in temporal 170 things; in trouble it looks to men for help; it even defies God's will and runs away from afflictions that it ought to bear because of God's command; and it doubts God's mercy. The Holy Spirit in our hearts battles against such feelings in order to suppress and destroy them and to give us new spiritual impulses. But later we shall assemble 171 more testimonies on this subject, though they are obvious throughout not only the Scriptures but also the holy Fathers.

Augustine says very clearly, "All the commandments of God 172 are kept when what is not kept is forgiven." [1] Therefore even in good works he requires our faith that for Christ's sake we please

---

[1] Augustine, *Retractions*, I, 19:3.

God and that the works in themselves do not have the value to
please God. Against the Pelagians, Jerome writes, "We are | 73
righteous, therefore, when we confess that we are sinners; and our
righteousness does not consist in our own merit, but in God's
mercy." [2] In the incipient keeping of the law, therefore, we | 74
need a faith which is sure that for Christ's sake we have a gracious
God. For mercy can be grasped only by faith, as we have said so
often. When Paul says, therefore, that the law is established | 75
through faith (Rom. 3:31), this should not be taken to mean only
that those who have been regenerated by faith receive the Holy Spirit
and that their impulses agree with God's law. Even more important,
it must be added that we should realize how far we are from the
perfection of the law. Therefore we dare not believe that we | 76
are accounted righteous before God on account of our keeping of
the law; for our conscience to be at peace we must seek justification
elsewhere. As long as we flee God's judgment and are angry at him,
we are not righteous before him.

We must conclude, therefore, that being reconciled by faith | 77
we are accounted righteous because of Christ, not because of the
law or our works. The incipient keeping of the law pleases God
because of faith; because of faith our failure to keep it is not imputed
to us, although the sight of our impurity thoroughly frightens us.
If, then, we must seek justification elsewhere, our love and works | 78
do not justify. Far above our purity—yes, far above the law itself—
should be placed the death and satisfaction of Christ, bestowed upon
us to assure us that because of this satisfaction and not because of
our keeping of the law we have a gracious God.

Paul teaches this when he says in Gal. 3:13, "Christ redeemed | 79
us from the curse of the law, being made a curse for us." That is,
the law condemns all men, but by undergoing the punishment of sin
and becoming a sacrifice for us, the sinless Christ took away the
right of the law to accuse and condemn those who believe in him,
because he himself is their propitiation, for whose sake they are now
accounted righteous. But when they are accounted righteous, the
law cannot accuse or condemn them, even though they have not really
satisfied the law. He writes to the same effect in Col. 2:10, "You
have come to fullness of life in him." It is as though he were saying,
"Though you are still far away from the perfection of the law, still
the remnants of your sin do not condemn you, because for Christ's
sake we have a firm and sure reconciliation through faith, though sin
still sticks to your flesh."

Because of his promise, because of Christ, God wishes to | 80

[2] Jerome, *Dialog against the Pelagians*, I, 5.

be favorably disposed to us and to justify us, not because of the
law or our works: this promise we must always keep in view. In
this promise timid consciences should seek reconciliation and justification, sustaining themselves with this promise and being sure that
because of Christ and his promise they have a gracious God. Thus
works can never pacify the conscience; only the promise can do
this. Therefore, if we are to seek justification and peace of con- |81
science elsewhere than in our love and works, love and works do not
justify; still they are virtues, in keeping with the righteousness of
the law, to the extent that they fulfill the law. And to that extent
this obedience of the law justifies by the righteousness of the law.
But God accepts this imperfect righteousness of the law only because
of faith. Therefore it does not justify; that is, it neither reconciles
nor regenerates nor of itself makes us acceptable before God.

From this it is evident that we are justified before God by faith |82
alone, since by faith alone we receive the forgiveness of sins and
reconciliation for Christ's sake, and reconciliation or justification is
something promised because of Christ, not because of the law. Therefore it is received by faith alone, though the keeping of the law follows
with the gift of the Holy Spirit.

REPLY TO THE OPPONENTS' ARGUMENTS

With the acknowledgment of the fundamentals in this issue |83
(namely, the distinction between the law and the promises or Gospel)
it will be easy to refute the opponents' objections. For they quote
passages about law and works but omit passages about the prom-
ises. To all their statements about the law we answer immedi- |84
ately that the law cannot be kept without Christ, and that if civil
works are done without Christ they do not please God. In commending
works, therefore, we must add that faith is necessary, and that they
are commended because of faith as its fruit or testimony.

Ambiguous and dangerous issues produce many and varied |85
solutions. For the word of the ancient poet is true, "Being sick in
itself, an unjust cause needs wise remedies." [3] But in just and sure
issues, one or two explanations, taken from the sources, will correct
everything that seems offensive. This is the case in our discussion.
The rule I have just stated interprets all the passages they quote on
law and works. For we concede that in some places the Scripture |86
presents the law, while in others it presents the Gospel, the free promise
of the forgiveness of sins for Christ's sake. But by their denial that
faith justifies and by their doctrine that because of our love and works
we receive the forgiveness of sins and reconciliation, our opponents

---

[3] Euripides. *Phoenissae*, vv. 474, 475.

simply abolish this free promise. If the forgiveness of sins were 187
conditional upon our works, it would be completely unsure and the
promise would be abolished. Therefore we call upon devout 188
minds to consider the promises, and we teach them about the free
forgiveness of sins and the reconciliation that comes through faith in
Christ. Later we add the teaching of the law. And we must distinguish between these, as Paul says (II Tim. 2:15). We must see what
the Scriptures ascribe to the law and what they ascribe to the promises. For they praise works in such a way as not to remove the free
promise.

Good works should be done because God has commanded 189
them and in order to exercise our faith, to give testimony, and to
render thanks. For these reasons good works must necessarily be
done. They take place in a flesh that is partly unregenerate and
hinders what the Holy Spirit motivates, fouling it with its impurity.
Because of faith they are nevertheless holy and divine works, sacrifices, and the reign of Christ, whereby he shows his rule before the
world. For in these works he sanctifies hearts and suppresses the
devil. And in order to keep the Gospel among men, he visibly pits
the witness of the saints against the rule of the devil; in our weakness
he displays his strength. The dangers, labors, and sermons of 190
the apostle Paul, Athanasius, Augustine, and other teachers of the
church are holy works, true sacrifices acceptable to God, battles by
which Christ restrained the devil and drove him away from the believers. David's labors in waging war and in governing the state 191
are holy works, true sacrifices, battles of God to defend the people
who had God's Word against the devil, that the knowledge of God
might not perish utterly from the earth.

We feel the same way about every work done in the most 192
humble occupation and in private life. Through these works Christ
shows his victory over the devil, just as the distribution of alms by
the Corinthians was a holy work (I Cor. 16:1), a sacrifice, and a
battle of Christ against the devil, who is determined that nothing
happen to the praise of God. To disparage works like the con- 193
fession of doctrine, afflictions, works of charity, and the mortification
of the flesh would be to disparage the outward administration of
Christ's rule among men. Let us add a word here about reward and
merit. We teach that rewards have been offered and promised 194
to the works of the faithful. We teach that good works are meritorious—not for the forgiveness of sins, grace, or justification (for we
obtain these only by faith) but for other physical and spiritual rewards
in this life and in that which is to come, as Paul says (I Cor. 3:8),
"Each shall receive his wages according to his labor." Therefore there
will be different rewards for different labors.

But the forgiveness of sins is the same and equal to all, as 195 Christ is one, and it is offered freely to all who believe that their sins are forgiven for Christ's sake. The forgiveness of sins and justification are received only by faith, not because of any works. This is evident in terrors of conscience, for we cannot set any works of ours against the wrath of God, as Paul clearly says (Rom. 5:1), "Since we are justified by faith, we have peace with God through our Lord Jesus Christ. Through him we have obtained access by faith." Because 196 faith makes us sons of God, moreover, it also makes us co-heirs with Christ. Because our works do not merit our justification, which makes us sons of God and co-heirs with Christ, we do not merit eternal life by our works. It is faith that obtains this because it justifies us and has a gracious God. Eternal life belongs to the justified, according to the saying, "Those whom he justified he also glorified" (Rom. 8:30).

Paul extols the commandment to honor our parents by re- 197 ferring to the reward that is connected to that commandment (Eph. 6:2, 3). He does not mean to say that obedience to parents justifies us before God, but rather that when it takes place in the justified it merits other great rewards. Yet God exercises his saints in dif- 198 ferent ways and often puts off the rewards for the righteousness of works. Thus they learn not to trust in their own righteousness, but to seek the will of God rather than the rewards, as is evident in Job, in Christ, and in other saints. Many Psalms teach us this as they console us against the good fortune of the wicked, like Psalm 37:1, "Be not envious." And Christ says (Matt. 5:10), "Blessed are those who are persecuted for righteousness' sake, for theirs is the kingdom of heaven." Such praise undoubtedly moves the faithful to good 199 works. At the same time the doctrine of penitence is preached 200 to the wicked, whose works are evil, and the wrath of God is revealed, threatening all the impenitent. Therefore we praise good works and require them, and we show many reasons why they 201 should be done.

Paul teaches the same thing about works when he says that Abraham did not receive circumcision in order to be justified (Rom. 4:9-22). By faith his justification was already accomplished, but circumcision was added to give him a sign written in his body by which he might be reminded and grow in faith, and through his witness testify to his faith before others and induce them to believe. By 202 faith Abel offered a more acceptable sacrifice (Heb. 11:4). Because he was righteous by faith, the sacrifice he made was acceptable to God—not to merit the forgiveness of sins and grace through this work, but to exercise his faith and display it to others, inviting them to believe.

Good works ought to follow faith in this way. But they are 203 put to a different use by anyone who cannot believe and be sure in his heart that for Christ's sake he is freely forgiven and freely has a gracious God. When such a person sees the works of the saints, he supposes, in human fashion, that through these works the saints merited grace and the forgiveness of sins. Then he imitates them in the delusion that by similar works he will merit grace and forgiveness of sins, appease the wrath of God, and achieve justification because of these works. We condemn this wicked idea about works. 204 First, it obscures the glory of Christ when men offer these works to God as a price and propitiation, thus giving our works an honor that belongs only to Christ. Secondly, they still do not find peace of conscience in these works, but in real terror they pile up works and ultimately despair because they cannot find works pure enough. The law always accuses them and brings forth wrath. Thirdly, such people never attain the knowledge of God, for in their anger they flee his judgment and never believe that he hears them. But faith gives 205 assurance of God's presence when it is sure that he freely forgives and hears us.

This wicked idea about works has always clung to the world. 206 The Gentiles had sacrifices which they took over from the patriarchs. They imitated their works but did not keep their faith, believing that these works were a propitiation and price that reconciled God to them. The people of the Old Testament imitated these sacrifices 207 with the notion that on account of them they had a gracious God, so to say, *ex opere operato*. Here we see how vehemently the prophets rebuke the people. Ps. 50:8, "I do not reprove you for your sacrifices." And Jer. 7:22, "I did not command concerning burnt offerings." Such passages do not condemn the sacrifices that God surely commanded as outward observances in the state, but they do condemn the wicked belief of those who did away with faith in the notion that through these works they placated the wrath of God. Because no 208 works can put the conscience at rest, they kept thinking up new works beyond God's commandment. The people of Israel had seen the prophets sacrifice on the high places.[4] The examples of the saints call forth imitation in those who hope that by similar actions they can obtain grace. Therefore the people began zealously to copy this action in order thereby to merit grace, righteousness, and the forgiveness of sins. But the prophets did not sacrifice on the high places to merit grace and forgiveness of sins by this deed, but because they were teaching in these places and thus gave evidence of their faith.

The people heard that Abraham had offered up his son.[5] 209 And so they put their sons to death in order by this cruel and painful

[4] I Sam. 9:12, 13; I Kings 18:20ff.
[5] Gen. 22.

deed to placate the wrath of God.[6] But Abraham did not offer up his son with the idea that this work was a price or propitiation for which he would be accounted righteous. Thus the Lord's Supper was 210 instituted in the church so that as this sign reminds us of the promises of Christ, the remembrance might strengthen our faith and we might publicly confess our faith and announce the blessings of Christ, as Paul says (I Cor. 11:26), "As often as you do this, you proclaim the Lord's death." But our opponents claim that the Mass is a work that justifies *ex opere operato* and removes the burden of guilt and punishment in those for whom it is offered, as Gabriel Biel writes.[7]

Anthony, Bernard, Dominic, Francis, and other holy Fathers 211 chose a certain kind of life for study or for other useful exercises. At the same time they believed that through faith they were accounted righteous and had a gracious God because of Christ, not because of their own spiritual exercises. But the crowd ever since has copied not the faith of the Fathers but only their behavior without their faith in order by such works to merit the forgiveness of sins, grace, and righteousness. They did not believe that they received these freely because of Christ, the propitiator. The world judges this way 212 about all works, that they are a propitiation by which God is appeased and a price because of which we are accounted righteous. It does not believe that Christ is the propitiator, or that freely by faith we are accounted righteous for Christ's sake. But because works cannot pacify the conscience, men constantly choose other works, make up new devotions, new vows, and new monastic orders beyond God's commandment in the hope of finding some great work that they can set against the wrath and judgment of God. Our opponents 213 maintain these wicked and unscriptural ideas about works. To credit our works with being a propitiation and to claim that they merit the forgiveness of sins and grace and that we are accounted righteous before God because of them rather than because of Christ by faith— what is this but to rob Christ of his honor as mediator and propitiator?

We believe and teach, therefore, that good works must neces- 214 sarily be done since our incipient keeping of the law must follow faith; but we still give Christ his honor. We are accounted righteous before God for Christ's sake by faith. We are not accounted righteous because of our works without Christ, the mediator. We do not merit the forgiveness of sins, grace, and righteousness through works. We cannot pit our works against the wrath and judgment of God. Our works cannot overcome the terrors of sin, but faith alone can overcome them. Only Christ, the mediator, can be pitted against God's wrath and judgment. This is what we believe and teach. Any- 215

⁶ Lev. 20:2ff.; II Kings 23:10; Jer. 7:31; 19:5; 32:35.
⁷ *Exposition of the Canon of the Mass*, 26:81.

one who believes otherwise does not give Christ the honor due him, for he has been set forth as the propitiator through whom we have access to the Father. We are talking now about the right- 216 eousness by which we deal with God, not with men, and by which we take hold of grace and peace of conscience. But the con- 217 science cannot find peace before God except by faith alone, by which it is sure that God is reconciled to us for Christ's sake, according to the saying (Rom. 5:1), "Since we are justified by faith, we have peace." For justification is something that is only promised freely because of Christ, and therefore it is always received before God by faith alone.

Now we shall answer the texts that our opponents quote[8] 218 to prove that we are justified by love and works. From I Cor. 13:2 they quote, "If I have all faith, etc., but have not love, I am nothing." Here they celebrate a great victory. Before the whole church, they say, Paul asserts that faith alone does not justify. Now that 219 we have shown what we believe about love and works, it will be easy to answer this. In this text Paul requires love. We require it, too. We have said above that we should be renewed and begin to keep the law, according to the statement (Jer. 31:33), "I will put my law within their hearts." Whoever casts away love will not keep his faith, be it ever so great, because he will not keep the Holy Spirit. But 220 in this text Paul is not discussing the mode of justification. He is writing to people who, upon being justified, needed urging to bear good fruits lest they lose the Holy Spirit. Our opponents pro- 221 ceed in reverse order. They quote this one text in which Paul teaches about the fruits, and they omit the many other texts in which he systematically discusses the mode of justification. Besides, to other texts that speak of faith they always add the correction that they should be understood in reference to "faith formed by love." [9] Here they do not add the correction: We need the faith that we are accounted righteous because of Christ, the propitiator. Thus our opponents exclude Christ from justification and teach only the righteousness of the law. But let us return to Paul.

No one can draw anything more from this text than that love 222 is necessary. This we grant. It is also necessary not to steal. It would be a fallacy to reason that because it is necessary not to steal, therefore not stealing justifies; for justification is not the approval of a particular act but of the total person. Hence this passage from Paul is not against us; only our opponents should not add their own

---

[8] In the Roman Confutation.

[9] Roman Confutation: "Their [the Lutheran princes'] reference here to faith is approved in so far as not faith alone (as some incorrectly teach) but faith which works by love is understood . ." (Pt. I, Art. V).

whims to it. For he is not saying that love justifies but that "I am nothing"; that is, faith is extinguished, no matter how great it may have been. He is not saying that love conquers the terrors of sin and death; that we can set our love against the wrath and judgment of God; that our love satisfies the law of God; that by our love we have access to God even without Christ, the propitiator; that by our love we receive the promised forgiveness of sins—Paul is saying none of these things. He does not believe that love justifies, for we are justified only when we take hold of Christ, the propitiator, and believe that for his sake God is gracious to us. Nor is justification even to be dreamed without Christ, the propitiator. Let our op- 223 ponents remove the promise about Christ, let them abolish the Gospel, if Christ is unnecessary and by our love we can conquer death and can have access to God without him as propitiator.

Our opponents twist many texts because they read their own 224 opinions into them instead of deriving the meaning from the texts themselves. There is no problem in this text if we remove the interpretation that our opponents add to it on their own, for they understand neither what justification is nor how it happens. Upon being justified, the Corinthians received many excellent gifts. As usual, their zeal was very fervent in the beginning. Then dissensions arose among them and, as Paul indicates, they began to dislike good teachers. Paul scolds them for this and calls them back to the duties of love. Even though these are necessary, it would be a foolish dream to imagine that we are justified before God by the works of the Second Table,[1] through which we deal with men and not specifically with God. In justification our business is with God; his wrath must be stilled and the conscience find peace before him. None of this happens through the works of the Second Table.

They object that love is preferred to faith and hope since 225 Paul says (I Cor. 13:13), "The greatest of these is love." Therefore it follows that the greatest and the main virtue should justify. In this passage, however, Paul speaks specifically about love to 226 our neighbor, and he indicates that love is the greatest because it has the most fruits. Faith and hope deal only with God, while love has infinite external duties to men. Nevertheless, we concede to our opponents that the love of God and neighbor is the greatest virtue because the great commandment is, "You shall love the Lord your God" (Matt. 22:27). How will they conclude from this that love justifies? The greatest virtue, they say, justifies. But as even the 227 the first and greatest law does not justify, neither does the greatest virtue of the law. But that virtue justifies which takes hold of Christ,

___
[1] Of the Ten Commandments.

communicating to us Christ's merits and, through them, grace and peace from God. This virtue is faith. As we have often said, faith is not merely knowledge but rather a desire to accept and grasp what is offered in the promise of Christ. This obedience toward God, 228 this desire to receive the offered promise, is no less an act of worship than is love. God wants us to believe him and to accept blessings from him; this he declares to be true worship.

Our opponents attribute justification to love because every- 229 where they teach and require the righteousness of the law. We cannot deny that love is the highest work of the law. Human wisdom looks at the law and seeks righteousness in it. Thus the great and learned scholastics proclaimed the highest work of the law, and to it they attributed justification. Deceived by human wisdom, they did not see the true face of Moses but only his veiled face,[2] just as the Pharisees, philosophers, and Mohammedans. We for our part 230 preach the foolishness of the Gospel,[3] which reveals another righteousness, namely, that because of Christ, the propitiator, we are accounted righteous when we believe that for Christ's sake God is gracious to us. We know how repulsive this teaching is to the judgment of reason and law and that the teaching of the law about love is more plausible; for this is human wisdom. But we are not ashamed of the foolishness of the Gospel.[4] Because of Christ's glory we defend it and we ask Christ for the help of his Holy Spirit to make it clear and distinct.

In the Confutation our opponents have also cited against us 231 Col. 3:14, "love, which is the bond of perfection." From this they argue that love justifies since it makes men perfect. Though we could give many answers about perfection, we shall simply present Paul's meaning. He is obviously discussing love of our neighbor. We have no right to suppose that Paul would ascribe either justification or perfection before God to the works of the Second Table rather than the First. If it is love that makes men perfect, Christ, the propitiator, will be unnecessary. Only faith takes hold of Christ, the propitiator. Paul would never permit Christ, the propitiator, to be excluded, and hence this view is far removed from his intention. So he is talk- 232 ing not about personal perfection but about fellowship in the church. He says that love is a bond and unbroken chain linking the many members of the church with one another. Similarly, in all families and communities harmony should be nurtured by mutual aid, for it is not possible to preserve tranquility unless men cover and forgive certain mistakes in their midst. In the same way Paul commands that

[2] II Cor. 3:12.
[3] Cf. I Cor. 3:23.
[4] Rom. 1:16.

there be love in the church to preserve harmony, to bear, if need be, with the crude behavior of the brethren, to cover up minor mistakes, lest the church disintegrate into various schisms and the hatreds, factions, and heresies that arise from such schisms.

For harmony will inevitably disintegrate if bishops impose 233 heavy burdens on the people or have no regard for their weakness. Dissensions also arise when the people judge their clergy's behavior too strictly or despise them because of some minor fault and then seek after some other kinds of doctrine and other clergy. On 234 the other hand, perfection (that is, the integrity of the church) is preserved when the strong bear with the weak, when the people put the best construction on the faults of their clergy, when the bishops take into account the weakness of the people. All the books 235 of the sages are full of these commands of fairness, that in everyday life we should put up with many things for the sake of mutual peace. Paul often enjoins this both here and elsewhere. And so it does not make sense when our opponents argue on the basis of the word "perfection" that love justifies, when Paul is speaking of unity and peace in the church. Ambrose interprets the text this way: "Just as a building is said to be perfect or whole when all its parts fit together properly."

Moreover, it comes in poor grace for our opponents to talk 236 so much about love when they never show it. What are they doing now? They are breaking up churches. They are writing laws in blood and are asking the emperor, this most clement prince, that these laws should be promulgated. They are slaughtering priests and other good men if they even intimate their disapproval of some open abuse. All this does not fit very well with their praises of love; if our opponents lived up to them, they would bring peace to both church and state. These tumults would die down if our opponents did not insist so bitterly on certain traditions which have no value for piety and most of which are not lived up to even by those who most violently defend them. For themselves they easily find forgiveness, but not for others, as the poet writes, "I forgive myself, says Maenius." [5] But this 237 is completely different from those praises of love which they recite from Paul; they have no more understanding than the walls that fling back an echo.

From Peter they quote this statement (I Pet. 4:8), "Love 238 covers a multitude of sins." Obviously Peter, too, is talking here about love to the neighbor, for he connects this statement with the commandment of mutual love. It could not have entered the mind of any apostle to say that our love conquers sin and death; or that in place of Christ, the mediator, love is the propitiation that recon-

---

[5] Horace, *Satires,* I, 3, 23.

ciles God to us; or that love is righteousness without Christ, the mediator. For even if there were such a love, it would be a righteousness of the law rather than of the Gospel which promises us reconciliation and righteousness if we believe that for the sake of Christ, the propitiator, the Father is gracious to us and that the merits of Christ are granted to us. Therefore a little earlier (I Pet. 2:4, 5) 239 Peter commands us to come to Christ and to be built upon Christ, and he adds (I Pet. 2:6), "He who believes in him will not be put to shame." Our love does not free us from shame when God judges and accuses us, but faith in Christ frees us in the midst of these fears because we know that for Christ's sake we are forgiven.

Furthermore, this statement about love is taken from Proverbs 240 (10:12), where the antithesis clearly shows what it means: "Hatred stirs up strife, but love covers all offenses." It teaches exactly 241 the same thing as Paul's statement in Col. 3:13, namely, that if any dissensions arise they should be quieted and settled by calmness and forbearance. Dissensions, it says, grow because of hatred, as we often see the greatest tragedies come from the most trifling offenses. Between Gaius Caesar and Pompey certain minor disagreements arose, which would never have brought on civil war if either had yielded the least bit to the other. When each one gave in to his hatred, 242 a major commotion emerged from an insignificant issue. Many heresies have arisen in the church simply from the hatred of the clergy. This text therefore speaks not of one's own sins but of other people's when it says, "Love covers all offenses," namely, other people's offenses and offenses between people. Even though these offenses occur, love covers them up, forgives, yields, and does not go to the limit of the law.

Peter does not mean that love merits the forgiveness of sins in relation to God; that in place of Christ the mediator it is our propitiation; or that it regenerates and justifies. He means that in human relations it is not peevish, harsh, or implacable; that it covers up some of the mistakes of its friends; and that it puts the best construction even on the more offensive actions of others, as the common proverb says, "Know, but do not hate, the manners of a friend." [6] It 243 is not without reason that the apostles speak so often about this duty of love which the philosophers call "leniency." [7] This virtue is necessary for the preservation of domestic tranquillity, which cannot endure unless pastors and churches overlook and forgive many things.

From James they quote the text, "You see that a man is 244 justified by works and not by faith alone" (James 2:24). No other passage is supposed to contradict our position more, but the answer is easy and clear. The words of James will cause no trouble if our

---

[6] Porphyry on Horace, *Satires,* I, 3, 32.

[7] Greek: *epieikeia.* Cf. above, Augsburg Confession, XXVI, 14.

opponents do not read into them their opinion about the merit of works. Wherever works are mentioned, our opponents falsely add their wicked opinions that by good works we merit the forgiveness of sins; that good works are a propitiation and price that reconciles God to us; that good works conquer the terrors of sin and death; that good works are accepted before God because of their intrinsic excellence; that we do not need mercy and Christ, the propitiator. None of this ever entered into James's mind, though our opponents uphold it under the pretext that this is what James meant.

First, we must note that this text is more against our opponents 245 than against us. They teach that a man is justified by love and works but say nothing about the faith by which we take hold of Christ, the propitiator. Not only do they condemn this faith in statements and writings, but they also try to wipe it out with sword and torture. How much better is James's teaching! For he does not omit faith nor exalt love in preference to it, but keeps it, lest Christ, the propitiator, be excluded from justification. Just so Paul includes faith and love in presenting a summary of the Christian life (I Tim. 1:5), "The aim of our charge is love that issues from a pure heart and a good conscience and sincere faith."

Second, the context demonstrates that the works spoken of 246 here are those that follow faith and show that it is not dead but living and active in the heart. James did not hold that by our good works we merit grace and the forgiveness of sins. He is talking about the works of the justified, who have already been reconciled and accepted and have obtained the forgiveness of sins. It is therefore fallacious for our opponents to argue from this text that James teaches we merit grace and forgiveness of sins by good works and that by our works we have access to God without Christ, the propitiator.

Third, James has just said that regeneration takes place 247 through the Gospel. He says (James 1:18), "Of his own will he brought us forth by the word of truth that we should be a kind of first fruits of his creatures." When he says that we have been regenerated by the Gospel, he teaches that we are regenerated and justified by faith. For it is only faith that takes hold of the promise of Christ when we set it against the terrors of sin and death. Thus James does not hold that we are regenerated by our works.

From this it is clear that James is not against us when he 248 distinguishes between dead and living faith and condemns the idle and smug minds who dream they have faith but do not. He 249 says that a faith which does not produce good works is dead, but it is alive when it brings forth good works. We have already shown often enough what we mean by faith. We are not talking about idle knowledge, such as even the demons have, but about a faith that resists the terrors of conscience and encourages and consoles terrified hearts. Such a faith is not an easy thing, as our opponents 250 imagine; nor is it a human power, but a divine power that makes us alive and enables us to overcome death and the devil. Just so Paul says that through the power of God faith is efficacious and overcomes death (Col. 2:12), "in which you were also raised with him through faith in the working of God." Since this faith is a new life, it necessarily produces new impulses and new works. Accordingly, James is correct in denying that we are justified by a faith without works. When he says we are justified by faith and works, he certainly 251 does not mean that we are regenerated by works. Nor does he say that our propitiation is due in part to Christ and in part to our works. Nor does he describe the manner of justification, but only the nature of the just who have already been justified and reborn.

"To be justified" here does not mean that a wicked man is 252 made righteous but that he is pronounced righteous in a forensic way, just as in the passage (Rom. 2:13), "the doers of the law will be justified." As these words, "the doers of the law will be justified," contain nothing contrary to our position, so we maintain the same about James's words, "A man is justified by works and not by faith alone," for men who have faith and good works are certainly pronounced righteous. As we have said, the good works of the saints are righteous and please God because of faith. James preaches only the works that faith produces, as he shows when he says of Abraham, "Faith was active along with his works" (2:22). In this sense it is said, "The doers of the law will be justified"; that is, God pronounces righteous those who belive him from their heart and then have good fruits, which please him because of faith and therefore are a keeping of the law. These words, spoken so simply, contain no error, 253 but our opponents twist them by reading into them their own wicked opinions. They do not warrant any of these conclusions: that works merit the forgiveness of sins; that works regenerate our hearts; that works are a propitiation; that works please God without Christ, the propitiator; that works do not need Christ, the propitiator. James says none of this, which our opponents shamelessly infer from his words.

Other statements about works are also quoted against us. 254 Luke 6:37, "Forgive, and you will be forgiven." Isa. 58:7, 9, "Share your bread with the hungry. Then you shall call, and the Lord will answer." Dan. 4:27, "Redeem your sins by showing mercy." Matt. 5:3, "Blessed are the poor in spirit, for theirs is the kingdom of heaven." And again (v. 7), "Blessed are the merciful, for they 255 shall obtain mercy." But these passages would say nothing against us if our opponents did not read something false into them. They contain two elements. One is the proclamation of the law or of penitence, wh:ch condemns wrongdoers and commands that they do right. The other is a promise that is added. They do not add that sins are forgiven without faith or that these works are themselves a propitiation.

In the preaching of the law there are two things we must   256 always keep in mind. First, we cannot keep the law unless we have been reborn by faith in Christ, as Christ says (John 15:5), "Apart from me you can do nothing." Secondly, though men can at most do certain outward works, this universal statement must be permitted to interpret the entire law (Heb. 11:6), "Without faith it is impossible to please God." We must keep the Gospel promise that through Christ we have access to the Father (Rom. 5:2). It is clear   257 that we are not justified by the law. Otherwise, if the preaching of the law were enough by itself, why would Christ and the Gospel be necessary? Thus in the preaching of penitence it is not enough to preach the law, the Word that convicts of sin. For the law works wrath; it only accuses; it only terrifies consciences. Consciences cannot find peace unless they hear the voice of God, clearly promising the forgiveness of sins. Therefore it is necessary to add the Gospel promise, that for Christ's sake sins are forgiven and that by faith in Christ we obtain the forgiveness of sins. If our opponents exclude the Gospel of Christ from the preaching of penitence, they deserve to be regarded as blasphemers against Christ.

This is evident in Isaiah's preaching of penitence: "Cease   258 to do evil, learn to do good; seek justice, correct oppression; defend the fatherless, plead for the widow. Come now, let us reason together, says the Lord: though your sins are like scarlet, they shall be white as snow" (Isa. 1:16-18). Thus the prophet urges penitence and adds a promise. It would be foolish in such a statement to look only at these works: "correct oppression, defend the fatherless." At the beginning he says, "Cease to do evil," as he denounces ungodly hearts and requires faith. The prophet does not say that through these works —"correct oppression, defend the fatherless"—they could merit the forgiveness of sins *ex opere operato,* but he commands these works as necessary to the new life. At the same time he wants the forgiveness of sins to be received by faith, and so he adds a promise.

We must interpret all similar passages in the same way.   259 Christ is preaching penitence when he says, "Forgive," and he adds the promise, "You will be forgiven" (Luke 6:37). He does not say that when we forgive, this merits the forgiveness of sins *ex opere operato,* but he requires a new life, which is certainly necessary. At the same time he wants the forgiveness of sins to be received by faith. Similarly, when Isaiah says (Isa. 58:7), "Share your bread with the hungry," he requires the new life. Nor does the prophet speak of this one work alone, but of all of penitence, as the text indicates; but at the same time he wishes the forgiveness of sins to be received by faith. For it is sure, and no gates of hell can over- 260 throw it (Matt. 16:18), that in the preaching of penitence the preaching of the law is not enough because the law works wrath and continually accuses. The preaching of the Gospel must be added, that is, that the forgiveness of sins is granted to us if we believe that our sins are forgiven for Christ's sake. Otherwise what need would there be of Christ, what need of the Gospel? We must always keep this important teaching in view. In this way we can oppose those who reject Christ, destroy the Gospel, and maliciously twist the Scriptures to suit the man-made theory that by our works we purchase the forgiveness of sins.

Thus in Daniel's sermon (4:24) faith is required. Daniel 261 did not only mean to say that the king should give alms, but he includes all of penitence when he says, "Redeem your iniquities by showing mercy to the oppressed," that is, redeem your sins by changing your heart and works. This presupposes faith. Daniel proclaimed many things to the king about the one God of Israel and converted him not only to the giving of alms but rather to faith. For there is the king's excellent confession about the God of Israel, "There is no other God who can save this way" (Dan. 3:29). Daniel's sermon contains two parts. One part instructs about the new life and its works. In the other part Daniel promises the king forgiveness of sins. This promise of the forgiveness of sins is not the preaching of the law, but a truly prophetic and evangelical voice which Daniel surely wanted to be received by faith. Daniel knew that the for- 262 giveness of sins in the Christ was promised not only to the Israelites but to all nations. Otherwise he could not have promised the king forgiveness of sins. Especially amid the terrors of sin, a human being must have a very definite Word of God to learn to know God's will, namely, that he is no longer angry. In his own language Daniel's words speak even more clearly about complete penitence and bring out the promise, "Redeem your sins by righteousness and your iniquities by favor to the poor." These words deal with the total scope of penitence. They command him to become righteous, then to do good and to defend the poor against injustice, as was the king's duty.

Righteousness is faith in the heart. Sins are redeemed by 263 penitence, that is, the obligation or debt is removed because God forgives those who are penitent, as is written in Ezek. 18:21, 22. We are not to reason from this that God forgives because of the works that follow or because of alms, but because of his promise he forgives those who take hold of that promise. They do not take hold of it unless they truly believe and by faith conquer sin and death. Reborn in this way, they bring forth fruits worthy of penitence, as John the Baptist says (Matt. 3:8). The promise is therefore added (Dan. 4:27), "Behold, there will be a healing of your offenses."

Here Jerome adds an extraneous particle expressing doubt, 264 and in his commentaries he maintains with even less authority that the forgiveness of sins is uncertain.[8] Let us remember that the Gospel promises the forgiveness of sins with certainty. It would clearly be an abolition of the Gospel if we were to deny that the forgiveness of sins must surely be given by a promise. Let us therefore dismiss Jerome in the interpretation of this text, though the promise is involved even in the word "redeem." It signifies that the forgiveness of sins is possible, that sins can be redeemed, that the obligation or debt can be removed, that the wrath of God can be stilled. Everywhere our opponents omit the promises and look only at the commandments, adding to them the human theory that forgiveness depends upon works. The text does not say this, but rather requires faith. Wherever there is a promise, there faith is required. Only faith can accept a promise.

In human eyes, works are very impressive. Human reason 265 naturally admires them; because it sees only works and neither looks at nor understands faith, it dreams that the merit of these works brings forgiveness of sins and justification. This legalistic opinion clings by nature to the minds of men, and it cannot be driven out unless we are divinely taught. The mind must be turned from such fleshly 266 opinions to the Word of God. We see that the Gospel and the promise of Christ are presented to us. We must not reject the promise of Christ when the law is preached and works are enjoined. We must first take hold of the promise so that we may be able to do good and that our works may be pleasing to God, as Christ says (John 15:5), "Apart from me you can do nothing." If Daniel had said, "Redeem your sins by penitence," our opponents would have passed over this passage. He uses other words to express this same thought, and our opponents immediately twist his words to mean the very opposite of the teaching of grace and faith, while Daniel most emphatically wants to include faith.

This, then, is how we reply to the words of Daniel: Since he 267 is preaching penitence he is teaching not only about works but about faith as well, as the narrative in the text shows. Secondly, because Daniel clearly sets forth a promise, he necessarily requires faith, which believes that God freely forgives sins. Although he mentions works in connection with penitence, therefore, Daniel does not say that by

---

[8] In his commentary Jerome translates Dan. 4:24, "Perhaps God will forgive your offenses."

these works we merit the forgiveness of sins. Daniel is not speaking about remission of punishment alone, because it is vain to seek remission of punishment unless the heart first receives remission of guilt. If our opponents understand Daniel as referring only to 268 remission of punishment, this text proves nothing against us, because then they will have to grant that first come forgiveness of sins and justification without works. Afterwards, as we readily admit, the punishments that chasten us are lightened by our prayers and good works, indeed by our complete penitence, according to the words, "If we judged ourselves, we would not be judged by the Lord" (I Cor. 11:31); "If you are converted, I will convert you" (Jer. 15:19); "Return to me and I will return to you" (Zech. 1:3); "Call upon me in the day of trouble" (Ps. 50:15).

Whenever good works are praised and the law preached, 269 therefore, we must hold fast to these rules: that the law is not kept without Christ—as he himself has said, "Apart from me you can do nothing" (John 15:5)—and that "without faith it is impossible to please God" (Heb. 11:6). The teaching of the law is certainly not intended to abolish the Gospel of Christ, the propitiator. Cursed be our opponents, those Pharisees, who interpret the law in such a way that they attribute Christ's glory to works and make of them a propitiation that merits the forgiveness of sins. It follows, therefore, that works are praised for pleasing God on account of faith, since they do not please him without Christ, the propitiator. "Through him we have obtained access" to the Father (Rom. 5:2), not by works without Christ, the mediator.

In the statement, "If you would enter life, keep the command- 270 ments" (Matt. 19:17), we must realize that no one can keep the commandments or please God without Christ. So the First Commandment of the Decalogue itself states, "Showing steadfast love to thousands of those who love me and keep my commandments" (Ex. 20:6), setting forth the most ample promise of the law. But without Christ this law is not kept. It always accuses the conscience, which does not satisfy the law and therefore flees in terror before the judgment and punishment of the law, "for the law brings wrath" (Rom. 4:15). But a man keeps the law as soon as he hears that God is reconciled to us for Christ's sake even though we cannot satisfy the law. When faith takes hold of Christ, the mediator, the heart is at peace and begins to love God and to keep the law. It knows that now it is pleasing to God for the sake of Christ, the mediator, even though its incipient keeping of the law is impure and far from perfect. In this way we must view the preaching of penitence. 271 Though the scholastics have said nothing at all about faith in their treatment of the doctrine of penitence, yet we think that none of our opponents is so mad as to deny that absolution is the spoken Gospel. Absolution should be received by faith, to cheer the terrified conscience.

Because the doctrine of penitence not only demands new 272 works but also promises the forgiveness of sins, it necessarily requires faith. Only faith accepts the forgiveness of sins. In passages about penitence we should understand that faith is required, not merely works, as in Matt. 6:14, "If you forgive men their trespasses, your heavenly Father also will forgive you." Here a work is required and a promise of the forgiveness of sins is added, depending not on the work but on Christ through faith. So the Scriptures testify in 273 many other places. Acts 10:43, "To him all the prophets bear witness that every one who believes in him receives forgiveness of sins through his name." I John 2:12, "Your sins are forgiven for his sake." Eph. 1:7, "In him we have redemption through his blood, the forgiveness of our trespasses." Why recite passages? This is 274 the essential proclamation of the Gospel, that we obtain forgiveness of sins by faith because of Christ and not because of our works. Our opponents try to silence this proclamation of the Gospel by twisting those passages which teach about the law or works. It is true that in teaching penitence works are required, since a new life is certainly required; but here our opponents maliciously maintain that by such works we merit forgiveness of sins or justification.

Nevertheless, Christ frequently connects the promise of for- 275 giveness of sins with good works. He does not mean that good works are a propitiation—for they follow reconciliation—but he does so for two reasons. One is that good fruits ought to follow of necessity, and so he warns that penitence is hypocritical and false if they do not follow. The other reason is that we need external signs of this exceedingly great promise, since a terrified conscience needs manifold consolations. Baptism and the Lord's Supper, for example, are 276 signs that constantly admonish, cheer, and confirm terrified minds to believe more firmly that their sins are forgiven. This same promise is written and pictured in good works, which thus urge us to believe more firmly. Those who fail to do good, do not arouse themselves to believe but despise these promises. But the faithful embrace them and are glad to have signs and testimonies of this great promise. Hence they exercise themselves in these signs and testimonies. Just as the Lord's Supper does not justify *ex opere operato* without faith, so almsgiving does not justify *ex opere operato* without faith.

The statement in Tob. 4:11 ought to be taken the same way, 277 "Alms free from every sin and from death." We shall not say that this is hyperbole; but that is how it ought to be understood so as not to take away from the glory of Christ, whose prerogative it is to free from sin and death. We must come back to the rule that without

Christ the teaching of the law has no value. Thus God is pleased 278 by that almsgiving which follows justification or reconciliation, not by that which precedes. Therefore almsgiving does not free from sin and death *ex opere operato*. As we said earlier that in penitence we must consider faith and fruits together, so here we say in reference to almsgiving that it is the whole newness of life which saves. Almsgiving is an exercise of that faith which accepts forgiveness of sins and overcomes death as it becomes ever stronger through such exercise. We also grant that alms merit many divine blessings, lighten our punishments, and merit a defense for us in the perils of sin and death, as we said a little earlier about penitence in general.

Taken in its entirety, Tobit's statement shows that faith is 279 required before almsgiving: "Have God in mind all the days of your life" (4:5), and later, "Bless God always, and ask him to direct your ways" (4:19). These actions properly belong to the kind of faith we have been discussing, one which believes that God is reconciled on account of his mercy and which wants to be justified, sanctified, and governed by God. But our opponents, clever men that they are, 280 pick out garbled sentences to put something over on the inexperienced. Then they add something from their own opinions. It is necessary to consider passages in their context, because according to the common rule it is improper in an argument to judge or reply to a single passage without taking the whole law into account. When passages are considered in their own context, they often yield their own interpretation.

Luke 11:41 is also quoted in a garbled form: "Give alms; and 281 behold, everything is clean for you." Our opponents must be deaf. Over and over we say that the Gospel of Christ must be added to the preaching of the law, that for his sake good works please God. Yet everywhere they exclude Christ and teach that we merit justification by the works of the law. An examination of the whole passage 282 shows that it requires faith. Christ is upbraiding the Pharisees for thinking that they are cleansed before God and justified by frequent washings. Just so some pope—I am not sure which—said that sprinkling water mixed with salt "sanctifies and cleanses the people," and the gloss says that it cleanses from venial sins.[9] Such were the opinions of the Pharisees, too. These Christ rejects, and in place of this false cleansing he puts a twofold cleanness, one internal and the other external. He commands that they be cleansed inwardly and then adds concerning the outward cleanness, "Give alms from what you have left over, and thus all things will be clean for you."

Our opponents misinterpret the universal particle "all." Christ 283 adds this conclusion to both clauses: all things will be clean if you

[9] Pseudo-Alexander I, in Gratian, *Decretum*, III, *De consecratione*, d. III, c.20.

are clean inwardly and if you give alms. He means that outward cleanness is to be sought in works commanded by God, not in human traditions like the ablutions in those days, or in our own time the daily sprinkling with water, the habit of the monks, the distinctions of foods, and similar pompous acts. Our opponents twist his meaning by sophistically transferring the universal particle to a single part: "All things will be clean when you have given alms." Yet Peter 284 says (Acts 15:9) that hearts are purified by faith. A study of the whole passage shows its agreement with the rest of the Scripture; for if hearts are clean and then the outward giving of alms is added (that is, all the works of love), then men are completely clean, outwardly as well as inwardly. Moreover, why do they not present the whole sermon? The admonition has many parts, some of which command faith, others works. An honest reader would not pick out the commands about works and skip the passages about faith.

Finally, we would remind our readers that our opponents coun- 285 sel pious consciences very badly when they teach that works merit the forgiveness of sins, because a conscience that seeks forgiveness through works cannot be sure that its work will satisfy God. It is always tormented and constantly invents other works and services until it despairs utterly. Describing this process in Rom. 4:5 ff., Paul proves that the promise of righteousness does not depend upon our works because we could never be sure that we have a gracious God. The law always accuses. Thus the promise would be vain and unsure. He concludes that not works but faith accepts the promised forgiveness of sins and righteousness of faith. This is what Paul really and truly means. This offers the greatest consolation to faithful consciences and illumines the glory of Christ, who was surely given to us that through him we might have grace, righteousness, and peace.

So far we have reviewed the main passages which our op- 286 ponents quote against us in arguing that faith does not justify and that by our works we merit grace and the forgiveness of sins. These passages do not conflict with our position. Our opponents maliciously twist the Scriptures to fit their own opinions. They quote many passages in a garbled form. They omit the clearest scriptural passages on faith, select the passages on works, and even distort these. Everywhere they add human opinions to what the words of Scripture say. They teach the law in such a way as to hide the Gospel of Christ. We hope we have shown all this to the satisfaction of pious consciences.

The opponents' whole system is derived either from human 287 reason or from the teaching of the law rather than the Gospel. They teach two modes of justification, one based upon reason, the other based upon the law, neither one based upon the Gospel or the promise of Christ.

The first mode of justification, according to them, is that men 288 merit grace by good works—first by the merit of congruity, then by the merit of condignity.[1] This mode is a doctrine of reason. Being blind to the uncleanness of the heart, reason thinks that it pleases God if it does good, but when men are in great peril they add other forms of worship to get rid of the terrors of conscience. The heathen and the Israelites sacrificed human victims and undertook many other painful works to appease the wrath of God. Later on men thought up monastic orders, which competed in the austerity of their observances to counteract the terrors of conscience and the wrath of God. Because this mode of gaining justification is reasonable and is preoccupied with outward works, it can be understood and, to some extent, its requirements can be met. For this reason the canonists have twisted ecclesiastical regulations. They did not understand why the Fathers had enacted them, namely, not that we should seek righteousness through these works but that for the sake of social tranquillity there should be some order in the church. In this way they have also distorted the sacraments, especially the Mass, through which they seek righteousness, grace, and salvation *ex opere operato.*

The other mode of justification, handed down by the scholastic 289 theologians,[2] teaches that we are righteous through a certain disposition (which is love) infused by God, that with the help of this disposition we obey the law of God both outwardly and inwardly, and that such obedience to the law is worthy of grace and eternal life. This is obviously a doctrine of the law. Truly the law says, "You shall love the Lord your God" (Deut. 6:5) and "You shall love your neighbor" (Lev. 19:18). Therefore love is the fulfilling of the law.

A Christian can easily evaluate both modes, since both exclude 290 Christ and therefore both are to be rejected. The ungodliness of the first is obvious because it teaches that our works are a propitiation for sin. The second contains much that is harmful. It does not teach us to avail ourselves of Christ in our regeneration. It does not teach that justification is the forgiveness of sins. It does not teach that the forgiveness of sins precedes our love, but it imagines that we produce an act of love whereby we merit the forgiveness of sins. It does not teach that by faith in Christ we overcome the terrors of sin and death. Without any warrant it teaches that men come to God through their own keeping of the law and not through Christ, the propitiator. Then it imagines that this very keeping of the law with Christ, the propitiator, is a righteousness worthy of grace and eternal life, although even a weak and feeble keeping of the law is rare, even among saints.

But the Gospel was not given to the world in vain. Christ was 291

---

[1] Merit of fitness and merit of worthiness respectively. See above, IV, 19.
[2] Cf. Thomas Aquinas, *Summa theologica,* II, 1, q.114, a.3.

not promised, revealed, born, crucified, and raised in vain. Whoever reflects on this will easily understand that we are justified neither by reason nor by the law. We are therefore obliged to disagree with our opponents on justification. The Gospel shows another way. It compels us to make use of Christ in justification. It teaches that through him we have access to God through faith (Rom. 5:2), and that we should set him, the mediator and propitiator, against the wrath of God. It teaches that by faith in Christ we receive the forgiveness of sins, reconciliation, and victory over the terrors of sin and death.

Thus Paul says, too, that righteousness is not by the law but 292 by the promise, in which the Father has given the assurance that he wishes to forgive and to be reconciled for Christ's sake. This promise is received by faith alone, as Paul declares in Rom. 4:13. Faith alone accepts the forgiveness of sins, justifies, and regenerates. Then love and other good fruits follow. As we have already stated, we teach that a man is justified when, with his conscience terrified by the preaching of penitence, he takes heart and believes that he has a gracious God for Christ's sake. This faith is accounted for righteousness before 293 God (Rom. 4:3, 5). When the heart is encouraged and quickened by faith in this way, it receives the Holy Spirit. Through his renewal we can keep the law, love God and his Word, obey God in the midst of afflictions, and practice chastity, love toward our neighbor, and so forth. Even though they are a long way from the perfection of the law, these works please God on account of the justifying faith that for Christ's sake we have a gracious God. These things are plain and in conformity with the Gospel, and any sound mind can grasp them.

From this fundamental article it is clear why we ascribe justi- 294 fication to faith rather than to love, though love follows faith since love is the keeping of the law. Paul teaches that we are justified not by the law but by the promise, which is received by faith only. We cannot come to God without Christ, the mediator; nor do we receive forgiveness of sin because of our love but because of Christ. We 295 cannot even love an angry God; the law always accuses us and thus always shows us an angry God. Therefore we must first take hold of the promise by faith, that for Christ's sake the Father is reconciled and forgiving. Later we begin to keep the law. Far 296 away from human reason, far away from Moses, we must turn our eyes to Christ, and believe that he was given for us to be justified on his account. In the flesh we never satisfy the law. Thus we are not accounted righteous because of the law but because of Christ, whose merits are conferred on us if we believe in him.

There are two basic facts: First, we are not justified by the law 297 because human nature cannot keep the law of God nor love God; and second, we are justified by the promise, in which reconciliation, righteousness, and eternal life are assured to us for Christ's sake. Christ was not promised, revealed. born, crucified, and raised in vain; the promise of grace in Christ was not given in vain, either, before the law and outside the law from the very beginning of the world. The promise is to be accepted by faith, as John says (1 John 5:10-12): "He who does not believe God, has made him a liar, because he has not believed in the testimony that God has borne to his Son. And this is the testimony, that God gave us eternal life, and this life is in his Son. He who has the Son, has life; he who has not the Son, has not life." Whoever reflects on all this will easily understand that justification must necessarily be attributed to faith. Christ says, "If the Son makes you free, you will be free indeed" (John 8:36). Paul says, "Through him we have obtained access" to God, adding, "through faith" (Rom. 5:2). By faith in Christ, therefore, we accept the promise of the forgiveness of sins and righteousness. We are not justified before God either by reason or by the law.

These things are so clear and evident that we are astonished 298 to see how furiously our opponents deny them. The proof is obvious: Since we are not justified before God by the law but by the promise, justification must necessarily be ascribed to faith. What argument can anybody possibly bring against this proof unless he wants utterly to abolish Christ and the Gospel? Christ's glory becomes brighter 299 when we teach men to make use of him as mediator and propitiator. In this teaching, faithful consciences see the most complete consolation offered them. They are taught to believe and to rely on the sure fact that they have a reconciled Father because of Christ, not because of our righteousness but because Christ still helps us to keep the law. Such great blessings our opponents take from the church in 300 condemning and trying to destroy the doctrine of righteousness by faith. Let all good men beware, therefore, of yielding to their ungodly counsels. Our opponents' teaching does not mention how we must set Christ against the wrath of God, as though we could overcome the wrath of God with our love or could love an angry God.

On these issues consciences are left in doubt. If they are 301 supposed to believe that they have a gracious God because they love and keep the law, they will have to doubt whether they have a gracious God. They either do not feel this love at all, as our opponents admit, or surely they feel that it is very weak. Much more often they feel angry at the judgment of God, who visits on human nature so many terrible evils, sufferings in this life and the fear of eternal wrath. When will the conscience be at rest, therefore, and when will it be pacified? When will it love God amid these doubts and terrors? What is this doctrine of the law but a doctrine of despair? Let any of 302 our opponents come forth to describe the love with which he loves

God. They do not know what they are talking about; like the walls of a house, they echo the word "love" without understanding it. How confused and unclear their teaching is! It transfers Christ's glory to human works; it leads consciences into either pride or despair.

We hope that pious minds will easily understand our teaching   303 and that it will bring godly and wholesome consolation to frightened consciences. In answer to our opponents' quibble that many wicked people and demons also believe (James 2:19), we have said several times that we are talking about faith in Christ and in the forgiveness of sins, a faith that truly and wholeheartedly accepts the promise of grace. This does not come without a great battle in the human heart. Sensible people can easily see that a faith which believes that God cares for us, forgives us, and hears us is a supernatural thing, for of itself the human mind believes no such thing about God. Therefore neither wicked people nor demons can have the faith we are discussing here.

Some sophist may quibble here that righteousness is in the will   304 and thus cannot be ascribed to faith, which is in the intellect. The answer to this is easy, since even the scholastics admit that the will commands the intellect to assent to the Word of God.[3] We say still more clearly: The terrors of sin and death are not merely thoughts in the intellect but are also a horrible turmoil in the will as it flees God's judgment; just so faith is not merely knowledge in the intellect but also trust in the will, that is, to desire and to accept what the promise offers—reconciliation and forgiveness of sins. This is how Scripture uses the word "faith," as this statement of Paul shows, "Since we are justified by faith, we have peace with God" (Rom. 5:1). In   305 this passage "justify" is used in a judicial way to mean "to absolve a guilty man and pronounce him righteous," and to do so on account of someone else's righteousness, namely, Christ's, which is communicated to us through faith. Since in this passage our right-   306 eousness is the imputation of someone else's righteousness, we must speak of righteousness in a different way here from the philosophical or judicial investigation of a man's own righteousness, which certainly resides in the will. Paul says (I Cor. 1:30), "He is the source of your life in Jesus Christ, whom God made our wisdom, our righteousness and sanctification and redemption." And II Cor. 5:21, "For our sake he made him to be sin who knew no sin, so that in him we might become the righteousness of God." Because the right-   307 eousness of Christ is given to us through faith, therefore faith is righteousness in us by imputation. That is, by it we are made acceptable to God because of God's imputation and ordinances, as Paul says (Rom. 4:5), "Faith is reckoned as righteousness."

³ Cf. *ibid.*, II, 1, q.56, a.3, c.

We must speak technically because of certain carping critics: 308
faith is truly righteousness because it is obedience to the Gospel.
Obedience to the edict of a superior is obviously a kind of distribu-
tive righteousness. Our good works or obedience to the law can be
pleasing to God only because this obedience to the Gospel takes
hold of Christ, the propitiator, and is reckoned for righteousness.
We do not satisfy the law, but for Christ's sake this is forgiven us,
as Paul says (Rom. 8:1), "There is now no condemnation for those
who are in Christ Jesus." This faith gives honor to God, gives   309
him what is properly his; it obeys him by accepting his promises.
As Paul says (Rom. 4:20), "No distrust made him waver concerning
the promise of God, but he grew strong in his faith as he gave glory
to God." Thus the service and worship of the Gospel is to   310
receive good things from God, while the worship of the law is to
offer and present our goods to God. We cannot offer anything to
God unless we have first been reconciled and reborn. The greatest
possible comfort comes from this doctrine that the highest worship
in the Gospel is the desire to receive forgiveness of sins, grace, and
righteousness. About this worship Christ speaks in John 6:40, "This
is the will of my Father, that everyone who sees the Son and believes
in him should have eternal life." And the Father says (Matt. 17:5),
"This is my beloved Son, with whom I am well pleased; listen to him."
Our opponents talk about obedience to the law; they do not   311
talk about obedience to the Gospel. Yet we cannot obey the law
unless we have been reborn through the Gospel, and we cannot love
God unless we have received the forgiveness of sins. As long as   312
we feel that he is wrathful against us, human nature flees his wrath
and judgment. Someone may quibble that if it is faith that wishes
for what the promise offers, then the dispositions of faith and hope
seem to be confused, since it is hope that expects what is promised.
To this we answer that these feelings cannot be divided in fact the
way they are in idle scholastic speculations. In Heb. 11:1 faith is
defined as "the assurance of things hoped for." If someone wants a
distinction anyway, we say that the object of hope is properly a
future event, while faith deals with both future and present things
and receives in the present the forgiveness of sins that the promise
offers.

We hope that from this the nature of faith will be clearly   313
understood, as well as the reasons that compel us to hold that we are
justified, reconciled, and reborn by faith, if indeed we want to teach
the righteousness of the Gospel and not of the law. Those who teach
that we are justified by love teach the righteousness of the law, they
do not teach us to use Christ as the mediator in justification. It   314
is evident that not with love but with faith we overcome the terrors

of sin and death since we cannot set our love and keeping of the law against the wrath of God. As Paul says (Rom. 5:2), "Through Christ we have obtained access to God by faith." We stress this statement so often because it is so clear. It summarizes our case very well, and a careful consideration of it will teach us much about the whole issue and bring consolation to well-disposed minds. Therefore it is well to have it at hand and keep it in mind, not only to refute the opponents' teaching that we come to God by love and merits without Christ, the mediator, rather than by faith, but also to cheer ourselves in the midst of fears and to exercise our faith. It is also clear 315 that without the help of Christ we cannot keep the law, as he himself says (John 15:5), "Apart from me you can do nothing." So before we can keep the law, our hearts must be reborn by faith.

From this it is understandable why we reject our opponents' 316 teaching on the merit of condignity.[4] This decision is easy. First, they do not mention faith or the fact that for Christ's sake we please God by faith. They imagine that good works, done with the help of a "disposition" of love, are a worthy righteousness that pleases God of itself and earns eternal life without needing Christ, the mediator. If we want to please God because of our works and not 317 because of Christ, what else is this but a transfer of Christ's glory to our works, a destruction of his glory as mediator? For he is the mediator continually and not just at the beginning of justification. Paul also says (Gal. 2:17) that if a man justified in Christ must then seek his righteousness elsewhere, he thereby makes Christ "an agent of sin" since he does not justify in full. It is highly absurd 318 when our opponents teach that good works earn grace by the merit of condignity, as though when our conscience terrifies us after justification, the way it often does, we must seek grace through a good work and not by faith in Christ.

Second, the opponents' teaching leaves consciences in doubt, 319 so that they can never be stilled; for the law always accuses us, even in good works. The flesh always lusts against the Spirit (Gal. 5:17). If a conscience believes that it ought to be pleasing to God because of its own work and not because of Christ, how will it have peace without faith? What work will it find that it will count worthy 320 of eternal life, if indeed hope ought to be sustained by merits? Against these doubts Paul says (Rom. 5:1), "Since we are justified by faith, we have peace with God"; we ought to be utterly sure that righteousness and eternal life are given us freely for Christ's sake. And of Abraham he says (Rom. 4:18), "In hope he believed against hope."

Third, how will the conscience know when a work has been 321 performed under the influence of this disposition of love, so that it

---

[4] See above, IV, 19.

can be sure of earning grace by the merit of condignity? This very distinction—that men sometimes acquire the merit of congruity and sometimes the merit of condignity—was made up to evade the Scriptures. For as we have said above, the intention of the one performing the work does not distinguish between the two kinds of merit. Rather, smug hypocrites simply believe that their works are worth enough to account them righteous, whereas terrified consciences are uncertain about all their works and therefore continually seek other works. To acquire the merit of condignity means to doubt and to work without faith until despair ensues. In short, everything our opponents teach on this question is full of errors and dangers.

Fourth, the whole church confesses that eternal life comes 322 through mercy. Speaking of the works that saints perform after justification, Augustine says in *Grace and Free Will*, "God leads us to eternal life, not by our merits, but according to his mercy." [5] In the ninth book of the *Confessions* he says, "Woe to the life of men, however praiseworthy, if it is to be judged without mercy." [6] Cyprian says in his commentary on the Lord's Prayer: "Lest anybody should flatter himself that he is innocent and by extolling himself should perish even more, he is instructed and taught that he sins daily, since he is commanded to pray daily for his sins." [7] But the point 323 is well known and has many clear testimonies in the Scriptures and in the Church Fathers, who declare unanimously that even if we have good works we need mercy in them. Looking at this mercy, 324 faith comforts and consoles us. Our opponents teach wrongly when they praise merits in such a way as to add nothing about this faith that takes hold of mercy. As we have said above that the promise and faith are correlative and that only faith can take hold of the promise, so we say here that the promised mercy correlatively requires faith and that only faith can take hold of this mercy. Properly, then, do we reject the doctrine of the merit of condignity since it teaches nothing about justifying faith and obscures Christ's glory and mediatorial work. Let no one think that we are teaching anything 325 new in this regard when the Church Fathers have so clearly handed down the doctrine that we need mercy even in our good works.

Scripture often stresses the same thing. Ps. 143:2, "Enter 326 not into judgment with thy servant, for no man living is righteous before thee." This absolutely denies any glory in man's righteousness, even to all the saints and servants of God, if God does not forgive but judges and condemns their hearts. When David elsewhere boasts of his righteousness, he is speaking of his cause against the

[5] Augustine, *Grace and Free Will*, 9:21.
[6] Augustine, *Confessions*, IX, 13.
[7] Cyprian, *The Lord's Prayer*, 22.

persecutors of God's Word, not of his personal purity. He prays for the defense of God's cause and his glory, as in Ps. 7:8, "Judge me, O Lord, according to my righteousness and according to the integrity that is in me." Similarly, in Ps. 130:3 he says that no one can stand the judgment of God if he observes our sins, "If thou, O Lord, shouldst mark iniquities, Lord, who could stand?" Job 9:28, 327 "I feared all my works"; vv. 30-31, "If I wash myself with snow, and cleanse my hands with lye, yet thou wilt plunge me into a pit." Prov. 20:9, "Who can say, 'I have made my heart clean, I am pure from my sin?'" I John 1:8, "If we say we have no sin, we 328 deceive ourselves, and the truth is not in us." And in the Lord's Prayer the saints pray for the forgiveness of sins; therefore saints have sins, too.

Num. 14:18, "And the innocent will not be innocent." Deut. 329 4:24, "Your God is a devouring fire." Zech. 2:13 says, "Be silent, all flesh, before the Lord." Isa. 40:6, 7, "All flesh is grass, and all its beauty is like the flower of the field. The grass withers, the flower fades, when the breath of the Lord blows upon it"; that is, the flesh and the righteousness of the flesh cannot stand the judgment of God. Jonah says (Jonah 2:8), "Those who forsake mercy observe 330 lying vanities"; that is, all trust is vain except a trust in mercy; mercy saves us, our own merits and efforts do not save us. Therefore 331 Daniel prays (9:18, 19), "For we do not present our supplications before thee on the ground of our righteousness, but on the ground of thy great mercy. O Lord, hear; O Lord, forgive; O Lord, give heed and act; delay not, for thy own sake, O my God, because thy city and thy people are called by thy name." So Daniel teaches us to take hold of mercy when we pray, that is, to trust the mercy of God and not our merits before him.

We wonder what our opponents do when they pray, if indeed 332 these profane men ever ask God for anything! If they declare that they are worthy because they have love and good works, and ask for grace as though they had earned it, then they pray like the Pharisee in Luke 18:11 who says, "I am not like other men." Such prayer, which relies on its own righteousness and not on the mercy of God, insults Christ, who intercedes for us as our high priest. There- 333 fore prayer relies upon the mercy of God when we believe that we are heard because of Christ the high priest, as he himself says (John 16:23), "If you ask anything of the Father, he will give it to you in my name." "In my name," he says, because without the high priest we cannot draw near to the Father.

Here Christ's statement (Luke 17:10) also applies, "When 334 you have done all that is commanded you, say, 'We are unworthy servants.'" These words clearly say that God saves through mercy and because of his promise, not as a payment which he owes to us for our good works. At this point our opponents make a mar- 335 velous play on Christ's words. They argue that if we are unworthy though we have done everything, much more must we say that we are unworthy though we have believed everything. Then they add that works are worthless to God, but that to us they are worth something. Look how this childish sophistry delights our opponents! 336 Though these absurdities do not deserve a refutation, we shall nevertheless give a brief answer. The argument is defective.

For one thing, our opponents are deceived with regard to 337 the term "faith." If it meant the knowledge of history that the wicked and demons also have (James 2:19), their argument that faith is worthless would be correct when they say: "When you have believed everything, say, 'We are unworthy servants.' " We are not talking about a knowledge of history, however, but about trust in God's promise and in his mercy. This trust in the promise confesses that we are unworthy servants. Indeed, this confession that our works are worthless is the very voice of faith, as is evident from the example of Daniel referred to above, "For we do not present our supplications before thee on the ground of our righteousness," etc. Faith 338 saves because it takes hold of mercy and the promise of grace, even though our works are worthless. On these grounds we are not bothered by the argument, "When you have believed everything, say, 'We are unworthy servants.' " For our works are worthless, and with the whole church we teach that we are saved by mercy.

Likewise, the argument from analogy is unwarranted: from 339 the statement, "When you have done everything, do not trust in your works," to the statement, "When you have believed everything, do not trust in the divine promise." The two statements are not analogous since the causes and objects of trust in the first are unlike those in the second. In the first, trust is a trust in our own works; in the second, trust is a trust in the divine promise. Christ condemns trust in our own works; he does not condemn trust in his promise. He does not want us to despair of God's grace and mercy. He denounces our works as worthless, but he does not denounce the promise that offers mercy gratis. Here Ambrose has clearly said, "Grace is to be 340 recognized, but nature is not to be ignored." [8] We should trust 341 the promise of grace, not our own nature. As usual, our opponents twist against faith statements made in support of faith. We leave these thorny questions to the schools. It is obviously a childish 342 quibble to interpret "unworthy servants" as meaning that works are worthless to God but worth something to us. Christ is speaking of that worthiness whereby God obligates himself to bestow his grace

---

[8] Ambrose, *Exposition of the Gospel according to Luke*, VIII, 32.

upon us, though it is out of place here to discuss what is worthy or worthless. "Unworthy servants" means "insufficient servants," since no one fears, loves, or trusts God as he ought. Let us have done   343 with these petty quibblings of our opponents which intelligent men can easily judge when they are brought to light. Everyone can see that this passage condemns trust in our own works.

Let us therefore hold to the church's confession that we are   344 saved through mercy. At this point someone may say, "Hope will be uncertain if we are saved through mercy and if, prior to salvation, there is nothing to distinguish those who are saved from those who are not." To this we must give a satisfactory answer. It seems that for some such reason the scholastics invented the term "merit of condignity." This can be a great problem to the human mind.   345 We shall therefore reply briefly. Precisely in order to make hope sure and to distinguish between those who are saved and those who are not, we must hold that we are saved through mercy. Unless it is qualified, this statement seems absurd. In courts of human judgment a right or debt is certain, while mercy is uncertain. The judgment of God is another thing altogether. Here mercy has God's clear and certain promise and his command. Properly speaking, the Gospel is the command to believe that we have a gracious God because of Christ. "God sent the Son into the world, not to condemn the world, but that the world might be saved through him. He who believes in him is not condemned," etc. (John 3:17, 18). So whenever   346 mercy is spoken of, faith in the promise must be added. This faith produces a sure hope, for it rests on the Word and commandment of God. If our hope were to rest on works, then it would really be unsure since works cannot still the conscience, as we have often said above. This faith makes the difference between those who are   347 saved and those who are not. Faith makes the difference between the worthy and the unworthy because eternal life is promised to the justified and it is faith that justifies.

Here our opponents will raise the cry that good works are un-   348 necessary if they do not merit eternal life. We have refuted this slander earlier. Of course, good works are necessary. We say that eternal life is promised to the justified, but those who walk according to the flesh can retain neither faith nor righteousness. We are justified for this very purpose, that, being righteous, we might begin to do good works and obey God's law. For this purpose we are reborn   349 and receive the Holy Spirit, that this new life might have new works and new impulses, the fear and love of God, hatred of lust, etc. The faith we speak of has its existence in penitence. It ought   350 to grow and become firmer amid good works as well as temptations and dangers, so that we become ever stronger in the conviction that

God cares for us, forgives us, and hears us for Christ's sake. No one learns this without many severe struggles. How often our aroused conscience tempts us to despair when it shows our old or new sins or the uncleanness of our nature! This handwriting[9] is not erased without a great conflict in which experience testifies how difficult a thing faith is.

While we are receiving encouragement and comfort in the   351 midst of our terrors, other spiritual impulses increase, such as knowledge and fear of God, love of God, and hope. We are renewed, as Paul says (Col. 3:10; II Cor. 3:18), "in knowledge," and "beholding the glory of the Lord, we are changed into his likeness"; that is, we acquire the true knowledge of God, enabling us truly to fear him and to trust that he cares for us and hears us. This rebirth is,   352 so to speak, the beginning of eternal life, as Paul says (Rom. 8:10), "If Christ is in you, although your bodies are dead because of sin, your spirits are alive because of righteousness." And again (II Cor. 5:2, 3), "We long to put on our heavenly dwelling, so that by putting it on we may not be found naked." From these statements the   353 fair-minded reader can judge that we very definitely require good works, since we teach that this faith arises in penitence and ought to grow continually in penitence. Here is Christian and spiritual perfection, if penitence and faith amid penitence grow together. The devout can understand this teaching better than what our opponents teach about contemplation or perfection. Just as justification   354 belongs to faith, so eternal life belongs to it. As Peter says (I Pet. 1:9), "As the outcome of your faith you obtain the salvation of your souls." Our opponents grant that the justified are children of God and fellow heirs with Christ (Rom. 8:17). Afterwards works   355 merit other bodily and spiritual rewards because they please God through faith. There will be distinctions in the glory of the saints.

Here our opponents reply that eternal life is called a reward   356 and that therefore it is merited by the merit of condignity through good works. We shall answer briefly and clearly. Paul calls eternal life a "gift" (Rom. 6:23) because the righteousness bestowed on us for Christ's sake at the same time makes us sons of God and fellow heirs with Christ (Rom. 8:17), as John says (John 3:36), "He who believes in the Son has eternal life." Augustine says, as do many later writers, "God crowns his gifts in us." [1] But elsewhere (Luke 6:23) it is written, "Your reward is great in heaven." If these passages seem to our opponents to be in conflict, let them see to it. But   357 they are not fair judges, for they omit the word "gift." They also omit the central thought of the discussion; they pick out the word

___

[9] Cf. Col. 2:14.
[1] Augustine, *Grace and Free Will*, VI, 9, 15.

"reward" and in their explanation do violence not only to Scripture but also to the very usage of the language. Because a "reward" is mentioned, they argue that our works ought to be counted so precious that eternal life is their due and that therefore they are worthy of grace and eternal life without needing mercy or the mediator Christ or faith. Such logic is completely new. We hear the term   358 "reward": therefore we need neither Christ the mediator nor the faith that has access to God for Christ's sake, not for our works' sake. Who cannot see that this is a fallacious conclusion?

We are not arguing about the term "reward." We do contend   359 about the issue whether good works of themselves are worthy of grace and eternal life or whether they please God only because of the faith that takes hold of Christ, the mediator. Not only do our op-   360 ponents attribute to works a worthiness of grace and eternal life. They even suppose that they have extra merits which they can give to justify others, as when monks sell the merits of their orders to others. Chrysippus-like,[2] they draw the following absurd conclusion when they hear this one word "reward": "It is called a reward, there-fore we have works that are precious enough to earn a reward; there-fore works please God for their own sake, not for the sake of Christ, the mediator. Since one has more merits than another, therefore some have extra merits. Those who merit them can transfer these merits to others." Look out, dear reader, you have not yet heard the whole sorites. We must add certain "sacraments" of this   361 transfer, as when a monk's hood is placed on a dead man. By such a series of arguments the blessings of Christ and the righteousness of faith are obscured.

We are not putting forward an empty quibble about the term   362 "reward." If our opponents will grant that we are accounted righteous by faith for Christ's sake and that good works are pleasing to God because of faith, then we will not argue much about the term "re-ward." We grant that eternal life is a reward because it is something that is owed—not because of our merits but because of the promise. We have shown above that justification is strictly a gift of God; it is a thing promised. To this gift the promise of eternal life has been added, according to Rom. 8:30, "Those whom he justified he also glorified." Here Paul's words apply, "There is laid up for me   363 the crown of righteousness, which the Lord, the righteous judge, will give me," etc. (II Tim. 4:8). The crown is owed to the justified because of the promise. This promise the saints must know. It   364 is not an incentive to work for their own advantage, since they should work for the glory of God. But to escape despair amid afflictions,

---

[2] Chrysippus was a brilliant dialectician of the third century before Christ who drew dubious conclusions from many indiscriminate citations.

they should know that it is the will of God to help, rescue, and save them. The strong hear the mention of punishments and rewards in one way, and the weak in another; for the weak work for their own advantage.

Yet the proclamation of rewards and punishments is necessary. 365 In the proclamation of punishments the wrath of God is displayed, and hence this belongs to the preaching of penitence. In the proclamation of rewards grace is displayed. When they talk about good works, the Scriptures often include faith, since they wish to include the righteousness of the heart with other fruits. Just so they sometimes offer grace with other rewards, as in Isa. 58:8, 9 and often in other places in the prophets. We also concede, and have often 366 declared, that though justification and eternal life belong to faith, still good works merit other rewards, both bodily and spiritual, in various degrees, according to I Cor. 3:8, "Each shall receive his wages according to his labor." The righteousness of the Gospel, which deals with the promise of grace, receives justification and new life gratis. The keeping of the law that follows faith deals with the law, in which a reward is offered and owed, not gratis but for our works. Those who merit this are justified before they keep the law. First they have been "transferred into the kingdom of God's Son," as Paul says (Col. 1:13), and made fellow heirs with Christ (Rom. 8:17).

Whenever merit is discussed, our opponents immediately apply 367 it not to the other rewards but to justification, though the Gospel offers justification freely because of Christ's merits, not ours, and Christ's merits are communicated to us by faith. Works and afflictions merit not justification but other rewards, as in these passages a reward is offered for works. "He who sows sparingly will also reap sparingly, he who sows bountifully will also reap bountifully" (II Cor. 9:6); here the degree of the reward is evidently commensurate with the degree of the work. "Honor your father and your mother, that your days may be long in the land" (Ex. 20:12); here, too, the law offers a reward for a certain work. Although keeping the law thus 368 merits a reward, since a reward properly belongs to the law, still we must remember that the Gospel offers justification freely for Christ's sake. We neither do nor can keep the law before we have been reconciled to God, justified, and reborn. This keeping of the law would not please God unless we had been accepted because of faith. Since men are accepted because of faith, this incipient keeping of the law pleases God and has its reward, both here and hereafter. We 369 might say more on the term "reward," based on the nature of the law, but since it would take too long we shall expound it in another connection.

Our opponents urge that good works properly merit eternal 370 life, since Paul says (Rom. 2:6), "He will render to every man according to his works"; and v. 10, "Glory and honor and peace for every one who does good." John 5:29, "Those who have done good will come forth to the resurrection of life"; Matt. 25:35, "I was hungry and you gave me food," etc. These passages and all 371 others like them where works are praised in the Scriptures must be taken to mean not only outward works but also the faith of the heart, since the Scriptures do not speak of hypocrisy but of righteousness in the heart and of its fruits. Whenever law and works are 372 mentioned, we must know that Christ, the mediator, should not be excluded. He is the end of the law (Rom. 10:4), and he himself says, "Apart from me you can do nothing" (John 15:5). By this rule, as we have said earlier, all passages on works can be interpreted. Therefore, when eternal life is granted to works, it is granted to the justified. None can do good works except the justified, who are led by the Spirit of Christ; nor can good works please God without the mediator Christ and faith, according to Heb. 11:6, "Without faith it is impossible to please God."

When Paul says, "He will render to every man according to 373 his works," we must understand not merely outward works but the entire righteousness or unrighteousness. That is to say, "Glory for him who does good," namely, for the righteous man. "You gave me food" [3] is cited as fruit and evidence of the righteousness of the heart and of faith, and for this reason eternal life is granted to righteousness. In this way the Scriptures lump together the righteousness 374 of the heart and its fruit. They often mention the fruit to make it clearer to the inexperienced and to show that a new life and new birth are required, not hypocrisy. Such a new birth comes by faith amid penitence.

No sane man can judge otherwise. We are not trying to be 375 overly subtle here in distinguishing the righteousness of the heart from its fruits, if only our opponents would grant that the fruits please God because of faith and the mediator Christ but in themselves are not worthy of grace and eternal life. This is what we condemn in our 376 opponents' position, that by interpreting such passages of the Scriptures in either a philosophical or a Jewish manner they eliminate from them the righteousness of faith and Christ, the mediator. From these passages they reason that works merit grace by the merit of congruity or, if love is added, by the merit of condignity;[4] that is, that they justify, and because they are righteousness that they are worthy of eternal life. This error obviously destroys the righteousness of faith, which believes that we have access to God not because of

---

[3] Matt. 25:35.
[4] See above, IV, 19.

our works but because of Christ, and that through his priestly mediation we are led to the Father and have a reconciled Father, as we have said often enough. This teaching about the righteousness 377 of faith dare not be neglected in the church of Christ; without it the work of Christ cannot be understood, and what is left of the doctrine of justification is nothing more than the teaching of the law. We are therefore obliged to hold fast to the Gospel and the teaching of the promise given for Christ's sake.

It is then no minor matter about which we are arguing here 378 with our opponents. We are not trying to be overly subtle when we condemn those who teach that we merit eternal life by works, omitting the faith that takes hold of the mediator Christ. About this faith, 379 which believes that the Father is propitious to us for Christ's sake, there is not a syllable in the scholastics. Everywhere they maintain that we are acceptable and righteous because of our works, either done by the reason or at least wrought by the impulse of the love they talk about. From ancient writers they have taken certain 380 sayings, decrees as it were, and these they quote in a twisted way, boasting in the schools that good works please God because of 381 grace and that therefore we must place our confidence in God's grace. Here they interpret grace as a disposition by which we love God, as though the ancients meant to say that we should put confidence in our love, which we know by experience is weak and unclean. Yet it is peculiar that they advise us to trust our love when they teach that we cannot know whether it is present. Why not expound here God's grace and mercy toward us? Whenever this is mentioned, faith should be added, since we take hold of God's mercy, reconciliation, and love toward us only by faith. If they understood it this way, they would be correct when they say that we must put our confidence in grace and that good works please God because of grace; for faith takes hold of grace.

In the schools they also boast that our good works are valid 382 by virtue of Christ's suffering. Well said! But why not say something about faith? Christ is a propitiation, as Paul says, through faith (Rom. 3:25). When frightened consciences are consoled by faith and believe that our sins are blotted out by Christ's death and that God has been reconciled to us because of Christ's suffering, then indeed Christ's suffering benefits us. If the doctrine of faith is omitted, it is vain to say that our works are valid by virtue of the suffering of Christ.

The scholastics do not teach the righteousness of faith. They 383 interpret faith as merely a knowledge of history or of dogmas, not as the power that grasps the promise of grace and righteousness, quickening the heart amid the terrors of sin and death. Therefore they corrupt many other statements. Paul says (Rom. 10:10), "Man believes with his heart and so is justified, and he confesses with his lips and so is saved." Here we think that our opponents will   384 grant that the mere act of confessing does not save, but that it saves only because of faith in the heart. Paul says that confession saves in order to show what kind of faith obtains eternal life, a faith that is firm and active. No faith is firm that does not show itself in con-   385 fession. Thus other good works please God because of faith, as the prayers of the church ask that everything be accepted because of Christ and request everything because of Christ. It is well known that every prayer closes with this phrase: "through Christ our Lord."

Therefore we conclude that we are justified before God,   386 reconciled to him, and reborn by a faith that penitently grasps the promise of grace, truly enlivens the fearful mind, and is convinced that God is reconciled and propitious to us because of Christ. Through this faith, Peter says (I Pet. 1:5), we are "guarded for a salvation ready to be revealed." Christians need to understand this faith,   387 for it brings the fullest comfort in all afflictions and shows us the work of Christ. Those who deny that men are justified by faith deny that Christ is the mediator and propitiator, deny the promise of grace and the Gospel. They teach a doctrine of justification derived either from reason or from the law.

As much as was possible here, we have pointed out the   388 sources of this conflict and have explained those issues on which our opponents had raised objections. These will be easy for good men to evaluate if they remember, whenever a passage on love or works is quoted, that the law cannot be kept without Christ, and that we are not justified by the law but by the Gospel, the promise of grace offered in Christ. However brief this discussion may be,   389 we hope that good men will find it useful for strengthening their faith and for teaching and comforting their conscience. We know that what we have said agrees with the prophetic and apostolic Scriptures, with the holy Fathers Ambrose, Augustine, and many others, and with the whole church of Christ, which certainly confesses that Christ is the propitiator and the justifier.

We ought not assume immediately that the church of Rome   390 accepts everything that the pope or cardinals or bishops or some theologians or monks advance. To the prelates their own authority is obviously more important than the Gospel of Christ, and everybody knows that most of them are openly Epicureans. It is also obvious that the theologians have mingled more than enough philosophy with Christian doctrine. Their authority ought not seem   391 so great as to end all argument, when there are so many manifest errors among them, such as the idea that we can love God above all things by purely natural powers. Despite its obvious falsehood, this teaching has spawned many errors. The Scriptures, the holy 392 Fathers, and the judgment of all the faithful are consistently against them. Therefore the knowledge of Christ has remained with some faithful souls. This in spite of the fact that prelates and some theologians and monks in the church have taught us to seek forgiveness of sins, grace, and righteousness through our works and new devotions, obscuring the work of Christ and making of him not the propitiator and justifier, but only a legislator.

Moreover, the Scriptures predicted that human traditions 393 and the teaching of works would obscure the righteousness of faith in this way. So Paul often complains[5] that even then there were some who in place of the righteousness of faith taught that men were reconciled to God and justified by their own works and devotions, not by faith for Christ's sake. By nature men judge that God ought to be appeased by works. The only righteousness that reason can 394 see is the righteousness of the law, understood as civic uprightness. So there have always been some in the world who taught only this outward righteousness to the exclusion of the righteousness of faith, and such teachers there will always be. The same thing hap- 395 pened among the people of Israel. The majority of the people believed that they merited the forgiveness of sins by their works, and so they multiplied sacrifices and devotions. The prophets, on the contrary, condemned this opinion and taught the righteousness of faith. The history of the people of Israel is a type of what was to happen in the church of the future.

Therefore let not pious minds be troubled by the crowd of 396 adversaries who condemn our teaching. It is easy to evaluate their spirit, for in some doctrines they have condemned a truth so manifest and clear that their ungodliness comes out into the open. The 397 bull of Leo X[6] has condemned a very necessary doctrine that all Christians should hold and believe, namely, "We ought to trust that we have been absolved, not because of our contrition but because of the word of Christ, 'Whatever you bind,' etc. (Matt. 16:19)." Now in this very gathering[7] the authors of the Confutation 398 have condemned us in clear words for saying faith is part of penance, by which we obtain forgiveness of sin, conquer the terrors of sin, and receive peace for our conscience. Who does not see that this doctrine —that by faith we obtain the forgiveness of sin—is most true and certain and indispensable for all Christians? When future generations

---

[5] Gal. 4:9; 5:7; Col. 2:8, 16, 17; I Tim. 4:2, 3.

[6] The bull *Exsurge Domine* of 1520.

[7] The Diet of Augsburg, 1530.

hear that such a doctrine was condemned, how can they ascribe any knowledge of Christ to those who condemned it?

One can also judge their spirit from the unheard of cruelty   399 which, as everyone knows, they have hitherto shown toward many godly men. We have heard in this assembly that when opinions were being expressed about our Confession, a reverend father said that no plan seemed better to him than to give an answer written in blood to our Confession written in ink. What would Phalaris[8] say that was more cruel? Some of the princes regarded this expression as unworthy of being spoken in such an assembly.

Although our opponents arrogate to themselves the name of   400 the church, therefore, we know that the church of Christ is among those who teach the Gospel of Christ, not among those who defend wicked opinions against the Gospel, as the Lord says, "My sheep hear my voice" (John 10:27). Augustine says: "The question is, where is the church? What then shall we do? Shall we seek it in our own words or in the words of its head, our Lord Jesus Christ? I think we should seek it in the words of him who is the truth and who knows his body best." [9] The judgments of our opponents will not bother us since they defend human opinions contrary to the Gospel, contrary to the authority of the holy Fathers, and contrary to the testimony of pious minds.

[ARTICLES VII AND VIII.] THE CHURCH

The authors of the Confutation have condemned the seventh   1 article of our Confession in which we said that the church is the assembly of saints.[1] And they have added a lengthy dissertation, that the wicked are not to be separated from the church since John compared the church to a threshing floor on which chaff and wheat are heaped together (Matt. 3:12) and Christ compared it to a net in which there are both good and bad fish (Matt. 13:47).

The saying is certainly true that there is no defense against   2 the attacks of slanderers. Nothing can be said so carefully that it can avoid misrepresentation. That was why we added the eighth   3 article, to avoid the impression that we separate evil men and hypocrites from the outward fellowship of the church or deny efficacy to the sacraments which evil men or hypocrites administer. Thus we do not need to defend ourselves at any length against this slander.

---

[8] A tyrant in Sicily about 560 B.C.

[9] Augustine, *Epistle against the Donatists* (concerning the Unity of the Church), VI, 15, 2.

[1] Roman Confutation: "The seventh article of the Confession, in which it is affirmed that the church is the assembly of saints, cannot be admitted without prejudice to faith if by this definition the wicked and sinners are separated from the church" (Pt. I, Art. VII).

The eighth article exonerates us enough. We concede that in this life hypocrites and evil men are mingled with the church and are members of the church according to the outward associations of the church's marks—that is, Word, confession, and sacraments—especially if they have not been excommunicated. The sacraments do not lose their efficacy when they are administered by evil men; indeed, we may legitimately use sacraments that are administered by evil men. Paul also predicts that Antichrist will "take his seat in the temple 4 of God" (II Thess. 2:4), that is, that he will rule and hold office in the church.

The church is not merely an association of outward ties and 5 rites like other civic governments, however, but it is mainly an association of faith and of the Holy Spirit in men's hearts. To make it recognizable, this association has outward marks, the pure teaching of the Gospel and the administration of the sacraments in harmony with the Gospel of Christ. This church alone is called the body of Christ, which Christ renews, consecrates, and governs by his Spirit, as Paul testifies when he says (Eph. 1:22, 23), "And he has made him the head over all things for the church, which is his body, the fullness," that is, the whole congregation "of him who fills all in all." Thus those in whom Christ is not active are not members of Christ. This much our opponents also admit, that the wicked are dead members of the church. We wonder why they criticize our description, 6 which speaks of living members.

We have not said anything new. Paul defined the church in 7 the same way in Eph. 5:25-27, saying that it should be purified in order to be holy. He also added the outward marks, the Word and the sacraments. He says, "Christ loved the church and gave himself up for it, that he might sanctify it, having cleansed it by the washing of water with the word, that the church might be presented before him in splendor, without spot or wrinkle or any such thing, that it might be holy and without blemish." We have repeated this statement almost verbatim in our Confession. The Creed also defines the church this way, teaching us to believe that there is a holy, catholic church. Certainly the wicked are not a holy church! The follow- 8 ing phrase, "the communion of saints," seems to have been added to explain what "church" means, namely, the assembly of saints who share the association of the same Gospel or teaching and of the same Holy Spirit, who renews, consecrates, and governs their hearts.

We set forth this doctrine for a very necessary reason. We 9 see the infinite dangers that threaten the church with ruin. There is an infinite number of ungodly within the church who oppress it. The church will abide nevertheless; it exists despite the great multitude of the wicked, and Christ supplies it with the gifts he has promised—

the forgiveness of sins, answer to prayer, and the gift of the Holy Spirit. The Creed offers us these consolations that we may not despair but may know all this. It says "the church catholic" lest we take 10 it to mean an outward government of certain nations. It is, rather, made up of men scattered throughout the world who agree on the Gospel and have the same Christ, the same Holy Spirit, and the same sacraments, whether they have the same human traditions or not. The gloss in the *Decrees* says that "the church in the larger sense includes both the godly and the wicked," and that the wicked are part of the church only in name and not in fact, while the godly are part of the church in fact as well as in name.[2] The Fathers say 11 the same thing in many places. For example, Jerome says, "Therefore the sinner who has been defiled by any spot cannot be called part of the church of Christ, nor can he be said to be subject to Christ."[3]

Hypocrites and evil men are indeed associated with the true 12 church as far as outward ceremonies are concerned. But when we come to define the church, we must define that which is the living body of Christ and is the church in fact as well as in name. We 13 must understand what it is that chiefly makes us members, and living members, of the church. If we were to define the church as only an outward organization embracing both the good and the wicked, then men would not understand that the kingdom of Christ is the righteousness of the heart and the gift of the Holy Spirit but would think of it as only the outward observance of certain devotions and rituals. Then, too, what difference will there be between the church 14 and the Old Testament people? Yet Paul distinguishes the church from the Old Testament people by the fact that the church is a spiritual people, separated from the heathen not by civil rites but by being God's true people, reborn by the Holy Spirit. Among the Old Testament people, those born according to the flesh had promises about physical well-being, political affairs, etc. in addition to the promise about Christ. Because of these promises even the wicked among them were called the people of God inasmuch as God had separated these physical descendants from other nations by certain outward ordinances and promises. Nevertheless, these evil people did not please God. But the Gospel brings not the shadow of eternal 15 things but the eternal blessings themselves, the Holy Spirit and the righteousness by which we are righteous before God.

According to the Gospel, therefore, only those are the true 16 people who accept this promise of the Spirit. Besides the church is the kingdom of Christ, the opposite of the kingdom of the devil. It is evident, moreover, that the wicked are in the power of the devil

---

[2] Gratian, *Decretum*, II, chap. 33, q.3, d.1, *De poenitentia*, c.70.
[3] Pseudo-Jerome, *On the Epistle to the Ephesians*, 5:24.

and are members of the devil's kingdom, as Paul teaches in Eph. 2:2 when he says that the devil "is now at work in the sons of disobedience." Certainly the Pharisees had an outward affiliation with the church (that is, with the saints among the Old Testament people), for they held high positions and they sacrificed and taught. To them Christ says (John 8:44), "You are of your father the devil." Thus the church, which is truly the kingdom of Christ, is, precisely speaking, the congregation of the saints. The wicked are ruled by the devil and are his captives; they are not ruled by the Spirit of Christ.

But why belabor the obvious? If the church, which is truly 17 the kingdom of Christ, is distinguished from the kingdom of the devil, it necessarily follows that since the wicked belong to the kingdom of the devil, they are not the church. In this life, nevertheless, because the kingdom of Christ has not yet been revealed, they are mingled with the church and hold office in the church. The fact that the 18 revelation has not yet come does not make the wicked the kingdom of Christ. What he quickens by his Spirit is always the same kingdom of Christ, whether it be revealed or hidden under the cross, just as Christ is the same, whether now glorified or previously afflicted. Christ's parables agree with this. He clearly says in Matt. 13:38 19 that "the good seed means the sons of the kingdom, the weeds are the sons of the evil one." The field, he says, is the world, not the church. Thus John speaks (Matt. 3:12) about the whole Jewish nation and says that the true church will be separated from it. Therefore this passage is more against our opponents than for them since it shows that the true and spiritual people will be separated from the physical people. Christ is talking about the outward appearance of the church when he says that the kingdom of God is like a net (Matt. 13:47) or like ten virgins (Matt. 25:1). He teaches us that the church is hidden under a crowd of wicked men so that this stumbling block may not offend the faithful and so that we may know that the Word and the sacraments are efficacious even when wicked men administer them. Meanwhile he teaches that though these wicked men participate in the outward marks, still they are not the true kingdom of Christ and members of Christ, for they are members of the kingdom of the devil.

We are not dreaming about some Platonic republic, as has 20 been slanderously alleged, but we teach that this church actually exists, made up of true believers and righteous men scattered throughout the world. And we add its marks, the pure teaching of the Gospel and the sacraments. This church is properly called "the pillar of truth" (I Tim. 3:15), for it retains the pure Gospel and what Paul calls the "foundation" (I Cor. 3:12), that is, the true knowledge of Christ and faith. Of course, there are also many weak people in it who build on this foundation perishing structures of stubble, that is, unprofitable opinions. But because they do not overthrow the foundation, these are forgiven them or even corrected. The writings 21 of the holy Fathers show that even they sometimes built stubble on the foundation but that this did not overthrow their faith. Most of what our opponents maintain, on the other hand, does overthrow faith, as when they condemn our doctrine that forgiveness of sins is received by faith. It is also an open and wicked error when our opponents teach that men merit the forgiveness of sins by their love for God before entering a state of grace. This, too, means to remove Christ as the foundation. Similarly, why will faith be necessary if sacraments justify *ex opere operato*,[4] without a good attitude in the one using them?

Just as the church has the promise that it will always have the 22 Holy Spirit, so it also has the warning that there will be ungodly teachers and wolves. But the church, properly speaking, is that which has the Holy Spirit. Though wolves and ungodly teachers may run rampant in the church, they are not, properly speaking, the kingdom of Christ. So Lyra testifies when he says: "The church is not made up of men by reason of their power or position, whether ecclesiastical or secular, because princes and supreme pontiffs as well as those in lesser stations have apostasized from the faith. Therefore the church is made up of those persons in whom there is true knowledge and the confession of faith and truth." [5] What have we said in our Confession that is different from what Lyra says here?

Perhaps our opponents demand some such definition of the 23 church as the following. It is the supreme outward monarchy of the whole world in which the Roman pontiff must have unlimited power beyond question or censure. He may establish articles of faith, abolish the Scriptures by his leave, institute devotions and sacrifices, enact whatever laws he pleases, excuse and exempt men from any laws, divine, canonical, or civil, as he wishes. From him the emperor and all kings have received their power and right to rule, and this at Christ's command; for as the Father subjected everything to him, so now this right has been transferred to the pope. Therefore the pope must be lord of the whole world, of all the kingdoms of the world, and of all public and private affairs. He must have plenary power in both the temporal and the spiritual realm, both swords, the temporal and the spiritual. Now, this definition of the papal kingdom rather than 24 of the church of Christ has as its authors not only the canonists but also Dan. 11:36-39.

If we defined the church that way, we would probably have 25

---

[4] See above, IV, 63.
[5] Nicholas of Lyra, *Postil on Matthew*, 16:10.

fairer judges. There are in existence many extravagant and wicked writings about the power of the Roman pope for which no one has ever been brought to trial. We alone are accused, because we preach the blessing of Christ, that we obtain forgiveness of sins through faith in him and not through devotions invented by the pope. Christ, 26 the prophets, and the apostles define the church as anything but such a papal kingdom. Nor should that be transferred to the 27 popes which is the prerogative of the true church: that they are pillars of the truth[6] and that they do not err. How many of them care anything for the Gospel or think it worth reading? Many openly ridicule all religions, or if they accept anything, accept only what agrees with human reason and regard the rest as mythology, like the tragedies of the poets.

In accordance with the Scriptures, therefore, we maintain that 28 the church in the proper sense is the assembly of saints who truly believe the Gospel of Christ and who have the Holy Spirit. Nevertheless, we grant that the many hypocrites and evil men who are mingled with them in this life share an association in the outward marks, are members of the church according to this association in the outward marks, and therefore hold office in the church. When the sacraments are administered by unworthy men, this does not rob them of their efficacy. For they do not represent their own persons but the person of Christ, because of the church's call, as Christ testifies (Luke 10:16), "He who hears you hears me." When they offer the Word of Christ or the sacraments, they do so in Christ's place and stead. Christ's statement teaches us this in order that we may not be offended by the unworthiness of ministers.

On this issue we have spoken out clearly enough in our Confes- 29 sion, where we condemn the Donatists and the Wycliffites,[7] who believed that men sinned if they received the sacraments from unworthy men in the church. For the time being this seemed enough to defend the definition of the church which we had given. Nor do we see how it could be defined otherwise, since the church, properly so called, is termed the body of Christ. It is clear that the wicked belong to the kingdom and body of the devil, who drives them on and holds them captive. All this is clearer than the light of noonday; if our opponents still continue to twist it, we shall not mind replying more fully.

Our opponents also condemn the part of the seventh article in 30 which we said, "For the true unity of the church it is enough to agree concerning the teaching of the Gospel and the administration of the

---

[6] I Tim. 3:15.

[7] John Wycliffe and his followers are not mentioned in Art. VIII of the Augsburg Confession, but the Roman Confutation mentions "John Wycliffe in England and John Hus in Bohemia" as having adopted Donatist views (Art. VIII).

sacraments. It is not necessary that human traditions or rites and ceremonies, instituted by men, should be alike everywhere." If we mean "particular rites" they approve our article, but if we mean "universal rites" they disapprove it.[8] We do not quite understand 31 what our opponents mean. We are talking about true spiritual unity, without which there can be no faith in the heart nor righteousness in the heart before God. For this unity, we say, a similarity of human rites, whether universal or particular, is not necessary. The righteousness of faith is not a righteousness tied to certain traditions, as the righteousness of the law was tied to the Mosaic ceremonies, because this righteousness of the heart is something that quickens the heart. To this quickening human traditions, whether universal or particular, contribute nothing; nor are they wrought by the Holy Spirit, as are chastity, patience, the fear of God, the love of our neighbor, and the works of love.

We certainly had weighty reasons for presenting this article, 32 for it is clear that many foolish opinions about traditions have crept into the church. Some have thought that human traditions are devotions necessary for meriting justification. Later they debated how it happened that they had come to worship God in so many ways, as though these observances were really acts of devotion rather than outward rules of discipline, completely unrelated to the righteousness of the heart or the worship of God. For good and valid reasons, these vary according to the circumstances, one way or another. Similarly, some churches have excommunicated others because of such traditions as the observance of Easter, the use of icons, and the like.[9] From this the uninitiated have concluded that there can be no righteousness of the heart before God without these observances. On this issue there are many foolish books by the summists and others.[1]

But as the different length of day and night does not harm the 33 unity of the church, so we believe that the true unity of the church is not harmed by differences in rites instituted by men, although we like it when universal rites are observed for the sake of tranquillity. So in our churches we willingly observe the order of the Mass, the Lord's day, and the other more important feast days. With a very

---

[8] Roman Confutation: "They [the Lutheran princes] are also commended for not regarding variety of rites as destroying unity of faith if they mean particular rites . . . But if they extend this part of the Confession to universal church rites, this also must be utterly rejected . . ." (Pt. I, Art. VII).

[9] In the Paschal Controversy at the end of the second century Roman Christians excommunicated Christians in Asia Minor. In the Iconoclastic Controversy in the eighth century the Lateran Synod condemned the Synod of Constantinople. In 1054 the pope excommunicated the Eastern Orthodox.

[1] Since the thirteenth century many casuistical handbooks of penance (e.g., Raimund of Pennaforte, *Summa de casibus conscientiae*) had been prepared.

thankful spirit we cherish the useful and ancient ordinances, especially when they contain a discipline that serves to educate and instruct the people and the inexperienced. Now, we are not discussing 34 whether it is profitable to observe them for the sake of tranquillity or bodily profit. Another issue is involved. The question is whether the observance of human traditions is an act of worship necessary for righteousness before God. This must be settled in this controversy, and only then can we decide whether it is necessary for the true unity of the church that human traditions be alike everywhere. If human traditions are not acts of worship necessary for righteousness before God, it follows that somebody can be righteous and a child of God even if he does not observe traditions that have been maintained elsewhere. Thus if the German style of dress is not a devotion to God necessary for righteousness before him, it follows that men can be righteous, children of God, and the church of Christ even though they dress according to the French rather than the German style.

Paul clearly teaches this in Colossians (2:16, 17): "Let no one 35 pass judgment on you in questions of food and drink or with regard to a festival or a new moon or a sabbath. These are only a shadow of what is to come; but the substance belongs to Christ." And again (vv. 20-23): "If with Christ you died to the elemental spirits of the universe, why do you live as if you still belonged to the world? Why do you submit to regulations, 'Do not handle, Do not taste, Do not touch' (referring to things which all perish as they are used), according to human precepts and doctrines? These have indeed an appearance of wisdom in promoting rigor of devotion and self-abasement." What he means is this. The righteousness of the heart is a spiritual 36 thing that quickens men's hearts. It is evident that human traditions do not quicken the heart, are not works of the Holy Spirit (like love of neighbor, chastity, etc.), and are not means by which God moves the heart to believe (like the divinely instituted Word and sacraments). Rather, they are customs that do not pertain to the heart and "perish as they are used." Therefore we must not believe that they are necessary for righteousness before God. He says the same in Rom. 14:17, "The kingdom of God does not mean food and drink but righteousness and peace and joy in the Holy Spirit."

But it is not necessary to cite a great deal of evidence since it is 37 obvious throughout the Scriptures and we have assembled much of it in the latter part of our Confession. Later on we must raise again and discuss more fully the issue in this controversy, namely, the question whether human traditions are acts of devotion necessary for righteousness before God.

Our opponents say that universal traditions should be observed 38

because they are supposed to have been handed down by the apostles.[2]
How devout they are! Apostolic rites they want to keep, apostolic
doctrine they do not want to keep. We should interpret those rites   39
just as the apostles themselves did in their writings. They did not
want us to believe that we are justified by such rites or that such rites
are necessary for righteousness before God. They did not want to
impose such a burden on consciences, nor to make the observance of
days, food, and the like a matter of righteousness or of sin. In   40
fact, Paul calls such opinions "doctrines of demons." [3] To determine
the apostles' wish and intention, therefore, we must consult their writings, not merely their example. They observed certain days, not because such observance was necessary for justification but to let the
people know when to assemble. When they assembled, they also
observed other rites and a sequence of lessons. Frequently the people
continued to observe certain Old Testament customs, which the apostles adapted in modified form to the Gospel history, like the Passover
and Pentecost, so that by these examples as well as by instruction they
might transmit to posterity the memory of these great events. But   41
if they were transmitted as something necessary for justification, why
did the bishops later change them in so many ways? If they were of
divine right, it was unlawful for men to assume the right to change
them.

Before the Council of Nicaea some people celebrated Easter   42
at one time and others at another,[4] but this difference did no harm
to faith. Later on came the arrangement by which our Passover falls
at a different time from the Jewish Passover. The apostles had commanded their churches to celebrate the Passover with the brethren who
had been converted from Judaism, and so, after the Council of Nicaea,
certain nations held tenaciously to the custom of using the Jewish
time. But as the words of this decree show, the apostles did not want
to impose an ordinance on the churches. For they say that no one
should mind if his brethren do not correctly compute the time in
celebrating Easter. The text of the decree is preserved in Epiphanius:
"Do not calculate, but whenever your brethren of the circumcision do,
celebrate it at the same time with them; even if they have made a
mistake, do not let this bother you." [5] According to Epiphanius, these
words are from an apostolic decree about Easter; from them the discerning reader can easily judge that the apostles wanted to disabuse

---

[2] Roman Confutation: "That universal rites should be observed by all the
faithful was well taught to Januarius by Augustine, for it must be presumed
that such rites were handed down from the apostles" (Pt. I, Art. VII).

[3] I Tim. 4:1.

[4] The Paschal Controversy.

[5] Epiphanius, *Panarion haer.*, 70:10.

the people of the foolish notion of having to observe a set time, since they tell them not to be bothered even if there has been a mistake in the calculations.

There were some in the East who maintained that because of   43
this apostolic decree the Passover should be celebrated with the Jews; they were called Audians,[6] from the originator of this idea. In his refutation of them[7] Epiphanius praises the decree and says that it contains nothing contrary to the faith or the rule of the church, and he criticizes the Audians for misunderstanding it. He interprets it the same way that we do; for the apostles did not intend it to refer to the time when Easter should be celebrated, but for the sake of harmony they wanted others to follow the example of the chief brethren who had been converted from Judaism but kept their customs. The   44
apostles wisely admonished the reader neither to destroy evangelical liberty nor to impose a necessity upon consciences, since they tell him not to be bothered even if there has been a mistake in the calculations.

Many similar instances can be gathered from the histories in   45
which it appears that a difference in human observances does not harm the unity of the faith. But why discuss it? Our opponents completely misunderstand the meaning of the righteousness of faith and of the kingdom of God if they regard as necessary a uniformity of observances in food, days, clothing, and similar matters without divine command. But see what religious men our opponents are! They   46
require uniform human ceremonies for the unity of the church while they themselves have changed the ordinance of Christ in the use of the Lord's Supper, which certainly was previously a universal ordinance. But if universal ordinances are necessary, why do they change the ordinance of Christ's Supper, which is not human but divine? But on this whole controversy we shall have a few things to say later.

They have approved the entire eighth article.[8] There we confess   47
that hypocrites and evil men have been mingled with the church and that the sacraments are efficacious even when evil men administer them, for ministers act in Christ's stead and do not represent their own persons, according to the word (Luke 10:16), "He who hears you hears me." We should forsake wicked teachers because they no   48
longer function in the place of Christ, but are antichrists. Christ says (Matt. 7:15), "Beware of false prophets"; Paul says (Gal. 1:9), "If anyone is preaching to you a gospel contrary to that which you received, let him be accursed."

[6] Monastic sect of the fourth century.

[7] Epiphanius, op. cit., 70:10.

[8] Roman Confutation: "The eighth article of the Confession, concerning wicked ministers of the church and hypocrites, . . . is accepted . . ." (Pt. I, Art. VIII).

Christ has also warned us in his parables on the church[9] that 49
when we are offended by the personal conduct of priests or people,
we should not incite schisms, as the Donatists wickedly did. We 50
regard as utterly seditious those who have incited schisms because they
denied to priests the right to hold property or other possessions. The
right to hold property is a civil ordinance. It is legitimate for Christians to use civil ordinances just as it is legitimate for them to use the
air, light, food, and drink. For as this universe and the fixed movements of the stars are truly ordinances of God and are preserved by
God, so lawful governments are ordinances of God and are preserved
and defended by God against the devil.

[ARTICLE IX. BAPTISM]

They approve the ninth article where we confess that Baptism |
is necessary for salvation; children are to be baptized; the Baptism of
children is not useless but is necessary and efficacious for salvation.[1]
Among us, the Gospel is taught purely and diligently. We have 2
therefore received this fruit from it, by God's favor, that no Anabaptists have arisen in our churches since our people have been armed by
God's Word against the wicked and seditious faction of these robbers.
Among the many errors of the Anabaptists that we condemn is also
their assertion that the Baptism of children is useless. It is most certain
that the promise of salvation also applies to little children. It does not
apply to those who are outside of Christ's church, where there is
neither Word nor sacrament, because Christ regenerates through Word
and sacrament. Therefore it is necessary to baptize children, so that
the promise of salvation might be applied to them according to
Christ's command (Matt. 28:19), "Baptize all nations." Just as there
salvation is offered to all, so Baptism is offered to all—men, women,
children, and infants. Therefore it clearly follows that infants should
be baptized because salvation is offered with Baptism.

Secondly, since it is evident that God approves the Baptism 3
of little children, the Anabaptists teach wickedly when they condemn
the Baptism of little children. That God does approve the Baptism of
little children is shown by the fact that God gives the Holy Spirit to
those who were baptized this way. For if this Baptism were useless,
the Holy Spirit would be given to none, none would be saved, and
ultimately there would be no church. This point by itself can effec-
tually confirm good and godly minds against the ungodly and fanatical
opinions of the Anabaptists.

---

[9] Matt. 13:24-50.
[1] Roman Confutation: "The ninth article, concerning Baptism, . . . is
approved and accepted, and they [the Lutheran princes] are right in condemning the Anabaptists . . ." (Pt. I, Art. IX).

[ARTICLE X. THE HOLY SUPPER]

They approve the tenth article, where we confess our belief that 1 in the Lord's Supper the body and blood of Christ are truly and substantially present and are truly offered with those things that are seen, the bread and the wine, to those who receive the sacrament.[2] After careful examination and consideration of it, we firmly defend this belief. For since Paul says[3] that the bread is "a participation in the Lord's body," it would follow that the bread would not be a participation in the body of Christ but only in his spirit if the Lord's body were not truly present.

We know that not only the Roman Church affirms the bodily 2 presence of Christ, but that the Greek Church has taken and still takes this position. Evidence for this is their canon of the Mass, in which the priest clearly prays that the bread may be changed and become the very body of Christ.[4] And Vulgarius, who seems to us to be a sensible writer, says distinctly that "the bread is not merely a figure but is truly changed into flesh."[5] There is a long exposition of 3 John 15 in Cyril which teaches that Christ is offered to us bodily in the Supper. He says: "We do not deny that we are joined to Christ spiritually by true faith and sincere love. But we do deny that we have no kind of connection with him according to the flesh, and we say that this would be completely foreign to the sacred Scriptures. Who has ever doubted that Christ is a vine in this way and that we are truly branches, deriving life from him for ourselves? Listen to Paul say, 'We are all one body in Christ' (Rom. 12:5); 'We who are many are one body, for we all partake of the same loaf' (I Cor. 10:17). Does he think perhaps that we do not know the power of the mystical benediction? Since this is in us, does it not also cause Christ to dwell in us bodily through the communication of the flesh of Christ?" A little later he says, "Therefore we must consider that Christ is in us, not only according to the habit which we understand as love, but also by a natural participation," etc.[6]

We have quoted all of this here, not to begin an argument on 4 this subject (his Imperial Majesty does not disapprove this article), but to make clear to all our readers that we defend the doctrine received in the whole church—that in the Lord's Supper the body and blood of Christ are truly and substantially present and are truly offered

[2] Roman Confutation: "The tenth article gives no offense in its words . . ." (Pt. I, Art. X).

[3] I Cor. 10:16.

[4] The reference is to the epiklesis in early Eastern liturgies.

[5] The eleventh century Theophylact, *Commentary on the Gospel of Mark,* 14:22.

[6] Cyril of Alexander, *John,* 10:2.

with those things that are seen, bread and wine. We are talking about the presence of the living Christ, knowing that "death no longer has dominion over him." [7]

[ARTICLE XI. CONFESSION]

They approve the eleventh article on retaining absolution in the | church. But on confession they add the correction that the regulation *Omnis utriusque*[8] should be observed, that confession should be made annually, and that even though all sins cannot be enumerated, one should diligently try to recall them and to enumerate those one does recall.[9] On this whole issue we shall speak more fully a little later when we explain our whole teaching on penitence.[1] It is well 2 known that we have so explained and extolled the blessing of absolution and the power of the keys that many troubled consciences have received consolation from our teaching. They have heard that it is the command of God—yes, the very voice of the Gospel—that we should believe the absolution and firmly believe that the forgiveness of sins is granted us freely for Christ's sake and that we should be sure that by this faith we are truly reconciled to God. This teaching has encouraged many devout minds, and in the beginning brought Luther the highest praise of all good men, since it discloses a sure and firm consolation for the conscience. Previously the whole power of absolution had been smothered by teachings about works, since the scholastics and monks teach nothing about faith and free forgiveness.

With regard to the time, it is certain that most people in our 3 churches use the sacraments, absolution and the Lord's Supper, many times in a year. Our clergy instruct the people about the worth and fruits of the sacraments in such a way as to invite them to use the sacraments often. On this subject our theologians have written many things which our opponents, if they are but honest, will undoubtedly approve and praise. The openly wicked and the despisers of the sacraments 4

---

[7] Rom. 6:9.

[8] *Decretum* of Gregory IX, Bk. V, 38, c.12.

[9] Roman Confutation: "In the eleventh article their [the Lutheran princes'] acknowledgment that private absolution with confession should be retained in the church is accepted . . . . Nevertheless, two things must be required of them in this connection: First, that they demand an annual observance of confession by their subjects according to the canon *Omnis utriusque* (concerning penance and remission) and the custom of the universal church. Second, that through their preachers they cause their subjects to be faithfully admonished before confession that, although they cannot state all their sins individually, nevertheless, a diligent examination of their conscience being made, they make an entire confession of their offenses—that is to say, of all which come to mind in such an investigation. With reference to the rest, which have been forgotten or escaped our mind, it is lawful to make a general confession . . ." (Pt. I, Art. XI).

[1] Below, XII, 98-178.

are excommunicated. We do this according to both the Gospel[2] and
the ancient canons. But we do not prescribe a set time because   5
not everyone is ready in the same way at the same time. In fact, if
everyone rushed in at the same time, the people could not be heard
and instructed properly. The ancient canons and the Fathers do not
appoint a set time. The canon says only this: "If any enter the church
of God and are found never to commune, let them be admonished.
If they still do not commune, let them come to penitence. If they
commune, let them not be permanently expelled. If they do not
commune, let them be expelled." [3] Christ says (I Cor. 11:29) that
those who receive in an unworthy manner receive judgment upon
themselves. Therefore our pastors do not force those who are not
ready to use the sacraments.

With regard to the enumeration of sins in confession we teach   6
men in such a way as not to ensnare their consciences. It is, of course,
a good practice to accustom the unlearned to enumerate certain things
so that they might be instructed more easily. Now, we are discussing
what is necessary according to divine law. Therefore our opponents
ought not cite against us the regulation *Omnis utriusque;* we are aware
of it. They ought rather show from divine law that the enumeration
of sins is necessary to obtain their forgiveness. The whole church   7
throughout Europe knows how consciences have been ensnared by the
part of the regulation that requires all sins to be confessed. The text
by itself has not done as much damage as what the summists[4] added
to it later, including the circumstances of the sins. What labyrinths!
What great tortures for the most pious minds! These terrors made no
impression on wild and profane men. What tragic spectacles were   8
enacted between the secular and the regular clergy over the question
of who was the proper priest, when brothers did not act as brothers
in their fight about jurisdiction over confessions! We hold therefore
that the enumeration of sins is not required by divine law. The same
viewpoint was approved by Panormitanus[5] and others learned in the
canon law. We do not want to impose on our people's consciences
the regulation *Omnis utriusque,* for we judge that it, like other human
traditions, is not an act of worship necessary for justification. This
regulation commands the impossible, namely, that we make confession
of all our sins. It is certain that we neither remember nor understand
most of our sins, according to the statement (Ps. 19:12), "Who can
discern his errors?"

Good pastors will know how profitable it is to examine the   9

[2] Matt. 18:17.
[3] Gratian, *Decretum,* III, *De consecratione,* d.2, c.20.
[4] See above, VII and VIII, 32.
[5] Nicholas de Tudeschi, archbishop of Palermo (d. 1445).

inexperienced. But we do not want to sanction the torture of the summists, which, in spite of everything, would be more tolerable if they had added one word on faith, which consoles and encourages consciences. Now, on this faith which obtains the forgiveness of sins there is not a syllable in this heap of constitutions, glosses, summae, and penitential letters.[6] They say nothing about Christ. They only recite lists of sins. The greater part deals with sins against human traditions, which is the height of vanity. This teaching 10 has driven many devout minds to hopeless despair because they believed that an enumeration of sins was necessary by divine law and yet experienced that it was impossible. In our opponents' teaching on penitence there are other major faults, and these we shall presently discuss.

[ARTICLE XII.]   PENITENCE

In the twelfth article they approve the first part, where we 1 explain that those who have fallen after Baptism can obtain the forgiveness of sins whenever, and as often as, they are converted. They condemn the second part, in which we say that contrition and faith are the parts of penitence, and they deny that faith is the second part of penitence.[7]

What shall we do here, O Charles, most invincible Emperor? 2 This is the very voice of the Gospel, that by faith we obtain the forgiveness of sins. This voice of the Gospel these writers of the Confutation condemn, and therefore we can in no way agree to the Confutation. We cannot condemn the voice of the Gospel, so exceedingly salutary and full of consolation. If we deny that by faith we obtain the forgiveness of sins, what is this but to insult the blood and death of Christ? We therefore beg you, most invincible Emperor Charles, 3 to hear us out patiently and to consider carefully this most important issue, involving the chief doctrine of the Gospel, the true knowledge of Christ, and the true worship of God. All good men will see that especially on this issue we have taught what is true, godly, salutary, and necessary for the universal church of Christ. They will see that the writings of our theologians have shed much light on the Gospel

---

[6] Ecclesiastical regulations, explanations of canon law, casuistical handbooks of penance, and letters of indulgence.

[7] Roman Confutation: "In the twelfth article their [the Lutheran princes'] Confession . . . that the church should give absolution to such as return to penitence is commended . . . . But the second part of this article is utterly rejected. For when they ascribe only two parts to penitence, they come into conflict with the whole church, which from the time of the apostles has held and believed that there are three parts in penitence: contrition, confession, and satisfaction . . . . This part of the article, therefore, can in no way be admitted, nor can that which asserts that faith is the second part of penitence, for it is known to all that faith precedes penitence inasmuch as nobody repents unless he believes . . ." (Pt. I, Art. XII).

and have corrected many vicious errors which through the opinions of the scholastics and canonists had overwhelmed the doctrine of penitence.

Before beginning the defense of our position, we must say 4 something by way of preface. All good men of all classes, even the theologians, admit that before Luther's writings the doctrine of penitence was very confused. The commentaries on the *Sentences* 5 are full of endless questions which the theologians could never explain satisfactorily. The people could grasp neither the sum of the matter nor the chief requirements of penitence nor the source of the peace of conscience. Let any one of our opponents step forward and 6 tell us when the forgiveness of sins takes place. Good God, how great is the darkness! They wonder whether the forgiveness of sins takes place in attrition or in contrition.[8] If it takes place because of contrition, what is the need of absolution and what does the power of the keys accomplish if the sin is forgiven already? Here they labor still more and wickedly minimize the power of the keys. Some 7 of them imagine that the power of the keys does not forgive guilt, but only changes eternal punishments into temporal ones.[9] Then the salutary power of the keys would be a ministry not of life and of the Spirit, but only of wrath and punishment. Others are more careful and suppose that the power of the keys forgives sins before the church but not before God.[1] This is also a vicious error. For if the power of the keys does not console us before God, what is there that will finally bring peace to the conscience? What follows is still more complicated.

They teach that by contrition we merit grace. Why did not 8 Saul, Judas, and men like them attain grace even though they were terribly contrite? If someone should ask this, the answer must be in reference to faith and the Gospel, that Judas did not believe nor strengthen himself with the Gospel and the promise of Christ. For faith makes the difference between the contrition of Judas and that of Peter. But our opponents give the legalistic reply that Judas did not love God but feared the punishments. When can a terrified 9 conscience judge whether it fears God for his own sake or is running away from eternal punishments—especially in those serious, true, and great terrors described in the Psalms and the prophets and certainly experienced by those who are truly converted? An academic distinction between these two motives is possible, but in fact they are

---

[8] At the close of the Middle Ages there was debate as to whether attrition (sorrow over sin resulting from fear of God) might be substituted for contrition (sorrow over sin resulting from love of God). See below, XII, 9.

[9] Cf. Richard of St. Victor, *Treatise on the Power of Binding and Loosing*, 4.

[1] E.g., Gabriel Biel.

not so separated as these clever sophists imagine. Here we appeal 10 to the judgment of all good and wise men. They will undoubtedly confess that our opponents' discussions are very confused and intricate. Yet the issue at hand is a great one, the chief doctrine of the Gospel, the forgiveness of sins. Our opponents' whole teaching on the questions we have listed is full of error and hypocrisy; it obscures the blessing of Christ, the power of the keys, and the righteousness of faith. All this happens in the first step.[2] What happens when we 11 come to confession? How much effort is devoted to the endless enumeration of sins, most of them against human traditions! And to torture godly minds still more, they imagine that this enumeration is a divine command. While they demand this enumeration under 12 the pretext that it is by divine right, they speak very coldly about absolution, which really is by divine right. They pretend that the sacrament grants grace *ex opere operato,* without a right attitude in the recipient, and they do not mention faith, which grasps the absolution and consoles the conscience. This is really what is called "departing before the mysteries."[3]

There remains the third step, satisfaction. Here their dis- 13 cussions really become confused. They imagine that eternal punishments are changed into the punishments of purgatory, that of these one part is forgiven by the power of the keys and another part is redeemed by satisfactions.[4] They add further that satisfactions 14 ought to be works of supererogation, and these consist of stupid observances like pilgrimages, rosaries, or similar observances that do not have divine command. As they buy off purgatory with satis- 15 factions, so later on a most profitable way of buying off satisfactions was invented. They sell indulgences, which they interpret as the remission of satisfactions, and collect this revenue not only from the living but even more from the dead. They buy off the satisfactions of the dead not only by indulgences but also by the sacrifice of the Mass. In short, the whole business of satisfactions is endless, and 16 we cannot list all the abuses. Beneath these scandalous and demonic doctrines the doctrine of the righteousness of faith in Christ and of the blessing of Christ lies buried. All good men will understand, therefore, that good and proper reasons prompted us to reject the doctrine of penitence as taught by the scholastics and canonists. The following teachings are clearly false and foreign to the Holy Scriptures as well as the Church Fathers:

[2] I.e., in contrition.
[3] Allusion to the dismissal of catechumens before the Lord's Supper in the ancient church.
[4] Cf. Thomas Aquinas, *Summa theologica,* II, 1, q.87, a.6c; III, q.86, a.4c.

1. On the basis of God's covenant, we merit grace by good   17
works done apart from grace.[5]

2. We merit grace through attrition.[6]   18

3. To blot out sin, it is enough to detest the sin.   19

4. We receive the forgiveness of sins because of contrition,   20
not by faith in Christ.[7]

5. The power of the keys has validity for the forgiveness of sins   21
before the church, but not before God.[8]

6. The power of the keys does not forgive sins before God, but   22
it was instituted to commute eternal to temporal punishments, to impose certain satisfactions upon consciences, to institute new acts of
devotion, and to make such satisfactions and acts of devotion binding
upon consciences.

7. The enumeration of sins in confession, as our opponents   23
command it, is necessary by divine right.

8. Canonical satisfactions are necessary to redeem the punish-   24
ment of purgatory, or they profit as a payment to blot out guilt. This
is how uninformed people understand it.[9]

9. The reception of the sacrament of penitence obtains grace   25
ex opere operato, without the proper attitude in the recipient, that is,
without faith in Christ.[1]

10. By the power of the keys, through indulgences, souls are   26
delivered from purgatory.[2]

11. In reserved cases, not only the canonical punishment but   27
also the guilt ought to be reserved in the case of someone who is
truly converted.[3]

In order to deliver pious consciences from these labyrinths of   28
the scholastics, we have given penitence two parts, namely, contrition
and faith. If someone wants to call fruits worthy of penitence (Matt.
3:8) and an improvement of the whole life and character a third part,
we shall not object. We eliminate from contrition those useless   29
and endless discussions as to when we are sorry because we love God
and when because we fear punishment. We say that contrition is the
genuine terror of a conscience that feels God's wrath against sin and
is sorry that it has sinned. This contrition takes place when the Word
of God denounces sin. For the sum of the proclamation of the
Gospel is to denounce sin, to offer the forgiveness of sins and righteous-

---

[5] See above, IV, 9.
[6] So Duns Scotus, *Commentary on the Sentences,* IV, d.1, q.2.
[7] See above, XII, 6.
[8] See above, XII, 7.
[9] The teaching of the scholastics since Abailard.
[1] See above, IV, 63.
[2] Cf. Leo X's indulgence bull of March 31, 1515.
[3] Cf. Council of Trent, Sess. XIV, chap. I.

ness for Christ's sake, to grant the Holy Spirit and eternal life, and to lead us as regenerated men to do good. Christ gives this summary 30 of the Gospel in the last chapter of Luke (24:47), "That penitence and forgiveness of sins should be preached in my name to all nations."

Scripture speaks of these terrors, as in Ps. 38:4, 8, "For my 31 iniquities have gone over my head; they weigh like a burden too heavy for me. I am utterly spent and crushed; I groan because of the tumult of my heart." And in Ps. 6:2, 3, "Be gracious to me, O Lord, for I am languishing; O Lord, heal me, for my bones are troubled. My soul also is sorely troubled. But thou, O Lord—how long?" And in Isa. 38:10, 13, "I said, In the noontide of my days I must depart; I am consigned to the gates of Sheol. I cry for help until morning; like a lion he breaks all my bones." In these terrors the conscience 32 feels God's wrath against sin, unknown to men who walk in carnal security. It sees the foulness of sin and is genuinely sorry that it has sinned; at the same time it flees God's horrible wrath, for human nature cannot bear it unless it is sustained by the Word of God. So 33 Paul says (Gal. 2:19), "I through the law died to the law." For 34 the law only accuses and terrifies the conscience. In these terrors our opponents say nothing about faith, but present only the Word that denounces sin. Taken alone, this is the teaching of the law, not of the Gospel. They say that by these sorrows and terrors men merit grace if they love God. Yet how will men love God amid such real terrors when they feel the terrible and indescribable wrath of God? What do they teach but despair, when amid such terrors they show men only the law?

As the second part of our consideration of penitence, we there- 35 fore add faith in Christ, that amid these terrors the Gospel of Christ ought to be set forth to consciences—the Gospel which freely promises the forgiveness of sins through Christ. They should believe therefore that because of Christ their sins are freely forgiven. This faith 36 strengthens, sustains, and quickens the contrite according to the passage (Rom. 5:1), "Since we are justified by faith, we have peace with God." This faith obtains the forgiveness of sins. This faith justifies before God, as the same passage attests, "We are justified by faith." This faith shows the difference between the contrition of Judas and Saul on the one hand and that of Peter and David on the other. The contrition of Judas and Saul did not avail because it lacked the faith that grasps the forgiveness of sins granted for Christ's sake. The contrition of David and Peter did avail because it had the faith that grasps the forgiveness of sins granted for Christ's sake. Nor is 37 love present before faith has effected the reconciliation. For the law is not kept without Christ, according to the passage (Rom. 5:2), "Through him we have obtained access." This faith gradually grows and throughout life it struggles with sin to conquer sin and death. But love follows faith, as we have said above. Filial fear can be 38 clearly defined as an anxiety joined with faith, where faith consoles and sustains the anxious heart, whereas in servile fear faith does not sustain the anxious heart.

The power of the keys administers and offers the Gospel 39 through absolution, which is the true voice of the Gospel. In speaking of faith, therefore, we also include absolution since "faith comes from what is heard," as Paul says (Rom. 10:17). Hearing the Gospel and hearing absolution strengthens and consoles the conscience. Be- 40 cause God truly quickens through the Word, the keys truly forgive sin before him, according to the statement (Luke 10:16), "He who hears you, hears me." Therefore we must believe the voice of the one absolving no less than we would believe a voice coming from heaven. Absolution may properly be called a sacrament of 41 penitence, as even the more learned of the scholastics say.[4] Mean- 42 while this faith is nourished in many ways, amid temptations, through the proclamation of the Gospel and the use of the sacraments. These are signs of the new testament, that is, signs of the forgiveness of sins. Therefore they offer the forgiveness of sins, as the words in the Lord's Supper clearly state, "This is my body which is given for you. This cup is the new testament" (Luke 22:19, 20). So faith is conceived and confirmed through absolution, through the hearing of the Gospel, so that it may not succumb in its struggles against the terrors of sin and death. This understanding of penitence is plain and clear, it 43 adds to the honor of the power of the keys and the sacraments, it illumines the blessing of Christ, and it teaches us to make use of Christ as our mediator and propitiator.

Since the Confutation condemns us for assigning these two parts 44 to penitence,[5] we must show that Scripture makes them the chief parts in the penitence or conversion of the wicked. Christ says in Matt. 11:28, "Come to me, all who labor and are heavy-laden, and I will give you rest." There are two parts here. Labor and being heavy-laden mean contrition, anxiety, and the terrors of sin and death. To come to Christ means to believe that for his sake sins are forgiven. When we believe, the Holy Spirit quickens our hearts through the Word of Christ. There are, then, two chief parts here, contrition 45 and faith. In Mark 1:15 Christ says, "Repent, and believe in the Gospel." In the first part he denounces our sins, in the latter part he consoles us and shows us the forgiveness of sins. For to believe in the Gospel is not to have the general faith that even the demons have (James 2:19), but, in the true sense, to believe that for Christ's sake

[4] So Duns Scotus, *Commentary on the Sentences*, IV, d.16, q.1, 7.
[5] See above, XII, 1.

the forgiveness of sins has been granted us; this is revealed in the Gospel. You see that here, too, the two parts are combined: contrition, when sins are denounced; and faith, when it is said, "Believe in the Gospel." We shall not argue if someone says that Christ also includes the fruits of penitence or the new life. For us it is enough that he names contrition and faith as the chief parts of penitence.

Wherever Paul describes conversion or renewal, he almost 46 always names these two parts, mortifying and quickening. Col. 2:11, "In him also you were circumcised with a circumcision made without hands, by putting off the body of the sins of the flesh." And later on, "You were also raised with him through faith in the working of God" (v. 12). There are two parts here. The one is putting off the body of sins, the other is being raised through faith. Mortifying, quickening, putting off the body of sins, being raised—we are not to understand these terms in a Platonic sense as counterfeit changes; but mortification means genuine terrors, like those of the dying, which nature could not bear without the support of faith. Thus what we usually call contrition Paul calls "putting off the body of sins" because in these troubles our natural lust is purged away. And quickening should not be understood as a Platonic figment but as consolation truly sustaining a life that flees in contrition. There are therefore two 47 parts here, contrition and faith. Because there is no peace for the conscience except by faith, therefore faith alone quickens, according to the word (Hab. 2:4), "The righteous shall live by his faith."

Paul says in Col. 2:14 that Christ cancels the bond which stood 48 against us with its legal demands. Here, too, there are two parts, the bond and the cancellation of the bond. The bond is the conscience denouncing and condemning us; it is the voice that says with David (II Sam. 12:13), "I have sinned against the Lord." Wicked and smug men do not say this seriously, for they neither see nor read the sentence of the law written in their hearts. The sentence is understood only amid genuine sorrows and terrors. The bond therefore is contrition itself, condemning us. The cancellation of the bond is the removal of the sentence which declares that we are condemned and the substitution of the sentence by which we know that we have been delivered from this condemnation. This new sentence is faith, abolishing the earlier sentence and restoring peace and life to the heart.

But what need is there to cite passages since there are so many 49 throughout Scripture? Ps. 118:18, "The Lord has chastened me sorely, but he has not given me over to death." Ps. 119:28, "My soul melts away for sorrow; strengthen me according to thy word!" Here the first part contains contrition, while the second describes how we are revived in contrition by the Word of God which offers us grace.

This sustains and quickens the heart. I Sam. 2:6, "The Lord 50 kills and brings to life; he brings down to Sheol and raises up." In each of these sentences the first part means contrition, the second faith. Isa. 28:21, "The Lord will be wroth, to do his deed— 51 strange is his deed! and to work his work—alien is his work!" He calls it God's alien work to terrify because God's own proper work is to quicken and console. But he terrifies, he says, to make room for consolation and quickening because hearts that do not feel God's wrath in their smugness spurn consolation. In this way Scripture 52 makes a practice of joining these two, terror and consolation, to teach that these are the chief parts of penitence, contrition and the faith that consoles and justifies. We cannot see how the nature of penitence could be presented more clearly and simply.

These are the two chief works of God in men, to terrify and to 53 justify and quicken the terrified. One or the other of these works is spoken of throughout Scripture. One part is the law, which reveals, denounces, and condemns sin. The other part is the Gospel, that is, the promise of grace granted in Christ. This promise is repeated continually throughout Scripture; first it was given to Adam, later to the patriarchs, then illumined by the prophets, and finally proclaimed and revealed by Christ among the Jews, and spread by the apostles throughout the world. For all the saints were justified by faith in this 54 promise, not by their own attrition or contrition.

These two parts also appear in the lives of the saints. Adam 55 was rebuked and terrified after his sin; this was contrition. Then God promised grace and said there would be a seed that would destroy the kingdom of the devil, death, and sin! this was the offer of the forgiveness of sins. These are the chief parts. Even when punishment is still added afterwards, this punishment does not merit the forgiveness of sin. We shall discuss this form of punishment later.[6]

Thus David is rebuked by Nathan, and in his terror he says 56 (II Sam. 12:13), "I have sinned against the Lord." This is contrition. Then he hears the absolution (II Sam. 12:14), "The Lord has put away your sin; you shall not die." This voice encourages David and by faith it sustains, justifies, and quickens him. A punishment is also added here, but it does not merit the forgiveness of sins. Nor are 57 special punishments always added, but contrition and faith there must always be in penitence, as in Luke 7:37ff. The woman who was a sinner came to Christ in tears, which showed her contrition. Later she heard the absolution (vv. 48, 50), "Your sins are forgiven. Your faith has saved you; go in peace." This was the second part of her penance, the faith that encouraged and consoled her. From all 58 these passages godly readers can see that we put into penitence the

---

[6] See below, XII, 148-178.

parts that properly belong to it in conversion or regeneration and the forgiveness of sin. Worthy fruits as well as punishments follow regeneration and the forgiveness of sin. We have put in these two parts in order to emphasize the faith that we require in penitence. It is easier to understand the faith proclaimed by the Gospel when it is contrasted with contrition and mortification.

Our opponents expressly condemn our statement that men 59 obtain the forgiveness of sins by faith. We shall therefore add a few proofs to show that the forgiveness of sins does not come *ex opere operato* because of contrition, but by that personal faith by which each individual believes that his sins are forgiven. For this is the chief issue on which we clash with our opponents and which we believe all Christians must understand. Since it is evident that we have said enough about this earlier, we shall be briefer at this point. For the doctrine of penitence and the doctrine of justification are very closely related.

When our opponents talk about faith and say that it precedes 60 penitence, they do not mean justifying but the general faith which believes that God exists, that punishments hang over the wicked, etc. Beyond such "faith" we require everyone to believe that his sins are forgiven him. We are contending for this personal faith, and we set it in opposition to the opinion that bids us trust not in the promise of Christ but in contrition, confession, and satisfaction *ex opere operato*. This faith follows on our terrors, overcoming them and restoring peace to the conscience. To this faith we attribute justification and regeneration, for it frees us from our terrors and brings forth peace, joy, and a new life in the heart. We insist that this faith is really necessary for the forgiveness of sins, and therefore we put it in as one of the parts of penitence. The church of Christ believes the same, in spite of our opponents' cries to the contrary.

First, we ask our opponents whether the reception of absolution 61 is part of penitence or not. If they try to make a subtle distinction separating absolution from confession, we fail to see what value there is in confession without absolution. If, on the other hand, they do not separate the reception of absolution from confession, then they must maintain that faith is part of penitence since only faith can accept the absolution. That only faith can accept the absolution can be proved from Paul, who teaches in Rom. 4:16 that only faith accepts a promise. Now, since absolution is the promise of the forgiveness of sins, it necessarily requires faith. We do not see how anyone can 62 be said to receive absolution unless he believes it. What else is the refusal to believe absolution but the accusation that God is a liar? If the heart doubts, it maintains that God's promises are uncertain and inane. So it is written in I John 5:10, "He who does not believe God has made him a liar because he has not believed in the testimony that God has borne to his Son."

Second, we suppose our opponents will grant that the forgiveness 63 of sins is either a part of penitence or its goal—the "terminus to which," as they call it.[7] Then that which accepts the forgiveness of sins should properly be included as one of the parts of penitence. But it is very sure, though all the gates of hell (Matt. 16:18) cry out against it, that the forgiveness of sins cannot be accepted by anything but faith alone, according to Rom. 3:25, "Whom God put forward as an expiation by his blood, to be received by faith," and Rom. 5:2, "Through him we have obtained access by faith to this grace," etc. For a terrified conscience cannot pit our works or our love against 64 the wrath of God, but it finds peace only when it takes hold of Christ, the mediator, and believes the promises given for his sake. Those who dream that the heart can find peace without faith in Christ do not understand what the forgiveness of sins is nor how it comes to us. Peter (I Pet. 2:6) quotes the words from Isaiah (28:16), "He 65 who believes in him will not be put to shame." Hypocrites therefore must be put to shame, for they trust in their own works and not in Christ to receive the forgiveness of sins. Peter also says in Acts 10:43, "To him all the prophets bear witness that every one who believes in him receives forgiveness of sins through his name." He could not have said it any more clearly: "through his name," and he adds: "every one who believes in him." We receive the forgiveness of sins, therefore, only through the name of Christ, that is, because of him and not because of any merits or works of our own. And this happens when we believe that our sins are forgiven because of Christ.

Our opponents cry out that they are the church and follow the 66 consensus of the church. But here Peter cites the consensus of the church in support of our position: "To him all the prophets bear witness that every one who believes in him receives forgiveness of sins through his name," etc. Surely the consensus of the prophets should be interpreted as the consensus of the universal church. Neither to the pope nor to the church do we grant the authority to issue decrees contrary to this consensus of the prophets. Leo quite openly 67 condemns this doctrine of the forgiveness of sins in his bull,[8] and our opponents condemn it in their Confutation. In their decrees they condemn this teaching that we obtain the forgiveness of sins by faith for Christ's sake and not for the sake of our works. But they go further and demand that this teaching be wiped out by force and the sword, and that good men who hold this faith be put to death with

[7] *Terminus ad quem.* Cf. Thomas Aquinas, *Summa theologica,* II, 1, q.113, a.6c.
[8] Leo X's bull *Exsurge Domine,* 1520.

all sorts of cruelties. From this we can judge what sort of church it is that is made up of such men.

They have on their side some theologians of great reputation, 68 like Duns Scotus, Gabriel Biel, and the like in addition to patristic statements which the decrees quote in garbled form. Certainly, if we were to count authorities, they would be right; for there is a great crowd of worthless commentators on the *Sentences*[9] who as though by a conspiracy defend the false notions we have been discussing about the merits of attrition and works and similar ideas. Lest anyone 69 be moved by this large number of quotations, it must be kept in mind that no great authority attaches to the statements of later theologians who did not produce their own books but only compiled them from earlier ones and transferred these opinions from one book to another. In this they showed no judgment, but like petty public officials they quietly approved the errors of their superiors, without understanding them. Let us not hesitate, therefore, to oppose this statement 70 of Peter, citing the consensus of the prophets, to the many legions of commentators on the *Sentences*. The testimony of the Holy Spirit 71 was added to this statement of Peter, for the text says (Acts 10:44), "While Peter was still saying this, the Holy Spirit fell on all who heard the word."

Let pious consciences know, therefore, that God commands 72 them to believe that they are freely forgiven because of Christ, not because of our works. Let them sustain themselves with this command of God against despair and against the terrors of sin and death. Let them know that this is what the saints in the church have 73 believed since the beginning of the world. Peter clearly cites the consensus of the prophets; the writings of the apostles attest that they believed the same thing; nor are testimonies of the Fathers lacking. For Bernard says the same in words that are not unclear at all: "You must believe, first of all, that you cannot have the forgiveness of sins except by the forbearance of God; but add further that you also believe that through him your sins are forgiven. This is the witness that the Holy Spirit brings in your heart, saying, 'Your sins are forgiven you.' For thus the apostle concludes, that a man is justified freely by faith." [1] These words of Bernard marvelously illumine 74 our case. He does not merely require that we believe in a general way that sins are forgiven by mercy, but he bids us add the personal faith that they are forgiven to us as well. And he teaches us how to be sure of the forgiveness of sins, namely, that faith encourages our hearts and the Holy Spirit grants them peace. What more do our opponents need?

---

[9] See above, IV, 65.

[1] Bernard of Clairvaux, *Sermon on the Feast of the Blessed Virgin Mary,* I, 1.

Do they still dare to deny that we obtain the forgiveness of sins by faith, or that faith is part of penitence?

Third, our opponents say that sins are forgiven in this way: 75 Because a person who has attrition or contrition elicits an act of love to God, he merits the attainment of the forgiveness of sins by this act.[2] This is nothing but the teaching of the law, the elimination of the Gospel, and the abolition of the promise of Christ. They require only the law and our works because the law demands love. Besides, they teach us to believe that we obtain the forgiveness of sins because of our contrition or love. What is this but to place our trust in our own works rather than in God's Word and the promise of Christ? But if the law is enough to achieve the forgiveness of sins, what need is there of the Gospel? What need is there of Christ if by our work we achieve the forgiveness of sins? We, on the contrary, call   76 men's consciences away from the law to the Gospel, away from trust in their own works to trust in the promise and in Christ; for the Gospel shows us Christ and promises the forgiveness of sins freely for his sake. This promise bids us trust that because of Christ we are reconciled to the Father, not because of our contrition or love, for there is no other mediator or propitiator but Christ. Nor can we keep the law before we have been reconciled through Christ. Even if we could do so to some extent, still we must believe that we obtain the forgiveness of sins not because of these works but because of Christ, the mediator and propitiator.

Truly, we insult Christ and abrogate the Gospel if we believe   77 that we obtain the forgiveness of sins because of the law or in any other way except by faith in Christ. We discussed this issue earlier, in the article on justification, where we gave our reasons for declaring that men are justified by faith and not by love.[3] Our opponents'   78 doctrine that men obtain the forgiveness of sins by their contrition and love, and should trust their contrition and love, is simply a doctrine of the law—and that misunderstood, as the Jews looked at Moses' face covered by a veil.[4] Even supposing that love and works are present, neither love nor works can be a propitiation for sin. We cannot set them against the wrath and judgment of God, according to the passage (Ps. 143:2), "Enter not into judgment with thy servant; for no man living is righteous before thee." Nor should the honor of Christ be transferred to our works.

For these reasons Paul contends that we are not justified by the   79 law; to the law he opposes the promise of the forgiveness of sins granted for Christ's sake, and he teaches us to accept the forgiveness

---

[2] E.g., Gabriel Biel, *Commentary on the Sentences*, IV, d.16, q.4a, 3, dub. 3.
[3] See above, IV, 61-74.
[4] Cf. II Cor. 3:13.

of sins by faith, freely for Christ's sake. Paul calls us away from the law to this promise. He asks us to look at this promise, which would certainly be useless if we were justified by the law before the promise or if we obtained the forgiveness of sins because of our righteousness. But clearly the promise was given and Christ revealed to us 80 precisely because we cannot keep the law, and therefore we must be reconciled by the promise before we keep the law. Only faith accepts the promise. Therefore it is necessary for the contrite by faith to take hold of the promise of the forgiveness of sins granted for Christ's sake, and to be sure that freely for Christ's sake they have a gracious Father. This is what Paul means when he says in Rom. 4:16, 81 "That is why it depends on faith, in order that the promise may rest on grace and be guaranteed"; and in Gal. 3:22, "The scripture consigned all things to sin, that what was promised to faith in Jesus Christ might be given to those who believe." That is, all men are under sin, and they cannot be freed in any other way than by taking hold through faith of the promise of the forgiveness of sins. We 82 must therefore accept the forgiveness of sins by faith before we keep the law although, as we said before, love follows faith, for the regenerate receive the Holy Spirit and therefore begin to keep the law.

We would cite more passages if they were not obvious to 83 every devout reader of Scripture, and we want to avoid being lengthy in order to make our case more easily understood. There is no 84 doubt that this is Paul's position that we are defending: by faith we receive the forgiveness of sins for Christ's sake, by faith we ought to set against the wrath of God not our works but Christ, the mediator. It ought not disturb devout minds if our opponents twist Paul's sentences, for nothing can be said so simply that some quibbler cannot pervert it. We know that what we have said is what Paul really and truly means; we know that this position of ours brings devout consciences a firm consolation without which no one can stand before the judgment of God.

Therefore we reject the Pharisaic opinions of our opponents 85 that we do not receive the forgiveness of sins by faith but merit it by our love and works, and that we ought to set our love and works against the wrath of God. This is a teaching of the law and not of the Gospel, to imagine that a man is justified by the law before being reconciled to God through Christ, though Christ says (John 15:5), "Apart from me you can do nothing," and "I am the vine, you are the branches." But our opponents imagine that we are members of Moses rather 86 than of Christ. They want to be justified by the law and to offer our works to God before being reconciled to God and becoming the branches of Christ. Paul, on the contrary, contends that we cannot keep the law without Christ. Therefore we must accept the promise that by faith we are reconciled to God before we keep the law. We think this is clear enough for devout consciences, and from 87 this they will see why we said above that men are justified by faith and not by love. For we must not set our love or works against the wrath of God or trust in our love or works, but only in Christ, the mediator. We must take hold of the promise of the forgiveness of sins before we keep the law.

Finally, when will the conscience find peace if we receive the 88 forgiveness of sins because we love or keep the law? For the law will always accuse us because we never satisfy the law of God. As Paul says (Rom. 4:15), "The law brings wrath." Chrysostom asks in connection with penitence, "How do we become sure that our sins are forgiven?" [5] In the *Sentences* our opponents ask the same question. This cannot be answered nor consciences quieted unless we know it is God's command and the Gospel itself that they should be sure that their sins are forgiven freely for Christ's sake, not doubting that they are forgiven them personally. If anybody doubts, he makes the divine promise a lie, as John says.[6] We teach that such a certainty of faith is required in the Gospel; our opponents leave consciences wavering and uncertain. Consciences do nothing from 89 faith if they always doubt whether they have forgiveness. In such doubt, how can they call upon God, how can they be sure that he hears them? So their whole life is without God and without the true worship of God. This is what Paul says (Rom. 14:23), "Whatever does not proceed from faith is sin." Constantly tossed about in such doubt, they never experience what faith is, and so it is that at last they rush into despair. Such is our opponents' doctrine—a doctrine of the law, an abrogation of the Gospel, a doctrine of despair. On this doctrine of penitence, which is quite clear, we are happy 90 to have all good men judge and decide whether our teaching or our opponents' teaching is more godly and salutary for consciences. These dissensions in the church certainly give us no pleasure; therefore if we did not have grave and important reasons for disagreeing with our opponents, we would very gladly keep quiet. But since they condemn the open truth, it is not right for us to forsake the cause— not our cause but the cause of Christ and the church.

We have said why we set forth contrition and faith as the two 91 parts of penitence. We were all the more willing to do this because many statements about penitence are circulating which are quoted in garbled form from the Fathers and which our opponents quote in a distorted form to obscure faith. For example, "Penitence means to lament past evils and not to commit again deeds that ought to be

---

[6] John Chrysostom, *An Exhortation to Theodore after his Fall,* I, 5.
[9] I John 5:10.

lamented." Again, "Penitence is a sort of revenge by a person who is sorry, punishing in himself what he is sorry for having done." [7] These statements make no mention of faith, and the scholastics add nothing about faith in their interpretation of them. Therefore we have 92 listed the doctrine of faith among the parts of penitence in order to make it more conspicuous. For there is obvious danger in these statements, requiring contrition or good works and making no mention of justifying faith. Discernment may rightly be demanded 93 of those who have compiled these centos of the sentences and decrees. Since the Fathers discuss sometimes one part, sometimes another part of penitence, it would have been in order to select and combine their opinions not only about one but about both parts, contrition and faith.

For Tertullian speaks excellently about faith, dwelling espe- 94 cially on the oath in the prophet (Ez. 33:11), "As I live, says the Lord God, I have no pleasure in the death of the wicked, but that the wicked turn from his way and live." By swearing that he has no pleasure in the death of the wicked, God shows that he requires the faith with which we believe him when he swears and are sure that he forgives us. Even by themselves, the authority of the divine promises ought to be sufficient for us, but this promise is confirmed with an oath. If anybody, therefore, is not sure that he is forgiven, he denies that God has sworn to the truth; a more horrible blasphemy than this cannot be imagined. This is what Tertullian says: "He invites us to salvation with an offer and even an oath. When God says, 'As I live,' he wants to be believed. Oh, blessed are we for whose sake God swears an oath! Oh, most miserable are we if we do not believe the Lord even when he swears an oath!" [8]

Certainly this faith must believe firmly that God freely for- 95 gives us because of Christ and because of his promise, not because of our works, contrition, confession, or satisfactions. For if faith relies on these works, it immediately becomes unsure because an anxious conscience sees that these works are not good enough. Ambrose makes this very clear statement about penitence: "We 96 should believe both that we should be penitent and that we shall be pardoned, in such a way that we hope for pardon from faith just as faith obtains it from the written agreement." [9] Again, "It is faith that covers up our sins." Thus there are statements in the Fathers 97 not only about contrition and works, but also about faith. But since our opponents understand neither the nature of penitence nor the language of the Fathers, they select sayings about a part of penitence,

[7] Gratian, *Decretum*, II, chap. 33, q.3, *De poenitentia*, d.3, c.1, 4.
[8] Tertullian, *Penitence*, 4.
[9] Ambrose, *On Penitence against the Novatians*, II, 9.

namely works. Since they do not understand the sayings elsewhere about faith, they omit them.

CONFESSION AND SATISFACTION

Good men can easily judge the great importance of preserving 98 the true teaching about contrition and faith, the two parts of penitence we have discussed above. We have therefore concentrated on the explanation of these doctrines and thus far have written nothing about confession and satisfaction. For we also keep confession, 99 especially because of absolution, which is the Word of God that the power of the keys proclaims to individuals by divine authority. It 100 would therefore be wicked to remove private absolution from the church. And those who despise private absolution understand 101 neither the forgiveness of sins nor the power of the keys. As 102 for the enumeration of sins in confession, we have said earlier[1] that we do not believe that it is necessary by divine right. When 103 someone objects that a judge must hear a case before pronouncing sentence, that is irrelevant because the ministry of absolution is in the area of blessing or grace, not of judgment or law. The min- 104 isters of the church therefore have the command to forgive sins; they do not have the command to investigate secret sins. In addition, 105 they absolve us of those which we do not remember; therefore absolution, which is the voice of the Gospel forgiving sins and consoling consciences, does not need an investigation.

It is silly to transfer here the saying of Solomon (Prov. 27:23), 106 "Know well the condition of your flocks." Solomon is not talking about confession. He is merely giving a bit of domestic advice to the head of a household, telling him to pay diligent attention to his own property and leave other people's alone, but warning him not to be so preoccupied with the increase of his holdings that he neglects the fear of God or faith or his concern for God's Word. By a marvelous transformation, our opponents make passages of Scripture mean whatever they want them to mean. According to their interpretation, "know" here means to hear confessions, "condition" means the secrets of conscience and not outward conduct, and "flocks" means men. The interpretation surely is a neat one, worthy of these men who despise grammar. But if anybody wants by analogy to apply the commandment given a father to the pastor of a church, he should surely interpret "condition" as meaning outward conduct. That at least would be more consistent.

But let us skip over things like this. The Psalms mention 107 confession from time to time; for example (Ps. 32:5), "I said, 'I will confess my transgressions to the Lord'; then thou didst forgive

---

[1] See above, XII, 6-8.

the guilt of my sin." Such confession, made to God, is itself contrition. For when confession is made to God, it must come from the
heart and not just from the voice, as in a play. Therefore such a
confession is contrition; feeling God's wrath, we confess that he is
justly wrathful and cannot be placated by our works, and yet we seek
mercy because of the promise of God. It is the same with this   108
confession (Ps. 51:4), "Against thee only have I sinned, so that thou
art justified in thy sentence and blameless in thy judgment." That is,
"I confess that I am a sinner worthy of eternal wrath, and I cannot
set my righteousness or my merits against Thy wrath. Therefore I
declare Thee to be justified in condemning and punishing us. I declare
Thee to be blameless when hypocrites judge Thee to be unrighteous
in punishing them or condemning those who have deserved it. Yes,
we cannot set our merits against Thy judgment, but we shall be justified when Thou dost justify us and account us righteous through Thy
mercy." Maybe someone will quote James 5:16, "Confess your   109
sins to one another." But this does not speak of the specific confession to be made to priests but of the reconciliation of brethren to each
other, for it commands that the confession be mutual.

If our opponents contend that the enumeration of sins in con-   110
fession is necessary by divine right, they will be condemning many
of the most generally accepted theologians. Although we approve
of confession and maintain that some examination is useful to instruct
men better, still it must be controlled, lest consciences be ensnared;
for they will never be at rest if they suppose that they cannot obtain
the forgiveness of sins without enumerating all their sins. In   111
the Confutation our opponents have maintained that complete confession is necessary for salvation;[2] this is completely false, as well
as being impossible. What snares this requirement of complete confession has cast upon consciences! When will the conscience be sure
that its confession is complete? The church writers do mention   112
confession, but they are talking about the public rite of penitence,
not about this enumeration of secret sins.[3] Because the lapsed[4] or
notorious sinners were not accepted without certain satisfactions, they
made confession to the priests so that these satisfactions might be
suited to their offenses. All of this is totally different from the enumeration we are discussing. The reason for the confession was not that
without it there could be no forgiveness of sins before God but that
satisfactions could not be prescribed without knowing the character
of the offense. Different offenses had different canons.

---

[2] See above, XI, 1, and note.
[3] Outside of monasticism and a few exceptional situations, the ancient
church knew nothing of private confession but only of public penitence.
[4] The *lapsi* of the ancient church who under persecution expressly re-
nounced their faith or gave the impression that they had.

Our word "satisfaction" is a relic from this rite of public   113
penitence. The holy Fathers did not want to accept the lapsed or
the notorious sinners unless they had given public evidence of their
penitence, as far as was possible. There seem to have been many
reasons for this. Chastising the lapsed served as an example, as the
gloss on the decree warns,[5] and admitting notorious people to communion immediately was improper. These practices have long since
become antiquated, nor need we bring them back because they are
not necessary for the forgiveness of sins before God. The Fathers   114
did not believe that by such practices or such works men merit the
forgiveness of sins. Still these spectacles tend to beguile the inexperienced into thinking that by these works they merit the forgiveness
of sins. Whoever believes this has a Jewish and heathen faith, for
even the heathen had certain expiations for sin by which they supposed they were reconciled to God. But now that the practice   115
has become obsolete, the word "satisfaction" still remains together
with a remnant of the custom in prescribing certain satisfactions in
confession. They define these as works that are not due; we call them
canonical satisfactions. About these we believe, as we do about   116
the enumeration of sins, that canonical satisfactions are not necessary
by divine law for the forgiveness of sins, just as those ancient exhibitions of satisfaction in public penitence were not necessary by divine
law for the forgiveness of sins. We must keep the doctrine that by
faith we obtain the forgiveness of sins because of Christ, not because
of our works, either preceding or following. For this reason we have
discussed satisfactions in particular, lest by their adoption the righteousness of faith be obscured or people think that because of these
works they obtain the forgiveness of sins. Such errors received   117
support from many statements of the scholastics; for example, in
defining satisfaction they say that it is done to placate the divine
displeasure.[6]

Still our opponents admit that satisfactions do not contribute   118
to the remission of guilt, though they imagine that they do contribute
to the redemption of purgatorial and other punishments. They teach
that in the forgiveness of sin God remits the guilt, and yet, because
it is fitting for divine righteousness to punish sin, he commutes the
eternal punishment to a temporal punishment.[7] They add further
that part of this temporal punishment is forgiven by the power of
the keys, and the rest must be bought off by satisfactions. We cannot
understand which punishments are partly forgiven by the power of
the keys, unless they say that part of the punishments of purgatory

[5] Gloss on Gratian, *Decretum*, II, chap. 24, q.3, c.18.
[6] E.g., Gabriel Biel, *Commentary on the Sentences*, IV, d.16, q.2, a.1, C.
[7] Thomas Aquinas, *Summa theologica*, III Suppl., q.18, a.2 ad 1.

is forgiven; in that case satisfactions would only be punishments redeeming from purgatory. They say that these satisfactions avail even when they are performed by those who have relapsed into mortal sin, as though those who are in mortal sin could placate the divine displeasure. This whole theory is a recent fiction, without authority 119 either in the Scriptures or in the ancient writers of the church. Not even Peter Lombard speaks this way about satisfactions.[8] The 120 scholastics saw that there were satisfactions in the church, but they did not notice that these public exhibitions had been instituted as an example and to test those who wanted to be accepted into the church; that is, they did not see that this was a discipline, and a secular one at that. Thus they superstitiously imagined that satisfactions were valid not for discipline in the church, but for placating God. And just as elsewhere they often confused the spiritual and the secular improperly, so also in the case of satisfactions. But the gloss 121 on the canons says several times that these observances were instituted for the sake of church discipline.[9]

Look how our opponents prove these fictions of theirs in the 122 Confutation that they dared to thrust upon his Imperial Majesty. They quote many Scripture passages to give the inexperienced the impression that this idea has authority in Scripture, though it was unknown in the time of Peter Lombard. These are passages they quote: "Bear fruit that befits penitence" (Matt. 3:8); "Yield your members to righteousness" (Rom. 6:19); Christ's preaching of penitence (Matt. 4:17), "Be penitent"; Christ's command to the apostles (Luke 24:47) "that penitence should be preached"; Peter's preaching of penitence (Acts 2:38). Then they quote certain statements from the Fathers and the canons and conclude that the abolition of satisfactions in the church would be contrary to the express commands of the Gospel, the councils, and the Fathers; and that even those who have been absolved by the priest should perform the prescribed penitence, following the statement of Paul, "He gave himself for us to redeem us from all iniquity and to purify himself a people of his own who are zealous for good deeds."[1]

May God destroy these wicked sophists who so sinfully twist 123 the Word of God to suit their vain dreams! What good man would not be moved by such dishonesty? Christ says, "Be penitent"; the apostles preach penitence. Therefore the punishments of purgatory compensate for eternal punishments; therefore the keys have the command to remit part of the punishments of purgatory; therefore satisfactions buy off the punishments of purgatory. Who ever taught

[8] Peter Lombard, *Sentences*, IV, d.14-19.
[9] Gloss on Gratian, *Decretum*, II, chap. 23, q.4, c.18, 19.
[1] Titus 2:14.

these asses such logic? This is not logic or even sophistry, but sheer dishonesty. They quote the word, "Be penitent," against us so that when the uninitiated hear this they will conclude that we deny all penitence. With such tricks they try to alienate men's minds and fan their hatred, so that the uninitiated may demand that such terrible heretics, who reject penitence, should be removed from their midst. We hope that among good men these slanders will not gain |24 any adherents. God will not long endure such impudence and malice. The Roman pontiff did not add anything to his dignity in making use of such defenders and turning over to these sophists such an important assignment. For since in our Confession we covered almost the sum total of all Christian doctrine, judges should have been found to deal with such important, numerous, and varied subjects in whose learning and faith men could have had greater confidence than in that of the sophists who wrote the Confutation.

It was up to you, Campegius,[2] in keeping with your wisdom, |25 to see to it that on such important issues they did not write anything that now or in the future might tend to diminish the prestige of the Roman See. If the Roman See thinks it is right for all nations to recognize her as the mistress of the faith, she should take care that men of learning and integrity do the investigating on religious questions. How will the world evaluate the Confutation—if it is ever published?[3] What will posterity think about these slanderous judgments? You see, Campegius, that these are the last times, in |26 which Christ predicted there would be the greatest danger for religion. You, therefore, who should sit as though on a watchtower to guide religious affairs, ought in such times to exercise unusual wisdom and diligence. There are many threats which, unless you take care, indicate a change in the Holy Roman Empire. You are mistaken if you |27 suppose that churches should be maintained only by force and arms. Men are demanding instruction in religion. In Germany, England, Spain, France, Italy, even in Rome itself—how many do you think there are in these places who have begun to doubt because of the controversies that have arisen on the most important questions? How much silent indignation is there because you refuse to examine these questions and adjudge them rightly, because you do not strengthen wavering consciences, because you command only that we be conquered and destroyed by armed might?

There are many good men to whom such doubt is worse than |28 death. You do not pay enough attention to the importance of religion if you suppose that the doctrinal doubts of good men are mere petty anxiety. Such doubt cannot help producing the most bitter hatred

²The papal legate, Lorenzo Campegi (d. 1539).
³The Confutation was not published until 1573.

against those who, though they ought to be healing consciences, refuse to let the issue be explained. We are not saying here |29 that you ought to fear the judgment of God; for the members of the hierarchy suppose that they can take care of this easily since they hold the keys and so, of course, can open heaven for themselves whenever they wish. We are talking about the judgments of men and the silent desires of all nations; they certainly demand that these issues be examined and settled now in order to heal devout minds and free them from doubt. As a wise man you can easily imagine what will happen if this hatred should erupt against you. But if you are kind and heal doubting consciences, you can bind all nations to yourself; for men of discretion will value this service highly. It |30 is not because we are in doubt about confession that we have said this. We know that it is true, godly, and beneficial to godly consciences. But there are probably many people in many places who are in doubt about important issues but do not hear teachers capable of setting their consciences at rest.

Let us return to the proposition. The Scripture passages |31 quoted by our opponents say nothing whatever about canonical satisfactions or the opinions of the scholastics because these are obviously later inventions. Therefore this is merely a trick and a distortion of the Scriptures to suit their opinions. We say that after penitence (that is, conversion or regeneration) must come good fruits and good works in every phase of life. There can be no true conversion or contrition where mortifying the flesh and good fruits do not follow. True terrors and sorrows of the soul do not permit the indulgence of the body in lusts, and true faith is not ungrateful to God or contemptuous of his commandments. In a word, there is no penitence inwardly which does not produce outwardly the punishing of the flesh. This, we say, is what John means when he says |32 (Matt. 3:8), "Bear fruit that befits penitence," and Paul when he says (Rom. 6:19), "Yield your members to righteousness," and elsewhere (Rom. 12:1), "Present your bodies as a living sacrifice, holy," etc. When Christ says (Matt. 4:17), "Be penitent," he is surely talking about total penitence and total newness of life and fruits. He is not talking about those hypocritical satisfactions which the scholastics imagine avail as a payment for the punishments of purgatory or other punishments even when they come from men in mortal sin.

Many other arguments could be assembled to prove that these |33 passages of Scripture apply in no way to scholastic satisfactions. They suppose that satisfactions are works that are not obligatory, but in these passages Scripture requires works that are obligatory. For this word of Christ is a word of command, "Be penitent." Secondly, |34 our opponents write that if a penitent refuses to assume the satisfactions he does not sin but will have to pay the penalties in purgatory. Now, these passages are unquestionably commandments referring to this life: "Be penitent," "Bear fruit that befits penitence," "Yield your members to righteousness." These passages cannot be applied to satisfactions that one may refuse, for one may not refuse the commandments of God. Thirdly, it is just such satisfactions that indul- 135 gences remit, as the chapter on "Penitence and Remission" teaches.[4] But indulgences do not release us from commandments like "Be penitent" and "Bear fruit that befits penitence." So it is clearly a wicked distortion to apply these passages to canonical satisfactions. Look what follows! If the penalties of purgatory are satisfac- 136 tions, or rather "satispassions," or if satisfactions are a redemption from the penalties of purgatory, do these passages command that souls should be punished in purgatory? Since this necessarily follows from our opponents' position, these passages will have to be interpreted in a new way. "Bear fruit that befits penitence" and "Be penitent" will mean "Suffer the penalties of purgatory after this life." We 137 hate to waste any more words in refuting these silly arguments of our opponents. Clearly Scripture is speaking about obligatory works, about the whole newness of life, and not about observances and works that are not obligatory such as our opponents are discussing. And yet by these fictions they defend monastic orders, the sale of Masses, and endless observances which make satisfaction for punishment, if not for guilt.

The Scripture passages they quote do not say that non-obliga- 138 tory works compensate for eternal punishments; it is rash for them to say, therefore, that canonical satisfactions compensate for these punishments. There is no command for the keys to commute certain punishments or to remit part of the punishments. Where does Scripture say this? Christ is talking about the remission of sins when he says (Matt. 18:18), "Whatever you loose," etc. This remission removes eternal death and brings eternal life. Nor do the words "Whatever you bind" refer to imposing penalties but to retaining the sins of the unconverted. Peter Lombard's statement about remitting 139 part of the punishments referred to canonical penalties, part of which the pastors remitted.[5] We believe that God's glory and command require penitence to produce good fruits, and that good fruits like true fasting, prayer, and charity have his command. But nowhere in Holy Scripture are we told that only non-obligatory works like the punishments of purgatory or canonical satisfactions can remit eternal punishments, or that the power of the keys carries with it the command

[4] In Gregory IX, *Decretum*, lib. V, tit. 38, c.14.
[5] Peter Lombard, *Sentences*, IV, d.18, 7.

to commute penalties or to remit them in part. This our opponents would have to prove.

The death of Christ, furthermore, is a satisfaction not only 140 for guilt but also for eternal death, according to the passage (Hos. 13:14), "O Death, I will be your death." How horrible it is, then, to say that Christ's satisfaction redeems our guilt but our penalties redeem us from eternal death! Thus the statement, "I will be your death," should be taken to mean not Christ but our works—and not even works that God has commanded but the vain works that men have devised. These are supposed to abolish death, even when they are done in mortal sin. We are very sorry to have to list these 141 silly opinions of our opponents, which must enrage anyone who considers the demonic doctrines that the devil has broadcast in the church to suppress the knowledge of law and Gospel, penitence and quickening, and the blessings of Christ. Regarding the law they say that 142 in condescension to our weakness God has fixed a certain limit which man is bound to observe, namely, the commandments; over and above this, that is by the works of supererogation, he can make satisfaction for the sins he commits. Here are men who imagine that we can keep the law in such a way as to do even more than it requires, but Scripture cries out everywhere that we are far away from the perfection that the law requires. These men imagine that God's law deals with external, civil righteousness. They do not see that it requires us to love God "with all our hearts," etc. (Deut. 6:5) and condemns every aspect of lust in human nature. Therefore no one does as much as the law requires, and it is foolish of them to imagine that we can do even more. For though we can do external works that God's law does not require, it is vain and wicked to trust that thereby we make satisfaction to God's law.

True prayer, charity, and fasting have God's command; and 143 where they do, it is a sin to omit them. But where they are not commanded by God's law but have a set form derived from human tradition, such works belong to the human traditions of which Christ says (Matt. 15:9), "In vain do they worship me with the precepts of men." Thus certain fasts were instituted not to control the flesh but, as Scotus says, to pay homage to God and to compensate for eternal death.[6] The same holds when a fixed number of prayers or certain acts of charity are performed as acts of worship which *ex opere operato* pay homage to God and compensate for eternal death. They attribute satisfaction to the mere performance of these acts. for they teach that they avail even for those in mortal sin. Some 144 works, like pilgrimages, depart even further from God's commands;

---

[6] Duns Scotus, *Commentary on the Sentences*, IV, d.15, q.1, a.3.

of these there is a great variety, with one making a trip in armor and another going barefoot. Christ calls these useless acts of worship, and so they do not serve to placate God's displeasure, as our opponents claim. Still they dress up these works with fancy titles; they call them works of supererogation, and they ascribe to them the honor of being a price paid in lieu of eternal death. Thus they rank them above | 45 the works of God's commandments. In this way they obscure the law of God in two ways: first, because they think that outward and civil works satisfy God's law; and second, because they add human traditions, whose works they rank above the works of the law.

In addition, they obscure penitence and grace. This payment | 46 of works does not atone for eternal death because it is useless and in this life does not even get a taste of death. When death assails us, we must set something else against it. Faith in Christ overcomes death, just as it overcomes the wrath of God. So Paul says (I Cor. 15:57), "Thanks be to God, who gives us the victory through our Lord Jesus Christ." He does not say, "Who gives us the victory if we set our satisfactions against death." Our opponents carry on idle specula- | 47 tions about the remission of guilt. They do not see how, in the remission of guilt, faith frees the heart from the wrath of God and eternal death. The satisfaction for eternal death is the death of Christ; our opponents admit that the works of satisfaction are not obligatory works but works of human tradition, which Christ calls useless acts of worship. From this we may safely conclude that canonical satisfactions are not necessary by divine law to remit either guilt or eternal punishment or the penalties of purgatory.

Our opponents object that revenge or punishment is neces- | 48 sary for penitence because Augustine says that "penitence is revenge punishing," etc.[7] We grant that revenge or punishment is necessary for penitence, but not as a merit or price, as our opponents imagine satisfactions to be. But in a formal sense revenge is part of penitence because regeneration itself takes place by constantly mortifying the old life. The saying of Scotus may be beautiful, that penitence is so called because it holds punishment.[8] But what punishment and revenge is Augustine discussing? Certainly true punishment and revenge, that is, contrition and true terrors. Nor do we exclude here outward mortification of the body which follows true sorrow in the mind. Our | 49 opponents are badly mistaken if they think that canonical satisfactions are more genuine punishments than are real terrors in the heart. It is a foolish distortion to apply the term "punishments" to those vain satisfactions and not to apply them to the fearful terrors of conscience of which David says, "The sorrows of death encom-

---

[7] Pseudo-Augustine, *True and False Penitence*, 19:35.
[8] Duns Scotus, *Commentary on the Sentences*, IV, d.14, q.1 a.3, concl. 2.

passed me" (II Sam. 22:5). Who would not put on armor and seek out the church of St. James[9] or the basilica of St. Peter rather than undergo the unspeakable power of the grief that comes over even the simplest people in true penitence?

They object that it is in accord with God's justice to punish 150 sin. He is certainly punishing it when amid the terrors of contrition he reveals his wrath. David attests to this when he prays (Ps. 6:1), "O Lord, rebuke me not in thy anger"; and Jer. 10:24, "Correct me, O Lord, but in just measure; not in thy anger, lest thou bring me to nothing." This certainly speaks of the most bitter punishments. Our opponents admit that contrition can be so great as to make satisfaction unnecessary; thus contrition is a more genuine punishment than is satisfaction. Furthermore, the saints are subject to death and to 151 all the common troubles, as Peter says (I Pet. 4:17), "For the time has come for judgment to begin with the household of God; and if it begins with us, what will be the end of those who do not obey the gospel?" As a rule, these troubles are punishments for sin. In the godly they have another and better purpose, that is, to exercise them so that in their temptations they may learn to seek God's help and to acknowledge the unbelief in their hearts. So Paul says of himself (II Cor. 1:9), "We felt that we had received the sentence of death; but that was to make us rely not on ourselves but on God who raises the dead." Isaiah says, "The distress in which they cry out is thy chastening upon them" (Isa. 26:16); that is, troubles are a discipline by which God exercises the saints. So troubles are inflicted on 152 account of present sin because in the saints they kill and wipe out lust so that the Spirit may renew them. As Paul says (Rom. 8:10), "Your body is dead because of sin"; that is, it is being killed because of the sin still present and remaining in the flesh. Death itself serves 153 this same purpose: to destroy this sinful flesh so that we may rise completely renewed. In the death of a believer even now, once his faith has overcome its terrors, there is no longer that sting and sense of wrath of which Paul says (I Cor. 15:56), "The sting of death is sin, and the power of sin is the law." This power of sin, this sense of wrath, is a real punishment as long as it is present; without this sense of wrath death is actually no punishment at all. Canonical 154 satisfactions, moreover, do not apply to these punishments because our opponents say that the power of the keys remits part of the punishment. They also say that the keys remit both the satisfactions and the penalties on account of which the satisfactions are made. Clearly the power of the keys does not remove these common troubles;

---

[9] Santiago de Compostela, in Spain, alleged location of the martyrdom of St. James, was a favorite place of pilgrimage in the Middle Ages.

but if this is what they mean, why do they add that we must make satisfaction in purgatory?

In rebuttal they bring up the case of Adam, and of David | 55 who was punished for his adultery. From these instances they construct the universal rule that for the forgiveness of sins there must be temporal punishments corresponding to particular sins. We | 56 have said before that the saints suffer penalties which are the work of God, like contrition or terrors of conscience, as well as other common troubles. Some of them suffer penalties which God imposes only on them, for the sake of example. These penalties have nothing to do with the power of the keys because the keys can neither impose nor remit them; God imposes and remits them apart from the administration of the keys.

From the particular penalty imposed on David it does not follow as a universal rule that over and above our common troubles there is a special penalty in purgatory, where the particular punishment fits the particular crime. Where does Scripture teach that we can be | 57 freed from eternal death only by the payment of certain penalties over and above our common troubles? On the contrary, it constantly teaches that we obtain the forgiveness of sins freely because of Christ, who is the victor over sin and death. Therefore we should not mingle the merit of satisfactions with this. And though we still have troubles, Scripture interprets them as the mortification of present sin, not as a payment for or a ransom from eternal death.

Scripture explains that Job's afflictions were not imposed on | 58 him because of his past misdeeds. So afflictions are not always punishments or signs of wrath. When in the midst of troubles terrified consciences see only God's punishment and wrath, they should not feel that God has rejected them but they should be taught that troubles have other and more important purposes. They should look at these other and more important purposes, that God is doing his alien work in order to do his proper work, as Isaiah teaches in a long sermon in his twenty-eighth chapter.[1] When the disciples asked who had | 59 sinned in the case of the blind man, Christ replied that the reason for his blindness was not sin but "that the works of God might be made manifest in him" (John 9:3). In Jeremiah (49:12) it is said, "Those who did not deserve to drink the cup must drink it." Thus the prophets were killed, and John the Baptist, and other saints. Therefore troubles are not always penalties for certain past | 60 deeds, but works of God, intended for our profit, that the power of God might be made more manifest in our weakness.

Thus Paul says, "The power of God is made perfect in weakness" (II Cor. 12:9). It is the will of God that our bodies should be sac-

[1] Isa. 28:21.

rifices, to show our obedience but not to pay for eternal death; for this God has another price, the death of his Son. This is how |6| Gregory interprets the punishment of David when he says: "If God had threatened that because of his sin he would be humiliated by his son, why did he carry out the threat even when the sin was forgiven? The answer is that the sin was forgiven so as not to prevent the man from obtaining eternal life, but the lesson of the threat followed so that especially through humiliation his piety might be exercised and tested. Thus God imposed physical death on man because of sin, and even after the forgiveness of sin he did not abolish it, for the sake of righteousness, that is, to exercise and test the righteousness of those who are sanctified." [2]

The performance of canonical satisfactions does not do away |62 with the calamities common to man—that is, the performance of human traditions which they say avails *ex opere operato* so that even those in mortal sin can buy off their punishments. They quote |63 Paul against us (I Cor. 11:31), "If we judged ourselves truly, we should not be judged" by the Lord; but the word "judge" refers to the whole process of penitence and the fruits that are due, not to "non-obligatory works." Our opponents are paying the penalty for their neglect of grammar when they explain "judge" as "to make a pilgrimage to St. James[3] dressed in armor or to perform similar works." "Judge" means all of penitence; it means "to condemn sins." Such condemnation really happens in contrition and in a changed |64 life. The whole process of penitence—contrition, faith, and good fruits —brings about the mitigation of public and private punishments and calamities, as Isa. 1:16-19 teaches: "Cease to do evil, learn to do good. Though your sins are like scarlet, they shall be white as snow. If you are willing and obedient, you shall eat the good of the land." A statement that is important and wholesome with regard |65 to the whole process of penitence and obligatory works commanded by God should not be transferred to the satisfaction and performance of human traditions. It is wholesome to teach that our common evils are mitigated by our penitence and its true fruits, good works done from faith, but not, as these men imagine, by works done in mortal sin. Here the example of the Ninevites is a case in point. By |66 their penitence—we mean the whole process of penitence—they were reconciled to God and saved their city from destruction.

As we have said before, the patristic discussions and conciliar |67 decisions about satisfactions were a matter of ecclesiastical discipline established for the sake of setting an example; they did not think that this discipline was necessary for the remission either of the guilt

---

[2] Augustine, *Merits and the Remission of Sins*, II, 34:56.
[3] See above, XII, 149.

or of the punishment. By their references to purgatory in this connection they did not mean a payment for eternal punishment, or a satisfaction, but the cleansing of imperfect souls. So Augustine says that venial sins are consumed,[4] that is, that distrust of God and similar attitudes are destroyed. Occasionally the Fathers take the word 168 "satisfaction" from the public rite and use it to denote the real mortification. So Augustine says, "True satisfaction means cutting off the causes of sin, that is, mortifying and restraining the flesh, not to pay for eternal punishments but to keep the flesh from alluring us to sin." [5]

Thus Gregory says about restitution that penitence is false 169 if it does not satisfy those whose property we have taken.[6] Anyone who keeps on stealing is not really sorry that he has stolen or robbed, for he is still a thief and a robber as long as he unjustly holds on to another man's property. Civil restitution is necessary, as it is written (Eph. 4:28), "Let the thief no longer steal." Similarly, Chry- 170 sostom says, "In the heart contrition, in the mouth confession, in the deed complete humility." [7] This proves nothing against us. Good works ought to follow penitence, and penitence ought to be not a fraud but an improvement of the total life.

Furthermore, the Fathers wrote that once in a lifetime was 171 enough for the sort of public or formal penitence described by the canons dealing with satisfactions.[8] From this it is clear that they did not regard these canons as necessary for the forgiveness of sins, for they often say that penitence should be shown in other ways besides this formal one required in the canons dealing with satisfactions.

The writers of the Confutation say it is intolerable to abolish 172 satisfactions contrary to the clear teaching of the Gospel.[9] As we have already shown, the Gospel does not command that these canonical satisfactions or non-obligatory works be done to compensate for punishment. This is obvious from the subject-matter itself. If 173 works of satisfaction are non-obligatory works, why cite the clear teaching of the Gospel? If the Gospel commanded us to buy off punishment by such works, then they would certainly be obligatory. All of this is intended to put something over on the uninitiated. They quote passages dealing with obligatory works, though in their satisfactions they impose non-obligatory works. In fact, they admit in

---

[4] Augustine, *The City of God*, XXI, 26:4.

[5] Pseudo-Augustine, *Ecclesiastical Dogma*, 24.

[6] Gratian, *Decretum*, II, chap. 33, q.3, *De poenitentia*, d.6, c.6.

[7] Pseudo-Chrysostom, in *ibid.*, II, chap. 33, q.3, *De poenitentia*, d.1, c.4.

[8] Probably a misunderstanding of such a passage as Ambrose, *Penitence*, II, 95.

[9] Roman Confutation: "Satisfactions should not be abolished in the church contrary to the express Gospel and the decrees of councils and Fathers . . ." (Pt. I, Art. XII).

their schools that it is not a sin to reject satisfactions. Clearly they are falsifying the matter when they say that the clear teaching of the Gospel compels us to assume these canonical satisfactions.

We have testified often enough that penitence ought to pro-   174 duce good fruits. What these fruits are, we learn from the command-ments—prayer, thanksgiving, the confession of the Gospel, the teach-ing of the Gospel, obedience to parents and magistrates, faithfulness to one's calling, peaceable conduct instead of murder and hatred, the greatest possible generosity to the needy, restraint and chastise-ment of the flesh instead of adultery and fornication, truthfulness— not to buy off eternal punishment but to keep from surrendering to the devil or offending the Holy Spirit. These fruits are commanded by God, they should be done to his glory and because of his com-mand, and they have their reward. But Scripture does not teach that only the observance of certain traditions and the penalties of pur-gatory can remit eternal punishments. Formerly indulgences   175 were the remission of public penitence so as not to burden men too heavily. Now, if human authority can remit satisfactions and penalties, this observance cannot be a necessity commanded by divine law, for human authority cannot abrogate divine law. Since the custom itself has now become obsolete, and that without objection from the bishops, there is no point in such remissions. Still the name indulgences re-mains. The term "satisfaction" no longer refers to civil discipline but to payment for penalties; so also "indulgence" has been misinterpreted as a liberation of souls from purgatory.

It is only on earth, however, that the keys have the power   176 to bind and loose, according to the statement (Matt. 16:19), "What-ever you bind on earth shall be bound in heaven, and whatever you loose on earth shall be loosed in heaven." As we have said above, the keys do not have the power to impose penalties or to institute forms of worship; they only have the command to forgive the sins of those who are converted and to denounce and excommunicate those who refuse to be converted. Just as "to loose" means to for-give sins, so "to bind" means not to forgive sins. It is of a spiritual kingdom that Christ is speaking. God's command is that the min-isters of the Gospel absolve those who are converted, according to the statement (II Cor. 10:8), "Our authority, which the Lord   177 gave for building you up." But the reservation of cases[1] is a secular matter. It is the reservation of canonical penalties, not the reservation of guilt before God in the case of the truly converted. Thus our opponents are right in their judgment when they grant that in the hour of death the reservation of cases should not be an obstacle to absolution.

[1] See Augsburg Confession, XXVIII, 2.

We have expounded here a summary of our doctrine on peni- | 78
tence; we are certain that it is godly and wholesome for the minds
of the devout. If devout men will compare our teaching with the
complicated discussions of our opponents, they will see that our
opponents have neglected to teach the faith that justifies and consoles
faithful hearts. They will see, too, that our opponents have made
up a great deal about the merit of attrition, the endless enumeration
of offenses, and satisfactions, and that these touch neither earth nor
heaven and they themselves cannot satisfactorily explain them.

[Article XIII.] The Number and Use of the Sacraments

In Article XIII our opponents approve the statement that the |
sacraments are no mere marks of profession among men, as some
imagine, but are rather signs and testimonies of God's will toward us,
through which he moves men's hearts to believe. But they insist that
we enumerate seven sacraments.[2] We believe we have the duty not 2
to neglect any of the rites and ceremonies instituted in Scripture, whatever their number. We do not think it makes much difference if, for
purposes of teaching, the enumeration varies, provided what is handed
down in Scripture is preserved. For that matter, the Fathers did not
always use the same enumeration.[3]

If we define sacraments as "rites which have the command 3
of God and to which the promise of grace has been added,"[4] we can
easily determine which are sacraments in the strict sense. By this
definition, rites instituted by men are not sacraments in the strict
sense since men do not have the authority to promise grace. Hence
signs instituted without God's command are not sure signs of grace,
even though they may instruct or admonish the simple folk. The 4
genuine sacraments, therefore, are Baptism, the Lord's Supper, and
absolution (which is the sacrament of penitence), for these rites have
the commandment of God and the promise of grace, which is the
heart of the New Testament. When we are baptized, when we eat
the Lord's body, when we are absolved, our hearts should firmly
believe that God really forgives us for Christ's sake. Through 5
the Word and the rite God simultaneously moves the heart to believe
and take hold of faith, as Paul says (Rom. 10:17), "Faith comes

[2] Roman Confutation: "We must request that what they [the Lutheran
princes] here ascribe to the seven sacraments in general they also confess
specifically concerning the seven sacraments of the church and take measures
for their observance by their subjects" (Pt. I, Art. XIII).

[3] In the ancient church the term "sacrament" was applied loosely to a
great variety of sacred teachings or acts. The enumeration of seven sacraments, proposed by Peter Lombard in the twelfth century, finally prevailed
in the late medieval church.

[4] Melanchthon's own definition in his *Loci* of 1521.

from what is heard." As the Word enters through the ears to strike the heart, so the rite itself enters through the eyes to move the heart. The Word and the rite have the same effect, as Augustine said so well when he called the sacrament "the visible Word," [5] for the rite is received by the eyes and is a sort of picture of the Word, signifying the same thing as the Word. Therefore both have the same effect.

Confirmation and extreme unction are rites received from the 6 Fathers which even the church does not require as necessary for salvation since they do not have the command of God.[6] Hence it is useful to distinguish these from the earlier ones which have an express command from God and a clear promise of grace.

Our opponents do not interpret the priesthood in reference 7 to the ministry of the Word or the administration of the sacraments to others, but in reference to sacrifice, as though the new covenant needed a priesthood like the Levitical to offer sacrifices and merit the forgiveness of sins for the people. We teach that the sacrificial 8 death of Christ on the cross was sufficient for the sins of the whole world and that there is no need for additional sacrifices as though this were not sufficient for our sins. Men are not justified, there- 9 fore, because of any other sacrifices, but because of this one sacrifice of Christ if they believe that it has redeemed them. Thus priests are not called to make sacrifices that merit forgiveness of sins for the people, as in the Old Testament, but they are called to preach the Gospel and administer the sacraments to the people. As the 10 Epistle to the Hebrews teaches clearly enough, we do not have a priesthood like the Levitical.[7] If ordination is interpreted in relation 11 to the ministry of the Word, we have no objection to calling ordination a sacrament. The ministry of the Word has God's command and glorious promises: "The Gospel is the power of God for salvation to every one who has faith" (Rom. 1:16), again, "My word that goes forth from my mouth shall not return to me empty, but it shall accomplish that which I purpose, and prosper in the thing for which I sent it" (Isa. 55:11). If ordination is interpreted this way, we 12 shall not object either to calling the laying on of hands a sacrament. The church has the command to appoint ministers; to this we must subscribe wholeheartedly, for we know that God approves this ministry and is present in it. It is good to extol the ministry of the 13 Word with every possible kind of praise in opposition to the fanatics who dream that the Holy Spirit does not come through the Word

---

[5] Augustine, *Tractate 80* on John 3.
[6] With a qualification in Thomas Aquinas, *Summa theologica*, III, q.72, a.1 ad 3: "Confirmation is necessary for salvation, although one can be saved without it."
[7] Heb. 7-9.

but because of their own preparations. They sit in a dark corner doing and saying nothing, but only waiting for illumination, as the enthusiasts taught formerly and the Anabaptists teach now.

Matrimony was first instituted not in the New Testament but 14 in the very beginning, at the creation of the human race. It has the commandment of God and also certain promises, but these apply to physical life and not strictly to the New Testament. If anybody therefore wants to call it a sacrament, he should distinguish it from the preceding ones which are, in the strict sense, "signs of the New Testament," testimonies of grace and of the forgiveness of sins. If 15 matrimony should be called a sacrament because it has God's command, then many other states or offices might also be called sacraments because they have God's command, as, for example, government.

Ultimately, if we should list as sacraments all the things that 16 have God's command and a promise added to them, then why not prayer, which can most truly be called a sacrament? It has both the command of God and many promises. If it were placed among the sacraments and thus given, so to speak, a more exalted position, this would move men to pray. Alms could be listed here, as well as 17 afflictions, which in themselves are signs to which God has added promises. But let us pass over all this. No intelligent person will quibble about the number of sacraments or the terminology, so long as those things are kept which have God's command and promises.

It is much more necessary to know how to use the sacraments. 18 Here we condemn the whole crowd of scholastic doctors who teach that unless there is some obstacle, the sacraments confer grace *ex opere operato*, without a good disposition in the one using them.[8] It is sheer Judaism to believe that we are justified by a ceremony without a good disposition in our heart, that is, without faith. Yet this ungodly and wicked notion is taught with great authority throughout the papal realm. In opposition to this, Paul denies that Abraham 19 was justified by circumcision, but says that circumcision was a sign given to exercise faith.[9] Thus we teach that in using the sacraments there must be a faith which believes these promises and accepts that which is promised and offered in the sacrament. The reason for 20 this is clear and well founded. A promise is useless unless faith accepts it. The sacraments are signs of the promises. When they are used, therefore, there must be faith, so that anyone who uses the Lord's Supper uses it this way. Because this is a sacrament of the New Testament, as Christ clearly says (I Cor. 11:25), the communicant should be certain that the free forgiveness of sins, promised in the New Testament, is being offered to him. He should accept this by

[8] See above, IV, 63.
[9] Rom. 4:9.

faith, comfort his troubled conscience, and believe that the testimonies are not false but as certain as though God, by a new miracle, promised his will to forgive. For that matter, what good would such miracles or promises do an unbeliever? Here we are talking about per- 21 sonal faith, which accepts the promise as a present reality and believes that the forgiveness of sins is actually being offered, not about a faith which believes in a general way that God exists. Such use of the 22 sacrament comforts devout and troubled minds.

Words cannot describe the abuses which this fanatical notion, 23 about the sacraments *ex opere operato* without a good disposition in the one using them, has spawned in the church. From it has come the endless desecration of Masses, which we shall discuss a little later.[1] No one can produce a single word from the Fathers that supports the scholastics on this question. In fact, Augustine says the opposite: that faith in the sacrament, and not the sacrament, justifies.[2] And Paul's statement is familiar (Rom. 10:10), "Man believes with his heart and so is justified."

[ARTICLE XIV. ECCLESIASTICAL ORDER]

With the proviso that we employ canonical ordination, they 1 accept Article XIV, where we say that no one should be allowed to administer the Word and the sacraments in the church unless he is duly called.[3] On this matter we have given frequent testimony in the assembly to our deep desire to maintain the church polity and various ranks of the ecclesiastical hierarchy, although they were created by human authority. We know that the Fathers had good and useful reasons for instituting ecclesiastical discipline in the manner described by the ancient canons. But the bishops either force 2 our priests to forsake and condemn the sort of doctrine we have confessed, or else, in their unheard of cruelty, they kill the unfortunate and innocent men. This keeps our priests from acknowledging such bishops. Thus the cruelty of the bishops is the reason for the abolition of canonical government in some places, despite our earnest desire to keep it. Let them see to it how they will answer to God for disrupting the church.

In this issue our consciences are clear and we dare not approve 3 the cruelty of those who persecute this teaching, for we know that our confession is true, godly, and catholic. We know that the 4 church is present among those who rightly teach the Word of God

[1] Below, Art. XXIV.
[2] Augustine, *Tractate 80* on John 3.
[3] Roman Confutation: "It ought to be understood that he is rightly called who is called in accordance with the form of law and the ecclesiastical ordinances and decrees hitherto observed everywhere in the Christian world . . ." (Pt. I, Art. XIV).

and rightly administer the sacraments. It is not present among those who seek to destroy the Word of God with their edicts, who even butcher anyone who teaches what is right and true, though the canons themselves are gentler with those who violate them. Furthermore, 5 we want at this point to declare our willingness to keep the ecclesiastical and canonical polity, provided that the bishops stop raging against our churches. This willingness will be our defense, both before God and among all nations, present and future, against the charge that we have undermined the authority of the bishops. Thus men may read that, despite our protest against the unjust cruelty of the bishops, we could not obtain justice.

[ARTICLE XV.] HUMAN TRADITIONS IN THE CHURCH

In Article XV they accept the first part, where we say that 1 we should observe those ecclesiastical rites which can be observed without sin and which are conducive to tranquillity and good order in the church. They completely condemn the second part, where we say that human traditions instituted to appease God, to merit grace, and to make satisfaction for sin are contrary to the Gospel.[4] Although we have discussed traditions at length in Article XXVI 2 of the Confession, we must repeat a few things here.

We expected our opponents to defend human traditions on 3 other grounds. We did not think that they would actually condemn the doctrine that we do not merit grace or the forgiveness of sins by the observance of human traditions. Now that they have condemned this doctrine, we have an easy and simple case. Here our op- 4 ponents are openly Judaizing; they are openly replacing the Gospel with doctrines of demons. Scripture calls traditions "doctrines of demons" (I Tim. 4:1) when someone teaches that religious rites are helpful in gaining grace and the forgiveness of sins. This obscures the Gospel, the blessing of Christ, and righteousness of faith. The 5 Gospel teaches that by faith, for Christ's sake, we freely receive the forgiveness of sins and are reconciled to God. Our opponents, on the other hand, set up these traditions as another mediator through which they seek to gain the forgiveness of sins and appease the wrath of God. But Christ clearly says (Matt. 15:9), "In vain do they worship me with the precepts of men."

We have previously shown at length that men are justified by 6 the faith that they have a gracious God not because of works but freely for Christ's sake. This is definitely the teaching of the Gospel,

---

[4] Roman Confutation: "The appendix to this article must be entirely removed, for it is false that human ordinances instituted to propitiate God and make satisfactions for sins are opposed to the Gospel, as will more amply be set forth hereafter concerning vows, the choice of food, and the like" (Pt. I, Art. XV).

for Paul clearly teaches (Eph. 2:8), "By grace you have been saved through faith; and this is not your own doing, it is the gift of God" and not of men. They say that men merit the forgiveness of sins 7 by these human observances. What is this but to set up another justifier and mediator instead of Christ? Paul says to the Galatians 8 (5:4), "You are severed from Christ, you who would be justified by the law." That is, if by the observance of the law you think you deserve to be accounted righteous before God, then Christ is of no use to you, for why does anyone need Christ if he believes he is righteous by his own observance of the law? God has appointed 9 Christ as the mediator; he wants to be gracious to us through him, not through our own righteousness. These men believe that God is reconciled and gracious because of the traditions and not because of Christ. Thus they rob Christ of his honor as the mediator.

From this point of view there is no difference between our 10 traditions and the ceremonies of Moses. Paul condemns the ceremonies of Moses as well as traditions because they were thought of as works meriting righteousness before God and therefore they obscured the work of Christ and the righteousness of faith. With the removal of the law and of the traditions, he therefore contends that the forgiveness of sins has been promised, not because of our works but freely because of Christ, provided that we accept it by faith; for only faith can accept a promise. Since it is by faith that we 11 accept the forgiveness of sins and by faith that we have a gracious God for Christ's sake, it is an ungodly error to maintain that we merit the forgiveness of sins by these observances. Someone 12 might say in this connection that though we do not merit the forgiveness of sins, those who are already justified do merit grace by observing these traditions. To this Paul replies that Christ would be "an agent of sins" (Gal. 2:17) if we were to believe that after justification we are not accounted righteous for his sake but must first merit this by other observances. "No one adds even to a man's covenant." [5] In other words, to the covenant of God, promising that he will be gracious to us for Christ's sake, we dare not add the condition that we must first earn our acceptance and justification through these observances.

What need is there of a long discussion? The holy Fathers 13 did not institute any traditions for the purpose of meriting the forgiveness of sins or righteousness. They instituted them for the sake of good order and tranquillity in the church. If somebody wants 14 to institute certain works to merit the forgiveness of sins or righteousness, how will he know that these works please God since they

---

[5] Gal. 3:15.

do not have support in God's Word? How will he inform men of God's will without the command and Word of God? Does not God throughout the prophets forbid the establishment of additional ceremonies without his command? In Ezek. 20:18, 19 it is written, "Do not walk in the statutes of your fathers, nor observe their ordinances, nor defile yourselves with their idols. I the Lord am your God; walk in my statutes, and be careful to observe my ordinances." If men   15 are allowed to establish new rites and if by such rites they merit grace, we shall have to approve the religious rites of all the heathen, as well as the rites established by Jeroboam[6] and others over and above the law. Where is the difference? If we are permitted to establish rites that serve to merit grace or righteousness, why did not the heathen and Israelites have the same privilege? Yet the   16 rites of the heathen and the Israelites were condemned precisely because, in their ignorance of the righteousness of faith, they believed that by these they merited the forgiveness of sins and righteousness. Finally, what assurance do we have that religious rites   17 established by men without God's command can justify since we can affirm nothing about the will of God without the Word of God? What if God does not approve these acts of worship? How, then, can our opponents maintain that they justify? They cannot maintain this without the Word and testimony of God, and Paul says (Rom. 14:23), "Whatever does not proceed from faith is sin." Since these rites have no testimony in the Word of God, the conscience must doubt whether they please God.

What need is there for words in a matter so clear? If our   18 opponents defend the notion that these human rites merit justification, grace, and the forgiveness of sins, they are simply establishing the kingdom of Antichrist. The kingdom of Antichrist is a new kind of worship of God, devised by human authority in opposition to Christ. Thus the kingdom of Mohammed has rites and works by which it seeks to be justified before God, denying that men are freely justified before God by faith for Christ's sake. So the papacy will also be a part of the kingdom of Antichrist if it maintains that human rites justify. They take honor away from Christ when they teach that we are not justified freely for his sake but by such rites, and especially when they teach that for justification such rites are not only useful but necessary. The Confutation condemns our statement in the article on the church that for the true unity of the church it is not necessary that rites instituted by men be everywhere alike.[7] In his eleventh   19 chapter Daniel says that the invention of human rites will be the very form and constitution of the kingdom of Antichrist. This is what he

---

[6] I Kings 12:28ff.
[7] See above, VII and VIII, 30.

says (11:38): "He shall honor the god of fortresses instead of these: a god whom his fathers did not know he shall honor with gold and silver, with precious stones and costly gifts." Here he is describing the invention of rites, for he says that a god will be worshiped whom the fathers did not know.

Although the holy Fathers themselves had rites and traditions, 20 they did not regard them as useful or necessary for justification. They did not obscure the glory or work of Christ but taught that we are justified by faith for Christ's sake, not for the sake of these human rites. They observed these human rites because they were profitable for good order, because they gave the people a set time to assemble, because they provided an example of how all things could be done decently and in order in the churches,[8] and finally because they helped instruct the common folk. For different seasons and various rites serve as reminders for the common folk. For these reasons the 21 Fathers kept ceremonies, and for the same reasons we also believe in keeping traditions. We are amazed when our opponents maintain that traditions have another purpose, namely, to merit the forgiveness of sins, grace and justification. What is this but honoring God "with gold and silver and precious stones." [9] believing that he is reconciled by a variety of vestments, ornaments, and innumerable similar observances in the human traditions.

In Col. 2:23 Paul writes that traditions "have an appearance 22 of wisdom," and indeed they have. This good order is very becoming in the church and is therefore necessary. But because human reason does not understand the righteousness of faith, it naturally supposes that such works justify men and reconcile God. Under this de- 23 lusion the common people among the Israelites expanded such ceremonies, just as they have been expanded among us in the monasteries. This is how human reason interprets fasting and bodily 24 discipline. Though their purpose is to restrain the flesh, reason imagines that they are to be rites which justify, as Thomas writes, "Fasting avails to destroy and prevent guilt." [1] This is what Thomas says. So men are deceived by the appearance of wisdom and righteousness in such works. Then there are the examples of the saints; when men strive to imitate them, they copy their outward behavior without copying their faith.

Once this appearance of wisdom and righteousness has deceived 25 men, all sorts of troubles follow. The Gospel of the righteousness of faith in Christ is obscured and replaced by a vain trust in such works. As a result, the commandments of God are obscured; for when men

[8] Cf. I Cor. 14:40.
[9] Dan. 11:38.
[1] Thomas Aquinas, *Summa theologica*, II, 2, q.147, a.3, c.

regard these works as perfect and spiritual, they will vastly prefer them to the works that God commands, like the tasks of one's calling, the administration of public affairs, the administration of the household, married life, and the rearing of children. Compared with 26 these ceremonies such tasks seem profane, so that many perform them with scruples of conscience. It is a matter of record that many have given up their administrative positions in the government and their marriages because they regarded these observances as better and holier.

Nor is this all. When minds are obsessed with the idea that 27 such observances are necessary for justification, consciences are sorely troubled because they cannot keep the requirements in every detail. Who could even list them all? There are huge tomes, even whole libraries, that do not contain a single syllable about Christ or faith in him or the good works to be performed in one's calling, but only the traditions together with interpretations that make them either stricter or easier. How the great Gerson suffers as he looks for 28 the degrees and limitations of these precepts and cannot fix the mitigation in any definite degree! Yet at the same time he deplores the danger to consciences that comes from this strict interpretation of the traditions.[2]

Against this deceptive appearance of wisdom and righteous- 29 ness in human rites, let us therefore arm ourselves with the Word of God. Let us know that they merit neither the forgiveness of sins nor justification before God, and that they are not necessary for justification. We have already quoted some proofs for this, and 30 Paul's letters abound in them. In Col. 2:16, 17 he says: "Let no one pass judgment on you in questions of food and drink or with regard to a festival or a new moon or a sabbath. These are only a shadow of what is to come; but the substance belongs to Christ." This includes both the law of Moses and the traditions of men, so that our opponents cannot use their customary evasion and say that Paul is talking only about the law of Moses. He makes it perfectly clear that he is talking about human traditions. Our opponents do not know what they are talking about. If, according to the Gospel, the divinely instituted ceremonies of Moses do not justify, how much less do the traditions of men justify!

Nor do bishops have the power to institute rites as though they 31 justified or were necessary for justification. In the apostolic statement in Acts 15:10, "Why do you make a trial of God by putting a yoke," etc., Peter charges that to put this burden on the church is a great sin. In Gal. 5:1 Paul forbids them to "submit again to slavery." True, 32 in the Old Testament ceremonies were necessary for the time

---

[2] John Gerson, *The Spiritual Life*, lectio 2, III, 16.

being. But the apostles insisted that Christian liberty remain in the church, lest the observances of the law or traditions be regarded as necessary. If men believe that these observances merit justification or are necessary for justification, they obscure the righteousness of faith. Many look for loopholes in the traditions to ease their 33 consciences, yet they do not find any sure standards by which to free themselves from these fetters. When Alexander could not untie 34 the Gordian knot, he solved it for good by cutting it with his sword. Just so the apostles have freed consciences from traditions for good, especially from the notion that they merit justification. By precept and example the apostles compel us to oppose this teaching. They compel us to teach that traditions do not justify; that they are not necessary for justification; that no one ought to create or accept traditions with the idea that they merit justification. Then if anybody 35 observes them, let him do so without claiming any value before God for them, just as there is no value before God in observing secular customs, if soldiers wear one kind of uniform and scholars another. The apostles violated traditions, and Christ excused them, for this 36 was to serve as an example to the Pharisees of the uselessness of these acts of worship.[3] If our people drop certain useless traditions, 37 they have excuse enough now that these are being required as a means of meriting justification. For such an idea of traditions is wicked.

We gladly keep the old traditions set up in the church because 38 they are useful and promote tranquillity, and we interpret them in an evangelical way, excluding the opinion which holds that they justify. Our enemies falsely accuse us of abolishing good or- 39 dinances and church discipline. We can truthfully claim that in our churches the public liturgy is more decent than in theirs, and if you look at it correctly we are more faithful to the canons than our opponents are. Among our opponents, unwilling celebrants and 40 hirelings perform Mass, and they often do so only for the money. When they chant the Psalms, it is not to learn or pray but for the sake of the rite, as if this work were an act of worship or at least worth some reward. Every Lord's Day many in our circles use the Lord's Supper, but only after they have been instructed, examined, and absolved. The children chant the Psalms in order to learn; the people sing, too, in order to learn or to worship. Among our 41 opponents there is no catechization of the children at all, though even the canons give prescriptions about it. In our circles the pastors and ministers of the churches are required to instruct and examine the youth publicly, a custom that produces very good results. Among 42 our opponents, there are many regions where no sermons are preached

[3] Cf. Matt. 12:1-8.

during the whole year, except in Lent. But the chief worship of God is the preaching of the Gospel.

When our opponents do preach, they talk about human traditions, the worship of the saints, and similar trifles. This the people rightly despise and walk out on them after the reading of the Gospel. A few of the better ones are now beginning to talk about good works, but they say nothing about the righteousness of faith or about faith in Christ or about comfort for the conscience. In their polemics they even attack this most salutary part of the Gospel. In our churches, 43 on the other hand, all sermons deal with topics like these: penitence, the fear of God, faith in Christ, the righteousness of faith, comfort for the conscience through faith, the exercise of faith, prayer and our assurance that it is efficacious and is heard, the cross, respect for rulers and for all civil ordinances, the distinction between the kingdom of Christ (or the spiritual kingdom) and political affairs, marriage, the education and instruction of children, chastity, and all the works of love. From this description of the state of our 44 churches it is evident that we diligently maintain church discipline, pious ceremonies, and the good customs of the church.

With regard to the mortifying of the body and the discipline 45 of the flesh we teach exactly what we said in the Confession,[4] that the cross and the troubles with which God disciplines us effect a genuine and not a counterfeit mortification. When this comes, we must obey God's will, as Paul says (Rom. 12:1), "Present your bodies as a sacrifice." This is the spiritual exercise of fear and faith. Be- 46 sides this mortification brought on by the cross, a voluntary kind of exercise is also necessary. Of this Christ says (Luke 21:34), "Take heed to yourselves lest your hearts be weighed down with dissipation," and Paul says (I Cor. 9:27), "I pommel my body and subdue it." We should undertake these exercises not as services that 47 justify but as restraints on our flesh, lest we be overcome by satiety and become complacent and idle with the result that we indulge and pamper the desires of our flesh. In this we must be diligent at all times because God commands it at all times. But their prescrip- 48 tion of certain foods and seasons contributes nothing to the subjection of the flesh. Their fasts are more luxurious and sumptuous than others' feasts, and our opponents do not even observe the canonical prescriptions.

This subject of traditions involves many difficult and contro- 49 versial questions, and we know from actual experience that traditions are real snares for consciences. When they are required as necessary, they bring exquisite torture to a conscience that has omitted some observance. On the other hand, their abrogation involves its own

[4] See above, Augsburg Confession, XXVI, 33-39.

difficulties and problems. But our case is plain and simple because 50
our opponents condemn us for teaching that human traditions do not
merit the forgiveness of sins, and they require so-called "universal
rites"[5] as necessary for salvation. Here Paul is our constant champion; everywhere he insists that these observances neither justify nor
are necessary over and above the righteousness of faith. Never- 51
theless, liberty in these matters should be used moderately, lest the
weak be offended and become more hostile to the true teaching of the
Gospel because of an abuse of liberty. Nothing should be changed
in the accustomed rites without good reason, and to foster harmony
those ancient customs should be kept which can be kept without sin
or without great disadvantage. This is what we teach. In this 52
very assembly we have shown ample evidence of our willingness to
observe adiaphora with others,[6] even where this involved some disadvantage to us. We believed that the greatest possible public harmony, without offense to consciences, should be preferred to all other
advantages, but we shall have more to say about this whole issue
when we discuss vows and ecclesiastical authority.[7]

[ARTICLE XVI. POLITICAL ORDER]

Our opponents approve Article XVI without exception.[8] There 1
we confessed that a Christian might legitimately hold public office,
render verdicts according to imperial or other established laws, prescribe legal punishments, engage in just wars, render military service,
enter into legal contracts, own property, take an oath when the government requires it, or contract marriage—in short, that lawful civil
ordinances are God's good creatures and divine ordinances in which
a Christian may safely take part. The writings of our theologians 2
have profitably illumined this whole question of the distinction between Christ's kingdom and a political kingdom. Christ's kingdom
is spiritual; it is the knowledge of God in the heart, the fear of God
and faith, the beginning of eternal righteousness and eternal life. At
the same time it lets us make outward use of the legitimate political
ordinances of the nation in which we live, just as it lets us make use
of medicine or architecture, food or drink or air. The Gospel does 3

---

[5] See above, VII and VIII, 30.

[6] During the Diet of Augsburg in 1530, after the public presentation of
the Augsburg Confession, Roman and Lutheran theologians had negotiations
looking toward a possible reconciliation of their differences, and Melanchthon
and his colleagues indicated willingness to make some concessions in church
practice.

[7] See below, Art. XXVII, XXVIII.

[8] Roman Confutation: "The sixteenth article, concerning civil magistrates,
is received with pleasure . . . . And the princes are praised for condemning
the Anabaptists . . ." (Pt. I, Art. XVI).

not introduce any new laws about the civil estate, but commands us to obey the existing laws, whether they were formulated by heathen or by others, and in this obedience to practice love. It was mad of Carlstadt to try to impose on us the judicial laws of Moses.[9] Our 4 theologians have written extensively on this subject because the monks had broadcast many dangerous ideas through the church. They called it an evangelical state to hold property in common, and they called it an evangelical counsel not to own property and not to go to court. These ideas seriously obscure the Gospel and the spiritual kingdom; they are also dangerous to the state. For the Gospel does not 5 destroy the state or the family but rather approves them, and it commands us to obey them as divine ordinances not only from fear of punishment but also "for the sake of conscience" (Rom. 13:5).

Julian the Apostate,[1] Celsus,[2] and many others opposed the 6 Christians on the grounds that their Gospel would destroy the commonwealth by its prohibition of legal redress and by other teachings that were not suited to civil relationships. These questions were very disturbing to Origen,[3] Nazianzus,[4] and others, though they are very easy to answer if we keep certain things in mind. The Gospel does not legislate for the civil estate but is the forgiveness of sins and the beginning of eternal life in the hearts of believers. It not only approves governments but subjects us to them, just as we are necessarily subjected to the laws of the seasons and to the change of winter and summer as ordinances of God. The Gospel forbids private revenge, 7 and Christ stresses this so often lest the apostles think that they should usurp the government from those who hold it, as in the Jewish dream of the messianic kingdom; instead, he would have them know their duty to teach that the spiritual kingdom does not change the civil government. Thus private revenge is forbidden not as an evangelical counsel but as a command (Matt. 5:39; Rom. 12:19). Public redress through a judge is not forbidden but expressly commanded, and it is a work of God according to Paul (Rom. 13:1ff.). Now the various kinds of public redress are court decisions, punishments, wars, military service. How poor the judgment of many writers in these matters 8 has been is evident from their erroneous view that the Gospel is something external, a new and monastic form of government. Thus they failed to see that the Gospel brings eternal righteousness to hearts, while it approves the civil government.

[9] Over against Andrew Carlstadt, Luther had asserted in his "Against the Heavenly Prophets" (1525) that "the judicial laws of Moses" were binding only on the Jews and that later peoples were bound to observe the civil laws of their nations.
[1] Emperor Julian (A.D. 361-363), *Against the Christians*, II, 12.
[2] Origen, *Against Celsus*, VII, 58.
[3] *Ibid.*, VII, 59-61.
[4] *Oration IV against Julian*, I, 97.

It is also false to claim that Christian perfection consists in 9 not holding property. What makes for Christian perfection is not contempt of civil ordinances but attitudes of the heart, like a deep fear of God and a strong faith. Though they were wealthy and held high positions, Abraham, David, and Daniel were no less perfect than any hermit. The monks impressed men with this outward hypoc- 10 risy and blinded them to the essence of real perfection. How they have praised the theory that the Gospel requires us to hold property in common! Such praise is dangerous, especially because it is so 11 out of harmony with the Scriptures. Scripture does not command holding property in common, but by its command, "You shall not steal," the Decalogue recognizes the right of ownership and commands everyone to possess his own. Wycliffe was obviously out of his mind in claiming that priests were not allowed to own property.[5] End- 12 less discussions about contracts will never satisfy good consciences unless they keep the rule in mind, that a Christian may legitimately make use of civil ordinances and laws. This rule safeguards consciences, for it teaches that if contracts have the approval of magistrates or of laws, they are legitimate in the sight of God as well.

Our theologians have explained this whole matter of political 13 affairs so clearly that many good men involved in politics and in business have testified how they were helped after the theories of the monks had troubled them and put them in doubt whether the Gospel permitted such public and private business. We have repeated our position here so that those outside our group may understand that our doctrine does not weaken but rather strengthens the authority of magistrates and the value of civil ordinances generally. The importance of this had been obscured by foolish monastic theories which put a hypocritical poverty and humility far above the state and the family, even though these have God's command while the Platonic commune does not have God's command.

[ARTICLE XVII. CHRIST'S RETURN TO JUDGMENT]

Our opponents accept Article XVII without exception.[6] There 1 we confess that at the consummation of the world Christ will appear and raise all the dead, granting eternal life and eternal joys to the godly but condemning the ungodly to endless torment with the devil.

[ARTICLE XVIII. FREE WILL]

Our opponents accept Article XVIII on free will, but they 1 add several proofs which are hardly applicable in this matter. They

---

[5] John Wycliffe, *The Church*, VIII.
[6] Roman Confutation: "The confession of the seventeenth article is received . . ." (Pt. I, Art. XVII).

also add a caution, lest too much be conceded to free will, as in Pelagianism, or all liberty be denied it, as in Manichaeism.[7] Well 2 and good; but what is the difference between the Pelagians and our opponents, since both believe that without the Holy Spirit men can love God and perform "the essence of the acts" required by his commandments and that without the Holy Spirit men can merit grace and justification by works that reason produces on its own? How 3 many absurdities follow from these Pelagian notions which the schools teach with great authority! In the article on justification[8] we quoted Augustine's emphatic refutation of these notions, based on Paul.

We are not denying freedom to the human will. The human will 4 has freedom to choose among the works and things which reason by itself can grasp. To some extent it can achieve civil righteousness or the righteousness of works. It can talk about God and express its worship of him in outward works. It can obey rulers and parents. Externally, it can choose to keep the hands from murder, adultery, or theft. Since human nature still has reason and judgment about the things that the senses can grasp, it also retains a choice in these things, as well as the liberty and ability to achieve civil righteousness. This righteousness which the carnal nature—that is, the reason—can achieve on its own without the Holy Spirit, Scripture calls the righteousness of the flesh. But so great is the power of concupiscence 5 that men obey their evil impulses more often than their sound judgment, while the devil, who as Paul says (Eph. 2:2) is at work in the ungodly, never stops inciting this feeble nature to various offenses. For these reasons even civil righteousness is rare among men, as we see from the fact that even philosophers who seem to have wanted this righteousness did not achieve it. Moreover, it is false to say 6 that a man does not sin if, outside the state of grace, he does the works prescribed in the commandments; to this they add that such works, by the merit of congruity, earn the forgiveness of sins and justification. Without the Holy Spirit human hearts have neither the fear of God nor trust in God nor the faith that God hears, forgives, helps, or saves them. Therefore they are ungodly; for "a bad tree cannot bear good fruit" (Matt. 7:18) and "without faith it is impossible to please" God (Heb. 11:6).

Although we concede to free will the liberty and ability to do 7 the outward works of the law, we do not ascribe to it the spiritual capacity for true fear of God, true faith in God, true knowledge and

---

[7] Roman Confutation: "This confession is received and approved, for it becomes Catholics to pursue the middle way so as not, with the Pelagians, to ascribe too much to free will, nor, with the godless Manichaeans, to deny the will all freedom . . ." (Pt. I, Art. XVIII).

[8] See above, IV, 29, 30.

trust that God considers, hears, and forgives us. These are the real works of the first table,[9] which the human heart cannot perform without the Holy Spirit. As Paul says (I Cor. 2:14), "The natural man," that is, the man who uses only his natural powers, "does not perceive the things of God." Men can easily determine this if they consider 8 what their hearts believe about God's will, whether they really believe that God regards and hears them. Even for the saints it is hard to keep this faith; for the ungodly it is impossible. As we have said before, it comes into being when terrified hearts hear the Gospel and receive consolation.

Therefore we may profitably distinguish between civil righteous- 9 ness and spiritual righteousness, attributing the former to the free will and the latter to the operation of the Holy Spirit in the regenerate. This safeguards outward discipline, because all men ought to know that God requires this civil righteousness and that, to some extent, we can achieve it. At the same time it shows the difference between human righteousness and spiritual righteousness, between philosophical teaching and the teaching of the Holy Spirit; and it points out the need for the Holy Spirit. This distinction is not our invention 10 but the clear teaching of the Scriptures. Augustine discusses it too,[1] and more recently William of Paris has discussed it very well.[2] But it has been criminally suppressed by those who dream that men can obey the law of God without the Holy Spirit and that the Holy Spirit is given to them out of regard for the merit of this obedience.

[ARTICLE XIX. THE CAUSE OF SIN]

Our opponents accept Article XIX.[3] There we confess that 1 God alone has established all of nature and preserves everything that exists. Nevertheless, the cause of sin is the will of the devil and of men turning away from God, as Christ said about the devil (John 8:44), "When he lies, he speaks according to his own nature."

[ARTICLE XX. GOOD WORKS]

In Article XX they expressly state their rejection and con- 1 demnation of our statement that men do not merit the forgiveness of sins by good works. This article they explicitly reject and condemn.[4] What can we say about an issue that is so clear? Here 2

---

[9] Of the Ten Commandments.
[1] See the passage cited above, Augsburg Confession, XVIII, 5, 6.
[2] William Peraldus, *Summa de virtutibus,* V.
[3] Roman Confutation: "The nineteenth article is likewise approved and accepted . . ." (Pt. I, Art. XIX).
[4] Roman Confutation: "In the twentieth article . . . there is only one thing that pertains to the princes and cities, namely, that good works do not merit the forgiveness of sins. As this has been rejected and disapproved before, so it is also rejected and disapproved now . . ." (Pt. I, Art. XX).

the framers of the Confutation have shown their true spirit. For what is more certain in the church than that the forgiveness of sins is given freely for Christ's sake, that not our works but Christ is the propitiation for sin? As Peter says (Acts 10:43), "To him all the prophets bear witness that every one who believes in him receives forgiveness of sins through his name." We would rather agree with this church of the prophets than with those damnable writers of the Confutation who so impudently blaspheme Christ. There have 3 indeed been theologians who held that after the forgiveness of sins men are righteous before God not through faith but through their own works; nevertheless, they did not mean to say that we receive the forgiveness of sins itself on account of our works and not freely on account of Christ.

Therefore the blasphemy of attributing the honor of Christ to 4 our works is intolerable. These theologians have lost all sense of shame if they dare to smuggle such a notion into the church. We are sure that His Most Excellent Imperial Majesty and many of the princes would have refused to let this statement of the Confutation stand if their attention had been called to it. Here we could quote endless 5 passages from Scripture and the Fathers, but we have already said enough on this subject. There is no need for proofs to anyone who knows that Christ was given to us to be a propitiation for our sins. Isaiah says (53:6), "The Lord has laid on him the iniquity of us all." Our opponents, on the other hand, teach that God has laid our iniquities on our works and not on Christ. We are not inclined to mention here the type of works they require. We see that a horrible decree 6 has been drawn up against us; this would frighten us more if we were arguing about dubious or trivial matters. Now that we see in our conscience that our opponents are condemning the obvious truth—truth which the church must defend and which increases the glory of Christ —we can easily ignore the terrors of the world and bravely bear whatever we have to suffer for Christ and the advancement of the church. Who would not gladly die in the confession of the article that we 7 receive the forgiveness of sins freely for Christ's sake and that our works do not merit the forgiveness of sins? Pious consciences will 8 have no sure foundation when sin and death terrify them and the devil tempts them to despair unless they know that they must believe in the forgiveness of sins freely given for Christ's sake. This faith gives support and life to the heart in its hardest struggle against despair.

This issue is so weighty that we shrink from no danger on account 9 of it. "Do not yield to the wicked, but go on still more boldly," [5] every one of you who has agreed to our Confession, when our opponents

---

[5] Vergil, *Aeneid*, VI, 95.

use their terrors, tortures, and punishments to try to drive you away from the consolation which this article of ours offers to the universal church. Anyone who looks will find many passages in Scripture 10 to set his mind at ease, for Paul fairly screams, as it were, that sins are freely forgiven for Christ's sake. He says, "We are justified by his grace as a gift" (Rom. 3:24) "in order that the promise may be guaranteed" (Rom. 4:16). That is, if the promise were conditional on our works, it would not be guaranteed. If the forgiveness of sins were given on account of our works, when would we know that we had attained it, when would a terrified conscience find a work that it thought adequate to placate the wrath of God? The reader can find our 11 proofs in our earlier discussion of this whole issue.[6] The shameful way in which our opponents have treated this issue has compelled us to register a complaint rather than compose a point-by-point refutation. They have gone on record as rejecting our doctrine that we obtain the forgiveness of sins not on account of our works but freely for Christ's sake.

Our opponents quote many Scripture passages to show why they 12 have condemned our article, and it is worthwhile to examine some of these. From Peter they quote (II Pet. 1:10), "Be zealous to confirm your call." Now you see, dear reader, that our opponents have indeed got the most out of their logic courses, for they have learned the trick of deducing from Scripture whatever suits them. "Confirm your call by good works"; therefore works merit the forgiveness of sins! By the same argument we could say to a man who was sentenced to die and then pardoned, "The magistrate commands that from now on you steal no more, and therefore you are pardoned." Such argumen- 13 tation is to make the effect the cause. Peter is talking about the works that follow the forgiveness of sins; he is giving instruction that they should be done in order to confirm their call, that is, lest they fall from their call by sinning again. Do good works to persevere in your call and not to lose its gifts, which were given to you before your works and not because of them and which are now kept by faith. Faith does not remain in those who lose the Holy Spirit and reject penitence; as we have said before,[7] faith has its existence in penitence.

They add other proofs that are no more relevant. Finally they 14 say that our opinion was condemned a thousand years ago, in the days of Augustine.[8] This is completely false. The church of Christ has always believed that the forgiveness of sins is free; in fact, the Pelagians

[6] See above, IV, 40-47.

[7] E.g., above, IV, 142.

[8] Roman Confutation: "This opinion concerning good works was condemned and rejected more than a thousand years ago, in the time of Augustine" (Pt. I, Art. XX).

were condemned for maintaining that grace is given because of our works. Furthermore, we have already given ample evidence of 15 our conviction that good works must necessarily follow faith. We do not overthrow the law, Paul says (Rom. 3:31), but uphold it; for when we have received the Holy Spirit by faith, the keeping of the law necessarily follows, by which love, patience, chastity, and other fruits of the Spirit gradually increase.

[ARTICLE XXI. THE INVOCATION OF THE SAINTS]

They absolutely condemn Article XXI because we do not require 1 the invocation of the saints.[9] Nowhere else do they expend so much sophistry, but all they manage to prove is that the saints should be honored and that the living saints should pray for others. They present this as though on this account the invocation of departed saints were also necessary. Cyprian asked Cornelius, while he was still alive, 2 to pray for his brothers after his departure.[1] They cite this example to prove the invocation of the dead. They also refer to Jerome's controversy with Vigilantius[2] and say, "On this field of battle Jerome conquered Vigilantius eleven hundred years ago." So our opponents stage a triumph as though the war were already over. These asses do not see that in the controversy between Jerome and Vigilantius there is not a syllable about invoking, but only about honoring, the saints. Nor do the rest of the ancient Fathers before Gregory mention 3 invocation. The theory of invocation, together with the theories our opponents now hold about the application of merits, surely has no support among the ancient Fathers.

Our Confession approves giving honor to the saints. This honor 4 is threefold. The first is thanksgiving: we should thank God for showing examples of his mercy, revealing his will to save men, and giving teachers and other gifts to the church. Since these are his greatest gifts, we should extol them very highly; we should also praise the saints themselves for using these gifts, just as Christ praises faithful businessmen (Matt. 25:21, 23). The second honor is the strength- 5 ening of our faith: when we see Peter forgiven after his denial, we are

[9] Roman Confutation: "They [the Lutheran princes] admit that the memory of saints may be set before us so that we may follow their faith and good works, but not that they be invoked and called on for aid . . . . This error . . . has often been condemned in the church, ever since on this field of battle Jerome conquered Vigilantius eleven hundred years ago . . . . Wherefore this article of the Confession, so frequently condemned, must be utterly rejected and, in harmony with the whole universal church, be condemned, for in favor of the invocation of saints we have not only the authority of the universal church but also the agreement of the holy Fathers . . ." (Pt. I, Art. XXI).

[1] Cyprian, *Epistles*, 60:5.

[2] Jerome, *Against Vigilantius*, 5:7.

encouraged to believe that grace does indeed abound more than sin (Rom. 5:20). The third honor is the imitation, first of their   6 faith and then of their other virtues, which each should imitate in accordance with his calling. Our opponents do not require these   7 real honors; they only argue about invocation, which, even if it were not dangerous, is certainly unnecessary.

Besides, we grant that the angels pray for us. This is attested to   8 by Zech. 1:12, where the angel prays, "O Lord of hosts, how long wilt thou have no mercy on Jerusalem?" We also grant that the   9 saints in heaven pray for the church in general, as they prayed for the church universal while they were on earth. Nevertheless, there is no passage in Scripture about the dead praying, except for the dream recorded in the Second Book of the Maccabees (15:14).

Even if the saints do pray fervently for the church, it does not   10 follow that they should be invoked. But our Confession affirms only this much, that Scripture does not teach us to invoke the saints or to ask their help. Neither a command nor a promise nor an example can be shown from Scripture for the invocation of the saints; from this it follows that consciences cannot be sure about such invocation. Since prayer ought to come from faith, how do we know that God approves such invocation? How do we know, without proof from Scripture, that the saints hear the individual's prayers? Evidently   11 some attribute divinity to the saints, the power to perceive the unspoken thoughts of our minds. They argue about morning and evening knowledge,[3] perhaps because they are not sure whether they hear us in the morning or in the evening. They have not thought this up to honor the saints but to defend their religious traffic. Our oppo-   12 nents can produce nothing against the argument that since invocation cannot be proved from the Word of God, we cannot affirm that the saints are aware of it or, even if they are, that God approves it. Therefore our opponents should not coerce us to adopt something   13 uncertain, for prayer without faith is not prayer. Since they refer to the example of the church, we reply that this is a novel custom in the church. The ancient prayers mention the saints, but they do not invoke them. Besides, this novel invocation in the church is not the same as the invocation of individuals.

Not only do our opponents require invocation in the veneration   14 of the saints; they even apply the merits of the saints to others and make the saints propitiators as well as intercessors. This is completely intolerable, for it transfers to the saints honor belonging to Christ alone. It makes them mediators and propitiators. Even though they distinguish between mediators of intercession and mediators of redemp-

---

[3] E.g., Gabriel Biel, *Exposition of the Canon of the Mass* (1488), 31.

tion,[4] they obviously make the saints mediators of redemption.
They do not even have proof from Scripture for calling them   15
mediators of intercession. To put it mildly, even this obscures the
work of Christ and transfers to the saints the trust we should have in
Christ's mercy. Men suppose that Christ is more severe and the
saints more approachable; so they trust more in the mercy of the
saints than in the mercy of Christ and they flee from Christ and turn
to the saints. Thus they actually make them mediators of redemption.

Now we shall prove that they actually make the saints not only   16
intercessors but propitiators, that is, mediators of redemption. For the
present we shall not list the abuses among the common people but
discuss only the views of the theologians. As to the rest even the
uninitiated can pass judgment.

Two qualifications must be present if one is to be a propitiator.   17
In the first place, there must be a Word of God to assure us that God
is willing to have mercy and to answer those who call upon him through
this propitiator. For Christ there is such a promise (John 16:23), "If
you ask anything of the Father, he will give it to you in my name."
But for the saints there is no such promise, and hence consciences
cannot be sure that we shall be heard if we invoke the saints. Such an
invocation, therefore, is not based on faith. Furthermore, we have   18
the command to call upon Christ, according to Matthew 11:28, "Come
to me, all who labor," which is certainly addressed to us. Isaiah says
(11:10), "In that day the root of Jesse shall stand as an ensign to the
peoples; him shall the nations seek." Ps. 45:12, 13, "The richest of
the people will sue your favor." Ps. 72:11, 15, "May all kings fall
down before him! May prayer be made for him continually!" In John
5:23 Christ says, "That all may honor the Son, even as they honor
the Father." In II Thess. 2:16, 17 Paul prays, "May our Lord Jesus
Christ himself, and God our Father, comfort your hearts and establish
them." But what precept or example can our opponents produce from
Scripture for the invocation of the saints?

The second qualification in a propitiator is this: His merits   19
must be authorized to make satisfaction for others and to be bestowed on them by divine imputation, so that through them we may
be accounted righteous as though the merits were our own. If one
pays a debt for one's friend, the debtor is freed by the merit of another
as though it were his own. Thus the merits of Christ are bestowed on
us so that when we believe in him we are accounted righteous by our
trust in Christ's merits as though we had merits of our own.

Both the promise and the bestowal of merits are therefore the   20

---

[4] Roman Confutation: "Although His Imperial Majesty, together with
the entire church, confesses that there is one mediator of redemption, yet
there are many mediators of intercession . . ." (Pt. I, Art. XXI).

sources of trust in mercy. Such trust in God's promise and Christ's merits must be the basis for prayer. We must be completely certain that we are heard for Christ's sake and that by his merits we have a gracious Father.

Our opponents tell us, first of all, to invoke the saints, though 21 they have neither God's promise nor a command nor an example from Scripture. Yet they would have us trust more in the mercy of the saints than in the mercy of Christ, though Christ commanded us to come to him and not to the saints. They tell us, secondly, to trust 22 in the merits of the saints. These they apply to others in the same way as Christ's, as though we were accounted righteous on account of them just as we are by Christ's merits. We are not making false charges here. In indulgences they claim to apply the merits of the saints. 23 Gabriel Biel's interpretation of the canon of the Mass confidently declares: "It is a divinely instituted order that we should take refuge in the help of the saints, so that we may be saved by their merits and vows." [5] These are Gabriel's own words. Here and there in our opponents' books and sermons there are even greater absurdities. What is this if not to make the saints propitiators? If we are to trust in them for our salvation, they are being put on the same level as Christ.

Where is the "divinely instituted order that we should take 24 refuge in the help of the saints," as this man says? Let him produce one example or precept from Scripture. Perhaps they derive this "order" from the usage at royal courts, where friends must be used as intercessors. But if a king has appointed a certain intercessor, he does not want appeals to be addressed to him through others. Since Christ has been appointed as our intercessor and high priest, why seek others?

In some places this form of absolution is used: "The passion 25 of our Lord Jesus Christ and the merits of the most blessed virgin Mary and of all the saints be to thee for the forgiveness of sins." According to this declaration of absolution, we are reconciled and accounted righteous not only by Christ's merits but also by the merits of other saints. Some of us have seen a certain monastic theolo- 26 gian, summoned to console a dying doctor of theology, do nothing but urge this prayer upon the dying man, "Mother of grace, protect us from the enemy and receive us in the hour of death."

Granted that blessed Mary prays for the church, does she re- 27 ceive souls in death, does she overcome death, does she give life? What does Christ do if blessed Mary does all this? Even though she is worthy of the highest honors, she does not want to be put on the same level as Christ but to have her example considered and followed. The 28 fact of the matter is that in popular estimation the blessed Virgin has

[5] Gabriel Biel, *Exposition of the Canon of the Mass*, 30.

completely replaced Christ. Men have invoked her, trusted in her mercy, and sought through her to appease Christ, as though he were not a propitiator but only a terrible judge and avenger. We main- 29 tain that we dare not trust in the transfer of the saints' merits to us, as though God were reconciled to us or accounted us righteous or saved us on this account. We obtain the forgiveness of sins only by Christ's merits when we believe in him. About the other saints it has been said (I Cor. 3:8), "Each shall receive his wages according to his labor"; that is, they cannot bestow their merits on one another, like the monks who peddle the merits of their orders. Hilary says of 30 the foolish virgins: "Since the foolish virgins could not go out with their lamps extinguished, they begged the wise ones to lend them oil. These replied that they could not give it for fear that there might not be enough for all. No one can be helped by the works or merits of others, for everyone must buy oil for his own lamp." [6]

Our opponents teach that we should put our trust in the invoca- 31 tion of the saints, though they have neither a Word of God nor an example from Scripture for this. They apply the merits of the saints in the same way as the merits of Christ and thus transfer to the saints the honor that belongs to Christ. Therefore we cannot accept either their ideas about venerating the saints or their practice of praying to them. We know that we must put our trust in the intercession of Christ because only this has God's promise. We know that the merits of Christ are our only propitiation. Because of them we are accounted righteous when we believe in him, as the text says (Rom. 9:33), "He who believes in him will not be put to shame." We must not believe that we are accounted righteous by the merits of the blessed Virgin or of the other saints.

Even the theologians hold to the error that each saint has a 32 special sphere of activity assigned to him. Thus Anne grants riches, Sebastian wards off pestilence, Valentine heals epilepsy, and George protects knights. Such notions are obviously of pagan origin. The Romans thought that Juno granted riches, Febris warded off fever, and Castor and Pollux protected knights. Even supposing that 33 the invocation of saints could be taught with great moderation, the precedent still would be dangerous. Why should it be defended if it has no command or proof in the Word of God? In fact, there is no proof for it either in the Fathers of the church. As I have said 34 earlier, our whole knowledge of Christ disappears if we seek out other mediators besides Christ and put our trust in them. Let us look at this as it really is. It seems that when the saints were first mentioned, as in the ancient prayers, this was not done in a reprehensible way.

[6] Hilary, *Commentary on the Gospel according to Matthew*, 27:5 (on Matt. 25:8, 9).

Afterwards came invocation, with abuses that were enormous and worse than pagan. From invocation the next step was to images. Men venerated these and thought they contained some sort of magical power, just as sorcerers imagine that horoscopes carved at a particular time contain power. In one monastery we saw a statue of the blessed Virgin which was manipulated like a puppet so that it seemed to nod Yes or No to the petitioners.

But all these marvelous tales about statues and pictures do not   35 even compare with the fairy tales about the saints which are being taught in public on the highest authority. In the midst of her tortures, Barbara asks for a reward—that no one who calls upon her should die without the Eucharist. Another one recited the whole Psalter every day while standing on one foot. Some smart person painted Christopher in such a way as to symbolize that those who would carry Christ, that is, those who would teach or confess the Gospel, must be strong of soul because they have to undergo great danger. Then the foolish monks taught the people to call on Christopher, as though there had really been such a Polyphemus. The great things that   36 the saints have done serve as examples to men in their public or private life, as a means of confirming their faith and as an incentive to imitate them in public affairs. But these no one has sought out in the true stories about the saints. The saints administered public affairs, underwent troubles and dangers, helped kings in times of great danger, taught the Gospel, battled against heretics. It is truly worthwhile to hear of these things and to see some examples of mercy. Peter was forgiven for denying Christ; Cyprian was forgiven for having been a sorcerer; Augustine experienced the power of faith in sickness and constantly affirmed that God hears the prayers of believers. It would be useful to recall such examples as these which talk about faith or fear or the administration of public affairs. But the inventors of   37 these fables, which imitate the epics and bring only superstitious examples of certain prayers, fasts, and other profitable ceremonies, are clowns who know nothing about either faith or public affairs. There is no point in listing here the miracles they have invented about rosaries and similar ceremonies, or the legends,[7] as they call them, and the mirrors and the rosaries,[8] all of which contain many things that resemble the "true stories" of Lucian.[9]

Bishops, theologians, and monks applaud these monstrous and   38 ungodly tales because they make money. And they refuse to tolerate us because we do not require the invocation of saints and condemn

[7] The most popular medieval collection was the *Golden Legends* of the thirteenth century.

[8] Popular titles, like *Speculum perfectionis*.

[9] Lucian of Samosata, Greek satirist of the second century.

abuses in the worship of saints in order to emphasize the honor and the work of Christ. Good men everywhere have been hoping that 39 the bishops would exert their authority and the preachers do their duty in correcting these abuses; but in the Confutation our opponents completely ignore even the obvious offenses, as though they intended, by forcing our acceptance of the Confutation, to compel us to approve of the most notorious abuses.

At this point, and almost everywhere else, the Confutation is a 40 deceitful document. Nowhere do they distinguish between their teachings and obvious abuses. Yet anyone in their party with a little sense would admit that the teachings of the scholastics and canonists contain many false opinions and that the ignorance and negligence of the pastors permitted many abuses to creep into the church. Luther 41 was not the first to complain about public abuses. Long before, there were many learned and outstanding men who deplored the abuses of the Mass, the trust in monastic observances, the mercenary worship of the saints, the confusion in the doctrine of penitence which ought to be as clear and plain as possible in the church. We ourselves have heard excellent theologians ask for limitations upon scholastic doctrine because it leads to philosophical disputes rather than to piety. The earlier scholastics are usually closer to Scripture than the more recent ones, so their theology has steadily degenerated. Those who sided with Luther from the outset did so because they saw that he was freeing human minds from the labyrinthine confusions and endless disputations of the scholastic theologians and canonists and was teaching things profitable for godliness.

Therefore it was dishonest of our opponents to ignore abuses 42 when they required us to accept the Confutation. If they really had the good of the church at heart at this point, they would ask that our most gracious emperor take steps to correct the abuses, for clearly he is most anxious for the healing and improving of the church. Instead of supporting this most honorable and holy desire of the emperor, our opponents are doing everything to crush us. They give many 43 indications that the state of the church does not concern them very much. They make no effort to provide a summary of the doctrines of the church for the people. They defend obvious abuses with new and illegal cruelty. They do not tolerate capable clergy in the churches. This way of doing things helps neither their position nor the church, and good men can easily gauge its outcome. After the good clergy have been killed and sound doctrine crushed, fanatical spirits will arise whom our opponents will be unable to restrain. They will trouble the church with their godless teachings and overthrow the whole organization of the church, which we are very anxious to maintain.

Therefore, gracious Emperor Charles, for the sake of the glory 44 of Christ, which we know you want to extol and advance, we implore you not to agree to the violent counsels of our opponents but to find other honorable ways of establishing harmony — ways that will not burden faithful consciences nor persecute innocent men, as has happened before, nor crush sound doctrine in the church. It is your special responsibility before God to maintain and propagate sound doctrine and to defend those who teach it. God demands this when he honors kings with his own name and calls them gods (Ps. 82:6), "I say, 'You are gods.'" They should take care to maintain and propagate divine things on earth, that is, the Gospel of Christ, and as vicars of God they should defend the life and safety of the innocent.

[ARTICLE XXII.] THE LORD'S SUPPER UNDER BOTH KINDS

There can be no doubt that the use of both kinds in the Lord's | Supper is godly and in accord with the institution of Christ and the words of Paul. For Christ instituted both kinds, and he did not do so only for part of the church, but for all of the church. By divine authority and not by human authority, as we suppose our opponents admit, all of the church uses the sacrament, not only the priests. If Christ instituted it for all of the church, why is one kind 2 taken away from part of the church and its use prohibited? Why is Christ's ordinance changed, especially since he himself calls it his testament? If it is illegal to annul a man's testament, it is much more illegal to annul Christ's. Paul says (I Cor. 11:23, 24) 3 that he had received from the Lord what he was delivering, but the text clearly shows that this was the use of both kinds. "Do this," Christ says first about the body; later he says the same about the cup. Later on he says, "Let a man examine himself, and so eat of the bread and drink of the cup." These are the words of him who instituted the sacrament; previously he had said that those who would use the Lord's Supper should use it jointly. It is evident, therefore, that 4 the entire sacrament was instituted for the whole church. In the Greek churches this practice still remains, and once it prevailed in the Latin church, as Cyprian[1] and Jerome attest. In his commentary on Zephaniah, Jerome says, "The priests who serve the Eucharist and distribute the blood of the Lord to the people."[2] The Council of Toledo gives the same testimony,[3] and it would not be hard to collect a great multitude of testimonies. We are not 5 exaggerating here, but we leave it to the prudent reader to decide what he should believe about a divine ordinance.

In the Confutation our opponents do not even try to explain 6

---

[1] *Epistles,* 57.

[2] Jerome, *Commentary on Zephaniah,* chap. 3.

[3] Council of Toledo (A.D. 633), canon 7.

to the church why one part of the sacrament has been withheld. This is what good religious men ought to do. They should have given the church a valid explanation to instruct those who were not permitted to receive the entire sacrament. These men maintain that it is right to deny one part, and they refuse to grant both kinds. They 7 cannot produce any ancient examples to prove their fiction that in the beginning of the church it was customary in some places to administer only one part. They quote passages that mention bread, like Luke 24:35, which says that the disciples recognized Christ in the breaking of the bread. They quote other passages that talk about the breaking of the bread.[4] We do not seriously object if someone takes these passages as referring to the sacrament. Still it does not follow that only one part was given; for by the ordinary usage of language, naming one part also signifies the other. They also 8 refer to "lay communion."[5] But this was not the use of only one kind. When priests were commanded to use lay communion, this indicated that they had been unfrocked and were no longer permitted to consecrate the elements. Our opponents know this very well, but they throw sand in the eyes of the uninitiated, who when they hear the phrase "lay communion" immediately imagine that it means our present custom of giving the laity only a part of the sacrament.

Look at the effrontery of the men! Among the reasons why 9 both kinds are not given, Gabriel says that a distinction should be made between laity and clergy.[6] This is no doubt the main reason for defending the denial of one part: to elevate the position of the clergy by a religious rite. To put it as mildly as possible, this is a human device and its purpose is quite evident. In the Confuta- 10 tion they also mention the case of Eli's sons; after the loss of the high priesthood, they were supposed to ask for the one part that belonged to the priests (I Sam. 2:36). They say this indicates the use of one kind, and they add, "Thus our laity should be satisfied with the one part offered by the priest, that is, with one kind." Our opponents are obviously clowning when they apply the story of Eli's sons to the sacrament. The story describes Eli's punishment. Do they also want to say that the laity has been kept from the one kind as a punishment? The sacrament was instituted to console and strengthen terrified hearts when they believe that Christ's flesh, given for the life of the world, is their food and that they come to life by

---

[4] Acts 2:42, 46; 20:7.

[5] Roman Confutation: "There has always been a distinction in the church between lay communion under one kind and priestly communion under both kinds" (Pt. II, Art. I).

[6] Gabriel Biel, *Exposition of the Canon of the Mass*, 84.

being joined to Christ. Our opponents argue that the laity has been kept from the one kind as a punishment. They say, "They should be satisfied."

This is the way a tyrant would act. But why should they be   11 satisfied? They should not ask for a reason; but whatever the theologians say, let that be law! These are the dregs of Eck.[7] We recognize these Thrasonian voices,[8] and if we wanted to answer them we would have enough to say. Look at the great effrontery of the man. Like some tyrant in a play, he commands, "Whether they like it or not, they should be satisfied!" In the judgment of God, 12 will the reasons he gives exonerate those who withhold a part of the sacrament and rage against good men who use the entire sacrament? If they withhold it to make a distinction of orders, this in 13 itself should keep us from agreeing with our opponents, even though otherwise we might want to maintain their practice. There are other distinctions of order between priest and people, but there is no mystery as to why they defend this distinction so zealously. But to avoid the impression that we are minimizing the real dignity of the order, we shall not say anything more about their crafty designs.

They also refer to the danger of spilling and similar factors[9] 14 which are not cogent enough to change Christ's ordinance. Even 15 if we grant the freedom to use one kind or both, how can they make the withholding of one kind mandatory? But the church cannot arrogate to itself the freedom to call Christ's ordinances matters of indifference. We do not blame the church, which has suffered 16 this injury because it could not obtain both parts; but we do blame the writers who defend the legitimacy of withholding both kinds in the sacrament and who even excommunicate and violently persecute anyone that uses the entire sacrament. Let them figure out how they will account to God for their decisions. Nor dare we assume that 17 the church immediately approves or accepts whatever the pontiffs decide, especially when Scripture prophesies about bishops and pastors in the words of Ezekiel (7:26), "The law perishes from the priest."

---

[7] John Eck was a leading opponent of the Lutherans at the Diet of Augsburg.

[8] Thraso was a loud-mouthed soldier in Terence's *The Eunuch*.

[9] Roman Confutation: ". . . On account of many dangers the custom of administering both kinds ceased. For when the multitude of people is considered, where there are old and young, tremulous and weak and awkward, if great care is not exercised harm is done to the sacrament by the spilling of the liquid. Because of the great multitude there would also be difficulty in giving the chalice cautiously for the species of wine. Moreover, when kept for a long time, this would sour and cause nausea or vomiting to those who received it. Nor could it be taken readily to the sick without danger of spilling . . ." (Pt. II, Art. I).

[ARTICLE XXIII. THE MARRIAGE OF PRIESTS]

Despite the notoriety of their defiled celibacy, our opponents 1
not only use the wicked and false pretext of divine authority for
their audacious defense of the pontifical law, but they even urge
the emperor and the princes not to let the Roman Empire be dis-
graced and shamed by the marriage of priests. This is exactly what
they say.[1]

Where in any history can one read of greater brazenness than 2
that of our opponents? We shall review their arguments in a moment.
First, let the intelligent reader consider the impudence of these good-
for-nothings who say that marriage disgraces and shames the empire,
as if the church were adorned by the public disgrace and the unnatural lusts of the holy fathers "who look like Curius and live like
Bacchantes." [2] Most of the things these men do with utter abandon
cannot even be mentioned without blushing. They ask you to 3
defend these libidos of theirs with your chaste right hand, Emperor
Charles—you whom even some of the ancient prophecies call the
king with the modest face, for the saying appears about you, "A
man with a modest face will reign everywhere." [3] In opposition to
divine law, the law of the nations, and the canons of the councils,
they demand that you dissolve marriages. And merely because of
their marriage, you sentence innocent men to cruel punishments,
slaughter priests whom even the barbarians reverently spare, and
banish deserted wives and orphaned children. To you, our most
chaste and excellent Emperor, they propose laws which no barbarous
country, however savage or cruel, would consider. Because your 4
conduct is free of disgrace and cruelty, we hope that you will deal
kindly with us in this case, especially when you learn that for our
position we have the most serious of reasons, taken from the Word
of God, while our opponents set against them their own foolish and
vain opinions.

But they are not serious in their defense of celibacy. They 5
know good and well how few practice chastity, but they use religion
as a pretext to maintain their authority, which they think celibacy
enhances. Now we see the correctness of Peter's warning (II Pet. 2:1)
that false prophets would deceive people with their fictions. Our
opponents will not speak, write, or act honestly, frankly, or openly

---

[1] Roman Confutation: ". . . They [the Lutheran princes] call sacerdotal
celibacy an abuse when the direct contrary, the violation of celibacy and
unlawful transition to marriage, deserves to be called the worst abuse in
priests . . . . The princes ought not tolerate it, to the perpetual shame and
disgrace of the Roman Empire, but should rather conform with the universal
church . . ." (Pt. II, Art. II).

[2] Juvenal, Satires, II, 3.

[3] Sibylline Oracles, VIII, 169, 170.

in this whole business. All they are actually fighting for is their authority; they imagine that this is in danger and they are trying to fortify it with a wicked pretense of godliness.

We cannot approve the law of celibacy put forth by our op- 6 ponents because it clashes with divine and natural law and conflicts with the very decrees of councils.[4] It obviously endangers religion and morality, for it produces endless scandals, sins, and the corruption of public morals. Our other controversies call for some theological discussion, but in this one the situation is so clear that no discussion is necessary, only the judgment of any honest and God-fearing man. In the face of the clear truth which we have advanced, our opponents have thought up some subterfuges to satirize our position.

First, Gen. 1:28 teaches that men were created to be fruitful 7 and that one sex should have a proper desire for the other. We are not talking about sinful lust but about so-called "natural love," the desire which was meant to be in uncorrupted nature. This love of one sex for the other is truly a divine ordinance. Since this ordinance of God cannot be suspended without an extraordinary work of God, it follows that neither regulations nor vows can abolish the right to contract marriage.

Our opponents reply with the silly argument that originally 8 there was a command to replenish the earth, but now that the earth has been replenished marriage is not commanded.[5] Look at their clever argument! The Word of God did not form the nature of men to be fruitful only at the beginning of creation, but it still does as long as this physical nature of ours exists. Just so this Word makes the earth fruitful (Gen. 1:11), "Let the earth put forth vegetation, plants yielding seed." Because of this ordinance, the earth did not begin to bring forth plants only at the beginning, but yearly the fields are clothed as long as this universe exists. Just as human regulations cannot change the nature of the earth, so neither vows nor human regulations can change the nature of man without an extraordinary act of God.

Second, because this creation or divine ordinance in man is a 9 natural right, the jurists have said wisely and correctly that the union of man and woman is by natural right. Now, since natural right is unchangeable, the right to contract marriage must always remain.

[4] The Council of Nicaea rejected a prohibition of sacerdotal marriage. Socrates, *Ecclesiastical History,* I, 11.

[5] Roman Confutation: "The command was then given, concerning the procreation of offspring, that the earth should be replenished. But since it has now been replenished so that there is a pressure of peoples, the commandment no longer pertains to those who are able to be continent . . ." (Pt. II, Art. II).

Where nature does not change, there must remain that ordinance which God has built into nature, and human regulations cannot abolish it. So it is ridiculous for our opponents to say that 10 originally marriage was commanded but that it is no longer commanded. This is the same as saying that formerly men were born with a sex and now they are not, or that originally they were born with a natural right and now they are not. No one could fabricate anything more crafty than this foolishness, thought up in order to circumvent the natural law. Let us therefore keep this fact in 11 mind, taught by Scripture and wisely put by the jurists: The union of man and woman is by natural right. Natural right is really 12 divine right, because it is an ordinance divinely stamped on nature. Since only an extraordinary act of God can change this right, the right to contract marriage necessarily remains. For the natural desire of one sex for the other is an ordinance of God, and therefore it is a right; otherwise, why would both sexes have been created? As we said, we are not talking about sinful lust but about 13 the desire which is called "natural love," which lust did not remove from nature but only inflamed. Now it needs a remedy even more, and marriage is necessary for a remedy as well as for procreation. This is so clear and firm as to be irrefutable.

Third, Paul says (I Cor. 7:2), "Because of the temptation to 14 immorality, each man should have his own wife." This is an express command, directed to anyone not suited for celibacy. Our 15 opponents demand to be shown a command requiring that priests should marry[6]—as though priests were not human beings. We maintain that whatever applies to human nature in general, applies to priests as well. Is not Paul here commanding those to marry who 16 do not have the gift of continence? He interprets himself a little later when he says (v. 9), "It is better to marry than to be aflame with passion." And Christ clearly said (Matt. 19:11), "Not all men can receive this precept, but only those to whom it is given." Ever since man sinned, natural desire and the lust that inflames it come together; therefore marriage is more necessary now than in the state of purity. Hence Paul speaks of marriage as a remedy and commands it because of these flaming passions. Because human authority, regulations, and vows cannot abolish either nature or lust, they cannot abolish the statement, "It is better to marry than to be aflame with passion." Thus anyone who is aflame retains the right to marry. Paul's command, "Because of the temptation of immorality, each 17

---

[6] Roman Confutation: "In vain, too, do they boast of God's express command. Let them show, if they can, where God has commanded priests to marry" (Pt. II, Art. II).

man should have his own wife," binds all those who are not truly continent. It is up to each man's conscience to decide this matter.

Here they order men to pray God for continence and to subdue 18 their bodies with labors and fasting.[7] Why do they not apply these magnificent commandments to themselves? As we said before, our opponents are only clowning; they do not mean this seriously. If 19 continence were possible for everyone, it would not require a special gift. Christ shows that it does require a special gift; therefore, it is not for everyone. God wants the rest to use the universal law of nature which he has instituted, for he does not want us to despise his ordinances, his creatures. He wants men to be chaste by using the remedy he offers, just as he wants to nourish our life by using food and drink. Gerson testifies that many good men have 20 tried to control their body but without much success.[8] Therefore Ambrose correctly observes, "Virginity is something that can only be recommended, but not commanded; it is voluntary rather than obligatory."[9] If someone raises the objection here that Christ 21 commends those "who have made themselves eunuchs for the sake of the kingdom of heaven" (Matt. 19:12), let him remember that Christ is praising those who have the gift of continence and therefore adds, "He who is able to receive this, let him receive it." Impure 22 continence does not please Christ. We, too, commend true continence, but now we are arguing about the regulation and about those who do not have the gift of continence. The matter should be left free, and no snares should be set for the weak through this regulation.

Fourth, the pontifical regulation also disagrees with the canons 23 of the councils. The ancient canons do not forbid marriage, nor dissolve marriages that have been contracted, though they remove those from the public ministry who married while in office. In those times such a dismissal was an act of kindness. These new canons do not represent the decision of the synods but the private judgment of the popes. They forbid the contracting of marriages and dissolve them once they have been contracted, and all this in open defiance of Christ's command (Matt. 19:6), "What God has joined together, let no man put asunder." In the Confutation our opponents 24

---

[7] Roman Confutation: ". . . Those who are consecrated to God have other remedies [than marriage] for infirmities. For example, let them avoid the society of women, shun idleness, mortify the flesh by fasting and vigils, keep the outward senses (especially sight and hearing) from things forbidden, turn away their eyes from beholding vanity, and finally dash their little ones (that is, their carnal thoughts) on a rock (and Christ is the rock), suppress their passions, and frequently and devoutly resort to God in prayer. These are undoubtedly the most effectual remedies for incontinence in ecclesiastics and servants of God . . ." (Pt. II, Art. II).

[8] Perhaps John Gerson, *On Celibacy,* 3.

[9] Ambrose, *Exhortation to Virginity,* 3:17.

shriek that the councils have commanded celibacy. We do not object to the councils, for they do allow marriage under certain circumstances; but we do object to the regulations which the Roman pontiffs have set up since the ancient synods and contrary to their authority. The pontiffs show contempt for the authority of the synods while they want others to accept it as sacrosanct. Thus the regulation   25 about perpetual celibacy is peculiar to this new pontifical tyranny, and with good reason; Daniel says that it is characteristic of Antichrist's kingdom to despise women (11:37).

Fifth, although our opponents do not defend this regulation   26 for religious reasons, since they see that it is not being observed, still they cloak it with pious-sounding phrases to give it a religious front. They claim that they require celibacy because it is pure, as though marriage were impure and sinful or as though celibacy merited justification more than marriage. For this they refer to the   27 ceremonies of the Mosaic law which prescribed that during the period of their ministration the priests of the Old Testament were to be separated from their wives; since the priests of the New Testament must pray continually, they must also preserve perpetual continence. This clumsy analogy is presented as a proof to force perpetual celibacy on priests, though in this very analogy marriage is permitted and intercourse is forbidden only during the period of ministration. Besides, prayer is one thing and ministration another. The saints prayed even when they were not carrying on their public ministry, and marital intercourse did not keep them from praying.

We shall reply to these figments one by one. In the first   28 place, our opponents must admit that for believers marriage is pure because it has been sanctified by the Word of God; that is, it is something which the Word of God permits and approves, as the Scriptures abundantly testify. Christ calls marriage a divine union   29 when he says in Matt. 19:6, "What God has joined together." Paul says marriage, food, and similar things are "consecrated by   30 the word of God and prayer" (I Tim. 4:5): by the Word which assures the conscience that God approves, and by prayer, that is, by faith which uses it gratefully as a gift of God. In I Cor. 7:14   31 he says, "The unbelieving husband is consecrated through his wife"; that is, the use of marriage is permissible and holy through faith in Christ just as the use of food, etc. is permissible. In I Tim. 2:15   32 he says, "Woman will be saved through bearing children." If our opponents could produce a passage like that about celibacy, they would stage a wonderful victory celebration. Paul says that woman is saved through bearing children. In contrast to the hypocrisy of celibacy, what greater honor could he bestow than to say that woman is saved by the marital functions themselves, by marital intercourse, by childbirth, and by her other domestic duties? What does Paul say? Let the reader note that he adds faith and does not praise domestic duties apart from faith: "if she continues," he says, "in faith." He is talking about the whole class of mothers, and above all he requires the faith by which a woman accepts the forgiveness of sins and justification. Then he adds a certain task of her calling, as performance of the tasks of a particular calling should follow everyone's faith, pleasing God because of faith. So a woman's duties please God because of faith, and a believing woman is saved if she serves faithfully in these duties of her calling.

These passages teach that marriage is a lawful thing. If purity 33 means that something has God's permission and approval, then marriages are pure since they are approved by the Word of God. Paul 34 says about lawful things (Tit. 1:15), "To the pure all things are pure," that is, to believers in Christ who are righteous by faith. As virginity is impure in the ungodly, therefore, so marriage is pure in the godly, through the Word of God and faith.

In the second place, the proper contrast is between lust and 35 purity understood as the purity of the heart and the mortification of lust; it is not marriage that the law forbids, but lust, adultery, and promiscuity. Therefore celibacy is not necessarily pure. There may be greater purity of heart in a married man like Abraham or Jacob than in many others who are truly continent.

Finally, if they interpret celibacy as a purity that merits justi- 36 fication more than marriage does, we shall really object. Neither by virginity nor by marriage are we justified, but freely for Christ's sake when we believe that for his sake God is gracious to us. Here they may cry out that we put marriage on the same 37 level with virginity, as Jovinian did.[1] But no such outcry will make us surrender the truth of the righteousness of faith, as we have expounded it above. We do not put marriage on the same level 38 with virginity. One gift surpasses another. Thus prophecy surpasses eloquence, military science surpasses agriculture, and eloquence surpasses architecture. So also virginity is a gift that surpasses marriage. But as eloquence does not make an orator more righteous 39 before God than building makes an architect, so the virgin does not merit justification by virginity any more than the married person does by performing the duties of marriage. Each should serve faithfully in what he has been given to do, believing that for Christ's sake he obtains the forgiveness of sins and that through faith he is accounted righteous before God.

Neither Christ nor Paul commends virginity because it justifies 40 but because it gives more time for praying, teaching, and serving

---

[1] See above, Augsburg Confession, XXVI, 30.

and is not so distracted by household chores. This is why Paul says (I Cor. 7:32), "The unmarried man is anxious about the affairs of the Lord." He commends virginity for the sake of meditation and study. Thus Christ does not simply commend those who make themselves eunuchs, but he adds, "for the sake of the kingdom of heaven" (Matt. 19:12), that is, to make room for hearing or teaching the Gospel. He does not say that virginity merits salvation or the forgiveness of sins.

As for the analogy with the Levitical priests, we have already 41 answered that this does not make it necessary to impose perpetual celibacy on priests. In addition, the Levitical laws about uncleanness do not apply to us. Intercourse contrary to these laws was uncleanness; now it is not, for Paul says (Titus 1:15), "To the pure all things are pure." The Gospel frees us from these Levitical regulations about impurity. If anybody supports the law of celibacy in order to 42 burden consciences with these Levitical observances, we must definitely resist him as the apostles in Acts 15 resisted those who required circumcision and tried to impose the law of Moses on Christians.

At the same time good men will know how to use marriage 43 moderately, especially when they are occupied with public service, which is often so burdensome to good men that domestic problems are excluded from their minds. Good men know, too, that Paul commands each one to possess his vessel in holiness (I Thess. 4:4). They know that sometimes they must withdraw to have opportunity for prayer, but Paul does not want this to be perpetual (I Cor. 7:5). Such continence is easy for the godly and busy. But it 44 is all too evident that the great crowd of lazy priests in the confraternities, where they can live voluptuously, cannot even keep this Levitical continence. We all know the verse, "The boy who is used to being lazy hates those who are busy." [2]

Many heretics have misunderstood the law of Moses; there- 45 fore they have spoken contemptuously about marriage and admiringly about celibacy. Epiphanius complains that this characteristic among the Encratites captured the imagination of the unwary.[3] They abstained from wine, even in the Lord's Supper; they abstained from the meat of all animals, thus surpassing the Dominican friars, who eat fish. They also abstained from marriage, and this called forth the most admiration. They thought they would merit grace by performing these works and services instead of using wine or meat or marriage, which seemed profane and unclean and hardly pleasing to God, even though it was not completely condemned.

[2] Ovid, *Cures for Love*, 149.
[3] The Encratites were ascetic vegetarians in the primitive church, some of whom were later influenced by Gnosticism. Epiphanius, *Heresies*, 46, 47.

Paul condemns such "worship of angels" in Colossians (2:18).   46
It surpasses the knowledge of Christ by making men believe that
through such hypocrisy they are pure and righteous. It obscures the
recognition of God's commands and gifts, which he wants us to use
devoutly. We could mention cases of godly consciences being   47
very troubled about the legitimacy of being married. The origin of
this evil is the exaggerated way the monks have praised celibacy.
We do not disparage temperance or continence; we have said   48
before that discipline and restraint of the body are necessary. But we
deny that one should trust in certain observances for righteousness.
In the excellent phrase of Epiphanius, such observances should   49
be praised "for the sake of discipline and the common weal" [4] (that is,
for the discipline of the body and for public morality), just as certain
rites were introduced as lessons for the ignorant and not as services
that justify.

Our opponents do not demand celibacy for religious reasons,   50
for they know that chastity is not the usual thing. They use religion
as a pretext to put something over on the ignorant. They are therefore more contemptible than the Encratites, who seem to have gone
astray through some sort of religion. These Epicureans[5] purposely
use religion as a pretext.

Sixth, we have many reasons for rejecting the law of per-   51
petual celibacy. But even if the law were not unjust, it is dangerous
to public and private morals; this alone should keep good men from
approving a burden that has destroyed so many souls.

Good men have been complaining about this burden for a long   52
time, either for themselves or for those whom they saw in danger,
but none of the popes listened to these complaints. It is no secret
how harmful this law has been to public morals and how productive
of vices and shameful lusts. In its satires Rome still reads and recognizes its own morals.[6]

So God takes revenge against those who despise his gift and   53
ordinance and forbid marriage. Since it has been customary to change
other laws if the common good demanded it, why was not the same
done to this law? There are so many good reasons for changing it,
especially in these last times. Nature is growing older and progres-
sively weaker, so that we ought to use the remedies God has given
us. The destruction in the flood and the burning of Sodom and   54
Gomorrah reveal God's wrath at human vice. Similar vices have
preceded the fall of many other cities, like Sybaris and Rome. This

---

[4] Epiphanius, *Panarion haer.,* 47:1, 6.

[5] *Sardanapal,* proverbial for effeminate or soft-living person.

[6] The reference is to satires of contemporary life, especially to those posted
in Rome during the annual Pasquino festival between 1504 and 1518.

has given us a picture of the times that will precede the end of all things. In a time like this it was appropriate to guard marriage 55 with the strictest laws and examples and to invite men to it. This is the duty of public officials, who ought to maintain public order. Meanwhile, preachers of the Gospel should exhort the incontinent to marry and also exhort others not to despise the gift of continence.

Daily the pontiffs dispense and change other good laws; on 56 this one law of celibacy they are adamant and inexorable, though it is obviously a matter of simple human right. Now they are 57 making the law even more unbearable in several ways. The canon commands that priests be suspended;[7] our canonists suspend them all right—not from office but from trees! They cruelly kill men just because they are married. Such murders show that this law is 58 a doctrine of demons (I Tim. 4:1-3); since the devil is a murderer (John 8:44), he uses these murders to defend his law.

We know we are laying ourselves open to the charge of 59 schism because we seem to have separated ourselves from those who are regarded as the regular bishops. But our consciences are at ease. Despite our most earnest desire to establish harmony, we know that to satisfy our opponents we would have to reject the clear truth. We would have to go along with our opponents in the defense of this unjust law, the dissolution of existing marriages, the murder of priests who refuse to submit, and the exile of poor women and orphaned children. Since these conditions are certainly displeasing to God, we do not regret our lack of an alliance with such murderous opponents.

We have explained why we cannot conscientiously agree with 60 our opponents in their defense of the pontifical law of perpetual celibacy. It conflicts with divine and natural law; it disagrees even with the canons; it is superstitious and full of danger; finally, the whole thing is a fraud. The real purpose of the law is not religion but domination, for which religion is just a wicked pretext. No sane man can argue with these cogent facts. The Gospel permits 61 marriage for those who need it, but it does not force marriage on anyone who wants to remain continent, as long as he is really continent. We believe that priests should have this same freedom; we refuse to force anyone into celibacy or to dissolve existing marriages.

In presenting our own arguments, we have incidentally recited 62 and refuted the silly counter-arguments of our opponents. Now we shall briefly review their weighty arguments in defense of the law. They say, first, that it was revealed by God.[8] Just look at these 63

---

[7] Synod of Rome (1078), canon 11.

[8] Roman Confutation: "The holy martyr Cyprian testifies that it was revealed to him by the Lord, and he was most solemnly enjoined earnestly to admonish the clergy not to occupy houses in common with women. Hence,

impudent rascals! They dare to claim divine revelation for the law of perpetual celibacy, though it conflicts with clear passages of Scripture commanding each man to have his own wife because of the temptation to immorality (I Cor. 7:2) and forbidding the dissolution of existing marriages (Matt. 19:6). Paul points out the real author of such a law when he calls it a "doctrine of demons" (I Tim. 4:1). The real author is evident in the results, the many unnatural lusts and the many murders for which this law provides an excuse.

The second argument of our opponents is that priests should 64 be pure, according to the statement (Isa. 52:11), "Purify yourselves, you who bear the vessels of the Lord." [9] They give many quotations to support this. We have already refuted this very specious argument. We have said that without faith virginity is not pure in the sight of God, and that because of faith marriage is pure, according to the statement (Titus 1:15), "To the pure all things are pure." We have also said that the outward ceremonies and purity laws of the Old Testament do not apply here because the Gospel requires purity of the heart and not ceremonies of the law. It is possible that the heart of married men like Abraham and Jacob, who were polygamists, was purer and less inflamed with lust than that of many celibates who are really continent. Isaiah's words, "Purify yourselves, you who bear the vessels of the Lord," must be taken to mean purity of the heart and total penitence. Besides, the saints will know the 65 value of moderation in marital intercourse and of what Paul calls possessing one's vessel in holiness (I Thess. 4:4). Finally, since 66 marriage is pure, it is right to say that those who are not continent in celibacy should marry in order to be pure. Thus the same law, "Purify yourselves, you who bear the vessels of the Lord," requires impure celibates to become pure husbands.

Their third argument is horrible: the marriage of priests is 67 the Jovinian heresy.[1] Fine talk! This is a new charge, that marriage is a heresy! In Jovinian's time the world still did not know the law of perpetual celibacy. So it is a shameless lie to say that the marriage of priests is the Jovinian heresy or that the church condemned marriage at that time. Such statements show our op- 68 ponents' purpose in writing the Confutation. They decided that the

---

since sacerdotal celibacy has been commanded by the pontiffs, revealed by God, and promised by the priest in a special vow, it must not be rejected ..." (Pt. II, Art II). Cf. Pseudo-Cyprian, *The Singularity of the Clergy*, 1.

[9] Roman Confutation: "Priests who frequently eat Christ our Passover ought to gird their loins with continence and cleanliness as the Lord commands them. 'Be ye clean,' he says, 'that bear the vessels of the Lord' (Isa. 52:11) ..." (Pt. II, Art. II).

[1] Roman Confutation: "This is manifestly the ancient heresy of Jovinian which the Roman Church condemned and Jerome refuted in his writings" (Pt. II, Art. II). Cf. above, Augsburg Confession, XXVI, 30.

best way to arouse the ignorant was to raise the cry of heresy against us over and over, and to give the impression that our cause had been tried and convicted by many previous tribunals of the church. So they often misquote these tribunals of the church. They are well aware of this; hence they refuse to show us a copy of the Confutation, lest their fraud and slander be exposed. We have previously 69 stated our position in the Jovinian controversy on the relative value of marriage and celibacy.[2] We do not put marriage and virginity on the same level, but neither virginity nor marriage merits justification.

With false arguments like these they defend a wicked and im- 70 moral law. With reasons like these they persuade the princes to take a position contrary to the judgment of God, who will call them to account for breaking up marriages and torturing and killing priests. Have no doubt that as the blood of Abel cried out in death (Gen. 4:10), so the blood of the many innocent victims of their rage will also cry out. God will avenge this cruelty. Then you will see the emptiness of our opponents' arguments and understand that in the judgment of God no perversion of God's Word will stand, as Isaiah says (40:6), "All flesh is grass, and all its beauty is like the flower of the field."

Whatever happens, our princes can have a clear conscience on 71 this matter. Even if the priests had done wrong in marrying, it is certainly contrary to God's will and Word to break up marriages and to issue savage and cruel prohibitions. Our princes do not delight in change for its own sake, but they have greater respect for the Word of God than for anything else, especially when the issue is so clear.

[ARTICLE XXIV.] THE MASS

To begin with, we must repeat the prefatory statement that 1 we do not abolish the Mass but religiously keep and defend it. In our churches Mass is celebrated every Sunday and on other festivals, when the sacrament is offered to those who wish for it after they have been examined and absolved. We keep traditional liturgical forms, such as the order of the lessons, prayers, vestments, etc.

In a long harangue about the use of Latin in the Mass, our 2 clever opponents quibble about how a hearer who is ignorant of the faith of the church benefits from hearing a Mass that he does not understand.[3] Apparently they imagine that mere hearing is a bene-

---

[2] See above, XXIII, 33, 34, 37f.

[3] Roman Confutation: "They perform ecclesiastical rites not in the Latin but in the German language and pretend that they do this on the authority of St. Paul, who taught that in church a language should be used that is understood by the people (I Cor. 14:19) . . . . If the words of the apostle are pondered, it is sufficient that the person responding occupy the place of the unlearned and say 'Amen,' the very thing that the canons prescribe. Nor is it necessary that he hear or understand all the words of the Mass,

ficial act of worship even where there is no understanding. We do 3 not want to belabor this point, but we leave it up to the judgment of the reader. We mention this only in passing in order to point out that our churches keep the Latin lessons and prayers.

The purpose of observing ceremonies is that men may learn the Scriptures and that those who have been touched by the Word may receive faith and fear and so may also pray. Therefore we keep Latin for the sake of those who study and understand it, and we insert German hymns to give the common people something to learn that will arouse their faith and fear. This has always been the 4 custom in the churches. Though German hymns have varied in frequency, yet almost everywhere the people sang in their own language. No one has ever written or suggested that men benefit 5 from hearing lessons they do not understand, or from ceremonies that do not teach or admonish, simply *ex opere operato*, by the mere doing or observing. Out with such pharisaic ideas!

There is nothing contrary to the church catholic in our having 6 only the public or common Mass. Even today, Greek parishes have no private Masses but only one public Mass, and this only on Sundays and festivals. The monasteries have public, though daily, Mass. These are remnants of ancient practice, for the Fathers of the church before Gregory make no mention of private Masses. For the 7 present, we forego any discussion of their origins. But it is clear that the prevalence of the mendicant friars brought on the multiplication of private Masses; so superstitious and so mercenary have they been that for a long time good men have wanted some limits set to them. Although St. Francis sought to regulate this with the provision that each community should be content with a single common daily Mass,[4] reasons of piety or of profit later changed this. So when 8 it suits them, they change the institutions of the Fathers and then quote the authority of the Fathers against us. Epiphanius writes that in Asia Minor there were no daily Masses but Communion was celebrated three times a week, and that this practice came from the apostles. He says, "Assemblies for Communion were appointed by the apostles to be held on the fourth day, on Sabbath eve, and on the Lord's Day."[5]

Our opponents have collected many statements to prove that 9 the Mass is a sacrifice. But all the quotations from the Fathers and

or always direct his attention to it with understanding. It is more important that he understand and be attentive to the purpose, for Mass is celebrated in order that the Eucharist may be offered in memory of Christ's passion" (Pt. II, Art. II).

[4] Francis of Assisi, *Letters to the General Chapter*, 3.
[5] Epiphanius, *Heresies*, Book III.

the arguments they adduce are silenced by the fact that the Mass does not confer grace *ex opere operato,* nor merit for others the forgiveness of venial or mortal sins, of guilt, or of punishment. This single answer refutes all our opponents' objections, both here in the Confutation and in all their other books about the Mass.

We want to remind our readers of the real issue. Aeschines 10 reminded the Jews that both parties in a controversy must deal only with the point at issue and not wander off into side issues, like wrestlers fighting for their position.[6] In the same way our opponents should be forced to discuss the point at issue. Once the real issue of the controversy is clear, it will be easy to evaluate the arguments both sides have presented.

In our Confession we have stated our position that the Lord's 11 Supper does not grant grace *ex opere operato* and does not merit for others, whether living or dead, forgiveness of sins or of guilt or of punishment *ex opere operato.* This position is established and 12 proved by the impossibility of our obtaining the forgiveness of sins *ex opere operato* through our works and by the necessity of faith to conquer the terrors of sins and death and to comfort our hearts with the knowledge of Christ; for his sake we are forgiven, his merits and righteousness are bestowed upon us. "Since we are justified by faith, we have peace" (Rom. 5:1). This is so firm and sure that it can prevail against all the gates of hell.[7]

If this were the whole problem, the case would be settled. 13 No sane person can approve this pharisaic and pagan notion about the working of the Mass *ex opere operato.* Yet this notion has taken hold among the people and has infinitely multiplied the Masses. With the work of these Masses they think they can placate God's wrath, gain the remission of guilt and punishment, secure whatever they need in this life, and even free the dead. The monks and scholastics have brought this pharisaic notion into the church.

Though we have already stated our case, we must add a few 14 things because of the way our opponents have twisted many passages of Scripture in defense of their errors. The Confutation has a great deal to say about sacrifice, though in our Confession we purposely avoided this term because of its ambiguity. We have already described the current understanding of sacrifice among those whose abuses we criticize. Now we shall explain the passages of Scripture which they have distorted, and to do this we must first set down the nature of a sacrifice. For the last ten years our opponents have 15 been publishing almost endless books about sacrifice, but none of them has defined it. They find the term "sacrifice" in either the

[6] *In Ctesiphontem,* 206.
[7] Matt. 16:18.

Scriptures or the Fathers and use it out of context, attaching their own ideas to it as if it meant whatever they want it to mean.

SACRIFICE, ITS NATURE AND TYPES

In Plato's *Phaedrus*, Socrates says that he is very fond of 16 distinctions because without them nothing can be explained or understood in a discussion, and that if he found someone skilled in making them he would follow in his footsteps as those of a god.[8] He tells the person making the distinctions to cut the members at the joint, lest like an unskilled cook he sever the member at the wrong place. Plato would really call our opponents "poor cooks," [9] for they despise these instructions and mutilate the various members of the concept "sacrifice," as our enumeration of the types of sacrifice will make clear. The theologians make a proper distinction between sac- 17 rament and sacrifice. The genus common to both could be "ceremony" or "sacred act." A sacrament is a ceremony or act in 18 which God offers us the content of the promise joined to the ceremony; thus Baptism is not an act which we offer to God but one in which God baptizes us through a minister functioning in his place. Here God offers and presents the forgiveness of sins according to the promise (Mark 16:16), "He who believes and is baptized will be saved." By way of contrast, a sacrifice is a ceremony or act which we render to God to honor him.

There are two, and only two, basic types of sacrifice. One is 19 the propitiatory sacrifice; this is a work of satisfaction for guilt and punishment that reconciles God or placates his wrath or merits the forgiveness of sins for others. The other type is the eucharistic sacrifice; this does not merit the forgiveness of sins or reconciliation, but by it those who have been reconciled give thanks or show their gratitude for the forgiveness of sins and other blessings received.

In this controversy as well as in many others, we must never 20 lose sight of these two types of sacrifice and be very careful not to confuse them. If the limits of this book permitted, we would enumerate the many proofs for this distinction found in the Epistle to the Hebrews and elsewhere.[1] All the Levitical sacrifices can be 21 classified under one or another of these heads. The Old Testament called certain sacrifices propitiatory because of what they signified and foreshadowed. They did not merit the forgiveness of sins in the sight of God, but they did on the basis of the justice of the law; thus those for whom they were offered did not have to be excluded from the commonwealth. They were accordingly called propitiatory sac-

---

[8] Plato, *Phaedrus*, 50:266.
[9] *Ibid.*, 49:265.
[1] Heb. 10:5-16; Ex. 32:6; II Sam. 6:17 *et passim*.

rifices for sin or burnt offerings for trespasses. The eucharistic sacrifices were the oblation, the drink offerings, the thank offering, the first fruits, and the tithes.[2]

There has really been only one propitiatory sacrifice in the 22 world, the death of Christ, as the Epistle to the Hebrews teaches (10:4), "It is impossible that the blood of bulls and goats should take away sins." A little later it says about the will of Christ (v. 10), "By that will we have been sanctified through the offering of the body of Jesus Christ once for all." Isaiah interprets the law to 23 mean that the death of Christ is a real satisfaction or expiation for our sins, as the ceremonies of the law were not; therefore he says (53:10), "When he makes himself an offering for sin, he shall see his offspring, he shall prolong his days." The word he uses here ('asam) means a victim sacrificed for transgression. In the Old Testament this meant that a victim was to come to reconcile God and make satisfaction for our sins, so that men might know that God does not want our own righteousness but the merits of another (namely, of Christ) to reconcile him to us. Paul interprets the same word as "sin" in Rom. 8:3, "As a sin offering he condemned sin," that is, through an offering for sin. We can understand the meaning of the word more readily if we look at the customs which the heathen adopted from their misinterpretation of the patriarchal tradition. The Latins offered a sacrificial victim to placate the wrath of God when, amid great calamities, it seemed to be unusually severe; this they called a trespass offering. Sometimes they offered up human sacrifices, perhaps because they had heard that a human victim was going to placate God for the whole human race. The Greeks called them either "refuse" or "offscouring." [3] Isaiah and Paul mean that Christ became a sacrificial victim or trespass offering to reconcile God by his merits instead of ours. Let this stand in this issue, then, that the death of Christ is the only real propitiatory sacrifice. The Levitical 24 propitiatory sacrifices were so called only as symbols of a future offering. By analogy they were satisfactions since they gained the righteousness of the ceremonial law and prevented the exclusion of the sinner from the commonwealth. But after the revelation of the Gospel they had to stop; therefore they were not really propitiations, since the Gospel was promised in order to set forth a propitiation.

The rest are eucharistic sacrifices, called "sacrifices of praise": 25 the proclamation of the Gospel, faith, prayer, thanksgiving, confession, the afflictions of the saints, yes, all the good works of the saints. These sacrifices are not satisfactions on behalf of those who bring them, nor can they be transferred to merit the forgiveness of sins or

[2] Lev. 1-7.
[3] Cf. I Cor. 4:13.

reconciliation for others *ex opere operato*. Those who bring them are already reconciled. The sacrifices of the New Testament are 26 of this type, as Peter teaches in I Pet. 2:5, "A holy priesthood, to offer spiritual sacrifices." Spiritual sacrifices are contrasted not only with the sacrifices of cattle but also with human works offered *ex opere operato*, for "spiritual" refers to the operation of the Holy Spirit within us. Paul teaches the same in Rom. 12:1, "Present your bodies as a living sacrifice, holy and acceptable to God, which is your spiritual worship." "Spiritual worship" is a worship in which the spirit knows and takes hold of God, as it does when it fears and trusts him. Therefore the contrast is not only with Levitical worship, where cattle were slaughtered, but with any worship where men suppose they are offering God a work *ex opere operato*. The Epistle to the Hebrews teaches the same (13:15): "Through him let us continually offer up a sacrifice of praise to God," with the interpretation, "that is, the fruit of lips that acknowledge his name." He commands them to offer praises, that is, prayer, thanksgiving, confession, and the like. These are valid, not *ex opere operato* but because of faith. We see this from the phrase, "Through him let us offer," namely, through faith in Christ.

In short, the worship of the New Testament is spiritual; it is 27 the righteousness of faith in the heart and the fruits of faith. Thus it abrogates Levitical worship. Christ says in John 4:23, 24, "The true worshipers will worship the Father in spirit and truth, for such the Father seeks to worship him. God is spirit, and those who worship him must worship in spirit and truth." This passage clearly condemns the notion that the sacrifices are valid *ex opere operato*, and it teaches that worship should be in spirit, in faith, and with the heart. The 28 Old Testament prophets also condemn the popular notion of worship *ex opere operato* and teach spiritual righteousness and sacrifice. Jer. 7:22, 23, "I did not speak to your fathers or command them concerning burnt offerings and sacrifices. But this command I gave them, 'Obey my voice, and I will be your God.'" How are we to think the Jews accepted this declaration, which seems to contradict Moses directly? Clearly God had commanded the fathers concerning burnt offerings and sacrifices, but what Jeremiah is condemning is an idea of sacrifices that did not come from God, namely, that such worship pleased him *ex opere operato*. He adds that God had commanded faith. "Obey me," that is, "Believe that I am your God and that this is the way I want you to know me when I show mercy and help you, for I do not need your sacrifices. Believe that I want to be God, the one who justifies and saves, because of my Word and promise, not because of works. Truly and wholeheartedly seek and expect help from me."

Ps. 50:13, 15 also condemns the idea of sacrifices *ex opere* 27
operato. It rejects sacrificial victims and requires prayer: "Do I eat
the flesh of bulls? Call upon me in the day of trouble; I will deliver
you, and you shall glorifiy me." It declares that calling upon God is
really worshiping and honoring him.

Ps. 40:6 says, "Sacrifice and offering thou dost not desire; but
thou hast given me an open ear." That is, "Thou hast offered me thy
Word to hear, and dost require me to believe it and thy promises of
willingness to show mercy and to help." Ps. 51:16, 17 says, "Thou
hast no delight in burnt offering. The sacrifice acceptable to God
is a broken spirit; a broken and contrite heart, O God, thou wilt not
despise." So also Ps. 4:5, "Offer right sacrifices, and put your trust
in the Lord." He commands us to trust and says that this is a right
sacrifice, indicating that other sacrifices are not true and right. And
Ps. 116:17, "I will offer to thee sacrifices of thanksgiving and call
on the name of the Lord." Prayer is called a sacrifice of thanksgiving.

But Scripture is full of such passages which teach that sacrifices 30
do not reconcile God *ex opere operato*. With the abrogation of
Levitical worship, the New Testament teaches that there should be
a new and pure sacrifice; this is faith, prayer, thanksgiving, confession
and proclamation of the Gospel, suffering because of the Gospel, etc.

About such sacrifices Malachi says (1:11), "From the rising 31
of the sun to its setting my name is great among the nations, and in
every place incense is offered to my name, and a pure offering."
Our opponents misinterpret this passage and apply it to the Mass,
and for this they quote patristic authority. The answer is easy. Even
if this were a reference to the Mass, it would not follow that the
Mass justifies *ex opere operato* or that it merits the forgiveness of
sins when it is transferred to others. The prophet says nothing about
these shameless fabrications of the monks and scholastics. Besides, 32
the prophet's own words give us his meaning. They say, first, that
the name of the Lord will be great. This takes place through the
proclamation of the Gospel, which makes known the name of Christ
and the Father's mercy promised in Christ. The proclamation of the
Gospel produces faith in those who accept it. They call upon God,
they give thanks to God, they bear afflictions in confession, they do
good works for the glory of Christ. This is how the name of the
Lord becomes great among the nations. Therefore "incense" and
"a pure offering" do not refer to a ceremony *ex opere operato* but to
all those sacrifices through which the name of the Lord becomes
great, like faith, prayer, proclamation of the Gospel, confession, etc.

If somebody wants to include the ceremony here, we shall 33
gladly concede this, so long as he does not mean that by itself, or
ex opere operato, the ceremony is beneficial. Among the praises of

God or sacrifices of praise we include the proclamation of the Word. In the same way, the reception of the Lord's Supper itself can be praise or thanksgiving, but it does not justify *ex opere operato* or merit the forgiveness of sins when it is transferred to others. In a moment we shall explain how even a ceremony is a sacrifice. Malachi is talking about all the worship of the New Testament, not only about the Lord's Supper, and he does not propound the pharisaic idea of ceremonies *ex opere operato;* therefore he does not refute our position but supports it. For he requires the worship of the heart, by which the name of the Lord really becomes great.

They quote another passage from Malachi (3:3), "And he   34 will purify the sons of Levi and refine them like gold and silver, till they present right offerings to the Lord." This passage clearly requires the offerings of the righteous; therefore it does not support the notion of ceremonies *ex opere operato.* The offerings of the sons of Levi (that is, of those who teach in the New Testament) are the proclamation of the Gospel and its good fruits. Thus Paul speaks in Rom. 15:16 of "the priestly service of the gospel of God, so that the offering of the Gentiles may be acceptable, sanctified by the Holy Spirit," that is, so that the Gentiles may become offerings acceptable to God through faith. The slaughter of animals in the Old Testament symbolized both the death of Christ and the proclamation of the Gospel, which should kill this old flesh and begin a new and eternal life in us.

But our opponents always apply the term "sacrifice" only to the ceremony. They omit the proclamation of the Gospel, faith, prayer, and things like that, though it was for these that the ceremony was instituted. The New Testament requires sacrifices of the heart, not the ceremonial sacrifices for sin offered by a Levitical priesthood.

They also refer to the daily sacrifice: as there was a daily   35 sacrifice in the Old Testament, so the Mass ought to be the daily sacrifice of the New Testament. Our opponents will really achieve something if we let them defeat us with allegories, but it is evident that allegory does not prove or establish anything. We are perfectly willing for the Mass to be understood as a daily sacrifice, provided this means the whole Mass, the ceremony and also the proclamation of the Gospel, faith, prayer, and thanksgiving. Taken together, these are the daily sacrifice of the New Testament; the ceremony was instituted because of them and ought not be separated from them. Therefore Paul says (I Cor. 11:26), "As often as you eat this bread and drink the cup, you proclaim the Lord's death." From the Levitical analogy it does not follow at all that there must be a ceremony that justifies *ex opere operato* or that merits the forgiveness of sins when applied to others.

This analogy symbolizes not only the ceremony but the procla-   36 mation of the Gospel. Num. 28:4ff. lists three parts of this daily sacrifice, the burning of the lamb, the drink offering, and the offering of flour. The Old Testament had pictures or shadows of what was to come;[4] thus this depicted Christ and the whole worship of the New Testament. The burning of the lamb symbolizes the death of Christ. The drink offering symbolizes the sprinkling, that is, the sanctifying of believers throughout the world with the blood of that lamb, by the proclamation of the Gospel, as Peter says (I Pet. 1:2); "Sanctified by the Spirit for obedience to Jesus Christ and for sprinkling with his blood." The offering of flour symbolizes faith, prayer, and thanksgiving in the heart. Therefore, as we discern the shadow in the 37 Old Testament, so in the New we should look for what it represents and not for another symbol that seems to be a sacrifice.

Although the ceremony is a memorial of the death of Christ, 38 therefore, it is not the daily sacrifice by itself; the commemoration is the real daily sacrifice, the proclamation and the faith which truly believes that by the death of Christ God has been reconciled. There must be a drink offering, namely, the effect of the proclamation, as we are sanctified, put to death, and made alive when the Gospel sprinkles us with the blood of Christ. There must also be an offering in thanksgiving, confession, and affliction.

With the rejection of the idea that ceremonies work *ex opere* 39 *operato*, we can see that their real meaning is spiritual worship and the daily sacrifice of the heart, for in the New Testament we should look for the substance of things, for the Holy Spirit who puts us to death and makes us alive. From this it is clear that the analogy 40 of the daily sacrifice does not refute but supports our stand because we require all the actions that it symbolizes. Our opponents imagine that it symbolizes the ceremony alone and not preaching the Gospel, being put to death and being made alive.

Now good men can easily see the falsity of the charge that we 41 do away with the daily sacrifice. Experience shows the sort of tyrants who rule the church. Under the pretext of religion they usurp the kingdom of the world, and they rule without regard for religion and the preaching of the Gospel. They wage war like the kings of the world, and they have instituted new worship in the church. For 42 in the Mass our opponents keep only the ceremony, which they put on in public as a money-making venture. Then they make the claim that this work can be transferred to someone else to merit for him grace and every good. In their sermons they do not preach 43 the Gospel or console consciences or point out that sins are freely forgiven for Christ's sake. Instead, they discuss the worship of saints, human satisfactions, and human traditions with the claim that these

[4] Cf. Col. 2:17.

justify men before God. Despite the obvious wickedness of some of this, they violently defend it. The preachers who want to look more learned take up philosophical questions, which neither they nor the people understand. The better ones teach the law and say nothing about the righteousness of faith.

In the Confutation our opponents wring their hands over "the 44 desolation of the temples" and the altars standing unadorned, without candles or statues. They call these trifles the ornament of the churches.[5] Daniel describes a vastly different desolation,[6] igno- 45 rance of the Gospel. The people were swamped by the many different traditions and ideas and could not grasp the sum of Christian doctrine. Who among the people has ever understood our opponents' 46 doctrine of penitence? Yet this is the principal doctrine of the Christian faith.

Satisfactions and the enumeration of sins were a torture for consciences. Our opponents never mentioned faith, by which we freely receive the forgiveness of sins. All their books and sermons were silent about the exercise of faith in its struggle with despair and about the free forgiveness of sins for Christ's sake. In addition, they 47 horribly profaned the Mass and introduced much wicked worship into the churches. This is the desolation that Daniel describes.

By the blessing of God, the priests in our churches pay 48 attention to the ministry of the Word, they teach the Gospel of the blessings of Christ, and they show that the forgiveness of sins comes freely for Christ's sake. This teaching really consoles consciences. They add to it the teaching of the good works which God commands, and they talk about the value and use of the sacraments.

If the use of the sacrament were the daily sacrifice, we could 49 lay more claim to observing it than our opponents because in their churches mercenary priests use the sacrament. In our churches the use is more frequent and more devout. It is the people who use it, and this only when they have been instructed and examined. They are instructed about the proper use of the sacrament as a seal and witness of the free forgiveness of sins and as an admonition to timid consciences really to trust and believe that their sins are freely forgiven. Thus, since we keep both the proclamation of the Gospel and the proper use of the sacraments, we still have the daily sacrifice.

[5] Roman Confutation: "The daily sacrifice of Christ will cease universally at the advent of the abomination (that is, of Antichrist), just as it has already ceased, especially in some churches, and thus will be unemployed in the place of desolation (that is, when churches will be desolated) in which the canonical hours will not be chanted or Masses celebrated or sacraments administered and in which there will be no altars, no images of saints, no candles, no furniture" (Pt. II, Art. III).
[6] Dan. 11:31.

And as for outward appearances, our church attendance is 50
greater than theirs. Practical and clear sermons hold an audience,
but neither the people nor the clergy have ever understood our
opponents' teaching. The real adornment of the churches is 51
godly, practical, and clear teaching, the godly use of the sacraments,
ardent prayer, and the like. Candles, golden vessels, and ornaments
like that are fitting, but they are not the peculiar adornment of the
church. If our opponents center their worship in such things rather
than in the proclamation of the Gospel, in faith, and in its struggles,
they should be classified with those whom Daniel (11:38) describes as
worshiping their God with gold and silver.

They also quote the Epistle to the Hebrews (5:1), "Every 52
high priest chosen from among men is appointed to act on behalf of
men in relation to God, to offer gifts and sacrifies for sins." From this
they conclude that since the New Testament has priests and high
priests, it must also have some sort of sacrifice for sins. This is a very
convincing argument for the ignorant, especially when the pomp of
the Old Testament priesthood and sacrifices is spread before their eyes.
The analogy deceives them, and they think that we should have some
ceremony or sacrifice for sins, just as the Old Testament did. The
services of the Mass and the rest of the papal order are nothing but
a misinterpretation of the Levitical order.

Though the main proofs for our position are in the Epistle to 53
the Hebrews, our opponents twist passages from this very epistle
against us—like this one, which says that "every high priest is
appointed to offer sacrifices for sins." The Scripture itself adds
immediately that Christ is the high priest. The preceding words
talk about the Levitical priesthood and say that it was a picture of
Christ's priesthood. The Levitical sacrifices for sin did not merit
the forgiveness of sins in the sight of God; as we have already said,
they were merely a picture of the sacrifice of Christ which was to be
the one propitiatory sacrifice. Therefore a large part of the epistle 54
is devoted to the theme that the ancient priesthood and the ancient
sacrifices were not instituted to merit the forgiveness of sins or reconciliation before God, but only to symbolize the future death of Christ
alone. In the Old Testament as in the New, the saints had to be 55
justified by faith in the promise of the forgiveness of sins given for
Christ's sake. Since the beginning of the world, all the saints have
had to believe that Christ would be the offering and the satisfaction
for sin, as Isa. 53:10 teaches, "When he makes himself an offering
for sin."

The Old Testament sacrifices, therefore, did not merit reconcilia- 56
tion—unless by analogy, since they merited civil reconciliation—
but only symbolized the coming sacrifice. From this it follows that

only the sacrifice of Christ can be valid for the sins of others, and that there is no other such sacrifice left in the New Testament except the one sacrifice of Christ on the cross.

It is completely erroneous to imagine that the Levitical sacrifices   57 merited the forgiveness of sins before God and that by analogy there must be sacrifices in the New Testament besides the death of Christ that are valid for the sins of others. This notion completely negates the merit of Christ's suffering and the righteousness of faith, it corrupts the teaching of both the Old and the New Testament, and it replaces Christ as our mediator and propitiator with priests and sacrificers who daily peddle their wares in the churches.

If anyone argues, therefore, that the New Testament must have   58 a priest who sacrifices for sin, this can only apply to Christ. The whole Epistle to the Hebrews supports this interpretation. We would be setting up other mediators besides Christ if we were to look for some other satisfaction that was valid for the sins of others and reconciled God. Since the priesthood of the New Testament is a   59 ministry of the Spirit, as Paul teaches in II Cor. 3:6, the only sacrifice of satisfaction it has for the sins of others is the sacrifice of Christ. It has no sacrifices like the Levitical which could be transferred to others *ex opere operato;* but it offers to others the Gospel and the sacraments so that thereby they may receive faith and the Holy Spirit and be put to death and made alive. The ministry of the Spirit contradicts any such transfer *ex opere operato.* Through the ministry of the Spirit, the Holy Spirit works in the heart. Therefore this ministry benefits people when he does work to give them new birth and life. This does not happen by the transfer of one man's work to another *ex opere operato.*

We have shown the conflict between the righteousness of   60 faith and the idea that the Mass justifies *ex opere operato* or that it merits the forgiveness of sins for others. There can be no forgiveness of sins and no conquest of the terrors of death and sin through any work or anything else but faith in Christ, as we read (Rom. 5:1), "Since we are justified by faith, we have peace."

We have also shown that the Scripture passages quoted against   61 us give no support to our opponents' wicked idea that the Mass justifies *ex opere operato.* Good men in every country can see this. We   62 therefore reject the error of Thomas when he writes, "The body of the Lord, once offered on the cross for the original debt, is daily offered on the altar for daily offenses so that in this the church might have a service that reconciles God." [7] We also reject other   63 common errors: that the Mass confers grace *ex opere operato* on one

---

[7] Thomas Aquinas, *Opuscula,* 58; *The Venerable Sacrament of the Altar,* c.1.

who uses it, or that it merits the remission of sins, guilt, and punishment for those to whom it is transferred, even for wicked people, if they do not put an obstacle in its way. These are the wicked and recent fictions of the ignorant monks; they destroy the glory of Christ's suffering and the righteousness of faith.

These errors have sired endless others, like the one that Masses   64 are valid when they are transferred to many just as when they are transferred to one. The scholastics have scales of merit, like the money-changers with gold or silver. They sell the Mass as a price for success, to merchants for good business, to hunters for good hunting, and things like that.[8] Finally, they even transfer it to the dead and free souls from purgatorial punishment by the application of the sacrament, though without faith the Mass does not even benefit living people. Our opponents cannot produce a syllable from the Scriptures in   65 support of the fairy tales which they teach so authoritatively in the church; nor do they have the support of the ancient church and the Fathers.

Patristic Teaching on Sacrifice

Now that we have explained the Scripture passages that they   66 quote against us, we must also discuss the Fathers. We are aware of the fact that the Fathers call the Mass a sacrifice; but they do not mean that the Mass confers grace *ex opere operato* or that it merits the remission of sins, of guilt, and of punishment for those to whom it is transferred. Where do the Fathers say anything so monstrous? They make clear that they are talking about thanksgiving; hence they call it "eucharist." We have already said that a eucharistic sacrifice   67 does not merit reconciliation but comes from the reconciled, just as afflictions do not merit reconciliation but are eucharistic sacrifices when the reconciled endure them.

This is enough of a general reply to our opponents regarding what the Fathers said. Certainly this fiction about merit *ex opere operato* is not to be found anywhere in the Fathers. But to make the whole matter as clear as possible, we shall say about the use of the sacrament what actually agrees with the Fathers and with Scripture.

Sacrifice and the Use of the Sacrament

Some clever people[9] imagine that the Lord's Supper was in-   68 stituted for two reasons. First, it was supposed to be a mark and witness of profession, just as a certain type of hood is the mark of a particular monastic profession. In the second place, Christ was

[8] Votive Masses for special intentions.
[9] Ulrich Zwingli and his followers. See above, Augsburg Confession, XIII, 1.

supposed to be very pleased with a mark that took the form of a meal symbolizing the mutual union and friendship among Christians because banquets are symbols of agreement and friendship. But this is a secular idea that ignores the chief use of what God has instituted. It talks only about the practice of love, which even profane and secular men understand; it does not talk about faith, whose true meaning very few understand.

The sacraments are not only signs among men, but signs of 69 God's will toward us; so it is correct to define the New Testament sacraments as signs of grace. There are two parts to a sacrament, the sign and the Word. In the New Testament, the Word is the added promise of grace. The promise of the New Testament is the promise of the forgiveness of sins, as the text says, "This is my body, which is given for you";[1] "this is the cup of the new testament with my blood, which is poured out for many for the forgiveness of sins." [2] Therefore the Word offers forgiveness of sins, while the ceremony 70 is a sort of picture or "seal," as Paul calls it (Rom. 4:11), showing forth the promise. As the promise is useless unless faith accepts it, so the ceremony is useless without the faith which really believes that the forgiveness of sins is being offered here. Such a faith encourages the contrite mind. As the Word was given to arouse this faith, so the sacrament was instituted to move the heart to believe through what it presents to the eyes. For the Holy Spirit works through the Word and the sacraments.

This use of the sacrament, when faith gives life to terrified 71 hearts, is the worship of the New Testament, because what matters in the New Testament is the spiritual motivation, dying and being made alive. For such use Christ instituted it, as he commanded (I Cor. 11:24), "Do this in remembrance of me." The remem- 72 brance of Christ is not the vain celebration of a show or a celebration for the sake of example, the way plays celebrate the memory of Hercules or Ulysses. It is rather the remembrance of Christ's blessings and the acceptance of them by faith, so that they make us alive. So the Psalm says (Ps. 111:4, 5), "He has caused his wonderful works to be remembered; the Lord is gracious and merciful. He provides food for those who fear him." This means that in the ceremony we should acknowledge the will and mercy of God. A faith 73 that acknowledges mercy makes alive. The principal use of the sacrament is to make clear that terrified consciences are the ones worthy of it, and how they ought to use it.

There is also a sacrifice, since one action can have several pur- 74 poses. Once faith has strengthened a conscience to see its liberation

[1] Luke 22:19.
[2] Matt. 26:28.

from terror, then it really gives thanks for the blessing of Christ's suffering. It uses the ceremony itself as praise to God, as a demonstration of its gratitude, and a witness of its high esteem for God's gifts. Thus the ceremony becomes a sacrifice of praise.

The Fathers speak of a twofold effect, of the comfort for the   75 conscience and of thanksgiving or praise; the first of these belongs to the nature of the sacrament, and the second to the sacrifice. Ambrose says about the comfort: "Go to him and be absolved, for he is the forgiveness of sins. Do you ask who he is? Hear his own words (John 6:35), 'I am the bread of life; he who comes to me shall not hunger, and he who believes in me shall never thirst.' " [3] This proves that the sacrament offers the forgiveness of sins and that it ought to be received by faith. There are many statements of this sort in the Fathers, all of which our opponents twist in support of their idea that sacraments work *ex opere operato* and can be transferred to others; but the Fathers clearly require faith and speak of the appropriation of the comfort, not of any transfer.

There are also statements about thanksgiving, like the beautiful   76 statement of Cyprian about the godly communicant, "Piety distinguishes between what is given and what is forgiven, and it gives thanks to the Giver of such a generous blessing." [4] That is, piety looks at what is given and at what is forgiven; it compares the greatness of God's blessings with the greatness of our ills, our sin and our death; and it gives thanks. From this the term "eucharist" arose in the church. The ceremony is not a thanksgiving that can be trans-   77 ferred to others *ex opere operato* to merit the forgiveness of sins for them or to free the souls of the dead. The theory that a ceremony can benefit either the worshiper or anyone else without faith conflicts with the righteousness of faith.

The Term "Mass"

Our opponents also refer us to philology. From the names   78 for the Mass they take arguments which do not deserve a lengthy discussion. It does not follow from the fact that the Mass is called a sacrifice that it grants grace *ex opere operato* or that it merits the forgiveness of sins for those to whom it is transferred.[5] The Greeks   79

---

[3] Ambrose, *Exposition of the Psalms*, 118, c.18, 28.

[4] Pseudo-Cyprian, *The Lord's Supper and the First Institution*, 7.

[5] Roman Confutation: "Applicable to this topic, too, is what is read according to the new translation in Acts 13:1, 2: Barnabas, Simeon, Lucius of Cyrene, Manaeen, and Saul sacrificed, that is, they offered an oblation . . . of the Mass, for by the Greeks it is called 'liturgy.' . . . In Hebrews St. Paul is speaking of the offering of a victim (that is, of a bloody sacrifice, of a lamb slain on the altar of the cross), which offering was indeed once made, and from it all sacraments, including the sacrifice of the Mass, have their efficacy . . . . The force of the word shows that the Mass is a sacrifice, for

call the Mass "liturgy," and this, they say, means "sacrifice." Why do they not mention the old term "communion," [6] which shows that formerly the Mass was the communion of many? But let us talk about the term "liturgy." It does not really mean a sacrifice but a 80 public service. Thus it squares with our position that a minister who consecrates shows forth the body and blood of the Lord to the people, just as a minister who preaches shows forth the gospel to the people, as Paul says (I Cor. 4:1), "This is how one should regard us, as ministers of Christ and dispensers of the sacraments of God," that is, of the Word and sacraments; and II Cor. 5:20, "We are ambassadors for Christ, God making his appeal through us. We beseech you on behalf of Christ, be reconciled to God."

Thus the term "liturgy" squares well with the ministry. It is 81 an old word, ordinarily used in public law. To the Greeks it meant "public duties," like the taxes collected for equipping a fleet. As Demosthenes' oration *Leptines* shows, it is completely taken up with public duties and immunities: "He will say that some unworthy men have found an immunity and have avoided public duty." [7] They used it this way in the time of the Romans, as the rescript of Pertinax on the law of immunity shows: "Even though the number of children does not excuse parents from public duties." [8] A commentator on Demosthenes says that "liturgy" is a kind of tax to pay for the games, ships, care of the gymnasium, and similar public responsibilities.[9]

In II Cor. 9:12 Paul uses this word for a collection. Taking 82 this collection not only supplies what the saints need but also causes many to thank God more abundantly. In Phil. 2:25 he calls Epaphroditus a "minister to my need," which surely does not mean a sacrificer. But further proofs are unnecessary since anyone who 83 reads the Greek authors can find examples everywhere of their use of "liturgy" to mean public duties or ministrations. Because of the diphthong, philologists do not derive it from *lite,* which means prayers, but from *leita,* which means public goods; thus the verb means to care for or to administer public goods.

It is silly to argue that since the Holy Scriptures mention an 84 altar, the Mass must be a sacrifice; for Paul uses the figure of an altar only for illustration. They also imagine that "Mass" is 85 derived from *mizbeach,* the Hebrew word for altar. Why such a farfetched etymology, except perhaps to show off their knowledge of Hebrew? Why go so far afield for the etymology when the term

'Mass' is nothing but 'oblation' and has received its name from the Hebrew word *mizbeach* . . ." (Pt. II, Art. III).

[6] Greek: *Synaxis.*

[7] Demosthenes, *Leptines,* 1:547.

[8] *Digest of Laws,* 6, 6, sec. 2.

[9] Ulpian, *Commentary on Demosthenes' Oration to Leptines,* 494, 26.

occurs in Deut. 16:10, where it means the collections or gifts of the people rather than the offering of the priest? Individuals coming to the celebration of the Passover had to bring some gift as a contribution. Originally the Christians kept this practice. The apos- 86 tolic canons show that when they gathered they brought bread, wine, and other things.[1] Part of this was taken to be consecrated, the rest was distributed to the poor. With this practice they also kept the term "Mass" as the name for the contributions. It seems that because of such contributions the Mass was called *agape* in some places, unless some one prefers to think it was called that because of the common banquet. But let us pass over these trifles. It is silly for our op- 87 ponents to raise such quibbles about such an important issue. For even though the Mass is called an offering, what does that term have to do with these dreams about the efficacy of the act *ex opere operato* and its supposed applicability to merit the forgiveness of sins for others? It can be called an offering, as it is called a eucharist, because prayers, thanksgivings, and the whole worship are offered there. But neither ceremonies nor prayers provide an advantage *ex opere operato* without faith. Nevertheless, we are arguing here not about prayers, but really about the Lord's Supper.

The Greek canon also says much about an offering; but it 88 clearly shows that it is not talking about the body and blood of the Lord in particular, but about the whole service, about the prayers and thanksgivings. This is what it says: "And make us worthy to come to offer Thee entreaties and supplications and bloodless sacrifices for all the people." [2] Properly understood, this is not offensive. It prays that we might be made worthy to offer prayers and supplications and bloodless sacrifices for the people. It calls even prayers "bloodless sacrifices." So it says a little later: "We offer Thee this reasonable and bloodless service." [3] It is a misinterpretation to translate this as "reasonable victim" and apply it to the body of Christ itself. For the canon is talking about the whole service; and by "reasonable service" (Rom. 12:1) Paul meant the service of the mind, fear, faith, prayer, thanksgiving, and the like, in opposition to a theory of *ex opere operato*.

[MASS FOR THE DEAD]

Our opponents defend the application of the ceremony to free 89 the souls of the dead, from which they make infinite profits. But for this they have no scriptural proof or command. It is no mere peccadillo to establish such services in the church without the command

---

[1] *Apostolic Constitutions*, VIII, 47.
[2] Prayer at the beginning of the *missa fidelium* in the liturgy of Chrysostom.
[3] The invocation in the same liturgy.

of God and the example of Scripture, and to apply to the dead the Lord's Supper which was instituted for commemoration and preaching among the living. This is an abuse of the name of God in violation of the Second Commandment.

For one thing, it is an insult to the Gospel to maintain that without faith, *ex opere operato,* a ceremony is a sacrifice that reconciles God and makes satisfaction for sins. It is horrible to attribute as much to the work of a priest as to the death of Christ. Then, too, sin and death cannot be conquered except by faith in Christ, as Paul teaches (Rom. 5:1), "Being justified by faith, we have peace." Therefore the penalty of purgatory cannot be overcome by the application of someone else's work.

Now we shall pass over the sort of proofs our opponents have 90 for purgatory, the sort of penalties they suppose purgatory has, the reasons they adduce in support of the doctrine of satisfaction, which we have refuted earlier.[4] In reply we shall say only this much. Surely the Lord's Supper was instituted for the sake of forgiving guilt. For it offers the forgiveness of sins, which necessarily implies real guilt. Nevertheless, it does not make satisfaction for guilt; otherwise, the Mass would be on a par with the death of Christ. The forgiveness of guilt can be accepted only by faith. Therefore the Mass is not a satisfaction but a promise and a sacrament requiring faith.

Indeed, the bitterest kind of sorrow must seize all the faithful 91 if they ponder the fact that the Mass has largely been transferred to the dead and to satisfactions for penalties. This is the abolition of the daily sacrifice in the church. It is the kingdom of tyrants who transferred the blessed promises of the forgiveness of guilt and faith to vain ideas of satisfactions. It is a contamination of the Gospel, a corruption of the use of the sacraments. These are the ones who, Paul said (I Cor. 11:27), are "guilty of the body and blood of the Lord." They have crushed the doctrine of faith, and under the pretext of satisfactions they have debased the forgiveness of guilt and the body and blood of the Lord for their own sacrilegious profit. Some day they will pay the penalty for this sacrilege. Therefore we and all faithful consciences should be careful not to support the abuses of our opponents.

But let us get back to the issue. Since the Mass is not a satis- 92 faction for either punishment or guilt, *ex opere operato* and without faith, it follows that it is useless to transfer it to the dead. There is no need here of a very lengthy discussion. Clearly this transference to the dead cannot be proved from the Scriptures, and it is not safe to institute services in the church without the authority of Scripture. If the need ever arises, we shall discuss this whole issue more fully.

[4] Above, XII, 113-130.

Why should we wrangle with our opponents who understand the meaning of neither sacrifice nor sacrament nor forgiveness of sins nor faith?

The Greek canon does not apply the offering as a satisfaction   93 for the dead because it applies it equally to all the blessed patriarchs, prophets, and apostles. Therefore it seems that the Greeks offer it only as a thanksgiving and do not apply it as a satisfaction for penalties. But they speak not only of offering the body and blood of the Lord, but about the other parts of the Mass, namely, prayers and thanksgivings. For after the consecration they pray that it may benefit the communicants; they do not talk about others. Then they add, "Yet we offer Thee this reasonable service for those who have departed in faith, forefathers, fathers, patriarchs, prophets," etc.[5] And "reasonable service" does not mean the host itself but the prayers and everything that goes on there. Our opponents quote the Fathers   94 on offerings for the dead. We know that the ancients spoke of prayer for the dead. We do not forbid this, but rather we reject the transfer of the Lord's Supper to the dead *ex opere operato*. The ancients do not support the opponents' idea of the transfer *ex opere operato*. Even though they have support at most from Gregory and the more recent theologians, we set against them the clearest and surest passages of Scripture. There is also great variety among the Fathers. They   95 were men and they could err and be deceived. If they came back to life now and saw their sayings being twisted to support the obvious lies which our opponents teach about transfer *ex opere operato*, they would express themselves far differently.

Our opponents also misapply against us the condemnation of   96 Aerius, who they say was condemned because he denied that in the Mass there was an offering for the living and the dead.[6] They often use this dodge. They cite ancient heresies and by falsely comparing them with our position they try to crush us. Epiphanius testifies that Aerius believed that prayers for the dead were useless.[7] This he rejects. We do not support Aerius either. But we are at suit with you for wickedly defending a heresy that clearly conflicts with the prophets, apostles, and holy Fathers, namely, that the Mass justifies *ex opere operato* and that it merits the forgiveness of guilt and punishment even for the wicked to whom it is applied, if they make no objection. We reject these wicked errors which rob Christ's suffering

---

[5] The intercession in the liturgy of Chrysostom.

[6] Roman Confutation: "Augustine says that this was a very ancient heresy of the Aerians, who denied that in the Mass an oblation was made for the living and the dead" (Pt. II, Art. III). Aerius, fourth century presbyter of Sebaste, in Pontus, attacked some of the legalistic and hierarchical tendencies of the church in his time.

[7] Epiphanius, *Panarion*, 75:2, 3, 7.

of its glory and utterly destroy the doctrine of righteousness by faith.

The wicked people in the Old Testament had a similar notion 97 that they merited the forgiveness of sins by sacrifices *ex opere operato* rather than receiving it freely through faith. Hence they increased the services and sacrifices. In Israel they introduced the worship of Baal; in Judah they even sacrificed in groves. When the prophets condemn this notion, therefore, they are battling not only against the worshipers of Baal but also against other priests who perform the sacrifices instituted by God with this wicked notion in mind.[8] But this notion clings to the world, and always will, that services and sacrifices are propitiations. Carnal men cannot stand it when only the sacrifice of Christ is honored as a propitiation. For they do not understand the righteousness of faith but give equal honor to other sacrifices and services. A false idea about sacrifices clung to the 98 wicked priests in Judah, and in Israel the worship of Baal continued; yet the church of God was there, condemning wicked services. So in the papal realm the worship of Baal clings—namely, the abuse of the Mass, which they apply in order by it to merit the forgiveness of guilt and punishment for the wicked. And it seems that this worship of Baal will endure together with the papal realm until Christ comes to judge and by the glory of his coming destroys the kingdom of Antichrist. Meanwhile all those who truly believe the Gospel should reject those wicked services invented against God's command to obscure the glory of Christ and the righteousness of faith.

We have briefly said this about the Mass to let all good men 99 understand that we most zealously preserve the dignity of the Mass, that we show its proper use, and that we have most valid reasons for disagreeing with our opponents. We want all good men to be warned not to help our opponents in defending their desecration of the Mass lest they burden themselves with other men's sin. This is a great cause and a great issue, not inferior to the work of the prophet Elijah in condemning the worship of Baal.[9] We have set forth such an important issue with the greatest moderation, and now we have replied without casting any reproach. But if our opponents make us compile all kinds of abuses of the Mass, we shall not handle the case so gently.

[ARTICLE XXVII.] MONASTIC VOWS

Thirty years ago, in the Thuringian town of Eisenach, there 1 was a Franciscan named John Hilten. He was thrown into prison by his order because he had condemned certain notorious abuses. We have seen his writings, and from them the nature of his teaching can be well understood. Those who knew him testify that he was a mild

---

[8] Cf. Jer. 2:8.
[9] I Kings 18:17-46.

old man, serious but not morose. He predicted many things. Some 2
of them have already happened, and others seem to be impending.
We do not want to recite them here lest we give the impression that
we are doing so out of anger or favor toward anyone. But at last,
when he became ill either on account of age or on account of the
filth of the prison, he sent for the guardian to tell him of his illness.
Inflamed with a pharisaical hatred, the guardian began to denounce
him for his doctrine, which seemed to be injuring his food. Then
with a sigh Hilten omitted all mention of his illness and said that he
was bearing these injuries with equanimity for Christ's sake inasmuch
as he had neither written nor taught anything that threatened the
monastic estate but had only denounced certain notorious abuses.
"But another one will come," he said, "in the year of our Lord 3
1516. He will destroy you, and you will be unable to resist him." Later
his friends found this same statement about the decline of the monastic
regime and this same number of years written down by him in the
commentaries he left on certain passages in Daniel.

History will show how much credence should be given to this 4
statement. But there are other signs, no less sure than oracles, which
threaten a change in the monastic regime. Everyone knows how
much hypocrisy, ambition, and greed there is in the monasteries; how
ignorant and cruel these illiterate men are; and how vain they are in
their sermons and in thinking up new ways of making money. There
are other vices, too, which we would rather not talk about. Though 5
once upon a time they were schools of Christian instruction, they
have degenerated as from a golden age to an iron age, or as the
Platonic cube degenerates into bad harmonies which, Plato says,
cause destruction.[1] Some of the richest monasteries just feed a lazy
crowd that gorges itself on the public alms of the church. But 6
Christ warns that tasteless salt is usually "thrown out and trodden
under foot" (Matt. 5:13). When they act this way, therefore, the
monks are signing their own fate. Another sign is the fact that 7
sometimes they are responsible for murdering good men. Without
doubt, God will soon avenge these murders. We are not blaming 8
everyone. We think that here and there in the monasteries there are
some good men who have a moderate opinion of human and "facti-
tious" services, as some writers call them, and who do not approve
of the cruelty which the hypocrites among them display.

The issue is the kind of doctrine which the architects of the 9
Confutation are now defending, not the question whether vows should
be kept. We maintain that legitimate vows should be kept, but we
are arguing about other questions. Do those services merit the for-

---

[1] Possibly Pseudo-Plato, *Timaeus Locrus*, 98 C.

giveness of sins and justification? Are they satisfactions for sins? Are they equal to Baptism? Are they the observance of commandments and counsels? Are they "evangelical perfection"? Do they have merits of supererogation? Do these merits save others when they are transferred to them? Are vows made with these notions in mind legitimate? Are vows legitimate that have been taken with the pretext of religion, but actually for the sake of appetite or hatred? Are vows really vows if they have been extorted from the unwilling, or from those who are not old enough to make up their own minds about their way of life, whom parents or friends pushed into the monastery to be supported at public expense without the loss of their private patrimony? Are vows legitimate if they openly point to an evil end, either because weakness prevents their observance or because the members of these orders are forced to approve and support the abuses of the Mass, the wicked services to the saints, and the conspiracies against good men? In the Confession we said much 10 about such vows, which even the papal canons condemn.[2] But still our opponents demand the rejection of everything that we have produced; these are the very words they used.[3]

It is worthwhile to hear how they twist our arguments and what they adduce to support their case. Therefore we shall briefly run through a few of our arguments, and in passing we shall refute our opponents' quibbles against them. Since Luther discussed this whole issue carefully and fully in his book called *Monastic Vows*,[4] we want to be interpreted here as reiterating that book.

First, it certainly is not a legitimate vow if the one making 11 it supposes that by it he merits the forgiveness of sins before God or makes satisfaction for sins before God. This idea is an open insult to the Gospel, which teaches that the forgiveness of sins is given us freely for Christ's sake, as we have said at length above. Thus it was fitting for us to quote Paul's statement from Galatians (Gal. 5:4), "You are severed from Christ, you who would be justified by the law; you have fallen away from grace." Those who seek the forgiveness of sins not by faith in Christ, but by monastic works, take away from Christ's honor and crucify him again. But listen how the architects of the Confutation slip away here! They apply the passage 12 in Paul only to the law of Moses. And they add that the monks observe everything for Christ's sake and try to live more closely according to the Gospel in order to merit eternal life. To this they append a

---

[2] See above, Augsburg Confession, XXVII.

[3] Roman Confutation: "All things which have been produced in this article against monasticism must be rejected" (Pt. II, Art. VI).

[4] Luther's *De votis monasticis* appeared in 1521, *WA*, 8:573-669.

horrible epilogue in the words: "Therefore what has here been charged against monasticism is wicked." [5]

O Christ, how long wilt Thou bear these insults with which 13 our enemies attack thy Gospel! In the Confession we said that the forgiveness of sins is received freely for Christ's sake, through faith. If this is not the true voice of the Gospel, if it is not the statement of the eternal Father which Thou who art in the bosom of the Father hast revealed to the world—then the charge against us is true. But thy death is a witness, thy resurrection is a witness, the Holy Spirit is a witness, thy whole church is a witness: this is truly the teaching of the Gospel that we receive the forgiveness of sins not because of our merits but because of Thee, through faith.

Since Paul denies that by the law of Moses men merit the 14 forgiveness of sins, he refuses even more to give this credit to human traditions, as he clearly shows in Col. 2:16. If the law of Moses, which was divinely revealed, did not merit the forgiveness of sins, how much less do these silly observances merit the forgiveness of sins, opposed as they are to the customs of public life?

Our opponents pretend that Paul abolished the law of Moses 15 and that Christ took its place, so that he does not give the forgiveness of sins freely but on account of the works of other laws that have now been thought up. By this wicked and fanatical notion they 16 bury the blessing of Christ. Then they pretend that among those who observe this law of Christ, the monks come closer in their observance than do others because of their poverty, chastity, and obedience—hypocrisies all, since they are all full of sham. They brag about poverty amid a bounty of everything. They brag about obedience though no class of men has greater license' than the monks. As for celibacy, we would rather not discuss it. Gerson indicates how pure this is in most of those who strive to be continent.[6] And how many of them strive to be continent?

By this sham, to be sure, the monks "pattern their lives more 17 closely after the Gospel"![7] Christ takes Moses' place, not by forgiving sins on account of our works but by setting his merits and his propitiation against the wrath of God for us so that we might be freely forgiven. Whoever sets his own merits, in addition to Christ's propitiation, against the wrath of God; whoever tries to attain to the for-

---

[5] Roman Confutation: "False, therefore, is the judgment by which they condemn monastic service as godless, when it is actually most Christian. For the monks have not fallen from God's grace like the Jews, of whom St. Paul speaks (Gal. 5:4), who continued to seek justification by the law of Moses. The monks try to pattern their lives more closely after the Gospel in order to merit eternal life. Therefore what has here been charged against monasticism is wicked" (Pt. II, Art. VI).

[6] John Gerson, On Celibacy, 3, II, 629 C.

[7] See note 5 above.

giveness of sins because of his own merits by doing the works of the Mosaic law or of the Decalogue or of the rule of Benedict or of the rule of Augustine[8] or of other rules—whoever does this abolishes the promise of Christ, has cast Christ away, and has fallen from Christ. This is the verdict of Paul.

But look, most clement Emperor Charles; look, princes; look, 18 all you estates! How impudent our opponents are! Though we have quoted Paul's statement in support of this, they have written, "What has been charged against monasticism here is wicked." But what 19 is surer than that men attain to the forgiveness of sins by faith for Christ's sake? These rascals have the audacity to call this statement wicked. We do not doubt that if you had been told about this passage, you would have seen to it that such blasphemy was removed from the Confutation.

Since we have above shown at length the wickedness of the 20 opinion that we attain to the forgiveness of sins because of our works, we shall be briefer here. From that the discerning reader will easily be able to conclude that we do not merit the forgiveness of sins by monastic works. Hence it is also an intolerable blasphemy when Thomas says that a monastic profession is equal to Baptism.[9] It is madness to put a human tradition, which has neither a command of God nor a promise, on the same level with an ordinance of Christ which has both a command and a promise of God, which contains a covenant of grace and eternal life.

Second, obedience, poverty, and celibacy, provided they are 21 not impure, are non-obligatory forms of discipline. Hence the saints can use them without sinning, as did Bernard, Francis,[1] and other holy men. They used them for their physical advantage, to have more leisure for teaching and other pious duties, not because the works themselves are services that justify or merit eternal life. Finally, they belong to the class of which Paul says (I Tim. 4:8), "Bodily training is of little value." It is likely that here and there in the mon- 22 asteries there are still some good men serving the ministry of the Word who follow these observances without wicked ideas. But 23 the notion that these observances are services because of which we are accounted righteous before God and through which we merit eternal life conflicts with the Gospel of the righteousness of faith, which teaches that for Christ's sake righteousness and eternal life are

---

[8] The rule of Benedict of Nursia, of the sixth century, became basic for western monasticism. The rule observed by Augustinian canons in the late Middle Ages was ascribed to Augustine; see his letter to the nuns of Hippo, *Epistles,* 211.

[9] Thomas Aquinas, *Summa theologica,* II, 2, q.189, a.3 ad 3.

[1] Bernard of Clairvaux and Francis of Assisi.

given to us. It also conflicts with Christ's statement (Matt. 15:9), "In vain do they worship me with the precepts of men." It also conflicts with this statement (Rom. 14:23): "Whatever does not proceed from faith is sin." How can they maintain that these are services which God approves as righteousness before him when they have no proof for this from the Word of God?

But look at the impudence of our opponents! Not only do they 24 teach that these observances are services that justify. They also say that they are more perfect services than other ways of life, that is, that they merit forgiveness of sins and justification more than the others. To this they add many other false and wicked ideas. They imagine that they observe both precepts and counsels.[2] Since they dream that they have merits of supererogation, these liberal men then sell them to others. All this is full of pharisaical vanity. It 25 is the height of wickedness to believe that they satisfy the Ten Commandments in such a way that there are merits left over, when these Commandments accuse all the saints, "You shall love the Lord your God with all your heart" (Deut. 6:5), and again, "You shall not covet" (Ex. 20:17). The prophet says (Ps. 116:11), "All men are liars"; that is, they do not think correctly about God, they do not fear him enough, they do not believe God enough. Therefore it is false for the monks to boast that the observance of a monastic life satisfies the Commandments and does more than the Commandments.

It is also false that monastic observances are the works of the 26 counsels of the Gospel. For the Gospel does not counsel distinctions among clothes or foods, nor the surrender of property. These are human traditions, about all of which it has been said (I Cor. 8:8), "Food does not commend us to God." Hence they are neither justifying services nor perfection. Indeed, when they are proposed under the cover of these titles, they are "doctrines of demons" (I Tim. 4:1).

Virginity is recommended—but to those who have the gift, 27 as has been said above. However, it is a most wicked error to believe that evangelical perfection is to be found in human traditions. If it were, even the monks among the Mohammedans could boast that they have evangelical perfection. Nor is it to be found in the observance of other things which are called "adiaphora."[3] Because the kingdom of God is righteousness (Rom. 14:17) and life in the heart, therefore perfection means to grow in the fear of God, in trust in the mercy promised in Christ, and in devotion to one's calling. Paul also describes perfection (II Cor. 3:18) thus: "We are changed from

[2] Medieval theologians distinguished between "precepts," which were deemed obligatory for all men, and "counsels," which were not deemed obligatory and hence earned additional merit.

[3] Matters of indifference, ethically neutral.

glory to glory, as by the Spirit of the Lord." He does not say, "We are constantly receiving another hood or other sandals or other girdles." It is terrible to read and hear such pharisaical and even Mohammedan expressions in the church, finding the perfection of the Gospel and of the kingdom of Christ, which is eternal life, in these silly observances of vestments and similar trifles.

Now listen to the unworthy verdict our judges have rendered 28 in the Confutation. This is what they say: "It has been stated in the Sacred Scriptures that the monastic life merits eternal life if it is maintained by a due observance, as by the grace of God any monk can maintain it. Indeed, Christ has promised this in abundance to those who have forsaken home and brothers (Matt. 19:29)." [4] These are our opponents' words in which, first of all, they make 29 the impudent claim that according to the statement of the Sacred Scriptures the monastic life merits eternal life. Where do the Sacred Scriptures talk about the monastic life? That is the way our opponents argue their case; that is the way these good-for-nothings quote the Scriptures. Though everyone knows that monasticism is a recent invention, they still cite the authority of Scripture and even say that this decree of theirs is stated in the Scriptures.

In addition, they insult Christ when they say that by a mo- 30 nastic life men merit eternal life. God does not even give his own law the honor of meriting eternal life, as he clearly says in Ezek. 20:25, "I gave them statutes that were not good and ordinances by which they could not have life." In the first place, it is sure that 31 the monastic life does not merit the forgiveness of sins but that we receive this freely by faith, as has been said. In the second 32 place, eternal life is given by mercy for Christ's sake to those who accept forgiveness by faith and do not set their merits against the judgment of God. As Bernard also says very powerfully, "First of all, you must believe that you cannot have the forgiveness of sins except by God's indulgence; secondly, that you cannot have any good work at all unless he has given this, too; finally, that by no works can you merit eternal life, but that this is freely given as well." [5] We have quoted earlier the other things that follow this sentence, but at the end Bernard adds: "Let nobody deceive himself; for if he considers carefully, he will undoubtedly discover that even with ten thousand soldiers he cannot stand up against the Lord who comes at him with twenty thousand." [6] Since we do not merit the forgiveness 33 of sins or eternal life even by the works of the divine law, but must

---

[4] Roman Confutation, Pt. II, Art. VI, 8.
[5] Bernard of Clairvaux, *Sermon on the Annunciation of the Blessed Virgin Mary*, I, 1.
[6] *Ibid.*, I, 2.

seek the mercy promised in Christ, much less do monastic observances, mere human traditions, deserve the credit for meriting the forgiveness of sins or eternal life.

Thus those who teach that the monastic life merits the for- 34 giveness of sins or eternal life are simply crushing the Gospel about the free forgiveness of sins and the promised mercy available in Christ and are transferring to their own foolish observances the trust that is due Christ. Instead of Christ they worship their own cowls and their own filth. Although they need mercy themselves, they wickedly fabricate works of supererogation and sell them to others.

We have discussed this briefly, for on the basis of what we 35 said earlier about justification, penance, and human traditions, it is quite clear that monastic vows are not a price for which the forgiveness of sins and eternal life are granted. And since Christ calls traditions "useless services," they are not evangelical perfection at all.

But our opponents slyly seek to give the impression that they 36 are modifying the common notion about perfection. They deny that the monastic life is perfection, but they say that it is a state for acquiring perfection.[7] Well said! We remember that this correction is found in Gerson.[8] It seems that wise men were offended by the immoderate praises of the monastic life; but since they did not dare to deny it the claim of perfection altogether, they added this correction, that it is a state for acquiring perfection. If we follow this, 37 the monastic life will be no more a state of perfection than the life of a farmer or an artisan. These, too, are states for acquiring perfection. All men, whatever their calling, ought to seek perfection, that is, growth in the fear of God, in faith, in the love of their neighbor, and similar spiritual virtues.

In the histories of the hermits there are stories of Anthony and 38 of others which put various ways of life on the same level. It is written that when Anthony asked God to show him what progress he was making in his way of life, God pointed in a dream to a certain shoemaker in the city of Alexandria as a basis for comparison. The next day Anthony went into the city and came to the shoemaker to find out about his exercises and gifts. In his conversation with the man he did not hear anything, except that in the morning he prayed in a few words for the whole city and then paid attention to his busi-

---

[7] Roman Confutation: "The malicious charge which is further added, that those in religious orders claim to be in a state of perfection, has never been heard of by them, for the religious do not claim perfection for themselves but only a state for acquiring perfection because their regulations are instruments of perfection and not perfection itself" (Pt. II, Art. VI).

[8] John Gerson, *Evangelical Counsels*, II, 679. The Roman Confutation also alludes to Gerson.

ness. Thus Anthony came to understand that justification was not to be attributed to the way of life he had undertaken.[9]

Although our opponents are now modifying their praises about 39 perfection, they really believe otherwise. They sell merits and transfer them to others under the pretext that they observe both precepts and counsels. Therefore they really believe that they have merits left over. If this is not arrogating perfection to oneself, what is? In the Confutation itself they say that monks try to pattern their lives more closely with the Gospel.[1] They are ascribing perfection to human traditions if they say that monks pattern their lives more closely after the Gospel because they do not have property, are unmarried, and obey the rule in trifles like clothing and food.

Again, the Confutation says that monks merit a more abundant 40 eternal life, and it quotes the passage (Matt. 19:29), "Every one who has left houses," etc. That is to say, here, too, it claims perfection for artificial religious acts. But this passage of Scripture has nothing to do with the monastic life. Christ does not mean to say that leaving parents or wife or brothers is a work we should do because it merits the forgiveness of sins and eternal life. Indeed, such leaving is accursed; for if someone leaves his parents or his wife in order by this act to merit the forgiveness of sins or eternal life, he is insulting Christ.

There are two kinds of leaving. One happens without a call, 41 without a command of God; this Christ does not approve, for works which we have chosen are "vain worship" (Matt. 15:9). The fact that Christ speaks of leaving wife and children makes it even clearer that he does not approve this kind of flight, since we know that the command of God forbids deserting wife and children. The other kind of leaving is that which happens by a command of God, when a government or a tyranny forces us either to leave or to deny the Gospel. Here we have the command rather to bear the injury, to let property, wife, and children, even life itself, be taken from us. This kind of leaving Christ approves. He adds the phrase "for the Gospel" (Mark 10:29) to show that he is talking not about those who do injury to wife and children but about those who bear injury because of the confession of the Gospel. We should leave our body, too, 42 for the Gospel. But it would be silly to conclude from this that it is a service to God to commit suicide and to leave our body without the command of God. So it is silly to maintain that it is a service to God to leave possessions, friends, wife, and children without the command of God.

It is evident, therefore, that they wickedly twist the saying 43 of Christ in applying it to monastic life, unless perhaps the statement

[9] *Lives of the Fathers*, III, *Verba seniorum*, 130.
[1] See above, XXVII, 12 and note.

that they will receive a hundredfold in this life applies here. Many become monks not for the sake of the Gospel but for the sake of food and leisure; instead of a slender inheritance they find the most ample riches. But as the whole monastic system is full of coun-   44 terfeits, so they quote passages of Scripture under false pretenses. Thus they are guilty of a double sin—deceiving men, and doing so under the pretext of the divine name.

They quote another passage on perfection (Matt. 19:21), "If   45 you would be perfect, go, sell what you possess and give to the poor; and come, follow me." This passage has exercised many people because they imagined that perfection consists in casting off possessions and the control of property. Let the philosophers praise   46 Aristippus for throwing a great weight of gold into the sea.[2] Such examples have nothing to do with Christian perfection. The distribution, control, and possession of property are civil ordinances, approved by the Word of God in the commandment (Ex. 20:15), "You shall not steal." The abandonment of property is neither commanded nor advised in the Scriptures. The poverty of the Gospel (Matt. 5:3) does not consist in the abandonment of property, but in the absence of greed and of trust in riches. Thus David was poor in a very rich kingdom.

Since the abandonment of property is therefore merely a   47 human tradition, it is a useless service. It is an exaggeration to praise it the way the *Extravagant* does, saying that renouncing the ownership of everything for God is meritorious and holy and the way of perfection.[3] It is highly dangerous to heap such extravagant praises upon something that conflicts with political order. Yet Christ calls   48 it perfection here! Yes, he does, but they do violence to the text when they quote it in a mutilated form. Perfection consists in that which Christ adds, "Follow me." This sets forth the example   49 of obedience in a calling. Since callings vary, this calling is not for everyone, but only for the person with whom Christ is talking here. Thus the call of David to rule, or of Abraham to sacrifice his son, are not for us to imitate. Callings are personal, just as matters of business themselves vary with times and persons; but the example of obedience is universal. It would have been perfection for this   50 young man to believe and obey this calling. So it is perfection for each of us with true faith to obey his own calling.

Third, in monastic vows chastity is promised. We have said   51 above in connection with the marriage of priests that the law of

---

[2] Actually, the ancient philosopher Aristippus threw his gold into the sea to prevent its falling into the hands of pirates.
[3] From a constitution of Pope Nicholas III.

nature in men cannot be repealed by vows or laws.[4] Since not everyone has the gift of continence, many fail in their continence because of weakness. Nor can any vows or any laws abolish the commandment of the Holy Spirit (I Cor. 7:2), "Because of the temptation to immorality, each man should have his own wife." Therefore such a vow is not lawful for anybody whose weakness causes him to defile himself because he does not have the gift of continence. On this 52 whole topic we have said enough earlier. It is indeed strange that with such dangers and scandals going on before their very eyes, our opponents should defend their traditions, contrary to the clear command of God. They are also undaunted by the voice of Christ upbraiding the Pharisees for setting up traditions contrary to the command of God.[5]

Fourth, those who live in monasteries are released by such 53 wicked ceremonies as the desecration of the Mass by its application to the dead for the sake of profit. Then there is the worship of saints which is guilty of a double fault: it arrogates Christ's place to the saints, and it worships them wickedly. Thus the Dominicans made up the rosary of the blessed Virgin,[6] which is mere babbling,[7] as stupid as it is wicked, nourishing a false confidence. This wickedness, too, is used only for the sake of profit. Meanwhile they neither 54 hear nor preach the Gospel about the free forgiveness of sins for Christ's sake, about the righteousness of faith, about true penitence, about works that have the command of God. But they spend their time either on philosophical discussions or on ceremonial traditions that obscure Christ.

Here we shall not discuss their whole ceremonial worship— 55 lessons, chants, and the like—which could be tolerated if they were used as exercises, the way lessons are in school, with the purpose of teaching the listeners and, in the process of teaching, prompting some of them to fear or faith. But now they imagine that these ceremonies are the worship of God to merit the forgiveness of sins for them and for others. That is why they multiply these ceremonies. If they undertook them in order to teach and exhort the hearers, brief and pointed lessons would be more useful than these endless babblings. Thus 56 the whole monastic life is full of hypocrisy and false opinions. In addition to all this, there is the danger that those who belong to these chapters are forced to agree with the persecutors of the truth. Therefore there are many serious and cogent reasons that release good men from this way of life.

---

[4] See above, XXIII, 6-27.
[5] Matt. 15:3.
[6] A legend of the fifteenth century ascribes the origin of the rosary to a vision of Mary by Dominic, founder of the Dominicans.
[7] Matt. 6:7.

Finally, the canons themselves release many who took their 57 vows without proper judgment because they were deceived by the tricks of the monks or because they were under duress from their friends. Not even the canons maintain that such vows are really vows. From all this it is apparent that there are many arguments for the stand that monastic vows, as made until now, are not vows, and that therefore it is proper to abandon a way of life so full of hypocrisy and false opinions.

Here they quote against us the example of the Nazarites from 58 the Old Testament.[8] But those men did not undertake their vows with the opinions which, as we have said, we condemn in the vows of the monks. The ritual of the Nazarites was intended to exercise or show faith before men, not to merit the forgiveness of sins before God or to justify before God. Furthermore, just as circumcision or the slaughter of victims would not be an act of worship now, so the ritual of the Nazarites should not be proposed as an act of worship but should be regarded simply as a matter of indifference. Hence it is not right to compare monasticism, thought up without a Word of God as an act of worship to merit forgiveness of sins and justification, with the ritual of the Nazarites, which had a Word of God and was not meant to merit the forgiveness of sins but to be an outward exercise like the other ceremonies of the Old Testament. The same can be said about other vows described in the Old Testament.

They also cite the case of the Rechabites who, as Jeremiah 59 writes (35:6), neither had any possessions nor drank any wine. Yes, indeed, the example of the Rechabites is a beautiful parallel to our monks, whose monasteries are fancier than kings' palaces and who live most sumptuously. Though they were poor in everything, the Rechabites were married; though our monks abound in every delight, they claim to be celibate.

Besides, examples ought to be interpreted according to the rule, 60 that is, according to sure and clear passages of Scripture, not against the rule or the passages. It is a sure thing that our observances 61 do not merit the forgiveness of sins or justification. When the Rechabites are praised, therefore, we must note that they did not observe their way of life out of the belief that they would merit forgiveness of sins by it, or that this work was itself an act of worship that justified, or that because of it—not because of the promised Seed, through the mercy of God—they would attain eternal life. But

---

[8] Roman Confutation: "In the Old Testament God approved the vows of the Nazarites (Num. 6:2) and the vows of the Rechabites, who neither drank wine nor ate grapes (Jer. 36:6, 19), while he strictly requires that a vow once made must be fulfilled (Deut. 23:21, 22) . . . God also teaches expressly through the prophet (Isa. 56:4, 5) that monastic vows please him . . ." (Pt. II, Art. VI).

because they had a command from their parents, they are praised for their obedience, which God commanded (Ex. 20:12), "Honor your father and your mother."

Then, too, the custom had an immediate purpose: since they 62 were nomads rather than Israelites, their father apparently wanted to distinguish them by certain marks from their countrymen, lest they fall back into the wickedness of their countrymen. By these marks he wanted to remind them of the teaching of faith and immortality— surely a lawful purpose. But vastly different purposes are set forth for monasticism. They imagine that the works of monasticism are acts of worship and that they merit forgiveness of sins and justification. Thus the example of the Rechabites does not resemble 63 monasticism. We shall not even discuss the other evils inherent in present-day monasticism.

They also cite I Tim. 5:11, 12 on the widows who served the 64 church and were supported from public funds, "They desire to marry, and so they incur condemnation for having violated their first faith." First, even if we suppose that Paul is talking here about 65 vows, this passage does not support monastic vows, taken for wicked acts of worship and with the idea that they merit forgiveness of sins and justification. For Paul loudly condemns all worship, all laws, all works, if they are observed in order to merit the forgiveness of sins or to secure eternal life for us instead of mercy for Christ's sake. Therefore the vows of the widows, if any, must have been different from monastic vows.

If our opponents insist upon misapplying this passage to vows, 66 they must also misapply the other one which forbids that anyone "be enrolled as a widow who is under sixty years of age" (I Tim. 5:9). Thus vows made before that age must be invalid. As a matter 67 of fact, the church did not yet know about these vows. Paul condemns the widows, not because they were getting married (he commands the younger ones to marry, v. 14), but because they became wanton while being supported from public funds and thus lost the faith. This is what he calls "first faith"—not a monastic vow, but Christianity. He uses "faith" this way in the same chapter (I Tim. 5:8), "If any one does not provide for his relatives, and especially for his own family, he has disowned the faith." He talks about faith differently 68 from the sophists. He does not attribute faith to people who have a mortal sin; therefore he says that those who do not provide for their relatives have rejected the faith. In the same way he says that the wanton women had rejected the faith.

We have run through a number of our arguments, and in passing 69 we have refuted the objections of our opponents. We have assembled all this not only for the sake of our opponents, but even more for the sake of showing pious hearts why they should reject the hypocrisy and the sham worship of the monks, which Christ cancels with one declaration when he says (Matt. 15:9), "In vain do they worship me with the precepts of men." Hence the vows themselves and the observance of foods, lessons, chants, vestments, sandals, cinctures— all these are unprofitable services before God. And let every pious heart know and be sure that such ideas as this are plain, damnable pharisaism: that these observances merit the forgiveness of sins; that because of them we are accounted righteous; that we attain eternal life because of them rather than because of Christ through mercy. Holy men who followed this way of life must have come to reject   70 any confidence in such observances, learning that they had forgiveness of sins freely for Christ's sake, that for Christ's sake by mercy they would attain eternal life and not for the sake of such services, and that God is pleased only with services instituted by his Word and done in faith.

[ARTICLE XXVIII.] ECCLESIASTICAL POWER

Here our opponents rant about the privileges and the ecclesiasti-   1 cal estate, and they conclude with the summary: "Everything is false that the present article states against the immunity of churches and priests." [9] This is sheer slander, for in this article we have been   2 arguing about something different. Besides, we have often testified that we do not criticize political ordinances nor the gifts and privileges of princes.[1]

But if our opponents would only listen to the complaints of   3 churches and pious hearts! Our opponents valiantly defend their own position and wealth. Meanwhile they neglect the state of the churches, and they do not see to it that there is proper preaching and administration of the sacraments in the churches. They admit all kinds of people to the priesthood quite indiscriminately. Then they impose intolerable burdens on them, as though they took pleasure in the destruction of their fellowmen. They demand greater strictness in the observance of their traditions than of the Gospel. In these   4 very serious and difficult controversies the people desperately want instruction in order to have a sure way to go. Instead of alleviating such minds tortured by doubt, they call to arms. In these evident questions they set forth an edict written in blood, threatening men with horrible punishments unless they act in clear opposition to God's commands. But here you should see the tears of the sufferers and   5 hear the pitiful complaints of many good men. God undoubtedly sees

[9] Roman Confutation, Pt. II, Art. VII, 5.
[1] E.g., Augsburg Confession, XXVIII.

and hears them, and it is to him that you will some day have to give account of your stewardship.

In this article of the Confession we included various subjects. 6 But our opponents' only reply is that bishops have the power to rule and to correct by force in order to guide their subjects toward the goal of eternal bliss, and that the power to rule requires the power to judge, define, distinguish, and establish what is helpful or conducive to the aforementioned goal.[2] These are the words of the Confutation, by which our opponents inform us that bishops have the authority to create laws which are useful for attaining eternal life. That is the issue in controversy.

In the church we must keep this teaching, that we receive 7 forgiveness of sins freely for Christ's sake by faith. We must also keep the teaching that human traditions are useless as acts of worship, and that therefore neither sin nor righteousness depends upon food, drink, clothing, and similar matters. Christ wanted to leave their use free when he said (Matt. 15:11), "What goes into the mouth does not defile a man." And Paul says (Rom. 14:17), "The kingdom of God is not food or drink." Thus bishops have no right to 8 create traditions apart from the Gospel as though they merited the forgiveness of sins or were acts of worship that pleased God as righteousness. Nor do the bishops have the right to burden consciences with such traditions so that it would be a sin to omit them. All this is taught by that one passage in Acts (15:9), where the apostles say that hearts are cleansed by faith and then go on to forbid the imposing of a yoke, showing how dangerous this is and enlarging on the sin of those who burden the church. "Why do you make a trial of God?" they say (Acts 15:10). But this thunderbolt does not scare our opponents, who vigorously defend their traditions and wicked notions.

Earlier they also condemned Article XV,[3] in which we main- 9 tained that traditions do not merit the forgiveness of sins; here they also say that traditions are conducive to eternal life.[4] Do they merit forgiveness of sins? Are they acts of worship which please God as righteousness? Do they make hearts alive? In Colossians (2:20- 10 23) Paul denies that traditions avail for eternal righteousness and eternal life since food, drink, clothing, and the like are things which perish as they are used. But it is eternal things, the Word of God and the Holy Spirit, that work eternal life in the heart. So let our opponents explain how traditions are conducive to eternal life.

---

[2] Roman Confutation, Pt. II, Art. VII, 4.

[3] See above, XV.

[4] Roman Confutation: ". . . Bishops have the power not only of the ministry of the Word but also of ruling and forcibly correcting in order to direct subjects to the goal of eternal bliss" (Pt. II, Art. VII).

The Gospel clearly testifies that traditions should not be   11
imposed on the church to merit forgiveness of sins or to be acts of
worship that please God as righteousness or to burden consciences so
that their omission is judged to be a sin. Therefore our opponents
will never be able to show that bishops have the power to institute
such acts of worship.

In the Confession we have said what power the Gospel grants   12
to bishops. Those who are now bishops do not perform the duties of
bishops according to the Gospel, though they may well be bishops
according to canonical polity, to which we do not object. But we are
talking about a bishop according to the Gospel. We like the old   13
division of power into the power of the order and the power of
jurisdiction.[5] Therefore a bishop has the power of the order, namely,
the ministry of Word and sacraments. He also has the power of
jurisdiction, namely, the authority to excommunicate those who are
guilty of public offenses or to absolve them if they are converted and
ask for absolution. A bishop does not have the power of a tyrant   14
to act without a definite law, nor that of a king to act above the
law. But he has a definite command, a definite Word of God, which
he ought to teach and according to which he ought to exercise his
jurisdiction. Therefore it does not follow that since they have a
certain jurisdiction bishops may institute new acts of worship, for
worship does not belong to their jurisdiction. They have the Word,
they have the command about when they should exercise their jurisdiction, namely, when anyone does something contrary to that Word
which they have received from Christ.

In the Confession we nevertheless added the extent to which   15
it is legitimate for them to create traditions, namely, that they must
not be necessary acts of worship but a means for preserving order
in the church, for the sake of peace. These must not ensnare consciences as though they were commanding necessary acts of worship.
This is what Paul teaches when he says (Gal. 5:1), "Stand fast in the
freedom with which Christ has set you free, and do not submit again
to a yoke of slavery." Therefore the use of such ordinances   16
ought to be left free, only that offenses should be avoided and that
they be not regarded as necessary acts of worship. Thus even the
apostles ordained many things that were changed by time, and they
did not set them down as though they could not be changed. For
they did not contradict their own writings, in which they worked
hard to free the church from the idea that human rites are necessary
acts of worship.

This is the simple way to interpret traditions. We should know   17
that they are not necessary acts of worship, and yet we should ob-

---

[5] *Potestas ordinis, potestas jurisdictionis.*

serve them in their place and without superstition, in order to avoid offenses. This is the way many great and learned men in the 18 church have felt about it. We do not see what possible objection there can be to this. Certainly the statement, "He who hears you hears me" (Luke 10:16), is not referring to traditions but is rather directed against traditions. It is not what they call a "commandment with unlimited authority," but rather a "caution about something prescribed," about a special commandment. It is a testimony given to the apostles so that we may believe them on the basis of another's Word rather than on the basis of their own. For Christ wants to assure us, as was necessary, that the Word is efficacious when it is delivered by men and that we should not look for another word from heaven. "He who hears you hears me" cannot be applied to 19 traditions. For Christ requires them to teach in such a way that he might be heard, because he says, "hears me." Therefore he wants his voice, his Word to be heard, not human traditions. Thus these asses take a statement that supports our position and contains the deepest kind of comfort and teaching, and they misapply it to these trifles, distinction of foods and clothing and the like.

They also quote the statement (Heb. 13:17), "Obey your 20 leaders."[6] This statement requires obedience to the Gospel; it does not create an authority for bishops apart from the Gospel. Bishops must not create traditions contrary to the Gospel, nor interpret their traditions in a manner contrary to the Gospel. When they do so, we are forbidden to obey them by the statement (Gal. 1:8), "If anyone preaches another Gospel, let him be accursed."

We give the same response to the passage (Matt. 23:3), 21 "Observe whatever they tell you." Clearly it does not set down the universal commandment that we are to observe everything, for elsewhere (Acts 5:29) Scripture commands that we must obey God rather than men. To the extent that they teach wicked things, they should not be heard. But these are wicked things: that human traditions are the worship of God; that they are necessary acts of worship; that they merit forgiveness of sins and eternal life.

They also raise an objection on the basis of the public offenses 22 and commotions which have arisen under the pretext of our teaching.[7] We shall respond to this in brief. If all the offenses are 23 put together, still the one doctrine of the forgiveness of sins, that by faith we freely obtain the forgiveness of sins for Christ's sake, brings

---

[6] Not in the Roman Confutation but elsewhere; e.g., Herborn, *Enchiridion*, 23, 27.

[7] Roman Confutation: "Nor does Christian liberty, which they adduce as an argument, avail them since this is not liberty but prodigious license which, inculcated in the people, excites them to fatal and most dangerous sedition" (Pt. II, Art. VII).

enough good to hide all the evils. Originally this gained for Luther 24
not only our good will but that of many who are now opposed to us.
"The former good will ceases, and mortals are forgetful," said Pindar.[8]
Still we will not forsake the truth which the church needs, nor can we
agree with our opponents who condemn it. For we must obey 25
God rather than men (Acts 5:29). Those who originally condemned
the clear truth, and are now most cruelly persecuting it, will give an
account for the schism that has been provoked. Besides, are there
no offenses among our opponents? What evil there is in the 26
sacrilegious desecration of the Mass for profit! What disgrace there
is in celibacy! But let us skip over the comparison. For the time being
we have made this reply to the Confutation. Now we leave it 27
to the judgment of all pious people whether our opponents are right
in boasting that they have really refuted our Confession with the
Scriptures.

[8] Pindar, *Isthmionikai*, VII, 23, 24.

IV

THE SMALCALD ARTICLES

Articles
of Christian doctrine

which were to have been presented by our party at
the council in Mantua, or wherever else the council
was to have been convened, and which were to
indicate what we could or could not accept or yield.
Written by Dr. Martin Luther in the year 1537

INTRODUCTION

*During the early years of the Reformation Luther and others
proposed again and again that a general council of the church be
convened to discuss and arbitrate the questions of doctrine and practice
that were in controversy. When sterner measures had failed to extirpate
the Protestant heresies, Pope Paul III finally called a council in June,
1536, to meet in Mantua the following May. Although the council
did not actually convene until 1545, and then in Trent, the papal
summons confronted the Lutherans with the necessity of deciding what
their attitude toward such a council should be. This was especially
necessary since the situation was no longer the same as it had been
when Luther first appealed to a council.*

*Under these circumstances the elector of Saxony instructed Luther
in a letter of Dec. 11, 1536, to prepare a statement indicating the
articles of faith in which concessions might be made for the sake of
peace and the articles in which no concessions could be made (see
below, Preface, 1). Luther set to work at once on what came to be
called "The Smalcald Articles." By Dec. 28 the document was ready
for review by a small group of theologians assembled in Wittenberg,
who, among other things, proposed the addition of the section on the
invocation of saints (see p. 297). The first eight signatures were
affixed at this time, Philip Melanchthon's with a reservation (see p. 316.
The elector of Saxony then took the Articles to Smalcald, where*

*representatives of the Smalcald League met on Feb. 8, 1537, in the
hope of having the document adopted. This hope was not realized,
partly because Luther's continued illness prevented him from attending
and throwing the weight of his personal influence behind the proposed
adoption and partly because Melanchthon succeeded in persuading the
princes that the Articles would only precipitate doctrinal disputes
among the members of the League. Although not officially endorsed
at Smalcald, the Articles were signed by many of the clergymen who
were present in token of their personal adherence to the faith expressed
therein. In later years the Articles were looked upon with growing
favor as a witness to genuine Lutheranism, and as such they were
finally incorporated in the Book of Concord.*

*The English translation is based on the German text. Only the most
significant variants from the later Latin version are indicated in the
footnotes.*

PREFACE OF DR. MARTIN LUTHER

Pope Paul III called a council to meet in Mantua last year,[1] in |
Whitsuntide. Afterwards he transferred the council from Mantua, and
it is not yet known where it will or can be held. In any case, we had
reason to expect that we might be summoned to appear before the
council or be condemned without being summoned. I was therefore
instructed[2] to draft and assemble articles of our faith to serve as a basis
for possible deliberations and to indicate, on the one hand, what and
in how far we were willing and able to yield to the papists and, on the
other hand, what we intended to hold fast to and persevere in.

Accordingly I assembled these articles and submitted them to our   2
representatives.[3] The latter accepted them, unanimously adopted them
as their confession, and resolved[4] that these articles should be presented
publicly as the confession of our faith if the pope and his adherents
ever became so bold as seriously, in good faith, and without deception

---

[1] This preface was written by Luther in 1538, when he prepared the
Articles for publication.

[2] By Elector John Frederick of Saxony, early in December, 1536.

[3] The Articles were reviewed and somewhat modified in a conference of
theologians held in Wittenberg in December, 1536, and they were considered
and signed by theologians at the meeting of the Smalcald League held in
Smalcald in February, 1537. However, the princes and free cities of the
Smalcald League ("our representatives") did not, as Luther mistakenly
supposed, adopt the Articles.

[4] Luther was still laboring in 1538 under the misapprehension that these
things had happened in Smalcald.

or treachery to hold a truly free council, as indeed the pope is in duty bound to do.

But the Roman court is dreadfully afraid of a free council and 3 flees from the light in a shameful fashion. Even adherents of that party have lost hope that the Roman court will ever permit a free council, to say nothing of calling one. They are deeply offended, as well they might be, and are not a little troubled on this account, for they perceive that the pope prefers to see all Christendom lost and all souls damned rather than suffer himself and his adherents to be reformed a little and allow limitations to be placed on his tyranny.

Nevertheless, I have decided to publish these articles so that, if I should die before a council meets (which I fully expect, for those knaves who shun the light and flee from the day take such wretched pains to postpone and prevent the council), those who live after me may have my testimony and confession (in addition to the confession[5] which I have previously given) to show where I have stood until now and where, by God's grace, I will continue to stand.

Why do I say this? Why should I complain? I am still alive. I 4 am still writing, preaching, and lecturing every day. Yet there are some who are so spiteful—not only among our adversaries, but also false brethren among those who profess to be adherents of our party—that they dare to cite my writings and teachings against me. They let me look on and listen, although they know very well that I teach otherwise. They try to clothe their venomous spirits in the garments of my labor and thus mislead the poor people in my name. Imagine what will happen after I am dead!

I suppose I should reply to everything while I am still living. But 5 how can I stop all the mouths of the devil? What, above all, can I do with those (for they are all poisoned) who do not pay attention to what I write and who keep themselves busy by shamefully twisting and corrupting my every word and letter? I shall let the devil—or ultimately the wrath of God—answer them as they deserve. I often think of 6 the good Gerson,[6] who doubted whether one ought to make good writings public. If one does not, many souls that might have been saved are neglected. On the other hand, if one does, the devil appears at once to poison and pervert everything by wagging countless venomous and malicious tongues and thus destroying the fruit. However, what such persons accomplish is manifest. For although 7 they slander us so shamefully and try by their lies to keep the people on their side, God has constantly promoted his work, has made their following smaller and smaller and ours ever larger, and has caused, and still causes, them and their lies to be put to shame.

[5] Luther's "Confession Concerning the Holy Supper" (1528).
[6] John Gerson (1363-1429) in his *De laude scriptorum,* XI.

Let me illustrate this. There was a doctor[7] here in Wittenberg, 8
sent from France, who reported in our presence that his king had been
persuaded beyond a doubt that among us there is no church, no
government, and no state of matrimony, but that all live promiscuously
like cattle and everybody does what he pleases. Imagine how those 9
will face us on the last day, before the judgment seat of Christ, who in
their writings have urged such big lies upon the king and foreign peoples
as if they were the unadulterated truth! Christ, the lord and judge of us
all, knows very well that they lie and have lied. I am sure that he will
pronounce sentence upon them. God convert those who are capable of
conversion and turn them to repentance! As for the rest, wretchedness
and woe will be their lot forever.

But let us return to the subject. I should be very happy to see a 10
true council assemble in order that many things and many people might
derive benefit from it. Not that we ourselves need such a council, for
by God's grace our churches have now been so enlightened and
supplied with the pure Word and the right use of the sacraments, with
an understanding of the various callings of life, and with true works,
that we do not ask for a council for our own sake, and we have no
reason to hope or expect that a council would improve our conditions.
But in the dioceses of the papists we see so many vacant and desolate
parishes everywhere that our hearts would break with grief.[8] Yet
neither the bishops nor the canons care how the poor people live or die,
although Christ died for them too. Those people cannot hear Christ
speak to them as the true shepherd speaking to his sheep. This 11
horrifies me and makes me fear that he may cause a council of angels
to descend on Germany and destroy us utterly, like Sodom and
Gomorrah, because we mock him so shamefully with the council.[9]

Besides such necessary concerns of the church, there are count- 12
less temporal matters that need reform. There is discord among princes
and political estates. Usury and avarice have burst in like a deluge and
have taken on the color of legality. Wantonness, lewdness, extravagance
in dress, gluttony, gambling, vain display, all manner of vice and
wickedness, disobedience of subjects, domestics, and laborers, extortion
in every trade and on the part of peasants—who can enumerate everything?—these have gained the ascendancy to such an extent that ten
councils and twenty diets would not be able to set things right again.
If members of a council were to consider such fundamental matters 13
of the ecclesiastical and secular estates as are contrary to God, their

---

[7] Dr. Gervasius Waim, or Wain, legate of King Francis I of France, was
in Saxony in 1531.

[8] In Luther's table talk of Sept. 10, 1538 (*WA, TR*, 4: No. 4002), it was
reported that 600 rich parishes in the diocese of Würzburg were vacant.

[9] Latin: pretext of a council.

hands would be so full that their trifling and tomfoolery with albs, great tonsures, broad cinctures, bishops' and cardinals' hats and crosiers, and similar nonsense would soon be forgotten. If we would first carry out God's commands and precepts in the spiritual and temporal estates, we would find enough time to reform the regulations concerning fasts, vestments, tonsures, and chasubles. But if we are willing to swallow camels and strain out gnats,[1] if we let logs stand and dispute about specks,[2] we might just as well be satisfied with such a council.

I have drafted only a few articles, for, apart from these, God has |4 laid so many tasks upon us in church, state, and family that we can never carry them out. What is the use of adopting a multitude of decrees and canons in a council, especially when the primary things, which are commanded by God, are neither regarded nor observed? It is as if we were to expect God to acquiesce in our mummeries while we trample his solemn commandments underfoot. But our sins oppress us and keep God from being gracious to us, for we do not repent and we even try to justify all our abominations.

Dear Lord Jesus Christ, assemble a council of thine own, and |5 by thy glorious advent deliver thy servants. The pope and his adherents are lost. They will have nothing to do with Thee. But help us, poor and wretched souls who cry unto Thee and earnestly seek Thee according to the grace which Thou hast given us by thy Holy Spirit, who with Thee and the Father liveth and reigneth, blessed forever. Amen.

[PART I]

The first part of the Articles treats the sublime articles of the divine majesty, namely:

1. That Father, Son, and Holy Spirit, three distinct persons in one divine essence and nature, are one God, who created heaven and earth, etc.

2. That the Father was begotten by no one, the Son was begotten by the Father, and the Holy Spirit proceeded from the Father and the Son.

3. That only the Son became man, and neither the Father nor the Holy Spirit.

4. That the Son became man in this manner: he was conceived by the Holy Spirit, without the cooperation of man, and was born of the

---

[1] Cf. Matt. 23:24.
[2] Cf. Matt. 7:3-5.

pure, holy, and virgin Mary.³ Afterwards he suffered, died, was buried, descended to hell, rose from the dead, and ascended to heaven; and he is seated at the right hand of God, will come to judge the living and the dead, etc., as the Apostles' Creed, the Athanasian Creed, and the Catechism in common use for children⁴ teach.

These articles are not matters of dispute or contention, for both parties confess them.⁵ Therefore, it is not necessary to treat them at greater length.

[PART II]

The second part treats the articles which pertain to the office and work of Jesus Christ, or to our redemption.

[ARTICLE I. CHRIST AND FAITH]

The first and chief article is this, that Jesus Christ, our God and   1 Lord, "was put to death for our trespasses and raised again for our justification" (Rom. 4:25). He alone is "the Lamb of God, who   2 takes away the sin of the world" (John 1:29). "God has laid upon him the iniquities of us all" (Isa. 53:6). Moreover, "all have sinned,"   3 and "they are justified by his grace as a gift, through the redemption which is in Christ Jesus, by his blood" (Rom. 3:23-25).

Inasmuch as this must be believed and cannot be obtained or   4 apprehended by any work, law, or merit, it is clear and certain that such faith alone justifies us, as St. Paul says in Romans 3, "For we hold that a man is justified by faith apart from works of law" (Rom. 3:28), and again, "that he [God] himself is righteous and that he justifies him who has faith in Jesus" (Rom. 3:26).

Nothing in this article can be given up or compromised,⁶ even if   5 heaven and earth and things temporal should be destroyed. For as St. Peter says, "There is no other name under heaven given among men by which we must be saved" (Acts 4:12). "And with his stripes we are healed" (Isa. 53:5).

On this article rests all that we teach and practice against the pope, the devil, and the world. Therefore we must be quite certain and have no doubts about it. Otherwise all is lost, and the pope, the devil, and all our adversaries will gain the victory.

---

³ Latin: ever virgin Mary.

⁴ The second article of the Creed in Luther's Small Catechism.

⁵ I.e., Roman and Lutheran parties alike acknowledged the creeds of the ancient church. What follows in Part II makes it clear that, despite this, the two parties disagreed in their interpretation and application of these creeds.

⁶ Latin adds: nor can any believer concede or permit anything contrary to it.

ARTICLE II. [THE MASS]

The Mass in the papacy must be regarded as the greatest and most 1 horrible abomination because it runs into direct and violent conflict with this fundamental article. Yet, above and beyond all others, it has been the supreme and most precious of the papal idolatries, for it is held that this sacrifice or work of the Mass (even when offered by an evil scoundrel) delivers men from their sins, both here in this life and yonder in purgatory, although in reality this can and must be done by the Lamb of God alone, as has been stated above.[7] There is to be no concession or compromise in this article either, for the first article does not permit it.

If there were reasonable papists, one would speak to them in the 2 following friendly fashion:

"Why do you cling so tenaciously to your Masses?

"1. After all, they are a purely human invention. They are not commanded by God. And we can discard all human inventions, for Christ says, 'In vain do they worship me, teaching as doctrines the precepts of men' (Matt. 15:9).

"2. The Mass is unnecessary, and so it can be omitted without 3 sin and danger.

"3. The sacrament can be had in a far better and more blessed 4 manner—indeed, the only blessed manner—according to the institution of Christ. Why, then, do you drive the world into wretchedness and woe on account of an unnecessary and fictitious matter when the sacrament can be had in another and more blessed way?

"Let the people be told openly that the Mass, as trumpery, can be 5 omitted without sin, that no one will be damned for not observing it, and that one can be saved in a better way without the Mass. Will the Mass not then collapse of itself—not only for the rude rabble, but also for all godly, Christian, sensible, God-fearing people—especially if they hear that it is a dangerous thing which was fabricated and invented without God's Word and will?

"4. Since such countless and unspeakable abuses have arisen 6 everywhere through the buying and selling of Masses, it would be prudent to do without the Mass for no other reason than to curb such abuses, even if it actually possessed some value in and of itself. How much the more should it be discontinued in order to guard forever against such abuses when it is so unnecessary, useless, and dangerous and when we can obtain what is more necessary, more useful, and more certain without the Mass.

"5. The Mass is and can be nothing else than a human work, 7 even a work of evil scoundrels (as the canon[8] and all books on the

---

[7] Pt. II, Art I, above.
[8] Roman canon of the Mass.

subject declare), for by means of the Mass men try to reconcile themselves and others to God and obtain and merit grace and the forgiveness of sins. It is observed for this purpose when it is best observed. What other purpose could it have? Therefore, it should be condemned and must be abolished because it is a direct contradiction to the fundamental article, which asserts that it is not the celebrant of a Mass and what he does but the Lamb of God and the Son of God who takes away our sin." [9]

Somebody may seek to justify himself by saying that he wishes to   8 communicate himself for the sake of his own devotion.[1] This is not honest, for if he really desires to commune, he can do so most fittingly and properly in the sacrament administered according to Christ's institution. To commune by himself is uncertain and unnecessary, and he does not know what he is doing because he follows a false human opinion and imagination without the sanction of God's Word. Nor is it right (even if everything else is in order) for   9 anyone to use the sacrament, which is the common possession of the church, to meet his own private need and thus trifle with it according to his own pleasure apart from the fellowship of the church.

This article concerning the Mass will be the decisive issue in the   10 council. Even if it were possible for the papists to make concessions to us in all other articles, it would not be possible for them to yield on this article. It is as Campegio[2] said in Augsburg: he would suffer himself to be torn to pieces before he would give up the Mass. So by God's help I would suffer myself to be burned to ashes before I would allow a celebrant of the Mass and what he does to be considered equal or superior to my Saviour, Jesus Christ. Accordingly we are and remain eternally divided and opposed the one to the other. The papists are well aware that if the Mass falls, the papacy will fall with it. Before they would permit this to happen, they would put us all to death.

Besides, this dragon's tail—that is, the Mass—has brought forth   11 a brood of vermin and the poison of manifold idolatries.

The first is purgatory. They were so occupied with requiem   12 Masses, with vigils, with the weekly, monthly, and yearly celebrations of requiems,[3] with the common week,[4] with All Souls' Day, and with

---

[9] Cf. John 1:29.

[1] Cf. *WA, Br,* 5:504, 505; *WA,* 8:438, 514.

[2] Lorenzo Campegio (1474-1539), the papal legate. The same anecdote also appears elsewhere.

[3] The celebration of Mass on the anniversary of the deceased is referred to as early as Tertullian (*De corona,* III), and celebrations on the week and month following death are mentioned by Ambrose (*De obitu Theodosii oratio,* III).

[4] The week following St. Michael's Day (Sept. 29), when many Masses were offered for the dead.

soul-baths[5] that the Mass was used almost exclusively for the dead although Christ instituted the sacrament for the living alone. Consequently purgatory and all the pomp, services, and business transactions associated with it are to be regarded as nothing else than illusions of the devil, for purgatory, too, is contrary to the fundamental article that Christ alone, and not the work of man, can help souls. Besides, nothing has been commanded or enjoined upon us with reference to the dead. All this may consequently be discarded, apart entirely from the fact that it is error and idolatry.

The papists here adduce passages from Augustine and some of 13 the Fathers[6] who are said to have written about purgatory. They suppose that we do not understand for what purpose and to what end the authors wrote these passages. St. Augustine[7] does not write that there is a purgatory, nor does he cite any passage of the Scriptures that would constrain him to adopt such an opinion. He leaves it undecided whether or not there is a purgatory and merely mentions that his mother asked that she be remembered at the altar or sacrament. Now, this is nothing but a human opinion of certain individuals and cannot establish an article of faith. That is the prerogative of God alone. But our papists make use of such human opinions to make men 14 believe their shameful, blasphemous, accursed traffic in Masses which are offered for souls in purgatory, etc. They can never demonstrate these things from Augustine. Only when they have abolished their traffic in purgatorial Masses (which St. Augustine never dreamed of) shall we be ready to discuss with them whether statements of St. Augustine are to be accepted when they are without the support of the Scriptures and whether the dead are to be commemorated in the sacrament. It will not do to make articles of faith out of the holy 15 Fathers' words or works. Otherwise what they ate, how they dressed, and what kind of houses they lived in would have to become articles of faith—as has happened in the case of relics. This means that[8] the Word of God shall establish articles of faith and no one else, not even an angel.[9]

The second is a consequence of this: evil spirits have introduced 16 the knavery of appearing as spirits of the departed[1] and, with unspeakable lies and cunning, of demanding Masses, vigils, pilgrimages, and other alms. We had to accept all these things as articles of faith 17

---

[5] Free baths endowed for the poor with the intention that the latter should pray for the donors' salvation.

[6] E.g., Gregory the Great, *Dialogs*, IV, 39.

[7] *Confessions*, IX, 11, 13.

[8] Latin: We have another rule, namely, that.

[9] Cf. Gal. 1:8.

[1] The reference is to spirit manifestations reported by Gregory the Great (*Dialogs*, IV, 40) and Peter Damiani (*Opusculum*, XXXIV, 5).

and had to live according to them. Moreover, the pope gave his approval to these things as well as to the Mass and all the other abominations. Here, too, there can be no concession or compromise.

The third are pilgrimages. Masses, forgiveness of sins, and 18 God's grace were sought here, too, for Masses dominated everything. It is certain that we have not been commanded to make pilgrimages, nor are they necessary, because we may obtain forgiveness and grace in a better way and may omit pilgrimages without sin and danger. Why do they neglect their own parishes, the Word of God, their wives and children, etc. and pursue these unnecessary, uncertain, harmful will-o'-the-wisps of the devil? They do so simply because the 19 devil has possessed the pope to praise and approve of these practices in order that great multitudes of people may turn aside from Christ to their own merits and (what is worst of all) become idolaters. Besides, it is an unnecessary, uncommanded, abortive, uncertain, and even harmful thing. Therefore there may be no concession or compro- 20 mise here either.

The fourth are fraternities.[2] Here monasteries, chapters, and 21 vicars have obligated themselves to transfer (by legal and open sale) all Masses, good works, etc. for the benefit of the living and the dead. Not only is this mere human trumpery, utterly unnecessary and without command, but it is contrary to the first article, concerning redemption.[3] Therefore, it is under no circumstances to be tolerated.

The fifth are relics. In this connection so many manifest lies 22 and so much nonsense has been invented about the bones of dogs and horses that even the devil has laughed at such knavery. Even if there were some good in them, relics should long since have been condemned. They are neither commanded nor commended. They are utterly unnecessary and useless. Worst of all, however, is the claim that 23 relics effect indulgences and the forgiveness of sin and that, like the Mass, etc., their use is a good work and a service of God.

The sixth place belongs to the precious indulgences, which are 24 granted to the living and the dead (for money) and by which the pope sells the merits of Christ together with the superabundant merits of all the saints and the entire church. These are not to be tolerated. Not only are they unnecessary and without commandment, but they are also contrary to the first article, for the merits of Christ are obtained by grace, through faith, without our work or pennies. They are offered to us without our money or merit, not by the power of the pope but by the preaching of God's Word.

---

[2] Since the eighth century members of certain monasteries obligated themselves to offer prayers and engage in works of piety in behalf of deceased monks. In the late Middle Ages similar obligations were assumed by groups of clergymen, clergymen and laymen, or only laymen.

[3] Pt. II, Art. I, above.

The Invocation of Saints

The invocation of saints is also one of the abuses of the Anti-   25
christ. It is in conflict with the first, chief article and undermines
knowledge of Christ. It is neither commanded nor recommended, nor
does it have any precedent in the Scriptures. Even if the invocation of
saints were a precious practice (which it is not), we have everything
a thousandfold better in Christ.

Although angels in heaven pray for us (as Christ himself also   26
does), and although saints on earth, and perhaps also in heaven, do
likewise, it does not follow that we should invoke angels and saints,
pray to them, keep fasts and festivals for them, say Masses and offer
sacrifices to them, establish churches, altars, and services for them,
serve them in still other ways, regard them as helpers in time of need,
and attribute all sorts of help to them, assigning to each of them a
special function,[4] as the papists teach and practice. This is idolatry.
Such honor belongs to God alone. As a Christian and a saint on   27
earth, you can pray for me, not in one particular necessity only, but
in every kind of need. However, I should not on this account pray to
you, invoke you, keep fasts and festivals and say Masses and offer
sacrifices in your honor, or trust in you for my salvation. There are
other ways in which I can honor, love, and thank you in Christ. If   28
such idolatrous honor is withdrawn from angels and dead saints, the
honor that remains will do no harm and will quickly be forgotten.
When spiritual and physical benefit and help are no longer expected,
the saints will cease to be molested in their graves and in heaven, for
no one will long remember, esteem, or honor them out of love when
there is no expectation of return.

In short, we cannot allow but must condemn the Mass, its   29
implications, and its consequences in order that we may retain the holy
sacrament in its purity and certainty according to the institution of
Christ and may use and receive it in faith.

Article III. [Chapters and Monasteries]

The chapters[5] and monasteries which in former times had been   1
founded with good intentions for the education of learned men and
decent women should be restored to such purposes in order that we
may have pastors, preachers, and other ministers in the church, others

---

[4] The notion that certain saints were specialists in intercession for specific
afflictions is discussed, for example, in Luther's "The Fourteen of Consolation" (1520).

[5] Associations of secular priests, called canons. There were also canonesses, women who lived under a rule without taking the perpetual vows of
nuns. Chapter schools were conducted for boys by canons and for girls
by canonesses.

who are necessary for secular government in cities and states, and also well trained girls to become mothers, housekeepers, etc.

If they are unwilling to serve this purpose, it would be better to   2 abandon them or tear them down rather than preserve them with their blasphemous services, invented by men, which claim to be superior to the ordinary Christian life and to the offices and callings established by God. All this, too, is in conflict with the first, fundamental article concerning redemption in Jesus Christ. Besides, like other human inventions, all this is without commandment, unnecessary, and useless. Moreover, it causes dangerous and needless effort, and accordingly the prophets call such service of God *aven*,[6] that is, vanity.

ARTICLE IV. [THE PAPACY]

The pope is not the head of all Christendom by divine right or   I according to God's Word, for this position belongs only to one, namely, to Jesus Christ. The pope is only the bishop and pastor of the churches in Rome and of such other churches as have attached themselves to him voluntarily or through a human institution (that is, a secular government).[7] These churches did not choose to be under him as under an overlord but chose to stand beside him as Christian brethren and companions, as the ancient councils[8] and the time of Cyprian[9] prove. But now no bishop dares to call the pope "brother," as was then   2 customary,[1] but must address him as "most gracious lord," as if he were a king or emperor. This we neither will nor should nor can take upon our consciences. Those who wish to do so had better not count on us!

Hence it follows that all the things that the pope has undertaken   3 and done on the strength of such false, mischievous, blasphemous, usurped authority have been and still are purely diabolical transactions and deeds (except what pertains to secular government,[2] where God sometimes permits much good to come to a people through a tyrant or scoundrel) which contribute to the destruction of the entire holy Christian church (in so far as this lies in his power) and come into conflict with the first, fundamental article which is concerned with redemption in Jesus Christ.

All the pope's bulls and books, in which he roars like a lion (as   4

[6] Cf. Zech. 10:2, Hab. 1:3, Isa. 1:13, etc.

[7] The secular power of the pope, the patrimony of Peter.

[8] Luther here refers to the Councils of Nicaea, Constantinople, Ephesus, and Chalcedon.

[9] See note 4, below, and also Melanchthon's "Treatise on the Power and Primacy of the Pope," below, 13-17.

[1] Luther often referred to the letters of Bishop Cyprian of Carthage (d. 258) to Pope Cornelius in which the pope is addressed as "very dear brother."

[2] See above, IV, 1, and note 1 at that place.

the angel in Rev. 10:3[3] suggests), are available. Here it is asserted that no Christian can be saved unless he is obedient to the pope and submits to him in all that he desires, says, and does.[4] This is nothing less than to say, "Although you believe in Christ, and in him have everything that is needful for salvation, this is nothing and all in vain unless you consider me your god and are obedient and subject to me." Yet it is manifest that the holy church was without a pope for more than five hundred years at the least[5] and that the churches of the Greeks and of many other nationalities have never been under the pope and are not at the present time. Manifestly (to repeat what has already 5 been said often) the papacy is a human invention, and it is not commanded, it is unnecessary, and it is useless. The holy Christian church can exist very well without such a head, and it would have remained much better if such a head had not been raised up by the devil. The papacy is of no use to the church because it exercises no 6 Christian office. Consequently the church must continue to exist without the pope.

Suppose that the pope would renounce the claim that he is the 7 head of the church by divine right or by God's command; suppose that it were necessary to have a head, to whom all others should adhere, in order that the unity of Christendom might better be preserved against the attacks of sects and heresies; and suppose that such a head would then be elected by men and it remained in their power and choice to change or depose this head. This is just the way in which the Council of Constance acted with reference to the popes when it deposed three and elected a fourth.[6] If, I say, the pope and the see of Rome were to concede and accept this (which is impossible), he would have to suffer the overthrow and destruction of his whole rule and estate, together with all his rights and pretensions. In short, he cannot do it. Even if he could, Christendom would not be helped in any way. There 8 would be even more sects than before because, inasmuch as subjection to such a head would depend on the good pleasure of men rather than on a divine command, he would very easily and quickly be despised and would ultimately be without any adherents at all. He would not always

---

[3] The reference in Luther's text, probably set down from memory, is mistakenly given as Rev. 12.

[4] The classic statement of extreme papal claims was Boniface VIII's bull *Unam Sanctam* (1302): "It is altogether necessarv to salvation for every human creature to be subject to the Roman pontiff."

[5] Luther often thought of Gregory I (590-604) as the last Roman bishop before the succession of popes began. See also Melanchthon's "Treatise on the Power and Primacy of the Pope," below, 19.

[6] John XXIII, Benedict XIV, and Gregory XII, rival claimants to the papacy, were removed from office (with the cooperation of the last-named) and Martin V was elected in their place by the Council of Constance (1414-1418).

have to have his residence in Rome or some other fixed place,[7] but it could be anywhere and in whatever church God would raise up a man fitted for such an office. What a complicated and confused state of affairs that would be!

Consequently the church cannot be better governed and main- 9 tained than by having all of us live under one head, Christ,[8] and by having all the bishops equal in office (however they may differ in gifts)[9] and diligently joined together in unity of doctrine, faith, sacraments, prayer, works of love, etc. So St. Jerome writes[1] that the priests of Alexandria governed the churches together and in common. The apostles did the same, and after them all the bishops throughout Christendom, until the pope raised his head over them all.

This[2] is a powerful demonstration that the pope is the real 10 Antichrist[3] who has raised himself over and set himself against Christ, for the pope will not permit Christians to be saved except by his own power, which amounts to nothing since it is neither established nor commanded by God. This is actually what St. Paul calls exalting 11 oneself over and against God.[4] Neither the Turks nor the Tartars, great as is their enmity against Christians, do this; those who desire to do so they allow to believe in Christ, and they receive bodily tribute and obedience from Christians.

However, the pope will not permit such faith but asserts that 12 one must be obedient to him in order to be saved.[5] This we are unwilling to do even if we have to die for it in God's name. All 13 this is a consequence of his wishing to be the head of the Christian church by divine right. He had to set himself up as equal to and above Christ and to proclaim himself the head, and then the lord of the church, and finally of the whole world. He went so far as to claim to be an earthly god[6] and even presumed to issue orders to the angels in heaven.[7]

[7] For example, the papal court was in Avignon from 1309 to 1377.

[8] Cf. Eph. 1:22; 4:15; 5:25; Col. 1:18.

[9] Cf. I Cor. 12:4, 8-10; Rom. 12:6-8.

[1] Quoting from memory, Luther here combines two citations from Jerome which he was fond of quoting: *Commentary on the Epistle to Titus*, 1:5, 6, and *Epistle to Euangelus the Presbyter*, No. 146.

[2] Latin: This doctrine.

[3] *Endechrist oder Widerchrist.*

[4] Cf. II Thess. 2:4.

[5] See IV, 4, above, and note 2 at that place.

[6] So Augustinus de Ancona (d. 1328), Zenzelinus de Cassanis (d. ca. 1350), Franciscus de Zabarellis (d. 1417).

[7] The reference is to the allegedly spurious bull of Pope Clement VI, *Ad memoriam reducendo*, of June 27, 1346, in which the pope is said to have commanded the angels "to lead to heaven the souls of the pilgrims who might die on their way to Rome" during the "holy year" of 1350.

When the teaching of the pope is distinguished from that of the   14 Holy Scriptures, or is compared with them, it becomes apparent that, at its best, the teaching of the pope has been taken from the imperial, pagan law[8] and is a teaching concerning secular transactions and judgments, as the papal decretals[9] show. In keeping with such teaching, instructions are given concerning the ceremonies of churches, vestments, food, personnel, and countless other puerilities, fantasies, and follies without so much as a mention of Christ, faith, and God's commandments.

Finally, it is most diabolical for the pope to promote his lies about Masses, purgatory, monastic life, and human works and services (which are the essence of the papacy) in contradiction to God, and to damn, slay, and plague all Christians who do not exalt and honor these abominations of his above all things. Accordingly, just as we cannot adore the devil himself as our lord or God, so we cannot suffer his apostle, the pope or Antichrist, to govern us as our head or lord, for deception, murder, and the eternal destruction of body and soul are characteristic of his papal government,[1] as I have demonstrated in many books.[2]

In these four articles they will have enough to condemn in the   15 council, for they neither can nor will concede to us even the smallest fraction of these articles. Of this we may be certain, and we must rely on the hope that Christ, our Lord, has attacked his adversaries and will accomplish his purpose by his Spirit and his coming.[3] Amen. In   16 the council we shall not be standing before the emperor or the secular authority, as at Augsburg,[4] where we responded to a gracious summons and were given a kindly hearing, but we shall stand before the pope and the devil himself, who does not intend to give us a hearing but only to damn, murder, and drive us to idolatry. Consequently we ought not here kiss his feet[5] or say, "You are my gracious lord," but we ought rather speak as the angel spoke to the devil in Zechariah, "The Lord rebuke you, O Satan" (Zech. 3:2).[6]

---

[8] That is, Roman law.

[9] Decisions of the popes in the form of letters.

[1] This passage is quoted below in the Formula of Concord, Solid Declaration, X, 20.

[2] E.g., *Resolutio super propositione de potestate papae* (1519).

[3] Cf. II Thess. 2:8.

[4] The diet of Augsburg in 1530, when the Augsburg Confession was presented. Here, as elsewhere, Luther spoke well of Emperor Charles V.

[5] All the faithful were required to kneel before the pope and kiss his foot in an act of homage (*adoratio*). This is still observed today at the election of a new pope. In 1520 Luther had written: "It is an unchristian, even anti-Christian, thing for a poor sinful man to allow his foot to be kissed by one who is a hundred times better than he is" (*WA*, 6:435).

[6] Originally Luther added here, *Pfui dein mal an*, "Shame on you!"

[PART III]

The following articles treat matters which we may discuss with learned and sensible men, or even among ourselves. The pope and his court do not care much about these things; they are not concerned about matters of conscience but only about money, honor, and power.

I. Sin

Here we must confess what St. Paul says in Rom. 5:12, namely, 1 that sin had its origin in one man, Adam, through whose disobedience all men were made sinners and became subject to death and the devil. This is called original sin, or the root sin.

The fruits of this sin are all the subsequent evil deeds which are 2 forbidden in the Ten Commandments, such as unbelief, false belief, idolatry, being without the fear of God, presumption, despair, blindness —in short, ignorance or disregard of God—and then also lying, swearing by God's name, failure to pray and call upon God, neglect of God's Word, disobedience to parents, murder, unchastity, theft, deceit, etc.

This hereditary sin[7] is so deep a corruption of nature that reason 3 cannot understand it. It must be believed because of the revelation in the Scriptures (Ps. 51:5, Rom. 5:12ff., Exod. 33:20, Gen. 3:6ff.). What the scholastic theologians taught concerning this article is therefore nothing but error and stupidity, namely,

1. That after the fall of Adam the natural powers of man have 4 remained whole and uncorrupted, and that man by nature possesses a right understanding and a good will, as the philosophers teach.[8]

2. Again, that man has a free will, either to do good and refrain 5 from evil or to refrain from good and do evil.

3. Again, that man is able by his natural powers to observe and 6 keep all the commandments of God.

4. Again, that man is able by his natural powers to love God 7 above all things and his neighbor as himself.

5. Again, if man does what he can, God is certain to grant him 8 his grace.

6. Again, when a man goes to the sacrament there is no need of 9 a good intention to do what he ought, but it is enough that he does not have an evil intention to commit sin, for such is the goodness of man's nature and such is the power of the sacrament.

---

[7] *Erbsunde; peccatum haereditarium.*
[8] E.g., Plato and Aristotle.

7. That it cannot be proved from the Scriptures that the Holy 10 Spirit and his gifts are necessary for the performance of a good work.

Such and many similar notions have resulted from misunder- 11 standing and ignorance concerning sin and concerning Christ, our Saviour. They are thoroughly pagan doctrines, and we cannot tolerate them. If such teachings were true, Christ would have died in vain, for there would be no defect or sin in man for which he would have had to die, or else he would have died only for the body and not for the soul inasmuch as the soul would be sound and only the body would be subject to death.

II. The Law

Here we maintain that the law was given by God first of all to 1 restrain sins by threats and fear of punishment and by the promise and offer of grace and favor. But this purpose failed because of the wickedness which sin has worked in man. Some, who hate the law 2 because it forbids what they desire to do and commands what they are unwilling to do, are made worse thereby. Accordingly, in so far as they are not restrained by punishment, they act against the law even more than before. These are the rude and wicked people who do evil whenever they have opportunity. Others become blind and pre- 3 sumptuous, imagining that they can and do keep the law by their own powers, as was just said above[9] concerning the scholastic theologians. Hypocrites and false saints are produced in this way.

However, the chief function or power of the law is to make 4 original sin manifest and show man to what utter depths his nature has fallen and how corrupt it has become. So the law must tell him that he neither has nor cares for God or that he worships strange gods —something that he would not have believed before without a knowledge of the law. Thus he is terror-stricken and humbled, becomes despondent and despairing, anxiously desires help but does not know where to find it, and begins to be alienated from God, to murmur, etc. This is what is meant by Rom. 4:15,[1] "The law brings wrath," and 5 Rom. 5:20, "Law came in to increase the trespass."

III. Repentance

This function of the law is retained and taught by the New 1 Testament. So Paul says in Rom. 1:18, "The wrath of God is revealed from heaven against all ungodliness and wickedness of men," and in Rom. 3:19, 20, "The whole world may be held accountable to God, for no human being will be justified in his sight." Christ also says in John 16:8, "The Holy Spirit will convince the world of sin."

[9] See Pt. III, Art. I, 3-10.
[1] Luther mistakenly wrote Rom. 3.

This, then, is the thunderbolt by means of which God with one 2 blow destroys both open sinners and false saints. He allows no one to justify himself. He drives all together into terror and despair. This is the hammer of which Jeremiah speaks, "Is not my word like a hammer which breaks the rock in pieces?" (Jer. 23:29). This is not *activa contritio* (artificial remorse), but *passiva contritio* (true sorrow of the heart, suffering, and pain of death).

This is what the beginning of true repentance is like. Here man 3 must hear such a judgment as this: "You are all of no account. Whether you are manifest sinners or saints,[2] you must all become other than you now are and do otherwise than you now do, no matter who you are and no matter how great, wise, mighty, and holy you may think yourselves. Here no one is godly," etc.

To this office of the law the New Testament immediately adds the 4 consoling promise of grace in the Gospel. This is to be believed, as Christ says in Mark 1:15, "Repent and believe in the Gospel," which is to say, "Become different, do otherwise, and believe my promise." John, who preceded Christ, is called a preacher of repentance—but 5 for the remission of sins. That is, John was to accuse them all and convince them that they were sinners in order that they might know how they stood before God and recognize themselves as lost men. In this way they were to be prepared to receive grace from the Lord and to expect and accept from him the forgiveness of sins. Christ him- 6 self says this in Luke 24:47, "Repentance and the forgiveness of sins should be preached in his name to all nations."

But where the law exercises its office alone, without the addition 7 of the Gospel, there is only death and hell, and man must despair like Saul and Judas.[3] As St. Paul says,[4] the law slays through sin. More- 8 over, the Gospel offers consolation and forgiveness in more ways than one, for with God there is plenteous redemption (as Ps. 130:7 puts it) from the dreadful captivity to sin, and this comes to us through the Word, the sacraments, and the like, as we shall hear.[5]

Now we must compare the false repentance of the sophists[6] with 9 true repentance so that both may be better understood.

THE FALSE REPENTANCE OF THE PAPISTS

It was impossible for them to teach correctly about repentance 10 because they did not know what sin really is. For, as stated above,[7]

---

[2] Latin adds: in your opinion.
[3] Cf. I Sam. 28:20 and 31:4; Matt. 27:3-5.
[4] Cf. Rom. 7:10.
[5] See Pt. III, Art. IV.
[6] Scholastic theologians.
[7] Pt. III, Art. I, 4, 8.

they did not have the right teaching concerning original sin but asserted that the natural powers of man have remained whole and uncorrupted, that reason is capable of right understanding and the will is capable of acting accordingly, and that God will assuredly grant his grace to the man who does as much as he can according to his free will.

From this it follows that people did penance only for actual sins, | 1 such as wicked thoughts to which they consented (for evil impulses, lust, and inclinations they did not consider sin), wicked words, and wicked works which man with his free will might well have avoided. Such repentance the sophists divided into three parts—contrition, | 2 confession, and satisfaction—with the added consolation that a man who properly repents, confesses, and makes satisfaction has merited forgiveness and has paid for his sins before God. In their teaching of penance the sophists thus instructed the people to place their confidence in their own works. Hence the expression in the pulpit when the | 3 general confession was recited to the people: "Prolong my life, Lord God, until I make satisfaction for my sins and amend my life." [8]

There was no mention here of Christ or of faith. Rather, men | 4 hoped by their own works to overcome and blot out their sins before God. With this intention we, too, became priests and monks, that we might set ourselves against sin.

As for contrition, this was the situation: Since nobody could | 5 recall all his sins (especially those committed during the course of a whole year),[9] the following loophole was resorted to, namely, that when a hidden sin was afterwards remembered, it had also to be repented of, confessed, etc., but meanwhile the sinner was commended to the grace of God. Moreover, since nobody knew how much | 6 contrition he had to muster in order to avail before God, this consolation was offered: If anybody could not be contrite (that is, really repentant), he should at least be attrite (which I might call half-way or partially repentant). They understood neither of these terms, and to this day they are as far from comprehending their meaning as I am. Nevertheless, such attrition was reckoned as a substitute for contrition when people went to confession. And when somebody said that | 7 he was unable to repent or be sorry for his sin (which might have been committed, let us say, in whoredom, revenge, or the like), such a person was asked if he did not wish or desire to be repentant. If he said Yes (for who but the devil himself would want to say No?) it was accounted as contrition and, on the basis of this good work of his,

---

[8] Words from the general confession of sins, spoken by the priest in behalf of the congregation. See "General Confession" in *New Schaff-Herzog Encyclopedia*, IV, 449.

[9] The obligation of confession at least once a year was imposed at the Fourth Lateran Council (1215) on all who had reached years of discretion.

his sin was forgiven. Here the example of St. Bernard, etc. was cited.[1]

Here we see how blind reason gropes about in matters which 18 pertain to God, seeking consolation in its own works, according to its own inventions, without being able to consider Christ and faith. If we examine this in the light, we see that such contrition is an artificial and imaginary idea evolved by man's own powers without faith and without knowledge of Christ. A poor sinner who reflected on his lust or revenge in this fashion would sooner have laughed than wept, unless perchance he was really smitten by the law or vainly vexed with a sorrowful spirit by the devil. Apart from cases like this, such repentance surely was pure hypocrisy. It did not extinguish the lust for sin. The person involved was obliged to grieve, but he would rather have sinned if he had been free to do so.

As for confession, the situation was like this: Everybody had to 19 give an account of all his sins—an impossibility and the source of great torture. The sins which had been forgotten were pardoned only when a man remembered them and thereupon confessed them. Accordingly he could never know when he had made a sufficiently complete or a sufficiently pure confession. At the same time his attention was directed to his own works, and he was told that the more completely he confessed, the more he was ashamed, and the more he abased himself before the priest, the sooner and the better he would make satisfaction for his sins, for such humiliation would surely earn grace before God. Here, again, there was neither faith nor Christ. A 20 man did not become aware of the power of absolution, for his consolation was made to rest on his enumeration of sins and on his self-abasement. But this is not the place to recount the torture, rascality, and idolatry which such confession has produced.

Satisfaction was even more complicated,[2] for nobody could 21 know how much he was to do for one single sin, to say nothing of all his sins. Here the expedient was resorted to of imposing small satisfactions which were easy to render, like saying five Our Fathers, fasting for a day, etc. For the penance that was still lacking man was referred to purgatory.

Here, too, there was nothing but anguish and misery. Some 22 thought that they would never get out of purgatory because, according to the ancient canons, seven years of penance were required for a single mortal sin.[3] Nevertheless, confidence was placed in man's 23 own works of satisfaction. If the satisfaction could have been perfect, full confidence would have been placed in it, and neither faith nor Christ would have been of any value. But such confidence was

---

[1] Cf. Bernard of Clairvaux, *Treatise on Grace and Free Will*, IV, 10.

[2] Latin: perplexing.

[3] Such statements were to be found in the so-called *47 canones poenitentiales* which were well known at the close of the Middle Ages.

impossible. Even if one had done penance in this way for a hundred years, one would still not have known whether this was enough. This is a case of always doing penance but never coming to repentance.

Here the holy see in Rome came to the aid of the poor church   24 and invented indulgences. By these satisfaction was remitted and canceled, first for seven years in a single case, then for a hundred, etc. The indulgences were distributed among the cardinals and bishops so that one could grant them for a hundred years, another for a hundred days, but the pope reserved for himself alone the right to remit the entire satisfaction.[4]

When this began to yield money and the bull market became   25 profitable, the pope invented the jubilee year and attached it to Rome.[5] This was called remission of all penalty and guilt,[6] and the people came running, for everyone was eager to be delivered from the heavy, unbearable burden. Here we have the discovery and digging up of the treasures of the earth.[7] The popes went further and quickly multiplied the jubilee years.[8] The more money they swallowed, the wider became their maws. So they sent their legates out into all lands until every church and house was reached by jubilee indulgences. Finally the   26 popes forced their way into purgatory, first by instituting Masses and vigils for the dead and afterwards by offering indulgences for the dead through bulls and jubilee years.[9] In time souls got to be so cheap that they were released at six pence a head.

Even this did not help, however, for although the pope taught   27 the people to rely on and trust in such indulgences, he again introduced uncertainty when he declared in his bulls, "Whoever wishes to benefit from the indulgence or jubilee year must be contrite, make confession, and pay money." [1] But the contrition and confession practiced by these people, as we have heard above,[2] are uncertain and hypocritical. Moreover, nobody knew which soul was in purgatory, and nobody knew which of those in purgatory had truly repented and properly confessed. So the pope took the money, consoled the people with his

---

[4] Plenary indulgences were first granted in 1095 in connection with the crusades.

[5] The jubilee or holy year was instituted by Pope Boniface VIII in 1300 for the benefit of pilgrims to Rome.

[6] The expression *remissio poenae et culpae* was frequently used.

[7] There was a saying in the Middle Ages, based on Dan. 11:43, that the devil would show the Antichrist the hidden treasures of the earth in order that men might be seduced by them.

[8] From once every hundred years to once every twenty-five years.

[9] The first papal indulgence for the dead seems to have been offered in 1476. After 1500 such indulgences were connected with holy years.

[1] Contrition and confession were often mentioned as conditions for receiving indulgences.

[2] See sec. 16, 19.

power and indulgences, and once again directed attention to uncertain human works.

There were some who did not think they were guilty of actual 28 sins—that is, of sinful thoughts, words, and deeds. I and others like myself who wished to be monks and priests in monasteries and chapters fought against evil thoughts by fasting, vigils, prayers, Masses, coarse clothing, and hard beds and tried earnestly and mightily to be holy, and yet the hereditary evil which is born in us did what is its nature to do, sometimes while we slept (as St. Augustine, St. Jerome, and others confess).[3] Each one, however, held that some of the others were, as we taught, without sin and full of good works, and so we shared our good works with others and sold them to others in the belief that they were more than we ourselves needed for heaven. This is certainly true, and there are seals, letters, and examples to show it. Such persons did not need to repent, for what were they to repent 29 of when they did not consent to evil thoughts? What should they confess when they refrained from evil words? What satisfaction should they render when they were innocent of evil deeds and could even sell their superfluous righteousness to other poor sinners? The scribes and Pharisees in Christ's time were just such saints.[4]

Here the fiery angel[5] St. John, the preacher of true repentance, 30 intervenes. With a single thunderbolt he strikes and destroys both. "Repent," he says.[6] On the one hand there are some who think, "We have already done penance," and on the other hand there are 31 others who suppose, "We need no repentance." But John says: 32 "Repent, both of you. Those of you in the former group are false penitents, and those of you in the latter are false saints. Both of you need the forgiveness of sins, for neither of you knows what sin really is, to say nothing of repenting and shunning sin. None of you is good. All of you are full of unbelief, blindness, and ignorance of God and God's will. For he is here present, and from his fullness have we all received, grace upon grace.[7] No man can be just before God without him. Accordingly, if you would repent, repent rightly. Your repentance accomplishes nothing. And you hypocrites who think you do not need to repent, you brood of vipers,[8] who has given you any assurance that you will escape the wrath to come?"

St. Paul teaches the same thing in Rom. 3:10-12: "None is 33 righteous, no, not one; no one understands, no one seeks for God. All have turned aside, together they have gone wrong." And in Acts 34

---

[3] Augustine, *Confessions,* II, 2; X, 30; Jerome, *Epistle to Eustochius,* 22:7.
[4] Latin adds: and hypocrites.
[5] Cf. Rev. 10:1.
[6] Matt. 3:2.
[7] John 1:16.
[8] Cf. Matt. 3:7.

17:30, "Now he commands all men everywhere to repent." He says "all men," that is, excepting no one who is a man. Such repentance 35 teaches us to acknowledge sin—that is, to acknowledge that we are all utterly lost, that from head to foot there is no good in us, that we must become altogether new and different men.

This repentance is not partial and fragmentary like repentance 36 for actual sins, nor is it uncertain like that. It does not debate what is sin and what is not sin, but lumps everything together and says, "We are wholly and altogether sinful." We need not spend our time weighing, distinguishing, differentiating. On this account there is no uncertainty in such repentance, for nothing is left that we might imagine to be good enough to pay for our sin. One thing is sure: We cannot pin our hope on anything that we are, think, say, or do. And so our repentance cannot be false, uncertain, or partial, for a 37 person who confesses that he is altogether sinful embraces all sins in his confession without omitting or forgetting a single one. Nor 38 can our satisfaction be uncertain, for it consists not of the dubious, sinful works which we do but of the sufferings and blood of the innocent Lamb of God who takes away the sin of the world.[9]

This is the repentance which John preaches, which Christ 39 subsequently preaches in the Gospel, and which we also preach. With this repentance we overthrow the pope and everything that is built on our good works, for all of this is constructed on an unreal and rotten foundation which is called good works or the law, although no good work but only wicked works are there and although no one keeps the law (as Christ says in John 7:19) but all transgress it. Accordingly the entire building, even when it is most holy and beautiful, is nothing but deceitful falsehood and hypocrisy.

In the case of a Christian such repentance continues until death, 40 for all through life it contends with the sins that remain in the flesh. As St. Paul testifies in Rom. 7:23, he wars with the law in his members, and he does this not with his own powers but with the gift of the Holy Spirit which follows the forgiveness of sins. This gift daily cleanses and expels the sins that remain and enables man to become truly pure and holy.

This is something about which the pope, the theologians, the 41 jurists, and all men understand nothing. It is a teaching from heaven, revealed in the Gospel, and yet it is called a heresy by godless saints.

Some fanatics may appear (and perhaps they are already 42 present, such as I saw with my own eyes at the time of the uprising)[1] who hold that once they have received the Spirit or the forgiveness of sins, or once they have become believers, they will persevere in faith

[9] Cf. John 1:29.
[1] The Peasants' War in 1525.

even if they sin afterwards, and such sin will not harm them. They cry out, "Do what you will, it matters not as long as you believe, for faith blots out all sins," etc. They add that if anyone sins after he has received faith and the Spirit, he never really had the Spirit and faith. I have encountered many foolish people like this and I fear that such a devil still dwells in some of them.

It is therefore necessary to know and to teach that when holy   43 people, aside from the fact that they still possess and feel original sin and daily repent and strive against it, fall into open sin (as David fell into adultery, murder, and blasphemy),[2] faith and the Spirit have departed from them. This is so because the Holy Spirit does not   44 permit sin to rule and gain the upper hand in such a way that sin is committed, but the Holy Spirit represses and restrains it so that it does not do what it wishes. If sin does what it wishes, the Holy Spirit and faith are not present, for St. John says, "No one born of God   45 commits sin; he cannot sin."[3] Yet it is also true, as the same St. John writes, "If we say we have no sin, we deceive ourselves, and the truth is not in us."[4]

IV. THE GOSPEL

We shall now return to the Gospel, which offers counsel and help against sin in more than one way, for God is surpassingly rich in his grace: First, through the spoken word, by which the forgiveness of sin (the peculiar function of the Gospel) is preached to the whole world; second,[5] through Baptism; third, through the holy Sacrament of the Altar; fourth, through the power of keys; and finally, through the mutual conversation and consolation of brethren. Matt. 18:20, "Where two or three are gathered," etc.[6]

V. BAPTISM

Baptism is nothing else than the Word of God in water, com-   1 manded by the institution of Christ; or as Paul says, "the washing of water with the word";[7] or, again, as Augustine puts it, "The Word is added to the element and it becomes a sacrament."[8] Therefore   2 we do not agree with Thomas[9] and the Dominicans who forget the Word (God's institution) and say that God has joined to the water a spiritual power which, through the water, washes away sin. Nor do   3

[2] Cf. II Sam. 11.
[3] I John 3:9; 5:18.
[4] I John 1:8.
[5] The order of succeeding topics is here indicated.
[6] Luther wrote: "Where two are gathered."
[7] Eph. 5:26.
[8] *Tractate 80*, on John 3.
[9] Cf. Thomas Aquinas, *Summa theologica*, III, q.62, a.4.

we agree with Scotus[1] and the Franciscans who teach that Baptism washes away sin through the assistance of the divine will, as if the washing takes place only through God's will and not at all through the Word and the water.

As for infant Baptism, we hold that children should be baptized, 4 for they, too, are included in the promise of redemption which Christ made,[2] and the church should administer Baptism to them.

VI. THE SACRAMENT OF THE ALTAR

We hold that the bread and the wine in the Supper are the true 1 body and blood of Christ and that these are given and received not only by godly but also by wicked Christians.

We also hold that it is not to be administered in one form only.[3] 2 We need not resort to the specious learning of the sophists[4] and the Council of Constance[5] that as much is included under one form as under both. Even if it were true that as much is included under 3 one form as under both, yet administration in one form is not the whole order and institution as it was established and commanded by Christ. Especially do we condemn and curse in God's name those 4 who not only omit both forms but even go so far as autocratically to prohibit, condemn, and slander the use of both as heresy and thus set themselves against and over Christ, our Lord and God, etc.

As for transubstantiation, we have no regard for the subtle 5 sophistry of those who teach that bread and wine surrender or lose their natural substance and retain only the appearance and shape of bread without any longer being real bread, for that bread is and remains there agrees better with the Scriptures, as St. Paul himself states, "The bread which we break" (I Cor. 10:16), and again, "Let a man so eat of the bread" (I Cor. 11:28).

VII. THE KEYS

The keys are a function and power given to the church by Christ[6] 1 to bind and loose sins, not only the gross and manifest sins but also those which are subtle and secret and which God alone perceives. So it is written, "Who can discern his errors?" (Ps. 19:12). And Paul himself complains (Rom. 7:23) that in his flesh he was a captive to "the law of sin." It is not in our power but in God's alone to judge 2

---

[1] Cf. Duns Scotus, *Sentences,* IV, dist. 1, q.2 ff.

[2] Cf. Matt. 19:14.

[3] That is, the bread alone, without the wine.

[4] Scholastic theologians.

[5] Decree of June 15, 1415, which defined the doctrine of sacramental concomitance, namely, that the whole body and the whole blood of Christ are under the form of the bread alone.

[6] Cf. Matt. 16:19; 18:18.

which, how great, and how many our sins are. As it is written, "Enter not into judgment with thy servant, for no man living is righteous before thee" (Ps. 143:2), and Paul also says in I Cor. 4:4, "I am 3 not aware of anything against myself, but I am not thereby acquitted."

VIII. Confession

Since absolution or the power of the keys, which was instituted I by Christ in the Gospel, is a consolation and help against sin and a bad conscience, confession and absolution should by no means be allowed to fall into disuse in the church, especially for the sake of timid consciences and for the sake of untrained young people who need to be examined and instructed in Christian doctrine.

However, the enumeration of sins should be left free to every- 2 body to do or not as he will. As long as we are in the flesh we shall not be untruthful if we say, "I am a poor man, full of sin. I see in my members another law," etc. (Rom. 7:23). Although private absolution is derived from the office of the keys, it should not be neglected; on the contrary, it should be highly esteemed and valued, like all other functions of the Christian church.

In these matters, which concern the external, spoken Word, we 3 must hold firmly to the conviction that God gives no one his Spirit or grace except through or with the external Word which comes before. Thus we shall be protected from the enthusiasts—that is, from the spiritualists who boast that they possess the Spirit without and before the Word and who therefore judge, interpret, and twist the Scriptures or spoken Word according to their pleasure. Münzer[7] did this, and many still do it in our day who wish to distinguish sharply between the letter and the spirit without knowing what they say or teach. The 4 papacy, too, is nothing but enthusiasm, for the pope boasts that "all laws are in the shrine of his heart," [8] and he claims that whatever he decides and commands in his churches is spirit and law, even when it is above and contrary to the Scriptures or spoken Word. All this 5 is the old devil and the old serpent who made enthusiasts of Adam and Eve. He led them from the external Word of God to spiritualizing and to their own imaginations, and he did this through other external words. Even so, the enthusiasts of our day condemn the external 6 Word, yet they do not remain silent but fill the world with their chattering and scribbling, as if the Spirit could not come through the Scriptures or the spoken word of the apostles but must come through their own writings and words. Why do they not stop preaching and writing until the Spirit himself comes to the people without and before their

---

[7] Thomas Münzer.

[8] *Corpus juris canonici*, Book VI, I, 2, c.1.

writings since they boast that the Spirit came upon them without the testimony of the Scriptures?[9] There is no time to dispute further about these matters. After all, we have treated them sufficiently elsewhere.[1]

Even those who have come to faith before they were baptized 7 and those who came to faith in Baptism came to their faith through the external Word which preceded. Adults who have attained the age of reason must first have heard, "He who believes and is baptized will be saved" (Mark 16:16), even if they did not at once believe and did not receive the Spirit and Baptism until ten years later. Cornelius 8 (Acts 10:1ff.) had long since heard from the Jews about the coming Messiah through whom he was justified before God, and his prayers and alms were acceptable to God in this faith (Luke calls him "devout" and "God-fearing"),[2] but he could not have believed and been justified if the Word and his hearing of it had not preceded. However, St. Peter had to reveal to him that the Messiah, in whose coming he had previously believed, had already come, and his faith concerning the coming Messiah did not hold him captive with the hardened, unbelieving Jews, but he knew that he now had to be saved by the present Messiah and not deny or persecute him as the Jews did.

In short, enthusiasm clings to Adam and his descendants from 9 the beginning to the end of the world. It is a poison implanted and inoculated in man by the old dragon, and it is the source, strength, and power of all heresy, including that of the papacy and Mohammedanism. Accordingly, we should and must constantly maintain that God 10 will not deal with us except through his external Word and sacrament. Whatever is attributed to the Spirit apart from such Word and sacrament is of the devil. For even to Moses God wished to appear 11 first through the burning bush and the spoken word,[3] and no prophet, whether Elijah or Elisha, received the Spirit without the Ten Commandments. John the Baptist was not conceived without the 12 preceding word of Gabriel, nor did he leap in his mother's womb 13 until Mary spoke.[4] St. Peter says that when the prophets spoke, they did not prophesy by the impulse of man but were moved by the Holy Spirit, yet as holy men of God.[5] But without the external Word they were not holy, and the Holy Spirit would not have moved them to speak while they were still unholy. They were holy, St. Peter says, because the Holy Spirit spoke through them.

[9] Literally: without the preaching of the Scriptures.
[1] E.g., Luther's "Against the Heavenly Prophets" (1525).
[2] Cf. Acts 10:2, 22.
[3] Cf. Ex. 3:2, 4.
[4] Cf. Luke 1:13-42.
[5] II Peter 1:21.

IX. Excommunication

We consider the greater excommunication,[6] as the pope calls it, to be merely a civil penalty which does not concern us ministers of the church. However, the lesser (that is, the truly Christian) excommunication excludes those who are manifest and impenitent sinners from the sacrament and other fellowship of the church until they mend their ways and avoid sin. Preachers should not mingle civil punishments with this spiritual penalty or excommunication.

X. Ordination and Vocation

If the bishops were true bishops and were concerned about the   1
church and the Gospel, they might be permitted (for the sake of love and unity, but not of necessity) to ordain and confirm us and our preachers,[7] provided this could be done without pretense, humbug, and unchristian ostentation. However, they neither are nor wish to be true bishops. They are temporal lords and princes who are unwill-   2
ing to preach or teach or baptize or administer Communion or discharge any office or work in the church. More than that, they expel, persecute, and condemn those who have been called to do these things. Yet the church must not be deprived of ministers on their account.

Accordingly, as we are taught by the examples of the ancient   3
churches and Fathers, we shall and ought ourselves ordain suitable persons to this office. The papists have no right to forbid or prevent us, not even according to their own laws, for their laws state that those who are ordained by heretics shall also be regarded as ordained and remain so.[8] St. Jerome, too, wrote concerning the church in Alexandria that it was originally governed without bishops by priests and preachers in common.[9]

XI. The Marriage of Priests

The papists had neither authority nor right to prohibit marriage   1
and burden the divine estate of priests with perpetual celibacy. On the contrary, they acted like antichristian, tyrannical, and wicked scoundrels, and thereby they gave occasion for all sorts of horrible, abominable, and countless sins, in which they are still involved. As little   2
as the power has been given to us or to them to make a woman out of a man or a man out of a woman or abolish distinctions of sex altogether, so little have they had the power to separate such creatures

---

[6] The Roman Church distinguished between a lesser ban, which excluded only from the sacraments, and a greater ban, which imposed civil disabilities in addition to spiritual penalties.

[7] See also above, Apology, Art. XIV.

[8] Gratian, *Decretum*, Pt. I, dist. 68, chap. 1; Pt. III, dist. 4, chap. 107.

[9] See above. Pt. II, Art. IV, 9.

of God or forbid them to live together honestly in marriage. We   3
are therefore unwilling to consent to their abominable celibacy, nor
shall we suffer it. On the contrary, we desire marriage to be free, as
God ordained and instituted it, and we shall not disrupt or hinder
God's work, for St. Paul says that to do so is a doctrine of demons.[1]

XII. THE CHURCH

We do not concede to the papists that they are the church, for   I
they are not. Nor shall we pay any attention to what they command   2
or forbid in the name of the church, for, thank God, a seven-year-old
child[2] knows what the church is, namely, holy believers and sheep
who hear the voice of their Shepherd.[3] So children pray, "I believe   3
in one holy Christian church." Its holiness does not consist of sur-
plices, tonsures, albs, or other ceremonies of theirs which they have
invented over and above the Holy Scriptures, but it consists of the
Word of God and true faith.

XIII. HOW MAN IS JUSTIFIED BEFORE GOD, AND HIS GOOD WORKS

I do not know how I can change what I have heretofore con-   I
stantly taught on this subject, namely, that by faith (as St. Peter says)[4]
we get a new and clean heart and that God will and does account us
altogether righteous and holy for the sake of Christ, our mediator.
Although the sin in our flesh has not been completely removed or
eradicated, he will not count or consider it.

Good works follow such faith, renewal, and forgiveness. What-   2
ever is still sinful or imperfect in these works will not be reckoned as
sin or defect for the sake of the same Christ. The whole man, in
respect both of his person and of his works, shall be accounted and
shall be righteous and holy through the pure grace and mercy which
have been poured out upon us so abundantly in Christ. Accordingly   3
we cannot boast of the great merit in our works if they are considered
apart from God's grace and mercy, but, as it is written, "Let him who
boasts, boast of the Lord" (I Cor. 1:31). That is to say, all is well if
we boast that we have a gracious God. To this we must add that if
good works do not follow, our faith is false and not true.

XIV. MONASTIC VOWS

Since monastic vows are in direct conflict with the first chief   I
article, they must be absolutely set aside. It is of these that Christ
says in Matt. 24:5, "I am the Christ," etc. Whoever takes the vows

---

[1] Cf. I Tim. 4:1-3.
[2] Seven years was the minimum age of discretion.
[3] John 10:3.
[4] Acts 15:9.

of monastic life believes that he is entering upon a mode of life that is better than that of the ordinary Christian and proposes by means of his work to help not only himself but also others to get to heaven. This is to deny Christ, etc. And on the authority of their St. Thomas, such people boast that a monastic vow is equal to Baptism.[5] This is blasphemy.

XV. HUMAN TRADITIONS

The assertion of the papists that human traditions effect forgive- | ness of sins or merit salvation is unchristian and to be condemned. As Christ says, "In vain do they worship me, teaching as doctrines the precepts of men" (Matt. 15:9), and it is written in Titus 1:14, "They are men who reject the truth." When the papists say that it is a 2 mortal sin to break such precepts of men, this, too, is false.

These are the articles on which I must stand and on which I will 3 stand, God willing, until my death. I do not know how I can change or concede anything in them. If anybody wishes to make some concessions, let him do so at the peril of his own conscience.

Finally, there remains the pope's bag of magic tricks which con- 4 tains silly and childish articles, such as the consecration of churches, the baptism of bells, the baptism of altar stones, the invitation to such ceremonies of sponsors who might make gifts, etc. Such baptizing is a ridicule and mockery of holy Baptism which should not be tolerated.[6] In addition, there are blessings of candles, palms, spices, oats, 5 cakes, etc.[7] These cannot be called blessings, and they are not, but are mere mockery and fraud. Such frauds, which are without number, we commend for adoration to their god and to themselves until they tire of them. We do not wish to have anything to do with them.

Dr. MARTIN LUTHER subscribed
Dr. JUSTUS JONAS, rector, subscribed with his own hand
Dr. JOHN BUGENHAGEN, of Pomerania, subscribed
Dr. CASPAR CREUTZIGER subscribed
NICHOLAS AMSDORF, of Magdeburg, subscribed
GEORGE SPALATIN, of Altenburg, subscribed

I, PHILIP MELANCHTHON, regard the above articles as right and Christian. However, concerning the pope I hold that, if he would allow the Gospel, we, too, may concede to him that superiority over the bishops which he possesses by human right, making this concession for

[5] Thomas Aquinas, *Summa theologica*, Pt. II, 2, q.189, a.3 ad 3.
[6] Bells were commonly named for saints, and when they were "blessed" with an order which closely resembled the order for the baptism of children, the "sponsors" who were present were obligated to pay fees.
[7] Priests "blessed" candles on Candlemas; palm branches on Palm Sunday; herbs, flowers, ears of corn, honey, and vines on the Feast of the Assumption; oats on St. Stephen's Day; unleavened Easter cakes on Easter Eve.

the sake of peace and general unity among the Christians who are now under him and who may be in the future.

JOHN AGRICOLA, of Eisleben, subscribed

GABRIEL DIDYMUS subscribed

I, Dr. URBAN RHEGIUS, superintendent of the churches in the Duchy of Lüneburg, subscribe in my own name and in the name of my brethren and of the church of Hanover

I, STEPHEN AGRICOLA, minister in Hof, subscribe

Also I, JOHN DRACH, professor and minister in Marburg, subscribe

I, CONRAD FIGENBOTZ, for the glory of God subscribe that I have thus believed and am still preaching and firmly believing as above.

I, ANDREW OSIANDER, minister in Nuremberg, subscribe

I, Master VEIT DIETRICH, minister in Nuremberg, subscribe

I, ERHARD SCHNEPF, preacher in Stuttgart, subscribe

CONRAD OETTINGER, preacher of Duke Ulric of Pforzheim

SIMON SCHNEEWEISS, pastor of the church in Crailsheim

I, JOHN SCHLAGENHAUFEN, pastor of the church in Köthen, subscribe

Master GEORGE HELT, of Forchheim

Master ADAM OF FULDA, preacher in Hesse

Master ANTHONY CORVINUS

I, Dr. John Bugenhagen of Pomerania, again subscribe in the name of Master JOHN BRENZ, who on his departure from Smalcald directed me orally and by a letter which I have shown to these brethren who have subscribed[8]

I, DIONYSIUS MELANDER, subscribe the Confession, the Apology, and the Concord[9] in the matter of the Eucharist

PAUL RHODE, superintendent of Stettin

GERARD OEMCKEN, superintendent of the church in Minden.

I, BRIXIUS NORTHANUS, minister of the church of Christ which is in Soest, subscribe the articles of the reverend father, Martin Luther, confess that I have hitherto thus believed and taught, and by the Spirit of Christ I will thus continue to believe and teach

MICHAEL CAELIUS, preacher in Mansfeld, subscribed

Master PETER GELTNER, preacher in Frankfurt, subscribed

WENDAL FABER, pastor of Seeburg in Mansfeld

I, JOHN AEPINUS, subscribe

Likewise I, JOHN AMSTERDAM, of Bremen

I, FREDERICK MYCONIUS, pastor of the church in Gotha, Thuringia, subscribe in my own name and in that of JUSTUS MENIUS, of Eisenach

---

[8] The letter was dated Feb. 23, 1537.

[9] The Wittenberg Concord of 1536, an attempt to bring about an understanding with the Swiss on the Lord's Supper.

I, Dr. JOHN LANG, preacher of the church in Erfurt, in my own name and in the names of my other co-workers in the Gospel, namely:

the Rev. Licentiate LOUIS PLATZ, of Melsungen

the Rev. Master SIGISMUND KIRCHNER

the Rev. WOLFGANG KISWETTER

the Rev. MELCHIOR WEITMANN

the Rev. JOHN THALL

the Rev. JOHN KILIAN

the Rev. NICHOLAS FABER

the Rev. ANDREW MENSER (I subscribe with my hand)

And I, EGIDIUS MELCHER, have subscribed with my hand

V

TREATISE ON THE POWER AND PRIMACY OF THE POPE

Compiled by the Theologians Assembled in Smalcald
in the Year 1537

INTRODUCTION

Although the representatives of the Smalcald League who met in
Smalcald early in February, 1537, did not adopt the Articles prepared
by Luther (see Introduction to the Smalcald Articles, above), it was
felt to be necessary to say something about the pope and his power,
especially in view of the fact that Pope Paul III had called a council
of the church to convene in Mantua later that year. It was pointed
out that it had originally been the intention to include a statement on
this subject in the Augsburg Confession and that such a statement had
been omitted only to avoid offending the emperor and causing him
to end the discussion of religious differences in Augsburg. Since cir-
cumstances now seemed to demand what had before been put off, the
clergymen who were present in Smalcald were instructed to prepare
a statement of this kind. They in turn entrusted the matter to Philip
Melanchthon, who within a few days completed the "Treatise on the
Power and Primacy of the Pope."

Unlike the Smalcald Articles, the Treatise was officially adopted in
Smalcald as a confession of faith. It was intended as a supplement to
the Augsburg Confession and was not, as used to be supposed, an
appendix to the Smalcald Articles. All the clergymen who were present
signed the Treatise; the signature of Luther is wanting because he was
too ill to attend the meeting.

The English translation is made from the Latin text. Only the most
significant variants from the later German version are indicated in
the footnotes.

TREATISE ON THE POWER AND PRIMACY
OF THE POPE

The Roman bishop arrogates to himself the claim that he is by   1
divine right above all bishops and pastors.[1] Then he adds that by   2
divine right he possesses both swords, that is, the authority to bestow
and transfer kingdoms.[2] Finally, he declares that it is necessary for   3
salvation to believe these things, and for such reasons the bishop of
Rome calls himself the vicar of Christ on earth.[3]

These three articles we acknowledge and hold to be false,   4
impious, tyrannical, and injurious to the church. In order that the   5
ground of this our assertion may be understood, we must at the outset
define what the papists mean when they say that the Roman bishop is
above all bishops by divine right. They mean that the pope is the
universal bishop or, as they put it, the ecumenical bishop. That is,
all bishops and pastors throughout the whole world should seek ordination and confirmation from him because he has the right to elect,
ordain, confirm, and depose all bishops. Besides this, he arrogates   6
to himself the authority to make laws concerning worship, concerning
changes in the sacraments, and concerning doctrine. He wishes his
articles, his decrees, and his laws to be regarded as articles of faith
or commandments of God, binding on the consciences of men, because
he holds that his power is by divine right and is even to be preferred
to the commandments of God. What is even more horrible is that he
adds that it is necessary to salvation to believe all these things.

[TESTIMONY OF THE SCRIPTURES]

1. First of all, therefore, let us show from the Gospel that the   7
Roman bishop is not by divine right above all other bishops and
pastors. In Luke 22:24-27 Christ expressly forbids lordship among
the apostles. For this was the very question the disciples were dis-   8
puting when Christ spoke of his passion: Who was to be the leader and,
as it were, the vicar of Christ after his departure? Christ reproved the
apostles for this error and taught them that no one should have lordship or superiority among them but that the apostles should be sent
forth as equals and exercise the ministry of the Gospel in common.
Accordingly he said, "The kings of the Gentiles exercise lordship over
them. But not so with you; rather let the greatest among you become

---

[1] Cf. Gratian, *Decretum*, Pt. I, dist. 21, chap. 3; dist. 22, chap. 1, 2.

[2] So especially in the bull *Unam Sanctam* (1301) of Boniface VIII.

[3] A designation used by popes after the time of Innocent III (1198-1216).

as one who serves." The antithesis here shows that lordship is disapproved. The same thing is taught by a parable when, in a similar dispute concerning the kingdom, Christ put a child in the midst of the disciples, signifying thereby that there was to be no primacy among ministers, just as a child neither seeks nor takes pre-eminence for himself.

2. According to John 20:21 Christ sent his disciples out as equals, without discrimination, when he said, "As the Father has sent me, even so I send you." He sent out each one individually, he said, in the same way in which he had himself been sent. Wherefore he granted to none a prerogative or lordship over the rest.   9

3. In Gal. 2:2, 6 Paul plainly asserts that he was neither ordained nor confirmed by Peter, nor does he acknowledge Peter as one from whom confirmation should be sought. From this fact he expressly argues that his call did not depend on the authority of Peter. But he should have acknowledged Peter as his superior if Peter had been his superior by divine right. He says, however, that he at once preached the Gospel without consulting Peter. "What they were who were reputed to be something," he says, "makes no difference to me," and again, "Those who were of repute added nothing to me" (Gal. 2:6). Since Paul clearly testifies that he did not desire to seek confirmation from Peter, even after he had come to him, he teaches that the authority of the ministry depends on the Word of God, that Peter was not superior to the other apostles, and that ordination or confirmation was not to be sought from Peter alone.   10

4. In I Cor. 3:4-8 Paul places ministers on an equality and teaches that the church is above the ministers. Therefore he does not attribute to Peter superiority or authority over the church or the other ministers. For he says, "All things are yours, whether Paul or Apollos or Cephas" (I Cor. 33:21, 22). This is to say that neither Peter nor the other ministers should assume lordship or authority over the church, nor burden the church with traditions, nor let anybody's authority count for more than the Word, nor set the authority of Cephas over against the authority of the other apostles. At that time, however, they reasoned thus: "Cephas observes this. He is an apostle of superior rank. Therefore Paul and the others ought to observe this." Paul deprives Peter of this pretext and denies that Peter's authority is superior to that of the others and of the church. I Peter 5:3, "Not domineering over the clergy." [4]   11

TESTIMONY FROM HISTORY

5. The Council of Nicaea decided that the bishop of Alexandria should administer the churches in the East and the bishop of Rome   12

[4] Rendering from the Vulgate.

should administer the suburban churches, that is, those that were in
the Roman provinces in the West.[5] Originally, therefore, the authority
of the Roman bishop grew out of a decision of a council and is of
human right, for if the bishop of Rome had his superiority by divine
right, it would not have been lawful for the council to withdraw any
right from him and transfer it to the bishop of Alexandria. In fact, all
the Eastern bishops should forever have sought ordination and confirmation from the Roman bishop.

6. Again, the Council of Nicaea decided that bishops should be   13
elected by their own churches in the presence of one or more
neighboring bishops.[6] This was also observed in the West and in   14
the Latin churches, as Cyprian and Augustine testify.[7] For Cyprian
states in his fourth letter to Cornelius:[8] "Wherefore you must diligently observe and practice, according to divine tradition and apostolic
usage, what is observed by us and in almost all provinces, namely, that
for the proper celebration of ordinations the neighboring bishops of
the same province should assemble with the people for whom a head
is to be ordained, and a bishop should be elected in the presence of
the people who are thoroughly acquainted with the life of each
candidate (as we have seen it done among you in the ordination of
our colleague Sabinus) in order that by the votes of all the brethren
and by the judgment of the bishops assembled in their presence, the
episcopate might be conferred and hands imposed on him." Cyp-   15
rian calls this custom a divine tradition and an apostolic usage, and he
asserts that it was observed in almost all provinces. Since, therefore,
neither ordination nor confirmation were sought from the bishop of
Rome in the greater part of the world, whether in Greek or Latin
churches, it is quite apparent that the churches did not attribute superiority and lordship to the bishop of Rome.

7. Such superiority is impossible, for it is not possible for one   16
bishop to be the overseer of all the churches in the world or for
churches situated in remote places to seek ordination from him alone.
It is evident that the kingdom of Christ is scattered over all the earth
and that there are many churches in the East today which do not seek
ordination or confirmation from the bishop of Rome. Consequently,
inasmuch as such superiority is impossible and the churches in the

----

[5] Canon 6 of the Nicene Council (325). The suburban bishoprics were
those of the ten provinces of Italy, not the later suburbicarian dioceses
around Rome.

[6] Canon 4 of the Nicene Council (325).

[7] Cyprian, *Epistles*, 67 to Presbyter Felix and Deacon Aelius; Augustine,
On Baptism, Against the Donatists, II, 2.

[8] In older editions Cyprian's Epistle 67, referred to above, was appended
to a letter to Cornelius.

greater part of the world never recognized or acted in accordance with it, it is quite apparent that it was not instituted.[9]

8. Many ancient synods were called and held in which the   17 bishop of Rome did not preside—as the Council of Nicaea and many others. This also shows that the church did not then acknowledge the primacy or superiority of the bishop of Rome.

9. Jerome says, "If it is authority that you want, the world is   18 greater than the city.[1] Wherever there is a bishop—whether in Rome or Eugubium[2] or Constantinople or Rhegium or Alexandria—he is of the same dignity and priesthood. It is the power of riches or the humility of poverty that makes a bishop superior or inferior." [3]

10. When writing to the patriarch of Alexandria, Gregory ob-   19 jected to having himself designated as universal bishop.[4] And in the records he states that at the Council of Chalcedon the primacy was offered to the bishop of Rome but he did not accept it.[5]

11. Finally, how can the pope be over the whole church by   20 divine right when the church elects him and the custom gradually prevailed that the bishops of Rome were confirmed by the emperors?[6]

Again, when there had for a long time been disputes between   21 the bishops of Rome and Constantinople over the primacy, Emperor Phocas had finally decided that the primacy should be assigned to the bishop of Rome.[7] But if the ancient church had acknowledged the primacy of the Roman pontiff, this dispute could not have occurred, nor would a decree of the emperor have been necessary.

[ARGUMENTS OF OPPONENTS REFUTED]

Here certain passages are quoted against us: "You are Peter,   22 and on this rock I will build my church" (Matt. 16:18). Again, "I will give you the keys" (Matt. 16:19). Again, "Feed my sheep" (John 21:17), and certain other passages. Since this whole contro-versy has been treated fully and accurately in the books of our theologians[8] and all the details cannot be reviewed here once more,

---

[9] German: was not instituted by Christ and does not come from divine right.

[1] German adds: That is, the world is greater than the city of Rome.

[2] The modern Gubbio, in Italy.

[3] Jerome, *Epistle to Euangelus*, No. 146.

[4] Gregory the Great, *Epistles*, Bk. VIII, No. 30, Epistle to Eulogius, bishop of Alexandria.

[5] *Epistles*, Bk. V, No. 43, Epistle to Eulogius and Anastasius.

[6] Emperors Lothair I (824) and Otto I (962) concluded agreements with the popes providing for such confirmation.

[7] In 607 Pope Boniface III received from the Byzantine Emperor Phocas an acknowledgment of Rome as "head of all the churches."

[8] Luther dealt with these passages often—for example, in *WA*, 2:187-194; 6:309-311; 7:409-415.

we refer to those writings and wish them to be regarded as reiterated. Nevertheless, we shall respond briefly by way of interpretation. In   23 all these passages Peter is representative of the entire company of apostles, as is apparent from the text itself, for Christ did not question Peter alone but asked, "Who do you say that I am?" (Matt. 16:15).[9] And what is here spoken in the singular number ("I will give you the keys" and "whatever you bind") is elsewhere given in the plural ("Whatever you bind"), etc.[1] In John, too, it is written, "If you forgive the sins," etc. (John 20:23).[2] These words show that the keys were given equally to all the apostles and that all the apostles were sent out as equals. In addition, it is necessary to acknowledge that   24 the keys do not belong to the person of one particular individual but to the whole church, as is shown by many clear and powerful arguments, for after speaking of the keys in Matt. 18:19, Christ said, "If two or three of you agree on earth," etc.[3] Therefore, he bestows the keys especially and immediately on the church, and for the same reason the church especially possesses the right of vocation. So it is necessary in these passages to regard Peter as the representative of the entire company of apostles, on which account these passages do not ascribe to Peter any special prerogative, superiority, or power.

As to the statement, "On this rock I will build my church"   25 (Matt. 16:18), it is certain that the church is not built on the authority of a man but on the ministry of the confession which Peter made when he declared Jesus to be the Christ, the Son of God. Therefore Christ addresses Peter as a minister and says, "On this rock," that is, on this ministry. Besides, the ministry of the New Testament is   26 not bound to places and persons, as the Levitical priesthood is, but is spread abroad through the whole world and exists wherever God gives his gifts, apostles, prophets, pastors, teachers. Nor is this ministry valid because of any individual's authority but because of the Word given by Christ.[4] Most of the holy Fathers (such as Origen,[5]   27 Ambrose,[6] Cyprian,[7] Hilary,[8] and Bede[9]) interpret the statement "on

[9] "You" (*vos*) is plural.

[1] Cf. Matt. 16:19 and Matt. 18:18.

[2] The plural form is used.

[3] Conflation of Matt. 18:19 and 20. German adds: Likewise Christ gives the supreme and final jurisdiction to the church when he says, "Tell it to the church" (Matt. 18:17).

[4] German adds: The person adds nothing to this Word and office commanded by Christ. No matter who it is who preaches and teaches the Word, if there are hearts that hear and adhere to it, something will happen to them according as they hear and believe because Christ commanded such preaching and demanded that his promises be believed.

[5] *Commentary on Matthew*, XII, 11.

[6] Ambrosiaster, *Commentary on the Epistle to the Ephesians*, II, 20.

[7] *The Unity of the Catholic Church*, IV.

[8] *The Trinity*, VI, 36, 37.

[9] *Exposition of the Gospel of Matthew*, III, 16.

this rock" in this way and not as applying to the person or superiority of Peter. So Chrysostom declares that Christ says "on this rock" 28 and not "on Peter," for he built his church not on the man but on the faith of Peter; and what was this faith other than "You are the Christ, the Son of the living God"?[1] Hilary declares: "The 29 Father revealed to Peter that he should say, 'You are the Son of the living God.' On this rock of confession, therefore, the church is built. This faith is the foundation of the church."[2]

As to the passages "Feed my sheep" (John 21:17) and "Do you 30 love me more than these?" (John 21:15), it in no wise follows that they bestow a special superiority on Peter, for Christ bids Peter to pasture the sheep, that is, to preach the Word or govern the church with the Word. This commission Peter holds in common with the rest of the apostles.

The second article is even clearer than the first because Christ 31 gave the apostles only spiritual power, that is, the command to preach the Gospel, proclaim the forgiveness of sins, administer the sacraments, and excommunicate the godless without physical violence. He did not give them the power of the sword or the right to establish, take possession of, or transfer the kingdoms of the world. For Christ said, "Go therefore and teach them to observe all that I have commanded you" (Matt. 28:19, 20), and also, "As the Father has sent me, even so I send you" (John 20:21). Moreover, it is manifest that Christ was not sent to wield a sword or possess a worldly kingdom, for he said, "My kingship is not of this world" (John 18:36). Paul also said, "Not that we lord it over your faith" (II Cor. 1:24), and again, "The weapons of our warfare are not worldly," etc. (II Cor. 10:4).

That Christ in his passion was crowned with thorns and that he 32 was led forth to be mocked in royal purple signified that the time would come after his spiritual kingdom was despised (that is, after the Gospel was suppressed) when another worldly kingdom would be set up on the pretext of ecclesiastical power. Wherefore the constitution of 33 Boniface VIII,[3] Distinction 22 of the chapter "Omnes,"[4] and other similar statements which claim that the pope is by divine right lord of the kingdoms of the world are false and impious. This notion 34 has caused horrible darkness to descend over the church, and afterwards great disturbances to arise in Europe. The ministry of the Gospel was neglected. Knowledge of faith and of a spiritual kingdom was extinguished. Christian righteousness was thought to be that external government which the pope had set up. Then the popes 35

---

[1] The exact citation cannot be ascertained, but the reference may be to Chrysostom's *Homilies on Matthew*, 54.
[2] See note 5 above.
[3] Boniface VIII's bull *Unam Sanctam* (1301).
[4] Gratian, *Decretum*, Pt. I, dist. 22, chap 1.

began to seize kingdoms for themselves,[5] transfer kingdoms,[6] and harass the kings of almost all the nations of Europe, but especially the emperors of Germany, with unjust excommunications[7] and wars,[8] sometimes in order to occupy Italian cities[9] and sometimes in order to make the German bishops subject to their power and deprive the emperors of the right to appoint bishops.[1] Indeed, it is even written in the Clementines, "When the imperial throne is vacant, the pope is the legitimate successor."[2] So the pope not only usurped dominion   36 contrary to the command of Christ,[3] but he even exalted himself tyrannically over all kings. In this matter the act itself is not to be deplored so much as the pretext is to be censured that he can transfer the keys of a worldly kingdom by the authority of Christ and that he can attach salvation to these impious and nefarious opinions by asserting that it is necessary for salvation to believe that such dominion belongs to the pope by divine right. Since these monstrous errors   37 obscure faith and the kingdom of Christ, they are under no circumstances to be ignored. The consequences demonstrate that they have been great plagues in the church.

On the third article this must be added: Even if the bishop of   38 Rome should possess primacy and superiority by divine right, obedience would still not be owing to those pontiffs who defend godless forms of worship,[4] idolatry, and doctrines which conflict with the Gospel. On the contrary, such pontiffs and such government ought to be regarded as accursed. So Paul clearly teaches, "If an angel from heaven should preach to you a gospel contrary to that which we preached to you, let him be accursed" (Gal. 1:8). And it is written in Acts, "We must obey God rather than men" (Acts 5:29). The canons likewise clearly teach that a heretical pope is not to be obeyed.[5] The Levitical high priest was the supreme pontifex by divine

---

[5] The papal states were expanded especially during and after the reign of Pope Alexander VI in the fifteenth century. Occupation of lands had long been justified by reference to the so-called Donation of Constantine.

[6] E.g., between 1077 and 1346 four counter-kings were set up in Germany by the popes.

[7] E.g., the excommunication of John the Landless of England and the imposition of the interdict on that country by Pope Innocent III in the thirteenth century.

[8] Between 1495 and 1513 three wars were waged by popes, the last against Emperor Charles V.

[9] In the Middle Ages popes and emperors were involved in almost continuous rivalry for possession of lands in Italy.

[1] The reference is to the Investiture Controversy which ended with the Concordat of Worms (1122).

[2] Corpus juris canonici Clementinae, II, ii, chap. 2.

[3] Cf. Mark 10:42, 43.

[4] Cultus; Gottesdienst.

[5] Gratian, Decretum, Pt. I, dist. 40, chap. 6.

right; nevertheless, godless high priests were not to be obeyed. So Jeremiah and other prophets dissented from them, and the apostles dissented from Caiaphas and were under no obligation to obey him.

[THE MARKS OF THE ANTICHRIST]

But it is manifest that the Roman pontiffs and their adherents   39 defend godless doctrines and godless forms of worship, and it is plain that the marks of the Antichrist coincide with those of the pope's kingdom and his followers. For in describing the Antichrist in his letter to the Thessalonians Paul calls him "an adversary of Christ who opposes and exalts himself against every so-called god or object of worship, so that he takes his seat in the temple of God, proclaiming himself to be God" (II Thess. 2:3, 4). He speaks therefore of one who rules in the church and not of the kings of nations, and he calls that man "an adversary of Christ" because he will devise doctrines which conflict with the Gospel and will arrogate to himself divine authority.

On the one hand, it is manifest that the pope rules in the church   40 and that he has set up this kingdom for himself on the pretext of the authority of the church and the ministry, offering as pretext these words, "I will give you the keys" (Matt. 16:19). On the other hand, the doctrine of the pope conflicts in many ways with the Gospel, and the pope arrogates to himself a threefold divine authority. First, because he assumes for himself the right to change the doctrine of Christ and the worship instituted by God, and he wishes to have his own doctrine and worship observed as divine. Second, because he assumes for himself not only the power to loose and bind in this life but also the jurisdiction over souls after this life. Third, because the pope is unwilling to be judged by the church or by anybody, and he exalts his authority above the decisions of councils and the whole church.[6] Such unwillingness to be judged by the church or by anybody is to make himself out to be God. Finally, he defends such horrible errors and such impiety with the greatest cruelty and puts to death those who dissent.[7]

Since this is the situation, all Christians ought to beware of   41 becoming participants in the impious doctrines, blasphemies, and unjust cruelties of the pope. They ought rather to abandon and execrate the pope and his adherents as the kingdom of the Antichrist. Christ commanded, "Beware of false prophets" (Matt. 7:15). Paul

[6] Pope Gelasius I had asserted, "The pope is to be judged by no one," as early as the end of the fifth century. The claims of the councils in the fifteenth century to superiority over the pope were condemned by Pope Leo X in 1516.

[7] The first Protestant martyrs were Henry Vos and John van den Esschen, slain in 1523.

also commanded that ungodly teachers should be shunned and exe-crated as accursed,[8] and he wrote in II Cor. 6:14, "Do not be mismated with unbelievers, for what fellowship has light with darkness?"

To dissent from the consensus of so many nations and to be 42 called schismatics is a serious matter. But divine authority commands us all not to be associated with and not to support impiety and unjust cruelty. Consequently our consciences are sufficiently excused. The errors of the pope's kingdom are manifest, and the Scriptures unanimously declare these errors to be doctrines of demons and of the Antichrist.[9] The idolatry in the profanation of Masses is manifest, 43 for in addition to other abuses they are shamelessly employed to secure disgraceful profits. The doctrine of repentance has been com- 44 pletely corrupted by the pope and his adherents, who teach that sins are forgiven on account of the worth of our work. Then they bid us to doubt whether forgiveness is obtained. Nowhere do they teach that sins are forgiven freely for Christ's sake and that by this faith we obtain the remission of sins. Thus they obscure the glory of Christ, deprive consciences of a firm consolation, and abolish true worship (that is, the exercise of faith struggling against despair).[1]

They have obscured the teaching concerning sin and have 45 invented a tradition concerning the enumeration of sins which has produced many errors and introduced despair. They have also invented satisfactions, by means of which they have further obscured the benefit of Christ. Out of these arose indulgences, which are nothing but 46 lies devised for the sake of gain. Then there is the invocation of 47 saints—how many abuses and what horrible idolatry it has produced! How many profligate acts have sprung from the tradition of 48 celibacy! With what darkness has the teaching about vows covered the Gospel! Here they have feigned that vows produce righteousness before God and merit forgiveness of sins. Thus they have transferred merit from Christ to human traditions and have utterly extinguished the teaching concerning faith. They have pretended that the most trivial traditions are services of God and perfection, and they have preferred these to works performed in callings which God requires and ordained. Such errors are not to be taken lightly, for they detract from the glory of God and bring destruction to souls. Accordingly they cannot be overlooked.

To these errors, then, two great sins must be added. The first is 49 that the pope defends these errors with savage cruelty and punishment. The other is that the pope wrests judgment from the church and does

---

[8] Cf. Titus 3:10.

[9] Cf. I Tim. 4:1.

[1] German: the exercise of faith which struggles against unbelief and despair over the promise of the Gospel.

not allow ecclesiastical controversies to be decided in the proper manner. In fact, he contends that he is above councils and can rescind the decrees of councils, as the canons sometimes impudently declare[2]— yet this was done much more impudently by the pontiffs, as examples show.[3] The ninth question of the third canon states, "No one shall 50 judge the supreme see, for the judge is judged neither by the emperor, nor by all the clergy, nor by kings, nor by the people."[4] Thus the 51 pope exercises a twofold tyranny: he defends his errors by force and murders, and he forbids a judicial examination. The latter does more harm than all the punishments, for when proper judicial process has been taken away, the churches are not able to remove impious teachings and impious forms of worship, and countless souls are lost generation after generation.

Therefore, let the godly consider the enormous errors of the 52 pope's kingdom and his tyranny. They should know, in the first place, that these errors must be rejected and that the true teaching must be embraced for the glory of God and the salvation of souls. Then, 53 in the second place, they should also know how great a crime it is to support unjust cruelty in the murder of saints,[5] whose blood God will undoubtedly avenge.

Especially does it behoove the chief members of the church, the 54 kings and the princes, to have regard for the interests of the church and to see to it that errors are removed and consciences are healed.[6] God expressly exhorts kings, "Now therefore, O kings, be wise; be warned, O rulers of the earth" (Ps. 2:10). For the first care of kings should be to advance the glory of God. Wherefore it would be most shameful for them to use their authority and power for the support of idolatry and countless other crimes and for the murder of saints.

Even if the pope should hold synods,[7] how can the church be 55 purified as long as the pope does not permit anything to be decreed contrary to his will and grants nobody the right to express an opinion, except his followers, whom he has bound by horrible oaths and curses to defend his tyranny and wickedness without any regard for the Word of God?[8] Since decisions of synods are decisions of the 56 church and not of the pontiffs, it is especially incumbent on the kings to restrain the license of the pontiffs and see to it that the church is not deprived of the power of making judgments and decisions according

[2] E.g., Gratian, *Decretum,* Pt. I, dist. 16, 17, 19, 21.
[3] Cf. the bull *Execrabilis* by Pius II (1460).
[4] Gratian, *Decretum,* Pt. II, chap. 9, q. 3:13.
[5] See 40 above, and note 7 at that place.
[6] The appeal is here made not to rulers as rulers but to rulers as "the chief members of the church."
[7] German: a council.
[8] Bishops were required to swear an oath of allegiance to the pope.

to the Word of God. And as other Christians ought to censure the rest of the pope's errors, so they ought also to rebuke the pope when he evades and obstructs true understanding and true judgment on the part of the church.

Accordingly, even if the bishop of Rome did possess the 57 primacy by divine right, he should not be obeyed inasmuch as he defends impious forms of worship and doctrines which are in conflict with the Gospel. On the contrary, it is necessary to resist him as Antichrist.

The errors of the pope are manifest, and they are not trifling. 58 Manifest, too, is the cruelty which he employs against the godly. And it is the clear command of God that we should flee from idolatry, impious doctrines, and unjust cruelty. Therefore all the godly have weighty, compelling, and evident reasons for not submitting to the pope, and these urgent reasons are a comfort to the godly when, as often happens, they are reproached for scandal, schism, and discord. On the other hand, those who agree with the pope and defend his 59 doctrines and forms of worship defile themselves with idolatry and blasphemous opinions, make themselves guilty of the blood of the godly whom the pope persecutes, detract from the glory of God, and hinder the welfare of the church by so strengthening errors and other crimes as to impose them on all posterity.

The Power and Jurisdiction of Bishops

In the Confession and in the Apology[9] we have set forth in general terms what we have to say about ecclesiastical power.

The Gospel requires of those who preside over the churches that 60 they preach the Gospel, remit sins, administer the sacraments, and, in addition, exercise jurisdiction, that is, excommunicate those who are guilty of notorious crimes and absolve those who repent. By the 61 confession of all, even of our adversaries, it is evident that this power belongs by divine right to all who preside over the churches, whether they are called pastors, presbyters, or bishops. Accordingly Jerome 62 teaches clearly that in the apostolic letters all who preside over the churches are both bishops and presbyters. He quotes from Titus, "This is why I left you in Crete, that you might appoint presbyters in every town," and points out that these words are followed by, "A bishop must be married only once" (Titus 1:5-7). Again, Peter and John call themselves presbyters.[1] And Jerome observes: "One man was chosen over the rest to prevent schism, lest several persons, by gathering separate followings around themselves, rend the church of

---

[9] Augsburg Confession, Art. XXVIII; Apology of the Augsburg Confession, Art. XXVIII.

[1] Cf. I Pet. 5:1; II John 1; III John 1.

Christ. For in Alexandria, from the time of Mark the Evangelist to the time of Bishops Heracles and Dionysius, the presbyters always chose one of their number, set him in a higher place, and called him bishop. Moreover, in the same way in which an army might select a commander for itself, the deacons may choose from their number one who is known to be active and name him archdeacon. For, apart from ordination, what does a bishop do that a presbyter does not do?" [2]

Jerome therefore teaches that the distinction between the grades 63 of bishop and presbyter (or pastor) is by human authority. The fact itself bears witness to this, for the power is the same, as I have already stated. Afterwards one thing made a distinction between bishops 64 and pastors, and this was ordination, for it was decided that one bishop should ordain the ministers in a number of churches. But 65 since the distinction between bishop and pastor is not by divine right, it is manifest that ordination administered by a pastor in his own church is valid by divine right. Consequently, when the regular 66 bishops become enemies of the Gospel and are unwilling to administer ordination,[3] the churches retain the right to ordain for themselves. For wherever the church exists, the right to administer the Gospel 67 also exists. Wherefore it is necessary for the church to retain the right of calling, electing, and ordaining ministers.

This right is a gift given exclusively to the church, and no human authority can take it away from the church. It is as Paul testifies to the Ephesians when he says, "When he ascended on high he gave gifts to men" (Eph. 4:8, 11, 12). He enumerates pastors and teachers among the gifts belonging exclusively to the church, and he adds that they are given for the work of ministry and for building up the body of Christ. Where the true church is, therefore, the right of electing and ordaining ministers must of necessity also be. So in an emergency even a layman absolves and becomes the minister and pastor of another. It is like the example which Augustine relates of two Christians in a ship, one of whom baptized the other (a catechumen), and the latter, after his Baptism, absolved the former.[4] Here the 68 words of Christ apply which testify that the keys were given to the church and not merely to certain individuals: "Where two or three are gathered in my name, there am I in the midst of them" (Matt. 18:20).

Finally, this is confirmed by the declaration of Peter, "You are 69 a royal priesthood" (I Pet. 2:9). These words apply to the true church which, since it alone possesses the priesthood, certainly has the right of electing and ordaining ministers. The most common 70

---

[2] Jerome, *Epistle to Euangelus*. Following an old text Melanchthon wrote "Esdras" instead of "Heracles" in the quotation.

[3] German: to ordain suitable persons.

[4] Gratian, *Decretum*, Pt. III, dist. 4, chap. 36, where a letter of Augustine to Fortunatus is cited.

custom of the church also bears witness to this, for there was a time when the people elected pastors and bishops. Afterwards a bishop, either of that church or of a neighboring church, was brought in to confirm the election with the laying on of hands; nor was ordination anything more than such confirmation. Later on new ceremonies 71 were added, many of which Dionysius describes; but he is a late and fictitious writer, whoever he may be,[5] just as the writings of Clement are spurious.[6] Still more recent writers added the words, "I give thee the power to sacrifice for the living and the dead." [7] But not even this is found in Dionysius!

From all these facts it is evident that the church retains the 72 right of electing and ordaining ministers. Wherefore, when the bishops are heretics or refuse to administer ordination, the churches are by divine right compelled to ordain pastors and ministers for themselves. And it is the wickedness and tyranny of the bishops that give occasion to schism and discord, for Paul commands that bishops who teach and defend impious doctrines and impious forms of worship should be regarded as anathema.[8]

We have spoken of ordination, which is the one thing (as 73 Jerome states) that distinguishes bishops from the rest of the presbyters. There is no need, therefore, for discussion of the other functions of bishops. Nor is it necessary to speak about confirmation[9] or the blessing of bells, which are almost the only things they have retained for themselves. Something, however, must be said about jurisdiction.

It is certain that the common jurisdiction of excommunicating 74 those who are guilty of manifest crimes belongs to all pastors. This the bishops have tyrannically reserved for themselves alone and have employed for gain. For it is evident that the officials[1] (as they are called) have exercised intolerable arbitrariness and, either on account of avarice or on account of other evil desires, have tormented men and excommunicated them without due process of law. What tyranny it is for civil officers to have the power to ban men arbitrarily without due process of law! And in what kinds of cases they have abused 75

---

[5] Pseudo-Dionysius the Areopagite, *The Celestial Hierarchy*, chap. V. A writer of the fifth century, the genuineness of his writings were questioned by humanists.

[6] The so-called *Recognitions*, attributed to Clement of Rome but probably written a century later.

[7] This formula, by which Roman priests were given the power to offer the sacrifice of the Mass, was introduced in the tenth century.

[8] Gal. 1:7-9.

[9] Here the reference is to the Roman sacrament of confirmation, not to the confirmation of elections, as above. The German text reads: confirmation [*Firmelung*], the blessing of the bells, and other humbug of this sort.

[1] Administrative officers in episcopal chancelleries who were responsible for disciplinary and matrimonial cases.

this power! Not in punishing real offenses, but in dealing with non-observance of fasts or festivals and similar trifles. To be sure, they sometimes punished persons involved in adultery, but in this connection they often harassed innocent and honest men. Besides, since this is a very serious charge, nobody should be condemned without due process of law. Since, therefore, the bishops have tyrannically reserved 76 this jurisdiction for themselves and have shamefully abused it, there is no need, on account of this jurisdiction, to obey the bishops. And since we have good reason for not obeying, it is right to restore this jurisdiction to godly pastors and see to it that it is used properly for the reformation of morals and the glory of God.

There remains jurisdiction in those cases which according to 77 canon law pertain to ecclesiastical courts (as they call them), especially matrimonial cases. This, too, the bishops have by human right only, and they have not had it for long, for it appears from the *Codex* and *Novellae* of Justinian[2] that decisions in matrimonial cases had formerly belonged to the magistrate. By divine right temporal magistrates are compelled to make these decisions if the bishops are negligent. This is conceded by the canons.[3] Wherefore it is not necessary to obey the bishops on account of this jurisdiction either. And since they have framed certain unjust laws concerning 78 marriage and apply them in their courts, there is additional reason why other courts should be established. For the traditions concerning spiritual relationship are unjust,[4] and equally unjust is the tradition which forbids an innocent person to marry after divorce. Unjust, too, is the law that in general approves all clandestine and underhanded betrothals in violation of the right of parents. The law concerning the celibacy of priests is likewise unjust. There are also other snares of conscience in their laws, but it would not be profitable to enumerate all of them here.

It is enough to have pointed out that there are many unjust papal laws on matrimonial questions and that on this account the magistrates ought to establish other courts.

Since therefore the bishops who are adherents of the pope 79 defend impious doctrines and impious forms of worship and do not ordain godly teachers but rather support the cruelty of the pope; since, in addition, they have wrested jurisdiction from the pastors and tyrannically exercise it alone; and since, finally, they observe unjust laws in matrimonial cases; there are sufficiently numerous and compelling reasons why the churches should not recognize them as bishops. They themselves should remember that riches have been 80

[2] Justinian Code, V, 1-27.
[3] Gregory, *Decretum,* IX, v, 26:2.
[4] German: the prohibition of marriage between sponsors is unjust.

given to bishops as alms for the administration and profit of the churches, as the rule states, "The benefice is given because of the office." [5] Wherefore they cannot possess these alms with a good conscience. Meanwhile they defraud the church, which needs these means for the support of ministers, the promotion of education, the care of the poor, and the establishment of courts, especially courts for matrimonial cases. The variety and number of matrimonial 81 disputes are so great that they require special courts, but these cannot be established without the endowments of the church. Peter 82 predicted that there would be wicked bishops in the future who would consume the alms of the churches for luxuries and would neglect the ministry. Let those who defraud the church know that God will require them to pay for their crime.

LIST OF THE DOCTORS AND PREACHERS WHO SUBSCRIBED THE CONFESSION AND APOLOGY, 1537

According to the command of the most illustrious princes and of the estates and cities professing the doctrine of the Gospel, we have re-read the articles of the Confession presented to the emperor in the diet of Augsburg and, by the favor of God, all the preachers who have been present in this assembly in Smalcald unanimously declare that in their churches they believe and teach in conformity with the articles of the Confession and Apology. They also declare that they approve the article concerning the primacy of the pope and the power and jurisdiction of the bishops which was presented to the princes here in this assembly in Smalcald. Accordingly they subscribe their names.

I, Dr. JOHN BUGENHAGEN, of Pomerania, subscribe the articles of the Augsburg Confession, the Apology, and the article concerning the papacy presented to the princes in Smalcald

I also, Dr. URBAN RHEGIUS, superintendent of the churches in the Duchy of Lüneburg, subscribe

NICHOLAS AMSDORF, of Magdeburg, subscribed

GEORGE SPALATIN, of Altenburg, subscribed

I, ANDREW OSIANDER, subscribe

Master VEIT DIETRICH, of Nuremberg, subscribes

STEPHEN AGRICOLA, minister in Chur, subscribed with his own hand

JOHN DRACH, of Marburg, subscribed

CONRAD FIGENBOTZ subscribes to all throughout

MARTIN BUCER

I, ERHARD SCHNEPF, subscribe

PAUL RHODE, preacher in Stettin

GERARD OEMCKEN, minister of the church in Minden

---

[5] *Corpus juris canonici,* **Book VI, I, 3, chap. 15.**

BRIXIUS NORTHANUS, minister in Soest

SIMON SCHNEEWEISS, pastor at Crailsheim

I, Pomeranus,[6] again subscribe in the name of Master JOHN BRENZ, as he commanded me

PHILIP MELANCHTHON subscribes with his own hand

ANTHONY CORVINUS subscribes with his own hand both in his name and in that of ADAM OF FULDA

JOHN SCHLAGENHAUFEN subscribes with his own hand

GEORGE HELT, of Forchheim

MICHAEL CAELIUS, preacher in Mansfeld

PETER GELTNER, preacher in the church in Frankfurt

DAVID MELANDER subscribed

PAUL FAGIUS, of Strasbourg

WENDEL FABER, pastor of Seeburg in Mansfeld

CONRAD OETTINGER, of Pforzheim, preacher of Ulric, duke of Württemberg

BONIFACE WOLFART, minister of the Word in the church in Augsburg

JOHN AEPINUS, superintendent in Hamburg, subscribed with his own hand

JOHN AMSTERDAM, of Bremen, did the same

JOHN FONTANUS, superintendent of Lower Hesse, subscribed

FREDERICK MYCONIUS subscribed for himself and for JUSTUS MENIUS

AMBROSE BLAUER

[6]John Bugenhagen, of Pomerania.

VI

Enchiridion[1]
THE SMALL CATECHISM
of Dr. Martin Luther
for Ordinary Pastors and Preachers

INTRODUCTION

Several years before he put his own hand to the task, Luther had suggested to some of his friends that they prepare a catechism for the instruction of children. Finally Luther himself undertook to fill the need, impelled especially by dismay over the ignorance of the people whom he encountered when he visited parishes in Saxony during the fall of 1528 (see Preface, below, 1-6). Before and after this visitation, as often in earlier years, Luther preached several series of sermons in Wittenberg on the Ten Commandments, the Creed, the Lord's Prayer, and the sacraments, and he used these sermons as a basis for the preparation of his Large Catechism.

In December, 1528, while he was still working on the Large Catechism, Luther also began on the text of the Small Catechism. As they were finished, its original five parts were printed on large charts, and about the middle of May, 1529, the completed Small Catechism was made available in an illustrated booklet. For this edition in book form Luther furnished the Preface at the beginning and the Table of Duties at the close. Other writings of Luther were later added, probably by the printers with or without Luther's consent: A Short Form for Marriage, A Short Form for Baptism, and the Litany.

Although prepared simultaneously and utilizing the same materials, the Small Catechism is not merely a condensation of the Large Catechism, nor is the Large Catechism simply an expansion of the Small Catechism. The tone is different, for there is not a trace in the Small Catechism of the polemics which punctuate the Large, and the intended audience is different, for the Small Catechism was written for use in the households of plain people while the Large was addressed particularly to the clergy. The high esteem in which the

[1] Greek: manual or handbook.

337

*Small Catechism was held is reflected in its incorporation in many
church orders of the sixteenth century and in several early collections
of confessional statements. It was quite natural, therefore, that it
should be taken up into the Book of Concord.*

*The English translation is made from the German text. Only the
most significant variants from the later Latin versions are indicated in
the footnotes.*

[PREFACE]

Grace, mercy, and peace in Jesus Christ, our Lord, from Martin
Luther to all faithful, godly pastors and preachers.

The deplorable conditions which I recently encountered when I   1
was a visitor[2] constrained me to prepare this brief and simple catechism
or statement of Christian teaching. Good God, what wretchedness   2
I beheld! The common people, especially those who live in the country,
have no knowledge whatever of Christian teaching, and unfortunately
many pastors are quite incompetent and unfitted for teaching.
Although the people are supposed to be Christian, are baptized, and   3
receive the holy sacrament, they do not know the Lord's Prayer, the
Creed, or the Ten Commandments,[3] they live as if they were pigs and
irrational beasts, and now that the Gospel has been restored they have
mastered the fine art of abusing liberty.

How will you bishops answer for it before Christ that you have   4
so shamefully neglected the people and paid no attention at all to the
duties of your office? May you escape punishment for this! You   5
withhold the cup in the Lord's Supper and insist on the observance of
human laws, yet you do not take the slightest interest in teaching the
people the Lord's Prayer, the Creed, the Ten Commandments, or a
single part of the Word of God. Woe to you forever!

I therefore beg of you for God's sake, my beloved brethren who   6
are pastors and preachers, that you take the duties of your office
seriously, that you have pity on the people who are entrusted to your
care, and that you help me to teach the catechism to the people,
especially those who are young. Let those who lack the qualifications
to do better at least take this booklet and these forms and read them
to the people word for word in this manner:

In the first place, the preacher should take the utmost care to   7

---

[2] Luther made visitations of congregations in Electoral Saxony and
Meissen between Oct. 22, 1528, and Jan. 9, 1529.

[3] This is the order in which these materials appeared in late medieval
manuals.

avoid changes or variations in the text and wording of the Ten Commandments, the Creed, the Lord's Prayer, the sacraments, etc. On the contrary, he should adopt one form, adhere to it, and use it repeatedly year after year. Young and inexperienced people must be instructed on the basis of a uniform, fixed text and form. They are easily confused if a teacher employs one form now and another form—perhaps with the intention of making improvements—later on. In this way all the time and labor will be lost.

This was well understood by our good fathers, who were 8 accustomed to use the same form in teaching the Lord's Prayer, the Creed, and the Ten Commandments. We, too, should teach these things to the young and unlearned in such a way that we do not alter a single syllable or recite the catechism differently from year to year. Choose the form that pleases you, therefore, and adhere to it henceforth. When you preach to intelligent and educated people, you are 9 at liberty to exhibit your learning and to discuss these topics from different angles and in such a variety of ways as you may be capable of. But when you are teaching the young, adhere to a fixed and unchanging form and method. Begin by teaching them the Ten 10 Commandments, the Creed, the Lord's Prayer, etc., following the text word for word so that the young may repeat these things after you and retain them in their memory.

If any refuse to receive your instructions, tell them that they 11 deny Christ and are no Christians. They should not be admitted to the sacrament, be accepted as sponsors in Baptism, or be allowed to participate in any Christian privileges.[4] On the contrary, they should be turned over to the pope and his officials,[5] and even to the devil himself. In addition, parents and employers should refuse to 12 furnish them with food and drink and should notify them that the prince is disposed to banish such rude people from his land.

Although we cannot and should not compel anyone to believe, 13 we should nevertheless insist that the people learn to know how to distinguish between right and wrong according to the standards of those among whom they live and make their living.[6] For anyone who desires to reside in a city is bound to know and observe the laws under whose protection he lives, no matter whether he is a believer or, at heart, a scoundrel or knave.

In the second place, after the people have become familiar with 14 the text, teach them what it means. For this purpose, take the explanations in this booklet, or choose any other brief and fixed

[4] Cf. Large Catechism, Short Preface, 1-5.
[5] Diocesan judges who decided disciplinary and other cases; now often called vicar-generals.
[6] Cf. Large Catechism, Short Preface, 2.

explanations which you may prefer, and adhere to them without   15
changing a single syllable, as stated above with reference to the text.
Moreover, allow yourself ample time, for it is not necessary to   16
take up all the parts at once. They can be presented one at a time.
When the learners have a proper understanding of the First Commandment, proceed to the Second Commandment, and so on. Otherwise
they will be so overwhelmed that they will hardly remember anything
at all.

In the third place, after you have thus taught this brief   17
catechism, take up a large catechism[7] so that the people may have a
richer and fuller understanding. Expound every commandment,
petition, and part, pointing out their respective obligations, benefits,
dangers, advantages, and disadvantages, as you will find all of this
treated at length in the many books written for this purpose. Lay   18
the greatest weight on those commandments or other parts which seem
to require special attention among the people where you are. For
example, the Seventh Commandment, which treats of stealing, must be
emphasized when instructing laborers and shopkeepers, and even
farmers and servants, for many of these are guilty of dishonesty and
thievery.[8] So, too, the Fourth Commandment must be stressed when
instructing children and the common people in order that they may be
encouraged to be orderly, faithful, obedient, and peaceful. Always
adduce many examples from the Scriptures to show how God punished
and blessed.

You should also take pains to urge governing authorities and   19
parents to rule wisely and educate their children. They must be
shown that they are obliged to do so, and that they are guilty of
damnable sin if they do not do so, for by such neglect they undermine
and lay waste both the kingdom of God and the kingdom of the world
and are the worst enemies of God and man. Make very plain to   20
them the shocking evils they introduce when they refuse their aid in the
training of children to become pastors, preachers, notaries, etc., and
tell them that God will inflict awful punishments on them for these
sins. It is necessary to preach about such things. The extent to which
parents and governing authorities sin in this respect is beyond telling.
The devil also has a horrible purpose in mind.

Finally, now that the people are freed from the tyranny of the   21
pope, they are unwilling to receive the sacrament and they treat it with
contempt. Here, too, there is need of exhortation, but with this
understanding: No one is to be compelled to believe or to receive the
sacrament, no law is to be made concerning it, and no time or place

---

[7] Luther here refers not only to his own Large Catechism but also to other
treatments of the traditional parts of the catechism. See the reference to
"many books" in the next sentence.

[8] Cf. Large Catechism, Ten Commandments, 225, 226.

should be appointed for it. We should so preach that, of their 22
own accord and without any law, the people will desire the sacrament
and, as it were, compel us pastors to administer it to them. This can
be done by telling them: It is to be feared that anyone who does not
desire to receive the sacrament at least three or four times a year
despises the sacrament and is no Christian, just as he is no Christian
who does not hear and believe the Gospel. Christ did not say, "Omit
this," or "Despise this," but he said, "Do this, as often as you drink it,"
etc.[9] Surely he wishes that this be done and not that it be omitted and
despised. "*Do* this," he said.

He who does not highly esteem the sacrament suggests thereby 23
that he has no sin, no flesh, no devil, no world, no death, no hell. That
is to say, he believes in none of these, although he is deeply immersed
in them and is held captive by the devil. On the other hand, he
suggests that he needs no grace, no life, no paradise, no heaven, no
Christ, no God, nothing good at all. For if he believed that he was
involved in so much that is evil and was in need of so much that is
good, he would not neglect the sacrament in which aid is afforded
against such evil and in which such good is bestowed. It is not
necessary to compel him by any law to receive the sacrament, for he
will hasten to it of his own accord, he will feel constrained to receive it,
he will insist that you administer it to him.

Accordingly you are not to make a law of this, as the pope has 24
done. All you need to do is clearly to set forth the advantage and
disadvantage, the benefit and loss, the blessing and danger connected
with this sacrament. Then the people will come of their own accord
and without compulsion on your part. But if they refuse to come, let
them be, and tell them that those who do not feel and acknowledge
their great need and God's gracious help belong to the devil. If 25
you do not give such admonitions, or if you adopt odious laws on the
subject, it is your own fault if the people treat the sacrament with
contempt. How can they be other than negligent if you fail to do
your duty and remain silent. So it is up to you, dear pastor and
preacher! Our office has become something different from what it 26
was under the pope. It is now a ministry of grace and salvation.
It subjects us to greater burdens and labors, dangers and tempta- 27
tions, with little reward or gratitude from the world. But Christ
himself will be our reward if we labor faithfully. The Father of all
grace grant it! To him be praise and thanks forever, through Christ,
our Lord. Amen.

[9] I Cor. 11:25.

[I]

THE TEN COMMANDMENTS

*in the plain form in which the head of the family
shall teach them to his household*[1]

THE FIRST

"You shall have no other gods." [2]   1
What does this mean?   2
Answer: We should fear,[3] love, and trust in God above all things.

THE SECOND

"You shall not take the name of the Lord your God in vain." [4]   3
What does this mean?   4
Answer: We should fear and love God, and so[5] we should not use
his name to curse, swear,[6] practice magic, lie, or deceive, but in every
time of need call upon him, pray to him, praise him, and give him
thanks.

THE THIRD

"Remember the Sabbath day,[7] *to keep it holy."*   5
What does this mean?   6
Answer: We should fear and love God, and so we should not
despise his Word and the preaching of the same, but deem it holy and
gladly hear and learn it.

---

[1] Latin title: Small Catechism for the Use of Children in School. How, in
a very Plain Form, Schoolmasters Should Teach the Ten Commandments to
their Pupils.

[2] The Nuremberg editions of 1531 and 1558 read: "I am the Lord your
God. You shall have no other gods before me." In some editions since the
sixteenth century "I am the Lord your God" was printed separately as an
introduction to the entire Decalogue. The Ten Commandments are from
Exod. 20:2-17 and Deut. 5:6-21.

[3] On filial and servile fear see Apology, XII, 38.

[4] The Nuremberg editions of 1531 and 1558 add: "for the Lord will not
hold him guiltless who takes his name in vain."

[5] On the translation of *dass* see M. Reu in *Kirchliche Zeitschrift*, L (1926),
pp. 626-689.

[6] For the meaning of "swear" see Large Catechism, Ten Commandments, 66.

[7] Luther's German word *Feiertag* means day of rest, and this is the
original Hebrew meaning of Sabbath, the term employed in the Latin text.
The Jewish observance of Saturday is not enjoined here, nor a Sabbatarian
observance of Sunday; cf. Augsburg Confession, XXVIII, 57-60; Large
Catechism, Ten Commandments, 79-82.

THE FOURTH

"Honor your father and your mother." 7
What does this mean? 8
Answer: We should fear and love God, and so we should not despise our parents and superiors, nor provoke them to anger, but honor, serve, obey, love, and esteem them.

THE FIFTH

"You shall not kill." **9**
What does this mean? 10
Answer: We should fear and love God, and so we should not endanger our neighbor's life, nor cause him any harm, but help and befriend him in every necessity of life.

THE SIXTH

"You shall not commit adultery." 11
What does this mean? 12
Answer: We should fear and love God, and so we should lead a chaste and pure life in word and deed, each one loving and honoring his wife or her husband.

THE SEVENTH

"You shall not steal." 13
What does this mean? 14
Answer: We should fear and love God, and so we should not rob our neighbor of his money or property, nor bring them into our possession by dishonest trade or by dealing in shoddy wares, but help him to improve and protect his income and property.

THE EIGHTH

"You shall not bear false witness against your neighbor." 15
What does this mean? 16
Answer: We should fear and love God, and so we should not tell lies about our neighbor, nor betray, slander, or defame him, but should apologize for him, speak well of him, and interpret charitably all that he does.

THE NINTH

"You shall not covet your neighbor's house." 17
What does this mean? 18
Answer: We should fear and love God, and so we should not seek

by craftiness to gain possession of our neighbor's inheritance or home, nor to obtain them under pretext of legal right, but be of service and help to him so that he may keep what is his.

THE TENTH

"You shall not covet your neighbor's wife, or his manservant, or   19
his maidservant, or his ox, or his ass,[8] or anything that is your
neighbor's."

What does this mean?   20

Answer: We should fear and love God, and so we should not abduct, estrange, or entice away our neighbor's wife, servants, or cattle, but encourage them to remain and discharge their duty to him.

[CONCLUSION]

What does God declare concerning all these commandments?   21

Answer: He says, "I the Lord your God am a jealous God, visiting the iniquity of the fathers upon the children to the third and the fourth generation of those who hate me, but showing steadfast love to thousands of those who love me and keep my commandments."

What does this mean?   22

Answer: God threatens to punish all who transgress these commandments. We should therefore fear his wrath and not disobey these commandments. On the other hand, he promises grace and every blessing to all who keep them. We should therefore love him, trust in him, and cheerfully do what he has commanded.

[II]

THE CREED

*in the plain form in which the head of the family
shall teach it to his household[9]*

THE FIRST ARTICLE: CREATION   1

"I believe in God, the Father almighty, maker of heaven and earth."

What does this mean?   2

---

[8] For "or his ox, or his ass" Luther's German text reads "or his cattle." The Latin text employs the fuller expression.

[9] Latin text: How, in a very Plain Form, Schoolmasters Should Teach the Apostles' Creed to their Pupils.

Answer: I believe that God has created me and all that exists; that he has given me and still sustains my body and soul, all my limbs and senses, my reason and all the faculties of my mind, together with food and clothing, house and home, family and property; that he provides me daily and abundantly with all the necessities of life, protects me from all danger, and preserves me from all evil. All this he does out of his pure, fatherly, and divine goodness and mercy, without any merit or worthiness on my part. For all of this I am bound to thank, praise, serve, and obey him. This is most certainly true.

THE SECOND ARTICLE: REDEMPTION   3

"And in Jesus Christ, his only son, our Lord: who was conceived by the Holy Spirit, born of the virgin Mary, suffered under Pontius Pilate, was crucified, dead, and buried: he descended into hell, the third day he rose from the dead, he ascended into heaven, and is seated on the right hand of God, the Father almighty, whence he shall come to judge the living and the dead."

What does this mean?   4

Answer: I believe that Jesus Christ, true God, begotten of the Father from eternity, and also true man, born of the virgin Mary, is my Lord, who has redeemed me, a lost and condemned creature, delivered me and freed me from all sins, from death, and from the power of the devil, not with silver and gold but with his holy and precious blood and with his innocent sufferings and death, in order that I may be his, live under him in his kingdom, and serve him in everlasting righteousness, innocence, and blessedness, even as he is risen from the dead and lives and reigns to all eternity. This is most certainly true.

THE THIRD ARTICLE: SANCTIFICATION   5

"I believe in the Holy Spirit, the holy Christian church, the communion of saints, the forgiveness of sins, the resurrection of the body, and the life everlasting. Amen."

What does this mean?   6

Answer: I believe that by my own reason or strength I cannot believe in Jesus Christ, my Lord, or come to him. But the Holy Spirit has called me through the Gospel, enlightened me with his gifts, and sanctified and preserved me in true faith, just as he calls, gathers, enlightens, and sanctifies the whole Christian church on earth and preserves it in union with Jesus Christ in the one true faith. In this Christian church he daily and abundantly forgives all my sins, and the sins of all believers, and on the last day he will raise me and all the dead and will grant eternal life to me and to all who believe in Christ. This is most certainly true.

[III]

THE LORD'S PRAYER

in the plain form in which the head of the family
shall teach it to his household[1]

[INTRODUCTION]

"Our Father who art in heaven." [2]   1
What does this mean?   2
Answer: Here God would encourage us to believe that he is truly
our Father and we are truly his children in order that we may approach
him boldly and confidently in prayer, even as beloved children
approach their dear father.

THE FIRST PETITION   3

"Hallowed be thy name."
What does this mean?   4
Answer: To be sure, God's name is holy in itself, but we pray in
this petition that it may also be holy for us.
How is this done?   5
Answer: When the Word of God is taught clearly and purely and
we, as children of God, lead holy lives in accordance with it. Help us
to do this, dear Father in heaven! But whoever teaches and lives
otherwise than as the Word of God teaches, profanes the name of God
among us. From this preserve us, heavenly Father!

THE SECOND PETITION   6

"Thy kingdom come."
What does this mean?   7
Answer: To be sure, the kingdom of God comes of itself, without
our prayer, but we pray in this petition that it may also come to us.
How is this done?   8
Answer: When the heavenly Father gives us his Holy Spirit so that
by his grace we may believe his holy Word and live a godly life, both
here in time and hereafter forever.

---

[1] Latin title: How, in a very Plain Form, Schoolmasters Should Teach the
Lord's Prayer to their Pupils.

[2] The "introduction" to the Lord's Prayer was not prepared by Luther
until 1531. It does not appear in the Latin text, which begins with the First
Petition. The text of the Prayer is from Matt. 6:9-13.

THE THIRD PETITION   9

"Thy will be done, on earth as it is in heaven."

What does this mean?   10

Answer: To be sure, the good and gracious will of God is done without our prayer, but we pray in this petition that it may also be done by us.

How is this done?   11

Answer: When God curbs and destroys every evil counsel and purpose of the devil, of the world, and of our flesh which would hinder us from hallowing his name and prevent the coming of his kingdom, and when he strengthens us and keeps us steadfast in his Word and in faith even to the end. This is his good and gracious will.

THE FOURTH PETITION   12

"Give us this day our daily bread."

What does this mean?   13

Answer: To be sure, God provides daily bread, even to the wicked, without our prayer, but we pray in this petition that God may make us aware of his gifts and enable us to receive our daily bread with thanksgiving.

What is meant by daily bread?   14

Answer: Everything required to satisfy our bodily needs, such as food and clothing, house and home, fields and flocks, money and property; a pious spouse and good children, trustworthy servants, godly and faithful rulers, good government; seasonable weather, peace and health, order and honor; true friends, faithful neighbors, and the like.

THE FIFTH PETITION   15

"And forgive us our debts, as we also have forgiven our debtors."

What does this mean?   16

Answer: We pray in this petition that our heavenly Father may not look upon our sins, and on their account deny our prayers, for we neither merit nor deserve those things for which we pray. Although we sin daily and deserve nothing but punishment, we nevertheless pray that God may grant us all things by his grace. And assuredly we on our part will heartily forgive and cheerfully do good to those who may sin against us.

THE SIXTH PETITION   17

"And lead us not into temptation."

What does this mean?   18

Answer: God tempts no one to sin, but we pray in this petition that God may so guard and preserve us that the devil, the world, and our flesh may not deceive us or mislead us into unbelief, despair, and other great and shameful sins, but that, although we may be so tempted, we may finally prevail and gain the victory.

THE SEVENTH PETITION   19

"But deliver us from evil."

What does this mean?   20

Answer: We pray in this petition, as in a summary, that our Father in heaven may deliver us from all manner of evil, whether it affect body or soul, property or reputation, and that at last, when the hour of death comes, he may grant us a blessed end and graciously take us from this world of sorrow to himself in heaven.

[CONCLUSION]

"Amen." [3]

What does this mean?   21

Answer: It means that I should be assured that such petitions are acceptable to our heavenly Father and are heard by him, for he himself commanded us to pray like this and promised to hear us. "Amen, amen" means "Yes, yes, it shall be so."

[IV]

THE SACRAMENT OF HOLY BAPTISM

in the plain form in which the head of the family shall teach it to his household[4]

FIRST

What is Baptism?   1

Answer: Baptism is not merely water, but it is water used   2 according to God's command and connected with God's Word.

What is this Word of God?   3

Answer: As recorded in Matthew 28:19, our Lord Christ said,   4 "Go therefore and make disciples of all nations, baptizing them in the name of the Father and of the Son and of the Holy Spirit."

SECOND

What gifts or benefits does Baptism bestow?   5

Answer: It effects forgiveness of sins, delivers from death and   6

---

[3] The Nuremberg edition of 1558, and many later editions, inserted "For thine is the kingdom, and the power, and the glory, for ever and ever" before "Amen."

[4] Latin title: How, in a very Plain Form, Schoolmasters Should Teach the Sacrament of Baptism to their Pupils.

the devil, and grants eternal salvation to all who believe, as the Word and promise of God declare.

What is this Word and promise of God? 7

Answer: As recorded in Mark 16:16, our Lord Christ said, "He 8 who believes and is baptized will be saved; but he who does not believe will be condemned."

THIRD

How can water produce such great effects? 9

Answer: It is not the water that produces these effects, but the 10 Word of God connected with the water, and our faith which relies on the Word of God connected with the water. For without the Word of God the water is merely water and no Baptism. But when connected with the Word of God it is a Baptism, that is, a gracious water of life and a washing of regeneration in the Holy Spirit, as St. Paul wrote to Titus (3:5-8), "He saved us by the washing of regeneration and renewal in the Holy Spirit, which he poured out upon us richly through Jesus Christ our Saviour, so that we might be justified by his grace and become heirs in hope of eternal life. The saying is sure."

FOURTH 11

What does such baptizing with water signify?

Answer: It signifies that the old Adam in us, together with all 12 sins and evil lusts, should be drowned by daily sorrow and repentance and be put to death, and that the new man should come forth daily and rise up, cleansed and righteous, to live forever in God's presence.

Where is this written? 13

Answer: In Romans 6:4, St. Paul wrote, "We were buried 14 therefore with him by baptism into death, so that as Christ was raised from the dead by the glory of the Father, we too might walk in newness of life."

[V]

[CONFESSION AND ABSOLUTION] 15

How Plain People Are to Be Taught to Confess[5]

What is confession? 16

Answer: Confession consists of two parts. One is that we confess our sins. The other is that we receive absolution or forgiveness from the confessor as from God himself, by no means doubting but firmly

---

[5] In 1531 this section replaced the earlier "A Short Method of Confessing" (1529), *WA*, 30I: 343-45. Luther intended confession especially for those who were about to receive Communion.

believing that our sins are thereby forgiven before God in heaven.

What sins should we confess?   17

Answer: Before God we should acknowledge that we are guilty   18
of all manner of sins, even those of which we are not aware, as we do
in the Lord's Prayer. Before the confessor, however, we should confess
only those sins of which we have knowledge and which trouble us.

What are such sins?   19

Answer: Reflect on your condition in the light of the Ten   20
Commandments: whether you are a father or mother, a son or
daughter, a master or servant; whether you have been disobedient,
unfaithful, lazy, ill-tempered, or quarrelsome; whether you have harmed
anyone by word or deed; and whether you have stolen, neglected, or
wasted anything, or done other evil.

Please give me a brief form of confession.   21

Answer: You should say to the confessor: "Dear Pastor, please hear
my confession and declare that my sins are forgiven for God's sake."

"Proceed."

"I, a poor sinner, confess before God that I am guilty of all sins.   22
In particular I confess in your presence that, as a manservant or maid-
servant, etc., I am unfaithful to my master, for here and there I have
not done what I was told. I have made my master angry, caused him to
curse, neglected to do my duty, and caused him to suffer loss. I have
also been immodest in word and deed. I have quarreled with my equals.
I have grumbled and sworn at my mistress, etc. For all this I am sorry
and pray for grace. I mean to do better."

A master or mistress may say: "In particular I confess in your   23
presence that I have not been faithful in training my children, servants,
and wife to the glory of God. I have cursed. I have set a bad example
by my immodest language and actions. I have injured my neighbor by
speaking evil of him, overcharging him, giving him inferior goods and
short measure." Masters and mistresses should add whatever else they
have done contrary to God's commandments and to their action in
life, etc.

If, however, anyone does not feel that his conscience is burdened   24
by such or by greater sins, he should not worry, nor should he search
for and invent other sins, for this would turn confession into torture;[6]
he should simply mention one or two sins of which he is aware. For
example, "In particular I confess that I once cursed. On one occasion
I also spoke indecently. And I neglected this or that," etc. Let this
suffice.

If you have knowledge of no sin at all (which is quite unlikely),   25
you should mention none in particular, but receive forgiveness upon the

---

[6] Luther was here alluding to the medieval practice of confession; see also
Smalcald Articles, Pt. II, Art. III, 19.

general confession[7] which you make to God in the presence of the confessor.

Then the confessor shall say: "God be merciful to you and 26 strengthen your faith. Amen."

Again he shall say: "Do you believe that this forgiveness 27 is the forgiveness of God?"

Answer: "Yes, I do."

Then he shall say: "Be it done for you as you have believed.[8] 28 According to the command of our Lord Jesus Christ, I forgive you your sins in the name of the Father and of the Son and of the Holy Spirit. Amen. Go in peace."[9]

A confessor will know additional passages of the Scriptures with 29 which to comfort and to strengthen the faith of those whose consciences are heavily burdened or who are distressed and sorely tried. This is intended simply as an ordinary form of confession for plain people.

[VI]

THE SACRAMENT OF THE ALTAR

in the plain form in which the head of the family shall teach it to his household[1]

What is the Sacrament of the Altar?   I

Answer: Instituted by Christ himself, it is the true body and 2 blood of our Lord Jesus Christ, under the bread and wine, given to us Christians to eat and to drink.

Where is this written?   3

Answer: The holy evangelists Matthew, Mark, and Luke, and 4 also St. Paul, write thus: "Our Lord Jesus Christ, on the night when he was betrayed, took bread, and when he had given thanks, he broke it, and gave it to the disciples and said, 'Take, eat; this is my body which is given for you. Do this in remembrance of me.' In the same way also he took the cup, after supper, and when he had given thanks he gave it to them, saying, 'Drink of it, all of you. This cup is the new covenant in my blood, which is poured out for many for the forgiveness of sins. Do this, as often as you drink it, in remembrance of me.' "[2]

---

[7] See article "General Confession" in *New Schaff-Herzog Encyclopedia of Religious Knowledge,* IV, 449. Cf. Smalcald Articles, Pt. III, Art. III, 13.

[8] Matt. 8:13.

[9] Mark 5:34; Luke 7:50; 8:48.

[1] Latin title: How, in very Plain Form, Schoolmasters Should Teach the Sacrament of the Altar to their Pupils.

[2] A conflation of texts from I Cor. 11:23-25; Matt. 26:26-28; Mark 14: 22-24; Luke 22:19, 20. Cf. Large Catechism, Sacrament of the Altar, 3.

What is the benefit of such eating and drinking?   5

Answer: We are told in the words "for you" and "for the   6
forgiveness of sins." By these words the forgiveness of sins, life, and
salvation are given to us in the sacrament, for where there is forgiveness
of sins, there are also life and salvation.

How can bodily eating and drinking produce such great effects?   7

Answer: The eating and drinking do not in themselves produce   8
them, but the words "for you" and "for the forgiveness of sins." These
words, when accompanied by the bodily eating and drinking, are the
chief thing in the sacrament, and he who believes these words has what
they say and declare: the forgiveness of sins.

Who, then, receives this sacrament worthily?   9

Answer: Fasting and bodily preparation are a good external   10
discipline, but he is truly worthy and well prepared who believes these
words: "for you" and "for the forgiveness of sins." On the other hand,
he who does not believe these words, or doubts them, is unworthy and
unprepared, for the words "for you" require truly believing hearts.

[VII]

[MORNING AND EVENING PRAYERS]

*How the head of the family shall teach his household
to say morning and evening prayers*[3]

In the morning, when you rise, make the sign of the cross and   1
say, "In the name of God, the Father, the Son, and the Holy Spirit.
Amen."

Then, kneeling or standing, say the Apostles' Creed and the   2
Lord's Prayer. Then you may say this prayer:

"I give Thee thanks, heavenly Father, through thy dear Son Jesus
Christ, that Thou hast protected me through the night from all harm
and danger. I beseech Thee to keep me this day, too, from all sin and
evil, that in all my thoughts, words, and deeds I may please Thee.
Into thy hands I commend my body and soul and all that is mine. Let
thy holy angel have charge of me, that the wicked one may have no
power over me. Amen."

After singing a hymn (possibly a hymn on the Ten Command-   3
ments)[4] or whatever your devotion may suggest, you should go to
your work joyfully.

---

[3] Latin title: How, in very Plain Form, Schoolmasters Should Teach their
Pupils to Say their Prayers in the Morning and in the Evening. (The material
in this section was adapted from the Roman Breviary.)

[4] See Large Catechism, Short Preface, 25.

In the evening, when you retire, make the sign of the cross and   4
say, "In the name of God, the Father, the Son, and the Holy Spirit.
Amen."

Then, kneeling or standing, say the Apostles' Creed and the   5
Lord's Prayer. Then you may say this prayer:

"I give Thee thanks, heavenly Father, through thy dear Son Jesus
Christ, that Thou hast this day graciously protected me. I beseech Thee
to forgive all my sin and the wrong which I have done. Graciously
protect me during the coming night. Into thy hands I commend my
body and soul and all that is mine. Let thy holy angels have charge
of me, that the wicked one may have no power over me. Amen."

Then quickly lie down and sleep in peace.

[VIII]

[GRACE AT TABLE]

How the head of the family shall teach his household   6
to offer blessing and thanksgiving at table[5]

[BLESSING BEFORE EATING]

When children and the whole household gather at the table, they   7
should reverently fold their hands and say:

"The eyes of all look to Thee, O Lord, and Thou givest them their
food in due season. Thou openest thy hand; Thou satisfiest the desire
of every living thing." [6]

(It is to be observed that "satisfying the desire of every living   8
thing" means that all creatures receive enough to eat to make them
joyful and of good cheer. Greed and anxiety about food prevent such
satisfaction.)

Then the Lord's Prayer should be said, and afterwards this   9
prayer:

"Lord God, heavenly Father, bless us, and these thy gifts which of
thy bountiful goodness Thou hast bestowed on us, through Jesus Christ
our Lord. Amen."

[THANKSGIVING AFTER EATING]   10

After eating, likewise, they should fold their hands reverently and
say:

---

[5] Latin title: How, in Plain Form, Schoolmasters Should Teach their
Pupils to Offer Blessing and Thanksgiving at Table. (The material in this
section was adapted from the Roman Breviary.)

[6] Ps. 145:15, 16. The gloss which follows, here given in parentheses, was
intended to explain the meaning of *Wohlgefallen* or *benedictio* in the German
and Latin translations of the Psalm.

"O give thanks to the Lord, for he is good; for his steadfast love endures forever. He gives to the beasts their food, and to the young ravens which cry. His delight is not in the strength of the horse, nor his pleasure in the legs of a man; but the Lord takes pleasure in those who fear him, in those who hope in his steadfast love." [7]

Then the Lord's Prayer should be said, and afterwards this   ‖ prayer:

"We give Thee thanks, Lord God, our Father, for all thy benefits, through Jesus Christ our Lord, who lives and reigns forever. Amen."

[IX]

TABLE OF DUTIES   ‖

consisting of certain passages of the Scriptures, selected
for various estates and conditions of men, by
which they may be admonished to do
their respective duties[8]

BISHOPS, PASTORS, AND PREACHERS   2

"A bishop must be above reproach, married only once, temperate, sensible, dignified, hospitable, an apt teacher, no drunkard, not violent but gentle, not quarrelsome, and no lover of money. He must manage his own household well, keeping his children submissive and respectful in every way. He must not be a recent convert," etc. (I Tim. 3:2-6).

DUTIES CHRISTIANS OWE THEIR TEACHERS AND PASTORS[9]   3

"Remain in the same house, eating and drinking what they provide, for the laborer deserves his wages" (Luke 10:7). "The Lord commanded that those who proclaim the gospel should get their living by the gospel" (I Cor. 9:14). "Let him who is taught the word share all good things with him who teaches. Do not be deceived; God is not mocked" (Gal. 6:6, 7). "Let the elders who rule well be considered worthy of double honor, especially those who labor in preaching and teaching; for the scripture says, 'You shall not muzzle an ox when it is treading out the grain,' and 'The laborer deserves his wages' " (I Tim. 5:17, 18). "We beseech you, brethren, to respect those who labor among you and are over you in the Lord and admonish you, and to

---

[7] Ps. 106:1; 136:26; 147:9-11.

[8] This table of duties was probably suggested to Luther by John Gerson's *Tractatus de modo vivendi omnium fidelium.*

[9] This section was not prepared by Luther, but was later taken up into the Small Catechism, probably with Luther's consent. The passages from Luke 10 and I Thess. 5 are not included in the Latin text.

esteem them very highly in love because of their work. Be at peace among yourselves" (I Thess. 5:12, 13). "Obey your leaders and submit to them; for they are keeping watch over your souls, as men who will have to give account. Let them do this joyfully, and not sadly, for that would be of no advantage to you" (Heb. 13:17).

GOVERNING AUTHORITIES[1]   4

"Let every person be subject to the governing authorities. For there is no authority except from God, and those that exist have been instituted by God. Therefore he who resists the authorities resists what God has appointed, and those who resist will incur judgment. He who is in authority does not bear the sword in vain; he is the servant of God to execute his wrath on the wrongdoer" (Rom. 13:1-4).

DUTIES SUBJECTS OWE TO GOVERNING AUTHORITIES   5

"Render therefore to Caesar the things that are Caesar's, and to God the things that are God's" (Matt. 22:21). "Let every person be subject to the governing authorities. Therefore one must be subject, not only to avoid God's wrath but also for the sake of conscience. For the same reason you also pay taxes, for the authorities are ministers of God, attending to this very thing. Pay all of them their dues, taxes to whom taxes are due, revenue to whom revenue is due, respect to whom respect is due, honor to whom honor is due" (Rom. 13:1, 5-7). "I urge that supplications, prayers, intercessions, and thanksgivings be made for all men, for kings and all who are in high positions, that we may lead a quiet and peaceable life, godly and respectful in every way" (I Tim. 2:1, 2). "Remind them to be submissive to rulers and authorities, to be obedient, to be ready for any honest work" (Tit. 3:1). "Be subject for the Lord's sake to every human institution, whether it be to the emperor as supreme, or to governors as sent by him to punish those who do wrong and to praise those who do right" (I Pet. 2:13, 14).

HUSBANDS   6

"You husbands, live considerately with your wives, bestowing honor on the woman as the weaker sex, since you are joint heirs of the grace of life, in order that your prayers may not be hindered" (I Pet. 3:7). "Husbands, love your wives, and do not be harsh with them" (Col. 3:19).

WIVES   7

"You wives, be submissive to your husbands, as Sarah obeyed Abraham, calling him lord. And you are now her children if you do right and let nothing terrify you" (I Pet. 3:1, 6).

[1] This section was not prepared by Luther, but was later taken up into the Small Catechism, probably with Luther's consent.

PARENTS   8

"Fathers, do not provoke your children to anger, lest they become discouraged, but bring them up in the discipline and instruction of the Lord" (Eph. 6:4; Col. 3:21).

CHILDREN   9

"Children, obey your parents in the Lord, for this is right. 'Honor your father and mother' (this is the first commandment with a promise) 'that it may be well with you and that you may live long on the earth' " (Eph. 6:1-3).

LABORERS AND SERVANTS, MALE AND FEMALE   10

"Be obedient to those who are your earthly masters, with fear and trembling, with singleness of heart, as to Christ; not in the way of eye-service, as men-pleasers, but as servants of Christ, doing the will of God from the heart, rendering service with a good will as to the Lord and not to men, knowing that whatever good anyone does, he will receive the same again from the Lord, whether he is a slave or free" (Eph. 6:5-8).

MASTERS AND MISTRESSES   11

"Masters, do the same to them, and forbear threatening, knowing that he who is both their Master and yours is in heaven, and that there is no partiality with him" (Eph. 6:9).

YOUNG PERSONS IN GENERAL   12

"You that are younger, be subject to the elders. Clothe yourselves, all of you, with humility toward one another, for 'God opposes the proud, but gives grace to the humble.' Humble yourselves therefore under the mighty hand of God, that in due time he may exalt you" (I Pet. 5:5, 6).

WIDOWS   13

"She who is a real widow, and is left all alone, has set her hope on God and continues in supplications and prayers night and day; whereas she who is self-indulgent is dead even while she lives" (I Tim. 5:5, 6).

CHRISTIANS IN GENERAL   14

"The commandments are summed up in this sentence, 'You shall love your neighbor as yourself' " (Rom. 13:9). "I urge that supplications, prayers, intercessions, and thanksgivings be made for all men" (I Tim. 2:1).

> Let each his lesson learn with care   15
> And all the household well will fare.[2]

---

[*] On this rhyme by Luther see *WA*, 35:580.

VII

THE LARGE CATECHISM
of
Dr. Martin Luther

INTRODUCTION

Once the Evangelical churches had achieved some external stability, the need was to strengthen them internally. Luther had already produced a number of sermons and pamphlets, beginning as far back as 1516, to present popular instruction on basic elements of Christian doctrine. In 1525 he assigned to his friends Justus Jonas and John Agricola the task of composing a book of religious instruction for children, which he referred to as a "catechism." When this work suffered delay, as did also an attempt in 1528 by Philip Melanchthon, Luther took the initiative again. He assigned to Melanchthon the composition of the "Instruction to the Visitors of the Clergy in the Electorate of Saxony" (1528) while he himself undertook the preparation of a catechism.

The immediate background material consists of three series of sermons which Luther preached in May, September, and November-December, 1528, and March, 1529. Before these sermons were ended Luther was at work writing the Large Catechism. Parts of it were sent to the press before the whole was completed, which helps to explain the discrepancies in the text of the Ten Commandments.

In April, 1529, the "German Catechism" appeared, printed by George Rhaw in Wittenberg. (The title "Large Catechism" is not Luther's.) Later the same year Luther issued a revised edition which added an "Exhortation to Confession," a lengthy insertion in the introduction to the explanation of the Lord's Prayer, and several marginal notes. This edition was the first to be illustrated, some of the cuts coming from Lucas Cranach the Elder. Another edition appeared in 1530, furnished with a second and longer preface which had probably been composed at the Coburg. The last revision corrected by Luther himself came out in 1538.

A Latin translation of the Large Catechism appeared in 1529 and a second edition in 1544, the work of a humanist, Vincent Obsopoeus, who undertook to make of it a stylistic showpiece by adorning it with classical citations and allusions to ancient history. Otherwise it is generally a slavish translation of Luther's German. It was not necessary, therefore, to reproduce here the Latin variations from the German text.

MARTIN LUTHER'S PREFACE[1]

It is not for trivial reasons that we constantly treat the Cate- 1 chism and strongly urge others to do the same. For we see to our sorrow that many pastors and preachers[2] are very negligent in this respect and despise both their office and this teaching itself. Some because of their great and lofty learning, others because of sheer laziness and gluttony, behave in this matter as if they were pastors or preachers for their bellies' sake and had nothing to do but live off the fat of the land all their days, as they used to do under the papacy.

Everything that they are to teach and preach is now available 2 to them in clear and simple form in the many excellent books which are in reality what the old manuals claimed in their titles to be: "Sermons That Preach Themselves," "Sleep Soundly," "Prepared!" and "Treasury." [3] However, they are not so upright and honest as to buy these books, or if they have them, to examine and read them. Such shameful gluttons and servants of their bellies would make better swineherds or dogkeepers than spiritual guides and pastors.

Now that they are free from the useless, bothersome babbling of 3 the Seven Hours,[4] it would be fine if every morning, noon, and evening they would read, instead, at least a page or two from the Catechism, the Prayer Book,[5] the New Testament, or something else from the Bible and would pray the Lord's Prayer for themselves and their parishioners. In this way they might show honor and gratitude to the Gospel, through which they have been delivered from so many burdens and troubles, and they might feel a little shame because, like pigs and dogs, they remember no more of the Gospel than this rotten,

---

[1] In the German edition of the Book of Concord, 1580, this Longer Preface (which dates from 1530) appeared after the Shorter Preface in accordance with the order observed in the fourth German volume of the Jena edition of Luther's Works (1556).

[2] Preachers (*Prediger*) were limited to preaching; pastors (*Pfarrherren*) exercised the full ministerial office.

[3] Titles of medieval sermon books.

[4] The seven canonical hours, daily prayers prescribed by the medieval Breviary.

[5] Luther published the "Little Prayer Book" (*Betbüchlein*) in 1522 to replace Roman Catholic devotional books.

pernicious, shameful, carnal liberty. As it is, the common people   4
take the Gospel altogether too lightly, and even our utmost exertions
accomplish but little. What, then, can we expect if we are sluggish
and lazy, as we used to be under the papacy?

Besides, a shameful and insidious plague of security and bore-   5
dom has overtaken us. Many regard the Catechism as a simple, silly
teaching which they can absorb and master at one reading. After
reading it once they toss the book into a corner as if they are ashamed
to read it again. Indeed, even among the nobility there are some   6
louts and skinflints who declare that we can do without pastors and
preachers from now on because we have everything in books and can
learn it all by ourselves. So they blithely let parishes fall into decay,
and brazenly allow both pastors and preachers to suffer distress and
hunger. This is what one can expect of crazy Germans. We Germans
have such disgraceful people among us and must put up with them.

As for myself, let me say that I, too, am a doctor and a preacher   7
—yes, and as learned and experienced as any of those who act so
high and mighty. Yet I do as a child who is being taught the Catechism. Every morning, and whenever else I have time, I read and
recite word for word the Lord's Prayer, the Ten Commandments, the
Creed, the Psalms, etc. I must still read and study the Catechism   8
daily, yet I cannot master it as I wish, but must remain a child and
pupil of the Catechism, and I do it gladly. These dainty, fastidious
fellows would like quickly, with one reading, to become doctors above
all doctors, to know all there is to be known. Well, this, too, is a
sure sign that they despise both their office and the people's souls, yes,
even God and his Word. They need not fear a fall, for they have
already fallen all too horribly. What they need is to become children
and begin learning their ABC's, which they think they have outgrown
long ago.

Therefore, I beg these lazy-bellies and presumptuous saints,   9
for God's sake, to get it into their heads that they are not really and
truly such learned and great doctors as they think. I implore them
not to imagine that they have learned these parts of the Catechism
perfectly, or at least sufficiently, even though they think they know
them ever so well. Even if their knowledge of the Catechism were
perfect (though that is impossible in this life), yet it is highly profitable
and fruitful daily to read it and make it the subject of meditation and
conversation. In such reading, conversation, and meditation the Holy
Spirit is present and bestows ever new and greater light and fervor, so
that day by day we relish and appreciate the Catechism more greatly.
This is according to Christ's promise in Matt. 18:20, "Where two or
three are gathered in my name, there am I in the midst of them."

Nothing is so effectual against the devil, the world, the flesh,   10
and all evil thoughts as to occupy oneself with the Word of God, talk

about it, and meditate on it. Psalm 1 calls those blessed who "meditate on God's law day and night." [6] You will never offer up any incense or other savor more potent against the devil than to occupy yourself with God's commandments and words and to speak, sing, and meditate on them. This, indeed, is the true holy water, the sign which routs the devil and puts him to flight.[7]

For this reason alone you should eagerly read, recite, ponder, | | and practice the Catechism, even if the only blessing and benefit you obtain from it is to rout the devil and evil thoughts. For he cannot bear to hear God's Word. God's Word is not like some empty tale, such as the one about Dietrich of Bern,[8] but as St. Paul says in Rom. 1:16, it is "the power of God," indeed, the power of God which burns the devil and gives us immeasurable strength, comfort, and help.

Why should I waste words? Time and paper would fail me if I | 2 were to recount all the blessings that flow from God's Word. The devil is called the master of a thousand arts. What, then, shall we call God's Word, which routs and destroys this master of a thousand arts with all his wiles and might? It must, indeed, be master of more than a hundred thousand arts. Shall we frivolously despise this | 3 might, blessing, power, and fruit—especially we who would be pastors and preachers? If so, we deserve not only to be refused food but also to be chased out by dogs and pelted with dung. Not only do we need God's Word daily as we need our daily bread; we also must use it daily against the daily, incessant attacks and ambushes of the devil with his thousand arts.

If this were not enough to admonish us to read the Catechism | 4 daily, there is God's command. That alone should be incentive enough. Deut. 6:7, 8 solemnly enjoins that we should always meditate upon his precepts whether sitting, walking, standing, lying down, or rising, and keep them before our eyes and in our hands as a constant token and sign. Certainly God did not require and command this so solemnly without good reason. He knows our danger and need. He knows the constant and furious attacks and assaults of the devil. So he wishes to warn, equip, and protect us against them with good "armor" against their "flaming darts," [9] and with a good antidote against their evil infection and poison. O what mad, senseless | 5 fools we are! We must ever live and dwell in the midst of such mighty enemies as the devils, and yet we despise our weapons and armor, too lazy to give them a thought!

[6] Ps. 1:2.
[7] I.e., the Word of God really does what holy water was formerly believed to accomplish.
[8] Luther frequently cited the legend of Dietrich of Bern as an example of lies and fables.
[9] Eph. 6:11, 16.

Look at these bored, presumptuous saints who will not or can- 16
not read and study the Catechism daily. They evidently consider
themselves much wiser than God himself, and wiser than all his holy
angels, prophets, apostles, and all Christians! God himself is not
ashamed to teach it daily, for he knows of nothing better to teach,
and he always keeps on teaching this one thing without varying it
with anything new or different. All the saints know of nothing better
or different to learn, though they cannot learn it to perfection. Are we
not most marvelous fellows, therefore, if we imagine, after reading
or hearing it once, that we know it all and need not read or study it
any more? Most marvelous fellows, to think we can finish learning
in one hour what God himself cannot finish teaching! Actually, he is
busy teaching it from the beginning of the world to the end, and all
prophets and saints have been busy learning it and have always remained pupils, and must continue to do so.

This much is certain: anyone who knows the Ten Command- 17
ments perfectly knows the entire Scriptures. In all affairs and circumstances he can counsel, help, comfort, judge, and make decisions in
both spiritual and temporal matters. He is qualified to sit in judgment
upon all doctrines, estates, persons, laws, and everything else in the
world.

What is the whole Psalter but meditations and exercises based 18
on the First Commandment? Now, I know beyond a doubt that such
lazy-bellies and presumptuous fellows do not understand a single
Psalm, much less the entire Scriptures, yet they pretend to know and
despise the Catechism, which is a brief compend and summary of all
the Holy Scriptures.

Therefore, I once again implore all Christians, especially pastors 19
and preachers, not to try to be doctors prematurely and to imagine
that they know everything. Vain imaginations, like new cloth, suffer
shrinkage! Let all Christians exercise themselves in the Catechism
daily, and constantly put it into practice, guarding themselves with the
greatest care and diligence against the poisonous infection of such
security or vanity. Let them continue to read and teach, to learn and
meditate and ponder. Let them never stop until they have proved by
experience that they have taught the devil to death and have become
wiser than God himself and all his saints.

If they show such diligence, then I promise them—and their 20
experience will bear me out—that they will gain much fruit and God
will make excellent men of them. Then in due time they themselves
will make the noble confession that the longer they work with the
Catechism, the less they know of it and the more they have to learn.
Only then, hungry and thirsty, will they truly relish what now they
cannot bear to smell because they are so bloated and surfeited. To
this end may God grant his grace! Amen.

PREFACE[1]

This sermon has been undertaken for the instruction of children   1
and uneducated people. Hence from ancient times it has been called,
in Greek, a "catechism"—that is, instruction for children. Its   2
contents represent the minimum of knowledge required of a Christian.
Whoever does not possess it should not be reckoned among Christians
nor admitted to a sacrament,[2] just as a craftsman who does not know
the rules and practices of his craft is rejected and considered incompetent. For this reason young people should be thoroughly in-   3
structed in the various parts of the Catechism or children's sermons
and diligently drilled in their practice.

Therefore, it is the duty of every head of a household to examine   4
his children and servants at least once a week and ascertain what they
have learned of it, and if they do not know it, to keep them faithfully
at it. I well remember the time when there were old people who   5
were so ignorant that they knew nothing of these things—indeed,
even now we find them daily—yet they come to Baptism and the
Sacrament of the Altar and exercise all the rights of Christians, although those who come to the sacrament ought to know more and
have a fuller understanding of all Christian doctrine than children and
beginners at school. As for the common people, however, we   6
should be satisfied if they learned the three parts[3] which have been
the heritage of Christendom from ancient times, though they were
rarely taught and treated correctly, so that all who wish to be Christians in fact as well as in name, both young and old, may be well-
trained in them and familiar with them.

I. THE TEN COMMANDMENTS OF GOD

1. You shall have no other gods before me.   1
2. You shall not take the name of God in vain.   2
3. You shall keep the Sabbath day holy.   3
4. You shall honor father and mother.   4
5. You shall not kill.   5
6. You shall not commit adultery.   6
7. You shall not steal.   7
8. You shall not bear false witness against your neighbor.   8

---

[1] The Shorter Preface is based on a sermon of May 18, 1528 (*WA*, 30I:2).

[2] This was not only a proposal of Luther, but also a medieval prescription;
cf. John Surgant, *Manuale Curatorum* (1502), etc.

[3] Ten Commandments, Creed, Lord's Prayer. From 1525 on catechetical
instruction in Wittenberg was expanded to include material on Baptism and
the Lord's Supper.

9. You shall not covet your neighbor's house.   9
10. You shall not covet his wife, man-servant, maid-servant, cattle,
or anything that is his.[4]   10

II. The Chief Articles of Our Faith

I believe in God, the Father almighty, maker of heaven and   11
earth:

And in Jesus Christ, his only Son, our Lord: who was conceived   12
by the Holy Spirit, born of the virgin Mary, suffered under Pontius
Pilate, was crucified, dead, and buried: he descended into hell, the
third day he rose from the dead, he ascended into heaven, and sits on
the right hand of God, the Father almighty, whence he shall come
to judge the living and the dead.

I believe in the Holy Spirit, the holy Christian church,[5] the   13
communion of saints, the forgiveness of sins, the resurrection of the
body, and the life everlasting. Amen.

III. The Prayer, or Our Father, Which Christ Taught

Our Father who art in heaven, hallowed be thy name. Thy   14
kingdom come, thy will be done, on earth as it is in heaven. Give us
this day our daily bread; and forgive us our debts, as we also have
forgiven our debtors; and lead us not into temptation, but deliver us
from evil. For thine is the kingdom and the power and the glory,
forever. Amen.[6]

These are the most necessary parts of Christian instruction.   15
We should learn to repeat them word for word. Our children   16
should be taught the habit of reciting them daily when they rise in
the morning, when they go to their meals, and when they go to bed
at night; until they repeat them they should not be given anything
to eat or drink. Every father has the same duty to his household;   17
he should dismiss man-servants and maid-servants if they do not know
these things and are unwilling to learn them. Under no circum-   18
stances should a person be tolerated if he is so rude and unruly that
he refuses to learn these three parts in which everything contained in
Scripture is comprehended in short, plain, and simple terms, for   19
the dear fathers or apostles, whoever they were,[7] have thus summed
up the doctrine, life, wisdom, and learning which constitute the Christian's conversation, conduct, and concern.

[4] Ex. 20:2-17; cf. Deut. 5:6-21.
[5] The translation of *ecclesiam catholicam* by *eine christliche Kirche* was
common in fifteenth century Germany.
[6] Matt. 6:9-13; cf. Luke 11:2-4.
[7] Luther was not interested in defending the apostolic authorship of the
Creed.

When these three parts are understood, we ought also to know   20
what to say about the sacraments which Christ himself instituted,
Baptism and the holy Body and Blood of Christ, according to the
texts of Matthew and Mark at the end of their Gospels where they
describe how Christ said farewell to his disciples and sent them forth.

BAPTISM   21

"Go and teach all nations, and baptize them in the name of the
Father and of the Son and of the Holy Spirit" (Matt. 28:19). "He
who believes and is baptized will be saved; but he who does not believe
will be condemned" (Mark 16:16).

It is enough for an ordinary person to know this much about   22
Baptism from the Scriptures. The other sacrament may be dealt with
similarly, in short, simple words according to the text of St. Paul.

THE SACRAMENT [OF THE ALTAR]   23

"Our Lord Jesus Christ on the night when he was betrayed took
bread, gave thanks, and broke it and gave it to his disciples, saying,
'Take and eat, this is my body, which is given for you. Do this in
remembrance of me.'

"In the same way also the cup, after supper, saying, 'This cup is
the new testament in my blood, which is shed for you for the forgiveness of sins. Do this, as often as you drink it, in remembrance of me'"
(I Cor. 11:23-25).

Thus we have, in all, five parts covering the whole of Christian   24
doctrine, which we should constantly teach and require young people
to recite word for word. Do not assume that they will learn and retain
this teaching from sermons alone. When these parts have been   25
well learned, you may assign them also some Psalms or some hymns,[8]
based on these subjects, to supplement and confirm their knowledge.
Thus our youth will be led into the Scriptures so that they make
progress daily.

However, it is not enough for them simply to learn and repeat   26
these parts verbatim. The young people should also attend preaching,
especially at the time designated for the Catechism,[9] so that they may
hear it explained and may learn the meaning of every part. Then they
will also be able to repeat what they have heard and give a good,
correct answer when they are questioned, and thus the preaching will
not be without benefit and fruit. The reason we take such care to   27
preach on the Catechism frequently is to impress it upon our youth,
not in a lofty and learned manner but briefly and very simply, so that
it may penetrate deeply into their minds and remain fixed in their
memories.

[8] Luther himself wrote six hymns based on the parts of the Catechism.
[9] Preaching and instruction on the Catechism especially during Lent.

Now we shall take up the above-mentioned parts one by one   28
and in the plainest possible manner say about them as much as is
necessary.

[FIRST PART: THE TEN COMMANDMENTS]

THE FIRST COMMANDMENT

"You shall have no other gods."

That is, you shall regard me alone as your God. What does this |
mean, and how is it to be understood? What is it to have a god? What
is God?

Answer: A god is that to which we look for all good and in   2
which we find refuge in every time of need. To have a god is nothing
else than to trust and believe him with our whole heart. As I have
often said, the trust and faith of the heart alone make both God and
an idol. If your faith and trust are right, then your God is the   3
true God. On the other hand, if your trust is false and wrong, then
you have not the true God. For these two belong together, faith and
God. That to which your heart clings and entrusts itself is, I say,
really your God.

The purpose of this commandment, therefore, is to require true   4
faith and confidence of the heart, and these fly straight to the one
true God and cling to him alone. The meaning is: "See to it that
you let me alone be your God, and never seek another." In other
words: "Whatever good thing you lack, look to me for it and seek it
from me, and whenever you suffer misfortune and distress, come and
cling to me. I am the one who will satisfy you and help you out of
every need. Only let your heart cling to no one else."

This I must explain a little more plainly, so that it may be   5
understood and remembered, by citing some common examples of
failure to observe this commandment. Many a person thinks he has
God and everything he needs when he has money and property; in
them he trusts and of them he boasts so stubbornly and securely that he
cares for no one. Surely such a man also has a god—mammon[1] by   6
name, that is, money and possessions—on which he fixes his whole
heart. It is the most common idol on earth. He who has money and   7
property feels secure, happy, fearless, as if he were sitting in the midst
of paradise. On the other hand, he who has nothing doubts and   8
despairs as if he never heard of God. Very few there are who are   9
cheerful, who do not fret and complain, if they do not have mammon.

[1] Cf. Matt. 6:24.

This desire for wealth clings and cleaves to our nature all the way to the grave.

So, too, if anyone boasts of great learning, wisdom, power, 10 prestige, family, and honor, and trusts in them, he also has a god, but not the one, true God. Notice, again, how presumptuous, secure, and proud people become because of such possessions, and how despondent when they lack them or are deprived of them. Therefore, I repeat, to have a God properly means to have something in which the heart trusts completely.

Again, consider what we used to do in our blindness under the 11 papacy. If anyone had a toothache, he fasted to the honor of St. Apollonia; if he feared fire, he sought St. Lawrence as his patron; if he feared the plague, he made a vow to St. Sebastian or Roch.[2] There were countless other such abominations, and every person selected his own saint and worshiped and invoked him in time of need. In this 12 class belong those who go so far as to make a pact with the devil in order that he may give them plenty of money, help them in love affairs, protect their cattle, recover lost possessions, etc., as magicians and sorcerers do. All these fix their heart and trust elsewhere than in the true God. They neither expect nor seek anything from him.

Thus you can easily understand the nature and scope of this 13 commandment. It requires that man's whole heart and confidence be placed in God alone, and in no one else. To have God, you see, does not mean to lay hands upon him, or put him into a purse, or shut him up in a chest. We lay hold of him when our heart embraces him 14 and clings to him. To cling to him with all our heart is nothing 15 else than to entrust ourselves to him completely. He wishes to turn us away from everything else, and to draw us to himself, because he is the one, eternal good. It is as if he said: "What you formerly sought from the saints, or what you hoped to receive from mammon or anything else, turn to me for all this; look upon me as the one who wishes to help you and to lavish all good upon you richly."

Behold, here you have the true honor and the true worship which 16 please God and which he commands under penalty of eternal wrath, namely, that the heart should know no other consolation or confidence than that in him, nor let itself be torn from him, but for him should risk and disregard everything else on earth. On the other hand, 17 you can easily judge how the world practices nothing but false worship

---

[2] On Feb. 9, 248 or 249, Apollonia was martyred, her teeth being knocked out; the medieval church therefore considered her a help against toothache. Lawrence was martyred by burning on Aug. 10, 258. Sebastian was put to death by arrows on Jan. 20, early in the fourth century (?). Roch, who died in 1327, gave himself to care for plague victims. Cf. Luther's first extended exposition of the Ten Commandments (1518) for references to these and other saints, and to magicians and sorcerers. Contemporaries of Luther such as Erasmus also ridiculed this cult of saints.

and idolatry. There has never been a people so wicked that it did not establish and maintain some sort of worship. Everyone has set up a god of his own, to which he looked for blessings, help, and comfort.

For example, the heathen who put their trust in power and 18 dominion exalted Jupiter as their supreme god. Others who strove for riches, happiness, pleasure, and a life of ease venerated Hercules, Mercury, Venus, or others, while pregnant women worshiped Diana or Lucina,[3] and so forth. Everyone made into a god that to which his heart was inclined. Even in the mind of all the heathen, therefore, to have a god means to trust and believe. The trouble is that their 19 trust is false and wrong, for it is not founded upon the one God, apart from whom there is truly no god in heaven or on earth. Accordingly the heathen actually fashion their fancies and dreams 20 about God into an idol and entrust themselves to an empty nothing. So it is with all idolatry. Idolatry does not consist merely of 21 erecting an image and praying to it. It is primarily in the heart, which pursues other things and seeks help and consolation from creatures, saints, or devils. It neither cares for God nor expects good things from him sufficiently to trust that he wants to help, nor does it believe that whatever good it receives comes from God.

There is, moreover, another false worship. This is the greatest 22 idolatry that has been practiced up to now, and it is still prevalent in the world. Upon it all the religious orders are founded. It concerns only that conscience which seeks help, comfort, and salvation in its own works and presumes to wrest heaven from God. It keeps account how often it has made endowments, fasted, celebrated Mass, etc. On such things it relies and of them it boasts, unwilling to receive anything as a gift from God, but desiring by itself to earn or merit everything by works of supererogation, just as if God were in our service or debt and we were his liege lords. What is this but making God into an 23 idol—indeed, an "apple-god"[4]—and setting up ourselves as God? This reasoning, however, is a little too subtle to be understood by young pupils.

This much, however, should be said to ordinary people so that 24 they may mark well and remember the meaning of this commandment: We are to trust in God alone and turn to him, expecting from him only good things; for it is he who gives us body, life, food, drink, nourishment, health, protection, peace, and all temporal and eternal blessings. It is he who protects us from evil, he who saves and

---

[3] Lucina was the Roman goddess of birth, often identified with Juno.

[4] "Apfelgott" is possibly a corruption of "Aftergott," sham god. Luther speaks of "Apfelkönige oder gemalete Herrn" (WA, 31[1]:234), the latter expression, literally "painted lords," being a term of derision somewhat like "plaster saint." Sebastian Franck uses the term "Apfelkaiser." The "Apfelbischof" was a Shrove Tuesday character in parts of Germany.

delivers us when any evil befalls. It is God alone, I have often enough repeated, from whom we receive all that is good and by whom we are delivered from all evil. This, I think, is why we Germans 25 from ancient times have called God by a name more elegant and worthy than any found in other languages, a name derived from the word "good" [5] because he is an eternal fountain which overflows with sheer goodness and pours forth all that is good in name and in fact.

Although much that is good comes to us from men, we receive 26 it all from God through his command and ordinance. Our parents and all authorities—in short, all people placed in the position of neighbors—have received the command to do us all kinds of good. So we receive our blessings not from them, but from God through them. Creatures are only the hands, channels, and means through which God bestows all blessings. For example, he gives to the mother breasts and milk for her infant, and he gives grain and all kinds of fruits from the earth for man's nourishment—things which no creature could produce by himself. No one, therefore, should presume to 27 take or give anything except as God has commanded it. We must acknowledge everything as God's gifts and thank him for them, as this commandment requires. Therefore, this way of receiving good through God's creatures is not to be disdained, nor are we arrogantly to seek other ways and means than God has commanded, for that would be not receiving our blessings from God but seeking them from ourselves.

Let everyone, then, take care to magnify and exalt this 28 commandment above all things and not make light of it. Search and examine your own heart thoroughly and you will find whether or not it clings to God alone. Do you have the kind of heart that expects from him nothing but good, especially in distress and want, and renounces and forsakes all that is not God? Then you have the one true God. On the contrary, does your heart cling to something else, from which it hopes to receive more good and help than from God, and does it flee not to him but from him when things go wrong? Then you have an idol, another god.

Consequently, in order to show that God will not have this 29 commandment taken lightly but will strictly watch over it, he has attached to it, first, a terrible threat and, then, a beautiful, comforting promise. These should be thoroughly stressed and impressed upon young people so that they may take them to heart and remember them.

[EXPLANATION OF THE APPENDIX TO THE FIRST COMMANDMENT][6]

"For I am the Lord your God, mighty and jealous, visiting the 30 *iniquity of the fathers upon the children to the third and fourth*

---

[5] Luther asserted this derivation more than once. But the two words, both in old German and in Gothic, are not etymologically connected.
[6] This subtitle is found only in the Latin version.

generation of those who hate me, and showing mercy to many thousands of those who love me and keep my commandments." [7]

Although these words apply to all the commandments (as we 31 shall hear later),[8] yet they are attached precisely to this one which stands at the head of the list because it is of the utmost importance for a man to have the right head. For where the head is right, the whole life must be right, and vice versa. Learn from these words, 32 then, how angry God is with those who rely on anything but himself, and again, how kind and gracious he is to those who trust and believe him alone with their whole heart. His wrath does not abate until the fourth generation. On the other hand, his kindness and goodness 33 extend to many thousands, lest men live in security and commit themselves to luck, like brutes who think that it makes no great difference how they live. He is a God who takes vengeance upon men who 34 turn away from him, and his anger continues to the fourth generation, until they are utterly exterminated. Therefore he wills to be feared and not to be despised.

This he has witnessed in all the records of history, as Scripture 35 amply shows and as daily experience can still teach us. From the beginning he has completely rooted out all idolatry, and on that account he has destroyed both heathen and Jews; just so in our day he overthrows all false worship so that all who persist in it must ultimately perish. Even now there are proud, powerful, and rich 36 pot-bellies who, not caring whether God frowns or smiles, boast defiantly of their mammon and believe that they can withstand his wrath. But they will not succeed. Before they know it they will be wrecked, along with all they have trusted in, just as all others have perished who thought themselves to be so high and mighty.

Just because such blockheads imagine, when God refrains from 37 disturbing their security, that he is unconcerned or uninterested in such matters, he must strike and punish them so severely that he will not forget his anger down to their children's children. He intends that everyone shall be impressed and see that this is no laughing matter with him. These are also the people he means when he says, 38 "who hate me," that is, those who persist in their stubbornness and pride. They refuse to hear what is preached or spoken to them. When they are rebuked, to bring them to their senses and cause them to mend their ways before punishment descends, they become so mad and foolish that they justly merit the wrath they receive. We observe this every day in the case of bishops and princes.

---

[7] This text is virtually the same as in Luther's Bible translation at Exod. 20:5. An entirely different German rendering appears in the conclusion of his exposition of the Ten Commandments, below, 320.

[8] See below, Ten Commandments, 321, 326.

Terrible as these threats are, much mightier is the comfort in   39
the promise that assures mercy to those who cling to God alone—sheer
goodness and blessing, not only for themselves but also for their
children to a thousand and even many thousands of generations.
Certainly, if we desire all good things in time and eternity, this   40
ought to move and impel us to fix our hearts upon God with perfect
confidence since the divine Majesty comes to us with so gracious an
offer, so cordial an invitation, and so rich a promise.

Therefore let everyone be careful not to regard this as if it   41
were spoken by man. For it brings you either eternal blessing,
happiness, and salvation, or eternal wrath, misery, and woe. What
more could you ask or desire than God's gracious promise that he will
be yours with every blessing and will protect and help you in every
need? The trouble is that the world does not believe this at all,   42
and does not recognize it as God's Word. For the world sees that
those who trust God and not mammon suffer grief and want and are
opposed and attacked by the devil. They have neither money, prestige,
nor honor, and can scarcely even keep alive; meanwhile, those who
serve mammon have power, prestige, honor, wealth, and every comfort
in the eyes of the world. Accordingly, we must grasp these words,
even in the face of this apparent contradiction, and learn that they
neither lie nor deceive but will yet prove to be true.

Reflect on the past, search it out, and tell me, When men have   43
devoted all their care and diligence to scraping together great wealth
and money, what have they gained in the end? You will find that they
have wasted their effort and toil or, if they have amassed great
treasures, that these have turned to dust and vanished. They themselves have never found happiness in their wealth, nor has it ever
lasted to the third generation.[9] Examples of this you will find   44
aplenty in all histories and in the recollections of elderly and experienced people. Just ponder and heed them. Saul was a great king,   45
chosen by God, and an upright man; but once he was secure on his
throne and he let his heart depart from God, placing his confidence
in his crown and power, he inevitably perished with all that he had;
not one of his children remained.[1] David, on the other hand, was   46
a poor, despised man, hunted down and persecuted, his life nowhere
secure, yet inevitably he remained safe from Saul and became king.[2]
These words must stand and prove to be true since God cannot lie or
deceive; just leave it to the devil and the world to deceive you with

---

[9] A late Latin proverb, often quoted by Luther, declares: "Ill-gotten gains
will not last to the third generation."

[1] Cf. I Sam. 10, 15, 16, 31; II Sam. 4.

[2] Cf. I Sam. 18 to II Sam. 2.

their appearance, which indeed endures for a time but in the end is nothing! [3]

Let us therefore learn the first commandment well and realize   47 that God will tolerate no presumption and no trust in any other object; he makes no greater demand of us than a hearty trust in him for all blessings. Then we shall be on the right path and walk straight ahead, using all of God's gifts exactly as a cobbler uses his needle, awl, and thread (for work, eventually to lay them aside) or as a traveler avails himself of an inn, food, and bed (only for his temporal need). Let each person be in his station in life according to God's order, allowing none of these good things to be his lord or idol.

Let this suffice for the First Commandment. We had to explain   48 it at length since it is the most important. For, as I said before,[4] where the heart is right with God and this commandment is kept, fulfillment of all the others will follow of its own accord.

The Second Commandment

"You shall not take the name of God in vain."   49

As the First Commandment has inwardly instructed the heart   50 and taught faith, so this commandment leads us outward and directs the lips and the tongue into the right relation to God. The first things that issue and emerge from the heart are words. As I have taught above how to answer the question, What it is to have a God, so you must learn to grasp simply the meaning of this and all the other commandments and apply them to yourself.

If you are asked, "How do you understand the Second Com-   51 mandment? What does it mean to misuse or take the name of God in vain?" you should answer briefly: "It is a misuse of God's name if we call upon the Lord God in any way whatsoever to support falsehood or wrong of any kind." Therefore what this commandment forbids is appealing to God's name falsely or taking his name upon our lips when our heart knows or should know that the facts are otherwise— for example, where men take oaths in court and one side lies against the other. God's name cannot be more grievously abused than for   52 purposes of falsehood and deceit. Let this stand as the plain and simple meaning of this commandment.

From this everyone can readily infer when and in how many   53 ways God's name is abused, though it is impossible to enumerate all its misuses. To discuss it briefly, misuse of the divine name occurs most obviously in worldly business and in matters involving money,

---

[3] The first Latin translator, Obsopoeus, and the German (1580) and Latin (1584) editions of the Book of Concord added a negative, thereby turning Luther's quip into a sober admonition.

[4] See above, Ten Commandments, 31.

property, and honor, whether publicly in court or in the market or elsewhere, when a person perjures himself, swearing by God's name or by his own soul. This is especially common in marriage matters when two persons secretly betroth themselves to each other and afterward deny it under oath.

The greatest abuse, however, occurs in spiritual matters, which 54 pertain to the conscience, when false preachers arise and peddle their lying nonsense as the Word of God.

See, all this is an attempt to embellish yourself with God's name 55 or to put up a good front and justify yourself, whether in ordinary worldly affairs or in sublime and difficult matters of faith and doctrine. Also to be counted among liars are blasphemers, not only the very crass ones who are well known to everyone and who disgrace God's name unabashedly (these belong in the hangman's school, not ours), but also those who publicly slander the truth and God's Word and consign it to the devil. Of this there is no need to speak further.

Let us take to heart how important this commandment is and 56 diligently shun and avoid every misuse of the holy name as the greatest sin that can be committed outwardly. For to lie and deceive is in itself a gross sin, but it is greatly aggravated when we attempt to justify and confirm it by invoking God's name and using it as a cloak to cover our shame. So from a single lie a double one results—indeed, manifold lies.

Therefore God has attached to this commandment a solemn 57 threat: "for the Lord will not hold him guiltless who takes his name in vain." This means that in no one shall a violation be condoned or left unpunished. As little as God will permit the heart that turns away from him to go unpunished, so little will he permit his name to be used to gloss over a lie. Unfortunately it is now a common 58 calamity all over the world that there are few who do not use the name of God for lies and all kinds of wickedness, just as there are few who trust in God with their whole heart.

By nature we all have this beautiful virtue that whenever we 59 commit a wrong we like to cover and gloss over our disgrace so that no one may see it or know it. No man is so arrogant as to boast before the whole world of the wickedness he has committed. We prefer to act in secret without anyone's being aware of it. Then if anyone is denounced, God and his name have to be dragged in to turn the villainy into righteousness and the disgrace into honor. This is the 60 common course of the world. Like a great deluge, it has flooded all lands. Hence we get what we deserve: plague, war, famine, fire, flood, wayward wives and children and servants, and troubles of every kind. Where else could so much misery come from? It is a great mercy that the earth still bears and sustains us.

Above all things, therefore, our young people should be strictly 61 required and trained to hold this as well as the other commandments in high regard. Whenever they transgress, we must be after them at once with the rod, confront them with the commandment, and continually impress it upon them, so that they may be brought up not merely with punishment but in the reverence and fear of God.

Now you understand what it means to take God's name in vain. 62 To repeat very briefly, it is either simply to lie and assert under his name something that is not so, or to curse, swear, conjure, and, in short, to practice wickedness of any sort.

In addition, you must also know how to use the name of God 63 aright. With the words, "You shall not take the name of God in vain," God at the same time gives us to understand that we are to use his name properly, for it has been revealed and given to us precisely for our use and benefit. Since we are forbidden here to use the 64 holy name in support of falsehood or wickedness, it follows, conversely, that we are commanded to use it in the service of truth and all that is good—for example, when we swear properly where it is necessary and required. So, also, when we teach properly; again, when we call on his name in time of need, or praise and thank him in time of prosperity, etc. All this is summarized in the command in Ps. 50:15, "Call upon me in the day of trouble: I will deliver you and you shall glorify me." All this is what we mean by calling upon his name in service of truth and using it devoutly. Thus his name is hallowed, as we pray in the Lord's Prayer.

Here you have the substance of the entire commandment 65 explained. If it is so understood, you have easily solved the question that has tormented so many teachers:[5] why swearing is forbidden in the Gospel,[6] and yet Christ, St. Paul,[7] and other saints took oaths. The explanation is briefly this: We are not to swear in support of 66 evil (that is, to a falsehood) or unnecessarily; but in support of the good and for the advantage of our neighbor we are to swear. This is a truly good work by which God is praised, truth and justice are established, falsehood is refuted, people are reconciled, obedience is rendered, and quarrels are settled. For here God himself intervenes and separates right from wrong, good from evil. If one party in 67 a dispute swears falsely, he will not escape punishment. Though it may take a long time, nothing he does will in the end succeed; everything he may gain by the false oath will slip through his fingers and will never be enjoyed. This I have seen in the case of many who broke their 68

[5] E.g., Augustine and Jerome. The issue had taken on new urgency with the rise of the Anabaptists.

[6] Matt. 5:33-37.

[7] Matt. 26:63f.; Gal. 1:20; II Cor. 1:23.

promise of marriage; they never enjoyed a happy hour or a healthful day thereafter, and thus they miserably perished, body, soul, and possessions.

Therefore I advise and urge, as I have before, that by means 69 of warning and threat, restraint and punishment, children be trained in due time to shun falsehood and especially to avoid calling upon God's name in its support. Where they are allowed to do as they please, no good will come of it. It is evident that the world today is more wicked than it has ever been. There is no government, no obedience, no fidelity, no faith—only perverse, unbridled men whom no teaching or punishment can help. All this is God's wrath and punishment upon such willful contempt of this commandment.

On the other hand, children should be constantly urged and 70 encouraged to honor God's name and keep it constantly upon their lips in all circumstances and experiences, for true honor to God's name consists of looking to it for all consolation and therefore calling upon it. Thus, as we have heard above, the heart by faith first gives God the honor due him and then the lips do so by confession.

This is a blessed and useful habit, and very effective against the 71 devil, who is ever around us, lying in wait to lure us into sin and shame, calamity and trouble. He hates to hear God's name and cannot long remain when it is uttered and invoked from the heart. Many a 72 terrible and shocking calamity would befall us if God did not preserve us through our calling upon his name. I have tried it myself and learned by experience that often sudden, great calamity was averted and vanished in the very moment I called upon God. To defy the devil, I say, we should always keep the holy name on our lips so that he may not be able to injure us as he is eager to do.

For this purpose it also helps to form the habit of commending 73 ourselves each day to God—our soul and body, wife, children, servants, and all that we have—for his protection against every conceivable need. Thus has originated and continued among us the custom of saying grace and returning thanks at meals and saying other prayers for both morning and evening.[8] From the same source came the 74 custom of children who cross themselves when they see or hear anything monstrous or fearful and exclaim, "Lord God, save us!" "Help, dear Lord Christ!" etc. Thus, too, if anyone meets with unexpected good fortune, however trivial, he may say, "God be praised and thanked!" "This God has bestowed upon me!" etc. Children used to be trained to fast and pray to St. Nicholas and other

---

[8] See the blessing before meals, the thanksgiving after meals, and the morning and evening blessings appended at the end of the Small Catechism, above.

saints, but the other practices would be more pleasing and acceptable to God than any monastic life and Carthusian holiness.[9]

With childish and playful methods like these we may bring up   75 our youth in the fear and honor of God so that the First and Second Commandments may become familiar and be constantly practiced. Then some good may take root, spring up, and bear fruit, and men may grow up of whom an entire land may be proud. This would be   76 the right way to bring up children, so long as they can be trained with kind and pleasant methods, for those who have to be forced by means of rods and blows will come to no good end; at best they will remain good only as long as the rod is on their backs.

This kind of training takes such root in their hearts that they   77 fear God more than they do rods and clubs. This I say plainly for the sake of the young, so that it may sink into their minds, for when we preach to children, we must also speak their language. Thus we have averted the misuse of the divine name and taught that its right use consists not only of words but also of practice and life. We want them to know that God is well pleased with the right use of his name and will as richly reward it, even as he will terribly punish its misuse.

THE THIRD COMMANDMENT

"You shall sanctify the holy day."   78

Our word "holy day" or "holiday" is so called from the Hebrew   79 word "Sabbath," which properly means to rest, that is, to cease from labor; hence our common expression for "stopping work" literally means "observing a holy day or holiday." [1] In the Old Testament   80 God set apart the seventh day and appointed it for rest, and he commanded it to be kept holy above all other days.[2] As far as outward observance is concerned, the commandment was given to the Jews alone. They were to abstain from hard work and to rest, so that both man and beast might be refreshed and not be exhausted by constant labor. In time, however, the Jews interpreted this commandment   81 too narrowly and grossly misused it. They slandered Christ and would not permit him to do what they themselves were in the habit of doing on that day, as we read in the Gospel[3]—as if the commandment

---

[9] Luther often cited the Carthusian Order (founded 1084) as an example of particularly strict asceticism and self-devised holiness.

[1] The ambiguity in the German word *Feiertag,* to which Luther refers, is discernible in the connection between the English words "holy day" and "holiday." *Feiern* (*feiern*) means to celebrate a festival, or simply to take time off from work. *Feierabend machen* or *heiligen Abend geben,* common expressions for "taking (or granting) time off," literally mean observing (or granting) a holy day, originally the eve of a festival.

[2] Gen. 2:3.

[3] Matt. 12:1ff.; Mark 2:23ff.; Luke 6:1ff, 13:10ff., 14:1ff.; John 5:9ff., 7:22f., 9:14ff.

could be fulfilled by refraining from manual labor of any kind. This was not its intention, but, as we shall hear, it meant that we should sanctify the holy day or day of rest.

Therefore, according to its literal, outward sense, this com-   82 mandment does not concern us Christians. It is an entirely external matter, like the other ordinances of the Old Testament connected with particular customs, persons, times, and places,[4] from all of which we are now set free through Christ.[5]

To offer ordinary people a Christian interpretation of what   83 God requires in this commandment, we point out that we keep holy days not for the sake of intelligent and well informed Christians, for these have no need of them. We keep them, first, for the sake of bodily need. Nature teaches and demands that the common people— man-servants and maid-servants who have attended to their work and trades the whole week long—should retire for a day to rest and be refreshed. Secondly and most especially, we keep holy days so   84 that people may have time and opportunity, which otherwise would not be available, to participate in public worship, that is, that they may assemble to hear and discuss God's Word and then praise God with song and prayer.

This, I say, is not restricted to a particular time, as it was among   85 the Jews, when it had to be precisely this or that day, for in itself no one day is better than another. Actually, there should be worship daily; however, since this is more than the common people can do, at least one day in the week must be set apart for it. Since from ancient times Sunday has been appointed for this purpose, we should not change it. In this way a common order will prevail and no one will create disorder by unnecessary innovation.

This, then, is the plain meaning of this commandment: Since   86 we observe holidays anyhow, we should devote their observance to learning God's Word. The special office of this day, therefore, should be the ministry of the Word for the sake of the young and the poor common people. However, the observance of rest should not be so narrow as to forbid incidental and unavoidable work.

Accordingly, when you are asked what "You shall sanctify the   87 holy day" means, answer: "It means to keep it holy." What is meant by "keeping it holy"? Nothing else than to devote it to holy words, holy works, holy life. In itself the day needs no sanctification, for it

---

[4] In his treatise "Against the Heavenly Prophets" (1525) Luther argued that whatever in the Mosaic Law exceeds the natural law is strictly binding on the Jews alone. The Mosaic Law is "the Jews' 'Saxon Code.'" France does not observe the Saxon Code, except in so far as it agrees with its own laws on the common ground of the natural law. Man's need for a day of rest is a testimony of nature. Just so, Christ placed the Sabbath law under man, Matt. 12, Mark 3 (*WA*, 18:81, 82).

[5] Cf. Col. 2:16f.

was created holy. But God wants it to be holy to you. So it becomes holy or unholy on your account, according as you spend the day in doing holy or unholy things.

How does this sanctifying take place? Not when we sit behind 88 the stove and refrain from external work, or deck ourselves with garlands and dress up in our best clothes, but, as has been said, when we occupy ourselves with God's Word and exercise ourselves in it.

Indeed, we Christians should make every day a holy day and 89 give ourselves only to holy activities—that is, occupy ourselves daily with God's Word and carry it in our hearts and on our lips. However, as we have said, since all people do not have this much time and leisure, we must set apart several hours a week for the young, and at least a day for the whole community, when we can concentrate upon such matters and deal especially with the Ten Commandments, the Creed, and the Lord's Prayer. Thus we may regulate our whole life and being according to God's Word. Wherever this practice is in 90 force, a holy day is truly kept. Where it is not, it cannot be called a Christian holy day. Non-Christians can spend a day in rest and idleness, too, and so can the whole swarm of clerics in our day who stand daily in the churches, singing and ringing bells, without sanctifying the holy day because they neither preach nor practice God's Word but teach and live contrary to it.

The Word of God is the true holy thing[6] above all holy things. 91 Indeed, it is the only one we Christians acknowledge and have. Though we had the bones of all the saints or all the holy and consecrated vestments gathered together in one heap, they could not help us in the slightest degree, for they are all dead things that can sanctify no one. But God's Word is the treasure that sanctifies all things. By it all the saints themselves have been sanctified. At whatever time God's 92 Word is taught, preached, heard, read, or pondered, there the person, the day, and the work are sanctified by it, not on account of the external work but on account of the Word which makes us all saints. Accordingly, I constantly repeat that all our life and work must be guided by God's Word if they are to be God-pleasing or holy. Where that happens the commandment is in force and is fulfilled.

Conversely, any conduct or work done apart from God's Word 93 is unholy in the sight of God, no matter how splendid and brilliant it may appear, or even if it be altogether covered with holy relics, as are the so-called spiritual estates[7] who do not know God's Word but seek holiness in their own works.

---

[6] *Heiligtum* is the word for "relic." To understand Luther's meaning, read something like this: We used to be taught to revere relics and other "holy things." But the Word of God is the true holy thing, etc.

[7] Cf. the title of Luther's treatise, "Against the Falsely So-called Spiritual Estate of the Pope and the Bishops" (1522).

Note, then, that the power and force of this commandment   94
consist not of the resting but of the sanctifying, so that this day
should have its own particular holy work. Other trades and occupations
are not properly called holy work unless the doer himself is first holy.
But here a work must be performed by which the doer himself is made
holy; this, as we have heard, takes place only through God's Word.
Places, times, persons, and the entire outward order of worship are
therefore instituted and appointed in order that God's Word may
exert its power publicly.

Since so much depends on God's Word that no holy day is   95
sanctified without it, we must realize that God insists upon a strict
observance of this commandment and will punish all who despise his
Word and refuse to hear and learn it, especially at the times appointed.

Therefore this commandment is violated not only by those who   96
grossly misuse and desecrate the holy day, like those who in their
greed or frivolity neglect to hear God's Word or lie around in taverns
dead drunk like swine, but also by that multitude of others who listen
to God's Word as they would to any other entertainment, who only
from force of habit go to hear preaching and depart again with as little
knowledge of the Word at the end of the year as at the beginning.

It used to be thought that Sunday had been properly hallowed if   97
one heard a Mass or the reading of the Gospel; no one asked about
God's Word, and no one taught it either. Now that we have God's
Word, we still fail to remove the abuse of the holy day, for we permit
ourselves to be preached to and admonished but we listen without
serious concern.

Remember, then, that you must be concerned not only about   98
hearing the Word but also about learning and retaining it. Do not
regard it as an optional or unimportant matter. It is the commandment
of God, and he will require of you an accounting of how you have
heard and learned and honored his Word.

In the same way those conceited fellows should be chastised   99
who, after hearing a sermon or two, become sick and tired of it and
feel that they know it all and need no more instruction. This is
precisely the sin that used to be classed among the mortal sins and was
called *acidia*[8]—that is, indolence or satiety—a malignant, pernicious
plague with which the devil bewitches and befuddles the hearts of many
so that he may take us by surprise and stealthily take the Word of God
away from us.

Let me tell you this. Even though you know the Word perfectly   100
and have already mastered everything, still you are daily under the
dominion of the devil, who neither day nor night relaxes his effort to
steal upon you unawares and to kindle in your heart unbelief and

---

⁸ The term *acedia* (or *acidia*) comes from Aristotle's Ethics, Book IV.

wicked thoughts against all these commandments. Therefore you must continually keep God's Word in your heart, on your lips, and in your ears. For where the heart stands idle and the Word is not heard, the devil breaks in and does his damage before we realize it. On the |101 other hand, when we seriously ponder the Word, hear it, and put it to use, such is its power that it never departs without fruit. It always awakens new understanding, new pleasure, and a new spirit of devotion, and it constantly cleanses the heart and its meditations. For these words are not idle or dead, but effective and living. Even if no |102 other interest or need drove us to the Word, yet everyone should be spurred on by the realization that in this way the devil is cast out and put to flight, this commandment is fulfilled, and God is more pleased than by any work of hypocrisy, however brilliant.

THE FOURTH COMMANDMENT

Thus far we have learned the first three commandments, which |103 are directed toward God. First, we should trust, fear, and love him with our whole heart all the days of our lives. Secondly, we should not misuse his holy name in support of lies or any evil purpose whatsoever, but use it for the praise of God and the benefit and salvation of our neighbor and ourselves. Thirdly, on holy days or days of rest we should diligently devote ourselves to God's Word so that all our conduct and life may be regulated by it. Now follow the other seven, which relate to our neighbor. Among these the first and greatest is:
"You shall honor your father and mother." |104

To fatherhood and motherhood God has given the special |105 distinction, above all estates that are beneath it, that he commands us not simply to love our parents but also to honor them. With respect to brothers, sisters, and neighbors in general he commands nothing higher than that we love them. Thus he distinguishes father and mother above all other persons on earth, and places them next to himself. For it is a much greater thing to honor than to love. |106 Honor includes not only love but also deference, humility, and modesty, directed (so to speak) toward a majesty hidden within them. It requires us not only to address them affectionately and |107 reverently, but above all to show by our actions, both of heart and of body, that we respect them very highly and that next to God we give them the very highest place. For anyone whom we are whole-heartedly to honor, we must truly regard as high and great.

Young people must therefore be taught to revere their parents |108 as God's representatives, and to remember that, however lowly, poor, feeble, and eccentric they may be, they are their own father and mother, given them by God. They are not to be deprived of their honor because of their ways or their failings. Therefore, we are not to think of their persons, whatever they are, but of the will of God, who has created and ordained them to be our parents. In other respects, indeed, we are all equal in the sight of God, but among ourselves there must be this sort of inequality and proper distinctions. God therefore commands you to be careful to obey me as your father and to acknowledge my authority.

First, then, learn what this commandment requires concerning 109 honor to parents. You are to esteem and prize them as the most precious treasure on earth. In your words you are to behave 110 respectfully toward them, and not address them discourteously, critically, and censoriously, but submit to them and hold your tongue, even if they go too far. You are also to honor them by your 111 actions (that is, with your body and possessions), serving them, helping them, and caring for them when they are old, sick, feeble, or poor; all this you should do not only cheerfully, but with humility and reverence, as in God's sight. He who has the right attitude toward his parents will not allow them to suffer want or hunger, but will place them above himself and at his side and will share with them all he has to the best of his ability.

In the second place, notice what a great, good, and holy work 112 is here assigned to children. Alas, it is utterly despised and brushed aside, and no one recognizes it as God's command or as a holy, divine word and precept. For if we had regarded it as such, it would have been apparent to all that they who lived according to these words must also be holy men. Then there would have been no need to institute monasticism or "spiritual estates." Every child would have remained faithful to this commandment and would have been able to set his conscience right toward God, saying: "If I am to do good and holy works, I know of none better than to show all honor and obedience to my parents, since God himself has commanded it. What God commands must be much nobler than anything we 113 ourselves may devise. And because there is no greater or better teacher to be found than God, there can also be no better teaching than his. Now, he amply teaches what we should do if we wish to perform truly good works, and by commanding them he shows that he is well pleased with them. So, if this is God's command, and it embodies his highest wisdom, then I shall never improve upon it."

In this way, you see, we should have had godly children, 114 properly taught, and reared in true blessedness; they would have remained at home in obedience and service to their parents, and we should have had an object lesson in goodness and happiness. However, men did not feel obliged to set forth God's commandment in its full glory. They were able to ignore it and skip lightly over it, and so children could not lay it to heart; they simply gaped in astonishment at all the arrangements we have devised without ever asking God's approval.

For the love of God, therefore, let us at last teach our young   115
people to banish all other things from sight and give first place to this
commandment. If they wish to serve God with truly good works, they
must do what is pleasing to their fathers and mothers, or to those
who have parental authority over them. Every child who knows and
does this has, in the first place, the great comfort of being able
joyfully to boast in the face of all who are occupied with works of
their own choice: "See, this work is well pleasing to my God in
heaven; this I know for certain." Let them all come forward   116
and boast of their many great, laborious, and difficult works; we shall
see whether they can produce a single work that is greater and nobler
than obedience to father and mother, which God has appointed and
commanded next to obedience to his own majesty. If God's Word
and will are placed first and observed, nothing ought to be considered
more important than the will and word of our parents, provided that
these, too, are subordinated to obedience toward God and are not set
into opposition to the preceding commandments.

You should rejoice heartily and thank God that he has chosen   117
and fitted you to perform a task so precious and pleasing to him.
Even though it seems very trivial and contemptible, make sure that you
regard it as great and precious, not on account of your worthiness but
because it has its place within that jewel and holy treasure, the Word
and commandment of God. O how great a price all the   118
Carthusian monks and nuns[9] would pay if in the exercise of their
religion they could bring before God a single work done in accordance
with his commandment and could say with a joyful heart in his
presence, "Now I know that this work is well pleasing to Thee!"
What will become of these poor wretched people when, standing before
God and the whole world, they shall blush with shame before a little
child that has lived according to this commandment and confess that
with the merits of their whole lives they are not worthy to offer him
a cup of water? It serves them right for their devilish perversity   119
in trampling God's commandment under foot that they must torture
themselves in vain with their self-devised works[1] and meanwhile have
only scorn and trouble for their reward.

Should not the heart leap and melt with joy when it can go to   120
work and do what is commanded, saying, "Lo, this is better than the
holiness of all the Carthusians, even though they kill themselves with
fasting and pray on their knees without ceasing"? Hence you have a
sure text and a divine testimony that God has commanded this;

---

[9] Here and elsewhere the translator of the Latin version, Obsopoeus,
altered "Carthusians" into "Carmelites," a hermit order founded *ca.* 1180
on Mt. Carmel in Palestine, later transformed into a mendicant order.

[1] Self-appointed works in contrast to God's commands—for example, the
injunction to strict silence, avoidance of meat, extreme vigils, etc.

concerning the other things he has commanded not a word. This is the plight and the miserable blindness of the world that no one believes this; so thoroughly has the devil bewitched us with the false holiness and glamor of our own works.

Therefore, I repeat, I should be very glad if we were to open | 21 our eyes and ears and take this to heart so that we may not again be led astray from the pure Word of God to the lying vanities of the devil. Then all would be well; parents would have more happiness, love, kindness, and harmony in their houses, and children would win their parents' hearts completely. On the other hand, when they | 22 are obstinate and never do their duty until a rod is laid on their backs, they anger both God and their parents. Thus they deprive themselves of this treasure and joy of conscience and lay up for themselves nothing but misfortune. That is the way things go in the world | 23 now, as everyone complains. Both young and old are altogether wayward and unruly; they have no sense of modesty or honor; they do nothing until they are driven with blows; and they defame and depreciate one another behind their backs in any way they can. God therefore punishes them so that they sink into all kinds of trouble and misery. Neither can parents, as a rule, do very much; one | 24 fool trains another, and as they have lived, so live their children after them.

This, I say, should be the first and strongest reason impelling | 25 us to keep this commandment. If we had no father and mother, we should wish, on account of the commandments, that God would set up a block or a stone which we might call father and mother. How much more, when he has given us living parents, should we be happy to show them honor and obedience. For we know that it is highly pleasing to the divine Majesty and all the angels, that it vexes all devils, and, besides, that it is the greatest work that we can do, next to the sublime worship of God described in the previous commandments. Even | 26 almsgiving and all other works for our neighbor are not equal to this. For God has exalted this estate of parents above all others; indeed, he has appointed it to be his representative on earth. This will and pleasure of God ought to provide us sufficient reason and incentive to do cheerfully and gladly whatever we can.

Besides this, it is our duty before the world to show gratitude | 27 for the kindness and for all the good things we have received from our parents. But here again the devil rules in the world; children | 28 forget their parents, as we all forget God, and no one takes thought how God feeds, guards, and protects us and how many blessings of body and soul he bestows upon us. Especially when an evil hour comes do we rage and grumble impatiently and forget all the blessings we have received throughout our life. Just so we act toward our parents, and there is no child that recognizes and considers this, unless he is led to it by the Holy Spirit.

The perversity of the world God knows very well. By means of 129 commandments, therefore, he reminds and impels everyone to consider what his parents have done for him. Then everybody recognizes that he has received his body and life from them and that he has been nourished and nurtured by them when otherwise he would have perished a hundred times in his own filth. The wise men of old 130 were right when they said, "God, parents, and teachers can never be sufficiently thanked and repaid." [2] He who views the matter in this light will, without compulsion, give all honor to his parents and esteem them as those through whom God has given him all blessings.

Over and above all this, another strong incentive for us to 131 keep this commandment is that God has attached to it a lovely promise, "That you may have long life in the land where you dwell." Here you see how important God considers this commandment. 132 He declares that it is not only an object of pleasure and delight to himself, but also an instrument intended for our greatest welfare, to lead us to a quiet, pleasant, and blessed life. St. Paul also highly 133 exalts and praises this commandment, saying in Eph. 6:2, 3, "This is the first commandment with a promise: that it may be well with you and that you may live long on the earth." Although the other commandments also have a promise implied, yet in none is it so plainly and explicitly stated.

This, then, is the fruit and the reward, that whoever keeps 134 this commandment will enjoy good days, happiness, and prosperity. On the other hand, the penalty for him who disobeys it is that he will perish sooner and never be happy in life. For, in the Scriptures, to have long life means not merely to grow old but to have everything that pertains to long life—health, wife and child, livelihood, peace, good government, etc., without which this life can neither be heartily enjoyed nor long endure. If you are unwilling to obey father and 135 mother or to submit to them, then obey the hangman; and if you will not obey him, then obey the grim reaper,[3] Death! This, in short, 136 is the way God will have it: render him obedience and love and service, and he will reward you abundantly with every blessing; on the other hand, if you provoke him to anger, he will send upon you both death and the hangman.

[2] Cf. *WA*, 30^{II}:579: "A diligent, upright schoolteacher or master, or anyone who faithfully trains and teaches boys, can never be sufficiently repaid, as the pagan Aristotle says."

[3] Luther often used the word *Streckebein,* primarily a Low German expression for death. A parallel word is *Streckefuss.* A seventeenth century explanation is that in mortal illness the legs give out before the head, i.e., the dying man is stretched out on his bed. Obsopoeus translated the word with *carnifex,* executioner.

Why do we have so many criminals who must daily be hanged, 137
beheaded, or broken on the wheel if not because of disobedience?
They will not allow themselves to be brought up in kindness; consequently, by the punishment of God they bring upon themselves the
misfortune and grief that we behold, for it seldom happens that such
wicked people die a natural and timely death.

The godly and the obedient, however, are blessed. They live long
in peace and quietness. They see their children's children, as we said
above, "to the third and fourth generation." Again, as we know 138
from experience, where there are fine old families who prosper and
have many children, it is certainly because some of them were brought
up well and revered their parents. On the other hand, it is written of
the wicked in Ps. 109:13, "May his posterity be cut off: and may
their name be cut off in one generation." Learn well, then, how 139
important God considers obedience, since he so highly exalts it, so
greatly delights in it, so richly rewards it, and besides is so strict about
punishing those who transgress it.

All this I say that it may be thoroughly impressed upon the 140
young people, for no one will believe how necessary is this commandment, which in the past was neither heeded nor taught under the
papacy. These are plain and simple words, and everyone thinks he
already knows them well. So he passes over them lightly, fastens
his attention on other things, and fails to perceive and believe how
angry he makes God when he neglects this commandment, and how
precious and acceptable a work he does when he observes it.

In connection with this commandment there is more to be said 141
about the various kinds of obedience due to our superiors, persons
whose duty it is to command and to govern. Out of the authority
of parents all other authority is derived and developed. Where a
father is unable by himself to bring up his child, he calls upon a
schoolmaster to teach him; if he is too weak, he enlists the help
of his friends and neighbors; if he passes away, he confers and
delegates his authority and responsibility to others appointed for the
purpose. Likewise he must have domestics (man-servants and 142
maid-servants) under him to manage the household. Thus all who are
called masters stand in the place of parents and derive from them
their power and authority to govern. In the Scriptures they are all
called fathers because in their responsibility they act in the capacity
of fathers and ought to have fatherly hearts toward their people. So
from ancient times the Romans and other peoples called the masters
and mistresses of the household *patres et matres familias* (that is,
house-fathers and house-mothers). Again, their princes and overlords
were called *patres patriae*[4] (that is, fathers of the country) to the

[4] Cicero received this title after exposing the conspiracy of Catiline. In
later times it became a part of the Roman emperor's official title.

great shame of us would-be Christians who do not speak of our rulers in the same way, or at least do not treat and honor them as such.

What a child owes to father and mother, the entire household 143 owes them likewise. Therefore man-servants and maid-servants should take care not only to obey their masters and mistresses, but also to honor them as their own parents and do everything that they know is expected of them, not from compulsion and reluctantly but gladly and cheerfully; and they should do it for the reason just mentioned, that it is God's commandment and is more pleasing to him than all other works. They ought even to be willing to pay for the privilege of 144 service and be glad to acquire masters and mistresses in order to have such joyful consciences and know how to do truly golden works. These works in the past have been neglected and despised; instead, everybody ran in the devil's name into monasteries, on pilgrimages, and after indulgences, to their own hurt and with a bad conscience.

If this truth could be impressed upon the poor people, a 145 servant girl would dance for joy and praise and thank God; and with her careful work, for which she receives sustenance and wages, she would gain a treasure such as all who pass for the greatest saints do not have. Is it not a wonderful thing to be able to boast to yourself, "If I do my daily housework faithfully, that is better than the holiness and austere life of all the monks"? You have the promise, 146 moreover, that you will prosper and fare well in everything. How can you lead a more blessed or holy life, as far as your works are concerned? In the sight of God it is really faith that makes a 147 person holy; faith alone serves him, while our works serve the people. Here you have everything that is good—shelter and protection 148 in the Lord and, what is more, a joyful conscience and a gracious God who will reward you a hundredfold. You are a true nobleman if you are upright and obedient. If you are not, you will have nothing but the wrath and displeasure of God; there will be no peace in your heart, and eventually you will have all kinds of trouble and misfortune.

Whoever will not be moved by this, and who will not be 149 inclined to godliness, we deliver to the hangman and the grim reaper. Therefore, let everyone who can take advice remember that God is not to be taken lightly. God speaks to you and demands obedience. If you obey him you are his dear child; if you despise this command-ment, then take shame, misery, and grief for your reward.

The same may be said of obedience to the civil government, 150 which, as we have said, is to be classed with the estate of fatherhood, the most comprehensive of all relations. In this case a man is father not of a single family, but of as many people as he has inhabitants, citizens, or subjects. Through civil rulers, as through our own parents, God gives us food, house and home, protection and security. Therefore, since they bear this name and title with all honor as their chief glory, it is our duty to honor and magnify them as the most precious treasure and jewel on earth.

He who is obedient, willing, ready to serve, and cheerfully |51 gives honor where it is due, knows that he pleases God and receives joy and happiness for his reward. On the other hand, if he will not do so in love, but despises or rebelliously resists authority, let him know that he shall have no favor or blessing from God. Where he counts on gaining a gulden[5] by his unfaithfulness, he will lose ten elsewhere. Or he will fall victim to the hangman, or perish through war, pestilence, or famine, or his children will turn out badly; servants, neighbors, or strangers and tyrants will inflict injury, injustice, and violence upon him. What we seek and deserve, then, is paid back to us in retaliation.

If we ever let ourselves be persuaded that works of obedience |52 are so pleasing to God and have so rich a reward, we shall be simply overwhelmed with our blessings and we shall have all that our hearts desire. But God's Word and commandment are despised, as if they came from some loutish peddler. Let us see, though, whether you are the man to defy him. How difficult do you think it will be for him to pay you back? You will live much better with God's favor, |53 peace, and blessing than you will with disfavor and misfortune. Why, do you think, is the world now so full of unfaithfulness, |54 shame, misery, and murder? It is because everyone wishes to be his own master, be free from all authority, care nothing for anyone, and do whatever he pleases. So God punishes one knave by means of another. When you defraud or despise your master, another person comes along and treats you likewise. Indeed, in your own household you must suffer ten times as much wrong from your own wife, children, or servants.

Of course, we keenly feel our misfortune, and we grumble and |55 complain of unfaithfulness, violence, and injustice; but we are unwilling to see that we ourselves are knaves who have roundly deserved punishment and that we are not one bit improved by it. We spurn favor and happiness; therefore, it is only fair that we have nothing but unhappiness without mercy. Somewhere on earth there must |56 still be some godly people, or else God would not grant us so many blessings! If it depended on our merits, we would not have a penny[6] in the house or a straw in the field. All this I have been obliged |57 to set forth with such a profusion of words in the hope that someone may take it to heart, so that we may be delivered from the blindness and misery in which we are so deeply sunk and may rightly understand

---

[5] The gulden was originally a large gold coin, later also silver, the equivalent of a florin.

[6] In popular expressions the heller, or penny, represented extreme insignificance in contrast with the groschen and other coins.

the Word and will of God and sincerely accept it. From God's Word we could learn how to obtain an abundance of joy, happiness, and salvation, both here and in eternity.

Thus we have three kinds of fathers presented in this com- 158 mandment: fathers by blood, fathers of a household, and fathers of the nation. Besides these, there are also spiritual fathers—not like those in the papacy who applied this title to themselves but performed no fatherly office. For the name spiritual father belongs only to those who govern and guide us by the Word of God. St. Paul boasts 159 that he is a father in I Cor. 4:15, where he says, "I became your father in Christ Jesus through the Gospel." Since such persons are 160 fathers, they are entitled to honor, even above all others. But they very seldom receive it, for the world's way of honoring them is to harry them out of the country and grudge them as much as a piece of bread. In short, as St. Paul says, they must be "the refuse of the world, and every man's offscouring." [7]

Yet there is need to impress upon the common people that 161 they who would bear the name of Christians owe it to God to show "double honor" [8] to those who watch over their souls and to treat them well and make provision for them. God will adequately recompense those who do so and will not let them suffer want. But here everybody resists and rebels; all are afraid that their 162 bellies will suffer, and therefore they cannot now support one good preacher although in the past they filled ten fat paunches. For 163 this we deserve to have God deprive us of his Word and his blessings and once again allow preachers of lies[9] to arise and lead us to the devil—and wring sweat and blood out of us besides.

Those who keep their eyes on God's will and commandment, 164 however, have the promise that they will be richly rewarded for all they contribute to their temporal and spiritual fathers, and for the honor they render them. Not only shall they have bread, clothing, and money for a year or two, but long life, sustenance, and peace, and afterwards abundance and blessedness forever. Do your duty, 165 then, and leave it to God how he will support you and provide for all your wants. Since he has promised it, and has never yet lied, he will not lie to you either.

This ought to encourage us and make our hearts so melt for 166 joy and love toward those to whom we owe honor that we lift our hands in joyful thanks to God for giving us such promises. We ought to be willing to run to the ends of the world to obtain them. For the

---

[7] I Cor. 4:13.
[8] I Tim. 5:17.
[9] "Preachers of lies" (cf. Mic. 2:11) was a favorite epithet in the sixteenth century.

combined efforts of the whole world cannot add an hour to our life or raise from the earth a single grain of wheat for us. But God can and will give you everything abundantly, according to your heart's desire. He who despises and disdains this is not worthy to hear a word from God.

More than enough has now been said to those to whom this commandment applies.

In addition, it would be well to preach to parents on the nature 167 of their office, how they should treat those committed to their authority. Although the duty of superiors is not explicitly stated in the Ten Commandments, it is frequently dealt with in many other passages of Scripture, and God intends it to be included in this commandment in which he speaks of father and mother. God 168 does not want to have knaves or tyrants in this office and responsibility; nor does he assign them this honor (that is, power and authority to govern) merely to receive homage. Parents should consider that they owe obedience to God, and that, above all, they should earnestly and faithfully discharge the duties of their office, not only to provide for the material support of their children, servants, subjects, etc., but especially to bring them up to the praise and honor of God. Therefore do not imagine that the parental office is a matter of 169 your pleasure and whim. It is a strict commandment and injunction of God, who holds you accountable for it.

The trouble is that no one perceives or heeds this. Everybody 170 acts as if God gave us children for our pleasure and amusement, gave us servants merely to put them to work like cows or asses, and gave us subjects to treat them as we please, as if it were no concern of ours what they learn or how they live. No one is willing to see that 171 this is the command of the divine Majesty, who will solemnly call us to account and punish us for its neglect, nor is it recognized how very necessary it is to devote serious attention to the young. If we 172 want qualified and capable men for both civil and spiritual leadership, we must spare no effort, time, and expense in teaching and educating our children to serve God and mankind. We must not think only of amassing money and property for them. God can provide for 173 them and make them rich without our help, as indeed he does daily. But he has given and entrusted children to us with the command that we train and govern them according to his will; otherwise God would have no need of father and mother. Therefore let everybody 174 know that it is his chief duty, on pain of losing divine grace, to bring up his children in the fear and knowledge of God, and if they are gifted to give them opportunity to learn and study so that they may be of service wherever they are needed.

If this were done, God would richly bless us and give us grace 175 so that men might be trained who would be a benefit to the nation and the people. We would also have soundly instructed citizens, virtuous and home-loving wives who would faithfully bring up their children and servants to be godly. Think what deadly harm you 176 do when you are negligent in this respect and fail to bring up your children to usefulness and piety. You bring upon yourself sin and wrath, thus earning hell by the way you have reared your own children, no matter how devout and holy you may be in other respects. Because this commandment is disregarded, God terribly punishes 177 the world; hence there is no longer any civil order, peace, or respect for authority. We all complain about this state of things, but we do not see that it is our own fault. Because of the way we train them, we have unruly and disobedient subjects.

This is enough to serve as a warning; a more extensive 178 explanation will have to await another occasion.[1]

THE FIFTH COMMANDMENT

"You shall not kill." 179

We have now dealt with both the spiritual and the civil govern- 180 ment, that is, divine and paternal authority and obedience. In this commandment we leave our own house and go out among our neighbors to learn how we should conduct ourselves individually toward our fellow men. Therefore neither God nor the government is included in this commandment, yet their right to take human life is not abrogated. God has delegated his authority of punishing evil-doers to civil 181 magistrates in place of parents; in early times, as we read in Moses,[2] parents had to bring their own children to judgment and sentence them to death. Therefore what is forbidden here applies to private individuals, not to governments.

This commandment is simple enough. We hear it explained 182 every year in the Gospel, Matthew 5,[3] where Christ himself explains and summarizes it: We must not kill, either by hand, heart, or word, by signs or gestures, or by aiding and abetting. It forbids anger except, as we have said, to persons who occupy the place of God, that is, parents and rulers. Anger, reproof, and punishment are the prerogatives of God and his representatives, and they are to be exercised upon those who transgress this and the other commandments.

The occasion and need for this commandment is that, as God 183 well knows, the world is evil and this life is full of misery. He has therefore placed this and the other commandments as a boundary between good and evil. There are many offenses against this command-

---

[1] Soon after this Luther wrote his "Sermon on Keeping Children in School" (1530).

[2] Deut. 21:18-20.

[3] Matt. 5:20-26 is the Gospel for the sixth Sunday after Trinity. We have 16 sermons of Luther on this text.

ment, as there are against all the others. We must live among many people who do us harm, and so we have reason to be at enmity with them. For instance, a neighbor, envious that you have received | 84 from God a better house and estate or greater wealth and good fortune than he, gives vent to his irritation and envy by speaking ill of you.

Thus by the devil's prompting you acquire many enemies who begrudge you even the least good, whether physical or spiritual. When we see such people, our hearts in turn rage and we are ready to shed blood and take revenge. Then follow cursing and blows, and eventually calamity and murder. Here God, like a kind father, | 85 steps in and intervenes to get the quarrel settled for the safety of all concerned. Briefly, he wishes to have all people defended, delivered, and protected from the wickedness and violence of others, and he has set up this commandment as a wall, fortress, and refuge about our neighbor so that no one may do him bodily harm or injury.

What this commandment teaches, then, is that no one should | 86 harm another for any evil deed, no matter how much he deserves it. Not only is murder forbidden, but also everything that may lead to murder. Many persons, though they may not actually commit murder, nevertheless call down curses and imprecations upon their enemy's head, which, if they came true, would soon put an end to him. This spirit or revenge clings to every one of us, and it is common | 87 knowledge that no one willingly suffers injury from another. Therefore God wishes to remove the root and source of this bitterness toward our neighbor. He wants us to keep this commandment ever before our eyes as a mirror in which to see ourselves, so that we may be attentive to his will and with hearty confidence and prayer commit to him whatever wrong we suffer. Then we shall be content to let our enemies rave and rage and do their worst. Thus we may learn to calm our anger and have a patient, gentle heart, especially toward those who have given us occasion for anger, namely, our enemies.

Briefly, then, to impress it unmistakably upon the common | 88 people, the import of the commandment against killing is this: In the first place, we should not harm anyone. This means, first, by hand or by deed; next, we should not use our tongue to advocate or advise harming anyone; again, we should neither use nor sanction any means or methods whereby anyone may be harmed; finally, our heart should harbor no hostility or malice toward anyone in a spirit of anger and hatred. Thus you should be blameless toward all people in body and soul, especially toward him who wishes or does you evil. For to do evil to somebody who desires and does you good is not human but devilish.

In the second place, this commandment is violated not only | 89 when a person actually does evil, but also when he fails to do good to his neighbor, or, though he has the opportunity, fails to prevent, protect,

and save him from suffering bodily harm or injury. If you send 190
a person away naked when you could clothe him, you have let him
freeze to death. If you see anyone suffer hunger and do not feed him,
you have let him starve. Likewise, if you see anyone condemned[4] to
death or in similar peril and do not save him although you know ways
and means to do so, you have killed him. It will do you no good to
plead that you did not contribute to his death by word or deed, for
you have withheld your love from him and robbed him of the service
by which his life might have been saved.

Therefore God rightly calls all persons murderers who do not 191
offer counsel and aid to men in need and in peril of body and life. He
will pass a most terrible sentence upon them in the day of judgment,
as Christ himself declares. He will say: "I was hungry and thirsty
and you gave me no food or drink, I was a stranger, and you did not
welcome me, I was naked and you did not clothe me, I was sick and in
prison, and you did not visit me." [5] That is to say, "You would have
permitted me and my followers to die of hunger, thirst, and cold, to be
torn to pieces by wild beasts, to rot in prison or perish from want."

What else is this but to reproach such persons as murderers and 192
bloodhounds? For although you have not actually committed all these
crimes, as far as you were concerned you have nevertheless permitted
your neighbor to languish and perish in his misfortune.

It is just as if I saw someone wearily struggling in deep water, or
fallen into a fire, and could extend him my hand to pull him out and
save him, and yet I did not do it. How would I appear before all the
world in any other light than as a murderer and a scoundrel?

Therefore it is God's real intention that we should allow no 193
man to suffer harm, but show to everyone all kindness and love.
And this kindness is directed, as I said, especially toward our 194
enemies. To show kindness to our friends is but an ordinary heathen
virtue, as Christ says in Matthew 5:46, 47.

Here again we have God's Word by which he wants to 195
encourage and urge us to true, noble, exalted deeds, such as gentleness,
patience, and, in short, love and kindness toward our enemies. He
always wants to remind us to think back to the First Commandment,
that he is our God; that is, he wishes to help and protect us, so that he
may subdue our desire for revenge.

If this could be thoroughly impressed on people's minds, we 196
would have our hands full of good works to do. But this would 197
be no preaching for monks. It would too greatly undermine the
"spiritual estate" and infringe upon the holiness of the Carthusians. It
would be practically the same as forbidding their good works and

[4] Variant reading: innocently condemned.
[5] Matt. 25:42, 43.

emptying the monasteries. For in this teaching the ordinary Christian life would be considered just as acceptable, and even more so. Everybody would see how the monks mock and mislead the world with a false, hypocritical show of holiness, while they have thrown this and the other commandments to the winds, regarding them as unnecessary, as if they were not commandments but mere counsels.[6] Moreover, they have shamelessly boasted and bragged of their hypocritical calling and works as "the most perfect life," so that they might live a nice, soft life without the cross and suffering. This is why they fled to the monasteries, so that they might not have to suffer wrong from anyone or do anyone any good. Know, however, that it is the works   198 commanded by God's Word which are the true, holy, and divine works in which he rejoices with all the angels. In contrast to them all human holiness is only stench and filth, and it merits nothing but wrath and damnation.

THE SIXTH COMMANDMENT

"You shall not commit adultery."   199

The following commandments are easily understood from the   200 preceding one. They all teach us to guard against harming our neighbor in any way They are admirably arranged. First they deal with our neighbor's person. Then they proceed to the person nearest and dearest to him, namely, his wife, who is one flesh and blood with him.[7] In no possession of his can we inflict a greater injury upon him. Therefore, it is explicitly forbidden here to dishonor his wife. Adultery is particularly mentioned because among the Jewish   201 people marriage was obligatory. Youths were married at the earliest age possible. The state of virginity was not commended, neither were public prostitution and lewdness tolerated as they are now. Accordingly adultery was the most common form of unchastity among them.

Inasmuch as there is a shameful mess and cesspool of all   202 kinds of vice and lewdness among us, this commandment applies to every form of unchastity, however it is called. Not only is the external act forbidden, but also every kind of cause, motive, and means. Your heart, your lips, and your whole body are to be chaste and to afford no occasion, aid, or encouragement to unchastity. Moreover,   203 you are to defend, protect, and rescue your neighbor whenever he is in danger or need, and on the contrary to aid and assist him so that he may retain his honor. Whenever you fail to do this (though you   204 could prevent a wrong) or wink at it as if it were no concern of yours,

---

[6] Luther here is making a sarcastic play on the Roman Catholic distinction between "commandments" and "(evangelical) counsels" according to which all men are unconditionally obligated to keep the "commandments," but a voluntary observance of the "counsels" brings special grace while their non-observance is no sin.

[7] Cf. Gen. 2:24.

you are just as guilty as the culprit himself. In short, everyone   205
is required both to live chastely himself and to help his neighbor do
the same. Thus God by his commandment wants every husband or
wife guarded and protected from any trespass.

Inasmuch as this commandment is concerned specifically with   206
the estate of marriage and gives occasion to speak of it, let us
carefully note, first, how highly God honors and glorifies the married
life, sanctioning and protecting it by his commandment. He sanctioned
it above in the fourth commandment, "You shall honor father and
mother"; but here, as I said, he has secured it and protected it.
Therefore he also wishes us to honor, maintain, and cherish it   207
as a divine and blessed estate. Significantly he established it as the
first of all institutions, and he created man and woman differently
(as is evident) not for lewdness but to be true to each other, be
fruitful, beget children, and support and bring them up to the glory
of God.

God has therefore most richly blessed this estate above all   208
others and, in addition, has supplied and endowed it with everything
in the world in order that this estate might be provided for richly and
adequately. Married life is no matter for jest or idle curiosity, but
it is a glorious institution and an object of God's serious concern.
For it is of the highest importance to him that persons be brought up
to serve the world, promote knowledge of God, godly living, and all
virtues, and fight against wickedness and the devil.

Therefore I have always taught that we should not despise or   209
disdain marriage, as the blind world and the false clergy do, but view
it in the light of God's Word, by which it is adorned and sanctified.
It is not an estate to be placed on a level with the others; it precedes
and surpasses them all, whether those of emperor, princes, bishops, or
anyone else. Important as the spiritual and civil estates are, these
must humble themselves and allow all people to enter the estate of
marriage, as we shall hear. It is not an exceptional estate, but   210
the most universal and the noblest, pervading all Christendom and
even extending throughout all the world.

In the second place, remember that it is not only an honorable   211
estate but also a necessary one, and it is solemnly commanded by God
that in general men and women in all conditions, who have been
created for it, shall be found in this estate. Yet there are some
(although few) exceptions whom God has especially exempted—some
who are unsuited for married life and others whom he has released by
a high supernatural gift so that they can maintain chastity outside of
marriage. Where nature has its way, as God implanted it, it is not   212
possible to remain chaste outside of marriage; for flesh and blood
remain flesh and blood, and the natural inclinations and stimulations
have their way without let or hindrance, as everyone's observation and

experience testify. Therefore, to make it easier for man to avoid unchastity in some measure, God has established marriage, so that everyone may have his allotted portion and be satisfied with it— although here, too, God's grace is still required to keep the heart pure.

From this you see how the papal rabble, priests, monks, and 213 nuns resist God's order and commandment when they despise and forbid marriage, and boast and vow that they will maintain perpetual chastity while they deceive the common people with lying words and wrong impressions. For no one has so little love and inclination 214 for chastity as those who under the guise of great sanctity avoid marriage and either indulge in open and shameless fornication or secretly do even worse—things too evil to mention, as unfortunately has been only too well proved. In short, even though they 215 abstain from the act, yet their hearts remain so full of unchaste thoughts and evil desires that they suffer incessant ragings of secret passion, which can be avoided in married life. Therefore all vows 216 of chastity apart from marriage are condemned and annulled by this commandment; indeed, all poor, captive consciences deceived by their monastic vows are even commanded to forsake their unchaste existence and enter the married life. Even granting that the monastic life is godly, yet it is not in their power to maintain chastity, and if they remain they will inevitably sin more and more against this commandment.

I say these things in order that our young people may be led 217 to acquire a love for married life and know that it is a blessed and God-pleasing estate. Thus it may in due time regain its proper honor, and there may be less of the filthy, dissolute, disorderly conduct which now is so rampant everywhere in public prostitution and other shameful vices resulting from contempt of married life. Therefore 218 parents and magistrates have the duty of so supervising youth that they will be brought up to decency and respect for authority and, when they are grown, will be married honorably in the fear of God. Then God will add his blessing and grace so that men may have joy and happiness in their married life.

Let it be said in conclusion that this commandment requires 219 everyone not only to live chastely in thought, word, and deed in his particular situation (that is, especially in the estate of marriage), but also to love and cherish the wife or husband whom God has given. For marital chastity it is above all things essential that husband and wife live together in love and harmony, cherishing each other whole-heartedly and with perfect fidelity. This is one of the chief ways to make chastity attractive and desirable. Under such conditions chastity always follows spontaneously without any command. This is why 220 St. Paul so urgently admonishes husbands and wives to love and honor

each other.[8] Here you have another precious good work—indeed,   221
many and great works—which you can joyfully set over against all
"spiritual estates" that are chosen without God's Word and
commandment.

THE SEVENTH COMMANDMENT

"You shall not steal."   222

Next to our own own person and our spouse, our temporal   223
property is dearest to us. This, too, God wants to have protected. He
has forbidden us to rob or pilfer the possessions of our neighbor.
For to steal is nothing else than to acquire another's property by   224
unjust means. In a few words, this includes taking advantage of our
neighbor in any sort of dealing that results in loss to him. Stealing is a
widespread, common vice, but people pay so little attention to it that
the matter is entirely out of hand. If all who are thieves, though they
are unwilling to admit it, were hanged on the gallows, the world would
soon be empty, and there would be a shortage of both hangmen and
gallows. As I have just said, a person steals not only when he robs a
man's strongbox or his pocket, but also when he takes advantage of
his neighbor at the market, in a grocery shop, butcher stall, wine- and
beer-cellar, work-shop, and, in short, wherever business is transacted
and money is exchanged for goods or labor.

Let us make it a little clearer for the common people so that   225
we may see how honest we are. Suppose, for example, that a man-
servant or maid-servant is unfaithful in his or her domestic duty and
does damage or permits damage to happen when it could have been
avoided. Or suppose that through laziness, carelessness, or malice a
servant wastes and neglects things to the vexation and annoyance of
his master or mistress. When this is done deliberately—for I am not
speaking of what happens inadvertently and unintentionally—a servant
can cheat his employer out of thirty or forty gulden or more a year.
If a thief had taken such sums he would be strangled with a noose,
but the servant may even become defiant and insolent and dare anyone
to call him a thief!

The same must be said of artisans, workmen, and day-laborers   226
who act high-handedly and never know enough ways to overcharge
people and yet are careless and unreliable in their work. All these are
far worse than sneak-thieves, against whom we can guard with lock
and bolt, or if we catch them we can deal with them so that they will
not repeat the offense. But against the others no one can guard. No
one even dares to give them a hard look or accuse them of theft. One
would ten times rather lose the money from one's purse. For these
are my neighbors, my good friends, my own servants, from whom I
expect good; but they are the first to defraud me.

[8] Cf. Eph. 5:22, 25; Col. 3:18f.

Furthermore, at the market and in everyday business the same   227
fraud prevails in full force. One person openly cheats another with
defective merchandise, false measures, dishonest weights, and bad
coins, and takes advantage of him by underhanded tricks and sharp
practices and crafty dealing. Or again, one swindles another in a
trade and deliberately fleeces, skins, and torments him. Who can even
describe or imagine it all? In short, thievery is the most common   228
craft and the largest guild on earth. If we look at mankind in all its
conditions, it is nothing but a vast, wide stable full of great thieves.

These men are called gentleman swindlers[9] or big operators.   229
Far from being picklocks and sneak-thieves who loot a cash box, they
sit in office chairs and are called great lords and honorable, good
citizens, and yet with a great show of legality they rob and steal.

Yes, we might well keep quiet here about various petty   230
thieves in order to launch an attack against the great, powerful arch-
thieves who consort with lords and princes and daily plunder not only
a city or two, but all Germany. Indeed, what would become of the
head and chief protector of all thieves, the Holy See at Rome, and
all its retinue, which has plundered and stolen the treasures of the
whole world and holds them to this day?

This, in short, is the way of the world. Those who can steal   231
and rob openly are safe and free, unmolested by anyone, even claiming
honor from men. Meanwhile the little sneak-thieves who have
committed one offense must bear disgrace and punishment so as to
make the others look respectable and honorable. But the latter
should be told that in the eyes of God they are the greatest thieves,
and that he will punish them as they deserve.

This commandment is very far-reaching, as we have shown. It   232
is necessary, therefore, to emphasize and explain it to the common
people in order that they may be restrained in their wantonness and
that the wrath of God may be continually and urgently kept before
their eyes. For we must preach this not to Christians but chiefly to
knaves and scoundrels, though it might be more fitting if the judge,
the jailer, or the hangman did the preaching. Let every one   233
know, then, that it is his duty, at the risk of God's displeasure, not to
harm his neighbor, take advantage of him, or defraud him by any
faithless or underhanded business transaction. More than that, he is
under obligation faithfully to protect his neighbor's property and
further his interests, especially when he takes remuneration for such
services.

---

[9] Luther's word is *Stuhlräuber*, a contemporary expression for "usurers."
He takes the term to refer to men whom we might call "swivel-chair
operators." Luther's etymology, however, is wrong; *Stuhlräuber* is derived
not from *Stuhl*, meaning chair, but from the Low German *Stôl*, meaning
capital let out for interest or "rent."

A person who willfully disregards this commandment may   234
indeed get by and escape the hangman, but he will not escape God's
wrath and punishment. Though he pursues his defiant and arrogant
course for a long time, still he will remain a tramp and a beggar and
will suffer all kinds of troubles and misfortunes. Now, you   235
servants ought to take care of your master's or mistress's property,
which enables you to stuff your craw and your belly. But you go your
own way, take your wages like a thief, and even expect to be revered
like noblemen. Many of you are even insolent toward masters and
mistresses and unwilling to do them the favor and service of protecting
them from loss. But see what you gain. When you come into   236
property yourself and have a house of your own—which God will
let you acquire to your undoing—there will come a day of reckoning
and retribution: for every penny you have taken and for every penny's
damage you have done you will have to pay back thirty-fold.

So will it be with artisans and day-laborers, from whom we are   237
obliged to suffer such intolerable insolence. They act as if they were
lords over others' possessions and entitled to whatever they demand.
Just let them keep on boldly fleecing people as long as they can.   238
God will not forget his commandment. He will pay them what they
deserve. He will hang them not on a green gallows but on a dry one.[1]
They will neither prosper nor gain anything their whole life long.
Of course, if our government were well regulated, such insolence   239
might soon be checked. The ancient Romans, for example, promptly
took such offenders by the scruff of the neck so that others took
warning.

The same fate will overtake those who turn the free public   240
market into a carrion-pit and a robbers' den. Daily the poor are
defrauded. New burdens and high prices are imposed. Everyone
misuses the market in his own willful, conceited, arrogant way, as if it
were his right and privilege to sell his goods as dearly as he pleases
without a word of criticism. We shall stand by and let such   241
persons fleece, grab, and hoard. But we shall trust God, who   242
takes matters into his own hands. After they have scrimped and scraped
for a long time, he will pronounce this kind of blessing over them:
"Your grain will spoil in the garner and your beer in the cellar. Your
cattle will die in the stall. Yes, where you have cheated and defrauded
anyone out of a gulden, your entire hoard will be consumed by rust
so that you will never enjoy it."

Indeed, we have the evidence before our very eyes every day   243
that no stolen or ill-gotten possession thrives. How many people scrape
and scratch day and night and yet grow not a penny richer! Though

---

[1] Death on the gallows was considered a more ignominious punishment
than death on a green tree ("green gallows").

they gather a great hoard, they must suffer so many troubles and misfortunes that they can never enjoy it or pass it on to their children. But because we ignore this and act as if it were none of our 244 business, God must punish us and teach us morals in a different way. He lays on us one affliction after another, or he quarters a troop of soldiers upon us; in one hour they clean out our chests and purse down to the last penny, and then by way of thanks they burn and ravage house and home and outrage and kill wife and children.

In short, however much you steal, depend on it that just as 245 much will be stolen from you. Anyone who robs and takes things by violence and dishonesty must put up with another who plays the same game. For God is a master of this art; since everyone robs and steals from the other, he punishes one thief by means of another. Otherwise, where would we find enough gallows and ropes?

Whoever is willing to learn a lesson, let him know that this 246 is God's commandment and must not be treated as a joke. We shall put up with those of you who despise, defraud, steal, and rob us. We shall endure your arrogance and show forgiveness and mercy, as the Lord's Prayer teaches. The upright, meanwhile, will not want, and you will hurt yourself more than others. But beware how you deal with the poor, of whom there are many now. If, when you meet a 247 poor man who must live from hand to mouth, you act as if everyone must live by your favor, you skin and scrape him right down to the bone, and you arrogantly turn him away whom you ought to give aid, he will go away wretched and dejected, and because he can complain to no one else, he will cry to heaven. Beware of this, I repeat, as of the devil himself. Such a man's sighs and cries will be no joking matter. They will have an effect too heavy for you and all the world to bear, for they will reach God, who watches over poor, sorrowful hearts, and he will not leave them unavenged. But if you despise and defy this, see whom you have brought upon yourself. If you succeed and prosper, before all the world you may call God and me liars.

We have now given sufficient warning and exhortation. He 248 who will not heed or believe this may go his own way until he learns it by experience. But it needs to be impressed upon the young people so that they may be on their guard and not follow the old, wayward crowd, but may keep their eyes fixed upon God's commandment, lest his wrath and punishment come upon them too. Our responsibility 249 is only to instruct and reprove by means of God's Word. To restrain open lawlessness is the responsibility of princes and magistrates. They should be alert and resolute enough to establish and maintain order in all areas of trade and commerce in order that the poor may not be burdened and oppressed and in order that they may not themselves be charged with other men's sins.

Enough has been said concerning the nature of stealing. It is 250 not to be confined to narrow limits but must extend to all our relations with our neighbors. To sum up, as we have done in the previous commandments: On one hand, we are forbidden to do our neighbor any injury or wrong in any way imaginable, whether by damaging, withholding, or interfering with his possessions and property. We are not even to consent to or permit such a thing, but are rather to avert and prevent it. On the other hand, we are 251 commanded to promote and further our neighbor's interests, and when he suffers want we are to help, share, and lend to both friends and foes.

Anyone who seeks and desires good works will here find 252 ample opportunity to do things which are heartily acceptable and pleasing to God. Moreover, he graciously lavishes upon them a wonderful blessing: We shall be richly rewarded for all the help and kindness we show to our neighbor, as King Solomon teaches in Prov. 19:17, "He who is kind to the poor lends to the Lord, and he will repay him for his deed." Here you have a rich Lord. 253 Surely he is sufficient for your needs and will let you lack or want for nothing. Thus with a happy conscience you can enjoy a hundred times more than you could scrape together by perfidy and injustice. Whoever does not desire this blessing will find wrath and misfortune enough.

THE EIGHTH COMMANDMENT

"You shall not bear false witness against your neighbor." 254

Besides our own body, our wife or husband, and our temporal 255 property, we have one more treasure which is indispensable to us, namely, our honor and good name, for it is intolerable to live among men in public disgrace and contempt. Therefore God will not 256 have our neighbor deprived of his reputation, honor, and character any more than of his money and possessions; he would have every man maintain his self-respect before his wife, children, servants, and neighbors. In its first and simplest meaning, as the words stand 257 ("You shall not bear false witness"), this commandment pertains to public courts of justice, where a poor, innocent man is accused and maligned by false witnesses and consequently punished in his body, property, or honor.

This problem appears to concern us only a little at present, but 258 among the Jews it was extremely common. That nation had an excellent, orderly government, and even now, where there is such a government, instances of this sin still occur. The reason is this: Where judges, mayors, princes, or others in authority sit in judgment, we always find that, true to the usual course of the world, men are loath to offend anyone. Instead, they speak dishonestly with an eye to gaining favor, money, prospects, or friendship. Consequently, a poor man is inevitably oppressed, loses his case, and suffers punishment. It is the universal misfortune of the world that men of integrity seldom preside in courts of justice.

A judge ought, above all, to be a man of integrity, and not   259 only upright but also a wise, sagacious, brave, and fearless man. Likewise, a witness should be fearless; more than that, he should be an upright man. He who is to administer justice equitably in all cases will often offend good friends, relatives, neighbors, and the rich and powerful who are in a position to help or harm him. He must therefore be quite blind, shutting his eyes and ears to everything but the evidence presented, and make his decision accordingly.

The first application of this commandment, then, is that   260 everyone should help his neighbor maintain his rights. He must not allow these rights to be thwarted or distorted but should promote and resolutely guard them, whether he be judge or witness, let the consequences be what they may. Here we have a goal set for our   261 jurists: perfect justice and equity in every case. They should let right remain right, not perverting or concealing or suppressing anything on account of anyone's money, property, honor, or power. This is one aspect of the commandment, and its plainest meaning, applying to all that takes place in court.

Next, it extends much further when it is applied to spiritual   262 jurisdiction or administration. Here, too, everyone bears false witness against his neighbor. Wherever there are godly preachers and Christians, they must endure having the world call them heretics, apostates, even seditious and accursed scoundrels. Moreover, the Word of God must undergo the most shameful and spiteful persecution and blasphemy; it is contradicted, perverted, misused, and misinterpreted. But let this pass; it is the blind world's nature to condemn and persecute the truth and the children of God and yet consider this no sin.

The third aspect of this commandment concerns us all. It   263 forbids all sins of the tongue by which we may injure or offend our neighbor. False witness is clearly a work of the tongue. Whatever is done with the tongue against a neighbor, then, is forbidden by God. This applies to false preachers with their corrupt teaching and blasphemy, to false judges and witnesses with their corrupt behavior in court and their lying and malicious talk outside of court. It   264 applies particularly to the detestable, shameful vice of back-biting or slander by which the devil rides us. Of this much could be said. It is a common vice of human nature that everyone would rather hear evil than good about his neighbor. Evil though we are, we cannot tolerate having evil spoken of us; we want the golden compliments of the whole world. Yet we cannot bear to hear the best spoken of others.

To avoid this vice, therefore, we should note that nobody has   265 the right to judge and reprove his neighbor publicly, even when he

has seen a sin committed, unless he has been authorized to judge
and reprove. There is a great difference between judging sin and 266
having knowledge of sin. Knowledge of sin does not entail the right
to judge it. I may see and hear that my neighbor sins, but to make
him the talk of the town is not my business. If I interfere and pass
sentence on him, I fall into a greater sin than his. When you become
aware of a sin, simply make your ears a tomb and bury it until you
are appointed a judge and authorized to administer punishment by
virtue of your office.

Those are called backbiters who are not content just to know 267
but rush ahead and judge. Learning a bit of gossip about someone else,
they spread it into every corner, relishing and delighting in it like pigs
that roll in the mud and root around in it with their snouts. This 268
is nothing else than usurping the judgment and office of God,
pronouncing the severest kind of verdict and sentence, for the harshest
verdict a judge can pronounce is to declare somebody a thief, a
murderer, a traitor, etc. Whoever therefore ventures to accuse his
neighbor of such guilt assumes as much authority as the emperor and
all magistrates. For though you do not wield the sword, you use your
venomous tongue to the disgrace and harm of your neighbor.

Therefore God forbids you to speak evil about another even 269
though, to your certain knowledge, he is guilty. All the more urgent
is the prohibition if you are not sure but have it only from hearsay.
But you say: "Why shouldn't I speak if it is the truth?" I reply: 270
"Why don't you bring it before the regular judge?" "Oh, I cannot
prove it publicly; I might be called a liar and sent away in disgrace."
Ah, now do you smell the roast? If you do not trust yourself to make
your charges before the proper authorities, then hold your tongue.
Keep your knowledge to yourself and do not give it out to others. For
when you repeat a story that you cannot prove, even if it is true, you
appear as a liar. Besides, you act like a knave, for no man should be
deprived of his honor and good name unless these have first been
taken away from him publicly.

Every report, then, that cannot be adequately proved is false 271
witness. No one should publicly assert as truth what is not 272
publicly substantiated. In short, what is secret should be allowed to
remain secret, or at any rate be reproved in secret, as we shall hear.
Therefore, if you encounter somebody with a worthless tongue 273
who gossips and slanders someone, rebuke him straight to his face
and make him blush for shame. Then you will silence many a one who
otherwise would bring some poor man into disgrace, from which he
could scarcely clear himself. For honor and good name are easily
taken away, but not easily restored.

So you see that we are absolutely forbidden to speak evil of 274
our neighbor. Exception is made, however, of civil magistrates,

preachers, and parents, for we must interpret this commandment in such a way that evil shall not go unpunished. We have seen that the Fifth Commandment forbids us to injure anyone physically, and yet an exception is made of the hangman. By virtue of his office he does not do his neighbor good but only harm and evil, yet he does not sin against God's commandment because God of his own accord instituted that office, and as he warns in the Fifth Commandment, he has reserved to himself the right of punishment. Likewise, although no one has in his own person the right to judge and condemn anyone, yet if they whose duty it is fail to do so, they sin as much as those who take the law into their own hands without such a commission. Necessity requires one to report evil, to prefer charges, to attest,   275 examine, and witness. It is no different from the situation of the physician who, to cure a patient, is sometimes compelled to examine and handle his private parts. Just so, magistrates, parents, even brothers and sisters and other good friends are under mutual obligation to reprove evil where it is necessary and beneficial.

But the right way to deal with this matter would be to observe   276 the order laid down by the Gospel, Matthew 19,[2] where Christ says, "If your brother sins against you, go and tell him his fault, between you and him alone." Here you have a fine, precious precept for governing the tongue which ought to be carefully noted if we are to avoid this detestable abuse. Let this be your rule, then, that you should not be quick to spread slander and gossip about your neighbor but admonish him privately so that he may amend. Likewise, if someone should whisper to you what this or that person has done, teach him, if he saw the wrongdoing, to go and reprove the man personally, otherwise to hold his tongue.

This lesson you can learn from the daily management of the   277 household. When the master of the house sees a servant failing to do his duty, he takes him to task personally. If he were so foolish as to leave the servant at home while he went out on the streets to complain to his neighbors, he would no doubt be told: "You fool! That is none of our business. Why don't you tell him yourself?" And that would be the brotherly thing to say, for the evil would   278 be corrected and the neighbor's honor maintained. As Christ himself says in the same passage, "If he listens to you, you have gained your brother." Then you have done a great and excellent work. Do you think it is an insignificant thing to gain a brother? Let all monks and holy orders step forth, with all their works heaped up together, and see if they can make the boast that they have gained one brother!

Christ teaches further: "If he does not listen, take one or two   279 others along with you, that every word may be confirmed by the

---

[2] Matt. 18:15. The reference was corrected in later editions.

evidence of two or three witnesses." [3] So the individual is to be dealt with personally and not gossiped about behind his back. If this 280 does not help, then bring the matter before the public, either before the civil or the ecclesiastical court. Then you do not stand alone. You have witnesses with you through whom you can convict the guilty one and on whose testimony the judge can base his decision and sentence. This is the right procedure for restraining and reforming a wicked person. But if you gossip about someone in every corner 281 and root around in the filth, nobody will be reformed. Moreover, when you are called upon to witness, you will probably deny having said anything. It would serve such gossips right to have their 282 sport spoiled, as a warning to others. If you were acting for 283 your neighbor's improvement or from love of the truth, you would not sneak about in secret, shunning the light of day.

All this refers to secret sins. But where the sin is so public 284 that the judge and the whole world are aware of it, you can without sin shun and avoid the person as one who has brought disgrace upon himself, and you may testify publicly concerning him. For when an affair is manifest to everybody there can be no question of slander or injustice or false witness. For example, we now censure the pope and his teaching, which is publicly set forth in books and shouted throughout the world. Where the sin is public, the punishment ought to be public so that everyone may know how to guard against it.

Now we have the sum and substance of this commandment: 285 No one shall harm his neighbor, whether friend or foe, with his tongue. No one shall speak evil of him, whether truly or falsely, unless it is done with proper authority or for his improvement. A person should use his tongue to speak only good of everyone, to cover his neighbor's sins and infirmities, to overlook them, and to cloak and veil them with his own honor. Our chief reason for doing so 286 should be the one which Christ indicates in the Gospel, and in which he means to embrace all the commandments concerning our neighbor, "Whatever you wish that men would do to you, do so to them." [4]

Even nature teaches the same thing in our own bodies, as 287 St. Paul says in I Cor. 12:22, 23, "The parts of the body which seem to be weaker are indispensable, and those parts of the body which we think less honorable we invest with the greater honor; and our unpresentable parts are treated with greater modesty." No one covers his face, eyes, nose, and mouth; we do not need to, for they are our most honorable members. But the weakest members, of which we are ashamed, we carefully conceal. Our hands and eyes, even the whole body, must help to cover and veil them. Thus in our relations 288

[3] Matt. 18:16.
[4] Matt. 7:12.

with one another, we should veil whatever blemishes and infirmities we find in our neighbor, doing our utmost to serve and help him to promote his honor. On the other hand, we should prevent everything that tends to his disgrace. It is a particularly fine, noble virtue   289 always to put the best construction upon all we may hear about our neighbor, as long as it is not a notorious evil, and to defend him against the poisonous tongues of those who are busy wherever they can pry out and pounce on something to criticize in their neighbor, misconstruing and twisting things in the worst way. This is what happens now especially to the precious Word of God and its preachers.

This commandment, then, embraces a great multitude of good   290 works which please God most highly and bring abundant blessings, if only the blind world and the false saints would recognize them. There is nothing about a man or in a man that can do greater   291 good or greater harm, in spiritual or in temporal matters, than this smallest and weakest of his members, the tongue.[5]

The Ninth and Tenth Commandments

"You shall not covet your neighbor's house."   292
"You shall not covet his wife, man-servant, maid-servant, cattle, or anything that is his."

These two commandments, taken literally, were given exclu-   293 sively to the Jews; nevertheless, in part they also apply to us. The Jews did not interpret them as referring to unchastity or theft, since these vices were sufficiently forbidden in commandments above. They thought they were keeping the commandments when they obeyed the injunctions and prohibitions contained in them. God therefore added these two commandments to teach them that it is sinful and forbidden to covet our neighbor's wife or property, or to have any designs upon them. Especially were these commandments needed   294 because under the Jewish government man-servants and maid-servants were not free, as now, to serve for wages according to their own choice; with their body and all they had they were their master's property, the same as his cattle and other possessions. Moreover,   295 every man had power to dismiss his wife publicly by giving her a bill of divorce[6] and to take another wife. So there was a danger among them that if anyone took a fancy to another's wife, he might on any flimsy excuse dismiss his own wife and estrange the other's from him so that he might legally take her. They considered this no more a sin or disgrace than it is now for a master to dismiss his servants or entice his neighbor's from him.

Therefore, I say, they interpreted these commandments   296

[5] Cf. James 3:5.
[6] Cf. Deut. 24:1.

correctly (though they also have a broader and higher application) to forbid anyone, even with a specious pretext, to covet or scheme to despoil his neighbor of what belongs to him, such as his wife, servants, house, fields, meadows, or cattle. Above, the seventh commandment prohibits seizing or withholding another's possessions to which you have no right. But here it is also forbidden to entice anything away from your neighbor, even though in the eyes of the world you could do it honorably, without accusation or blame for fraudulent dealing.

Such is nature that we all begrudge another's having as much   297 as we have. Everyone acquires all he can and lets others look out for themselves. Yet we all pretend to be upright. We know how to   298 put up a fine front to conceal our rascality. We think up artful dodges and sly tricks (better and better ones are being devised daily) under the guise of justice. We brazenly dare to boast of it, and insist that it should be called not rascality but shrewdness and business acumen. In this we are abetted by jurists and lawyers who twist and stretch   299 the law to suit their purpose, straining words and using them for pretexts, without regard for equity or for our neighbor's plight. In short, whoever is sharpest and shrewdest in such affairs gets most advantage out of the law, for as the saying has it, "The law favors the vigilant."

This last commandment, then, is addressed not to those whom   300 the world considers wicked rogues, but precisely to the most upright— to people who wish to be commended as honest and virtuous because they have not offended against the preceding commandments. To this class the Jews especially claimed to belong, as many great nobles, lords, and princes do now. For the common masses belong much farther down in the scale, where the Seventh Commandment applies, since they are not much concerned about questions of honor and right when it comes to acquiring possessions.

This situation occurs most frequently in lawsuits in which   301 someone sets out to gain and squeeze something out of his neighbor. For example, when people wrangle and wrestle over a large inheritance, real estate, etc., they resort to whatever arguments have the least semblance of right, so varnishing and garnishing them that the law supports them, and they gain such secure title to the property as to put it beyond complaint or dispute. Similarly, if anyone covets   302 a castle, city, county, or other great estate, he practices bribery, through friendly connections and by any other means at his disposal, until the property is taken away from the owner and legally awarded to him with letters patent and the seal of the prince attesting that it was acquired lawfully.

The same thing happens in ordinary business affairs, where one   303 cunningly slips something out of another's hand so that the victim is helpless to prevent it. Or, seeing an opportunity for profit—let us say, when a man because of adversity or debt cannot hold on to his property, nor yet sell it without loss—he hurries and worries him until he acquires a half or more of it; and yet this must not be considered as illegally acquired, but rather as honestly purchased. Hence the sayings, "First come, first served," and "Every man must look out for himself while others shift for themselves." Who is ingenious   304 enough to imagine how much he can acquire by such specious pretexts? The world does not consider this wrong, and it does not see that the neighbor is being taken advantage of and forced to sacrifice what he cannot spare without injury. Yet no one wishes this to happen to himself. From this it is clear that all these pretexts and shams are false.

This was also the case in ancient times with respect to wives.   305 They knew tricks like this: If a man took a fancy to another woman, he managed, either personally or through others and by any of a number of ways, to make her husband displeased with her, or she became so disobedient and hard to live with that her husband was obliged to dismiss her and leave her to the other man. That sort of thing undoubtedly was quite prevalent in the time of the law, for we read even in the Gospel[7] that King Herod took his brother's wife while the latter was still living, and yet posed as an honorable, upright man, as St. Mark testifies. Such examples, I trust, will not be   306 found among us, except that someone may by trickery entice a rich bride away from another, for in the New Testament[8] married people are forbidden to be divorced. But it is not uncommon among us for a person to lure away another's man-servant or maid-servant or otherwise estrange them with fair words.

However these things may be, you must learn that God does   307 not wish you to deprive your neighbor of anything that is his, letting him suffer loss while you gratify your greed, even though in the eyes of the world you might honorably retain the property. To do so is dark and underhanded wickedness, and, as we say, it is all done "under the hat"[9] so as to escape detection. Although you may act as if you have wronged no one, you have trespassed on your neighbor's rights. It may not be called stealing or fraud, yet it is coveting—that is, having designs upon your neighbor's property, luring it away from him against his will, and begrudging what God gave him. The   308 judge and the public may have to leave you in possession of it, but God will not, for he sees your wicked heart and the deceitfulness of the world. If you give the world an inch, it will take a yard, and at length open injustice and violence follow.

Let these commandments therefore retain their general appli-   309

[7] Matt. 14:3f.; Mark 6:17ff.
[8] Matt. 5:31f., 19:3-9; Mark 10:2-12; Luke 16:18; I Cor. 7:10f.
[9] An expression derived from sorcery.

cation. We are commanded not to desire harm to our neighbor, nor become accessory to it, nor give occasion for it; we are willingly to leave him what is his, and promote and protect whatever may be profitable and serviceable to him, as we wish that he would do to us. Thus these commandments are directed especially against envy 310 and miserable covetousness, God's purpose being to destroy all the roots and causes of our injuries to our neighbors. Therefore he sets it forth in plain words: "You shall not covet," etc. Above all, he wants our hearts to be pure, even though as long as we live here we cannot reach that ideal. So this commandment remains, like all the rest, one that constantly accuses us and shows just how upright we really are in God's sight.

Conclusion of the Ten Commandments[1]

Here, then, we have the Ten Commandments, a summary of 311 divine teaching on what we are to do to make our whole life pleasing to God. They are the true fountain from which all good works must spring, the true channel through which all good works must flow. Apart from these Ten Commandments no deed, no conduct can be good or pleasing to God, no matter how great or precious it may be in the eyes of the world.

Let us see, now, how our great saints can boast of their 312 spiritual orders and the great, difficult works which they have fashioned while they neglect these commandments as if they were too insignificant or had been fulfilled long ago.

It seems to me that we shall have our hands full to keep these 313 commandments, practicing gentleness, patience, love toward enemies, chastity, kindness, etc., and all that these virtues involve. But such works are not important or impressive in the eyes of the world. They are not unusual and pompous, restricted to special times, places, rites, and ceremonies, but are common, everyday domestic duties of one neighbor toward another, with no show about them. On the other 314 hand, those other works captivate all eyes and ears. Aided by great pomp, splendor, and magnificent buildings, they are so adorned that everything gleams and glitters. There is burning of incense, singing and ringing of bells, lighting of tapers and candles until nothing else can be seen or heard. For when a priest stands in a gold-embroidered chasuble[2] or a layman remains on his knees a whole day in church, this is considered a precious work that cannot be sufficiently extolled. But when a poor girl tends a little child, or faithfully does what she is told, that is regarded as nothing. Otherwise, why should monks and nuns go into cloisters?

---

[1] This title was inserted later.

[2] An elaborate vestment for the officiant at Mass. Cf. Smalcald Articles, Preface, 13.

Just think, is it not a devilish presumption on the part of those   315
desperate saints to dare to find a higher and better way of life than
the Ten Commandments teach? They pretend, as we have said, that
this is a simple life for the ordinary man, whereas theirs is for the
saints and the perfect. They fail to see, these miserable, blind   316
people, that no man can achieve so much as to keep one of the Ten
Commandments as it ought to be kept. Both the Creed and the Lord's
Prayer must help us, as we shall hear. Through them we must seek
and pray for help and receive it continually. Therefore all their
boasting amounts to as much as if I boasted, "Of course, I haven't a
single groschen to pay, but I promise to pay ten gulden." [3]

All this I say and repeat in order that men may get rid of the   317
pernicious abuse which has become so deeply rooted and still clings to
every man, and that all classes of men on earth may accustom themselves to look only to these precepts and heed them. It will be a long
time before men produce a doctrine or social order equal to that
of the Ten Commandments, for they are beyond human power to
fulfill. Anyone who does fulfill them is a heavenly, angelic man, far
above all holiness on earth. Just concentrate upon them and   318
test yourself thoroughly, do your very best, and you will surely find
so much to do that you will neither seek nor pay attention to any
other works or other kind of holiness.

Let this suffice concerning the first part,[4] both for instruction   319
and for admonition. In conclusion, however, we must repeat the text
which we have already treated above in connection with the First
Commandment[5] in order to show how much effort God requires us to
devote to learning how to teach and practice the Ten Commandments.

"I the Lord, your God, am a jealous God, visiting the iniquity   320
of the fathers upon the children to the third and fourth generation of
them that hate me; but to those who love me and keep my commandments,
I show mercy unto a thousand generations."

Although primarily attached to the First Commandment, as we   321
heard above, this appendix was intended to apply to all the commandments, and all of them as a whole ought to be referred and directed
to it. For this reason I said that we should keep it before the young
and insist that they learn and remember it so that we may see why we
are constrained and compelled to keep these Ten Commandments.
This appendix ought to be regarded as attached to each individual
commandment, penetrating and pervading them all.

Now, as we said before, these words contain both a wrathful   322
threat and a friendly promise, not only to terrify and warn us but also

---

[3] There were 21 groschen, small gold or silver coins (English: groat), to a
gulden.
[4] I.e., the first part of the Catechism.
[5] Section 30, above.

to attract and allure us. These words, therefore, ought to be received and esteemed as a serious matter to God because he himself here declares how important the commandments are to him and how strictly he will watch over them, fearfully and terribly punishing all who despise and transgress his commandments; and again, how richly he will reward, bless, and bestow all good things on those who prize them and gladly act and live in accordance with them. Thus he 323 demands that all our actions proceed from a heart that fears and regards God alone and, because of this fear, avoids all that is contrary to his will, lest he be moved to wrath; and, conversely, trusts him alone and for his sake does all that he asks of us, because he shows himself a kind father and offers us every grace and blessing.

This is exactly the meaning and right interpretation of the 324 first and chief commandment, from which all the others proceed. This word, "You shall have no other gods," means simply, "You shall fear, love, and trust me as your one true God." Wherever a man's heart has such an attitude toward God, he has fulfilled this commandment and all the others. On the other hand, whoever fears and loves anything else in heaven and on earth will keep neither this nor any other. Thus the entire Scriptures have proclaimed and presented 325 this commandment everywhere, emphasizing these two things, fear of God and trust in God. The prophet David particularly teaches it throughout the Psalter, as when he says, "The Lord takes pleasure in those who fear him, in those who hope in his mercy" (Ps. 147:11). He seems to explain the whole commandment in one verse, as if to say, "The Lord takes pleasure in those who have no other gods."

Thus the First Commandment is to illuminate and impart its 326 splendor to all the others. In order that this may be constantly repeated and never forgotten, therefore, you must let these concluding words run through all the commandments, like the clasp or the hoop of a wreath that binds the end to the beginning and holds everything together. For example, in the Second Commandment we are told to fear God and not take his name in vain by cursing, lying, deceiving, and other kinds of corruption and wickedness, but to use his name properly by calling upon him in prayer, praise, and thanksgiving, which spring from that love and trust which the First Commandment requires. Similarly, this fear, love, and trust should impel us not to despise his Word, but learn it, hear it gladly, keep it holy, and honor it.

So, through the following commandments which concern our 327 neighbor, everything proceeds from the force of the First Commandment: We are to honor father and mother, masters, and all in authority, being submissive and obedient to them not on their own account but for God's sake. For you dare not respect or fear father or mother wrongly, doing or omitting to do things simply in order to please them. Rather, ask what God wants of you and what he will quite surely demand of you. If you omit that, you have an angry judge; otherwise, you have a gracious father.

Again, you are to do your neighbor no harm, injury, or 328 violence, nor in any way molest him, either in his person, his wife, his property, his honor or rights, as these things are commanded in that order, even though you have the opportunity and occasion to do so and no man may reprove you. On the contrary, you should do good to all men, help them and promote their interests, however and whenever you can, purely out of love to God and in order to please him, in the confidence that he will abundantly reward you for all you do. Thus you see how the First Commandment is the chief 329 source and fountainhead from which all the others proceed; again, to it they all return and upon it they depend, so that end and beginning are all linked and bound together.

It is useful and necessary always to teach, admonish, and 330 remind young people of all this so that they may be brought up, not only with blows and compulsion, like cattle, but in the fear and reverence of God. These are not trifles of men but the commandments of the most high God, who watches over them with great earnestness, who vents his wrath upon those who despise them, and, on the contrary, abundantly rewards those who keep them. Where men consider this and take it to heart, there will arise a spontaneous impulse and desire gladly to do God's will. Therefore it is not without 331 reason that the Old Testament commands men to write the Ten Commandments on every wall and corner, and even on their garments.[6] Not that we are to have them there merely for a display, as the Jews did,[7] but we are to keep them incessantly before our eyes and constantly in our memory, and practice them in all our works and ways. Everyone is to make them his daily habit in all 332 circumstances, in all his affairs and dealings, as if they were written everywhere he looks, and even wherever he goes or wherever he stands. Thus, both for himself at home, and abroad among his neighbors, he will find occasion enough to practice the Ten Commandments, and no one need search far for them.

From all this it is obvious once again how highly these Ten 333 Commandments are to be exalted and extolled above all orders, commands, and works which are taught and practiced apart from them. Here we can fling out the challenge: Let all wise men and saints step forward and produce, if they can, any work like that which God in these commandments so earnestly requires and enjoins under threat of his greatest wrath and punishment, while at the same time he adds such glorious promises that he will shower us with all good things and

[6] Deut. 6:8f., 11:3f.
[7] Cf. Matt. 23:5

blessings. Therefore we should prize and value them above all other teachings as the greatest treasure God has given us.

SECOND PART: THE CREED

Thus far we have heard the first part of Christian doctrine. In it   1 we have seen all that God wishes us to do or not to do. The Creed properly follows, setting forth all that we must expect and receive from God; in brief, it teaches us to know him perfectly. It is given   2 in order to help us do what the Ten Commandments require of us For, as we said above, they are set on so high a plane that all human ability is far too feeble and weak to keep them. Therefore it is as necessary to learn this part as it is the other so that we may know where and how to obtain strength for this task. If we could by our   3 own strength keep the Ten Commandments as they ought to be kept, we would need neither the Creed nor the Lord's Prayer. But before   4 we explain the advantage and necessity of the Creed, it is sufficient, as a first step, for very simple persons to learn to understand the Creed itself.

In the first place, the Creed used to be divided into twelve   5 articles.[8] Of course, if all the thoughts contained in the Scriptures and belonging to the Creed were gathered together, there would be many more articles, nor could they all be clearly expressed in so few words. But to make it most clear and simple for teaching to children, we   6 shall briefly sum up the entire Creed in three articles,[9] according to the three persons of the Godhead, to whom all that we believe is related. The first article, of God the Father, explains creation; the second, of the Son, redemption; the third, of the Holy Spirit, sanctification. Hence the Creed may be briefly comprised in these few words: "I   7 believe in God the Father, who created me; I believe in God the Son, who redeemed me; I believe in the Holy Spirit, who sanctifies me." One God and one faith, but three persons, and therefore three articles or confessions. Let us briefly comment on these words.   8

THE FIRST ARTICLE

"I believe in God, the Father almighty, maker of heaven and   9 *earth."*

These words give us a brief description of God the Father, his   10 nature, his will, and his work. Since the Ten Commandments have explained that we are to have no more than one God, it may be asked:

---

[8] Tradition, dating to about A.D. 400, held that each of the twelve apostles contributed one article to the Creed.

[9] Luther proposed the three-fold division in "A Brief Form of the Creed" (1520), *WA*, 7:214.

"What kind of being is God? What does he do? How can we praise or portray or describe him in such a way as to make him known?" This is taught here and in the following articles. Thus the Creed is nothing else than a response and confession of Christians based on the First Commandment. If you were to ask a young child, "My boy, 11 what kind of God have you? What do you know about him?" he could say, "First, my God is the Father, who made heaven and earth. Apart from him alone I have no other God, for there is no one else who could create heaven and earth."

For the somewhat more advanced and the educated, however, 12 all three articles can be treated more fully and divided into as many parts as there are words. But for young pupils it is enough to indicate the most necessary points, namely, as we have said, that this article deals with creation. We should emphasize the words, "maker of heaven and earth." What is meant by these words, "I believe in 13 God, the Father almighty, maker," etc.? Answer: I hold and believe that I am a creature of God; that is, that he has given and constantly sustains my body, soul, and life, my members great and small, all the faculties of my mind, my reason and understanding, and so forth; my food and drink, clothing, means of support, wife and child, servants, house and home, etc. Besides, he makes all creation help 14 provide the comforts and necessities of life—sun, moon, and stars in the heavens, day and night, air, fire, water, the earth and all that it brings forth, birds and fish, beasts, grain and all kinds of produce. Moreover, he gives all physical and temporal blessings—good 15 government, peace, security. Thus we learn from this article that 16 none of us has his life of himself, or anything else that has been mentioned here or can be mentioned, nor can he by himself preserve any of them, however small and unimportant. All this is comprehended in the word "Creator."

Moreover, we confess that God the Father not only has given 17 us all that we have and see before our eyes, but also daily guards and defends us against every evil and misfortune, warding off all sorts of danger and disaster. All this he does out of pure love and goodness, without our merit, as a kind father who cares for us so that no evil may befall us. But further discussion of this subject belongs in 18 the other two parts of this article, where we say, "Father almighty."

Hence, since everything we possess, and everything in heaven 19 and on earth besides, is daily given and sustained by God, it inevitably follows that we are in duty bound to love, praise, and thank him without ceasing, and, in short, to devote all these things to his service, as he has required and enjoined in the Ten Commandments.

Much could be said if we were to describe in detail how few 20 people believe this article. We all pass over it, hear it, and recite it, but we neither see nor consider what the words enjoin on us. For 21 if we believed it with our whole heart, we would also act accordingly, and not swagger about and brag and boast as if we had life, riches, power, honor, and such things of ourselves, as if we ourselves were to be feared and served. This is the way the wretched, perverse world acts, drowned in its blindness, misusing all the blessings and gifts of God solely for its own pride and greed, pleasure and enjoyment, and never once turning to God to thank him or acknowledge him as Lord and Creator.

Therefore, this article would humble and terrify us all if we 22 believed it. For we sin daily with eyes and ears, hands, body and soul, money and property, and with all that we have. This is especially true of those who even fight against the Word of God. Yet Christians have this advantage, that they acknowledge themselves in duty bound to serve and obey him for all these things.

For this reason we ought daily to study this article and impress 23 it upon our minds. Everything we see, and every blessing that comes our way, should remind us of it. When we escape distress or danger, we should recognize that this is God's doing. He gives us all these things so that we may sense and see in them his fatherly heart and his boundless love toward us. Thus our hearts will be warmed and kindled with gratitude to God and a desire to use all these blessings to his glory and praise.

Such, very briefly, is the meaning of this article. It is all that 24 ordinary people need to learn at first, both about what we have and receive from God and about what we owe him in return. This is an excellent knowledge, but an even greater treasure. For here we see how the Father has given himself to us, with all his creatures, has abundantly provided for us in this life, and, further, has showered us with inexpressible eternal treasures through his Son and the Holy Spirit, as we shall hear.

THE SECOND ARTICLE

"And in Jesus Christ, his only Son, our Lord: who was conceived 25 *by the Holy Spirit, born of the virgin Mary, suffered under Pontius Pilate, was crucified, dead, and buried: he descended into hell, the third day he rose from the dead, he ascended into heaven, and is seated on the right hand of God, the Father almighty, whence he shall come to judge the living and the dead."*

Here we learn to know the second person of the Godhead, and 26 we see what we receive from God over and above the temporal goods mentioned above—that is, how he has completely given himself to us, withholding nothing. This article is very rich and far-reaching, but in order to treat it briefly and simply, we shall take up one phrase which contains the substance of the article; from it we shall learn how we are redeemed. We shall concentrate on these words, "in Jesus Christ, our Lord."

If you are asked, "What do you believe in the Second Article,   27 concerning Jesus Christ?" answer briefly, "I believe that Jesus Christ, true Son of God, has become my Lord." What is it to "become a Lord"? It means that he has redeemed me from sin, from the devil, from death, and from all evil. Before this I had no Lord and King but was captive under the power of the devil. I was condemned to death and entangled in sin and blindness.

When we were created by God the Father, and had received   28 from him all kinds of good things, the devil came and led us into disobedience, sin, death, and all evil. We lay under God's wrath and displeasure, doomed to eternal damnation, as we had deserved. There was no counsel, no help, no comfort for us until this only   29 and eternal Son of God, in his unfathomable goodness, had mercy on our misery and wretchedness and came from heaven to help us. Those tyrants and jailers now have been routed, and their place   30 has been taken by Jesus Christ, the Lord of life and righteousness and every good and blessing. He has snatched us, poor lost creatures, from the jaws of hell, won us, made us free, and restored us to the Father's favor and grace. He has taken us as his own, under his protection, in order that he may rule us by his righteousness, wisdom, power, life, and blessedness.

Let this be the summary of this article, that the little word   31 "Lord" simply means the same as Redeemer, that is, he who has brought us back from the devil to God, from death to life, from sin to righteousness, and now keeps us safe there. The remaining parts of this article simply serve to clarify and express how and by what means this redemption was accomplished—that is, how much it cost Christ and what he paid and risked in order to win us and bring us under his dominion. That is to say, he became man, conceived and born without sin, of the Holy Spirit and the Virgin, that he might become Lord over sin; moreover, he suffered, died, and was buried that he might make satisfaction for me and pay what I owed, not with silver and gold but with his own precious blood. All this in order to become my Lord. For he did none of these things for himself, nor had he any need of them. Afterward he rose again from the dead, swallowed up[1] and devoured death, and finally ascended into heaven and assumed dominion at the right hand of the Father. The devil and all powers, therefore, must be subject to him and lie beneath his feet until finally, at the last day, he will completely divide and separate us from the wicked world, the devil, death, sin, etc.

But the proper place to explain all these different points is not   32

[1] Cf. Isa. 25:8.

the brief children's sermons, but rather the longer sermons throughout
the year, especially at the times appointed[2] for dealing at length with
such articles as the birth, passion, resurrection, and ascension of Christ.

Indeed, the entire Gospel that we preach depends on the proper   33
understanding of this article. Upon it all our salvation and blessedness
are based, and it is so rich and broad that we can never learn it fully.

THE THIRD ARTICLE

"I believe in the Holy Spirit, the holy Christian church, the   34
communion of saints, the forgiveness of sins, the resurrection of the
body, and the life everlasting. Amen."

To this article, as I have said, I cannot give a better title than   35
"Sanctification." In it is expressed and portrayed the Holy Spirit and
his office, which is that he makes us holy. Therefore, we must
concentrate on the term "Holy Spirit," because it is so precise that we
can find no substitute for it. Many other kinds of spirits are   36
mentioned in the Scriptures, such as the spirit of man,[3] heavenly
spirits,[4] and the evil spirit.[5] But God's Spirit alone is called Holy Spirit,
that is, he who has sanctified and still sanctifies us. As the Father is
called Creator and the Son is called Redeemer, so on account of his
work the Holy Spirit must be called Sanctifier, the One who makes
holy. How does this sanctifying take place? Answer: Just as the   37
Son obtains dominion by purchasing us through his birth, death, and
resurrection, etc., so the Holy Spirit effects our sanctification through
the following: the communion of saints or Christian church, the
forgiveness of sins, the resurrection of the body, and the life everlasting. In other words, he first leads us into his holy community,
placing us upon the bosom of the church, where he preaches to us
and brings us to Christ.

Neither you nor I could ever know anything of Christ, or believe   38
in him and take him as our Lord, unless these were first offered to
us and bestowed on our hearts through the preaching of the Gospel
by the Holy Spirit. The work is finished and completed, Christ has
acquired and won the treasure for us by his sufferings, death, and
resurrection, etc. But if the work remained hidden and no one knew
of it, it would have been all in vain, all lost. In order that this
treasure might not be buried but put to use and enjoyed, God has
caused the Word to be published and proclaimed, in which he has given
the Holy Spirit to offer and apply to us this treasure of salvation.
Therefore to sanctify is nothing else than to bring us to the Lord   39

---

[2] Christmas, Lent, Easter, Ascension.
[3] E.g., I Cor. 2:11.
[4] Cf. II Macc. 11:6, 15:23. Luther interpreted these as the good angels.
[5] Cf. I Sam. 16:14, 23; Tobit 3:8; Acts 19:12, 15.

Christ to receive this blessing, which we could not obtain by ourselves.

Learn this article, then, as clearly as possible. If you are asked, 40 What do you mean by the words, "I believe in the Holy Spirit"? you can answer, "I believe that the Holy Spirit makes me holy, as his name implies." How does he do this? By what means? Answer: 41 "Through the Christian church, the forgiveness of sins, the resurrection of the body, and the life everlasting." In the first place, he has a 42 unique community in the world. It is the mother that begets and bears every Christian through the Word of God. The Holy Spirit reveals and preaches that Word, and by it he illumines and kindles hearts so that they grasp and accept it, cling to it, and persevere in it.

Where he does not cause the Word to be preached and does not 43 awaken understanding in the heart, all is lost. This was the case under the papacy, where faith was entirely shoved under the bench and no one recognized Christ as the Lord, or the Holy Spirit as the Sanctifier. That is, no one believed that Christ is our Lord in the sense that he won for us this treasure without our works and merits and made us acceptable to the Father. What was lacking here? There was no 44 Holy Spirit present to reveal this truth and have it preached. Men and evil spirits there were, teaching us to obtain grace and be saved by our works. Therefore there was no Christian church. For where 45 Christ is not preached, there is no Holy Spirit to create, call, and gather the Christian church, and outside it no one can come to the Lord Christ. Let this suffice concerning the substance of this 46 article. But since various points in it are not quite clear to the common people, we shall run through them also.

The Creed calls the holy Christian church a *communio sanc-* 47 *torum,* "a communion of saints." Both expressions have the same meaning. In early times the latter phrase was missing,[6] and it is unintelligible in our translation. If it is to be rendered idiomatically, we must express it quite differently. The word *ecclesia* properly means an assembly. We, however, are accustomed to the term 48 *Kirche,* "church," by which simple folk understand not a group of people but a consecrated house or building. But the house should not be called a church except for the single reason that the group of people assembles there. For we who assemble select a special place and give the house its name by virtue of the assembly. Thus the word "church" (*Kirche*) really means nothing else than a common assembly; it is not of German but of Greek origin, like the word *ecclesia.* In that language the word is *kyria,* and in Latin *curia.*[7] In our mother tongue

---

[6] In 1519 Luther expressed the opinion that the expression "communion of saints" was a late addition to the Creed, in apposition to "holy catholic Church" (*WA,* 2:190). The earliest extant version of the Creed containing the phrase is that attributed to Bishop Nicetas of Remesiana (ca. 400?).

[7] Luther was mistaken. *Kirche* comes not from the Greek *kyria* or *kyriake* but from the Celtic word *kyrk* (the circumscribed), related to the Latin

therefore it ought to be called "a Christian congregation or assembly," [8] or best and most clearly of all, "a holy Christian people." [9]

Likewise the word *communio*, which is appended, should not be 49 translated "communion" but "community." [1] It is nothing but a comment or interpretation by which someone wished to explain what the Christian church is. But some among us, who understand neither Latin nor German, have rendered this "communion of saints," although no German would use or understand such an expression. To speak idiomatically, we ought to say "a community of saints," that is, a community composed only of saints, or, still more clearly, "a holy community." This I say in order that the expression may be 50 understood; it has become so established in usage that it cannot well be uprooted, and it would be next to heresy to alter a word.

This is the sum and substance of this phrase: I believe that 51 there is on earth a little holy flock or community of pure saints under one head, Christ. It is called together by the Holy Spirit in one faith, mind, and understanding. It possesses a variety of gifts, yet is united in love without sect or schism. Of this community I also am a 52 part and member, a participant and co-partner[2] in all the blessings it possesses. I was brought to it by the Holy Spirit and incorporated into it through the fact that I have heard and still hear God's Word, which is the first step in entering it. Before we had advanced this far, we were entirely of the devil, knowing nothing of God and of Christ. Until the last day the Holy Spirit remains with the holy community 53 or Christian people. Through it he gathers us, using it to teach and preach the Word. By it he creates and increases sanctification, causing it daily to grow and become strong in the faith and in the fruits of the Spirit.

Further we believe that in this Christian church we have the 54 forgiveness of sins, which is granted through the holy sacraments and absolution as well as through all the comforting words of the entire Gospel. Toward forgiveness is directed everything that is to be preached concerning the sacraments and, in short, the entire Gospel and all the duties of Christianity. Forgiveness is needed constantly, for although God's grace has been won by Christ, and holiness has been wrought by the Holy Spirit through God's Word in the unity of

circus and *carcer*. Again, curia is related not to the Greek *kyria* but to *Quiris* (Roman citizen).

[8] *Eine christliche Gemeine oder Sammlung.* In the Bible Luther always translated *ekklesia* with *Gemeine* (cf. Matt. 16:18; Acts 19:39f.; I Cor. 1:2; Gal. 1:2).

[9] *Eine heilige Christenheit.* In the treatise, "On the Councils and the Church" (1539), Luther urged substitution of *Christenheit* or *christliches Volk* for the "un-German" and "blind" word *Kirche. WA*, 50:624f.

[1] Not *Gemeinschaft* but *Gemeine.*

[2] Cf. I Cor. 1:9.

the Christian church, yet because we are encumbered with our flesh we are never without sin.

Therefore everything in the Christian church is so ordered that   55 we may daily obtain full forgiveness of sins through the Word and through signs[3] appointed to comfort and revive our consciences as long as we live. Although we have sin, the Holy Spirit sees to it that it does not harm us because we are in the Christian church, where there is full forgiveness of sin. God forgives us, and we forgive, bear with, and aid one another.

But outside the Christian church (that is, where the Gospel is   56 not) there is no forgiveness, and hence no holiness. Therefore, all who seek to merit holiness through their works rather than through the Gospel and the forgiveness of sin have expelled and separated themselves from the church.

Meanwhile, since holiness has begun and is growing daily, we   57 await the time when our flesh will be put to death, will be buried with all its uncleanness, and will come forth gloriously and arise to complete and perfect holiness in a new, eternal life. Now we are   58 only halfway pure and holy. The Holy Spirit must continue to work in us through the Word, daily granting forgiveness until we attain to that life where there will be no more forgiveness. In that life are only perfectly pure and holy people, full of goodness and righteousness, completely freed from sin, death, and all evil, living in new, immortal, and glorified bodies.

All this, then, is the office and work of the Holy Spirit, to   59 begin and daily to increase holiness on earth through these two means, the Christian church and the forgiveness of sins. Then, when we pass from this life, he will instantly perfect our holiness and will eternally preserve us in it by means of the last two parts of this article.

The term "resurrection of the flesh," however, is not well   60 chosen. When we Germans hear the word *Fleisch* (flesh), we think no farther than the butcher shop. Idiomatically we would say "resurrection of the body."[4] However, this is not of great importance, as long as the words are rightly understood.

---

[3] The sacraments.

[4] *Auferstehung des Leibs oder Leichnams.* In the early church, the word *sarkos* (flesh) apparently was inserted deliberately to combat the Gnostic tendency to assert that only the "spirit" was capable of being saved, that the body or flesh was by nature evil. In his exposition of John 1:14 (*WA*, 10[1]: 235) Luther wrote: "By 'flesh' we should understand the whole human nature, body and soul, in the manner of the Scriptures, which call man 'flesh,' . . . and in the Creed we say, 'I believe in the resurrection of the flesh,' i.e., 'of all men.'" Older English translations of the Creed also read "resurrection of the flesh" until 1543, when in "The Necessary Doctrine and Erudition for any Christian Man," issued by Henry VIII, "resurrection of the body" was introduced.

This, then, is the article which must always remain in force. 61 Creation is past and redemption is accomplished, but the Holy Spirit carries on his work unceasingly until the last day. For this purpose he has appointed a community on earth, through which he speaks and does all his work. For he has not yet gathered together all his 62 Christian people, nor has he completed the granting of forgiveness. Therefore we believe in him who daily brings us into this community through the Word, and imparts, increases, and strengthens faith through the same Word and the forgiveness of sins. Then when his work has been finished and we abide in it, having died to the world and all evil, he will finally make us perfectly and eternally holy. We now wait in faith for this to be accomplished through the Word.

Here in the Creed you have the entire essence of God, his will, 63 and his work exquisitely depicted in very short but rich words. In them consists all our wisdom, which surpasses all the wisdom, understanding, and reason of men. Although the whole world has sought painstakingly to learn what God is and what he thinks and does, yet it has never succeeded in the least. But here you have everything in richest measure. In these three articles God himself has revealed 64 and opened to us the most profound depths of his fatherly heart, his sheer, unutterable love. He created us for this very purpose, to redeem and sanctify us. Moreover, having bestowed upon us everything in heaven and on earth, he has given us his Son and his Holy Spirit, through whom he brings us to himself. As we explained before, 65 we could never come to recognize the Father's favor and grace were it not for the Lord Christ, who is a mirror of the Father's heart. Apart from him we see nothing but an angry and terrible Judge. But neither could we know anything of Christ, had it not been revealed by the Holy Spirit.

These articles of the Creed, therefore, divide and distinguish us 66 Christians from all other people on earth. All who are outside the Christian church, whether heathen, Turks, Jews, or false Christians and hypocrites, even though they believe in and worship only the one, true God, nevertheless do not know what his attitude is toward them. They cannot be confident of his love and blessing. Therefore they remain in eternal wrath and damnation, for they do not have the Lord Christ, and, besides, they are not illuminated and blessed by the gifts of the Holy Spirit.

Now you see that the Creed is a very different teaching from 67 the Ten Commandments. The latter teach us what we ought to do; the Creed tells what God does for us and gives to us. The Ten Commandments, moreover, are inscribed in the hearts of all men.[5]

---

[5] Cf. Rom. 2:15. Luther was thinking of the natural law. See also above, Third Commandment, 82 and footnote.

No human wisdom can comprehend the Creed; it must be taught by the Holy Spirit alone. Therefore the Ten Commandments do not 68 by themselves make us Christians, for God's wrath and displeasure still remain on us because we cannot fulfill his demands. But the Creed brings pure grace and makes us upright and pleasing to God. Through this knowledge we come to love and delight in all the 69 commandments of God because we see that God gives himself completely to us, with all his gifts and his power, to help us keep the Ten Commandments: the Father gives us all creation, Christ all his works, the Holy Spirit all his gifts.

For the present this is enough concerning the Creed to lay a 70 foundation for the common people without overburdening them. After they understand the substance of it, they may on their own initiative learn more, relating to these teachings of the Catechism all that they learn in the Scriptures, and thus advance and grow richer in understanding. For as long as we live we shall have enough to preach and learn on the subject of faith.

THIRD PART: THE LORD'S PRAYER

We have heard what we are to do and believe. The best and most 1 blessed life consists of these things. Now follows the third part, how we are to pray. Mankind is in such a situation that no one can 2 keep the Ten Commandments perfectly, even though he has begun to believe. Besides, the devil, along with the world and our flesh, resists our efforts with all his power. Consequently nothing is so necessary as to call upon God incessantly and drum into his ears our prayer that he may give, preserve, and increase in us faith and obedience to the Ten Commandments and remove all that stands in our way and hinders us from fulfilling them. That we may know what and how to pray, 3 our Lord Christ himself has taught us both the way and the words, as we shall see.

Before we explain the Lord's Prayer part by part, it is very 4 necessary to exhort and draw the people to prayer, as Christ and the apostles also did.[6] The first thing to know is this: It is our duty to 5 pray because God has commanded it. We were told in the Second Commandment, "You shall not take God's name in vain." Thereby we are required to praise the holy name and pray or call upon it in every need. For to call upon it is nothing else than to pray. Prayer, 6 therefore, is as strictly and solemnly commanded as all the other commandments, such as having no other God, not killing, not stealing,

---

[6] Cf. Matt. 7:7; Luke 18:1, 21:36; Rom. 12:12; Col. 4:2; I Thess. 5:17; I Tim. 2:1; James 1:6, 5:13; I Pet. 4:8; Jude 20.

etc. Let no one think that it makes no difference whether I pray or not, as vulgar people do who say in their delusion: "Why should I pray? Who knows whether God heeds my prayer or cares to hear it? If I do not pray, someone else will." Thus they fall into the habit of never praying, alleging that since we reject false and hypocritical prayers we teach that there is no duty or need to pray.

It is quite true that the kind of babbling and bellowing that used   7 to pass for prayers in the church was not really prayer. Such external repetition, when properly used, may serve as an exercise for young children, pupils, and simple folk; while it may be called singing or reading exercise, it is not real prayer. To pray, as the Second   8 Commandment teaches, is to call upon God in every need. This God requires of us; he has not left it to our choice. It is our duty and obligation to pray if we want to be Christians, just as it is our duty and obligation to obey our fathers and mothers and the civil authorities. By invocation and prayer the name of God is glorified and used to good purpose. This you should note above all, so that you may silence and repel any thoughts that would prevent or deter us from praying. It would be improper for a son to say to his father: "What is the use   9 of being obedient? I will go and do as I please; what difference does it make?" But there stands the commandment, "You shall and must obey!" Just so, it is not left to my choice here whether to pray or not, but it is my duty and obligation [on pain of God's wrath and displeasure].[7]

[This should be kept in mind above all things so that you may   10 silence and repel thoughts which would prevent or deter us from praying, as though it made no great difference if we do not pray, or as though prayer were commanded for those who are holier and in better favor with God than we are. Indeed, the human heart is by nature so desperately wicked that it always flees from God, thinking that he neither wants nor cares for our prayers because we are sinners and have merited nothing but wrath. Against such thoughts, I say, we   11 should respect this commandment and turn to God so that we may not provoke his anger by such disobedience. By this commandment he makes it clear that he will not cast us out or drive us away, even though we are sinners; he wishes rather to draw us to himself so that we may humble ourselves before him, lament our misery and plight, and pray for grace and help. Therefore we read in the Scriptures that he is angry because those who were struck down for their sin did not return to him and assuage his wrath and seek grace by their prayers.]

[7] The text in square brackets here and in the following paragraph (sections 10, 11) does not appear in the first edition of the Large Catechism, in the Jena edition of Luther's works, or in the 1580 German edition of the Book of Concord. It is found in revised editions of the Catechism (1529 and later), in the Latin translation of 1544, and freshly translated in the Latin Book of Concord, 1584.

From the fact that prayer is so urgently commanded, we ought 12
to conclude that we should by no means despise our prayers, but
rather prize them highly. Take an illustration from the other commandments. A child should never despise obedience to his father 13
and mother, but should always reflect: "This is a work of obedience,
and what I do has no other purpose than that it befits obedience and
the commandment of God. On this I can rely and depend, and I can
revere it highly, not because of my worthiness, but because of the
commandment." So, too, here. What we shall pray, and for what, we
should regard as demanded by God and done in obedience to him.
We should think, "On my account this prayer would amount to
nothing; but it is important because God has commanded it." So, no
matter what he has to pray for, everybody should always approach God
in obedience to this commandment.

We therefore urgently beg and exhort everyone to take these 14
words to heart and in no case to despise prayer. Prayer used to be
taught, in the devil's name, in such a way that no one paid any
attention to it, and men supposed it was enough if the act was
performed, whether God heard it or not. But that is to stake prayer
on luck and to mumble aimlessly. Such a prayer is worthless.

We allow ourselves to be hindered and deterred by such 15
thoughts as these: "I am not holy enough or worthy enough; if I were
as godly and holy as St. Peter or St. Paul, then I would pray." Away
with such thoughts! The very commandment that applied to St. Paul
applies also to me. The Second Commandment is given just as much
on my account as on his. He can boast of no better or holier
commandment than I.

Therefore you should say: "The prayer I offer is just as 16
precious, holy, and pleasing to God as those of St. Paul and the holiest
of saints. The reason is this: I freely admit that he is holier in respect
to his person, but not on account of the commandment. God does not
regard prayer on account of the person, but on account of his Word
and the obedience accorded it. On this commandment, on which all
the saints base their prayer, I, too, base mine. Moreover, I pray for
the same thing for which they all pray, or ever have prayed." [8]

This is the first and most important point, that all our prayers 17
must be based on obedience to God, regardless of our person, whether
we be sinners or saints, worthy or unworthy. We must learn that 18
God will not have this commandment treated as a jest but will be
angry and punish us if we do not pray, just as he punishes all other
kinds of disobedience. Nor will he allow our prayers to be frustrated
or lost, for if he did not intend to answer you, he would not have

---

[8] Later edition adds: And I have just as great a need for it as those great
saints—indeed, a greater need than they.

ordered you to pray and backed it up with such a strict commandment.

In the second place, we should be all the more urged and   19
encouraged to pray because God has promised that our prayer will
surely be answered, as he says in Ps. 50:15, "Call upon me in the day
of trouble, and I will deliver you," and Christ says in Matt. 7:7, 8, "Ask
and it will be given you," etc. "For every one who asks receives."
Such promises certainly ought to awaken and kindle in our hearts   20
a desire and love to pray. For by his Word God testifies that our
prayer is heartily pleasing to him and will assuredly be heard and
granted, so that we may not despise or disdain it or pray uncertainly.

This you can hold up to him and say, "I come to Thee, dear   21
Father, and pray not of my own accord or because of my own
worthiness, but at thy commandment and promise, which cannot fail
or deceive me." Whoever does not believe this promise should realize
once again that he angers God, grossly dishonoring him and accusing
him of falsehood.

Furthermore, we should be encouraged and drawn to pray   22
because, in addition to this commandment and promise, God takes the
initiative and puts into our mouths the very words we are to use.
Thus we see how sincerely he is concerned over our needs, and we
shall never doubt that our prayer pleases him and will assuredly be
heard. So this prayer is far superior to all others that we might   23
ourselves devise. For in the latter our conscience would always be in
doubt, saying, "I have prayed, but who knows whether it pleased him,
or whether I have hit upon the right form and mode?" Thus there
is no nobler prayer to be found on earth,[9] for it has the excellent
testimony that God loves to hear it. This we should not trade for all
the riches in the world.

It has been prescribed for this reason, also, that we should   24
reflect on our needs, which ought to drive and impel us to pray
without ceasing. A person who wants to pray must present a petition,
naming and asking for something which he desires; otherwise it
cannot be called a prayer.

Therefore we have rightly rejected the prayers of monks and   25
priests, who howl and growl frightfully day and night; not one of them
thinks of asking for the least thing. If we gathered all the churches
together, with all their clergy, they would have to confess that they
never prayed whole-heartedly for so much as a drop of wine. None
of them has ever undertaken to pray out of obedience to God and faith
in his promise, or out of consideration for his own needs. They only
thought, at best, of doing a good work as a payment to God, not
willing to receive anything from him, but only to give him something.

But where there is true prayer there must be earnestness. We   26

[9] Later edition adds: than the daily Lord's Prayer.

must feel our need, the distress that impels and drives us to cry out. Then prayer will come spontaneously, as it should, and we shall not need to be taught how to prepare for it or how to generate devotion. The need which ought to be the concern of both ourselves and 27 others is quite amply indicated in the Lord's Prayer. Therefore it may serve to remind us and impress upon us not to become negligent about praying. We all have needs enough, but the trouble is that we do not feel or see them. God therefore wishes you to lament and express your needs and wants, not because he is unaware of them, but in order that you may kindle your heart to stronger and greater desires and spread your cloak wide to receive many things.

Each of us should form the habit from his youth up to pray 28 daily for all his needs, whenever he is aware of anything that affects him or other people around him, such as preachers, magistrates, neighbors, servants; and, as we have said, he should always remind God of his commandment and promise, knowing that he will not have them despised. This I say because I would like to see the people 29 brought again to pray rightly and not act so crudely and coldly that they become daily more inept at praying. This is just what the devil wants and works for with all his might, for he is well aware what damage and harm he suffers when prayer is in proper use.

This we must know, that all our safety and protection consist 30 in prayer alone. We are far too weak to cope with the devil and all his might and his forces arrayed against us, trying to trample us under foot. Therefore we must carefully select the weapons with which Christians ought to arm themselves in order to stand against the devil. What do you think has accomplished such great results in the 31 past, parrying the counsels and plots of our enemies and checking their murderous and seditious designs by which the devil expected to crush us, and the Gospel as well, except that the prayers of a few godly men intervened like an iron wall on our side? Otherwise they would have witnessed a far different drama: the devil would have destroyed all Germany in its own blood. Now they may confidently ridicule and mock. But by prayer alone we shall be a match both for them and for the devil, if we only persevere diligently and do not become slack. For whenever a good Christian prays, "Dear 32 Father, thy will be done," God replies from on high, "Yes, dear child, it shall indeed be done in spite of the devil and all the world."

Let this be said as an admonition in order that men may learn 33 above all to value prayer as a great and precious thing and may clearly distinguish between vain babbling and praying for something definite. We by no means reject prayer, but we do denounce the utterly useless howling and growling, as Christ himself rejects and forbids great

wordiness.[1] Now we shall treat the Lord's Prayer very briefly and   34
clearly. In seven successive articles or petitions are comprehended
all the needs that continually beset us, each one so great that it should
impel us to keep praying for it all our lives.

THE FIRST PETITION

"Hallowed be thy name."   35
This is rather obscure. It is not idiomatic German. In our   36
mother tongue we would say, "Heavenly Father, grant that thy name
alone may be holy." But what is it to pray that his name may   37
become holy? Is it not already holy? Answer: Yes, in itself it is
holy, but not in our use of it. God's name was given to us when we
became Christians at Baptism, and so we are called children of God
and enjoy the sacraments, through which he so incorporates us with
himself that all that is God's must serve for our use.

So we should realize that we are under the great necessity of   38
duly honoring his name and keeping it holy and sacred, regarding it
as the greatest treasure and most sacred thing we have, and praying,
as good children, that his name, which is already holy in heaven, may
also be kept holy on earth by us and all the world.

How does it become holy among us? The plainest answer is: 39
When both our teaching and our life are godly and Christian. Since in
this prayer we call God our Father, it is our duty in every way to
behave as good children so that he may receive from us not shame
but honor and praise.

Now, the name of God is profaned by us either in words or in   40
deeds; everything we do on earth may be classified as word or deed,
speech or act. In the first place, then, it is profaned when men   41
preach, teach, and speak in God's name anything that is false and
deceptive, using his name to cloak lies and make them acceptable; this
is the worst profanation and dishonor of the divine name. Like-   42
wise, when men grossly misuse the divine name as a cloak for their
shame, by swearing, cursing, conjuring, etc. In the next place, it is 43
also profaned by an openly evil life and wicked works, when those
who are called Christians and God's people are adulterers, drunkards,
gluttons, jealous persons, and slanderers. Here again God's name must
be profaned and blasphemed because of us.

Just as it is a shame and disgrace to an earthly father to have   44
a bad, unruly child who antagonizes him in word and deed with the
result that on his account the father suffers scorn and reproach, so God
is dishonored if we who are called by his name and enjoy his manifold
blessings fail to teach, speak, and live as godly and heavenly children

---

[1] Matt. 6:7, 23:14.

with the result that he must hear us called not children of God but children of the devil.

So you see that in this petition we pray for exactly the same   45 thing that God demands in the Second Commandment: that his name should not be taken in vain by swearing, cursing, deceiving, etc., but used rightly to the praise and glory of God. Whoever uses God's name for any sort of wrong profanes and desecrates this holy name, as in the past a church was said to be desecrated when a murder or any other crime had been committed in it, or when a monstrance[2] or a relic was profaned, thus rendering unholy by misuse that which is holy in itself. This petition, then, is simple and clear as soon as we understand   46 the language, namely, that "to hallow" means the same as in our idiom "to praise, extol, and honor" in word and deed.

See, then, what a great need there is for this kind of prayer!   47 Since we see that the world is full of sects and false teachers, all of whom wear the holy name as a cloak and warrant for their devilish doctrine, we ought constantly to cry out against all who preach and believe falsely and against those who attack and persecute our Gospel and pure doctrine and try to suppress it, as the bishops, tyrants, fanatics, and others do. Likewise, this petition is for ourselves who have the Word of God but are ungrateful for it and fail to live according to it as we ought. If you pray the petition whole-heartedly, you can be   48 sure that God is pleased. For there is nothing he would rather hear than to have his glory and praise exalted above everything else and his Word taught in its purity and cherished and treasured.

THE SECOND PETITION

"Thy kingdom come."

We prayed in the first petition that God would prevent the   49 world from using his glory and name to cloak its lies and wickedness, but would rather keep God's name sacred and holy in both doctrine and life so that he may be praised and exalted in us. Here we ask that his kingdom may come. Just as God's name is holy in itself   50 and yet we pray that it may be holy among us, so also his kingdom comes of itself without our prayer and yet we pray that it may come to us. That is, we ask that it may prevail among us and with us, so that we may be a part of those among whom his name is hallowed and his kingdom flourishes.

What is the kingdom of God? Answer: Simply what we learned   51 in the Creed, namely, that God sent his Son, Christ our Lord, into the world to redeem and deliver us from the power of the devil and to bring us to himself and rule us as a king of righteousness, life, and

---

[2] The monstrance was the vessel in which the host was displayed for adoration.

salvation against sin, death, and an evil conscience. To this end he also gave his Holy Spirit to teach us this through his holy Word and to enlighten and strengthen us in faith by his power.

We pray here at the outset that all this may be realized in us 52 and that God's name may be praised through his holy Word and our Christian lives. This we ask, both in order that we who have accepted it may remain faithful and grow daily in it and in order that it may gain recognition and followers among other people and advance with power throughout the world. So we pray that, led by the Holy Spirit, many may come into the kingdom of grace and become partakers of salvation, so that we may all remain together eternally in this kingdom which has now made its appearance among us.

God's kingdom comes to us in two ways: first, it comes here, in 53 time, through the Word and faith, and secondly, in eternity, it comes through the final revelation.[3] Now, we pray for both of these, that it may come to those who are not yet in it, and that it may come by daily growth here and in eternal life hereafter to us who have attained it. All this is simply to say: "Dear Father, we pray Thee, give us thy 54 Word, that the Gospel may be sincerely preached throughout the world and that it may be received by faith and may work and live in us. So we pray that thy kingdom may prevail among us through the Word and the power of the Holy Spirit, that the devil's kingdom may be overthrown and he may have no right or power over us, until finally the devil's kingdom shall be utterly destroyed and sin, death, and hell exterminated, and that we may live forever in perfect righteousness and blessedness."

You see that we are praying here not for a crust of bread or 55 for a temporal, perishable blessing, but for an eternal, priceless treasure and everything that God himself possesses. It would be far too great for any human heart to dare to desire if God himself had not commanded us to ask for it. But because he is God, he claims 56 the honor of giving far more abundantly and liberally than anyone can comprehend—like an eternal, inexhaustible fountain which, the more it gushes forth and overflows, the more it continues to give. He desires of us nothing more ardently than that we ask many and great things of him; and on the contrary, he is angered if we do not ask and demand confidently.

Imagine a very rich and mighty emperor who bade a poor 57 beggar to ask for whatever he might desire and was prepared to give great and princely gifts, and the fool asked only for a dish of beggar's broth. He would rightly be considered a rogue and a scoundrel who had made a mockery of his imperial majesty's command and was unworthy to come into his presence. Just so, it is a great reproach

---

[3] I.e., the return of Christ.

and dishonor to God if we, to whom he offers and pledges so many inexpressible blessings, despise them or lack confidence that we shall receive them and scarcely venture to ask for a morsel of bread.

The fault lies wholly in that shameful unbelief which does not   58 look to God even for enough to satisfy the belly, let alone expect, without doubting, eternal blesings from God. Therefore we must strengthen ourselves against unbelief and let the kingdom of God be the first thing for which we pray. Then, surely, we shall have all the other things in abundance, as Christ teaches, "Seek first the kingdom of God, and all these things shall be yours as well." [4] For how could God allow us to suffer want in temporal things when he promises that which is eternal and imperishable?

The Third Petition

"Thy will be done on earth, as it is in heaven."   59

Thus far we have prayed that God's name may be hallowed by   60 us and that his kingdom may prevail among us. These two points embrace all that pertains to God's glory and to our salvation, in which we appropriate God with all his treasures. But there is just as great need that we keep firm hold of these two things and never allow ourselves to be torn from them. In a good government there is   61 need not only for good builders and rulers, but also for defenders, protectors, and vigilant guardians. So here also; although we have prayed for what is most essential—for the Gospel, for faith, and for the Holy Spirit, that he may govern us who have been redeemed from the power of the devil—we must also pray that God's will may be done. If we try to hold fast these treasures, we must suffer an astonishing amount of attacks and assaults from all who venture to hinder and thwart the fulfillment of the first two petitions.

It is unbelievable how the devil opposes and obstructs their   62 fulfillment. He cannot bear to have anyone teach or believe rightly. It pains him beyond measure when his lies and abominations, honored under the most specious pretexts of God's name, are disclosed and exposed in all their shame, when he himself is driven out of men's hearts and a breach is made in his kingdom. Therefore, like a furious foe, he raves and rages with all his power and might, marshaling all his subjects and even enlisting the world and our own flesh as his allies. For our flesh is in itself vile and inclined to evil, even when   63 we have accepted and believe God's Word. The world, too, is perverse and wicked. These he stirs up, fanning and feeding the flames, in order to hinder us, put us to flight, cut us down, and bring us once more under his power. This is his only purpose, his desire and   64

[4] Matt. 6:33.

thought. For this end he strives without rest day and night, using all the arts, tricks, ways, and means that he can devise.

Therefore we who would be Christians must surely count on 65 having the devil with all his angels[5] and the world as our enemies and must count on their inflicting every possible misfortune and grief upon us. For where God's Word is preached, accepted or believed, and bears fruit, there the blessed holy cross will not be far away. Let nobody think that he will have peace; he must sacrifice all he has on earth—possessions, honor, house and home, wife and children, body and life. Now, this grieves our flesh and the old Adam, for it 66 means that we must remain steadfast, suffer patiently whatever befalls us, and let go whatever is taken from us.

Therefore, there is just as much need in this case as in every 67 other case to pray without ceasing: "Thy will be done, dear Father, and not the will of the devil or of our enemies, nor of those who would persecute and suppress thy holy Word or prevent thy kingdom from coming; and grant that whatever we must suffer on its account, we may patiently bear and overcome, so that our poor flesh may not yield or fall away through weakness or indolence."

Observe that in these three petitions interests which concern 68 God himself have been very simply expressed, yet we have prayed in our own behalf. What we pray for concerns only ourselves when we ask that what otherwise must be done without us may also be done in us. As God's name must be hallowed and his kingdom must come even without our prayer, so must his will be done and prevail even though the devil and all his host storm and rage furiously against it in their attempt utterly to exterminate the Gospel. But for our own sake we must pray that his will may be done among us without hindrance, in spite of their fury, so that they may accomplish nothing and we may remain steadfast in the face of all violence and persecution, submitting to the will of God.

Such prayer must be our protection and defense now to repulse 69 and beat down all that the devil,[6] bishops, tyrants, and heretics can do against our Gospel. Let them all rage and do their worst, let them plot and plan how to suppress and exterminate us so that their will and scheme may prevail. One or two Christians, armed with this single petition, shall be our bulwark, against which the others shall dash themselves to pieces. It is our solace and boast that the will and 70 purpose of the devil and of all our enemies shall and must fail and come to naught, no matter how proud, secure, and powerful they think they are. For if their will were not broken and frustrated, the kingdom of God could not abide on earth nor his name be hallowed.

---

[5] On the devil's angels, cf. Matt. 25:41.
[6] Later version adds: pope.

THE FOURTH PETITION

"Give us this day our daily bread."   71

Here we consider the poor bread-basket—the needs of our body   72
and our life on earth. It is a brief and simple word, but very
comprehensive. When you pray for "daily bread" you pray for everything that is necessary in order to have and enjoy daily bread and, on
the contrary, against everything that interferes with enjoying it. You
must therefore enlarge and extend your thoughts to include not only
the oven or the flour bin, but also the broad fields and the whole land
which produce and provide for us our daily bread and all kinds of
sustenance. For if God did not cause grain to grow and did not
bless and preserve it in the field, we could never take a loaf of bread
from the oven to set on the table.

To put it briefly, this petition includes everything that belongs   73
to our entire life in this world; only for its sake do we need daily bread.
Now, our life requires not only food and clothing and other necessities
for our body, but also peace and concord in our daily business and
in associations of every description with the people among whom we
live and move—in short, everything that pertains to the regulation of
our domestic and our civil or political affairs. For where these two
relations are interfered with and prevented from functioning properly,
there the necessities of life are also interfered with, and life itself cannot
be maintained for any length of time. Indeed, the greatest need of   74
all is to pray for our civil authorities and the government, for chiefly
through them does God provide us our daily bread and all the comforts
of this life. Although we have received from God all good things in
abundance, we cannot retain any of them or enjoy them in security
and happiness unless he gives us a stable, peaceful government. For
where dissension, strife, and war prevail, there our daily bread is taken
away, or at least reduced.

It would therefore be fitting if the coat-of-arms of every upright   75
prince were emblazoned with a loaf of bread instead of a lion or a
wreath of rue, or if a loaf of bread were stamped on coins, to remind
both princes and subjects that through the office of the princes we
enjoy protection and peace and that without them we could not have
the steady blessing of daily bread.[7] Rulers are worthy of all honor,
and we should render them the duties we owe and do all we can for
them, as to those through whom we enjoy our possessions in peace
and quietness, since otherwise we could not keep a penny. Moreover,
we should pray for them, that through them God may bestow on us
still more blessings and good things.

[7] A black lion on gold appeared on the coat-of-arms of the March of
Meissen, a red and white striped lion on blue on that of the County of
Thuringia, a wreath of rue on that of Electoral Saxony. The *Löwenpfennig*
of Saxony and of Brunswick showed a lion on the coat-of-arms.

Let us outline very briefly how comprehensively this petition 76 covers all kinds of relations on earth. Out of it one might make a long prayer, enumerating with many words all the things it includes. For example, we might ask God to give us food and drink, clothing, house, home, and a sound body; to cause the grain and fruits of the field to grow and yield richly; to help us manage our household well and give and preserve to us a good wife, children, and servants; to cause our work, craft, or occupation, whatever it may be, to prosper and succeed; to grant us faithful neighbors and good friends, etc. Again, to ask God to endow the emperor, kings, and all estates of 77 men, and especially our princes, counselors, magistrates, and officials, with wisdom, strength, and prosperity to govern well and to be victorious over the Turks and all our enemies; to grant their subjects and the people at large to live together in obedience, peace, and concord. On the other hand, to protect us from all kinds of harm 78 to our body and our livelihood, from tempest, hail, fire, and flood; from poison, pestilence, and cattle-plague; from war and bloodshed, famine, savage beasts, wicked men, etc. It is good to impress upon 79 the common people that all these things come from God and that we must pray for them.

But especially is this petition directed against our chief enemy, 80 the devil, whose whole purpose and desire it is to take away or interfere with all we have received from God. He is not satisfied to obstruct and overthrow spiritual order, so that he may deceive men with his lies and bring them under his power, but he also prevents and hinders the establishment of any kind of government or honorable and peaceful relations on earth. This is why he causes so much contention, murder, sedition, and war, why he sends tempest and hail to destroy crops and cattle, why he poisons the air, etc. In short, 81 it pains him that anyone receives a morsel of bread from God and eats it in peace. If it were in his power, and our prayer to God did not restrain him, surely we would not have a straw in the field, a penny in the house, or even our life for one hour—especially those of us who have the Word of God and would like to be Christians.

Thus, you see, God wishes to show us how he cares for us in 82 all our needs and faithfully provides for our daily existence. Although he gives and provides these blessings bountifully, even 83 for wicked men and rogues, yet he wishes us to pray for them so we may realize that we have received them from his hand and may recognize in them his fatherly goodness toward us. When he withdraws his hand, nothing can prosper or last for any length of time, as indeed we see and experience every day. How much trouble there now 84 is in the world simply on account of false coinage, yes, on account of daily exploitation and usury in public business, trading, and labor on the part of those who wantonly oppress the poor and deprive them of

their daily bread! This we must put up with, of course; but let
exploiters and oppressors beware lest they lose the common intercession
of the church,[8] and let them take care lest this petition of the Lord's
Prayer be turned against them.

THE FIFTH PETITION

"And forgive us our debts, as we forgive our debtors."   85

This petition has to do with our poor, miserable life. Although   86
we have God's Word and believe, although we obey and submit to
his will and are supported by God's gift and blessing, nevertheless we
are not without sin. We still stumble daily and transgress because
we live in the world among people who sorely vex us and give us
occasion for impatience, wrath, vengeance, etc. Besides, Satan is   87
at our backs, besieging us on every side and, as we have heard,
directing his attacks against all the previous petitions, so that it is not
possible always to stand firm in such a ceaseless conflict.

Here again there is great need to call upon God and pray,   88
"Dear Father, forgive us our debts." Not that he does not forgive sin
even without and before our prayer; and he gave us the Gospel, in
which there is nothing but forgiveness, before we prayed or even
thought of it. But the point here is for us to recognize and accept this
forgiveness. For the flesh in which we daily live is of such a   89
nature that it does not trust and believe God and is constantly aroused
by evil desires and devices, so that we sin daily in word and deed, in
acts of commission and omission. Thus our conscience becomes
restless; it fears God's wrath and displeasure, and so it loses the
comfort and confidence of the Gospel. Therefore it is necessary
constantly to turn to this petition for the comfort that will restore our
conscience.

This should serve God's purpose to break our pride and keep   90
us humble. He has reserved to himself this prerogative, that if anybody
boasts of his goodness and despises others he should examine himself
in the light of this petition. He will find that he is no better than others,
that in the presence of God all men must humble themselves and be
glad that they can attain forgiveness. Let no one think that he   91
will ever in this life reach the point where he does not need this
forgiveness. In short, unless God constantly forgives, we are lost.

Thus this petition is really an appeal to God not to regard our   92
sins and punish us as we daily deserve, but to deal graciously with us,
forgive as he has promised, and thus grant us a happy and cheerful
conscience to stand before him in prayer. Where the heart is not right
with God and cannot achieve such confidence, it will never dare to

_____

[8] The general prayer in the church. This was a kind of proverbial
expression, meaning "lose public respect."

pray. But such a confident and joyful heart can only come from the knowledge that our sins are forgiven.

Meanwhile, a necessary but comforting clause is added, "as we 93 forgive our debtors." God has promised us assurance that everything is forgiven and pardoned, yet on the condition that we also forgive our neighbor. Inasmuch as we sin greatly against God everyday 94 and yet he forgives it all through grace, we must always forgive our neighbor who does us harm, violence, and injustice, bears malice toward us, etc. If you do not forgive, do not think that God 95 forgives you. But if you forgive, you have the comfort and assurance that you are forgiven in heaven. Not on account of your forgiving, 96 for God does it altogether freely, out of pure grace, because he has promised it, as the Gospel teaches. But he has set up this condition for our strengthening and assurance as a sign along with the promise which is in agreement with this petition, Luke 6:37, "Forgive, and you will be forgiven." Therefore Christ repeats it immediately after the Lord's Prayer in Matt. 6:14, saying, "If you forgive men their trespasses, your heavenly Father also will forgive you," etc.

This sign is attached to the petition, therefore, that when we 97 pray we may recall the promise and think, "Dear Father, I come to Thee praying for forgiveness, not because I can make satisfaction or merit anything by my works, but because Thou hast given the promise and hast set thy seal to it, making it as certain as an absolution pronounced by thyself." Whatever can be effected by Baptism 98 and the Lord's Supper, which are appointed as outward signs, this sign also can effect to strengthen and gladden our conscience. And it has been especially instituted for us to use and practice every hour, keeping it with us at all times.

THE SIXTH PETITION

"And lead us not into temptation." 99

We have now heard enough about the trouble and effort 100 required to retain and persevere in all the gifts for which we pray. This, however, is not accomplished without failures and stumbling. Moreover, although we have acquired forgiveness and a good conscience, and have been wholly absolved, yet such is life that one stands today and falls tomorrow. Therefore, even though at present we are upright and stand before God with a good conscience, we must pray again that he will not allow us to fall and yield to trials and temptations.

Temptation (or, as the ancient Saxons called it, *Bekörunge*)[9] 101 is of three kinds: of the flesh, the world, and the devil. We live 102

[9] By Saxony Luther meant Lower Saxony; in the sixteenth century *Plattdeutsch* was spoken in Wittenberg. In the Latin Book of Concord *Bekörunge* was misunderstood as *Bekehrung, conversio.*

in the flesh and we have the old Adam hanging around our necks; he goes to work and lures us daily into unchastity, laziness, gluttony and drunkenness, greed and deceit, into acts of fraud and deception against our neighbor—in short, into all kinds of evil lusts which by nature cling to us and to which we are incited by the association and example of other people and by things we hear and see. All this often wounds and inflames even an innocent heart.

Next comes the world, which assails us by word and deed and   103 drives us to anger and impatience. In short, there is in it nothing but hatred and envy, enmity, violence and injustice, perfidy, vengeance, cursing, reviling, slander, arrogance, and pride, along with fondness for luxury, honor, fame, and power. No one is willing to be the least, but everyone wants to sit in the chief seat and be seen by all.

Then comes the devil, who baits and badgers us on all sides,   104 but especially exerts himself where the conscience and spiritual matters are at stake. His purpose is to make us scorn and despise both the Word and the works of God, to tear us away from faith, hope, and love, to draw us into unbelief, false security, and stubbornness, or, on the contrary, to drive us into despair, atheism, blasphemy, and countless other abominable sins. These are snares and nets; indeed, they are the real "flaming darts" [1] which are venomously shot into our hearts, not by flesh and blood but by the devil.

These are the great, grievous perils and temptations which   105 every Christian must bear, even if they come one by one. As long as we remain in this vile life in which we are attacked, hunted, and harried on all sides, we are constrained to cry out and pray every hour that God may not allow us to become faint and weary and to fall back into sin, shame, and unbelief. Otherwise it is impossible to overcome even the least temptation.

This, then, is "leading us not into temptation" when God   106 gives us power and strength to resist, even though the tribulation is not removed or ended. For no one can escape temptations and allurements as long as we live in the flesh and have the devil prowling about us. We cannot help but suffer tribulations, and even be entangled in them, but we pray here that we may not fall into them and be overwhelmed by them.

To feel temptation, therefore, is quite a different thing from   107 consenting and yielding to it. We must all feel it, though not all to the same degree; some have more frequent and severe temptations than others. Youths, for example, are tempted chiefly by the flesh; older people are tempted by the world. Others, who are concerned with spiritual matters (that is, strong Christians) are tempted by the devil. But we cannot be harmed by the mere feeling of temptation as   108

---

[1] Cf. Eph. 6:16.

long as it is contrary to our will and and we would prefer to be rid of it. If we did not feel it, it could not be called a temptation. But to consent to it is to give it free rein and neither resist it nor pray for help against it.

Accordingly we Christians must be armed and prepared for   109 incessant attacks. Then we shall not go about securely and heedlessly as if the devil were far from us but shall at all times expect his blows and parry them. Even if at present I am chaste, patient, kind, and firm in faith, the devil is likely in this very hour to send such a shaft into my heart that I can scarcely stand, for he is an enemy who never stops or becomes weary; when one attack ceases, new ones always arise.

At such times your only help or comfort is to take refuge in   110 the Lord's Prayer and to appeal to God from your heart, "Dear Father, Thou hast commanded me to pray; let me not fall because of temptation." Then you will see the temptation cease and eventually   111 admit defeat. Otherwise, if you attempt to help yourself by your own thoughts and counsels, you will only make the matter worse and give the devil a better opening. For he has a serpent's head; if it finds an opening into which it can slip, the whole body will irresistibly follow. But prayer can resist him and drive him back.

The Last Petition

"But deliver us from evil. Amen."   112

In the Greek[2] this petition reads, "Deliver or keep us from   113 the Evil One, or the Wicked One." The petition seems to be speaking of the devil as the sum of all evil in order that the entire substance of our prayer may be directed against our arch-enemy. It is he who obstructs everything that we pray for: God's name or glory, God's kingdom and will, our daily bread, a good and cheerful conscience, etc.

Therefore we sum it all up by saying, "Dear Father, help us to   114 get rid of all this misfortune." Nevertheless, this petition includes   115 all the evil that may befall us under the devil's kingdom: poverty, shame, death, and, in short, all the tragic misery and heartache of which there is so incalculably much on earth. Since the devil is not only a liar but also a murderer,[3] he incessantly seeks our life and vents his anger by causing accidents and injury to our bodies. He breaks many a man's neck and drives others to insanity; some he drowns, and many he hounds to suicide or other dreadful catastrophes. Therefore there is nothing for us to do on earth but to pray   116 constantly against this arch-enemy. For if God did not support us, we would not be safe from him for a single hour.

[2] The first edition of the Large Catechism reads erroneously, "In the Hebrew."

[3] John 8:44.

Thus you see how God wants us to pray to him for every-   117
thing that affects our bodily welfare and directs us to seek and expect
help from no one but him. But this petition he has put last, for   118
if we are to be protected and delivered from all evil, his name must
first be hallowed in us, his kingdom come among us, and his will be
done. Then he will preserve us from sin and shame and from everything else that harms or injures us.

Thus God has briefly set before us all the afflictions that may   119
ever beset us in order that we may never have an excuse for failing
to pray. But the efficacy of prayer consists in our learning also to say
"Amen" to it—that is, not to doubt that our prayer is surely heard and
will be granted. This word is nothing else than an unquestioning   120
affirmation of faith on the part of one who does not pray as a matter of
chance but knows that God does not lie since he has promised to grant
his requests. Where such faith is wanting, there can be no true prayer.

It is therefore a pernicious delusion when people pray in such   121
a way that they dare not whole-heartedly add "yes" and conclude with
certainty that God hears their prayer but remain in doubt, saying,
"Why should I be so bold as to boast that God hears my prayer? I am
only a poor sinner," etc. That means that they have their eye   122
not on God's promise but on their own works and worthiness, so that
they despise God and accuse him of lying. Therefore they receive   123
nothing, as St. James says, "If anyone prays, let him ask in faith, with
no doubting, for he who doubts is like a wave of the sea that is driven
and tossed by the wind. For that person must not suppose that he
will receive anything from God." [4] Behold, such is the impor-   124
tance that God attaches to our being certain that we do not pray in
vain and that we must not in any way despise our prayers.

FOURTH PART: BAPTISM

We have now finished with the three chief parts[5] of our common   1
Christian teaching. It remains for us to speak of our two sacraments,
instituted by Christ. Every Christian ought to have at least some brief,
elementary instruction in them because without these no one can be
a Christian, although unfortunately in the past nothing was taught
about them. First we shall take up Baptism, through which we   2
are first received into the Christian community. In order that it may
be readily understood, we shall treat it in a systematic way and confine
ourselves to that which is necessary for us to know. How it is to be

---

[4] James 1:6, 7.

[5] Luther used the word *Hauptstücke* in a double sense: "major divisions"
but also "chief articles" or "the most essential." Cf. above, Large Catechism,
II, 6, and Small Catechism, VI, 8.

maintained and defended against heretics and sectarians we shall leave to the learned.

In the first place, we must above all be familiar with the words 3 upon which Baptism is founded and to which everything is related that is to be said on the subject, namely, where the Lord Christ says in Matt. 28:19,

"Go into all the world, and teach all nations, baptizing them in 4 the name of the Father and of the Son and of the Holy Spirit."

Likewise in Mark 16:16,

"He who believes and is baptized will be saved; but he who 5 does not believe will be condemned."

Observe, first, that these words contain God's commandment 6 and ordinance. You should not doubt, then, that Baptism is of divine origin, not something devised or invented by men. As truly as I can say that the Ten Commandments, the Creed, and the Lord's Prayer are not spun out of any man's imagination but revealed and given by God himself, so I can also boast that Baptism is no human plaything but is instituted by God himself. Moreover, it is solemnly and strictly commanded that we must be baptized or we shall not be saved. We are not to regard it as an indifferent matter, then, like putting on a new red coat. It is of the greatest importance that we regard 7 Baptism as excellent, glorious, and exalted. It is the chief cause of our contentions and battles because the world now is full of sects who proclaim that Baptism is an external thing and that external things are of no use.[6] But no matter how external it may be, here stand 8 God's Word and command which have instituted, established, and confirmed Baptism. What God institutes and commands cannot be useless. It is a most precious thing, even though to all appearances it may not be worth a straw. If people used to consider it a great 9 thing when the pope dispensed indulgences with his letters and bulls and consecrated altars and churches solely by virtue of his letters and seals, then we ought to regard Baptism as much greater and more precious because God has commanded it and, what is more, it is performed in his name. So the words read, "Go, baptize," not in your name but "in God's name."

To be baptized in God's name is to be baptized not by men 10 but by God himself. Although it is performed by men's hands, it is nevertheless truly God's own act. From this fact everyone can easily conclude that it is of much greater value than the work of any man or saint. For what work can man do that is greater than God's work?

Here the devil sets to work to blind us with false appearances 11 and lead us away from God's work to our own. It makes a much

[6] This was an argument used by some left-wing radicals in the sixteenth century.

more splendid appearance when a Carthusian[7] does many great and
difficult works, and we all attach greater importance to our own
achievements and merits. But the Scriptures teach that if we piled   12
together all the works of all the monks, no matter how precious and
dazzling they might appear, they would not be as noble and good as
if God were to pick up a straw. Why? Because the person performing
the act is nobler and better. Here we must evaluate not the person
according to the works, but the works according to the person, from
whom they must derive their worth. But mad reason rushes forth[8]   13
and, because Baptism is not dazzling like the works which we do,
regards it as worthless.

Now you can understand how to answer properly the question,   14
What is Baptism? It is not simply common water, but water comprehended in God's Word and commandment and sanctified by them.
It is nothing else than a divine water, not that the water in itself is
nobler than other water but that God's Word and commandment are
added to it.

Therefore it is sheer wickedness and devilish blasphemy when   15
our new spirits, in order to slander Baptism, ignore God's Word and
ordinance, consider nothing but the water drawn from the well, and
then babble, "How can a handful of water help the soul?" Of   16
course, my friend! Who does not know that water is water, if such a
separation is proper? But how dare you tamper thus with God's ordinance and tear from it the precious jeweled clasp with which God has
fastened and enclosed it and from which he does not wish his ordinance
to be separated? For the nucleus in the water is God's Word or commandment and God's name, and this is a treasure greater and nobler
than heaven and earth.

Note the distinction, then: Baptism is a very different thing   17
from all other water, not by virtue of the natural substance but because
here something nobler is added. God himself stakes his honor, his
power, and his might on it. Therefore it is not simply a natural water,
but a divine, heavenly, holy, and blessed water—praise it in any other
terms you can—all by virtue of the Word, which is a heavenly, holy
Word which no one can sufficiently extol, for it contains and conveys
all the fullness of God. From the Word it derives its nature as a   18
sacrament, as St. Augustine taught, *"Accedat verbum ad elementum et
fit sacramentum."* [9] This means that when the Word is added to the
element or the natural substance, it becomes a sacrament, that is, a
holy, divine thing and sign.

Therefore, we constantly teach that the sacraments and all the   19

---

[7] See above, Ten Commandments, 74 and footnote.
[8] Later version: But mad reason will not listen to this.
[9] *Tractate 80,* on John 3.

external things ordained and instituted by God should be regarded not according to the gross, external mask (as we see the shell of a nut) but as that in which God's Word is enclosed. In the same way 20 we speak about the parental estate and civil authority. If we regard these persons with reference to their noses, eyes, skin and hair, flesh and bones, they look no different from Turks and heathen. Someone might come and say, "Why should I think more of this person than of others?" But because the commandment is added, "You shall honor father and mother," I see another man, adorned and clothed with the majesty and glory of God. The commandment, I say, is the golden chain about his neck, yes, the crown on his head, which shows me how and why I should honor this particular flesh and blood.

In the same manner, and even much more, you should honor 21 and exalt Baptism on account of the Word, since God himself has honored it by words and deeds and has confirmed it by wonders from heaven. Do you think it was a jest that the heavens opened when Christ allowed himself to be baptized, that the Holy Spirit descended visibly,[1] and that the divine glory and majesty were manifested everywhere?

I therefore admonish you again that these two, the Word and 22 the water, must by no means be separated from each other. For where the Word is separated from the water, the water is no different from that which the maid cooks with and could indeed be called a bathkeeper's baptism.[2] But when the Word is present according to God's ordinance, Baptism is a sacrament, and it is called Christ's Baptism. This is the first point to be emphasized: the nature and dignity of this holy sacrament.

In the second place, since we now know what Baptism is and 23 how it is to be regarded, we must also learn for what purpose it was instituted, that is, what benefits, gifts, and effects it brings. Nor can we understand this better than from the words of Christ quoted above, "He who believes and is baptized shall be saved."[3] To put it 24 most simply, the power, effect, benefit, fruit, and purpose of Baptism is to save. No one is baptized in order to become a prince, but as the words say, to "be saved." To be saved, we know, is nothing 25 else than to be delivered from sin, death, and the devil and to enter into the kingdom of Christ and live with him forever.

Here you see again how precious and important a thing Baptism 26 should be regarded as being, for in it we obtain such an inexpressible treasure. This shows that it is not simple, ordinary water, for ordinary

---

[1] Matt. 3:16.

[2] Cf. Luther's "Sermon on Baptism" (1534): "a mere watery or earthly water, or (as the sectarians call it) a bath-water or dog's bath." *WA*, 37:642.

[3] Mark 16:16.

water could not have such an effect. But the Word has. It shows also (as we said above) that God's name is in it. And where God's 27 name is, there must also be life and salvation. Hence it is well described as a divine, blessed, fruitful, and gracious water, for through the Word Baptism receives the power to become the "washing of regeneration," as St. Paul calls it in Titus 3:5.

Our know-it-alls, the new spirits,[4] assert that faith alone saves 28 and that works and external things contribute nothing to this end. We answer: It is true, nothing that is in us does it but faith, as we shall hear later on. But these leaders of the blind are unwilling 29 to see that faith must have something to believe—something to which it may cling and upon which it may stand. Thus faith clings to the water and believes it to be Baptism in which there is sheer salvation and life, not through the water, as we have sufficiently stated, but through its incorporation with God's Word and ordinance and the joining of his name to it. When I believe this, what else is it but believing in God as the one who has implanted his Word in this external ordinance and offered it to us so that we may grasp the treasure it contains?

Now, these people are so foolish as to separate faith from 30 the object to which faith is attached and bound on the ground that the object is something external. Yes, it must be external so that it can be perceived and grasped by the senses and thus brought into the heart, just as the entire Gospel is an external, oral proclamation. In short, whatever God effects in us he does through such external ordinances. No matter where he speaks—indeed, no matter for what purpose or by what means he speaks—there faith must look and to it faith must hold. We have here the words, "He who believes and 31 is baptized will be saved." To what do they refer but to Baptism, that is, the water comprehended in God's ordinance? Hence it follows that whoever rejects Baptism rejects God's Word, faith, and Christ, who directs us and binds us to Baptism.

In the third place, having learned the great benefit and power 32 of Baptism, let us observe further who receives these gifts and benefits of Baptism. This again is most beautifully and clearly expressed 33 in these same words, "He who believes and is baptized will be saved," that is, faith alone makes the person worthy to receive the salutary, divine water profitably. Since these blessings are offered and promised in the words which accompany the water, they cannot be received unless we believe them whole-heartedly. Without faith Baptism 34 is of no use, although in itself it is an infinite, divine treasure. So this single expression, "He who believes," is so potent that it excludes and rejects all works that we may do with the intention of meriting salva-

---

[4] Zwinglians or Anabaptists.

tion through them. For it is certain that whatever is not faith contributes nothing toward salvation, and receives nothing.

However, it is often objected, "If Baptism is itself a work, and 35 you say that works are of no use for salvation, what becomes of faith?" To this you may answer: Yes, it is true that our works are of no use for salvation. Baptism, however, is not our work but God's (for, as was said, you must distinguish Christ's Baptism quite clearly from a bath-keeper's baptism). God's works, however, are salutary and necessary for salvation, and they do not exclude but rather demand[5] faith, for without faith they could not be grasped. Just by 36 allowing the water to be poured over you, you do not receive Baptism in such a manner that it does you any good. But it becomes beneficial to you if you accept it as God's command and ordinance, so that, baptized in the name of God, you may receive in the water the promised salvation. This the hand cannot do, nor the body, but the heart must believe it.

Thus you see plainly that Baptism is not a work which we do 37 but is a treasure which God gives us and faith grasps, just as the Lord Christ upon the cross is not a work but a treasure comprehended and offered to us in the Word and received by faith. Therefore they are unfair when they cry out against us as though we preach against faith. Actually, we insist on faith alone as so necessary that without it nothing can be received or enjoyed.

Thus we have considered the three things that must be known 38 about this sacrament, especially that it is God's ordinance and is to be held in all honor. This alone would be enough, even though Baptism is an entirely external thing. Similarly the commandment, "You shall honor your father and mother," refers only to human flesh and blood, yet we look not at the flesh and blood but at God's commandment in which it is comprehended and on account of which this flesh is called father and mother. Just so, if we had nothing more than these words, "Go and baptize," we would still have to accept and observe Baptism as an ordinance of God. But here we have not 39 only God's commandment and injunction, but also his promise. Therefore, it is far more glorious than anything else God has commanded and ordained; in short, it is so full of comfort and grace that heaven and earth cannot comprehend it. It takes special understanding 40 to believe this, for it is not the treasure that is lacking; rather, what is lacking is that it should be grasped and held firmly.

In Baptism, therefore, every Christian has enough to study and 41 to practice all his life. He always has enough to do to believe firmly what Baptism promises and brings—victory over death and the devil,

---

[5] Luther's word *fodern* may mean both "demand" (*forden*) and "further" (*fördern*). Obsopoeus' Latin translation of the Catechism understood the word here as "demand."

forgiveness of sin, God's grace, the entire Christ, and the Holy Spirit
with his gifts. In short, the blessings of Baptism are so boundless   42
that if timid nature considers them, it may well doubt whether they
could all be true. Suppose there were a physician who had such   43
skill that people would not die, or even though they died[6] would afterward live forever. Just think how the world would snow and rain
money upon him! Because of the pressing crowd of rich men no one
else could get near him. Now, here in Baptism there is brought free
to every man's door just such a priceless medicine which swallows up
death[7] and saves the lives of all men.

To appreciate and use Baptism aright, we must draw strength   44
and comfort from it when our sins or conscience oppress us, and we
must retort, "But I am baptized! And if I am baptized, I have the
promise that I shall be saved and have eternal life, both in soul and
body." This is the reason why these two things are done in   45
Baptism: the body has water poured over it, though it cannot receive
anything but the water, and meanwhile the Word is spoken so that
the soul may grasp it.

Since the water and the Word together constitute one Baptism,   46
body and soul shall be saved and live forever: the soul through the
Word in which it believes, the body because it is united with the soul
and apprehends Baptism in the only way it can. No greater jewel,
therefore, can adorn our body and soul than Baptism, for through it
we obtain perfect holiness and salvation, which no other kind of life
and no work on earth can acquire.

Let this suffice concerning the nature, benefits, and use of Baptism
as answering the present purpose.

[INFANT BAPTISM] [8]

Here we come to a question by which the devil confuses the   47
world through his sects, the question of infant Baptism. Do children
also believe, and is it right to baptize them? To this we reply   48
briefly: Let the simple dismiss this question from their minds and
refer it to the learned. But if you wish to answer, then say:

That the Baptism of infants is pleasing to Christ is sufficiently   49
proved from his own work. God has sanctified many who have been
thus baptized and has given them the Holy Spirit. Even today there
are not a few whose doctrine and life attest that they have the Holy
Spirit. Similarly by God's grace we have been given the power to
interpret the Scriptures and to know Christ, which is impossible without the Holy Spirit. Now, if God did not accept the Baptism of   50

---

[6] Later version adds: would be restored to life and.

[7] Isa. 25·8.

[8] Title added in the German Book of Concord.

infants, he would not have given any of them the Holy Spirit nor any part of him; in short, all this time down to the present day no man on earth could have been a Christian. Since God has confirmed Baptism through the gift of his Holy Spirit, as we have perceived in some of the fathers, such as St. Bernard, Gerson, John Hus, and others,[9] and since the holy Christian church will abide until the end of the world, our adversaries must acknowledge that infant Baptism is pleasing to God. For he can never be in conflict with himself, support lies and wickedness, or give his grace and Spirit for such ends. This 51 is the best and strongest proof for the simple and unlearned. For no one can take from us or overthrow this article, "I believe one holy Christian church, the communion of saints," etc.

Further, we are not primarily concerned whether the baptized 52 person believes or not, for in the latter case Baptism does not become invalid. Everything depends upon the Word and commandment 53 of God. This, perhaps, is a rather subtle point, but it is based upon what I have already said, that Baptism is simply water and God's Word in and with each other; that is, when the Word accompanies the water, Baptism is valid, even though faith be lacking. For my faith does not constitute Baptism but receives it. Baptism does not become invalid even if it is wrongly received or used, for it is bound not to our faith but to the Word.

Even though a Jew should today come deceitfully and with 54 an evil purpose, and we baptized him in all good faith, we should have to admit that his Baptism was valid. For there would be water together with God's Word, even though he failed to receive it properly. Similarly, those who partake unworthily of the Lord's Supper receive the true sacrament even though they do not believe.

So you see that the objection of the sectarians is absurd. As 55 we said, even if infants did not believe—which, however, is not the case, as we have proved—still their Baptism would be valid and no one should rebaptize them. Similarly, the Sacrament of the Altar is not vitiated if someone approaches it with an evil purpose, and he would not be permitted on account of that abuse to take it again the selfsame hour, as if he had not really received the sacrament the first time. That would be to blaspheme and desecrate the sacrament in the worst way. How dare we think that God's Word and ordinance should be wrong and invalid because we use it wrongly?

Therefore, I say, if you did not believe before, then believe 56 afterward and confess, "The Baptism indeed was right, but unfortunately I did not receive it rightly." I myself, and all who are baptized, must say before God: "I come here in my faith, and in the faith of others, nevertheless I cannot build on the fact that I believe and

[9] Later version adds: who were baptized in infancy.

many people are praying for me. On this I build, that it is thy Word and command." Just so, I go to the Sacrament of the Altar not on the strength of my own faith, but on the strength of Christ's Word. I may be strong or weak; I leave that in God's hands. This I know, however, that he has commanded me to go, eat, and drink, etc. and that he gives me his body and blood; he will not lie or deceive me.

We do the same in infant Baptism. We bring the child with 57 the purpose and hope that he may believe, and we pray God to grant him faith. But we do not baptize him on that account, but solely on the command of God. Why? Because we know that God does not lie. My neighbor and I—in short, all men—may err and deceive, but God's Word cannot err.

Therefore only presumptuous and stupid persons draw the 58 conclusion that where there is no true faith, there also can be no true Baptism. Likewise I might argue, "If I have no faith, then Christ is nothing." Or again, "If I am not obedient, then father, mother, and magistrates are nothing." Is it correct to conclude that when anybody does not do what he should, the thing that he misuses has no existence or no value? My friend, rather invert the argument and conclude, 59 Precisely because Baptism has been wrongly received, it has existence and value. The saying goes, *"Abusus non tollit, sed confirmat substantiam,"* that is, "Misuse does not destroy the substance, but confirms its existence." Gold remains no less gold if a harlot wears it in sin and shame.

Let the conclusion therefore be that Baptism always remains 60 valid and retains its integrity, even if only one person were baptized and he, moreover, did not have true faith. For God's ordinance and Word cannot be changed or altered by man. But these fanatics 61 are so blinded that they do not discern God's Word and commandment. They regard Baptism only as water in the brook or in the pot, and magistrates only as ordinary people. And because they see neither faith nor obedience, they conclude that these ordinances are in themselves invalid. Here lurks a sneaky, seditious devil who would 62 like to snatch the crown from the rulers and trample it under foot and would, in addition, pervert and nullify all God's work and ordinances. We must therefore be watchful and well armed and not 63 allow ourselves to be turned aside from the Word, regarding Baptism merely as an empty sign, as the fanatics dream.

Finally, we must know what Baptism signifies and why God 64 ordained just this sign and external observance for the sacrament by which we are first received into the Christian church. This act or 65 observance consists in being dipped into the water, which covers us completely, and being drawn out again. These two parts, being dipped under the water and emerging from it, indicate the power and effect of Baptism, which is simply the slaying of the old Adam and the resurrection of the new man, both of which actions must continue in us our whole life long. Thus a Christian life is nothing else than a daily Baptism, once begun and ever continued. For we must keep at it incessantly, always purging out whatever pertains to the old Adam, so that whatever belongs to the new man may come forth. What is the old man? He is what is born in us from Adam, 66 irascible, spiteful, envious, unchaste, greedy, lazy, proud, yes, and unbelieving; he is beset with all vices and by nature has nothing good in him. Now, when we enter Christ's kingdom, this corruption 67 must daily decrease so that the longer we live the more gentle, patient, and meek we become, and the more free from greed, hatred, envy, and pride.

This is the right use of Baptism among Christians, signified by 68 baptizing with water. Where this amendment of life does not take place but the old man is given free rein and continually grows stronger, Baptism is not being used but resisted. Those who are outside of 69 Christ can only grow worse day by day. It is as the proverb says very truly, "Evil unchecked becomes worse and worse." If a year 70 ago a man was proud and greedy, this year he is much more so. Vice thus grows and increases in him from his youth up. A young child, who has no particular vice, becomes vicious and unchaste as he grows. When he reaches full manhood, the real vices become more and more potent day by day.

The old man therefore follows unchecked the inclinations of 71 his nature if he is not restrained and suppressed by the power of Baptism. On the other hand, when we become Christians, the old man daily decreases until he is finally destroyed. This is what it means to plunge into Baptism and daily come forth again. So the external 72 sign has been appointed not only on account of what it confers, but also on account of what it signifies. Where faith is present with its 73 fruits, there Baptism is no empty symbol, but the effect accompanies it; but where faith is lacking, it remains a mere unfruitful sign.

Here you see that Baptism, both by its power and by its 74 signification, comprehends also the third sacrament, formerly called Penance,[1] which is really nothing else than Baptism. What is 75 repentance but an earnest attack on the old man and an entering upon a new life? If you live in repentance, therefore, you are walking in Baptism, which not only announces this new life but also produces, begins, and promotes it. In Baptism we are given the grace, Spirit, 76

---

[1] *Penitentia* (*Busse*) in the Roman Catholic system meant both the sacrament (Penance) and the act of satisfaction enjoined by the priest (penance) and the inward attitude of repentance.

and power to suppress the old man so that the new may come forth
and grow strong.

Therefore Baptism remains forever. Even though we fall from   77
it and sin, nevertheless we always have access to it so that we may
again subdue the old man. But we need not again have the water   78
poured over us. Even if we were immersed in water a hundred times, it
would nevertheless be only one Baptism, and the effect and signification
of Baptism would continue and remain. Repentance, therefore, is   79
nothing else than a return and approach to Baptism, to resume and
practice what had earlier been begun but abandoned.

I say this to correct the opinion, which has long prevailed   80
among us, that our Baptism is something past which we can no longer
use after falling again into sin. We have such a notion because we
regard Baptism only in the light of a work performed once for all.
Indeed, St. Jerome is responsible for this view, for he wrote,   81
"Repentance is the second plank[2] on which we must swim ashore after
the ship founders" in which we embarked when we entered the
Christian church.[3] This interpretation deprives Baptism of its   82
value, making it of no further use to us. Therefore the statement is
incorrect.[4] The ship does not founder since, as we said, it is God's
ordinance and not a work of ours. But it does happen that we slip
and fall out of the ship. If anybody does fall out, he should immediately
head for the ship and cling to it until he can climb aboard again and
sail on in it as he had done before.

Thus we see what a great and excellent thing Baptism is, which   83
snatches us from the jaws of the devil and makes God our own,
overcomes and takes away sin and daily strengthens the new man,
always remains until we pass from this present misery to eternal glory.

Therefore let everybody regard his Baptism as the daily   84
garment which he is to wear all the time. Every day he should be
found in faith and amid its fruits, every day he should be suppressing
the old man and growing up in the new. If we wish to be   85
Christians, we must practice the work that makes us Christians.
But if anybody falls away from his Baptism let him return to it.   86
As Christ, the mercy-seat,[5] does not recede from us or forbid us to
return to him even though we sin, so all his treasures and gifts remain.
As we have once obtained forgiveness of sins in Baptism, so forgiveness
remains day by day as long as we live, that is, as long as we carry
the old Adam about our necks.

---

[2] Baptism was regarded as the first plank.
[3] Epistle 130 to Demetrias. Cf. also Epistle 122 to Rusticus, Epistle 147 to
Fallen Sabinianus, and Commentary on Isaiah, ch. 3, 8-9.
[4] Later version adds: or else was never rightly understood.
[5] Cf. Rom. 3:25; Heb. 4:16.

[FIFTH PART:] THE SACRAMENT OF THE ALTAR

As we treated Holy Baptism under three headings, so we must 1
deal with the second sacrament in the same way, stating what it is,
what its benefits are, and who is to receive it. All these are established
from the words by which Christ instituted it. So everyone who 2
wishes to be a Christian and go to the sacrament should be familiar
with them. For we do not intend to admit to the sacrament and
administer it to those who do not know what they seek or why they
come. The words are these:

"Our Lord Jesus Christ on the night when he was betrayed took 3
bread, gave thanks, broke it, and gave it to his disciples and said,
'Take, eat; this is my body, which is given for you. Do this in
remembrance of me.'"

"In the same way also he took the cup, after supper, gave thanks,
and gave it to them, saying, 'This cup is the new testament in my
blood, which is poured out for you for the forgiveness of sins. Do this,
as often as you drink it, in remembrance of me.'" [6]

We have no wish on this occasion to quarrel and dispute with 4
those who blaspheme and desecrate this sacrament; but as in the case
of Baptism, we shall first learn what is of greatest importance, namely,
God's Word and ordinance or command, which is the chief thing
to be considered. For the Lord's Supper was not invented or devised
by any man. It was instituted by Christ without man's counsel or
deliberation. Therefore, just as the Ten Commandments, the 5
Lord's Prayer, and the Creed retain their nature and value even if we
never keep, pray, or believe them, so also does this blessed sacrament
remain unimpaired and inviolate even if we use and handle it unworthily. Do you think God cares so much about our faith and 6
conduct that he would permit them to affect his ordinance? No, all
temporal things remain as God has created and ordered them, regardless
of how we treat them. This must always be emphasized, for thus 7
we can thoroughly refute all the babbling of the seditious spirits who
regard the sacraments, contrary to the Word of God, as human
performances.

Now, what is the Sacrament of the Altar? Answer: It is the 8
true body and blood of the Lord Christ in and under the bread and
wine which we Christians are commanded by Christ's word to eat and
drink. As we said of Baptism that it is not mere water, so we say 9
here that the sacrament is bread and wine, but not mere bread or wine
such as is served at the table. It is bread and wine comprehended in
God's Word and connected with it.

[6] I Cor. 11:23-25; Matt. 26:26-28; Mark 14:22-24; Luke 22:19f.

It is the Word, I maintain, which distinguishes it from mere   10
bread and wine and constitutes it a sacrament which is rightly called
Christ's body and blood. It is said, *"Accedat verbum ad elementum et
fit sacramentum,"* that is, "When the Word is joined to the external
element, it becomes a sacrament." [7] This saying of St. Augustine is so
accurate and well put that it is doubtful if he has said anything better.
The Word must make the element a sacrament; otherwise it remains a
mere element. Now, this is not the word and ordinance of a   11
prince or emperor, but of the divine Majesty at whose feet every knee
should bow and confess that it is as he says and should accept it with
all reverence, fear, and humility.

With this Word you can strengthen your conscience and declare: 12
"Let a hundred thousand devils, with all the fanatics, rush forward
and say, 'How can bread and wine be Christ's body and blood?' Still
I know that all the spirits and scholars put together have less wisdom
than the divine Majesty has in his little finger. Here we have   13
Christ's word, 'Take, eat; this is my body.' 'Drink of it, all of you,
this is the new covenant in my blood,' etc. Here we shall take our
stand and see who dares to instruct Christ and alter what he has
spoken. It is true, indeed, that if you take the Word away from   14
the elements or view them apart from the Word, you have nothing but
ordinary bread and wine. But if the words remain, as is right and
necessary, then in virtue of them they are truly the body and blood
of Christ. For as we have it from the lips of Christ, so it is; he cannot
lie or deceive."

Hence it is easy to answer all kinds of questions which now   15
trouble men — for example, whether even a wicked priest can
administer the sacrament, and like questions. Our conclusion is: 16
Even though a knave should receive or administer it, it is the true
sacrament (that is, Christ's body and blood) just as truly as when one
uses it most worthily. For it is not founded on the holiness of men
but on the Word of God. As no saint on earth, yes, no angel in
heaven can transform bread and wine into Christ's body and blood, so
likewise no one can change or alter the sacrament, even if it is misused.
For the Word by which it was constituted a sacrament is not   17
rendered false because of an individual's unworthiness or unbelief.
Christ does not say, "If you believe, or if you are worthy, you receive
my body and blood," but, "Take, eat and drink, this is my body and
blood." Likewise, he says, "Do this," namely, what I now do, what I
institute, what I give you and bid you take. This is as much as to   18
say, "No matter whether you are unworthy or worthy, you here have
Christ's body and blood by virtue of these words which are coupled
with the bread and wine." Mark this and remember it well. For   19

---

[7] Cf. above, IV, Baptism, 18.

upon these words rest our whole argument, protection, and defense against all errors and deceptions that have ever arisen or may yet arise.

We have briefly considered the first part, namely, the essence   20 of this sacrament. Now we come to its power and benefit, the purpose for which the sacrament was really instituted, for it is most necessary that we know what we should seek and obtain there. This is   21 plainly evident from the words just quoted, "This is my body and blood, given and poured out *for you* for the forgiveness of sins." In other words, we go to the sacrament because we receive there   22 a great treasure, through and in which we obtain the forgiveness of sins. Why? Because the words are there through which this is imparted! Christ bids me eat and drink in order that the sacrament may be mine and may be a source of blessing to me as a sure pledge and sign—indeed, as the very gift he has provided for me against my sins, death, and all evils.

Therefore, it is appropriately called the food of the soul since   23 it nourishes and strengthens the new man. While it is true that through Baptism we are first born anew, our human flesh and blood have not lost their old skin. There are so many hindrances and temptations of the devil and the world that we often grow weary and faint, at times even stumble. The Lord's Supper is given as a   24 daily food and sustenance so that our faith may refresh and strengthen itself and not weaken in the struggle but grow continually stronger. For the new life should be one that continually develops and   25 progresses. Meanwhile it must suffer much opposition. The devil   26 is a furious enemy; when he sees that we resist him and attack the old man, and when he cannot rout us by force, he sneaks and skulks about everywhere, trying all kinds of tricks, and does not stop until he has finally worn us out so that we either renounce our faith or yield hand and foot and become indifferent or impatient. For such   27 times, when our heart feels too sorely pressed, this comfort of the Lord's Supper is given to bring us new strength and refreshment.

Here again our clever spirits contort themselves with their   28 great learning and wisdom, bellowing and blustering, "How can bread and wine forgive sins or strengthen faith?" Yet they know that we do not claim this of bread and wine—since in itself bread is bread—but of that bread and wine which are Christ's body and blood and with which the words are coupled. These and no other, we say, are the treasure through which forgiveness is obtained. This treasure is conveyed   29 and communicated to us in no other way than through the words, "given and poured out for you." Here you have both truths, that it is Christ's body and blood and that these are yours as your treasure and gift. Christ's body can never be an unfruitful, vain thing, impotent   30 and useless. Yet, however great the treasure may be in itself, it must be comprehended in the Word and offered to us through the Word, otherwise we could never know of it or seek it.

Therefore it is absurd to say that Christ's body and blood are 31 not given and poured out for us in the Lord's Supper and hence that we cannot have forgiveness of sins in the sacrament. Although the work was accomplished and forgiveness of sins was acquired on the cross, yet it cannot come to us in any other way than through the Word. How should we know that this has been accomplished and offered to us if it were not proclaimed by preaching, by the oral Word? Whence do they know of forgiveness, and how can they grasp and appropriate it, except by steadfastly believing the Scriptures and the Gospel? Now, the whole Gospel and the article of the Creed, "I 32 believe in the holy Christian church, the forgiveness of sins," are embodied in this sacrament and offered to us through the Word. Why, then, should we allow this treasure to be torn out of the sacrament? Our opponents[8] must still confess that these are the very words which we hear everywhere in the Gospel. They can say that these words in the sacrament are of no value just as little as they dare say that the whole Gospel or Word of God apart from the sacrament is of no value.

So far we have treated the sacrament from the standpoint both 33 of its essence and of its effect and benefit. It remains for us to consider who it is that receives this power and benefit. Briefly, as we said above concerning Baptism and in many other places, the answer is: It is he who believes what the words say and what they give, for they are not spoken or preached to stone and wood but to those who hear them, those to whom Christ says, "Take and eat," etc. And 34 because he offers and promises forgiveness of sins, it cannot be received except by faith. This faith he himself demands in the Word when he says, "Given *for you*" and "poured out *for you*," as if he said, "This is why I give it and bid you eat and drink, that you may take it as your own and enjoy it." Whoever lets these words be addressed 35 to him and believes that they are true has what the words declare. But he who does not believe has nothing, for he lets this gracious blessing be offered to him in vain and refuses to enjoy it. The treasure is opened and placed at everyone's door, yes, upon everyone's table, but it is also your responsibility to take it and confidently believe that it is just as the words tell you.

This, now, is the preparation required of a Christian for 36 receiving this sacrament worthily. Since this treasure is fully offered in the words, it can be grasped and appropriated only by the heart. Such a gift and eternal treasure cannot be seized with the hand. Fasting and prayer and the like may have their place as an 37

---

[8] Zwinglians and Anabaptists.

external preparation and children's exercise so that one's body may behave properly and reverently toward the body and blood of Christ. But what is given in and with the sacrament cannot be grasped and appropriated by the body. This is done by the faith of the heart which discerns and desires this treasure.

Enough has been said now for all ordinary instruction on the 38 essentials of this sacrament. What may further be said about it belongs to another occasion.

In conclusion, now that we have the right interpretation and 39 doctrine of the sacrament, there is great need also of an admonition and entreaty that so great a treasure, which is daily administered and distributed among Christians, may not be heedlessly passed by. What I mean is that those who claim to be Christians should prepare themselves to receive this blessed sacrament frequently. For we see 40 that men are becoming listless and lazy about its observance. A lot of people who hear the Gospel, now that the pope's nonsense has been abolished and we are freed from his oppression and authority, let a year, or two, three, or more years go by without receiving the sacrament, as if they were such strong Christians that they have no need of it. Some let themselves be kept and deterred from it 41 because we have taught that no one should go unless he feels a hunger and thirst impelling him to it. Some pretend that it is a matter of liberty, not of necessity, and that it is enough if they simply believe. Thus the majority go so far that they become quite barbarous, and ultimately despise both the sacrament and the Word of God.

Now it is true, we repeat, that no one should under any 42 circumstances be coerced or compelled, lest we institute a new slaughter of souls. Nevertheless, let it be understood that people who abstain and absent themselves from the sacrament over a long period of time are not to be considered Christians. Christ did not institute it to be treated merely as a spectacle, but commanded his Christians to eat and drink and thereby remember him.

Indeed, true Christians who cherish and honor the sacrament 43 will of their own accord urge and impel themselves to come. However, in order that the common people and the weak, who also would like to be Christians, may be induced to see the reason and the need for receiving the sacrament, we shall devote a little attention to this point. As in other matters pertaining to faith, love, and patience it is 44 not enough simply to teach and instruct, but there must also be daily exhortation, so on this subject we must be persistent in preaching, lest people become indifferent and bored. For we know from experience that the devil always sets himself against this and every other Christian activity, hounding and driving people from it as much as he can.

In the first place, we have a clear text in the words of Christ, 45 "*Do this* in remembrance of me." These are words of precept and command, enjoining all who would be Christians to partake of the sacrament. They are words addressed to disciples of Christ; hence whoever would be one of them, let him faithfully hold to this sacrament, not from compulsion, coerced by men, but to obey and please the Lord Christ. However, you may say, "But the words are 46 added, 'as often as you do it'; so he compels no one, but leaves it to our free choice." I answer: That is true, but it does not say that 47 we should never partake. Indeed, the very words, "as often as you do it," imply that we should do it often. And they are added because Christ wishes the sacrament to be free, not bound to a special time like the Passover, which the Jews were obliged to eat only once a year, precisely on the evening of the fourteenth day of the first full moon,[9] without variation of a single day. Christ means to say: "I institute a Passover or Supper for you, which you shall enjoy not just on this one evening of the year, but frequently, whenever and wherever you will, according to everyone's opportunity and need, being bound to no special place or time" (although the pope afterward perverted it 48 and turned it back into a Jewish feast).[1]

Thus you see that we are not granted liberty to despise the 49 sacrament. When a person, with nothing to hinder him, lets a long period of time elapse without ever desiring the sacrament, I call that despising it. If you want such liberty, you may just as well take the further liberty not to be a Christian; then you need not believe or pray, for the one is just as much Christ's commandment as the other. But if you wish to be a Christian, you must from time to time satisfy and obey this commandment. For this commandment should ever 50 move you to examine your inner life and reflect: "See what sort of Christian I am! If I were one, I would surely have at least a little longing to do what my Lord has commanded me to do."

Indeed, since we show such an aversion toward the sacrament, 51 men can easily sense what sort of Christians we were under the papacy when we attended the sacrament merely from compulsion and fear of men's commandments, without joy and love and even without regard for Christ's commandment. But we neither force nor compel 52 anyone, nor need anyone partake of the sacrament to serve or please us. What should move and impel you is the fact that Christ desires it, and it pleases him. You should not let yourself be forced by men either to faith or to any good work. All we are doing is to urge you to do what you ought to do, not for our sake but for your own. He invites and incites you; if you despise this, you must answer for it yourself.

---

[9] Lev. 23:5.

[1] Cf. Fourth Lateran Council (1215): "receiving reverently the sacrament of the Eucharist at least in Paschal time. . . ." Henry Denzinger, *The Sources of Catholic Dogma,* tr. R. J. Deferrari (1957), p. 173.

This is the first point, especially for the benefit of the cold and 53 indifferent, that they may come to their senses and wake up. It is certainly true, as I have found in my own experience, and as everyone will find in his own case, that if a person stays away from the sacrament, day by day he will become more and more callous and cold, and eventually spurn it altogether. To avoid this, we must 54 examine our heart and conscience and act like a person who really desires to be right with God. The more we do this, the more will our heart be warmed and kindled, and it will not grow entirely cold.

But suppose you say, "What if I feel that I am unfit?" Answer: 55 This also is my temptation, especially inherited from the old order under the pope when we tortured ourselves to become so perfectly pure that God might not find the least blemish in us. Because of this we became so timid that everyone was thrown into consternation, saying, "Alas, I am not worthy!" Then nature and reason begin 56 to contrast our unworthiness with this great and precious blessing, and it appears like a dark lantern in contrast to the bright sun, or as dung in contrast to jewels. Because nature and reason see this, such people refuse to go to the sacrament and wait until they become prepared, until one week passes into another and one half year into yet another. If you choose to fix your eye on how good and pure 57 you are, to work toward the time when nothing will prick your conscience, you will never go.

For this reason we must make a distinction among men. Those 58 who are shameless and unruly must be told to stay away, for they are not fit to receive the forgiveness of sins since they do not desire it and do not want to be good. The others, who are not so callous 59 and dissolute but would like to be good, should not absent themselves, even though in other respects they are weak and frail. As St. Hilary has said, "Unless a man has committed such a sin that he has forfeited the name of Christian and has to be expelled from the congregation, he should not exclude himself from the sacrament," lest he deprive himself of life.[2] No one will make such progress 60 that he does not retain many common infirmities in his flesh and blood.

People with such misgivings must learn that it is the highest 61 wisdom to realize that this sacrament does not depend upon our worthiness. We are not baptized because we are worthy and holy, nor do we come to confession pure and without sin; on the contrary, we come as poor, miserable men, precisely because we are unworthy. The only exception is the person who desires no grace and absolution and has no intention to amend his life.

---

[2] Gratian, *Decretum*, Pt. III, D. 2, c. 15, quotes Hilary: "If a man's sins are not so great as to require excommunication, he must not exclude himself from the medicine of the Lord's body." The passage, however, is to be found in Augustine, Epistle 54, c. 3.

He who earnestly desires grace and consolation should compel   62
himself to go and allow no one to deter him, saying, "I would really
like to be worthy, but I come not on account of any worthiness of
mine, but on account of thy Word, because Thou hast commanded it
and I want to be thy disciple, no matter how insignificant my
worthiness." This is difficult, for we always have this obstacle and   63
hindrance to contend with, that we concentrate more upon ourselves
than upon the words that proceed from Christ's lips. Nature would like
to act in such a way that it may rest and rely firmly upon itself;
otherwise it refuses to take a step. Let this suffice for the first point.

In the second place, a promise is attached to the commandment,   64
as we heard above, which should most powerfully draw and impel us.
Here stand the gracious and lovely words, "This is my body, given
for you," "This is my blood, poured out *for you* for the forgiveness
of sins." These words, I have said, are not preached to wood or   65
stone but to you and me; otherwise Christ might just as well have
kept quiet and not instituted a sacrament. Ponder, then, and include
yourself personally in the "you" so that he may not speak to you in
vain.

In this sacrament he offers us all the treasure he brought from   66
heaven for us, to which he most graciously invites us in other places,
as when he says in Matt. 11:28, "Come to me, all who labor and are
heavy-laden, and I will refresh you." Surely it is a sin and a shame   67
that, when he tenderly and faithfully summons and exhorts us to our
highest and greatest good, we act so distantly toward it, neglecting it
so long that we grow quite cold and callous and lose all desire and
love for it. We must never regard the sacrament as a harmful   68
thing from which we should flee, but as a pure, wholesome, soothing
medicine which aids and quickens us in both soul and body. For
where the soul is healed, the body has benefited also. Why, then,
do we act as if the sacrament were a poison which would kill us if
we ate of it?

Of course, it is true that those who despise the sacrament and   69
lead unchristian lives receive it to their harm and damnation. To
such people nothing can be good or wholesome, just as when a sick
person willfully eats and drinks what is forbidden him by the
physician. But those who feel their weakness, who are anxious to   70
be rid of it and desire help, should regard and use the sacrament as a
precious antidote against the poison in their systems. For here in the
sacrament you receive from Christ's lips the forgiveness of sins, which
contains and conveys God's grace and Spirit with all his gifts,
protection, defense, and power against death and the devil and all evils.

Thus you have on God's part both the commandment and the   71
promise of the Lord Christ. Meanwhile, on your part, you ought to be
impelled by your own need, which hangs around your neck and which

is the very reason for this command and invitation and promise. Christ himself says, "Those who are well have no need of a physician, but those who are sick," [3] that is, those who labor and are heavy-laden with sin, fear of death, and the assaults of the flesh and the devil. If you are heavy-laden and feel your weakness, go joyfully to the *72* sacrament and receive refreshment, comfort, and strength. If you *73* wait until you are rid of your burden in order to come to the sacrament purely and worthily, you must stay away from it forever. In such a case Christ pronounces the judgment, "If you are pure *74* and upright, you have no need of me and I have no need of you." Therefore they alone are unworthy who neither feel their infirmities nor admit to being sinners.

Suppose you say, "What shall I do if I cannot feel this need or *75* experience hunger and thirst for the sacrament?" Answer: For persons in such a state of mind that they cannot feel it, I know no better advice than to suggest that they put their hands to their bosom and ask whether they are made of flesh and blood. If you find that you are, then for your own good turn to St. Paul's Epistle to the Galatians and hear what are the fruits of the flesh: "The works of the flesh are plain: adultery, immorality, impurity, licentiousness, idolatry, sorcery, enmity, strife, jealousy, anger, selfishness, dissension, party spirit, envy, murder, drunkenness, carousing, and the like." [4]

If you cannot feel the need, therefore, at least believe the *76* Scriptures. They will not lie to you, and they know your flesh better than you yourself do. Yes, and St. Paul concludes in Rom. 7:18, "For I know that nothing good dwells within me, that is, in my flesh." If St. Paul can speak thus of his flesh, let us not pretend to be better or more holy. But the fact that we are insensitive to our sin is all *77* the worse, for it is a sign that ours is a leprous flesh which feels nothing though the disease rages and rankles. As we have said, *78* even if you are so utterly dead in sin, at least believe the Scriptures, which pronounce this judgment upon you. In short, the less you feel your sins and infirmities, the more reason you have to go to the sacrament and seek a remedy.

Again, look about you and see whether you are also in the *79* world. If you do not know, ask your neighbors about it. If you are in the world, do not think that there will be any lack of sins and needs. Just begin to act as if you want to become good and cling to the Gospel, and see whether you will not acquire enemies who harm, wrong, and injure you and give you occasion for sin and wrong-doing. If you have not experienced this, then take it from the Scriptures, which everywhere give this testimony about the world.

[3] Matt. 9:12.
[4] Gal. 5:19, 20.

Besides the flesh and the world, you will surely have the devil   80
about you. You will not entirely trample him under foot because
our Lord Christ himself could not entirely avoid him. Now, what   81
is the devil? Nothing else than what the Scriptures call him, a liar
and a murderer.[5] A liar who seduces the heart from God's Word and
blinds it, making you unable to feel your needs or come to Christ. A
murderer who begrudges you every hour of your life. If you could   82
see how many daggers, spears, and arrows are at every moment aimed
at you, you would be glad to come to the sacrament as often as
possible. The only reason we go about so securely and heedlessly is
that we neither acknowledge nor believe that we are in the flesh, in
this wicked world, or under the kingdom of the devil.

Try this, therefore, and practice it well. Just examine yourself,   83
look around a little, cling to the Scriptures. If even then you feel
nothing, you have all the more need to lament both to God and to
your brother. Take others' advice and seek their prayers, and never
give up until the stone is removed from your heart. Then your   84
need will become apparent, and you will perceive that you have sunk
twice as low as any other poor sinner and are much in need of the
sacrament to combat your misery. This misery, unfortunately, you
do not see, though God grants his grace that you may become more
sensitive to it and more hungry for the sacrament. This happens
especially because the devil so constantly besieges you and lies in wait
to trap and destroy you, soul and body, so that you cannot be safe
from him one hour. How quickly can he bring you into misery and
distress when you least expect it!

Let this serve as an exhortation, then, not only for us who are   85
grown and advanced in years, but also for the young people who
ought to be brought up in Christian doctrine and a right understanding
of it. With such training we may more easily instill the Ten
Commandments, the Creed, and the Lord's Prayer into the young
so that they will receive them with joy and earnestness, practice them
from their youth, and become accustomed to them. For it is   86
clearly useless to try to change old people. We cannot perpetuate
these and other teachings unless we train the people who come after
us and succeed us in our office and work, so that they in turn may
bring up their children successfully. Thus the Word of God and the
Christian church will be preserved. Therefore let every head of a   87
household remember that it is his duty, by God's injunction and
command, to teach or have taught to his children the things they
ought to know. Since they are baptized and received into the Christian
church, they should also enjoy this fellowship of the sacrament so that

[5] John 8:44.

they may serve us and be useful. For they must all help us to believe, to love, to pray, and to fight the devil.

Here follows an exhortation to confession.[6]

A Brief Exhortation to Confession

Concerning confession, we have always taught that it should be 1 voluntary and purged of the pope's tyranny. We have been set free from his coercion and from the intolerable burden he imposed upon the Christian church. Up to now, as we all know from experience, there has been no law quite so oppressive as that which forced everyone to make confession on pain of the gravest mortal sin. Moreover, it so greatly burdened and tortured consciences with the 2 enumeration of all kinds of sin that no one was able to confess purely enough. Worst of all, no one taught or understood what confession 3 is and how useful and comforting it is. Instead, it was made sheer anguish and a hellish torture since people had to make confession even though nothing was more hateful to them. These three things 4 have now been removed and made voluntary so that we may confess without coercion or fear, and we are released from the torture of enumerating all sins in detail. Moreover, we have the advantage of knowing how to use confession beneficially for the comforting and strengthening of our conscience.

Everyone knows this now. Unfortunately, men have learned it 5 only too well; they do whatever they please and take advantage of their freedom, acting as if they will never need or desire to go to confession any more. We quickly understand whatever benefits us, and we grasp with uncommon ease whatever in the Gospel is mild and gentle. But such pigs, as I have said, are unworthy to appear in the presence of the Gospel or to have any part of it. They ought to remain under the pope and submit to being driven and tormented to confess, fast, etc., more than ever before. For he who will not believe the Gospel, live according to it, and do what a Christian ought to do, should enjoy none of its benefits. What would happen if 6 you wished to enjoy the Gospel's benefits but did nothing about it and paid nothing for it? For such people we shall provide no preaching, nor will they have our permission to share and enjoy any part of our liberty, but we shall let the pope or his like bring them back into subjection and coerce them like the tyrant he is. The rabble who will not obey the Gospel deserve just such a jailer as God's devil and hangman. To others who hear it gladly, however, we must always 7 preach, exhorting, encouraging, and persuading them not to lose this

---

[6] The section on confession was added first in the 1529 revised edition of the Catechism. It was omitted in the Jena edition of Luther's Works and in the German Book of Concord, hence also in several later editions of the Catechism.

precious and comforting treasure which the Gospel offers. Therefore we must say something about confession to instruct and admonish the simple folk.

To begin with, I have said that in addition to the confession 8 which we are discussing here there are two other kinds, which have an even greater right to be called the Christians' common confession. I refer to the practice of confessing to God alone or to our neighbor alone, begging for forgiveness. These two kinds are expressed in the Lord's Prayer when we say, "Forgive us our debts, as we forgive our debtors," etc. Indeed, the whole Lord's Prayer is nothing else than 9 such a confession. For what is our prayer but a confession that we neither have nor do what we ought and a plea for grace and a happy conscience? This kind of confession should and must take place incessantly as long as we live. For this is the essence of a genuinely Christian life, to acknowledge that we are sinners and to pray for grace.

Similarly the second confession, which each Christian makes 10 toward his neighbor, is included in the Lord's Prayer. We are to confess our guilt before one another and forgive one another before we come into God's presence to beg for forgiveness. Now, all of us are debtors one to another, therefore we should and we may confess publicly in everyone's presence, no one being afraid of anyone else. For it is true, as the proverb says, "If one man is upright, so are 11 they all"; no one does to God or his neighbor what he ought. However, besides our universal guilt there is also a particular one, when a person has provoked another to anger and needs to beg his pardon. Thus we have in the Lord's Prayer a twofold absolution: 12 our debts both to God and to our neighbor are forgiven when we forgive our neighbor and become reconciled with him.

Besides this public, daily, and necessary confession, there is 13 also the secret confession which takes place privately before a single brother. When some problem or quarrel sets us at one another's throats and we cannot settle it, and yet we do not find ourselves sufficiently strong in faith, we may at any time and as often as we wish lay our complaint before a brother, seeking his advice, comfort, and strength. This type of confession is not included in the command- 14 ment like the other two but is left to everyone to use whenever he needs it. Thus by divine ordinance Christ himself has entrusted absolution to his Christian church and commanded us to absolve one another from sins.[7] So if there is a heart that feels its sin and desires consolation, it has here a sure refuge when it hears in God's Word that through a man God looses and absolves him from his sins.

Note, then, as I have often said, that confession consists of 15 two parts. The first is my work and act, when I lament my sin and

[7] Matt. 18:15-19.

desire comfort and restoration for my soul. The second is a work
which God does, when he absolves me of my sins through a word
placed in the mouth of a man. This is the surpassingly grand and
noble thing that makes confession so wonderful and comforting.
In the past we placed all the emphasis on our work alone, and we   16
were only concerned whether we had confessed purely enough. We
neither noticed nor preached the very necessary second part; it was
just as if our confession were simply a good work with which we could
satisfy God. Where the confession was not made perfectly and in
complete detail, we were told that the absolution was not valid and
the sin was not forgiven. Thereby the people were driven to the   17
point that everyone inevitably despaired of confessing so purely
(which was impossible), and nobody could feel his conscience at peace
or have confidence in his absolution. Thus the precious confession was
not only made useless to us but it also became burdensome and bitter,
to the manifest harm and destruction of souls.

We should therefore take care to keep the two parts clearly   18
separate. We should set little value on our work but exalt and magnify
God's Word. We should not act as if we wanted to perform a
magnificent work to present to him, but simply to accept and receive
something from him. You dare not come and say how good or how
wicked you are. If you are a Christian, I know this well enough   19
anyway; if you are not, I know it still better. But what you must do
is to lament your need and allow yourself to be helped so that you may
attain a happy heart and conscience.

Further, no one dare oppress you with requirements. Rather,   20
whoever is a Christian, or would like to be one, has here the faithful
advice to go and obtain this precious treasure. If you are no Christian,
and desire no such comfort, we shall leave you to another's power.
Hereby we abolish the pope's tyranny, commandments, and   21
coercion since we have no need of them. For our teaching, as I have
said, is this: If anybody does not go to confession willingly and for the
sake of absolution, let him just forget about it. Yes, and if anybody
goes about relying on the purity of his confession, let him just stay
away from it. We urge you, however, to confess and express your   22
needs, not for the purpose of performing a work but to hear what God
wishes to say to you. The Word or absolution, I say, is what you
should concentrate on, magnifying and cherishing it as a great and
wonderful treasure to be accepted with all praise and gratitude.

If all this were clearly explained, and meanwhile if the needs   23
which ought to move and induce us to confession were clearly indicated,
there would be no need of coercion and force. A man's own conscience
would impel him and make him so anxious that he would rejoice and
act like a poor, miserable beggar who hears that a rich gift, of money

or clothes, is to be given out at a certain place; he would need no bailiff to drive and beat him but would run there as fast as he could so as not to miss the gift. Suppose, now, that the invitation were 24 changed into a command that all beggars should run to the place, no reason being given and no mention of what they were to look for or receive. How else would the beggar go but with repugnance, not expecting to receive anything but just letting everyone see how poor and miserable he is? Not much joy or comfort would come from this, but only a greater hostility to the command.

In the same way the pope's preachers have in the past kept 25 silence about this wonderful, rich alms and this indescribable treasure; they have simply driven men together in hordes just to show what impure and filthy people they were. Who could thus go to confession willingly? We, on the contrary, do not say that men should look 26 to see how full of filthiness you are, making of you a mirror for contemplating themselves. Rather we advise: If you are poor and miserable, then go and make use of the healing medicine. He who 27 feels his misery and need will develop such a desire for confession that he will run toward it with joy. But those who ignore it and do not come of their own accord, we let go their way. However, they ought to know that we do not regard them as Christians.

Thus we teach what a wonderful, precious, and comforting 28 thing confession is, and we urge that such a precious blessing should not be despised, especially when we consider our great need. If you are a Christian, you need neither my compulsion nor the pope's command at any point, but you will compel yourself and beg me for the privilege of sharing in it. However, if you despise it and 29 proudly stay away from confession, then we must come to the conclusion that you are no Christian and that you ought not receive the sacrament. For you despise what no Christian ought to despise, and you show thereby that you can have no forgiveness of sin. And this is a sure sign that you also despise the Gospel.

In short, we approve of no coercion. However, if anyone 30 refuses to hear and heed the warning of our preaching, we shall have nothing to do with him, nor may he have any share in the Gospel. If you are a Christian, you should be glad to run more than a hundred miles for confession, not under compulsion but rather coming and compelling us to offer it. For here the compulsion must be 31 inverted; we must come under the command and you must come into freedom. We compel no man, but allow ourselves to be compelled, just as we are compelled to preach and administer the sacrament.

Therefore, when I urge you to go to confession, I am simply 32 urging you to be a Christian. If I bring you to this point, I have also brought you to confession. Those who really want to be good Christians, free from their sins, and happy in their conscience, already have the true hunger and thirst. They snatch at the bread just like a hunted hart, burning with heat and thirst, as Ps. 42:2 says, "As a 33 hart longs for flowing streams, so longs my soul for thee, O God." That is, as a hart trembles with eagerness for a fresh spring, so I yearn and tremble for God's Word, absolution, the sacrament, etc. In 34 this way, you see, confession would be rightly taught, and such a desire and love for it would be aroused that people would come running after us to get it, more than we would like. We shall let the papists torment and torture themselves and other people who ignore such a treasure and bar themselves from it. As for ourselves, however, let us lift our 35 hands in praise and thanks to God that we have attained to this blessed knowledge of confession.

VIII

FORMULA OF CONCORD

A Thorough, Pure, Correct, and Final Restatement
and Explanation of a Number of Articles of the Augsburg
Confession on Which for Some Time There Has Been Disagreement
among Some of the Theologians Adhering to this Confession,
Resolved and Reconciled under the Guidance of the Word of God
and the Comprehensive Summary of our Christian Teaching

INTRODUCTION

*In the wake of Luther's death (1546) and the military defeat (1547)
of Lutheran princes and estates, a series of controversies about the
"pure doctrine" of the Reformation threatened to split the Lutherans
into two camps: an increasingly isolated "Gnesio-Lutheran" party
claiming to adhere to the original teachings of Martin Luther and
initially led by Matthias Flacius, and a "Philippist" party composed
of followers of Philip Melanchthon who carried their mentor's insights
to extremes. The desire for unification was abetted by strong political
pressures from both Roman Catholic and Calvinist sides.*

*The open breach among Lutherans that the Colloquy of Worms
(1557) revealed led to two ineffective conferences of princes at Frankfurt-on-the-Main (1558) and Naumburg (1561). Beginning in 1568, a
theological solution for the rift was attempted with generous moral
and financial support from the princes. The first formula proposed
was James Andreae's five-article "Confession and Brief Explanation,"
expanded in 1573 in his "Six Christian Sermons." A recasting of the
contents in the latter year produced the "Swabian Concord." A re-
working of this document, largely by Martin Chemnitz in the light of
comments from theological faculties and conferences and individual
theologians, resulted in the "Swabian-[Lower] Saxon Concord" (1575).
In the following year Luke Osiander and Balthasar Bidembach were
directed to draft another proposal, the so-called "Maulbronn Formula."
With the exposure of the Crypto-Calvinist Conspiracy in Electoral
Saxony, Elector August joined the movement for unification; in the
late spring of 1576 he convoked a conference of theologians in Torgau,*

where the Swabian-Saxon Concord and the Maulbronn Formula were combined into the so-called "Torgau Book," which Andreae summarized in the Epitome (or first part) of the Formula of Concord. After being sent to all interested territories for comment, the Torgau Book was reworked at Bergen Abbey into the Solid Declaration (or second part) of the Formula of Concord, the so-called "Bergen Book" (1577).

During the next three years, while the Preface went through draft after draft, 8,188 theologians, ministers, and teachers in the participating territories signed the Solid Declaration. Finally, on June 25, 1580, fifty years to the day after the reading of the Augsburg Confession before Charles V, the complete Book of Concord was placed on sale. The signatures to the Preface (reproduced at the beginning of this volume as the Preface to the Book of Concord) identify the princes and estates then committed to it.

The English translation was made from the German original. Latin quotations, which were reproduced and then translated into the vernacular at the insistence of some princes, are here rendered from the German. Only the more significant Latin expressions are indicated in the footnotes.

[PART I: EPITOME]

A SUMMARY EPITOME OF THE ARTICLES IN CONTROVERSY AMONG THE THEOLOGIANS OF THE AUGSBURG CONFESSION EXPOUNDED AND SETTLED IN CHRISTIAN FASHION IN CONFORMITY WITH GOD'S WORD IN THE RECAPITULATION HERE FOLLOWING

THE COMPREHENSIVE SUMMARY, RULE, AND NORM ACCORDING TO WHICH ALL DOCTRINES SHOULD BE JUDGED AND THE ERRORS WHICH INTRUDED SHOULD BE EXPLAINED AND DECIDED IN A CHRISTIAN WAY

1. We believe, teach, and confess that the prophetic and apos- 1 tolic writings of the Old and New Testaments are the only rule and norm according to which all doctrines and teachers alike must be appraised and judged, as it is written in Ps. 119:105, "Thy word is a lamp to my feet and a light to my path." And St. Paul says in Gal. 1:8, "Even if an angel from heaven should preach to you a gospel contrary to that which we preached to you, let him be accursed."

Other writings of ancient and modern teachers, whatever their 2 names, should not be put on a par with Holy Scripture. Every single one of them should be subordinated to the Scriptures and should be received in no other way and no further than as witnesses to the fashion in which the doctrine of the prophets and apostles was preserved in post-apostolic times.

2. Immediately after the time of the apostles—in fact, already 3 during their lifetime—false teachers and heretics invaded the church. Against these the ancient church formulated symbols (that is, brief and explicit confessions) which were accepted as the unanimous, catholic, Christian faith and confessions of the orthodox and true church, namely, the Apostles' Creed, the Nicene Creed, and the Athanasian Creed. We pledge ourselves to these, and we hereby reject all heresies and teachings which have been introduced into the church of God contrary to them.

3. With reference to the schism in matters of faith which has 4 occurred in our times, we regard, as the unanimous consensus and exposition of our Christian faith, particularly against the false worship, idolatry, and superstition of the papacy and against other sects, and as the symbol of our time, the first and unaltered Augsburg Confession, which was delivered to Emperor Charles V at Augsburg during the great Diet in the year 1530, together with the Apology thereof and the Articles drafted at Smalcald in the year 1537, which the leading theologians approved by their subscription at that time.[1]

Since these matters also concern the laity and the salvation 5 of their souls, we subscribe Dr. Luther's Small and Large Catechisms as both of them are contained in his printed works. They are "the layman's Bible" and contain everything which Holy Scripture discusses at greater length and which a Christian must know for his salvation.

All doctrines should conform to the standards set forth above. 6 Whatever is contrary to them should be rejected and condemned as opposed to the unanimous declaration of our faith.

In this way the distinction between the Holy Scripture of the 7 Old and New Testaments and all other writings is maintained, and Holy Scripture remains the only judge, rule, and norm according to which as the only touchstone all doctrines should and must be understood and judged as good or evil, right or wrong.

Other symbols and other writings are not judges like Holy 8 Scripture, but merely witnesses and expositions of the faith, setting forth how at various times the Holy Scriptures were understood by contemporaries in the church of God with reference to controverted articles, and how contrary teachings were rejected and condemned.

[1] Meant are Luther's Smalcald Articles plus Melanchthon's Treatise on the Power and Primacy of the Pope; see introductions to these documents, above.

I. ORIGINAL SIN

THE QUESTION AT ISSUE

The principal question in this controversy is if, strictly and 1 without any distinction, original sin is man's corrupted nature, substance, and essence, or indeed the principal and best part of his being (that is, his rational soul in its highest form and powers). Or if there is a distinction, even after the Fall, between man's substance, nature, essence, body, and soul on the one hand, and original sin on the other hand, so that man's nature is one thing and original sin, which inheres in the corrupted nature and corrupts it, is something else.

AFFIRMATIVE THESES

The Pure Doctrine, Faith, and Confession according to the aforesaid Standard and Comprehensive Exposition

1. We believe, teach, and confess that there is a distinction 2 between man's nature and original sin, not only in the beginning when God created man pure and holy and without sin, but also as we now have our nature after the Fall. Even after the fall our nature is and remains a creature of God. The distinction between our nature and original sin is as great as the difference between God's work and the devil's work.

2. We also believe, teach, and confess that we must preserve 3 this distinction most diligently, because the view that admits no distinction between our corrupted human nature and original sin militates against and cannot co-exist with the chief articles of our Christian faith, namely, creation, redemption, sanctification, and the resurrection of our flesh.

God not only created the body and soul of Adam and Eve 4 before the Fall, but also our bodies and souls after the Fall, even though they are corrupted, and God still acknowledges them as his handiwork, as it is written, "Thy hands fashioned and made me, all that I am round about" (Job 10:8).[2]

Furthermore, the Son of God assumed into the unity of his 5 person this same human nature, though without sin, and thus took on himself not alien flesh, but our own, and according to our flesh has truly become our brother. Heb. 2:14-17, "Since therefore the children share in flesh and blood, he himself likewise partook of the same nature. . . . For surely it is not with angels that he is concerned but with the descendants of Abraham. Therefore he had to be made like his brethren in every respect," sin excepted.

Thus Christ has redeemed our nature as his creation, sanctifies 6

[2] Cf. Deut. 32:6; Isa. 45:9; 54:5; 64:8; Acts 17:25-28; Ps. 100:3; 139:14; Eccl. 12:1.

it as his creation, quickens it from the dead as his creation, and adorns it gloriously as his creation. But he has not created original sin, has not assumed it, has not redeemed it, has not sanctified it, will not quicken it in the elect, will not glorify it or save it. On the contrary, in the resurrection it will be utterly destroyed. These points clearly 7 set forth the distinction between the corrupted nature itself and the corruption which is in the nature and which has corrupted the nature.

3. On the other hand, we believe, teach, and confess that 8 original sin is not a slight corruption of human nature, but that it is so deep a corruption that nothing sound or uncorrupted has survived in man's body or soul, in his inward or outward powers. It is as the church sings, "Through Adam's fall man's nature and essence are all corrupt." [3]

This damage is so unspeakable that it may not be recognized 9 by a rational process, but only from God's Word.

No one except God alone can separate the corruption of our 10 nature from the nature itself. This will take place wholly by way of death in the resurrection. Then the nature which we now bear will arise and live forever, without original sin and completely separated and removed from it, as Job 19:26, 27 asserts, "I shall be covered by this my skin, and in my flesh I shall see God; him I shall see for myself, and mine eyes shall behold him."

ANTITHESES

Rejection of the Contrary False Teaching

1. Accordingly we reject and condemn the teaching that 11 original sin is only a debt[4] which we owe because of someone else's wrongdoing, without any kind of corruption of our own nature.[5]

2. Likewise the teaching that evil desires are not sin but 12 concreated and essential properties of human nature, or the teaching that the cited defect and damage is not truly sin on account of which man outside of Christ is a child of wrath.[6]

3. We likewise reject the Pelagian error which asserts that 13 man's nature is uncorrupted even after the Fall, and especially that in spiritual things its natural powers remained wholly good and pure.

4. Likewise the teaching that original sin is a slight, insignificant 14

---

[3] A hymn (1524) by Lazarus Spengler which begins, "Durch Adams Fall ist ganz vorderbet menschlich Natur und Wesen." ·

[4] Latin, reatus.

[5] This view was held by some Latin theologians, notably Albert Pighius (1490-1542).

[6] The Council of Trent confirmed the identification of concupiscence with a tinder (fomes) and declared that it is not to be called sin in the sense that "it is truly and strictly sin in the regenerate." Council of Trent, Session V. See also above, Apology, II, 42-44.

spot or blemish that has only been sprinkled or splashed on externally and that underneath man's nature has retained unimpaired its powers for good even in spiritual things.

5. Furthermore, that original sin is only an external impediment 15 to man's good spiritual powers and not the complete deprivation or loss of the same, just as garlic juice, smeared upon a magnet, impedes but does not remove the natural powers of the magnet;[7] likewise the view that this blemish may be removed as readily as a spot can be washed from the face or color from the wall.

6. Furthermore, that the human nature and essence in man is 16 not entirely corrupted, but that man still has something good about him even in spiritual matters—for example, the capacity, skill, capability, or power to initiate, to effect, or to cooperate in something spiritual.[8]

7. We also reject the Manichaean error that original sin is 17 an essential, self-existing something which Satan infused into and mingled with human nature, as when poison and wine are mixed.

8. Likewise, that it is not the natural man himself who com- 18 mits sin but something extraneous and alien within man, and that therefore not the nature of man but only the original sin which is in the nature is being accused.

9. We also reject and condemn as a Manichaean error the 19 teaching that original sin is strictly and without any distinction corrupted man's substance, nature, and essence, so that no distinction should be made, even in the mind, between man's nature itself after the Fall and original sin, and that the two cannot be differentiated in the mind.[9]

Luther calls original sin "nature-sin," "person-sin," "essential 20 sin," not in order to identify without any distinction man's nature, person, or essence itself with original sin but by such terminology to indicate the difference between original sin, which inheres in human nature, and the other so-called actual sins.

For original sin is not a sin which man commits; it inheres 21 in the nature, substance, and essence of man in such a way that even if no evil thought would ever arise in the heart of corrupted man, no idle word were spoken, or no wicked act or deed took place, nevertheless man's nature is corrupted through original sin, innate in us through our sinful seed and the source of all other, actual sins, such as evil thoughts, words, and deeds, as it is written, "Out of the heart

---

[7] This view was voiced by Victorine Strigel in his disputation with Matthias Flacius at Weimar in 1560.

[8] The Synergists held that there are three concurring efficient causes of man's conversion: the Holy Spirit, the Word of God, and man's will.

[9] This was the position of Matthias Flacius in his controversy with Victorine Strigel. See below, Solid Declaration, I, 6.

come evil thoughts," etc.,[1] and "The imagination of man's heart is evil from his youth." [2]

It is important to observe that the word "nature" has several 22 meanings. This enables the Manichaeans to conceal their error and to mislead many simple people. Sometimes the term means man's essence, as when we say, "God has created human nature." At other times the word means the good or bad quality which inheres in the nature or essence of a thing, as when we say, "It is the nature of a serpent to sting," and, "It is the nature or quality of a man to sin," or, "Man's nature is sin." Here the word "nature" does not mean the substance of man but something which inheres in the nature or substance.

As far as the Latin words *substantia* and *accidens* are con- 23 cerned, they are not biblical terms and, besides, they are unknown to the common man. They should therefore not be employed in sermons delivered to common, unlearned people, but simple folk should be spared them.

In schools and learned circles these words can profitably be 24 retained in the discussion of original sin because they are familiar and convey no false impressions, and they clearly show the distinction between the essence of a particular thing and that which pertains to it only accidentally.

This terminology sets forth very clearly the distinction between 25 God's work and Satan's work. Satan cannot create a substance; he can only, with God's permission, corrupt accidentally the substance which God has created.

II. FREE WILL

The Question at Issue in This Controversy

The will of man may be discussed in four different states: I (1) before the Fall, (2) after the Fall, (3) after regeneration, (4) after the resurrection of the flesh. In this controversy the primary question revolves exclusively about man's will and ability in the second state. The question is, What powers does man possess in spiritual matters after the fall of our first parents and before his regeneration? Can man by his own powers, before he is reborn through the Holy Spirit, dispose and prepare himself for the grace of God? Can he or can he not accept the grace of God offered in the Word and the holy sacraments?

[1] Matt. 15:19.
[2] Gen. 8:21; 6:5.

AFFIRMATIVE THESES

The Pure Teaching concerning this Article on the Basis of God's Word

1. It is our teaching, faith, and confession that in spiritual 2 matters man's understanding and reason are blind and that he understands nothing by his own powers, as it is written in I Cor. 2:14, "The unspiritual man does not receive the gifts of the Spirit of God, for they are folly to him, and he is not able to understand them" when he is examined concerning spiritual things.

2. Likewise we believe, teach, and confess that man's unre- 3 generated will is not only turned away from God, but has also become an enemy of God, so that he desires and wills only that which is evil and opposed to God, as it is written, "The imagination of man's heart is evil from his youth." [3] Likewise, "The mind that is set on the flesh is hostile to God; it does not submit to God's law, indeed it cannot." [4] As little as a corpse can quicken itself to bodily, earthly life, so little can man who through sin is spiritually dead raise himself to spiritual life, as it is written, "When we were dead through our trespasses, he made us alive together with Christ." [5] Therefore we are not of ourselves "sufficient to claim anything as coming from us; our sufficiency is from God" (II Cor. 3:5).

3. God the Holy Spirit, however, does not effect conversion 4 without means; he employs to this end the preaching and the hearing of God's Word, as it is written that the Gospel is a "power of God" for salvation;[6] likewise, that faith comes from the hearing of God's Word (Rom. 10:17). It is God's will that men should hear his 5 Word and not stop their ears.[7] The Holy Spirit is present with this Word and opens hearts so that, like Lydia in Acts 16:14, they heed it and thus are converted solely through the grace and power of the Holy Spirit, for man's conversion is the Spirit's work alone. With- 6 out his grace our "will and effort," [8] our planting, sowing, and watering are in vain unless he "gives the growth." [9] Christ also states, "Apart from me you can do nothing." [1] In these few words he denies all power to free will and ascribes everything to the grace of God, so that no one might boast in the presence of God (I Cor. 9:16).

ANTITHESES

Contrary False Doctrine

Accordingly we reject and condemn all the following errors 7 as being contrary to the norm of the Word of God:

1. The mad dream of the so-called Stoic philosophers and of 8

³ Gen. 8:21.
⁴ Rom. 8:7.
⁵ Eph. 2:5.
⁶ Rom. 1:16.

⁷ Ps. 95:8.
⁸ Rom. 9:16.
⁹ I Cor. 3:7.
¹ John 15:5.

Manichaeans who taught that whatever happens must so happen and could not happen otherwise, that man always acts only under compulsion, even in his external acts, and that he commits evil deeds and acts like fornication, robbery, murder, theft, and similar sins under compulsion.

2. We also reject the error of the crass Pelagians who taught 9 that by his own powers, without the grace of the Holy Spirit, man can convert himself to God, believe the Gospel, whole-heartedly obey God's law, and thus merit forgiveness of sins and eternal life.

3. We also reject the error of the Semi-Pelagians who teach 10 that man by virtue of his own powers could make a beginning of his conversion but could not complete it without the grace of the Holy Spirit.[2]

4. Likewise the teaching that while before his conversion man 11 is indeed too weak by his free will to make a beginning, convert himself to God, and whole-heartedly obey God's law by his own powers, yet after the Holy Spirit has made the beginning through the preaching of the Word and in it has offered his grace, man's will is forthwith able by its own natural powers to add something (though it be little and feeble) to help, to cooperate, to prepare itself for grace, to dispose itself, to apprehend and accept it, and to believe the Gospel.

5. Likewise that after his conversion man is able to keep the 12 law of God perfectly and entirely and that this fulfilling constitutes our righteousness before God whereby we merit eternal life.

6. Likewise we reject and condemn the error of the Enthu- 13 siasts[3] who imagine that God draws men to himself, enlightens them, justifies them, and saves them without means, without the hearing of God's Word and without the use of the holy sacraments.

7. Likewise that in conversion and rebirth God wholly destroys 14 the substance and essence of the Old Adam, especially the rational soul, and that in conversion and rebirth he creates out of nothing a new essence of the soul.

8. Likewise when these statements are made without explana- 15 tion that man's will before, in, and after conversion resists the Holy Spirit, and that the Holy Spirit is given to such as resist him purposely and persistently. For as Augustine says, in conversion God makes willing people out of unwilling people and dwells in the willing ones.[4]

---

[2] This is the only instance in the Book of Concord where the term Semi-Pelagians (*halbe Pelagianer*) is employed. Cf. below, Solid Declaration, II, 76.

[3] A marginal note at this point reads: Enthusiasts is the term for people who expect the Spirit's heavenly illumination without the preaching of God's Word.

[4] *Against Two Letters of Pelagius to Boniface*, I, 19, 37.

Some ancient and modern teachers have used expressions such 16 as, "God draws, but draws the person who is willing," or, "Man's will is not idle in conversion, but does something." Since these expressions have been introduced to confirm the role of natural free will in conversion contrary to the doctrine of the grace of God, we hold that these expressions do not agree with the form of sound doctrine and that accordingly it is well to avoid them in a discussion of conversion to God.

On the other hand, it is correct to say that in conversion, 17 through the attraction of the Holy Spirit, God changes stubborn and unwilling people into willing people, and that after conversion, in the daily exercise of repentance, the reborn will of man is not idle but cooperates in all the works which the Holy Spirit performs through us.

9. Likewise Luther's statement that man's will in conversion 18 behaves "altogether passively" [5] (that is, that it does nothing at all) must be understood as referring to the action of divine grace in kindling new movements within the will, that is, when the Spirit of God through the Word that has been heard or through the use of the holy sacraments takes hold of man's will and works the new birth and conversion. But after the Holy Spirit has performed and accomplished this and the will of man has been changed and renewed *solely by God's power and activity,* man's new will becomes an instrument and means of God the Holy Spirit, so that man not only lays hold on grace but also cooperates with the Holy Spirit in the works that follow.

Prior to man's conversion there are only two efficient causes, 19 namely, the Holy Spirit and the Word of God as the Holy Spirit's instrument whereby he effects conversion. Man should hear this Word, though he cannot give it credence and accept it by his own powers but solely by the grace and operation of God the Holy Spirit.

III. THE RIGHTEOUSNESS OF FAITH BEFORE GOD

THE QUESTION AT ISSUE

It is the unanimous confession of our churches according to 1 the Word of God and the content of the Augsburg Confession that we poor sinners are justified before God and saved solely by faith in Christ, so that Christ alone is our righteousness. He is truly God and man since in him the divine and human natures are personally united to one another (Jer. 23:6; I Cor. 1:30, II Cor. 5:21). Because of the foregoing a question has arisen, According to which nature is

[5] E.g., *WA,* 18:697.

Christ our righteousness? Two false and mutually contradictory teachings have invaded some churches.

One party has held that Christ is our righteousness only 2 according to his Godhead. When he dwells in us by faith, over against this indwelling Godhead, the sins of all men are esteemed like a drop of water over against the immense ocean. Others, however, held that Christ is our righteousness before God only according to the human nature.[6]

AFFIRMATIVE THESES

The Pure Doctrine of the Christian Church
Against Both These Errors

1. In opposition to these two errors just recounted, we believe, 3 teach, and confess unanimously that Christ is our righteousness neither according to the divine nature alone nor according to the human nature alone. On the contrary, the entire Christ according to both natures is our righteousness solely in his obedience which as God and man he rendered to his heavenly Father into death itself. Thereby he won for us the forgiveness of sins and eternal life, as it is written, "For as by one man's disobedience many were made sinners, so by *one man's obedience* many will be made righteous" (Rom. 5:19).

2. Accordingly we believe, teach, and confess that our right- 4 eousness before God consists in this, that God forgives us our sins purely by his grace, without any preceding, present, or subsequent work, merit, or worthiness, and reckons to us the righteousness of Christ's obedience, on account of which righteousness we are accepted by God into grace and are regarded as righteous.

3. We believe, teach, and confess that faith is the only means 5 and instrument whereby we accept Christ and in Christ obtain the "righteousness which avails before God," and that for Christ's sake such faith is reckoned for righteousness (Rom. 4:5).

4. We believe, teach, and confess that this faith is not a mere 6 knowledge of the stories about Christ, but the kind of gift of God by which in the Word of the Gospel we recognize Christ aright as our redeemer and trust in him, so that solely because of his obedience, by grace, we have forgiveness of sins, are regarded as holy and righteous by God the Father, and shall be saved eternally.

5. We believe, teach, and confess that according to the usage 7 of Scripture the word "justify" means in this article "absolve," that is, pronounce free from sin. "He who justifies the wicked and he who condemns the righteous are both alike an abomination to the

---

[6] Andrew Osiander propounded the former view, Francis Stancaro the latter.

Lord" (Prov. 17:15); likewise, "Who shall bring any charge against God's elect? It is God who justifies" (Rom. 8:33). Sometimes, as 8 in the Apology,[7] the words *regeneratio* (rebirth) and *vivificatio* (making alive) are used in place of justification, and then they mean the same thing, even though otherwise these terms refer to the renovation of man and distinguish it from justification by faith.

6. We also believe, teach, and confess that, although the 9 genuinely believing and truly regenerated persons retain much weakness and many shortcomings down to their graves, they still have no reason to doubt either the righteousness which is reckoned to them through faith or the salvation of their souls, but they must regard it as certain that for Christ's sake, on the basis of the promises and the Word of the holy Gospel, they have a gracious God.

7. We believe, teach, and confess that if we would preserve 10 the pure doctrine concerning the righteousness of faith before God, we must give special attention to the "exclusive terms," [8] that is, to those words of the holy apostle Paul which separate the merit of Christ completely from our own works and give all glory to Christ alone. Thus the holy apostle Paul uses such expressions as *"by grace,"* "without merit," "without the law," "without works," "not by works," etc.[9] All these expressions say in effect that we become righteous and are saved "alone by faith" in Christ.

8. We believe, teach, and confess that the contrition that pre- 11 cedes justification and the good works that follow it do not belong in the article of justification before God. Nevertheless, we should not imagine a kind of faith in this connection that could coexist and co-persist with a wicked intention to sin and to act contrary to one's conscience. On the contrary, after a person has been justified by faith, a true living faith becomes "active through love" (Gal. 5:6). Thus good works always follow justifying faith and are certainly to be found with it, since such faith is never alone but is always accompanied by love and hope.

ANTITHESES

Rejection of the Contrary Doctrine

Accordingly we reject and condemn all the following errors: 12

1. That Christ is our righteousness only according to the 13 divine nature, etc.

2. That Christ is our righteousness only according to the 14 human nature, etc.

3. That when the righteousness of faith is spoken of in the 15

---

[7] Cf. above, Apology, IV, 72, 78, 117, 161, 250, 313; VII 31.
[8] Latin, *particulas exclusivas.*
[9] Rom. 6:46; 3:20, 21, 24, 28; 11:6; Gal. 2:16; Eph. 2:9; Titus 3:5.

pronouncements of the prophets and apostles, the words "to justify" and "to be justified" do not mean to absolve or to be absolved from sin and to obtain the forgiveness of sins, but mean to be made righteous in fact before God on account of the love and virtue that the Holy Spirit has infused and the works resulting therefrom.

4. That faith does not look alone to Christ's obedience, but 16 also to his divine nature (in so far as it dwells and works within us), and that by such indwelling our sins are covered up.

5. That faith is a kind of trust in the obedience of Christ that 17 can exist and remain in a person though he does not truly repent and gives no evidence of resulting love, but continues to sin against his conscience.

6. That not God himself but only divine gifts dwell in believers. 18

7. That faith saves because by faith there is begun in us the 19 renewal which consists in love toward God and our fellowman.

8. That faith indeed has the most prominent role in justifica- 20 tion, but that also renewal and love belong to our righteousness before God, not indeed as if it were the primary cause of our righteousness, but that nevertheless our righteousness before God is incomplete and imperfect without such love and renewal.

9. That believers are justified before God and saved both by 21 the righteousness of Christ reckoned to them and by the incipient new obedience, or in part by the reckoning to them of Christ's righteousness and in part by our incipient new obedience.

10. That the promise of grace becomes our own by faith in 22 the heart and by the confession of the lips, along with other virtues.

11. That faith does not justify without good works, in such a 23 way that good works are necessary for righteousness and that unless they are present a person cannot be justified.

IV. GOOD WORKS

THE CHIEF ISSUE IN THE CONTROVERSY CONCERNING GOOD WORKS

1. Two controversies have arisen in some churches concern- 1 ing the doctrine of good works:

The first division among some theologians was occasioned 2 when one party asserted that good works are necessary to salvation; that it is impossible to be saved without good works; and that no one has ever been saved without good works. The other party asserted that good works are detrimental to salvation.[1]

2. The second controversy arose among certain theologians 3

---

[1] George Major and others represented the first party, Nicholas von Amsdorf the second.

concerning the use of the words "necessary" and "free." The one party contended that we should not use the word "necessary" when speaking of the new obedience, since it does not flow from necessity or coercion but from a spontaneous spirit. The other party held with reference to the word "necessary" that the new obedience is not a matter of our choice but that regenerated persons are bound to render such obedience.

At first this was merely a semantic issue. Later on, a real 4 controversy developed. The one party contended that the law should not be preached at all to Christians but that people should be admonished to do good works solely on the basis of the Gospel. This the other party denied.

AFFIRMATIVE THESES
The Pure Doctrine of the Christian Church in this Controversy

In order to explain this controversy from the ground up and 5 to resolve it, this is our doctrine, faith, and confession:

1. That good works, like fruits of a good tree, certainly and 6 indubitably follow genuine faith—if it is a living and not a dead faith.

2. We believe, teach, and confess that good works should be 7 completely excluded from a discussion of the article of man's salvation as well as from the article of our justification before God. The Apostle affirms in clear terms, "So also David declares that salvation pertains only to the man to whom God reckons righteousness apart from works,[2] saying, 'Blessed are those whose iniquities are forgiven, and whose sins are covered' " (Rom. 4:6-8). And again, "For by grace you have been saved through faith; and this is not your own doing, it is the gift of God—not because of works, lest any man should boast" (Eph. 2:8, 9).

3. We believe, teach, and confess further that all men, but 8 especially those who are regenerated and renewed by the Holy Spirit, are obligated to do good works.

4. In this sense the words "necessary," "ought," and "must" 9 are correctly and in a Christian way applied to the regenerated and are in no way contrary to the pattern of sound words and terminology.

5. However, when applied to the regenerated the words "neces- 10 sity" and "necessary" are to be understood as involving not coercion but the due obedience which genuine believers, in so far as they are reborn, render not by coercion or compulsion of the law but from a spontaneous spirit because they are "no longer under the law but under grace."[3]

6. Therefore we also believe, teach, and confess that the 11

---

[2] Literal translation.
[3] Rom. 6:14; 7:6; 8:14.

statement, "The regenerated do good works from a free spirit," should not be understood as though it were left to the regenerated person's option whether to do or not to do good and that he might keep his faith even if he deliberately were to persist in sin.

7. This, however, should be understood exactly as our Lord and | 2 the apostles themselves explain it, as applying only to the liberated spirit which does good works not from a fear of punishment, like a slave, but out of a love of righteousness, like a child (Rom. 8:15).

8. However, in the elect children of God this spontaneity is | 3 not perfect, but they are still encumbered with much weakness, as St. Paul complains of himself in Rom. 7:14-25 and Gal. 5:17.

9. Nevertheless, for Christ's sake the Lord does not reckon | 4 this weakness against his elect, as it is written, "There is therefore now no condemnation for those who are in Christ Jesus" (Rom. 8:1).

10. We also believe, teach, and confess that not our works | 5 but only the Holy Spirit, working through faith, preserves faith and salvation in us. The good works are testimonies of the Holy Spirit's presence and indwelling.

FALSE ANTITHESES

1. Accordingly we reject and condemn spoken and written | 6 formulations which teach that good works are necessary to salvation; likewise, that no one has ever been saved without good works; likewise, that it is impossible to be saved without good works.

2. We also reject and condemn as offensive and as subversive | 7 of Christian discipline that bald statement that good works are detrimental to salvation.[4]

Especially in these last times, it is just as necessary to exhort | 8 people to Christian discipline and good works, and to remind them how necessary it is that they exercise themselves in good works as an evidence of their faith and their gratitude toward God, as it is to warn against mingling good works in the article of justification. Such an Epicurean dream concerning faith can damn people as much as a papistic and Pharisaic confidence in one's own works and merit.

3. We also reject and condemn the teaching that faith and the | 9 indwelling of the Holy Spirit are not lost through malicious sin, but that the holy ones and the elect retain the Holy Spirit even though they fall into adultery and other sins and persist in them.

V. LAW AND GOSPEL

THE CHIEF QUESTION AT ISSUE IN THIS CONTROVERSY

The question has been, Is the preaching of the Holy Gospel | strictly speaking only a preaching of grace which proclaims the for-

[4] The position of Nicholas von Amsdorf; see above, IV, 2.

giveness of sins, or is it also a preaching of repentance and reproof that condemns unbelief, since unbelief is condemned not in the law but wholly through the Gospel?

Affirmative Theses
The Pure Doctrine of God's Word

1. We believe, teach, and confess that the distinction between 2 law and Gospel is an especially glorious light that is to be maintained with great diligence in the church so that, according to St. Paul's admonition, the Word of God may be divided rightly.[5]

2. We believe, teach, and confess that, strictly speaking, the 3 law is a divine doctrine which teaches what is right and God-pleasing and which condemns everything that is sinful and contrary to God's will.

3. Therefore everything which condemns sin is and belongs 4 to the proclamation of the law.

4. But the Gospel, strictly speaking, is the kind of doctrine 5 that teaches what a man who has not kept the law and is condemned by it should believe, namely, that Christ has satisfied and paid for all guilt and without man's merit has obtained and won for him forgiveness of sins, the "righteousness that avails before God," [6] and eternal life.

5. The word "Gospel" is not used in a single sense in Holy 6 Scripture, and this was the original occasion of the controversy. Therefore we believe, teach, and confess that when the word "Gospel" means the entire doctrine of Christ which he proclaimed personally in his teaching ministry and which his apostles also set forth (examples of this meaning occur in Mark 1:15 and Acts 20:24), then it is correct to say or write that the Gospel is a proclamation both of repentance and of forgiveness of sins.

6. But when law and Gospel are opposed to each other, as 7 when Moses is spoken of as a teacher of the law in contrast to Christ as a preacher of the Gospel, then we believe, teach, and confess that the Gospel is not a proclamation of contrition and reproof but is, strictly speaking, precisely a comforting and joyful message which does not reprove or terrify but comforts consciences that are frightened by the law, directs them solely to the merit of Christ, and raises them up again by the delightful proclamation of God's grace and favor acquired through the merits of Christ.

7. Now as to the disclosure of sin, as long as men hear only 8 the law and hear nothing about Christ, the veil of Moses[7] covers their

[5] The reference is to a false etymology of the verb which the Revised Standard Version renders "rightly handling" in II Tim. 2:15.
[6] Rom. 1:17; II Cor. 5:21.
[7] II Cor. 3:13-16.

eyes, as a result they fail to learn the true nature of sin from the law, and thus they become either conceited hypocrites, like the Pharisees, or they despair, as Judas did, etc. Therefore Christ takes the law into his own hands and explains it spiritually (Matt. 5:21-48; Rom 7:14). Then "God's wrath is revealed from heaven" over all sinners[8] and men learn how fierce it is. Thus they are directed back to the law, and now they learn from it for the first time the real nature of their sin, an acknowledgment which Moses could never have wrung from them.

Therefore the proclamation of the suffering and death of Christ, 9 the Son of God, is an earnest and terrifying preaching and advertisement of God's wrath which really directs people into the law, after the veil of Moses has been removed for them, so they now know for the first time what great things God demands of us in the law, none of which we could fulfill, and that we should now seek all our righteousness in Christ.

8. Nevertheless, as long as all this—namely, the passion and 10 death of Christ—proclaims God's wrath and terrifies people, it is not, strictly speaking, the preaching of the Gospel but the preaching of Moses and the law, and therefore it is an "alien work" [9] of Christ by which he comes to his proper office—namely, to preach grace, to comfort, to make alive. And this is the preaching of the Gospel, strictly speaking.

ANTITHESIS

Rejected Contrary Doctrine

1. Hence we reject and deem it as false and detrimental when 11 men teach that the Gospel, strictly speaking, is a proclamation of conviction and reproof and not exclusively a proclamation of grace. Thereby the Gospel is again changed into a teaching of the law, the merit of Christ and the Holy Scriptures are obscured, Christians are robbed of their true comfort, and the doors are again opened to the papacy.

VI. THE THIRD FUNCTION OF THE LAW

THE CHIEF QUESTION AT ISSUE IN THIS CONTROVERSY

The law has been given to men for three reasons: (1) to 1 maintain external discipline against unruly and disobedient men, (2) to lead men to a knowledge of their sin, (3) after they are reborn, and although the flesh still inheres in them, to give them on that account a definite rule according to which they should pattern and

---

[8] Rom. 1:18.
[9] Isa. 28:21; see Luther, *WA*, 15:228.

regulate their entire life. It is concerning the third function of the law that a controversy has arisen among a few theologians. The question therefore is whether or not the law is to be urged upon reborn Christians. One party said Yes, the other says No.

The Correct Christian Teaching in this Controversy

1. We believe, teach, and confess that although people who 2 genuinely believe and whom God has truly converted are freed through Christ from the curse and the coercion of the law, they are not on that account without the law; on the contrary, they have been redeemed by the Son of God precisely that they should exercise themselves day and night in the law (Ps. 119:1). In the same way our first parents even before the Fall did not live without the law, for the law of God was written into their hearts when they were created in the image of God.[1]

2. We believe, teach, and confess that the preaching of the 3 law is to be diligently applied not only to unbelievers and the impenitent but also to people who are genuinely believing, truly converted, regenerated, and justified through faith.

3. For although they are indeed reborn and have been renewed 4 in the spirit of their mind, such regeneration and renewal is incomplete in this world. In fact, it has only begun, and in the spirit of their mind the believers are in a constant war against their flesh (that is, their corrupt nature and kind), which clings to them until death.[2] On account of this Old Adam, who inheres in people's intellect, will, and all their powers, it is necessary for the law of God constantly to light their way lest in their merely human devotion they undertake self-decreed and self-chosen acts of serving God. This is further necessary lest the Old Adam go his own self-willed way.[3] He must be coerced against his own will not only by the admonitions and threats of the law, but also by its punishments and plagues, to follow the Spirit and surrender himself a captive. I Cor. 9:27; Rom. 6:12; Gal. 6:14; Ps. 119:1; Heb. 13:21.

4. Concerning the distinction between works of the law and 5 fruits of the Spirit we believe, teach, and confess that works done according to the law are, and are called, works of the law as long as they are extorted from people only under the coercion of punishments and the threat of God's wrath.

5. Fruits of the Spirit, however, are those works which the 6 Spirit of God, who dwells in the believers, works through the re-

---

[1] Gen. 2:16; 3:3.
[2] Gal. 5:17; Rom. 7:21, 23.
[3] Rom. 12:7, 8.

generated, and which the regenerated perform in so far as they are reborn and do them as spontaneously as if they knew of no command, threat, or reward. In this sense the children of God live in the law and walk according to the law of God. In his epistles St. Paul calls it the law of Christ and the law of the mind. Thus God's children are "not under the law, but under grace" (Rom. 7:23; 8:1, 14).

6. Therefore both for penitent and impenitent, for regenerated 7 and unregenerated people the law is and remains one and the same law, namely, the unchangeable will of God. The difference, as far as obedience is concerned, rests exclusively with man, for the unregenerated man—just like the regenerated according to the flesh— does what is demanded of him by the law under coercion and unwillingly. But the believer without any coercion and with a willing spirit, in so far as he is reborn, does what no threat of the law could ever have wrung from him.

ANTITHESIS

1. Accordingly we condemn as dangerous and subversive of 8 Christian discipline and true piety the erroneous teaching that the law is not to be urged, in the manner and measure above described, upon Christians and genuine believers, but only upon unbelievers, non-Christians, and the impenitent.

VII. THE HOLY SUPPER OF CHRIST

The Zwinglian teachers cannot be numbered among the theo- 1 logians identified with the Augsburg Confession since they separated themselves from the latter at the very outset when the Augsburg Confession[4] was being submitted. Nevertheless, they endeavored surreptitiously to insinuate themselves and to disseminate their errors under the name of this Christian Confession, and therefore we have wished to report as far as necessary concerning this controversy also.

THE CHIEF QUESTION AT ISSUE BETWEEN OUR DOCTRINE AND THE SACRAMENTARIAN DOCTRINE IN THIS ARTICLE

The question is, In the Holy Communion are the true body 2 and blood of our Lord Jesus Christ truly and essentially present if they are distributed with the bread and wine and if they are received orally by all those who use the sacrament, be they worthy or unworthy, godly or godless, believers or unbelievers, the believers for

[4] Four southwestern German cities (Strasbourg, Memmingen, Constance, and Lindau) submitted the *Confessio Tetrapolitana* to Charles V. at Augsburg in 1530, and Ulrich Zwingli sent in the *Ratio Fidei* as his personal confession.

life and salvation, the unbelievers for judgment? The Sacramentarians[5] say No; we say Yes.

In order to explicate this controversy, it is necessary to men- 3 tion, first of all, that there are two kinds of Sacramentarians. Some are crass Sacramentarians who set forth in clear German words what they believe in their hearts, namely, that in the Holy Supper only bread and wine are present, distributed, and received orally. Others, 4 however, are subtle Sacramentarians, the most harmful kind, who in part talk our language very plausibly and claim to believe a true presence of the true, essential, and living body and blood of Christ in the Holy Supper but assert that this takes place spiritually by faith. But under this plausible terminology they really retain the former crass opinion that in the Holy Supper nothing but bread and wine are present and received with the mouth.

To them the word "spiritual" means no more than the presence 5 of Christ's spirit, or the power of Christ's absent body, or his merit. They deny that the body of Christ is present in any manner or way, since in their opinion it is confined to the highest heaven above, whither we should ascend with the thoughts of our faith and there, but not in the bread and wine of the Holy Supper, seek the body and blood of Christ.

AFFIRMATIVE THESES

*Confession of the Pure Doctrine of the Holy Supper
Against the Sacramentarians*

1. We believe, teach, and confess that in the Holy Supper 6 the body and blood of Christ are truly and essentially present and are truly distributed and received with the bread and wine.

2. We believe, teach, and confess that the words of the testa- 7 ment of Christ are to be understood in no other way than in their literal sense, and not as though the bread symbolized the absent body and the wine the absent blood of Christ, but that because of the sacramental union they are truly the body and blood of Christ.[6]

3. Concerning the consecration we believe, teach, and confess 8 that no man's work nor the recitation of the minister effect this presence of the body and blood of Christ in the Holy Supper, but it is to be ascribed solely and alone to the almighty power of our Lord Jesus Christ.

4. But at the same time we believe, teach, and confess with 9

---

[5] A term frequently used by Lutherans in the sixteenth century to designate left-wing opponents of their teaching concerning the Lord's Supper.

[6] Many copies of the Dresden edition of 1580 have the word "truly" twice in this sentence. A proofreader's query on the margin of the proof, "if one of them should not be omitted," was inserted in the text proper by a careless compositor; this is the famous *pudendum erratum* which has survived in a few copies of this early edition.

one accord that in the celebration of the Holy Supper the words of Christ's institution should under no circumstances be omitted, but should be spoken publicly, as it is written, "the cup of blessing which we bless" (I Cor. 10:16; 11:23-25). This blessing occurs through the recitation of the words of Christ.

5. The grounds on which we stand in this controversy with the 10 Sacramentarians are those which Dr. Luther proposed in his *Great Confession:*[7]

"The first ground is this article of our Christian faith: Jesus 11 Christ is true, essential, natural, complete God and man in one person, inseparable and undivided.

"The second ground is: "God's right hand is everywhere. 12 Christ, really and truly set at this right hand of God according to his human nature, rules presently and has in his hands and under his feet everything in heaven and on earth. No other human being, no angel, but only Mary's Son, is so set down at the right hand of God, whence he is able to do these things.

"The third ground is that God's Word is not false nor does 13 it lie.

"The fourth ground is that God has and knows various modes 14 of being at a given place, and not only the single mode which the philosophers call *local*[8] or spatial."

6. We believe, teach, and confess that with the bread and 15 wine the body and blood of Christ are received not only spiritually, by faith, but also orally—however, not in a Capernaitic[9] manner, but because of the sacramental union in a supernatural and heavenly manner. The words of Christ teach this clearly when they direct us to take, eat, and drink, all of which took place in the case of the apostles, since it is written, "And they all drank of it" (Mark 14:23). Likewise, St. Paul says, "The bread which we break, is it not a participation in the body of Christ?" (I Cor. 10:16)—that is, whoever eats this bread eats the body of Christ. This has also been the unanimous teaching of the leading Church Fathers, such as Chrysostom, Cyprian, Leo I, Gregory, Ambrose, Augustine.[1]

7. We believe, teach, and confess that not only the genuine 16 believers and those who are worthy but also the unworthy and the

---

[7] *Vom Abendmahl Christi, Bekenntnis,* in *WA,* 26:261-509.

[8] Latin, *localem.* See *WA,* 26:326, 327. "Local" refers to the quality in any substance which restricts it to a definitely fixed and clearly circumscribed space that it does not share with any other substance.

[9] The Sacramentarians charged that as the people in Capernaum interpreted Christ's words in John 6:26, 52 as referring to a physical eating, so the Lutheran doctrine could only mean that the communicants "rend the flesh of Christ with their teeth and digest it as other food." Some even condemned the Lutheran teaching as "cannibalistic."

[1] The references are listed below, Solid Declaration, VII, 37, 66.

unbelievers receive the true body and blood of Christ; but if they are not converted and do not repent, they receive them not to life and salvation but to their judgment and condemnation.

For although they reject Christ as a redeemer, they must   17 accept him even contrary to their will as a strict judge. He is just as much present to exercise and manifest his judgment on unrepentant guests as he is to work life and consolation in the hearts of believing and worthy guests.

8. We believe, teach, and confess that there is only one kind   18 of unworthy guest, namely, those who do not believe. Of such it is written, "He who does not believe is condemned already" (John 3:18). The unworthy use of the holy sacrament increases, magnifies, and aggravates this condemnation (I Cor. 11:27, 29).

9. We believe, teach, and confess that no genuine believer,   19 no matter how weak he may be, as long as he retains a living faith, will receive the Holy Supper to his condemnation, for Christ instituted this Supper particularly for Christians who are weak in faith but repentant, to comfort them and to strengthen their weak faith.

10. We believe, teach, and confess that the entire worthiness   20 of the guests at this heavenly feast is and consists solely and alone in the most holy obedience and complete merit of Christ, which we make our own through genuine faith and of which we are assured through the sacrament. Worthiness consists not at all in our own virtues or in our internal and external preparations.

ANTITHESES

The Contrary and Condemned Doctrine of the Sacramentarians

On the other side, we unanimously reject and condemn all the   21 following errors, which are contrary and contradictory to the doctrine set forth above and to our simple faith and confession about Christ's Supper:

1. The papistic transubstantiation, when it is taught in the   22 papacy that the bread and wine in the Holy Supper lose their substance and natural essence and are thus annihilated, in such a way that they are transmuted into the body of Christ and that only the exterior appearance remains.

2. The papistic sacrifice of the Mass for the sins of the living   23 and the dead.

3. The administration of only one kind of the sacrament to   24 the laity and the withholding of the cup from them, contrary to the clear Word of Christ's testament, so that they are deprived of the blood of Christ.

4. The teaching that the words of Christ's testament are not   25 to be understood or believed in their simple sense, as they read, but

that they are dark sayings whose meaning must first be sought in other passages.

5. That in the holy sacrament the body of Christ is not received   26 orally with the bread, but that with the mouth we receive only bread and wine and that we receive the body of Christ only spiritually by faith.[2]

6. That bread and wine in the Holy Supper are no more   27 than tokens whereby Christians recognize one another.[3]

7. That the bread and wine are only figures, images, and types   28 of the far-distant body and blood of Christ.

8. That the bread and wine are no more than reminders, seals,   29 and pledges to assure us that when our faith ascends into heaven, it there partakes of the body and blood of Christ as truly as we eat and drink bread and wine in the Supper.[4]

9. That the assurance and strengthening of our faith in the   30 Holy Supper is effected solely by the external signs of bread and wine and not by the truly present body and blood of Christ.

10. That in the Holy Supper only the power, operation,   31 and merit of the absent body and blood of Christ are distributed.[5]

11. That the body of Christ is so enclosed in heaven that it   32 can in no way be present at one and the same time in many places, still less in all places, where his Holy Supper is observed.[6]

12. That Christ could not have promised that his body and   33 blood would be essentially present in the Holy Supper, nor could he have kept such a promise, since the nature and properties of his assumed human nature could neither permit nor admit this.

13. That God, even with all his omnipotence, is unable (a   34 dreadful statement!) to cause his body to be essentially present at more than one place at a single given time.[7]

14. That faith, and not the omnipotent words of Christ's   35 testament, effect and cause the presence of the body and blood of Christ in the Holy Supper.

15. That the believers should not seek the body of Christ in   36 the bread and wine of the Holy Supper, but should lift their eyes from the bread to heaven and there seek the body of Christ.[8]

16. That in the Holy Supper unbelieving and impenitent   37

---

[2] View set forth by *Consensus Tigurinus*, Art. IX.

[3] View expressed by Zwingli, *De vera et falsa religione* (*Opera*, III, 145ff.).

[4] View of Calvin on I Cor. 11:23 (*C.R.*, 49:483).

[5] Calvin, *Institutes*, IV, 22, 18.

[6] Calvin, *Consensus Tigurinus*, Art. XXI.

[7] Theodore Beza in *Creophagia*, and Peter Martyr Vermigli in *Dialogus de utraque in Christo natura*, p. 14.

[8] Calvin, *Consensus Tigurinus*, Art. XXI and XXV.

Christians do not receive the body and blood of Christ, but only bread and wine.[9]

17. That the worthiness of the guests at this heavenly meal 38 does not consist only in true faith in Christ, but also depends on people's outward preparation.

18. That genuine believers, who have a genuine and living 39 faith[1] in Christ, can also receive this sacrament to their condemnation because they are still imperfect[2] in their external behavior.

19. That the external visible elements of bread and wine in the 40 holy sacrament should be adored.[3]

20. By the same token we commend to the righteous judg- 41 ment of God all presumptuous, sarcastic, and blasphemous questions and statements, which decency forbids us to recite and which the Sacramentarians advance most blasphemously and offensively in a coarse, carnal, Capernaitic, and abhorrent way concerning the supernatural and celestial mysteries of this sacrament.

21. Accordingly, we herewith condemn without any qualifica- 42 tion the Capernaitic eating of the body of Christ as though one rent Christ's flesh with one's teeth and digested it like other food. The Sacramentarians deliberately insist on crediting us with this doctrine, against the witness of their own consciences over our many protests, in order to make our teaching obnoxious to their hearers. On the contrary, in accord with the simple words of Christ's testament, we hold and believe in a true, though supernatural, eating of Christ's body and drinking of his blood, which we cannot comprehend with our human sense or reason. Here we take our intellect captive in obedience to Christ, as we do in other articles also, and accept this mystery in no other way than by faith and as it is revealed in the Word.

VIII. THE PERSON OF CHRIST

In connection with the controversy on the Holy Supper a disagreement has arisen between the authentic theologians of the Augsburg Confession and the Calvinists (who have misled some other theologians also) concerning the person of Christ, the two natures in Christ, and their properties.

---

[9] The denial of sacramental eating on the part of the unworthy (*manducatio indignorum*) has been a traditional point of divergence between Lutheran and Reformed theology.

[1] The German printed text has *wahrhaftigen, lebendigen, reinen Glauben* (genuine, living, pure faith). According to Chemnitz this was a compositor's mistake, who set *reinen* for *einen,* an error that proofreaders failed to catch. The manuscript copies appear not to have the added word.

[2] Council of Trent, Session XIII, chap. 7.

[3] *Ibid.,* chap. 5, 6.

The Chief Question at Issue in this Controversy

The chief question has been, Because of personal union in the 2 person of Christ, do the divine and human natures, together with their properties, *really* (that is, in deed and truth) share with each other, and how far does this sharing extend?

The Sacramentarians have asserted that in Christ the divine and 3 human natures are personally united in such a way that neither of the two *really* (that is, in deed and in truth) shares in the properties of the other but have in common only the name. They declare boldly that the "personal union makes merely the names common," so that God is called man and a man is called God, but that God really (that is, in deed and in truth) has nothing in common with the humanity and that the humanity really has nothing in common with the deity, its majesty, and its properties. Dr. Luther and his followers have contended for the opposite view against the Sacramentarians.

Affirmative Theses

The Pure Teaching of the Christian Church concerning the Person of Christ

To explain and to settle this controversy according to our 4 Christian faith we teach, believe, and confess the following:

1. That the divine and the human natures are personally united 5 in Christ in such a way that there are not two Christs, one the Son of God and the other the Son of man, but a single individual is both the Son of God and the Son of man (Luke 1:35; Rom. 9:5).

2. We believe, teach, and confess that the divine and the human 6 nature are not fused into one essence and that the one is not changed into the other, but that each retains its essential properties and that they never become the properties of the other nature.

3. The properties of the divine nature are omnipotence, eternity, 7 infinity, and (according to its natural property, by itself) omnipresence, omniscience, etc., which never become properties of the human nature.

4. The attributes of the human nature are to be a corporeal 8 creature, to be flesh and blood, to be finite and circumscribed, to suffer, to die, to ascend and to descend, to move from place to place, to endure hunger, thirst, cold, heat, and the like, which never become the properties of the divine nature.

5. Since both natures are united personally (that is, in one 9 person) we believe, teach, and confess that this personal union is not a combination or connection of such a kind that neither nature has anything in common with the other personally (that is, on account of the personal union), as when two boards are glued together and neither gives anything to or takes anything from the other. On the contrary, here is the highest communion which God truly has with man. Out

of this personal union and the resultant exalted and ineffable sharing there flows everything human that is said or believed about God and everything divine that is said or believed about Christ the man. The ancient Fathers have illustrated this union and sharing of the natures by the analogy of incandescent iron and the union of body and soul in man.[4]

6. Therefore we believe, teach, and confess that God is man   10 and man is God, which could not be the case if the divine and human natures did not have a real and true communion with each other.

For how could the man, Mary's son, truly be called or be God,   11 or the Son of the most high God, if his humanity were not personally and truly united with the Son of God and hence really (that is, in deed and in truth) shared only the name of God with the divine nature?

7. Therefore we believe, teach, and confess that Mary con-   12 ceived and bore not only a plain, ordinary, mere man but the veritable Son of God; for this reason she is rightly called, and truly is, the mother of God.[5]

8. Therefore we also believe, teach, and confess that it was   13 not a plain, ordinary, mere man who for us suffered, died, was buried, descended into hell, rose from the dead, ascended into heaven, and was exalted to the majesty and omnipotent power of God, but a man whose human nature has such a profound and ineffable union and communion with the Son of God that it has become one person with him.

9. Therefore the Son of God has truly suffered for us, but   14 according to the property of the human nature which he assumed into the unity of his divine person and made his own, so that he could suffer and be our high priest for our reconciliation with God, as it is written in I Cor. 2:8, They have "crucified the Lord of glory," and in Acts 20:28, We are purchased with God's own blood.

10. Therefore we believe, teach, and confess that the Son of   15 man according to his human nature is really (that is, in deed and in truth) exalted to the right hand of the omnipotent majesty and power of God, because he was assumed into God when he was conceived by the Holy Spirit in his mother's womb and his human nature was personally united with the Son of the Most High.[6]

11. According to the personal union he always possessed this   16

[4] The references are listed below, Solid Declaration, VIII, 18.

[5] Against the views ascribed to Nestorius it was asserted that Mary is *theotokos*.

[6] Andreae's original draft adds the following: "Accordingly he could not be exalted more highly after his resurrection, since he did not have to wait until after his resurrection to become God, or to have his human nature united personally with the Son of God, but he was God and man as soon as he was conceived in his mother's womb."

majesty. But in the state of his humiliation he dispensed with it and could therefore truly increase in age, wisdom, and favor with God and men, for he did not always disclose this majesty, but only when it pleased him. Finally, after his resurrection he laid aside completely the form of a slave[7] (not the human nature) and was established in the full use, revelation, and manifestation of his divine majesty. Thus he entered into his glory in such a way that now not only as God, but also as man, he knows all things, can do all things, is present to all creatures, and has all things in heaven and on earth and under the earth beneath his feet and in his hands,[8] as he himself testifies, "All authority in heaven and on earth has been given to me," [9] and as St. Paul states, He ascended "far above all the heavens that he might fill all things." [1] He exercises his power everywhere omnipresently, he can do everything, and he knows everything.

12. Therefore he is able and it is easy for him to impart to us   17 his true body and blood which are present in the Holy Supper, *not according to the mode or property of the human nature* but *according to the mode* and property of God's right hand, as Dr. Luther says on the basis of our Christian faith as we teach this to our children.[2] This presence is not mundane or Capernaitic[3] although it is true and essential, as the words of Christ's testament declare, *"This is, is, is my body,"* etc.

Our doctrine, faith, and confession do not divide the person   18 of Christ, as Nestorius did. He denied the genuine sharing of the properties[4] of the two natures in Christ and thus he actually divided the person, as Luther explains it in his treatise *On the Councils.*[5] Nor do we mingle the natures and their properties together in one essence, as Eutyches erroneously taught. Nor do we deny or abolish the human nature in the person of Christ, or change the one nature into the other.[6] Christ is, and remains to all eternity, God and man in one indivisible person. Next to the holy Trinity this is the highest mystery, as the apostle testifies,[7] and the sole foundation of our comfort, life, and salvation.

[7] Phil. 2:7.
[8] John 13:3.
[9] Matt. 28:18.
[1] Eph. 4:10.
[2] *WA,* 26:326ff.; 23:131ff.
[3] See above, Epitome, VII, 15.
[4] Latin, *communicatio idiomatum.*
[5] *Von den Konziliis und Kirchen* (1539), *WA,* 50:584ff.
[6] Calvinists claimed that the Lutheran Christology must lead to one or the other view.
[7] I Tim. 3:16.

ANTITHESES

Contrary False Doctrine concerning the Person of Christ

Accordingly we reject and condemn as contrary to the Word   19
of God and our simple Christian Creed the following erroneous
articles:

1. That in Christ God and man are not one person, but that   20
the Son of God is one person and the Son of man another, as
Nestorius foolishly asserted.

2. That the divine and human natures are mingled into one   21
essence and that the human nature has been changed into the deity,
as Eutyches dreamed.

3. That Christ is not true, natural, and eternal God, as Arius   22
held.

4. That Christ did not have a true human nature with a body   23
and a soul, as Marcion imagined.

5. That personal union achieves only common names and   24
titles.[8]

6. That it is only a verbalism and figure of speech when we   25
say "God is man, man is God," since really (that is, in fact) the deity
has nothing in common with the humanity, nor the humanity with
the deity.[9]

7. That it is a sheer matter of words when we say that the Son   26
of God died for the sins of the world or that the Son of man has
become almighty.[1]

8. That Christ's human nature has become an infinite essence,   27
like the divine nature; that it is omnipresent in the same manner as the
divine nature, because this essential power and property has been
severed from God and communicated to and infused into the human
nature.

9. That the human nature has been raised to the level of, and   28
has become equal to, the divine nature in its substance and essence,
or in its essential properties.

10. That the human nature of Christ is locally extended to every   29
place in heaven and earth (something that is not true of the divine
nature either).

11. That because of the property of the human nature it is   30
impossible for Christ to be present at the same time at more than one
place, still less to be present with his body everywhere.[2]

12. That only the mere humanity suffered for us and redeemed   31

---

[8] Zwingli's *alloeosis;* see below, Solid Declaration, VIII, 21, 39-43.
[9] Cf. below, Solid Declaration, VIII, 63.
[1] Cf. Zwingli, *Opera,* II, 1, 449.
[2] Cf. Calvin, *Institutes,* IV, 17, 26, 29.

us, and that in the passion the Son of God had no communion with the human nature in fact, as though it did not concern him at all.

13. That Christ is present with us on earth in the Word, in the 32 sacraments, and in all our necessities only according to his deity, and that this presence does not at all concern his human nature; and that after Christ had redeemed us by his suffering and death he no longer has anything to do with us according to his human nature.

14. That the Son of God who assumed the human nature, after 33 he laid aside the form of a slave, does not perform all works of his omnipotence in, through, and with his human nature, but only a few and only at the place where the human nature is locally present.

15. That in spite of Christ's express assertion, "All authority 34 in heaven and on earth has been given to me," [3] and St. Paul's statement, "In him dwells the whole fullness of deity bodily" (Col. 2:9), Christ, according to the human nature, is wholly incapable of omnipotence and other properties of the divine nature.

16. That according to his human nature Christ has indeed been 35 given greater power in heaven and on earth, that is, greater and more than all angels and other creatures; but that he does not share in the omnipotence of God, and that this has not been given to him. Therefore they invent an intermediate power (that is, a power that lies somewhere between God's omnipotence and the power of other creatures) and they imagine that through the exaltation the human nature of Christ received a power which is less than God's omnipotence but greater than the power of other creatures.

17. That according to his human spirit Christ has certain limi- 36 tations as to how much he is supposed to know, and that he does not know more than is fitting and necessary to perform his office as judge.

18. That Christ does not as yet have a perfect knowledge of 37 God and all his works, though it is written that in him are hid "all the treasures of wisdom and knowledge" (Col. 2:3).

19. That according to his human spirit Christ cannot know 38 what has existed from eternity, what is happening everywhere today, nor what will yet take place in eternity.

20. They misinterpret and blasphemously pervert the words 39 of Christ, "All authority has been given to me" (Matt. 28:18), to mean that in the resurrection and his ascension all power in heaven and on earth was restored or again returned to Christ according to the divine nature, as though in the state of humiliation he had laid it aside and forsaken it even according to his deity. This doctrine not only perverts the words of Christ's testament, but it opens a way for the accursed Arian heresy. Hence, unless we refute these errors on the firm basis of the divine Word and our simple Christian faith,

[3] Matt. 28:18.

we shall finally have Christ's eternal deity denied and we shall lose Christ altogether along with our salvation.

IX. CHRIST'S DESCENT INTO HELL

THE CHIEF QUESTION AT ISSUE IN THE CONTROVERSY ABOUT THIS ARTICLE

There has been a dispute among some theologians of the Augs- 1 burg Confession concerning this article also. The questions raised were: When and how, according to our simple Christian Creed, did Christ go to hell? Did it happen before or after his death? Did it occur only according to the soul, or only according to the deity, or according to body and soul, spiritually or corporeally? Does this article belong to Christ's suffering or to his glorious victory and triumph?

This article, like the preceding one, cannot be comprehended with 2 our senses and reason, but must be apprehended by faith alone. Therefore it is our unanimous opinion that we should not engage in disputations concerning this article, but believe and teach it in all sim- 3 plicity, as Dr. Luther of blessed memory taught in his sermon preached at Torgau in the year 1533, where he explains this article in a wholly Christian manner, eliminates all unnecessary questions, and admonishes all Christians to simplicity of faith.[4]

It is enough to know that Christ went to hell, destroyed hell for 4 all believers, and has redeemed them from the power of death, of the devil, and of the eternal damnation of the hellish jaws. How this took place is something that we should postpone until the other world, where there will be revealed to us not only this point, but many others as well, which our blind reason cannot comprehend in this life but which we simply accept.

X. CHURCH USAGES, CALLED ADIAPHORA OR INDIFFERENT THINGS

There has also been a division among theologians of the Augs- 1 burg Confession concerning those ceremonies or church usages which are neither commanded nor forbidden in the Word of God but have been introduced into the church in the interest of good order and the general welfare.

THE CHIEF QUESTION AT ISSUE IN THIS CONTROVERSY

The chief question has been, In times of persecution, when a 2 confession is called for, and when the enemies of the Gospel have not

4 *WA*, 37:62-67.

come to an agreement with us in doctrine, may we with an inviolate conscience yield to their pressure and demands, reintroduce some ceremonies that have fallen into disuse and that in themselves are indifferent things and are neither commanded nor forbidden by God, and thus come to an understanding with them in such ceremonies and indifferent things? One party said Yes to this, the other party said No.

AFFIRMATIVE THESES
The Correct, True Doctrine and Confession about this Article

1. To settle this controversy we believe, teach, and confess 3 unanimously that the ceremonies or church usages which are neither commanded nor forbidden in the Word of God, but which have been introduced solely for the sake of good order and the general welfare, are in and for themselves no divine worship or even a part of it. "In vain do they worship me, teaching as doctrines the precepts of men" (Matt. 15:9).

2. We believe, teach, and confess that the community of God[5] 4 in every locality and every age has authority to change such ceremonies according to circumstances, as it may be most profitable and edifying to the community of God.

3. But in this matter all frivolity and offenses are to be avoided, 5 and particularly the weak in faith are to be spared (I Cor. 8:9-13; Rom. 14:13ff.).

4. We believe, teach, and confess that in time of persecution, 6 when a clear-cut confession of faith is demanded of us, we dare not yield to the enemies in such indifferent things, as the apostle Paul writes, "For freedom Christ has set us free; stand fast therefore, and do not submit again to a yoke of slavery" (Gal. 5:11). "Do not be mismated with unbelievers, for what fellowship has light with darkness?" (II Cor. 6:14). "To them we did not yield submission even for a moment, that the truth of the Gospel might be preserved for you" (Gal. 2:5). In such a case it is no longer a question of indifferent things, but a matter which has to do with the truth of the Gospel, Christian liberty, and the sanctioning of public idolatry, as well as preventing offense to the weak in faith. In all these things we have no concessions to make, but we should witness an unequivocal confession and suffer in consequence what God sends us and what he lets the enemies inflict on us.

5. We believe, teach, and confess that no church should con- 7 demn another because it has fewer or more external ceremonies not commanded by God, as long as there is mutual agreement in doctrine and in all its articles as well as in the right use of the holy sacraments,

⁵ The Latin reads "churches of God."

according to the familiar axiom, "Disagreement in fasting does not destroy agreement in faith." [6]

ANTITHESES

False Doctrine concerning this Article

Therefore we reject and condemn as false and contrary to God's 8 Word the following teachings:

1. That human precepts and institutions in the church are to 9 be regarded as in themselves divine worship or a part of it.

2. When such ceremonies, precepts, and institutions are forcibly 10 imposed upon the community of God as necessary things, in violation of the Christian liberty which it has in external matters.

3. That in a time of persecution and when a public confession 11 is required, one may make concessions to or come to an understanding with the enemies of the holy Gospel (which serve to impair the truth) in such indifferent things and ceremonies.

4. When such external ceremonies and indifferent things are 12 abolished in a way which suggests that the community of God does not have the liberty to avail itself of one or more such ceremonies according to its circumstances and as it may be most beneficial to the church.

XI. GOD'S ETERNAL FOREKNOWLEDGE AND ELECTION

No public dissension has developed among the theologians of 1 the Augsburg Confession concerning this article. But since it is such a comforting article when it is correctly treated, we have included an explanation of it in this document, lest at some future date offensive dissension concerning it might be introduced into the church.

AFFIRMATIVE

Pure and True Doctrine concerning this Article

1. To start with, the distinction between the foreknowledge 2 and the eternal election of God is to be diligently noted.

2. God's foreknowledge is nothing else than that God knows 3 all things before they happen, as it is written, "There is a God in heaven who reveals mysteries, and he has made known to King Nebuchadnezzar what will be in the latter days" (Daniel 2:28).

3. This foreknowledge extends alike over good people and evil 4 people. But it is not a cause of evil or of sin which compels anyone to do something wrong; the original source of this is the devil and

---

[6] Irenaeus, "Epistle to Victor," quoted in Eusebius, *Church History*, V, 24, 13.

man's wicked and perverse will. Neither is it the cause of man's perdition; for this man himself is responsible. God's foreknowledge merely controls the evil and imposes a limit on its duration, so that in spite of its intrinsic wickedness it must minister to the salvation of his elect.

4. Predestination or the eternal election of God, however, is 5 concerned only with the pious children of God in whom he is well pleased. It is a cause of their salvation, for he alone brings it about and ordains everything that belongs to it. Our salvation is so firmly established upon it that the "gates of Hades cannot prevail against" it (John 10:28; Matt. 16:18).

5. We are not to investigate this predestination in the secret 6 counsel of God, but it is to be looked for in his Word, where he has revealed it.

6. The Word of God, however, leads us to Christ, who is "the 7 book of life" [7] in which all who are to be eternally saved are inscribed and elected, as it is written, "He chose us in him before the foundation of the world" (Eph. 1:4).

7. This Christ calls all sinners to himself and promises them 8 refreshment. He earnestly desires that all men should come to him and let themselves be helped.[8] To these he offers himself in his Word, and it is his will that they hear the Word and do not stop their ears or despise it. In addition he promises the power and operation of the Holy Spirit and divine assistance for steadfastness and eternal life.

8. Therefore we should not judge this election of ours to eternal 9 life on the basis either of reason or of God's law. This would either lead us into a reckless, dissolute, Epicurean life, or drive men to despair and waken dangerous thoughts in their hearts. As long as men follow their reason, they can hardly escape such reflections as this: "If God has elected me to salvation I cannot be damned, do as I will." Or, "If I am not elected to eternal life, whatever good I do is of no avail; everything is in vain in that case."

9. We must learn about Christ from the holy Gospel alone, 10 which clearly testifies that "God has consigned all men to disobedience, that he may have mercy upon all" (Rom. 11:32), and that he does not want anyone to perish (Ezek. 33:11; 18:23), but that everyone should repent and believe on the Lord Jesus Christ (I Tim. 2:6; I John 2:2).

10. The doctrine of God's eternal election is profitable and 11 comforting to the person who concerns himself with the revealed will of God and observes the order which St. Paul follows in the

[7] Phil. 4:3; Rev. 3:5; 20:15.
[8] Matt. 9:2, 9, 13, 22, 29, 35, 37; 11:28.

Epistle to the Romans. He there directs men first to repent, to acknowledge their sins, to believe in Christ, and to obey God, and only then does he speak of the mystery of God's eternal election.

11. The passage, "Many are called, but few are chosen," [9]   12 does not mean that God does not desire to save everyone. The cause of condemnation is that men either do not hear the Word of God at all but willfully despise it, harden their ears and their hearts, and thus bar the ordinary way for the Holy Spirit, so that he cannot work in them; or, if they do hear the Word, they cast it to the wind and pay no attention to it. The fault does not lie in God or his election, but in their own wickedness.[1]

12. The Christian is to concern himself with the doctrine of   13 the eternal election of God only in so far as it is revealed in the Word of God, which shows us Christ as the "book of life." Through the proclamation of the holy Gospel, Christ opens and reveals this book for us, as it is written, "Those he predestined, he also called." [2] In Christ we should seek the eternal election of the Father, who has decreed in his eternal counsel that he would save no one except those who acknowledge his Son, Christ, and truly believe on him. The Christian should banish all other opinions since they do not proceed from God but are inspired by the evil foe in an attempt to weaken for us or to rob us entirely of the glorious comfort which this salutary doctrine gives us, namely, that we know that we have been elected to eternal life out of pure grace in Christ without any merit of our own, and that no one can pluck us out of his hand. God assures us of this gracious election not only in mere words, but also with his oath, and has sealed it with his holy sacraments, of which we can remind ourselves and with which we can comfort ourselves in our greatest temptations and thus extinguish the flaming darts of the devil.

13. Furthermore, we are to put forth every effort to live ac-   14 cording to the will of God and "to confirm our call," as St. Peter says.[3] Especially are we to abide by the revealed Word which cannot and will not deceive us.

14. This brief exposition of the doctrine of God's eternal elec-   15 tion gives God his glory entirely and completely, because he out of pure grace alone, without any merit of ours, saves us "according to the purpose" of his will.[4] Nor will this doctrine ever give anyone occasion either to despair or to lead a reckless and godless life.

[9] Matt. 20:16.
[1] II Pet. 2:2ff.; Luke 11:49, 52; Heb. 12:25.
[2] Rom. 8:30.
[3] II Pet. 1:10.
[4] Eph. 1:11.

ANTITHESES

False Doctrine concerning this Article

Accordingly we believe and maintain that if anybody teaches 16 the doctrine of the gracious election of God to eternal life in such a way that disconsolate Christians can find no comfort in this doctrine but are driven to doubt and despair, or in such a way that the impenitent are strengthened in their self-will, he is not teaching the doctrine according to the Word and will of God, but in accord with his reason and under the direction of the devil, since everything in Scripture, as St. Paul testifies, was written for our instruction that by steadfastness and by the encouragement of the Scriptures we might have hope. Therefore we reject the following errors:

1. The doctrine that God does not want all men to come to 17 repentance and to believe the Gospel.[5]

2. Furthermore, the doctrine that God is not serious about 18 wanting all men to come to him when he calls us to him.

3. Furthermore, that God does not want everybody to be saved, 19 but that merely by an arbitrary counsel, purpose, and will, without regard for their sin, God has predestined certain people to damnation so that they cannot be saved.[6]

4. Likewise that it is not only the mercy of God and the most 20 holy merit of Christ, but that there is also within us a cause of God's election, on account of which he has elected us to eternal life.

These are all blasphemous and terrible errors, for they rob 21 Christians of all the comfort that they have in the holy Gospel and in the use of the holy sacraments. Hence they should not be tolerated in God's church.

This is a brief and simple explanation of the various articles 22 which for a time the theologians of the Augsburg Confession have been discussing and teaching in mutually contradictory terms. From it, under the guidance of the Word of God and the plain Catechism, every simple Christian can understand what is right and what is wrong, since we have not only set forth the pure doctrine but have also exposed the contrary errors. In this way the offensive controversies that have developed receive a basic settlement.

May the almighty God and Father of our Lord Jesus Christ grant us the grace of his Holy Spirit that we may all be of one heart in him and constantly abide in this Christian and God-pleasing concord. Amen.

---

[5] This is directed against the Calvinistic "special vocation." Cf. Calvin, *Institutes*, III, 21, 5.

[6] The Calvinistic doctrine of the double election was developed most fully by supralapsarian Theodore Beza; cf. Gallic Confession (1561), XII.

XII. OTHER FACTIONS AND SECTS WHICH HAVE NOT COM-
MITTED THEMSELVES TO THE AUGSBURG CONFESSION

In the preceding explanation we have made no mention of the   1
errors held by these factions. But lest as a result of our silence these
errors be attributed to us, we wish here at the end merely to enumerate
the articles in which they err and contradict our repeatedly cited
Christian Creed and Confession.

ERRORS OF THE ANABAPTISTS

The Anabaptists have split into many factions, some of which   2
teach many errors, others teach fewer. But in general they profess
doctrines of a kind that cannot be tolerated either in the church, or
in the body politic and secular administration, or in domestic society.

Errors which Cannot be Tolerated in the Church

1. That Christ did not assume his body and blood from the   3
virgin Mary, but brought them with him from heaven.

2. That Christ is not true God but that he only has more gifts   4
of the Holy Spirit than any other holy person.

3. That our righteousness before God does not consist wholly   5
in the unique merit of Christ, but in renewal and in our own pious
behavior. For the most part this piety is built on one's own individual
self-chosen spirituality, which in fact is nothing else but a new kind
of monkery.

4. That in the sight of God unbaptized children are not sinners   6
but are righteous and innocent, and that as long as they have not
achieved the use of reason they will be saved in this innocence without
Baptism (which according to this view they do not need). They thus
reject the entire doctrine of original sin and everything that pertains
to it.

5. That children are not to be baptized until they have achieved   7
the use of reason and can confess their faith personally.

6. That without and prior to Baptism the children of Christian   8
parents are holy and the children of God by virtue of their birth from
Christian and pious parents. For this reason, too, the Anabaptists
neither think highly of infant Baptism nor encourage it, in spite of
the expressed word of God's promise which extends only to those
who keep his covenant and do not despise it (Gen. 17:4-8; 19-21).

7. That a congregation is not truly Christian if sinners are still   9
found in it.

8. That no one should hear sermons or attend services in those   10
temples where formerly papistic Masses were read and celebrated.

9. That one is to have nothing to do with clergymen who preach   11

the Gospel according to the Augsburg Confession and reprove the preaching and the errors of the Anabaptists; nor should one serve them or work for them in any way, but flee and avoid them as perverters of God's Word.

Intolerable Articles in the Body Politic

1. That government is not a God-pleasing estate in the New 12 Testament.

2. That no Christian can serve or function in any civic office 13 with a good and clear conscience.

3. That as occasion arises no Christian, without violating his 14 conscience, may use an office of the government against wicked people, and that subjects may not call upon the government to use the power that it possesses and that it has received from God for their protection and defense.

4. That a Christian cannot swear an oath with a good con- 15 science nor pay oath-bound feudal homage to his territorial sovereign or liege-lord.

5. That in the New Testament the government cannot with 16 a clear conscience inflict capital punishment upon criminals.

Intolerable Errors which Undermine Domestic Society

1. That a Christian cannot with a good conscience hold or 17 possess private property but is in conscience bound to put it into a common treasury.

2. That a Christian cannot with a good conscience be an inn- 18 keeper, a merchant, or a cutler.

3. That difference of faith is sufficient ground for married/ 19 people to divorce one another, each go his own way, and marry someone else belonging to the same faith.

ERRORS OF THE SCHWENKFELDERS

1. That all who say that Christ according to the flesh is a 20 creature do not have a right understanding of Christ as the reigning king of heaven.

2. That in Christ's glorification his flesh received all the divine 21 properties in such a way that Christ as man is fully equal in rank and essential estates to the Father and to the Word as far as might, power, majesty, and glory are concerned, and that now both natures in Christ possess only one divine essence, property, will, and glory and that the flesh of Christ belongs to the essence of the holy Trinity.

3. That the ministry of the church—the Word preached and 22 heard—is not a means through which God the Holy Spirit teaches people and creates in them the saving knowledge of Christ, conversion, repentance, faith, and new obedience.

4. That the water of Baptism is not a means through which   23
the Lord God seals the adoption of children and effects rebirth.

5. That bread and wine in the Holy Supper are not means   24
through and by which Christ distributes his body and blood.

6. That a Christian who is truly born again through the Spirit   25
of God can perfectly keep and fulfill the law of God in this life.

7. That it is no true Christian congregation in which public   26
expulsion and the orderly process of excommunication do not take
place.

8. That a minister of the church cannot teach profitably or   27
administer true and genuine sacraments unless he is himself truly reborn,
righteous, and pious.

ERROR OF THE NEW ARIANS[7]

That Christ is not a true, essential, natural God, of one divine   28
essence with God the Father and the Holy Spirit, but is merely
adorned with divine majesty and is inferior to and beside God the
Father.

ERROR OF THE ANTI-TRINITARIANS

This is an entirely new sect, unknown in Christendom until   29
now, which believes, teaches, and confesses that there is not only one
eternal, divine essence, belonging to the Father, Son, and Holy Spirit,
but as God the Father, Son, and Holy Spirit are three distinct persons,
so each person has its distinct divine essence, separate from the other
persons of the Deity. Some maintain that each of the three has the
same power, wisdom, majesty, and glory, just like any three individual
people who are essentially separate from one another. Others maintain that the three are unequal in essence and properties and that only
the Father is rightly and truly God.

All these and similar articles, together with their erroneous   30
implications and conclusions, we reject and condemn as wrong, false,
heretical, and contrary to the Word of God, the three Creeds, the
Augsburg Confession, the Apology, the Smalcald Articles, and the
Catechisms of Luther. All pious Christians, of high degree and low,
must guard against these if they dearly love their soul's eternal welfare
and salvation.

In testimony that this is the doctrine, faith, and confession of all   31
of us as we shall give account of it on the Last Day before the righteous
judge, our Lord Jesus Christ, and that we shall neither secretly nor
publicly say or write anything contrary to it but intend by the grace
of God to abide by it, we have advisedly, in true fear and invocation

' Unitarians of the sixteenth century.

of God, subscribed our signatures with our own hands. Done at Bergen, May 29, 1577.

Dr. JAMES ANDREAE subscribed
Dr. NICHOLAS SELNECKER subscribed
Dr. ANDREW MUSCULUS subscribed
Dr. CHRISTOPHER KOERNER subscribed
DAVID CHYTRAEUS
Dr. MARTIN CHEMNITZ

[PART II: SOLID DECLARATION]

A GENERAL, PURE, CORRECT, AND DEFINITIVE RESTATEMENT AND EXPOSITION OF A NUMBER OF ARTICLES OF THE AUGSBURG CONFESSION CONCERNING WHICH THERE HAS BEEN A CONTROVERSY AMONG SOME THEOLOGIANS FOR A TIME, RESOLVED AND SETTLED ACCORDING TO THE WORD OF GOD AND THE SUMMARY FORMULATION OF OUR CHRISTIAN DOCTRINE

By the special grace and mercy of the Almighty, the teaching 1 concerning the chief articles of our Christian faith (which had been hideously obscured by human doctrines and ordinances under the papacy) was once more clearly set forth on the basis of the Word of God and purified by Dr. Luther, of blessed and holy memory, and the popish errors, abuses, and idolatry were condemned. The 2 opponents, however, regarded this pious reformation as a new doctrine and as wholly contrary to the Word of God and Christian institutions, attacked it violently (although unwarrantedly), and raised no end of slanders and insinuations against it. At that time a 3 number of Christian electors,[1] princes, and estates who had then accepted the pure doctrine of the holy Gospel and had allowed their churches to be reformed according to the Word of God, ordered the preparation of a Christian Confession on the basis of God's Word and submitted it to Emperor Charles V at the great Diet of Augsburg in 1530. In this document they gave a clear and unequivocal Christian witness, setting forth the faith and the teaching of the Evangelical

[1] Actually, John of Saxony (1525-1532) was the only elector who signed the Augsburg Confession.

Christian churches concerning the chief articles, especially those which were in controversy between them and the pope's adherents. The adversaries took a jaundiced view of this Confession, but, thank God, it has remained unrefuted and unimpregnable until this day.

Herewith we again whole-heartedly subscribe this Christian and 4 thoroughly scriptural Augsburg Confession, and we abide by the plain, clear, and pure meaning of its words. We consider this Confession a genuinely Christian symbol which all true Christians ought to accept next to the Word of God, just as in ancient times Christian symbols and confessions were formulated in the church of God when great controversies broke out, and orthodox teachers and hearers pledged themselves to these symbols with heart and mouth. Similarly we 5 are determined by the grace of the Almighty to abide until our end by this repeatedly cited Christian Confession as it was delivered to Emperor Charles in 1530. And we do not intend, either in this or in subsequent doctrinal statements, to depart from the aforementioned Confession or to set up a different and new confession.

Although the Christian doctrine set forth in this Confession has 6 remained practically unchallenged—except for the charges of the papists—it can nevertheless not be denied that some theologians did depart from it in several important and significant articles, either because they failed to grasp their true meaning or because they did not abide by them. Some, while boasting of and benefiting from their adherence to the Augsburg Confession, even dared to give a false interpretation to these articles. This caused serious and 7 dangerous schisms in the true Evangelical churches, just as during the very lifetime of the holy apostles frightful errors arose among those who pretended to be Christians and gloried in the doctrine of Christ. Some wanted to become righteous and to be saved by the works of the law (Acts 15:1-5, 10, 24); some denied the resurrection of the dead (I Cor. 15:12); and others even denied that Christ was eternal and true God.[2] The holy apostles were compelled vigorously to denounce all of these in their sermons and in their writings, though they knew that these titanic errors and the subsequent bitter controversies would involve serious offense for both the unbelievers and the weak believers. Similarly at the present time our adversaries, 8 the papists, rejoice over the schisms which have occurred among us, in the unchristian but futile hope that these disagreements will ultimately lead to the ruin of the pure doctrine. The weak in faith, on the other hand, will be scandalized; some will doubt if the pure doctrine can coexist among us with such divisions, while others will not know which of the contending parties they should support. After all, 9

---

[2] Possibly the authors of the Formula had in mind Jude 4:8; II Pet. 2:1-10; Col. 1 and 2; and I Tim. 2:5.

these controversies are not, as some may think, mere misunderstandings or contentions about words, with one party talking past the other, so that the strife reflects a mere semantic problem of little or no consequence. On the contrary, these controversies deal with weighty and important matters, and they are of such a nature that the opinions of the erring party cannot be tolerated in the church of God, much less be excused and defended. For that reason necessity requires 10 that such controverted articles be explained on the basis of God's Word and of approved writings in such a way that anybody with Christian intelligence can see which opinion in the controverted issues agrees with the Word of God and the Christian Augsburg Confession, and so that well-meaning Christians who are really concerned about the truth may know how to guard and protect themselves against the errors and corruptions that have invaded our midst.

THE SUMMARY FORMULATION,[3] BASIS, RULE, AND NORM, INDICATING HOW ALL DOCTRINES SHOULD BE JUDGED IN CONFORMITY WITH THE WORD OF GOD AND ERRORS ARE TO BE EXPLAINED AND DECIDED IN A CHRISTIAN WAY

The primary requirement for basic and permanent concord 1 within the church is a summary formula and pattern, unanimously approved, in which the summarized doctrine commonly confessed by the churches of the pure Christian religion is drawn together out of the Word of God. For this same purpose the ancient church always had its dependable symbols. It based these not on mere private writings, but on such books as had been written, approved, and accepted in the name of those churches which confessed the same doctrine and religion. In the same way we have from our hearts 2 and with our mouths declared in mutual agreement that we shall neither prepare nor accept a different or a new confession of our faith. Rather, we pledge ourselves again to those public and well-known symbols or common confessions which have at all times and in all places been accepted in all the churches of the Augsburg Confession before the outbreak of the several controversies among the adherents of the Augsburg Confession and which were kept and used during that period when people were everywhere and unanimously faithful to the pure doctrine of the Word of God as Dr. Luther of blessed memory had explained it:

1. We pledge ourselves to the prophetic and apostolic writings of 3 the Old and New Testaments as the pure and clear fountain of Israel,

---

[3] The Torgau Book had used the term "body of doctrine" (*corpus doctrinae*) at this point. The Formula was regarded as a new *corpus doctrinae* which would supplant the several territorial doctrinal summaries, notably the Crypto-Calvinist *Corpus doctrinae Misnicum* or *Philippicum*.

which is the only true norm according to which all teachers and teachings are to be judged and evaluated.

2. Since in ancient times the true Christian doctrine as it was 4 correctly and soundly understood was drawn together out of God's Word in brief articles or chapters against the aberrations of heretics, we further pledge allegiance to the three general Creeds,[4] the Apostles'; the Nicene, and the Athanasian, as the glorious confessions of the faith—succinct, Christian, and based upon the Word of God—in which all those heresies which at that time had arisen within the Christian church are clearly and solidly refuted.

3. By a special grace our merciful God has in these last days 5 brought to light the truth of his Word amid the abominable darkness of the papacy through the faithful ministry of that illustrious man of God, Dr. Luther. This doctrine, drawn from and conformed to the Word of God, is summarized in the articles and chapters of the Augsburg Confession against the aberrations of the papacy and of other sects. We therefore declare our adherence to the first, unaltered Augsburg Confession (in the form in which it was set down in writing in the year 1530 and submitted to Emperor Charles V at Augsburg by a number of Christian electors, princes, and estates of the Roman Empire as the common confession of the reformed[5] churches) as our symbol in this epoch, not because this confession was prepared by our theologians but because it is taken from the Word of God and solidly and well grounded therein. This symbol distinguishes our reformed churches from the papacy and from other condemned sects and heresies. We appeal to it just as in the ancient church it was traditional and customary for later synods and Christian bishops and teachers to appeal and confess adherence to the Nicene Creed.

4. After the repeatedly cited Augsburg Confession had been 6 submitted, an extensive Apology was prepared and published in 1531[6] to set forth clearly the true and genuine meaning of the Augsburg Confession, with a view both to presenting the doctrines against the papacy more clearly and effectively and to forestalling the possibility that under the name of the Augsburg Confession someone might surreptitiously undertake to insinuate into the church errors that had already been rejected. We therefore unanimously pledge our adherence to this Apology also, because in it the cited Augsburg Confession is clearly expounded and defended against errors and also because it is

[4] Latin: "those three catholic and general Creeds, possessed of the highest authority."

[5] The general use of "Reformed" as a proper noun to denote Zwinglian-Calvinistic churches is of later origin.

[6] The intention of this qualification is to establish the exclusive authority of the first edition.

supported with clear and irrefutable testimonies from the Holy Scriptures.

5. In the fifth place, we also commit ourselves to the Articles 7 which we prepared in the great assembly of theologians at Smalcald in 1537 and there approved and accepted.[7] We follow the version as it was initially prepared and published for presentation, in the name of the illustrious and most illustrious electors, princes, and estates, before the Council in Mantua (or wherever it would ultimately be held) as an explication of the Augsburg Confession, to which the electors, princes, and estates were resolved by God's grace to remain faithful. In these articles the doctrine of the cited Augsburg Confession is repeated, several articles are further explained on the basis of God's Word, and in addition the grounds and reasons are set forth at necessary length for renouncing the papistic errors and idolatries, for having no communion with the papists, and for neither expecting nor planning to come to an understanding with the pope about these matters.

6. Since these important matters also concern ordinary people 8 and laymen who for their eternal salvation must as Christians know the difference between true and false doctrine, we declare our unanimous adherence to Dr. Luther's Small and Large Catechisms, as he prepared them and incorporated them in his published works,[8] since they have been unanimously sanctioned and accepted and are used publicly in the churches, the schools, and the homes of those churches which adhere to the Augsburg Confession and since they formulate Christian doctrine on the basis of God's Word for ordinary laymen in a most correct and simple, yet sufficiently explicit, form.

The pure churches and schools have everywhere recognized 9 these publicly and generally accepted documents as the sum and pattern of the doctrine which Dr. Luther of blessed memory clearly set forth in his writings on the basis of God's Word and conclusively established against the papacy and other sects. We also wish to be regarded as appealing to further extensive statements in his doctrinal and polemical writings, but in the necessary and Christian terms and manner in which he himself refers to them in the Preface to the Latin edition of his collected works.[9] Here he expressly asserts by way of distinction that the Word of God is and should remain the sole rule and norm of all doctrine, and that no human being's writings dare be put on a par with it, but that everything must be subjected to it.

[7] As Art. X, 20-23, below, clearly shows, this commitment to the Smalcald Articles includes Melanchthon's Treatise on the Power and Primacy of the Pope.

[8] It had been argued by some that modifications had been made in the Small Catechism to accommodate the Zwinglians.

[9] *Opera Latina* (Wittenberg, 1545), Vol I. Cf. *WA*, 54:179-87.

This, of course, does not mean that other good, useful, and pure 10 books, such as interpretations of the Holy Scriptures, refutations of errors, and expositions of doctrinal articles, should be rejected. If they are in accord with the aforementioned pattern of doctrine they are to be accepted and used as helpful expositions and explanations. Our intention was only to have a single, universally accepted, certain, and common form of doctrine which all our Evangelical churches subscribe and from which and according to which, because it is drawn from the Word of God, all other writings are to be approved and accepted, judged and regulated.

The reason why we have embodied the writings above listed— 11 the Augsburg Confession, the Apology, the Smalcald Articles, and Luther's Large and Small Catechisms—in the cited summary of our Christian doctrine[1] is that they have always and everywhere been accepted as the common and universally accepted belief of our churches, that the chief and most illustrious theologians of that time subscribed them, and that all Evangelical churches and schools received them. We have included these confessions also because all were 12 prepared and published before the dissensions arose among the theologians of the Augsburg Confession. They are therefore regarded as impartial, none of the parties in the various controversies can or should reject them, nor can anyone who sincerely adheres to the Augsburg Confession object to these documents but will gladly admit and accept them as witnesses to the truth. No one can blame us 13 if we derive our expositions and decisions in the controverted articles from these writings, for just as we base our position on the Word of God as the eternal truth, so we introduce and cite these writings as a witness to the truth and as exhibiting the unanimous and correct understanding of our predecessors who remained steadfastly in the pure doctrine.

ANTITHESES IN THE CONTROVERTED ARTICLES

In order to preserve the pure doctrine and to maintain a thor- 14 ough, lasting, and God-pleasing concord within the church, it is essential not only to present the true and wholesome doctrine correctly, but also to accuse the adversaries who teach otherwise (I Tim. 3:9; Titus 1:9; II Tim. 2:24; 3:16). "Faithful shepherds," as Luther states, "must both pasture or feed the lambs and guard against wolves so that they will flee from strange voices and separate the precious from the vile" (John 10:12-16, 27; Jer. 15:19).

On this point we have reached a basic and mutual agreement 15 that we shall at all times make a sharp distinction between needless

[1] The plan to publish all previously adopted symbolical documents together with the prepared Formula of Concord was suggested by several groups.

and unprofitable contentions (which, since they destroy rather than edify, should never be allowed to disturb the church) and necessary controversy (dissension concerning articles of the Creed or the chief parts of our Christian doctrine, when the contrary error must be refuted in order to preserve the truth). It is true that the 16 Christian reader who really delights in the truth of God's Word will find in the previously mentioned writings what he should accept as correct and true in each of the controverted articles of our Christian faith, according to the prophetic and apostolic writings of God's Word, and what he should reject, flee, and avoid as false and wrong. Nevertheless, to insure that the truth may be established the most distinctly and clearly and may be distinguished from all error, and likewise to insure that familiar terminology may not hide and conceal something, we have collectively and severally come to a clear and express mutual agreement concerning the chief and most significant articles which were in controversy at this time. This agreement we have set forth as a certain and public testimony, not only to our contemporaries but also to our posterity, of that which our churches believe and accept with one accord as the correct and abiding answer in the controverted issues, to wit:

1. In the first place, we reject and condemn all heresies and 17 errors which the primitive, ancient, orthodox church rejected and condemned on the certain and solid basis of the holy and divine Scriptures.

2. In the second place, we reject and condemn all the sects and 18 heresies that are rejected in the aforementioned documents.

3. In the third place, since within the past twenty-five years[2] a 19 number of divisions have occurred among some of the theologians of the Augsburg Confession on account of the Interim and for other reasons, we wanted to set forth and explain our faith and confession unequivocally, clearly, and distinctly in theses and antitheses, opposing the true doctrine to the false doctrine, so that the foundation of divine truth might be made apparent in every article and that every incorrect, dubious, suspicious, and condemned doctrine might be exposed, no matter where or in what books it might be found or who may have said it or supported it. We did this so that we might thereby faithfully forewarn everyone against the errors contained here and there in the writings of certain theologians, lest anyone be misled by the high regard in which these theologians were held. This explanation 20 will enable the pious reader, as far as is necessary, to compare our present position with the aforementioned doctrinal writings. Such a

[2] The "twenty-five" years are reckoned from the Augsburg Interim (June 30, 1548) to the *Swabian Concord* (Nov. 29, 1573). Early editions of the Book of Concord (1580) read "thirty."

comparison will show him clearly that there is no contradiction between what we taught and confessed originally and afterward expounded as occasion demanded and what we now repeat in this document, but that it is the same simple, unchanging, constant truth. We do not, as our adversaries charge, veer from one doctrine to another. On the contrary, we want to be found faithful to the commonly accepted Christian meaning of the Augsburg Confession as it was originally submitted. By God's grace we shall continue to abide in it loyally and faithfully against all the aberrations that have arisen.

I. ORIGINAL SIN

.In the first place,[3] there has been dissension among a number of | theologians of the Augsburg Confession about what original sin, strictly understood, is. One side contended that "man's nature and essence are wholly corrupt as a result of the fall of Adam," [4] so that ever since the Fall the nature, substance, and essence of fallen man, at least the foremost and noblest part of his essence (namely, his rational soul in its highest degree and foremost powers) is original sin itself, which has been called "nature-sin" or "person-sin" because it is not a thought, a word, or a deed but the very nature itself out of which, as the root and source, all other sins proceed. For this reason there is now after the Fall allegedly no difference whatsoever between man's nature or essence and original sin.[5] The other party,[6] 2 however, took a contrary view and taught that original sin, strictly speaking, is not man's nature, substance, or essence (that is, man's body or soul), which even after the Fall are and remain God's handiwork and creation in us. They maintained that original sin is something in man's nature, in his body, soul, and all his powers, and that it is an abominable, deep, and inexpressible corruption thereof, in the sense that man lacks the righteousness in which he was originally created, that in spiritual matters he is dead to that which is good and is turned to everything evil, and that, because of this corruption and

---

[3] The "first" does not refer to the chronological sequence of the controversies, but to the order in which the disputed doctrines are presented. An effort was made to conform to the sequence of articles in the Augsburg Confession. The controversy treated in Article I originated in certain statements of Matthias Flacius in his disputation with Victorine Strigel at Weimar in August, 1560.

[4] The opening lines of Lazarus Spengler's hymn, "Durch Adams Fall ist ganz vorderbt menschlich Natur und Wesen."

[5] The spokesmen for this party were Matthias Flacius, Cyriacus Spangenberg, Christian Irenaeus, Francis Coelestinus, and others.

[6] The "other party" was led by Martin Chemnitz, Joachim Mörlin, Tilemann Heshusius, John Wigand, and Nicholas Selnecker, supported by Simon Musaeus, James Andreae, and others.

this inborn sin which inheres in his nature, all actual sins flow out of his heart. Hence, they say, we must preserve the distinction between the nature and essence of fallen man (that is, between his body and soul, which are God's handiwork and creatures in us even after the Fall) and original sin (which is a work of the devil by which man's nature has become corrupted).

This controversy concerning original sin is not a useless conten- 3 tion about words. On the contrary, when it is presented clearly from and according to the Word of God and is purged of all Pelagian and Manichaean errors, then (as the Apology declares) we are led to understand better and to magnify more fully Christ's benefits, his precious merits, and the Holy Spirit's gracious activity. Furthermore, we are extolling God's honor properly when we carefully distinguish his work and creation in man from the devil's work, the corruption of human nature. Hence, in order to explain this controversy 4 in a Christian fashion and according to the Word of God and to preserve the true and correct doctrine concerning original sin, we shall use the aforementioned writings to set forth in short chapters the true doctrine and its opposite in theses and antitheses.

In the first place, it is an established truth that Christians must 5 regard and recognize as sin not only the actual transgression of God's commandments but also, and primarily, the abominable and dreadful inherited disease which has corrupted our entire nature. In fact, we must consider this as the chief sin, the root and fountain of all actual sin.[7] Dr. Luther calls this sin "nature-sin" or "person-sin"[8] in 6 order to indicate that even though a man were to think no evil, speak no evil, or do no evil—which after the Fall of our first parents is of course impossible for human nature in this life—nevertheless man's nature and person would still be sinful. This means that in the sight of God original sin, like a spiritual leprosy, has thoroughly and entirely poisoned and corrupted human nature. On account of this corruption and because of the fall of the first man, our nature or person is under the accusation and condemnation of the law of God, so that we are "by nature the children of wrath,"[9] of death, and of damnation unless we are redeemed from this state through Christ's merit.

[7] The term "actual" is used in its basic Latin meaning, an "acted" sin in contrast to so-called inherited or inherent sin. The German translates the Latin *peccatum actuale* with *wirkliche* or *gewirkte Sünde*, the adjective being derived from the verb *wirken* (related to the English word "work").

[8] In a sermon on the Gospel for the Feast of Our Lord's Circumcision Luther stated, in diametrical opposition to every form of Pelagianism, that there would be no "acted sin" without this "nature-sin," and that for our redemption from this nature-sin Christ was circumcised—not on the hand or the tongue—to indicate that sin does not consist in words and deeds but in our depraved nature. *WA*, 51:354; 46:39, 40.

 Eph. 2:3.

In the second place, it is also a clearly established truth, as 7 Article XIX of the Augsburg Confession teaches, that God is not the creator, author, or cause of sin. Through Satan's scheme, "by one man sin (which is the work of the devil) entered into the world" (Rom. 5:12; I John 3:8). And even today, in this corruption, God does not create and make sin in us. Rather, along with the nature which God still creates and makes at the present time, original sin is transmitted through our carnal conception and birth out of sinful seed from our father and mother.[1]

Thirdly, reason does not know and understand the true nature 8 of this inherited damage. As the Smalcald Articles point out,[2] it is something that has to be learned and believed from the revelation of the Scriptures. The Apology[3] summarizes the matter under these heads:

1. That this inherited damage is the reason why all of us, 9 because of the disobedience of Adam and Eve, are in God's disfavor and are children of wrath by nature, as St. Paul says (Rom. 5:12).

2. Furthermore, that original sin is the complete lack or ab- 10 sence of the original concreated righteousness of paradise or of the image of God according to which man was originally created in truth, holiness, and righteousness, together with a disability and ineptitude as far as the things of God are concerned. As the Latin words put it, "The description of original sin denies to unrenewed human nature the gifts and the power, or the faculty and the concrete acts, to begin and to effect anything in spiritual matters." [4]

3. That original sin in human nature is not only a total lack of 11 good in spiritual, divine things, but that at the same time it replaces the lost image of God in man with a deep, wicked, abominable, bottomless, inscrutable, and inexpressible corruption of his entire nature in all its powers, especially of the highest and foremost powers of the soul in mind, heart, and will. As a result, since the Fall man inherits an inborn wicked stamp, an interior uncleanness of the heart and evil desires and inclinations. By nature every one of us inherits from Adam a heart, sensation, and mind-set which, in its highest powers and the light of reason, is by nature diametrically opposed to God and his highest commands and is actually enmity against God, especially in divine and spiritual matters. True, in natural and external 12 things which are subject to reason man still possesses a measure of reason, power, and ability, although greatly weakened since the inherited malady has so poisoned and tainted them that they amount to nothing in the sight of God.

---

[1] On traducianism vs. creationism, see below, 28.
[2] Smalcald Articles, Part III, Art. I.
[3] Apology, II, 2-50.
[4] Cf. Apology, II, 2, 3.

4. The punishment and penalty of original sin which God im-   13
poses upon Adam's children and upon original sin is death, eternal
damnation,[5] together with other bodily, spiritual, temporal, and eternal
misery, the tyranny and dominion of the devil, so that human nature
is subject to the devil's dominion, abandoned to his power, and held
captive in his servitude. He misleads many influential and wise men
of the world with terrible errors and heresies, strikes them with other
kinds of blindness, and drives them headlong into all sorts of vice.

5. This inherited damage is so great and terrible that in bap-   14
tized believers it can be covered up and forgiven before God only
for the Lord Christ's sake. Likewise, only the Holy Spirit's regeneration and renovation can heal man's nature, which original sin has
perverted and corrupted. Of course, this process is only begun in this
life, not to be completed until the life yonder.

These points, which we have given in summary form, are   15
explained in greater detail in the aforementioned Confessions of our
Christian doctrine.

It is incumbent upon us to maintain and preserve this doctrine   16
in such a way that we fall neither into Pelagian nor into Manichaean
errors. For this reason we shall briefly enumerate the contrary doctrines which are rejected and condemned in our churches.

1. First, in opposition to both old and new Pelagians, we   17
condemn and reject as false the opinion and doctrine that original sin
is only an obligation resulting from someone else's action without any
corruption of our own nature.[6]

2. Again, that the sinful wicked desires are not sin but con-   18
created and essential attributes of man's nature.[7]

3. Or that the above-mentioned lack and damage allegedly are   19
not really and truly such a sin in the sight of God that apart from
Christ every person on that account is necessarily a child of wrath
and of damnation and is in the kingdom and under the dominion
of Satan.

4. We likewise reject and condemn the following and related   20
Pelagian errors: That human nature even after the Fall is incorrupt
and, especially, that in spiritual matters it is good, pure, and in its
natural powers perfect.

5. Or that original sin is only a simple, insignificant, external   21

---

[5] The critique of the Prussian theologians requested that eternal damnation
be especially mentioned "so that people would know that original sin merits
not only temporal but also eternal death and condemnation."

[6] Cf. Peter Lombard (*Sentences*, II, dist. 30, c. 6) and others. For a
refutation see Martin Chemnitz, *Examen Concilii Tridentini*, ed. Preuss
(Berlin, 1861), p. 100.

[7] Cf. Council of Trent, Session V, Decree on original sin, chap. 5; Ulrich
Zwingli, *Fidei ratio* (1530).

spot or blemish, merely splashed on, or a corruption only of certain accidental elements in human nature, in spite of which and beneath which human nature has and retains its goodness and powers also in spiritual matters.[8]

6. Or that original sin is not a deprivation or absence of man's   22 spiritual good powers, but only an external impediment to them, just as garlic juice smeared on a magnet does not destroy the magnet's natural power but only impedes it;[9] or that the spots spoken of can easily be washed off, like a smudge of dirt from one's face or paint from the wall.

7. Likewise, we also reject and condemn those who teach that,   23 though man's nature has been greatly weakened and corrupted through the Fall, it has nevertheless not entirely lost all the goodness that belongs to spiritual and divine matters, or that the situation is not the way the hymn which we sing in our churches describes it, "Through Adam's fall man's nature and being are wholly corrupted," but that human nature has of and from man's natural birth something that is good—even though in only a small, limited, and poor degree— such as the faculty, aptitude, skill, or ability to initiate and effect something in spiritual matters or to cooperate therein.[1] We shall   24 give our exposition concerning the external, temporal, and civil affairs which are subject to human reason in the next article.

We condemn and reject these and similar false doctrines be-   25 cause God's Word teaches that man's corrupted nature can of and by itself do no good thing in spiritual, divine matters, not even the least thing (such as, for example, producing a good thought). Worse than that, in the sight of God it can by and of itself do nothing but sin (Gen. 6:5; 8:21).

1. On the other hand, this doctrine must also be protected   26 against any Manichaean aberrations. For that reason the following and similar errors are rejected: That now, since the Fall, human nature is initially created perfect and pure, and that afterward Satan infuses and blends original sin (as something essential) into man's nature, as when poison is blended with water.[2]

Although in the case of Adam and Eve man's nature was   27 originally created pure, good, and holy, sin did not invade their nature in such a way that Satan created or made something essentially

[8] Matthias Flacius (*Clavis Scripturae*, II, 481), among others, charged Victorine Strigel with this view.

[9] This is directed again against Victorine Strigel, who had employed this analogy in the Weimar Disputation.

[1] This is directed in part against Strigel and Philip Melanchthon (*C.R.*, XXI, 658, 659).

[2] Heshusius charged Flacius with this teaching.

evil and blended this with their nature, as the Manichaeans imagined in their enthusiasm. The fact is, that Satan misled Adam and Eve through the Fall, and that by God's judgment and verdict man lost the concreated righteousness as a punishment. This deprivation and lack, this corruption and wounding which Satan brought about, this loss has so perverted and corrupted human nature (as was indicated above) that all men, conceived and born in the natural way from a father and a mother, now inherit a nature with the same lack and corruption. For since the Fall human nature is not at first created 28 pure and holy and is corrupted only subsequently through original sin, but in the first moment of our conception the seed from which man is formed is sinful and corrupted.[3] Hence original sin is not something which exists independently within or apart from man's corrupted nature, just as it is not itself the proper essence, body, or soul of man or man himself. Nor are original sin and the human nature that 29 has been thereby corrupted to be distinguished from each other in such a way that man's nature is allegedly pure, holy, righteous, and incorrupt in the sight of God, and only the original sin which dwells in it is evil.

2. We also condemn the error which Augustine attributes to 30 the Manichaeans,[4] that it is not the corrupted man himself who sins because of his inborn original sin but a strange and foreign something within man, so that God by his law does not accuse and condemn man's nature, corrupted by sin, but only the original sin. As stated in a foregoing thesis when we discussed the correct doctrine of original sin, the whole nature of every human being born in the natural way from a father and a mother is corrupted and perverted by original sin in body and in soul, in all its powers from beginning to end, down to the ultimate part involving and affecting the goodness, truth, holiness, and righteousness imparted at creation to our nature in paradise. This does not mean that human nature has been totally destroyed, or has been transformed into some other substance essentially different from our nature and accordingly not coessential with us.

Because of this corruption the law accuses and condemns man's 31 entire corrupted nature unless the sin is forgiven for Christ's sake.

The law, however, accuses and condemns our nature, not be- 32 cause we are human beings created by God but because we are sinful and evil; not because and in so far as our nature and essence are the work, the product, and the creature of God even after the Fall but because and in so far as our nature has been poisoned and corrupted

---

[3] This statement has often been interpreted to support the view that the theology of the Formula of Concord leans toward traducianism.

[4] Augustine, *Confessions,* V, 10, 18; *Exposition of Psalm 140:9,* and generally throughout his writings against the Manichaeans and Pelagians.

by sin.

Although, in Luther's words,[5] original sin, like a spiritual 33 poison and leprosy, has so poisoned and corrupted man's whole nature that within the corrupted nature we are not able to point out and expose the nature by itself and original sin by itself as two manifestly separate things, nevertheless our corrupted nature or the essence of corrupted man, our body and soul or man himself created by God (within which original sin, by which the nature, essence, or total man is corrupted, dwells) are not identical with original sin (which dwells in man's nature or essence and corrupts it). Just as in a case of external leprosy the body which is leprous and the leprosy on or in the body are not one and the same thing, so, if one wishes to speak strictly, one must maintain a distinction between (a) our nature as it is created and preserved by God and in which sin dwells and (b) original sin itself which dwells in the nature. According to the Holy Scriptures we must and can consider, discuss, and believe these two as distinct from each other.

The chief articles of our Christian faith constrain and compel 34 us to maintain such a distinction. In the first place, in the article of creation Scripture testifies not only that God created human nature before the Fall, but also that after the Fall human nature is God's creature and handiwork (Deut. 32:6; Isa. 45:11; 54:9; 64:8; Acts 17: 25, 26; Rev. 4:11). Job says: "Thy hands fashioned and made 35 me together round about, and thou dost destroy me? Remember that thou hast made me of clay, and wilt thou turn me to dust again? Didst thou not pour me out like milk and curdle me like cheese? Thou didst clothe me with skin and flesh, and knit me together with bones and sinews. Thou hast granted me life and steadfast love; and thy care has preserved my spirit" (Job, 10:8-12). David says: "I 36 will praise thee, for I am wonderfully made.[6] Wonderful are thy works! Thou knowest me right well; my frame was not hidden from thee when I was being made in secret, intricately wrought in the depths of the earth. Thy eyes behold my uniformed substance; in thy book were written, every one of them, the days that were formed for me, when as yet there was none of them" (Ps. 139:14-16). And in Ecclesiastes we read, "And the dust returns to the earth 37 as it was, and the spirit returns to God who gave it" (Eccl. 12:7).

These passages indicate clearly that even after the Fall God is 38 man's creator who creates body and soul for him. Therefore the corrupted man cannot be identified unqualifiedly with sin itself, for in that case God would be the creator of sin. In the exposition of the First Article of the Creed in the Small Catechism we confess, "I believe

---

[5] *WA*, 36:682; 44:472, 489, 506, etc.
[6] Literal rendering.

that God has created *me* and all that exists, that he has given me and still sustains my body and soul, eyes, ears, and all my members, my reason and all my senses." Similarly we confess in the Large Catechism, "I hold and believe that I am a creature of God; that is, that he has given and constantly sustains my body, soul, and life, my members great and small, all the faculties of my mind, my reason and understanding," etc.[7] It is of course true that this creature and handiwork of God has been miserably corrupted by sin, for the dough out of which God forms and makes man has been corrupted and perverted in Adam and is transmitted to us in this condition. At 39 this point all Christian hearts may well ponder God's inexpressible kindness in that he does not immediately cast this corrupted, perverted, and sinful dough into hell-fire, but out of it he makes and fashions our present human nature, which is so miserably corrupted by sin, in order that through his beloved Son he might cleanse it from sin, sanctify it, and save it. This article shows the difference 40 irrefutably and clearly, because original sin does not come from God, nor is God the creator or author of sin. Neither is original sin the creature or handiwork of God; on the contrary, it is the devil's work. If there were no difference whatever between the nature and 41 essence of our body and soul (which are corrupted by original sin) and original sin itself (by which our nature is corrupted), we should be compelled to conclude: Either that, since God is the creator of this our nature, he has created and made original sin, which thus would also become his handiwork and creature; or that, since the devil is the author of sin, Satan is the creator of our nature, our body and soul, which would also necessarily have to be Satan's handiwork or creature if our corrupted nature were unqualifiedly identical with sin itself. Both conclusions are contrary to the first[8] article of our Christian faith.

For that reason and in order to distinguish God's creature and 42 handiwork in man from the devil's work, we declare that it is by God's creation that man has a body and soul; likewise, that it is God's work that man is able to think, to speak, to act, and to do anything, for "in him we live and move and are" (Acts 17:28). But the fact that our nature is corrupted, that our thoughts, words, and deeds are evil, is in its origin the handiwork of Satan, who through sin has in this fashion corrupted God's handiwork in Adam. This corruption has come upon us by inheritance.

Secondly, in the article of our redemption we have the mighty 43 testimony of Scripture that God's Son assumed our nature, though without sin, so that in every respect he was made like us, his brethren,

---

[7] Above, Large Catechism, Pt. II, 13.

[8] The German text has *den Artikel*, the Latin translation has *primo articulo*.

sin alone excepted (Heb. 2:17). Hence all the ancient orthodox teachers held that according to his assumed human nature Christ is of one and the same essence with us, his brethren, because the human nature which he assumed is in its essence and all its essential attributes —sin alone excepted—identical with ours; they also rejected the contrary doctrine as patent heresy. Now, if there were no differ- 44 ence between the nature or essence of corrupted man and original sin, it would have to follow that Christ either did not assume our nature inasmuch as he did not assume sin, or that Christ assumed sin inasmuch as he assumed our nature. Both statements are contrary to the Scriptures. Since, however, God's Son assumed our nature, but not original sin, it is evident that even after the Fall[9] human nature and original sin are not identical with but must be distinguished from each other.

Thirdly, in the article of sanctification we have the testimony 45 of Scripture that God cleanses man from sin, purifies him, and sanctifies him and that Christ has saved his people from their sins. Sin thus cannot be identified with man himself, since God receives man for Christ's sake into his grace but remains the enemy of sin throughout eternity! Hence it is unchristian and abominable to say that original sin is baptized in the name of the holy Trinity, is sanctified and saved, and other similar expressions with which we do not want to scandalize the uninstructed people although they are found in the writings of the modern Manichaeans.[1]

Fourthly, concerning the doctrine of the resurrection Scripture 46 testifies that precisely the substance of this our flesh, but without sin, shall arise, and that in eternal life we shall have and keep precisely this soul, although without sin. If there were no difference what- 47 ever between our corrupted body and soul on the one hand and original sin on the other, then it would follow, contrary to this article of our Christian faith, either that our flesh would not rise on Judgment Day and that in eternal life, instead of this essence of our body and soul, we should have another substance or another soul since we there shall be without sin, or else that sin would be raised and would be and remain in the elect in eternal life.

From this it is evident that we must reject this doctrine with all 48 its implications and conclusions, as when it is said that original sin is the very nature of corrupted man, its substance, its essence, its

---

[9] Chemnitz declared that it was necessary to add the seemingly superfluous "even after the Fall" on account of Spangenberg's extreme position.

[1] Christian Irenaeus, in his *Examen Libri Concordiae*, seems to take this position (Frank, *Die Theologie der Konkordienformel*, I, 101ff.). Flacius did not explicitly teach these extreme views (see, for instance, *Clavis Scripturae*, I, 1299), but contemporaries attributed the "paradox" that "original sin must be baptized in the name of the holy Trinity" to him.

body or soul, so that there is allegedly no distinction whatever between our corrupted nature or substance or being and original sin. The chief articles of our Christian faith show powerfully and mightily why we must maintain a distinction between the nature or substance of man, which is corrupted by sin, and the sin by and through which man is corrupted.

Let this suffice as a simple exposition of the doctrine and the 49 contrary doctrine, the thesis and antithesis, as far as the chief points in this controversy are concerned. We are not discussing it here at length but are treating only the chief points in summary fashion.

With specific reference to vocabulary and phraseology, how- 50 ever, the best and safest procedure is to use and keep the pattern of sound words, as the Holy Scriptures and the above-mentioned books use them in treating this article. In order to avoid all contentions 51 about words, it is necessary to explain carefully and distinctly all equivocal terms, that is, words and formulas that have two or more accepted meanings in common use. Thus in the statement, "God creates man's nature," the word "nature" means man's essence, body, and soul. But in the statement, "It is the serpent's nature to bite and poison," the term "nature" means—as it often does—a disposition or characteristic. It is in this latter sense that Luther writes that sin and sinning are man's disposition and nature.[2]

Strictly speaking, therefore, original sin is the deep corruption 52 of our nature as it is described in the Smalcald Articles. Sometimes, however, the term is applied in a wider sense to include the concrete person or subject (that is, man himself with the body and soul in which sin is and inheres) because through sin man is corrupted, poisoned, and sinful. Thus Luther can say, "Your birth, your nature, your entire essence is sin, that is, sinful and unclean."[3]

Luther himself explains that he uses the terms "nature-sin," 53 "person-sin," "essential sin" to indicate that not only thoughts, words, and deeds are sin but that the entire nature, person, and essence of man is wholly corrupted through original sin to its very foundation.[4]

Concerning the use of the Latin terms *substantia* and *accidens*, 54 we maintain that the assemblies of the uninstructed ought rightly be spared these terms in sermons, since they are not in the common man's vocabulary. But when scholars use the terms among themselves or in

---

[2] In his exposition of Ps. 51:3 (*WA*, 2:728; 18:501) Luther says that the concept "nature of man" varies with the profession of the observer: The lawyer sees man as one in legal difficulty; for the physician man's nature is his impaired health; in the eyes of philosophers man's nature is his reason. The theologian finds the nature and essence of man in his sinfulness.

[3] *WA*, 12-403; 40^{II}:322, 325, 380. Each party had appealed to Luther's usage to justify its use of these equivocal terms.

[4] *WA*, 10^{I,1}:508; 40^{II}:327, 385.

the company of persons to whom these words are not unfamiliar, as did Eusebius, Ambrose, and especially Augustine,[5] as well as many other prominent doctors of the church, under the necessity of explaining this doctrine against heretics, they use them in the sense of a perfect dichotomy (that is, a division without a middle term), so that every existing thing must either be a substance (that is, a self-subsisting essence) or an accident (that is, an accidental thing that is not self-subsistent but that subsists in another self-subsistent essence and can be distinguished from it).[6] This dichotomy was also used by Cyril and Basil.

It is one of the unquestioned and irrefutable axioms in theology   55 that every substance or self-subsisting essence, in as far as it is a substance, is either God himself or a product and creature of God. Thus in many of his writings against the Manichaeans, Augustine, in accord with all dependable teachers, deliberately and seriously condemned and rejected the statement, "Original sin is the nature or essence of man." On this basis all scholars and intelligent people have always held that whatever does not subsist by itself and is not a part of another self-subsisting essence, but is present in another thing mutably, is not a substance (that is, something self-subsistent) but an accident (that is, something accidental). Augustine therefore   56 constantly speaks in this fashion: Original sin is not man's nature itself, but an accidental defect and damage in the nature. In the same way, prior to this controversy, the theologians in our schools and churches, following the rules of logic, used the same terminology freely and without incurring suspicion, and for that reason without ever being corrected either by Dr. Luther or by any other dependable teacher of our pure Evangelical churches.

Since it is irrefutably true, attested and demonstrated by the   57 testimonies of the church's teachers, and never questioned by any really intelligent person that every existing thing is either a substance or an accident (that is, either a self-subsisting essence or something accidental thereto), if anyone were to ask if original sin is a substance (that is, a thing that subsists by itself and not in another thing) or if it is an accident (that is, a thing that does not subsist by itself but is in another thing and cannot exist or subsist by itself), then necessity compels us to answer simply and roundly that original sin is not a substance but an accident.

---

[5] Eusebius, *Praep. Evangel.*, VII, 22; Ambrose, *Hexaemeron*, I, 8, 28; *Commentary on Romans* (*ad* 7:18); Augustine, *De natura et gratia*, 19, 21; 20, 22, etc.

[6] This definition was accepted in preference to the "schoolboy" definition favored by Strigel: "An accident is that which is present or absent without the subject's corruption." The word "corruption" in this definition is equivocal.

For this reason the churches of God will never attain abiding 58 peace in this controversy but, on the contrary, the discord will only be increased and deepened if the clergy are in doubt whether or not original sin is a substance or an accident in the right and strict sense of the word. Really to settle this offensive and highly detrimental 59 controversy for our churches and schools therefore requires that every one be rightly instructed in these issues. It involves another 60 question, however, when someone inquires further, What kind of accident is original sin? No philosopher, no papist, no sophist, indeed, no human reason, be it ever so keen, can give the right answer. Holy Scripture alone can lead to a right understanding and give a correct definition of original sin. It testifies that original sin is an inexpressible impairment and such a corruption of human nature that nothing pure nor good has remained in itself and in all its internal and external powers, but that it is altogether corrupted, so that through original sin man is in God's sight spiritually lifeless and with all his powers dead indeed to that which is good.

Thus the term "accident" does not in any way minimize origi- 61 nal sin if the term is explained in harmony with the Word of God, just as Dr. Luther in his Latin exposition of Genesis 3[7] likewise writes earnestly against a minimizing of original sin. The term serves only to set forth the distinction between God's handiwork, our nature in spite of its being corrupted, and the devil's handiwork, the sin which inheres in and most profoundly and inexpressibly corrupts God's handiwork.

In this fashion Luther used both the term "accident" and the 62 term "quality" when treating this issue. But at the time he explained with special seriousness and great zeal and impressed on everyone how abominable and dreadful this quality and accident is, which did not simply sully human nature but corrupted it so deeply that nothing in it remained pure and uncorrupted. In his exposition of Ps. 90:12 he wrote, "Whether we call original sin a quality or a disease, ultimately the worst damage is that we shall not only endure God's eternal wrath and death but that we do not even realize what we are suffering." [8] And again on Gen. 3, "The venom of original sin has poisoned us from the soles of our feet to the crown of our head, inasmuch as this befell a hitherto perfect nature." [9]

II. FREE WILL OR HUMAN POWERS

There has been a controversy concerning free will, not only be- 1 tween the papists and our theologians but also among a number of

[7] *WA*, 42:123-125.
[8] *EA, Opera Exegetica*, XVIII, 320, 321.
[9] *WA*, 42:122.

theologians of the Augsburg Confession. We shall therefore first of all set forth the real issue in this controversy.

Man with his free will can be found and viewed as being in four 2 distinct and dissimilar states.[1] In this controversy the question is not concerning the state of man's will before the Fall, nor what man after the Fall and prior to his conversion can do in external things affecting this temporal life, nor what man can do in spiritual things after the Holy Spirit has regenerated him and rules him, nor what man's free will is going to be like after he will have risen from the dead. The chief issue is solely and alone what the unregenerated man's intellect and will can do in his conversion and regeneration, by those powers of his own that have remained after the Fall, when the Word of God is preached and the grace of God is offered to him. Can man prepare himself for such grace, accept it and give his assent to it? This is the issue which has been argued by some of the theologians of the churches of the Augsburg Confession for quite a few years.[2]

The one party[3] held and taught that, although by his own powers 3 and without the gift of the Holy Spirit man is unable to fulfill the commandment of God, to trust God truly, to fear and to love him, man nevertheless still has so much of his natural powers prior to his conversion that he can to some extent prepare himself for grace and give his assent to it, though weakly, but that without the gift of the Holy Spirit he could accomplish nothing with these powers but would succumb in the conflict.

On the other hand, both ancient and modern enthusiasts[4] have 4 taught that God converts man through the Holy Spirit without any means or created instruments (that is, without the external preaching and hearing of the Word of God) and brings them to the saving understanding of Christ.

Against both of these parties the pure teachers of the Augsburg 5 Confession[5] have taught and argued that through the fall of our first

---

[1] This fourfold distinction follows Peter Lombard, *Sentences,* II, dist. 25, cap. 6. Augustine also distinguishes four steps: before the law, under the law, under grace, in peace (*Exposition of Certain Propositions from Romans 13-18; Handbook for Laurence,* 118).

[2] The outbreak of the Synergistic Controversy is dated either 1556 (when Nicholas von Amsdorf attacked John Pfeffinger) or 1558 (when many controversial publications signaled a concerted attack on Pfeffinger).

[3] The chief exponents of this view were Philip Melanchthon (in the 1535 and later editions of his *Loci,* Article XVIII of the 1540 variata edition of the Augsburg Confession, and elsewhere), John Pfeffinger, Victorine Strigel, Paul Eber, George Major, and the theological faculties of the universities in Wittenberg and Leipzig during the sixties and early seventies.

[4] Among the ancients, the Messalians or Euchites; in the sixteenth century the Lutherans accused Caspar Schwenkfeld and Ulrich Zwingli of this error.

[5] Among them, Matthias Flacius (until 1560), Nicholas von Amsdorf,

parents man is so corrupted that in divine things, concerning our conversion and salvation, he is by nature blind and does not and cannot understand the Word of God when it is preached, but considers it foolishness; nor does he of himself approach God, but he is and remains an enemy of God until by the power of the Holy Spirit, through the Word which is preached and heard, purely out of grace and without any cooperation on his part, he is converted, becomes a believer, is regenerated and renewed.

In order to settle this controversy in a Christian way according 6 to the Word of God, and by God's grace to bring it to an end, we submit the following as our teaching, belief, and confession: We 7 believe that in spiritual and divine things the intellect, heart, and will of unregenerated man cannot by any native or natural powers in any way understand, believe, accept, imagine, will, begin, accomplish, do, effect, or cooperate, but that man is entirely and completely dead and corrupted as far as anything good is concerned. Accordingly, we believe that after the Fall and prior to his conversion not a spark of spiritual powers has remained or exists in man by which he could make himself ready for the grace of God or to accept the proffered grace, nor that he has any capacity for grace by and for himself or can apply himself to it or prepare himself for it, or help, do, effect, or cooperate toward his conversion by his own powers, either altogether or half-way or in the tiniest or smallest degree, "of himself as coming from himself," 6 but is a slave of sin (John 8:34), the captive of the devil who drives him (Eph. 2:2; II Tim. 2:26). Hence according to its perverse disposition and nature the natural free will is mighty and active only in the direction of that which is displeasing and contrary to God.

The following reasons from the Word of God support and 8 confirm the foregoing explanation of and summary reply to the questions and issues stated at the beginning of this article. It is true that they are contrary to proud reason and philosophy, but we also know that "the wisdom of this perverse world is folly with God" 7 and that it is only from the Word of God that judgments on articles of faith are to be pronounced.

In the first place, although man's reason or natural intellect 9 still has a dim spark of the knowledge that there is a God, as well as of the teaching of the law (Rom. 1:19-21, 28, 32), nevertheless, it is so ignorant, blind, and perverse that when even the most gifted and the most educated people on earth read or hear the Gospel of the

Tilemann Heshusius, John Wigand, Simon Musaeus, Joachim Mörlin, and Nicholas Gallus.
6 II Cor. 3:15.
7 I Cor. 3:19.

Son of God and the promise of eternal salvation, they cannot by their own powers perceive this, comprehend it, understand it, or believe and accept it as the truth. On the contrary, the more zealously and diligently they want to comprehend these spiritual things with their reason, the less they understand or believe, and until the Holy Spirit enlightens and teaches them they consider it all mere foolishness and fables. It is as St. Paul says in I Cor. 2:14, "The unspiritual 10 man does not receive the gifts of the Spirit of God, for they are folly to him, and he is not able to understand them because they are spiritually discerned." Again, "Since, in the wisdom of God, the world did not know God through its wisdom, it pleased God through the folly of the Gospel that we preach to save those who believe" (I Cor. 1:21). The others, who are not reborn through God's Spirit, "walk in the futility of their minds; they are darkened in their understanding, alienated from the life of God because of the ignorance that is in them, due to their hardness of heart" (Eph. 4:17, 18). "Seeing they do not see, and hearing they do not hear, nor do they understand. To you it has been given to know the secrets of the kingdom of God" (Matt. 13:13, 11). "No one understands, no one seeks for God. All have turned aside, together they have gone wrong; no one does good, not even one" (Rom. 3:11-12). In this way Scripture calls the natural man simply "darkness" in spiritual and divine things (Eph. 5:8; Acts 26:18). "The light shines in the darkness (that is, in the dark, blind world which neither knows nor regards God) and the darkness has not comprehended it" (John 1:5).[8] Moreover, Scripture teaches that the man who is "in sin" is not only weak and sick, but that he is truly lifeless and "dead" (Eph. 2:1, 5; Col. 2:13).

Just as little as a person who is physically dead can by his own 11 powers prepare or accommodate himself to regain temporal life, so little can a man who is spiritually dead, in sin, prepare or address himself by his own power to obtain spiritual and heavenly righteousness and life, unless the Son of God has liberated him from the death of sin and made him alive.

Thus Scripture denies to the intellect, heart, and will of the 12 natural man every capacity, aptitude, skill, and ability to think anything good or right in spiritual matters, to understand them, to begin them, to will them, to undertake them, to do them, to accomplish or to cooperate in them as of himself. "Not that we are sufficient of ourselves to claim anything as coming from us; our sufficiency is from God" (II Cor. 3:5). "They are all incompetent" (Rom. 3:12).[9] "My Word finds no place in you" (John 8:37). "The darkness comprehended it not" (John 1:5). "The unspiritual man does not receive

[8] Literal rendering.
[9] Literal rendering.

(or, as the Greek word actually has it, does not grasp, take hold of, or apprehend) the gifts of the Spirit of God (that is, he has no capacity for spiritual things) for they are folly to him, and he is not able to understand them" (I Cor. 2:14). Much less will he be able 13 truly to believe the Gospel, give his assent to it, and accept it as truth. For the mind that is set on the flesh (the natural man's understanding) "is hostile to God; it does not submit to God's law, indeed it cannot" (Rom. 8:7). Summing up everything, what the Son of God says 14 remains eternally true, "Apart from me you can do nothing" (John 15:5), and what St. Paul says is also true, "For God is at work in you, both to will and to work for his good pleasure" (Phil. 2:13). This appealing passage is of very great comfort to all devout Christians who perceive and discover a little spark and a longing for the grace of God and eternal salvation in their hearts. They know that God, who has kindled this beginning of true godliness in their heart, wills to continue to support them in their great weakness and to help them to remain in true faith until their end.

Here, too, belong all the petitions of the saints for divine 15 instruction, illumination, and sanctification. By these petitions they indicate that what they ask of God they cannot obtain by their own natural powers. In Ps. 119, for example, David asks God more than ten times to give him understanding so that he might rightly comprehend and learn the divine doctrine.[1] We find similar prayers in St. Paul's letters (Eph. 1:17, 18; Col. 1:9, 11; Phil. 1:9, 10). Of course, such prayers and passages about our ignorance and impotence were not written so that we might become remiss and lazy in reading, hearing, and meditating on the Word of God, but were written in order that above all things we should thank God from our hearts for having liberated us from the darkness of ignorance and the bondage of sin and death through his Son, and for having reborne and illuminated us through Baptism and the Holy Spirit.

And after God, through the Holy Spirit in Baptism, has kindled 16 and wrought a beginning of true knowledge of God and faith, we ought to petition him incessantly that by the same Spirit and grace, through daily exercise in reading his Word and putting it into practice, he would preserve faith and his heavenly gifts in us and strengthen us daily until our end. Unless God himself is our teacher, we cannot study and learn anything pleasing to him and beneficial to us and others.

In the second place, the Word of God testifies that in divine 17 matters the intellect, heart, and will of a natural, unregenerated man is not only totally turned away from God, but is also turned and perverted against God and toward all evil. Again, that man is not

[1] Ps. 119:18, 19, 26, 27, 33, 34, 66, 124, 125, 135, 144, 169.

only weak, impotent, incapable, and dead to good, but also that by
original sin he is so miserably perverted, poisoned, and corrupted
that by disposition and nature he is thoroughly wicked, opposed and
hostile to God, and all too mighty, alive, and active for everything
which is displeasing to God and contrary to his will. "The imagination of man's heart is evil from his youth" (Gen. 8:21). "The heart
of man is deceitful and desperately wicked," that is, is so perverted
and full of misery that no one can fathom it (Jer. 17:9). St. Paul explains this text: "The mind that is set on the flesh is hostile to God"
(Rom. 8:7), and again, "The desires of the flesh are against the Spirit,
and these are opposed to each other" (Gal. 5:17). "We know that the
law is spiritual; but I am carnal, sold under sin" (Rom. 7:14), and
shortly thereafter St. Paul says, "I know that nothing good dwells
within me, that is, in my flesh, for I delight in the law of God in my
inmost self (which the Holy Spirit has regenerated), but I see in my
members another law at war with the law of my mind and making me
captive to the law of sin" (Rom. 7:18, 22, 23).

If the natural or carnal free will of St. Paul and other regener-   18
ated persons wars against the law of God even after their regeneration,
the will of man prior to his conversion will be much more obstinately
opposed and hostile to God's law and will. From this it is evident, as
we have pointed out at greater length in the article on original sin (to
which for the sake of brevity we only refer), that the free will by its
own natural powers can do nothing for man's conversion, righteousness, peace, and salvation, cannot cooperate, and cannot obey, believe,
and give assent when the Holy Spirit offers the grace of God and
salvation through the Gospel. On the contrary, because of the wicked
and obstinate disposition with which he was born, he defiantly resists
God and his will unless the Holy Spirit illuminates and rules him.

For this reason the Holy Scriptures compare the heart of unre-   19
generated man to a hard stone[2] which resists rather than yields in
any way to human touch, or to an unhewn timber,[3] or to a wild,
unbroken animal[4]—not that man since the Fall is no longer a rational
creature, or that he is converted to God without hearing and meditating upon the divine Word, or that in outward or external secular
things he cannot have a conception of good or evil or freely choose to
act or not to act.

It is as Luther says in his comments on Ps. 91:[5] "In secular   20
and external matters affecting the nurture and needs of the body, man

[2] Ezek. 36:26; Jer. 5:3.
[3] Hos. 6:5.
[4] Ps. 73:22.
[5] This is not an exact quotation from Luther's *Exposition of Psalm 90*
but rather a paraphrase, amplified by insights from his comments on Hosea 6

is indeed very clever, intelligent, and extremely busy. In spiritual and divine things, however, which concern the salvation of his soul, man is like a pillar of salt, like Lot's wife, yes, like a log or a stone, like a lifeless statue which uses neither mouth nor eyes nor senses nor heart, inasmuch as man does not see or recognize the dreadful, 21 cruel wrath of God over sin and death but continues in his carnal security—even knowingly and willingly—and thereby runs into a thousand dangers and finally into eternal death and damnation. All pleas, all appeals, all admonitions are in vain. It is useless to threaten, to scold, or even to teach and preach" until the Holy Spirit enlightens, converts, and regenerates man, a destiny for which only man, no 22 stone or log, was created. And while God in his righteous and severe judgment cast away forever the wicked spirits who fell, he has nevertheless willed, out of particular and pure grace, that our poor, fallen, and corrupted human nature should again become and be capable of and a partaker in conversion, in the grace of God, and in eternal life, not by its own natural and efficient aptitude, capacity, or capability—our human nature is in recalcitrant enmity against God—but out of pure grace through the gracious and efficacious working of the Holy Spirit. Dr. Luther calls this a "capacity," [6] which he 23 explains as follows: "When the Fathers defend free will, they affirm a capacity for this freedom in such a way that by divine grace it can be converted to God and become truly free, a condition for which it was originally created." [7] Augustine has written in a similar vein in his second book *Against Julian*.[8]

But before man is illuminated, converted, reborn, renewed, and 24 drawn by the Holy Spirit, he can do nothing in spiritual things of himself and by his own powers. In his own conversion or regeneration he can as little begin, effect, or cooperate in anything as a stone, a

and his sermons in the *Church Postil* on the Epistle for Christmas Day (Tit. 3) and the Gospel for the Third Sunday after the Epiphany (Matt. 8:1-13). A marginal note in the Latin version of 1584 conscientiously lists all these references.

[6] In preparing the final copy, the parenthetic words *non activam sed passivam* were omitted from the German text of the 1580 edition after *capacitatem*. The earlier drafts have the missing words; so does the Latin version of 1584. It is difficult to reproduce the exact meaning of *passiva* in English. The emphasis is on the fact that man does nothing, but that something is done to him. The term itself does not indicate that this passivity is a deliberate, hence a good and meritorious, attitude. It merely means that man is a creature who can again be converted (*subjectum convertendum*). The word *capacitas* is also open to misunderstanding. Some sixteenth century theologians took it to imply a supernatural endowment; the authors of the Formula of Concord, on the other hand, understood it as a natural endowment involved in man's rationality and persisting in man in spite of the Fall and distinguishing man from a log, a stone, or a wild beast.

[7] *WA*, 2:647.

[8] *Contra Julianum*, II, 8, 23-30.

block, or a lump of clay could. Although he can direct the members of his body, can hear the Gospel and meditate on it to a certain degree, and can even talk about it, as Pharisees and hypocrites do, yet he considers it folly and cannot believe it. In this respect he is worse than a block because he is resistant and hostile to the will of God unless the Holy Spirit is active in him and kindles and creates faith and other God-pleasing virtues and obedience in him.

In the third place, Holy Scriptures ascribe conversion, faith in   25 Christ, regeneration, renewal, and everything that belongs to its real beginning and completion in no way to the human powers of the natural free will, be it entirely or one-half or the least and tiniest part, but altogether and alone to the divine operation and the Holy Spirit, as the Apology declares.[9] To some extent reason and free will are   26 able to lead an outwardly virtuous life. But to be born anew, to receive inwardly a new heart, mind, and spirit, is solely the work of the Holy Spirit. He opens the intellect and the heart to understand the Scriptures and to heed the Word, as we read in Luke 24:45, "Then he opened their minds to understand the Scriptures." Likewise, "Lydia heard us; the Lord opened her heart to give heed to what was said by Paul" (Acts 16:14). "For God is at work in you, both to will and to work" (Phil. 2:13). God "gives the repentance" (Acts 5:51; II Tim. 2:25). He works faith, for "It has been granted to you by God that you should believe on him" (Phil. 1:29). "It is the gift of God" (Eph. 2:8). "This is the work of God, that you believe in him whom he has sent" (John 6:29). God gives an understanding heart, seeing eyes, and hearing ears (Deut. 29:4; Matt. 13:15). The Holy Spirit in a Spirit "of regeneration and renewal" (Titus 3:5, 6). God removes the hard, stony heart and bestows a new and tender heart of flesh that we may walk in his commandments (Ezek. 11:19; 36:26; Deut. 30:6; Ps. 51:12); creates us in Christ Jesus for good works (Eph. 2:10); and makes us new creatures (II Cor. 5:17; Gal. 6:15). In short, every good gift comes from God (James 1:17). No one can come to Christ unless the Father draws him (John 6:44). "No one knows the Father except the Son and any one to whom the Son chooses to reveal him" (Matt. 11:27). "No one can say, Jesus is Lord, except by the Holy Spirit" (I Cor. 12:3). "Apart from me," says Christ, "you can do nothing" (John 15:5). "All our sufficiency is from God" (II Cor. 3:6). "What have you that you did not receive? If then you received it, why do you boast as if it were not a gift?" (I Cor. 4:7). It was   27 this passage in particular which, by St. Augustine's own statement, persuaded him to recant his former erroneous opinion as he had set it forth in his treatise *Concerning Predestination*,[1] "The grace of God

---

[9] Apology, XVIII, 7, 8.

consists merely in this, that God in the preaching of the truth reveals his will; but to assent to this Gospel when it is preached is our own work and lies within our own power." And St. Augustine says further on, "I have erred when I said that it lies within our power to believe and to will, but that it is God's work to give the ability to achieve something to those who believe and will."

This doctrine is founded upon the Word of God and accords 28 with the Augsburg Confession and the other writings before mentioned, as the following testimonies will indicate.

Article XX of the Augsburg Confession declares: "People 29 outside of Christ and without faith and the Holy Spirit are in the power of the devil. He drives them into many kinds of manifest sin. For that reason we begin our teaching with faith, through which the Holy Spirit is given, and by pointing out that Christ helps us and protects us against the devil." And shortly afterward the article states that "human reason and power without Christ is much too weak for Satan, who incites men to sin." [2] These statements indicate clearly that the 30 Augsburg Confession does not in any way recognize the freedom of the human will in spiritual matters. On the contrary, it declares that man is the captive of Satan. This being the case, how can man by his own powers turn to the Gospel or to Christ?

The Apology teaches as follows concerning free will:[3] "We also 31 declare that to a certain extent reason has a free will. For in those matters which can be comprehended by reason we have a free will." And shortly thereafter: "Hearts which are without the Holy Spirit are without fear of God, without faith, do not trust or believe that God will hear them, that he forgives their sin, or that he will help them in their troubles; therefore they are without God. An evil tree 32 cannot bear good fruit, and without faith no one can please God. Therefore, though we grant that it lies within our power to perform such external works, we declare that in spiritual things our free will and reason can do nothing." From this we see clearly that the Apology does not ascribe to man's will any ability either to initiate something good or by itself to cooperate.

The Smalcald Articles reject the following errors concerning 33 free will: "That man has a free will to do good and to avoid evil," and shortly thereafter, "That there is no scriptural basis for the position that the Holy Spirit and his grace are necessary for good works." [4] The Smalcald Articles state further: "This repentance continues 34 in Christians until death, for it contends with the sin remaining in the

---

[1] *De praedestinatione,* III, 7.
[2] Quoted according to the 1531 Wittenberg quarto edition.
[3] This is not an exact translation. See above, Apology, XVIII, 4, 5.
[4] See above, Smalcald Articles, Pt. III, Art. I.

flesh throughout life, as St. Paul says in Rom. 7:23, that he wars with the law in his members and that he does so not by his own powers but through the gift of the Holy Spirit which follows upon the forgiveness of sins. This gift purifies us and daily sweeps out the remaining sin and operates to make man truly pure and holy." [5] These words say nothing at all about our will, nor do they say that 35 even in the regenerated the will can do something of itself. On the contrary, they ascribe everything to the gift of the Holy Spirit, who purifies and daily makes man more pious and holy, to the complete exclusion of our own powers.

In his Large Catechism Dr. Luther writes: "I am also a part 36 and member of this Christian church, a shareholder and partaker in it of all the goods which it possesses. The Holy Spirit has brought me thereto and has incorporated me therein through this, that I have heard the Word of God and still hear it, which is the beginning of my entrance into it. For before we became members of the Christian 37 church we belonged entirely to the devil and were completely ignorant of God and Christ. Until the Last Day, the Holy Spirit remains with the holy community of Christendom, through which he heals us and which he uses to proclaim and propagate his Word, whereby he initiates and increases sanctification so that we grow daily and become strong in faith and in its fruits, which he creates." [6] In these words 38 the Catechism makes no mention whatever of our free will or of our contribution, but ascribes everything to the Holy Spirit, namely, that through the ministry he brings us into the church, sanctifies us therein, and effects in us a daily increase in faith and good works. Although 39 the regenerated, while still in this life, reach the point where they desire to do the good and delight in it (indeed, actually do good deeds and grow in sanctification), nevertheless, as mentioned above, we do this not of our own will and power, but the Holy Spirit, as St. Paul says, creates such willing and doing (Phil. 2:13), just as the apostle ascribes this work alone to God when he says, "We are his workmanship, created in Christ Jesus for good works, which God prepared beforehand, that we should walk in them" (Eph. 2:10).

In Dr. Luther's Small Catechism we read: "I believe that by my 40 own reason or strength I cannot believe in Jesus Christ, my Lord, or come to him. But the Holy Spirit has called me through the Gospel, enlightened me with his gifts, and sanctified and preserved me in true faith, just as he calls, gathers, enlightens, and sanctifies the whole Christian church on earth and preserves it in union with Jesus Christ in the one true faith." [7]

---

[5] Smalcald Articles, Pt. III, Art. III.
[6] Large Catechism, Pt. II, Art. III, 51-53.
[7] See above, Small Catechism, Creed, 6.

And in the exposition of the second petition of the Lord's 41
Prayer Luther answers the question, "How does the kingdom of God
come to us?" as follows: "When the heavenly Father gives us his Holy
Spirit so that by his grace we may believe his holy Word and live a
godly life."

These testimonies indicate clearly that we cannot by our own 42
powers come to Christ, but that God must give us his Holy Spirit, who
enlightens, sanctifies, and brings us to Christ in true faith and keeps us
with him. These testimonies make no mention whatever of our will
and cooperation.

We shall also include a statement from Dr. Luther's *Grea*ᵗ 43
Confession Concerning the Holy Supper in which he solemnly declares
that he will not deviate from his doctrine until his death. "I herewith
reject and condemn as sheer error every doctrine which glorifies our
free will, as directly and diametrically contrary to the help and grace
of our Lord Jesus Christ. Outside of Christ death and sin are our
masters and the devil is our god and lord, and there is no power or
ability, no cleverness or reason, with which we can prepare ourselves
for righteousness and life or seek after it. On the contrary, we must
remain the dupes and captives of sin and the property of the devil to do
and to think what pleases them and what is contrary to God and his
commandments." [8]

In these words Dr. Luther, of sacred and holy memory, grants 44
our free will no power of its own to prepare itself and to strive for
righteousness. On the contrary, he states that blind and captive man
performs only the devil's will and what is contrary to the Lord God.
There is therefore no cooperation on the part of our will in man's
conversion. God himself must draw man and give him new birth.
Without this our heart of itself does not once think to turn to the holy
Gospel and to accept it. Dr. Luther discusses this entire matter in his
book *The Bondage of the Will*,[9] in which he writes concerning the
enslaved will of man against Erasmus and carefully and in great detail
presents and demonstrates his case. Again, in his splendid exposition
of Genesis, especially of Chapter 26,[1] he repeats and explicates the
same thought. In these writings he also takes up several special disputed
points which Erasmus raised (for example, the question of "absolute
necessity"), indicates how he intended his statements to be understood,
and defends them diligently and to the best of his ability against all
misunderstanding and misinterpretation. We hereby appeal to these
writings and refer others to them.

[8] *WA*, 26:502, 503.
[9] *De servo arbitrio*, in *WA*, 18:600-727.
[1] *WA*, 43:457-463.

Therefore men teach wrongly when they pretend that unre-   45
generated man still has enough powers to want to accept the Gospel
and to comfort himself with it, and that thus the human will cooperates
in conversion. Such erroneous views are contrary to the Holy Scriptures
of God, the Christian Augsburg Confession, its Apology, the Smalcald
Articles, the Large and Small Catechisms of Luther, and other writings
of this eminent and enlightened theologian.

Both enthusiasts and Epicureans have in an unchristian fashion   46
misused the doctrine of the impotence and the wickedness of our
natural free will, as well as the doctrine that our conversion and
regeneration are exclusively the work of God and not of our own
powers. As a result of their statements many people have become
dissolute and disorderly, lazy and indifferent to such Christian exercises
as prayer, reading, and Christian meditation. They argue that since
they cannot convert themselves by their own natural powers, they will
continue wholly to resist God or wait until God forcibly converts them
against their will. Or they argue that since everything is altogether the
work of the Holy Spirit and they can do nothing of themselves in these
spiritual matters, they will refuse to heed, hear, or read the Word and
the sacraments but will wait until God pours his gifts into them out of
heaven, without means, and they are able actually to feel and to
perceive that God has truly converted them.

On the other hand, despondent hearts may fall into grave   47
anxiety and doubt, and wonder if God has really elected them and
actually purposes through his Holy Spirit to work these gifts of his
within them, since they feel no strong, ardent faith and cordial
obedience but only weakness and anxiety and misery.

We shall now set forth from the Word of God how man is   48
converted to God, how and by what means (namely, the oral Word
and the holy sacraments) the Holy Spirit wills to be efficacious in us
by giving and working true repentance, faith, and new spiritual power
and ability for good in our hearts, and how we are to relate ourselves
to and use these means.

It is not God's will that anyone should be damned but that all   49
men should turn themselves to him and be saved forever. "As I live, I
have no pleasure in the death of the wicked, but that the wicked turn
from his way and live" (Ezek. 33:11). "For God so loved the world
that he gave his only Son, that whoever believes on him should not
perish but have eternal life." [2]

To this end, in his boundless kindness and mercy, God provides   50
for the public proclamation of his divine, eternal law and the wonderful
counsel concerning our redemption, namely, the holy and only saving
Gospel of his eternal Son, our only Saviour and Redeemer, Jesus Christ.

[2] John 3:16.

Thereby he gathers an eternal church for himself out of the human race and works in the hearts of men true repentance and knowledge of their sins and true faith in the Son of God, Jesus Christ. And it is God's will to call men to eternal salvation, to draw them to himself, convert them, beget them anew, and sanctify them through this means and in no other way—namely, through his holy Word (when one hears it preached or reads it)[3] and the sacraments (when they are used according to his Word). "For since, in the wisdom of God, the   51 world did not know God through wisdom, it pleased God through the folly of what we preach to save those who believe" (I Cor. 1:21). "Peter will declare to you a message by which you will be saved, you and your household" (Acts 11:14). "Faith comes from what is heard, and what is heard comes by the preaching of Christ" (Rom. 10:17). "Sanctify them in the truth; thy Word is truth. I pray for those who are to believe in me through their Word" (John 17:17, 20). Therefore the eternal Father calls out from heaven concerning his beloved Son and concerning all who in his name preach repentance and the remission of sins, "Listen to him" (Matt. 17:5).

All who would be saved must hear this preaching, for the   52 preaching and the hearing of God's Word are the Holy Spirit's instrument in, with, and through which he wills to act efficaciously, to convert men to God, and to work in them both to will and to achieve.

The person who is not yet converted to God and regenerated   53 can hear and read this Word externally because, as stated above, even after the Fall man still has something of a free will in these external matters, so that he can go to church, listen to the sermon, or not listen to it.

Through this means (namely, the preaching and the hearing of   54 his Word) God is active, breaks our hearts, and draws man, so that through the preaching of the law man learns to know his sins and the wrath of God and experiences genuine terror, contrition, and sorrow in his heart, and through the preaching of and meditation upon the holy Gospel of the gracious forgiveness of sins in Christ there is kindled in him a spark of faith which accepts the forgiveness of sins for Christ's sake and comforts itself with the promise of the Gospel. And in this way the Holy Spirit, who works all of this, is introduced into the heart.

On the one hand, it is true that both the preacher's planting and   55 watering and the hearer's running and willing would be in vain, and no conversion would follow, if there were not added the power and operation of the Holy Spirit, who through the Word preached and

---

[3] The Torgau Book spoke of hearing, reading, and meditating on the Word, but the reference to meditation was deleted to avoid the implication that an unconverted man could meditate on the Word in a salutary way.

heard illuminates and converts hearts so that men believe this Word and give their assent to it. On the other hand, neither the preacher nor the hearer should question this grace and operation of the Holy Spirit, but should be certain that, when the Word of God is preached, pure and unalloyed according to God's command and will, and when the people diligently and earnestly listen to and meditate on it, God is certainly present with his grace and gives what man is unable by his own powers to take or to give. We should not and cannot pass   56 judgment on the Holy Spirit's presence, operations, and gifts merely on the basis of our feeling, how and when we perceive it in our hearts. On the contrary, because the Holy Spirit's activity often is hidden, and happens under cover of great weakness, we should be certain, because of and on the basis of his promise, that the Word which is heard and preached is an office and work of the Holy Spirit, whereby he assuredly is potent and active in our hearts (II Cor. 2:14ff.).

If a person will not hear preaching or read the Word of God,   57 but despises the Word and the community of God, dies in this condition, and perishes in his sins, he can neither comfort himself with God's eternal election nor obtain his mercy. For Christ, in whom we are elected, offers his grace to all men in the Word and the holy sacraments, earnestly wills that we hear it, and has promised that, where two or three are gathered together in his name and occupy themselves with his holy Word, he is in the midst of them.[4] But if such a person   58 despises the instruments of the Holy Spirit and will not hear, no injustice is done him if the Holy Spirit does not illuminate him but lets him remain in the darkness of his unbelief and be lost, as it is written, "How often would I have gathered your children together as a hen gathers her brood under her wings, and you would not!" (Matt. 23:37).

In this case it is correct to say that man is not a stone or a block.   59 A stone or a block does not resist the person who moves it, neither does it understand or perceive what is being done to it, as a man does who with his will resists the Lord God until he is converted. And it is equally true that prior to his conversion man is still a rational creature with an intellect and will (not, however, an intellect in divine things or a volition that wills what is good and wholesome). Yet he can do nothing whatsoever toward his conversion, as was mentioned above, and in this respect is much worse than a stone or block, for he resists the Word and will of God until God raises him from the death of sin, illuminates him, and renews him.

It is true that God does not coerce[5] anyone to piety, for those   60

---

[4] Matt. 18:20.

[5] At the Weimar Disputation Victorine Strigel maintained that the complete exclusion of human powers in conversion inevitably makes conversion nothing but coercion. He therefore stressed man's mode of acting (*modus*

who always resist the Holy Spirit and oppose and constantly rebel against acknowledged truth, as Stephen describes the obstinate Jews (Acts 7:51), will not be converted. Nevertheless, the Lord God draws the person whom he wills to convert, and draws him in such a way that man's darkened reason becomes an enlightened one and his resisting will becomes an obedient will. This the Scriptures call the creation of a new heart.

For this same reason it is not quite right to say that before his 61 conversion man has a mode of acting[6] in the sense of a mode of doing something good and wholesome in divine matters. Prior to his conversion man is dead in sin (Eph. 2:5); hence there can be in him no power to do something good in divine matters, and he cannot have a mode of acting in divine matters. But if one is discussing the 62 question how God operates in man, it is correct to say that the Lord God indeed has one mode of acting in man as a rational creature and another mode of action to work in irrational creatures or in a stone or block.[7] Nevertheless, one cannot ascribe to man prior to his conversion any mode of acting by which he does anything good in spiritual matters.

But after a man is converted, and thereby enlightened, and his 63 will is renewed, then he wills that which is good, in so far as he is reborn or a new man, and he delights in the law of God according to his inmost self (Rom. 7:22). And immediately he does good, as much and as long as the Holy Spirit motivates him, as St. Paul says, "For all who are led by the Spirit of God are sons of God." [8] This 64 impulse of the Holy Spirit is no coercion or compulsion because the converted man spontaneously does that which is good, as David says, "Your people will offer themselves freely on the day you lead your host." [9] Nevertheless, the words of St. Paul apply also to the regenerated, "For I delight in the law of God in my inmost self, but I see in my members another law at war with the law of my mind and making me captive to the law of sin which dwells in my members." Again, "So then, I of myself serve the law of God with my mind, but with my flesh the law of sin" (Rom. 7:22, 23, 25). And again, "For the desires of the flesh are against the Spirit, and the desires of the Spirit are against the flesh; for these are opposed to each other, to prevent you from doing what you would" (Gal. 5:17).

---

agendi), the rationality that distinguishes him from the beasts, and held that it depends on man's use of this mode of action whether or not he responds to the call of the Gospel.

[6] See preceding note.

[7] This was directed especially against the statement of Nicholas von Amsdorf, who in an over-zealous attempt to demonstrate the enslavement of man's will condemned Strigel's statement "that God works differently with man than with the other creatures."

[8] Rom. 8:14.

[9] Ps. 110:3.

From this it follows that as soon as the Holy Spirit has initiated   65
his work of regeneration and renewal in us through the Word and the
holy sacraments, it is certain that we can and must cooperate by the
power of the Holy Spirit, even though we still do so in great weakness.
Such cooperation does not proceed from our carnal and natural powers,
but from the new powers and gifts which the Holy Spirit has begun in
us in conversion, as St. Paul expressly and earnestly reminds us,   66
"Working together with him, then, we entreat you not to accept the
grace of God in vain." [1] This is to be understood in no other way
than that the converted man does good, as much and as long as God
rules him through his Holy Spirit, guides and leads him, but if God
should withdraw his gracious hand man could not remain in obedience
to God for one moment. But if this were to be understood as though
the converted man cooperates alongside the Holy Spirit, the way two
horses draw a wagon together, such a view could by no means be
conceded without detriment to the divine truth.

There is therefore a great difference between baptized people   67
and unbaptized people because, according to the teaching of St. Paul,
"all who have been baptized have put on Christ" (Gal. 3:27), are
thus truly born again, and now have a liberated will—that is, as Christ
says, they have again been made free.[2] As a result, they not only
hear the Word of God but also are able to assent to it and accept it,
even though it be in great weakness. But since in this life we have   68
received only the first fruits of the Spirit, and regeneration is not as yet
perfect but has only been begun in us, the conflict and warfare of the
flesh against the Spirit continues also in the elect and truly reborn.
Again, there is not only a great difference between Christians, one being
weak and the other strong in the Spirit, but even the individual Christian
in his own life discovers that at one moment he is joyful in the Spirit
and at another moment fearful and terrified, at one time ardent in love,
strong in faith and in hope, and at another time cold and weak.

But if those who have been baptized act contrary to their   69
conscience and permit sin to rule in themselves and thus grieve the
Holy Spirit within them and lose him, they dare not be baptized again,
though they must certainly be converted again, as we have sufficiently
reported above on this matter.

It is, of course, self-evident that in true conversion there must be   70
a change, there must be new activities and emotions in the intellect,

---

[1] II Cor. 6:1. In spite of the objection of a number of theologians, this
exegetically dubious reference was retained, probably because the synergists
had employed this text in the interest of their own theology. Cf. Melanchthon, *Loci* (1543), in *C.R.*, XXI, 761. The Latin edition of 1584 attempted
to redress the situation by supplementing this reference with marginal
quotations from I Cor. 3:9, 16 and 15:20.
[2] John 8:36.

will, and heart, so that the heart learns to know sin, to fear the wrath of God, to turn from sin, to understand and accept the promise of grace in Christ, to have good spiritual thoughts, Christian intentions, and diligence, and to fight against the flesh, etc. For if none of these things takes place or exists, there is no true conversion.

But since the question is asked concerning the efficient cause 71 (that is, who works these things in us, from where man acquires these things, and how he comes by them),[3] our doctrine answers in this way: Man's natural powers cannot contribute anything or help in any way (I Cor. 2:4-12; II Cor. 3:4-12) to bring it about that God in his immeasurable kindness and mercy anticipates[4] us and has his holy Gospel preached to us, through which the Holy Spirit wills to work such conversion and renewal in us, and through the preaching of his Word and our meditation upon it kindles faith and other God-pleasing virtues in us, so that they are gifts and works of the Holy Spirit alone. This doctrine directs us to the means through which the Holy Spirit 72 wills to begin and accomplish all this, reminds us also how he preserves, strengthens, and increases these gifts, and admonishes us not to receive this grace of God in vain but to exercise ourselves in considering what a grievous sin it is to hinder and resist such operations of the Holy Spirit.

On the basis of this thorough presentation of the entire doctrine 73 of free will it is possible to decide the questions that for a considerable number of years have been agitated in the churches of the Augsburg Confession: Whether man before, in, or after his conversion resists the Holy Spirit, and if he does nothing at all, but merely suffers what God accomplishes in him? Whether man in his conversion behaves and is like a block? Whether the Holy Spirit is given to those who resist him? Whether conversion is brought about through coercion, so that God forcibly compels a man to be converted against his will? In the light of the previous discussion one can readily recognize, expose, reject, and condemn such false doctrines and errors as these:

1. The absurdity of the Stoics[5] and Manichaeans[6] in holding 74 that everything must happen as it does; that man acts only under coercion; that even in external works man's will has no freedom or power whatever to achieve a measure of external righteousness and honorable behavior and to avoid manifest sins and vices; or that the

---

[3] This discussion was designed to answer Victorine Strigel's theory of the mode of acting that unregenerate man possesses. In philosophical terms the question centered around the *causa efficiens:* Is God the sole efficient cause of man's conversion, or does man have a *modus agendi?*

[4] The German has *zuvorkommen,* the Latin *praevenire;* the original meaning is preserved in the Augustinian expression "prevenient grace."

[5] The Stoics, especially Seneca and Cicero, held the doctrine of an inexorable fate in the form of a *series implexa causarum.*

[6] See above, Solid Declaration, I, 26.

will of man is coerced into doing such wicked acts as lechery, robbery, and murder.

2. The error of the coarse Pelagians, that by his own natural   75 powers, without the Holy Spirit, the free will can convert itself to God, believe the Gospel, and obey the law of God from the heart, and by this spontaneous obedience earn the forgiveness of sin and eternal life.

3. The error of the papists and scholastics,[7] whose doctrine was   76 slightly more subtle and who taught that by his natural powers man can start out toward that which is good and toward his own conversion, and that thereupon, since man is too weak to complete it, the Holy Spirit comes to the aid of the good work which man began by his natural powers.

4. The teaching of the synergists,[8] who maintain that in   77 spiritual things man is not wholly dead toward that which is good, but only grievously wounded and half-dead. As a result, his free will is too weak to make a beginning and by its own powers to convert itself to God and to obey the law of God from the heart. Nevertheless, after the Holy Spirit has made the beginning and has called us by the Gospel and offers his grace, the forgiveness of sins, and eternal life, then the free will by its own natural powers can meet God and to some degree—though only to a small extent and in a weak way—help and cooperate and prepare itself for the grace of God, embrace and accept it, believe the Gospel, and by its own powers cooperate with the Holy Spirit in the continuation and preservation of this work within us. But we have shown above[9] that such a capacity naturally to prepare   78 oneself for grace does not come from man's own natural powers but solely through the operation of the Holy Spirit.

5. Likewise we reject the teachings of the papists and the   79 monks[1] that man after his conversion can keep the law of God perfectly in this life and by such perfect obedience of the law merit righteousness before God and eternal life.

6. On the other hand, we must condemn with all seriousness   80 and zeal, and in no wise tolerate in the church of God, the enthusiasts who imagine that without means, without the hearing of the divine Word and without the use of the holy sacraments, God draws man to himself, illuminates, justifies, and saves him.

7. Likewise those who imagine that in conversion and regener-   81

[7] Peter Lombard, *Sentences,* II, 26-28; Council of Trent, Session VI, chap. 1 and 5.

[8] There was some objection to the use of the term "synergists," but its retention was justified by the assertion that it referred to a teaching, not specifically to certain persons. The chief proponents of the "synergist" position among the Lutherans were Pfeffinger and Strigel, while Erasmus was generally held to be the real author of sixteenth century synergism.

[9] Solid Declaration, II, 5-15.

[1] Council of Trent, Session VI, canon 32.

ation God creates a new heart and a new man in such a way that the substance and essence of the Old Adam, and especially the rational soul, are completely destroyed and a new substance of the soul is created out of nothing.[2] This error St. Augustine condemns in express words in his commentary on Ps. 25, where he adduces and explains St. Paul's words, "Put off the old man," as follows: "Lest anyone might think that the substance or essence of man must be laid aside, he himself explains what it means to lay off the old man and put on the new man by adding, 'Therefore lay aside lies and speak the truth.' Behold, this is laying off the old man and putting on the new man." [3]

8. We also reject the following formulas if they are used 82 without explanation: that man's will before, in, and after conversion resists the Holy Spirit, and that the Holy Spirit is given to those who resist him. From the foregoing exposition it is clear that when 83 the Holy Spirit's activity produces no change at all for good in the intellect, will, and heart, when man in no way believes the promise and is not prepared by God for grace, but wholly resists the Word, conversion does not and cannot take place. For conversion is that kind of change through the Holy Spirit's activity in the intellect, will, and heart of man whereby man through such working of the Holy Spirit is able to accept the offered grace. All who stubbornly and perseveringly resist the Holy Spirit's activities and impulses, which take place through the Word, do not receive the Holy Spirit but grieve and lose him.

Of course, there remains also in the regenerated a resistance, of 84 which the Scriptures say that the desires of the flesh are against the Spirit, and likewise that the passions of the flesh wage war against the soul, and the law in our members is at war with the law of our mind.[4]

Hence the unregenerated man resists God entirely and is com- 85 pletely the servant of sin. But the regenerated man delights in the law of God according to the inmost self, though he also sees in his members the law of sin at war with the law of his mind. For that reason with the law of his mind he serves the law of God, but with his flesh he serves the law of sin (Rom. 7:22, 23, 25). In this way one can and should explain and teach the correct opinion in this matter thoroughly, clearly, and definitively.

The formulas, "Man's will is not idle in conversion but also does 86 something," and, "God draws, but he draws the person who wills," [5]

---

[2] This was directed against Flacius.

[3] Augustine, *Enarratio in Ps. XXV*, II, 1.

[4] Gal. 5:17; I Pet. 2:11; Rom. 7:23.

[5] These expressions were used by John Chrysostom and Pseudo-Basil and were quoted frequently by Melanchthon; for example, in his *Loci* of 1543 (*C.R.*, XXI, 658). Their inclusion was the subject of vehement discussion among Lutheran theologians.

were introduced to support the view that man's naturally free will cooperates in his conversion, contrary to the article of God's grace. It is evident from the preceding discussion that this position does not conform to the form of sound doctrine but rather opposes it and therefore is rightly to be avoided in the discussion of man's conversion to God. For the conversion of our corrupted will, which is 87 nothing else but a resurrection of the will from spiritual death, is solely and alone the work of God, just as the bodily resurrection of the flesh is to be ascribed to God alone, as was thoroughly demonstrated above from clear passages of Holy Scripture.

It has also been explained in sufficient detail above that in 88 conversion, through the drawing of the Holy Spirit, God makes willing people out of resisting and unwilling people, and that after such conversion man's reborn will is not idle in the daily exercise of repentance but cooperates in all the works that the Holy Spirit does through us.

Again, when Luther says that man behaves in a purely passive 89 way[6] in his conversion (that is, that man does not do anything toward it and that man only suffers that which God works in him), he did not mean that conversion takes place without the preaching and the hearing of the divine Word, nor did he mean that in conversion the Holy Spirit engenders no new impulses and begins no spiritual operations in us. On the contrary, it is his understanding that man of himself or by his natural powers is unable to do anything and cannot assist in any way toward his conversion, and that man's conversion is not only in part, but entirely, the operation, gift, endowment, and work of the Holy Spirit alone, who accomplishes and performs it by his power and might through the Word in the intellect, will, and heart of man. Man is, as it were, the subject which suffers. That is, man does or works nothing; he only suffers—though not as a stone does when a statue is carved out of it, or wax when a seal is impressed into it, for these do not know anything about what is going on or perceive or will anything in connection with it, but in the way and after the manner set forth and explained above.

The young students at our universities have been greatly misled 90 by the doctrine of the three efficient causes of unregenerated man's conversion to God, particularly as to the manner in which these three (the Word of God preached and heard, the Holy Spirit, and man's will)

---

[6] Luther employed the terms *pure passive, mere passive,* and *subjectum convertendum* in their formal scholastic sense solely to show that man does not cooperate in his conversion but is the subject which is converted. *WA,* 18:697. Cf. Martin Chemnitz, *Examen Concilii Tridentini,* I, 5 (ed. Preuss, 144). The enthusiasts appealed to this phrase to support their view that the Holy Spirit converts without means.

concur.[7] From the previous explanation it is evident that conversion to God is solely of God the Holy Spirit, who is the true craftsman who alone works these things, for which he uses the preaching and the hearing of his holy Word as his ordinary means and instrument. The unconverted man's intellect and will are only that which is to be converted, since they are the intellect and will of a man who is spiritually dead, in whom the Holy Spirit works conversion and renewal. Toward this work the will of the person who is to be converted does nothing, but only lets God work in him, until he is converted. Then he cooperates with the Holy Spirit in subsequent good works by doing that which is pleasing to God, in the manner and degree set forth in detail above.

III. THE RIGHTEOUSNESS OF FAITH BEFORE GOD

The third controversy which has arisen among several theologians | of the Augsburg Confession concerns the righteousness of Christ or of faith which God by grace through faith reckons to poor sinners as righteousness.

The one party[8] contended that the righteousness of faith, which 2 St. Paul calls the righteousness of God,[9] is the essential righteousness of God (namely, Christ himself as the true, natural, essential Son of God, who through faith dwells in the elect, impels them to do what is right, and is in this way their righteousness), and that in comparison with this righteousness the sins of all men are like a drop of water compared to the mighty ocean.

On the other side some have held and taught that Christ is our 3 righteousness only according to his human nature.[1]

Against both parties the other teachers of the Augsburg Con- 4 fession[2] held unanimously that Christ is our righteousness, not

---

[7] Melanchthon's *Loci* of 1535 and 1543 (*C.R.*, XXI, 376, 658) refer to "three concurring causes of our good action," and the phrase was at first generally applied to sanctification in the narrow sense. The three causes are called "efficient" in his *Elementa Rhetorices* (*C.R.*, XIII, 426f.). The "Philippists" speak of three concurring efficient causes in man's conversion, although they frequently have the continuing, lifelong conversion of man in mind. The authors of the Formula of Concord conceded three concurring causes in conversion, provided the human will is described as the *causa materialis in qua et circa quam.*

[8] Andrew Osiander.

[9] Rom. 1:22.

[1] Francis Stancaro, who, like Peter Lombard, held that Christ is our mediator only according to his human nature.

[2] Notably Philip Melanchthon, Joachim Mörlin, Justus Menius, Matthias Flacius, Nicholas von Amsdorf, Nicholas Gallus, and Matthew Lauterwaldt. Upon the request of Albert of Prussia for theological opinions on Osiander's *Confession*, a large number of theologians from all parts of the empire submitted criticisms of Osiander's position.

according to the divine nature alone or according to the human nature alone but according to both natures; as God and man he has by his perfect obedience redeemed us from our sins, justified and saved us. Therefore they maintained that the righteousness of faith is forgiveness of sins, reconciliation with God, and the fact that we are adopted as God's children solely on account of the obedience of Christ, which, through faith alone, is reckoned by pure grace to all true believers as righteousness, and that they are absolved from all their unrighteousness because of this obedience.

Several other controversies concerning the article of justification   5 were occasioned and evoked by the Interim and otherwise, which will be set forth below in the antitheses,[3] that is, in the enumeration of those who contradict the pure doctrine.

In the words of the Apology,[4] this article of justification by   6 faith is "the chief article of the entire Christian doctrine," "without which no poor conscience can have any abiding comfort or rightly understand the riches of the grace of Christ." In the same vein Dr. Luther declared: "Where this single article remains pure, Christendom will remain pure, in beautiful harmony, and without any schisms. But where it does not remain pure, it is impossible to repel any error or heretical spirit.[5]

And St. Paul says specifically of this doctrine that a little leaven   7 ferments the whole lump.[6] Therefore he stresses the exclusive terms, that is, the terms by which all human works are excluded, such as "without the law," "without works," "by grace alone."[7] He stresses these terms with such zeal in order to indicate how very important it is that in this article, side by side with the true doctrine, we clearly segregate, expose, and condemn the false contrary doctrine.

Therefore to explain this controversy in a Christian way accord-   8 ing to the Word of God and to settle it by his grace, we affirm our teaching, belief, and confession as follows: Concerning the right-   9 eousness of faith before God we believe, teach, and confess unanimously, in accord with the summary formulation of our Christian faith and confession described above,[8] that a poor sinner is justified before God (that is, he is absolved and declared utterly free from all his sins, and from the verdict of well deserved damnation, and is adopted as a child of God and an heir of eternal life) without any merit or

---

[3] Sections 45-51 of this article.
[4] Apology, German version, IV, 2, 3.
[5] *WA*, 31^1:255.
[6] I Cor. 5:6.
[7] I Cor. 5:6; Gal. 5:9.
[8] That is, the Creeds, Augsburg Confession and its Apology, Smalcald Articles, and the two Catechisms of Luther. See above, Solid Declaration, "The Summary Formulation," 1-9.

worthiness on our part, and without any preceding, present, or subsequent works, by sheer grace, solely through the merit of the total obedience, the bitter passion, the death, and the resurrection of Christ, our Lord, whose obedience is reckoned to us as righteousness. The Holy Spirit offers these treasures to us in the promise of the 10 Gospel, and faith is the only means whereby we can apprehend, accept, apply them to ourselves, and make them our own. Faith is a gift 11 of God whereby we rightly learn to know Christ as our redeemer in the Word of the Gospel and to trust in him, that solely for the sake of his obedience we have forgiveness of sins by grace, are accounted righteous and holy by God the Father, and are saved forever. Thus the following statements of St. Paul are to be considered 12 and taken as synonymous: "We are justified by faith" (Rom 3:28), or "faith is reckoned to us as righteousness" (Rom. 4:5), or when he says that we are justified by the obedience of Christ, our only mediator, or that "one man's act of righteousness leads to acquittal and life for all men" (Rom. 5:18).[9] For faith does not justify because it is so 13 good a work and so God-pleasing a virtue, but because it lays hold on and accepts the merit of Christ in the promise of the holy Gospel. This merit has to be applied to us and to be made our own through faith if we are to be justified thereby. Therefore the righteousness 14 which by grace is reckoned to faith or to the believers is the obedience, the passion, and the resurrection of Christ when he satisfied the law for us and paid for our sin. Since Christ is not only man, but God 15 and man in one undivided person, he was as little under the law— since he is the Lord of the law—as he was obligated to suffer and die for his person.[1] Therefore his obedience consists not only in his suffering and dying, but also in his spontaneous subjection to the law in our stead and his keeping of the law in so perfect a fashion that, reckoning it to us as righteousness, God forgives us our sins, accounts us holy and righteous, and saves us forever on account of this entire obedience which, by doing and suffering, in life and in death, Christ rendered for us to his heavenly Father. This righteousness is 16 offered to us by the Holy Spirit through the Gospel and in the sacraments, and is applied, appropriated, and accepted by faith, so that thus believers have reconciliation with God, forgiveness of sins, the grace of God, adoption, and the inheritance of eternal life.

Accordingly the word "justify" here means to declare righteous 17

---

[9] The German edition of 1580 follows Luther's original translation, "Through one man's righteousness the righteousness of faith has come upon all men." The Latin text, however, following the Greek, has "righteousness of life."

[1] This is evidently directed against George Karg (Parsimonius), who maintained that the "active obedience" of Christ has no vicarious value since the incarnate Christ was obligated to keep the law.

and free from sins and from the eternal punishment of these sins on account of the righteousness of Christ which God reckons to faith (Phil. 3:9). And this is the usual usage and meaning of the word in the Holy Scriptures of the Old and the New Testaments. "He who justifies the wicked and he who condemns the righteous are both alike an abomination to the Lord" (Prov. 17:15). "Woe to those who acquit the godless for a bribe, and deprive the innocent of his right" (Isa. 5:22). "Who shall bring any charge against God's elect? It is God who justifies" (Rom. 8:33), that is, absolves and acquits from sins.

Since the word "regeneration" is sometimes used in place of 18 "justification," it is necessary to explain the term strictly so that the renewal which follows justification by faith will not be confused with justification and so that in their strict senses the two will be differentiated from one another.

The word "regeneration" is used, in the first place, to include 19 both the forgiveness of sins solely for Christ's sake and the subsequent renewal which the Holy Spirit works in those who are justified by faith. But this word is also used in the limited sense of the forgiveness of sins and our adoption as God's children. In this latter sense it is frequently used in the Apology, where the statement is made, "Justification is regeneration," [2] that is, justification before God is regeneration, just as St. Paul uses the terms discriminately when he states, "He saved us by the washing of regeneration and renewing in the Holy Spirit" (Titus 3:5).

Likewise the term "vivification," that is, being made alive, has 20 sometimes been used in the same sense.[3] For when the Holy Spirit has brought a person to faith and has justified him, a regeneration has indeed taken place because he has transformed a child of wrath into a child of God and thus has translated him from death into life, as it is written, "When we were dead through our trespasses, he made us alive together with Christ" (Eph. 2:5). "He who through faith is righteous shall live" (Rom. 1:17). The Apology often uses the term in this sense.[4]

Frequently the word "regeneration" means the sanctification or 21 renewal which follows the righteousness of faith, as Dr. Luther used the term in his book *On the Councils and the Church* and elsewhere.[5]

---

[2] This phrase does not occur in the Apology, although the idea finds expression in Apology, IV, 72, 78, 117, and the phrase is Melanchthonian (Cf. *C.R.*, XXVII, 466, 468, 470).

[3] At the Altenburg Colloquy the Jena theologians objected to the Wittenberg faculty's coordination of *iustificatio* and *vivificatio* as an undiscriminating confusion of terms.

[4] For example, Apology, IV, 250; VII, 31.

[5] *WA*, 50:599; 625ff.

When we teach that through the Holy Spirit's work we are re- 22
born and justified, we do not mean that after regeneration no unrighteousness in essence and life adheres to those who have been
justified and regenerated, but we hold that Christ with his perfect
obedience covers all our sins which throughout this life still inhere in
our nature. Nevertheless, they are regarded as holy and righteous
through faith and for the sake of Christ's obedience, which Christ
rendered to his Father from his birth until his ignominious death on
the cross for us, even though, on account of their corrupted nature,
they are still sinners and remain sinners until they die. Nor, on the
other hand, does this mean that we may or should follow in the ways
of sin, abide and continue therein without repentance, conversion, and
improvement. For genuine contrition must precede. And to those 23
who by sheer grace, for the sake of the only mediator, Christ, through
faith alone, without any work or merit, are justified before God (that
is, accepted into grace) there is given the Holy Spirit, who renews and
sanctifies them and creates within them love toward God and their
fellowman. But because the inchoate renewal remains imperfect in
this life and because sin still dwells in the flesh even in the case of the
regenerated, the righteousness of faith before God consists solely in the
gracious reckoning of Christ's righteousness to us, without the addition
of our works, so that our sins are forgiven and covered up and are not
reckoned to our account (Rom. 4:6-8).

Here, too, if the article of justification is to remain pure, we 24
must give especially diligent heed that we do not mingle or insert that
which precedes faith or follows faith into the article of justification,
as if it were a necessary or component part of this article, since we
cannot talk in one and the same way about conversion and about
justification. For not everything that belongs to conversion is 25
simultaneously also a part of justification. The only essential and
necessary elements of justification are the grace of God, the merit of
Christ, and faith which accepts these in the promise of the Gospel,
whereby the righteousness of Christ is reckoned to us and by which we
obtain the forgiveness of sins, reconciliation with God, adoption, and
the inheritance of eternal life. Thus there cannot be genuine 26
saving faith in those who live without contrition and sorrow and have
a wicked intention to remain and abide in sin, for true contrition
precedes and genuine faith exists only in or with true repentence.

Love is a fruit which certainly and necessarily follows true 27
faith. For if a person does not love, this indicates certainly that he is
not justified but is still in death, or that he has again lost the righteousness of faith, as St. John says (I John 3:14). But when St. Paul says,
"We are justified by faith apart from works" (Rom. 3:28), he indicates
thereby that neither the preceding contrition nor the subsequent works
belong in the article or matter of justification by faith. For good works

do not precede justification; rather they follow it, since a person must first be righteous before he can do good works. Similarly, although 28 renewal and sanctification are a blessing of Christ, the mediator, and a work of the Holy Spirit, it does not belong in the article or matter of justification before God; it rather follows justification, because in this life sanctification is never wholly pure and perfect on account of our corrupted flesh. In his beautiful and exhaustive exposition of the Epistle to the Galatians Dr. Luther well states: "We certainly grant 29 that we must teach about love and good works too. But it must be done at the time and place where it is necessary, namely, when we deal with good works apart from this matter of justification. At this point the main question with which we have to do is not whether a person should also do good works and love, but how a person may be justified before God and be saved. And then we answer with St. Paul that we are justified alone through faith in Christ, and not through the works of the law or through love—not in such a way as if we thereby utterly rejected works and love (as the adversaries falsely slander and accuse us) but so that we may not be diverted (as Satan would very much like) from the main issue with which we here have to do into another extraneous matter which does not belong in this article at all. Therefore, while and as long as we have to do with this article of justification, we reject and condemn works, since the very nature of this article cannot admit any treatment or discussion of works. For this reason we summarily cut off every reference to the law and the works of the law in this conjunction." [6] So far Luther.

Not only on this account but also in order to afford saddened 30 consciences dependable and reliable comfort and to give due honor to the merit of Christ and the grace of God, Scripture teaches that the righteousness of faith before God consists solely in a gracious reconciliation or the forgiveness of sins, which is bestowed upon us by pure grace because of the unique merit of Christ, the mediator, and which we receive only by faith in the promise of the Gospel. Accordingly in justification before God faith trusts neither in contrition nor in love nor in other virtues, but solely in Christ and (in him) in his perfect obedience with which he fulfilled the law of God in our stead and which is reckoned to the believers as righteousness. Neither is 31 contrition nor love nor any other virtue the means and instrument with and through which we could receive and accept the grace of God, the merit of Christ, and the forgiveness of sins offered to us in the promise of the Gospel, but only faith.

It is indeed correct to say that believers who through faith in 32 Christ have been justified possess in this life, first, the reckoned righteousness of faith and, second, also the inchoate righteousness of

* *WA*, 40I:240.

the new obedience or of good works. But these two dare not be confused with one another or introduced simultaneously into the article of justification by faith before God. For because this inchoate righteousness or renewal in us is imperfect and impure in this life on account of the flesh, no one can therewith and thereby stand before the tribunal of God. Only the righteousness of the obedience, passion, and death of Christ which is reckoned to faith can stand before God's tribunal. Hence even after his renewal, after he has done many good works and leads the best kind of life, a person is pleasing and acceptable to God and is adopted to sonship and the inheritance of eternal life only on account of Christ's obedience. At this point St. Paul's 33 statement concerning Abraham is apposite. He says that Abraham was justified before God through faith alone for the sake of the Mediator without the addition of his own works, not only when he was first converted from idolatry and had no good works, but also afterward when the Holy Spirit had renewed and adorned him with many resplendent good works (Rom. 4:3; Gen. 15:6; Heb. 11:8). And St. Paul raises this question (Rom. 4:1): On what did the righteousness of Abraham before God, whereby he had a gracious God and was pleasing and acceptable to him to eternal life, rest? To this he 34 answers: "To one who does not work, but trusts him who justifies the ungodly, his faith is reckoned as righteousness" (Rom. 4:5, 6), and David also says that salvation belongs solely to that person to whom God reckons righteousness without the addition of works. From 35 this it follows that although converted persons and believers possess the beginning of renewal, sanctification, love, virtues, and good works, these should and must not be drawn or mingled into the article of justification before God, in order to preserve the glory due to Christ, the redeemer, and, because our new obedience is imperfect and impure, in order to supply tempted consciences with abiding comfort. And 36 this is St. Paul's intention when in this article he so earnestly and diligently stresses such exclusive terms (that is, terms that exclude works from the article of justification by faith) as "without works," "without the law," "freely," "not of works," all of which exclusive terms may be summarized in the assertion that we are justified before God and saved "through faith alone." This terminology does not exclude works, however, as though there could well be true faith without true contrition, or as though good works should, must, and dare not follow true faith as certain and unquestioned fruits, or as though believers must or dare do nothing good. The point is that good works are excluded from the article of justification so that in the treatment of the justification of poor sinners before God they should not be drawn, woven, or mingled in. And the right understanding of the exclusive terms in the article of justification (that is, of the terms in the article of justification listed above) consists solely therein. The same points should be urged with all diligence and seriousness in the treatment of this article:

1. That thereby there are excluded completely from the article 37 of justification all our own works, merit, worthiness, glory, and trust in any of our works, so that we might or should not view our works as either the cause or the meritorious basis of our justification which God takes into consideration in this article or matter, or rely on them, or make or regard them as entirely or one-half or even only to the smallest degree factors in our justification.

2. That faith's sole office and property is to serve as the only 38 and exclusive means and instrument with and through which we receive, grasp, accept, apply to ourselves, and appropriate the grace and the merit of Christ in the promise of the Gospel. From this office and property of application and appropriation we must exclude love and every other virtue or work.

3. That neither renewal, sanctification, virtues, nor other good 39 works are our righteousness before God, nor are they to be made and posited to be a part or a cause of our justification, nor under any kind of pretense, title, or name are they to be mingled with the article of justification as pertinent or necessary to it. The righteousness of faith consists solely in the forgiveness of sins by sheer grace, entirely for the sake of Christ's merit, which treasures are offered to us in the promise of the Gospel and received, accepted, applied to us, and made our own solely through faith.

In this way, too, the proper order between faith and good works 40 is bound to be maintained and preserved, as well as between justifica- tion and renewal or sanctification. For good works do not precede 41 faith, nor is sanctification prior to justification. First the Holy Spirit kindles faith in us in conversion through the hearing of the Gospel. Faith apprehends the grace of God in Christ whereby the person is justified. After the person is justified, the Holy Spirit next renews and sanctifies him, and from this renewal and sanctification the fruits of good works will follow. This is not to be understood, however, as though justification and sanctification are separated from each other in such a way as though on occasion true faith could coexist and survive for a while side by side with a wicked intention, but this merely shows the order in which one thing precedes or follows the other. For Dr. Luther's excellent statement remains true: "There is a beautiful agreement between faith and good works; nevertheless, it is faith alone which apprehends the blessing without works. And yet faith is at no time ever alone." [7] This has been set forth above.

This correct distinction explains usefully and well the various 42 disputed issues which the Apology discusses in connection with James

7 *WA*, 43:255.

2:24.[8] If we speak of the manner in which faith justifies, it is St. Paul's doctrine that faith alone justifies without works when, as we have said above, it applies to us and makes our own the merits of Christ. When, however, the question is asked, how a Christian can identify, either in his own case or in the case of others, a true living faith and distinguish it from a simulated and dead faith (since many lazy and secure Christians delude themselves into thinking that they have faith when they do not have true faith), the Apology gives the following answer: "James calls that faith dead where all kinds of good works and the fruits of the Spirit do not follow," and the Latin text of the Apology states, "James teaches correctly when he denies that we are justified by such a faith as is without works, which is a dead faith." [9] But, as the Apology declares, James is speaking of the good works   43 of those who are already justified through Christ, who are reconciled with God, and who have obtained forgiveness of sins through Christ.[1] But when we ask where faith gets the power to justify and save, and what belongs thereto, then it is false and incorrect to answer: Faith cannot justify without works; or, faith justifies or makes righteous in so far as it is associated with love, on account of which love the power to justify is ascribed to faith; or, the presence of good works along with faith is necessary if men are to be justified by it before God; or, the presence of good works is necessary in the article of justification, or for our justification, as a cause without which a person cannot be justified, and that the exclusive terms which St. Paul employs, such as "apart from works," [2] do not exclude works from the article of justification. Faith justifies solely for this reason and on this account, that as a means and instrument it embraces God's grace and the merit of Christ in the promise of the Gospel.

Let this suffice as a summary exposition of the doctrine of   44 justification by faith, since it meets the requirements of this document. The doctrine has been set forth in detail in the previously mentioned writings. From these, too, the false antitheses become clear, namely, that in addiiton to the errors already named we must criticize, expose, and reject the following and similar errors as contrary to the preceding explanation:[3]

1. That our love or our good works are a meritorious basis or   45 cause of our justification before God, either entirely or in part.[4]

---

[8] Apology, IV, 244.
[9] Apology, IV, 249.
[1] Apology, IV, 252.
[2] Rom. 3:28.
[3] The antitheses are allegedly directed against "Romanist errors," though Andrew Osiander was also the target.
[4] Cf. Martin Chemnitz, *Examen Concilii Tridentini*, I, 9 (ed. Preuss, 178ff.).

2. That by good works man must make himself worthy and fit   46
to have the merit of Christ applied to him.[5]

3. That our real righteousness before God is our love or the   47
renewal which the Holy Spirit works and is within us.[6]

4. That righteousness by faith before God consists of two pieces   48
or parts, namely, the gracious forgiveness of sins and, as a second
element, renewal or sanctification.

5. That faith justifies only because righteousness is begun in us   49
by faith, or that faith has priority in justification but that renewal and
love likewise belong to our righteousness before God, in such a way,
however, that they are not the principal cause but that our justification
before God is incomplete or imperfect without such love and renewal.

6. Likewise that the believers are justified before God and are   50
righteous both through the reckoned righteousness of Christ and
through their own inchoate new obedience, or in part by the
reckoning of Christ's righteousness and in part by the inchoate new
obedience.

7. Likewise that the promise of grace is made our own through   51
faith in the heart, through the confession which we make with our
mouth, and through other virtues.

It is also an error when it is taught that man is saved in a   52
different way or by a different thing from the one by which he is
justified before God, as though we are indeed justified solely through
faith without works but that we cannot be saved without works or that
salvation cannot be obtained without works. This is wrong because   53
it is diametrically opposed to Paul's statement that salvation belongs
to that man to whom God reckons righteousness without works
(Rom. 4:6). Paul's reason is that we receive both our righteousness
and our salvation in one and the same way; in fact, that when we are
justified through faith we simultaneously receive adoption and the
inheritance of eternal life and salvation. For this reason Paul uses and
urges exclusive terms (that is, terms that wholly exclude works and our
own merit, such as "by grace" and "without works") just as emphatically in the article of salvation as he does in the article of justification.

We must also explain correctly the discussion concerning the   54
indwelling of God's essential righteousness in us.[7] On the one hand,
it is true indeed that God the Father, Son, and Holy Spirit, who is the
eternal and essential righteousness, dwells by faith in the elect who
have been justified through Christ and reconciled with God, since all

[5] Council of Trent, Session VI, chap. 6, 9, 16; canons 7 and 9.

[6] Osiander had defined *formalis justitia* thus: "Righteousness is precisely
that which prompts the righteous to act rightly." Cf. Council of Trent,
Session VI, chap. 7; canons 10 and 11.

[7] This involved the basic metaphor of Osiander's doctrine of justification,
which he affirmed against an exclusive "reckoning" (*imputatio*) doctrine.

Christians are temples of God the Father, Son, and Holy Spirit, who impels them to do rightly. But, on the other hand, this indwelling of God is not the righteousness of faith of which St. Paul speaks[8] and which he calls the righteousness of God, on account of which we are declared just before God. This indwelling follows the preceding righteousness of faith, which is precisely the forgiveness of sins and the gracious acceptance of poor sinners on account of the obedience and merit of Christ.

Hence, since in our churches the theologians of the Augsburg   55 Confession accept the principle that we must seek our entire righteousness apart from our own and all other human merits, works, virtues, and worthiness and that our righteousness rests solely and alone on the Lord Christ, it is important to consider carefully in what way Christ is called our righteousness in this matter of justification: Our righteousness rests neither upon his divine nature nor upon his human nature but upon the entire person of Christ, who as God and man in his sole, total, and perfect obedience is our righteousness.

For even though Christ had been conceived by the Holy Spirit   56 without sin and had been born and had in his human nature alone fulfilled all righteousness but had not been true, eternal God, the obedience and passion of the human nature could not be reckoned to us as righteousness. Likewise, if the Son of God had not become man, the divine nature alone could not have been our righteousness. Therefore we believe, teach, and confess that the total obedience of Christ's total person, which he rendered to his heavenly Father even to the most ignominious death of the cross, is reckoned to us as righteousness. For neither the obedience nor the passion of the human nature alone, without the divine nature, could render satisfaction to the eternal and almighty God for the sins of all the world. Likewise, the deity alone, without the humanity, could not mediate between God and us.

Since, as was mentioned above,[9] it is the obedience of the entire   57 person, therefore it is a perfect satisfaction and reconciliation of the human race, since it satisfied the eternal and immutable righteousness of God revealed in the law.[1] This obedience is our righteousness which avails before God and is revealed in the Gospel, upon which faith depends before God and which God reckons to faith, as it is written, "For as by one man's disobedience many will be made sinners, so by

---

[8] Rom. 1:17, 3:5, 22, 25; II Cor. 5:21, etc.

[9] Sections 15 and 16.

[1] In opposing Osiander, Flacius, for instance, insisted that the righteousness which avails before God must be something which honors and praises God, an active and sincere obedience and honest life—in short, a righteousness "which the creature owes the Creator, and not a righteousness which the Creator gives to the creature. It is a bounden service of the creature given to the Creator and not a blessing which God bestows upon the creature."

one man's obedience many will be made righteous" (Rom. 5:19), and "the blood of Jesus, his Son, cleanses us from all sin" (I John 1:7), and again, "The righteous shall live by his faith" (Hab. 2:4).

For this reason neither the divine nor the human nature of 58 Christ by itself is reckoned to us as righteousness, but only the obedience of the person who is God and man at the same time. Faith thus looks at the person of Christ, how this person was placed under the law for us, bore our sin, and in his path to the Father rendered to his Father entire, perfect obedience from his holy birth to his death in the stead of us poor sinners, and thus covered up our disobedience, which inheres in our nature, in its thoughts, words, and deeds, so that our disobedience is not reckoned to us for our damnation but is forgiven and remitted by sheer grace for Christ's sake alone.

Accordingly we unanimously reject and condemn, in addition 59 to the previously mentioned errors, the following and all similar errors as contrary to the Word of God, the teaching of the prophets and apostles, and our Christian faith:

1. The doctrine that Christ is our righteousness before God 60 only according to his divine nature;

2. That Christ is our righteousness only according to his human 61 nature.

3. That when the prophets and the apostles speak of the 62 righteousness of faith, the words "to justify" and "to be justified" do not mean "to absolve from sins" and "to receive forgiveness of sins," but to be made really and truly righteous on account of the love and virtues which are poured into them by the Holy Spirit and the consequent good works.

4. That faith does not look solely to the obedience of Christ, 63 but also to his divine nature in so far as it dwells and works within us, and that by such indwelling our sins are covered up in the sight of God.

5. That faith is such a kind of trust in the obedience of Christ 64 that it can be and remain in a person who has no true repentance (and upon which no love follows) but against his conscience remains in sin.[2]

6. That not God but only the gifts of God dwell in believers.[3] 65

These and all similar errors we reject unanimously as contrary 66 to the clear Word of God, and by God's grace we shall remain steadfastly and constantly with the doctrine of justification by faith before God as it is set forth, explained, and demonstrated from God's Word in the Augsburg Confession and its subsequent Apology.

[2] Thus the Council of Trent, Session VI, chap. 15; canon 28.
[3] It is not certain against whom specifically this statement is directed. Stancaro allegedly held this view (cf. Peter Lombard, Sentences, I, 14). In refuting Osiander's doctrinal treatise, the Hamburg ministerium said that there is no indwelling of the Trinity in believers but only an indwelling of the divine power.

If anybody regards anything more as necessary by way of a 67
detailed explanation of this high and important article of justification
before God, on which the salvation of our souls depends, we direct him
for the sake of brevity to Dr. Luther's beautiful and splendid exposition
of St. Paul's Epistle to the Galatians.

IV. GOOD WORKS

A controversy concerning good works has likewise arisen among 1
the theologians of the Augsburg Confession. One party[4] employed
such words and formulas as "Good works are necessary to salvation,"
and "It is impossible to be saved without good works," and "No one
has been saved without good works," since good works are required
of true believers as fruits of faith and since faith without love is dead,
although such love is not a cause of salvation.

The other party[5] contended on the contrary that good works are 2
indeed necessary—not for salvation, however, but for other reasons.
They held that therefore the preceding propositions and formulas are
contrary to the form of sound doctrine and words and have been used
by the papists, now as well as formerly, to oppose that article of our
Christian faith in which we confess that faith alone justifies and saves.
Hence, they held, these propositions should not be tolerated in the
church, lest the merit of Christ, our redeemer, be diminished and in
order to retain for believers the firm and certain promise of salvation.

In this controversy a very few[6] asserted the provocative proposi- 3
tion or principle "that good works are detrimental to salvation." A few
theologians also maintained that good works are not necessary but
spontaneous, since they are not extorted by fear and punishment of the
law but flow from a spontaneous spirit and a joyful heart. Another
party took the contrary view that good works are necessary. At 4
first this latter controversy arose about the words "necessary" and
"free," especially the word "necessary." This word may refer to the
immutable order which obligates and binds all men to be obedient to
God, but at times it implies the coercion with which the law forces men
to do good works. In the course of time, however, the issue ceased 5
to be only a semantic problem and became a vehemently argued
theological controversy when some contended that, because of the

---

[4] Philip Melanchthon, in his *Loci*, 1535 (*C.R.*, XXI, 479); George Major.
especially in his *Sermon von S. Pauli und aller Gottfürchtigen menschen
bekerung zu Gott* (Leipzig, 1553); and Justus Menius.

[5] Nicholas von Amsdorf and Matthias Flacius (in various treatises against
Major and Menius), Nicholas Gallus, John Wigand.

[6] Nicholas von Amsdorf was the only theologian of importance who
maintained this view.

divine order referred to above, new obedience is not necessary in the regenerated.[7]

In order to explain this disagreement in a Christian way and   6 according to the Word of God, and by God's grace to arrive at a complete settlement, we shall state our teaching, belief, and confession.

First of all, there is in this article no disagreement among us   7 concerning the following points: That it is God's will, ordinance, and command that believers walk in good works; that only those are truly good works which God himself prescribes and commands in his Word, and not those that an individual may devise according to his own opinion or that are based on human traditions; that truly good works are not done by a person's own natural powers but only after a person has been reconciled to God through faith and renewed through the Holy Spirit, or, as St. Paul says, "has been created in Christ Jesus for good works."[8]

Neither is there a controversy among us as to how and why the   8 good works of believers are pleasing and acceptable to God, even though they are still impure and imperfect in this flesh of ours. We agree that this is so for the sake of the Lord Christ through faith, because the person is acceptable to God. For works which belong to the maintenance of outward discipline and which unbelievers and the unconverted are also able and required to perform, are indeed praiseworthy in the sight of the world, and even God will reward them with temporal blessings in this world, but since they do not flow from true faith, they are sinful (that is, spattered with sins in the sight of God), and God regards them as sin and as impure because of our corrupted nature and because the person is not reconciled with God. A bad tree cannot bear good fruit,[9] and "Whatsoever does not proceed from faith is sin" (Rom. 14:23). The person must first be pleasing to God—and that alone for Christ's sake—before that person's works are pleasing.

Hence faith alone is the mother and source of the truly good and   9 God-pleasing works that God will reward both in this and in the next world. For this reason St. Paul calls them fruits of faith or of the Spirit.[1]

For, as Luther writes in his Preface to the Epistle of St. Paul to   10 the Romans, "Faith is a divine work in us that transforms us and begets us anew from God, kills the Old Adam, makes us entirely different people in heart, spirit, mind, and all our powers, and brings the Holy Spirit with it. Oh, faith is a living, busy, active, mighty thing, so that

[7] The so-called Second Antinomian Controversy, chiefly between Andrew Musculus and Obadiah Praetorius (see below Articles V and VI).

[8] Eph. 2:10.

[9] Matt. 7:18.

[1] Gal. 5:22; Eph. 5:9.

it is impossible for it not to be constantly doing what is good. Likewise, faith does not ask if good works are to be done, but 11 before one can ask, faith has already done them and is constantly active. Whoever does not perform such good works is a faithless man, blindly tapping around in search of faith and good works without knowing what either faith or good works are, and in the meantime he chatters and jabbers a great deal about faith and good works. Faith 12 is a vital, deliberate trust in God's grace, so certain that it would die a thousand times for it. And such confidence and knowledge of divine grace makes us joyous, mettlesome, and merry toward God and all creatures. This the Holy Spirit works by faith, and therefore without any coercion a man is willing and desirous to do good to everyone, to serve everyone, to suffer everything for the love of God and to his glory, who has been so gracious to him. It is therefore as impossible to separate works from faith as it is to separate heat and light from fire." [2]

But since on these points there has been no controversy among 13 us, we shall discuss them no further but shall explain only the controverted points simply and clearly.

In the first place, it is evident that in discussing the question 14 whether good works are necessary or free, both the Augsburg Confession and its Apology often employ formulas like these: "Good works are necessary"; again, "It is necessary to do good works because they necessarily follow faith and reconciliation"; again, "We should and must of necessity do good works that God has commanded." [3] Likewise, Holy Scripture itself uses words like "necessity," "necessary," "needful," "should," and "must" to indicate what we are bound to do because of God's ordinance, commandment, and will (Rom. 13:5, 6, 9; I Cor. 9:9; Acts 5:29; John 15:12; I John 4:11).

It is wrong, therefore, to criticize and reject the cited proposi- 15 tions and formulas when they are used in their strict and Christian sense, as some have done. They should rightly be used and urged to criticize and reject a complacent Epicurean delusion, since many people dream up for themselves a dead faith or superstition, without repentance and without good works, as if there could simultaneously be in a single heart both a right faith and a wicked intention to continue and abide in sin, which is impossible. Or as if a person could have and retain true faith, righteousness, and salvation even though he still is and continues to be a barren, unfruitful tree since no good fruits appear, yes, even though he were to persist in sins against conscience or embark deliberately on such sins again, which is impious and false.

[2] *EA*, 63:124, 125.
[3] See above, Augsburg Confession, VI, XX; Apology, IV, 141, 189, 200, 214.

Here, however, it is necessary to keep a distinction in mind,   16
namely, that when the word "necessary" is used in this context, it is not
to be understood as implying compulsion but only as referring to the
order of God's immutable will, whose debtors we are, as his commandment indicates when it enjoins the creature to obey its Creator.

Elsewhere, as in II Cor. 9:7, Philem. 14, and I Pet. 5:2, "neces-   17
sity" is used with reference to that which is extorted from a person
against his will, by coercion or otherwise, so that he does externally,
for a pretence, something that is really unwilled by him or even
contrary to his will. Such works of pretence God does not want. On
the contrary, the people of the New Testament are to be a people who
offer themselves freely (Ps. 110:3), who bring free-will offerings (Ps.
54:6), not reluctantly or under compulsion but with obedience from
the heart (II Cor. 9:7, Rom. 6:7) because God loves a cheerful giver
(II Cor. 9:7). With this meaning and in this sense it is right to say   18
and teach that truly good works are to be done willingly or from a
spontaneous spirit by those whom the Son of God has set free. It was
chiefly in this interest that many defended the proposition that good
works are spontaneous.

Here again careful attention must be given to the distinction   19
which Paul makes when he says on the one hand (Rom. 7:22, 23) that
he is willing and delights in the law of God in his inmost self, and on
the other that in his flesh he finds another law which is not only
unwilling or unenthusiastic but actually wars against the law of his
mind. Concerning this unwilling and recalcitrant flesh, Paul says, "I
pommel my body and subdue it" (I Cor. 9:27), and again, they who
belong to Christ have crucified (that is, killed) their flesh with its
passions, desires, and deeds (Gal. 5:24; Rom. 8:13). But we   20
reject and condemn as false the view that good works are free to
believers in the sense that it lies within their free option if they may
or want to do or not do them or to act in a contrary fashion and
nonetheless still retain faith and God's mercy and his grace.

Secondly, when we teach that good works are necessary we must   21
also explain why and for what causes they are necessary, as the
Augsburg Confession and the Apology have done.[4] But here we   22
must be extremely careful that works are not drawn into and mingled
with the article of justification and salvation. Therefore we correctly
reject the propositions that good works are necessary for the believers'
salvation, or that it is impossible to be saved without good works, since
such propositions are directly contrary to the doctrine of exclusive
terms in the articles of justification and salvation (that is, they are
diametrically opposed to St. Paul's words which exclude our works and
merit completely from the article of justification and salvation and

---

[4] Augsburg Confession, VI, XX; Apology, IV, 183-400.

ascribe everything solely to the grace of God and the merit of Christ, as was explained in the preceding article).[5] Furthermore, these 23 propositions deprive tempted and troubled consciences of the consolation of the Gospel, give occasion for doubt, are dangerous in many ways, confirm presumptuous trust in one's own righteousness and confidence in one's own good works, and are adopted by the papists and used to their own advantage against the pure doctrine of salvation by faith alone.[6] Thus they are contrary to the pattern of sound 24 words, like the Scripture passage which ascribes the bliss of salvation solely to the man to whom God reckons righteousness apart from works (Rom. 4:6), or the statement in Article VI of the Augsburg Confession, "We are saved without works solely by faith." Luther also has rejected and condemned these propositions:

1. In the case of the false prophets among the Galatians;[7] 25
2. In his writings against the papists at many places; 26
3. In his writings against the Anabaptists, who advanced this 27 interpretation: We should indeed not put our faith in the merit of our works, but we must nevertheless have them as something necessary for salvation;
4. Furthermore, in the case of some of his own followers who 28 attempted to explain the proposition by saying that, although we require good works as necessary to salvation, we nevertheless do not teach people to put their trust in their work (in his *Commentary on Genesis*, Chapter 22).

Hence and for these reasons it is right for our churches to 29 continue to insist that the aforementioned propositions are not to be taught, defended, or condoned but are to be expelled and rejected by our churches as false and incorrect and as issues which in times of persecution, when it was particularly important to have a clear and correct confession against all sorts of corruptions and counterfeiting of the article of justification, were raised again as a result of the Interim,[8] flowed forth from it, and were made matters of controversy.

In the third place, a disputation has arisen as to whether good 30 works preserve salvation or are necessary to preserve faith, righteousness, and salvation. This, of course, is a serious and important question since only he who endures to the end will be saved (Matt. 24:13) and "We share in Christ only if we hold our first confidence firm to the end" (Heb. 3:14). For this reason it is important to declare well and

---

[5] Above, Solid Declaration, III, 36, 43.

[6] Council of Trent, Session VI, canon 32.

[7] *Commentary on Galatians*, in *WA*, 40I: 220, 223 230, 236, 240, 249, etc.

[8] The Leipzig Interim (1548), a provisional arrangement which under political pressure made concessions to Roman Catholic doctrine and practice.

in detail how righteousness and salvation are preserved in us so that we do not lose them again.

Therefore we must begin by earnestly criticizing and rejecting 31 the false Epicurean delusion which some dream up that it is impossible to lose faith and the gift of righteousness and salvation, once it has been received, through any sin, even a wanton and deliberate one, or through wicked works; and that even though a Christian follows his evil lusts without fear and shame, resists the Holy Spirit, and deliberately proceeds to sin against his conscience, he can nevertheless retain faith, the grace of God, righteousness, and salvation. We should 32 often, with all diligence and earnestness, repeat and impress upon Christians who have been justified by faith these true, immutable, and divine threats and earnest punishments and admonitions: "Do you not know that the unrighteous will not inherit the kingdom of God? Do not be deceived; neither the immoral, nor idolaters, nor adulterers will inherit the kingdom of God" (I Cor. 6:9). "Those who do such things shall not inherit the kingdom of God" (Gal. 5:21; Eph. 5:5). "If you live according to the flesh you will die" (Rom. 8:13). "On account of these the wrath of God is coming upon the sons of disobedience" (Col 3:6).

The Apology offers a fine example as to when and how, on the 33 basis of the preceding, the exhortation to do good works can be instilled without darkening the doctrine of faith and justification. In explaining II Pet. 1:10, "Be the more zealous to confirm your call and election," the Apology states in Article XX: "Peter teaches why we should do good works, namely, that we confirm our calling, that is, that we do not fall from our calling by lapsing again into sin. He says: 'Do good works so that you remain in your heavenly calling, lest you fall away and lose the Spirit and his gifts, which you have not received because of your subsequent works but which have come to you by grace through Christ and which you retain through faith! Faith, however, does not remain in those who lead a wicked life, lose the Holy Spirit, and reject repentance.' " [9]

It does not, however, mean that faith accepts righteousness and 34 salvation only at the beginning, and then delegates this function to works, as if works should henceforth preserve faith, the righteousness that has been received, and salvation. On the contrary, in order that the promise that we shall not only receive but also retain righteousness and salvation may be very certain to us, Paul ascribes to faith not only our entry into grace but also our present state of grace and our hope of sharing the glory of God (Rom. 5:2). In other words, he attributes to faith alone the beginning, the middle, and the end of everything. Likewise, he says, "They were broken off because of their unbelief, and

* Apology XX, 13.

you stand fast only through faith" (Rom. 11:20). "He will present you holy and blameless and irreproachable before him, provided you continue in the faith" (Col. 1:22). "By God's power we are guarded through faith for a salvation," and again, "As the outcome of your faith, you obtain the salvation of your souls" (I Pet. 1:5, 9).

Since it is evident from the Word of God that faith is the proper 35 and the only means whereby righteousness and salvation are not only received but also preserved by God, we rightly reject the decree of the Council of Trent[1] and anything else that tends toward the same opinion, namely, that our good works preserve salvation, or that our works either entirely or in part sustain and preserve either the righteousness of faith that we have received or even faith itself.

For although, prior to this controversy, not a few orthodox 36 teachers used these and similar formulas in expounding Holy Scripture without in any way intending to confirm the aforementioned error of the papists, yet, since a controversy subsequently arose on this point which led to many offensive exaggerations, it is safest to follow the advice of St. Paul to maintain the pattern of sound words as well as the true doctrine itself (II Tim. 1:13). This would eliminate much useless wrangling and preserve the church from many offenses.

In the fourth place, concerning the proposition that good works 37 are supposed to be detrimental to salvation,[2] we give the following clear answer: If anyone draws good works into the article of justification and rests his righteousness or his assurance of salvation on good works in order to merit the grace of God and to be saved thereby, it is not we, but Paul himself, who declares no less than three times in Phil. 3:7ff. that good works not only are useless and an impediment to such a person but are actually harmful. The fault, however, lies not with the good works themselves, but with the false confidence which, contrary to the express Word of God, is being placed upon good works. But 38 it does not follow herefrom that one may say without any qualifications that good works are detrimental to believers as far as their salvation is concerned. For when good works are done on account of right causes and for right ends (that is, with the intention that God demands of the regenerated), they are an indication of salvation in believers (Phil. 1:28). It is God's will and express command that believers should do good works which the Holy Spirit works in them, and God is willing to be pleased with them for Christ's sake and he promises to reward them gloriously in this and in the future life. Hence our 39 churches condemn and reject this proposition, too, because when asserted without explanation it is false and offensive, might weaken discipline and decency, and might introduce and confirm a wicked,

---

[1] Council of Trent, Session VI, canons 24, 32.
[2] Nicholas von Amsdorf made this extravagant claim.

wild, complacent, and Epicurean way of life. For one ought to avoid
with the greatest diligence whatever is detrimental to one's salvation.
But since Christians are not to be deterred from good works, but   40
are most diligently to be admonished and urged to apply themselves to
good works, we cannot and should not tolerate, teach, or defend this
proposition, unqualifiedly stated, in our churches.

V. LAW AND GOSPEL

The distinction between law and Gospel is an especially brilliant   1
light which serves the purpose that the Word of God may be rightly
divided[3] and the writings of the holy prophets and apostles may be
explained and understood correctly. We must therefore observe this
distinction with particular diligence lest we confuse the two doctrines
and change the Gospel into law. This would darken the merit of
Christ and rob disturbed consciences of the comfort which they would
otherwise have in the holy Gospel when it is preached purely and
without admixture, for by it Christians can support themselves in their
greatest temptations against the terrors of the law.

On this point, too, there has been a controversy among some   2
theologians of the Augsburg Confession. The one party claimed that,
strictly speaking, the Gospel is not only a proclamation of grace but
also at the same time a proclamation of repentance, which rebukes the
greatest sin, unbelief.[4] The other party, however, maintained and
contended that, strictly speaking, the Gospel is not a proclamation of
repentance or reproof. This, they said, is strictly a function of the law
of God, which reproves all sins, including unbelief, whereas the Gospel
in its strict sense is a proclamation of the grace and mercy of God for
Christ's sake, which proclamation assures those who have been
converted to Christ that their unbelief, in which they formerly had been
mired and which the law of God reproved, has been pardoned and
forgiven.[5]

When we rightly reflect on this controversy, we find that it was   3
chiefly occasioned by the fact that the little word "Gospel" does not
always have one and the same meaning but is used in a twofold way,
both in the Holy Scripture of God and by ancient and modern
theologians. In the one case the word is used in such a way that we   4
understand by it the entire teaching of Christ, our Lord, which in his
public ministry on earth and in the New Testament he ordered to be
observed. Here the term includes both the exposition of the law and

---

[3] An allusion to II Tim. 2:15.

[4] The reference is less to Agricola's Antinomianism than to Melanchthon's
thesis that the Gospel is also *doctrina poenitentiae*.

[5] The chief advocates of this position were Matthias Flacius, Matthew
Judex, and John Wigand.

the proclamation of the mercy and grace of God, his heavenly Father, as it is written in Mark 1:1, "The beginning of the Gospel of Jesus Christ, the Son of God." Shortly thereafter the chief parts are announced, namely, repentance and forgiveness of sins (Mark 1:4). Similarly when Christ after his resurrection commands his apostles to preach the Gospel in all the world (Mark 16:15), he summarizes his doctrine in a few words, "Thus it is written, that the Christ should suffer and on the third day rise from the dead, and that repentance and forgiveness of sin should be preached in his name to all nations" (Luke 24:46, 47). Likewise, Paul calls his entire teaching the "Gospel" (Acts 20:24) and summarizes it under these heads: repentance to God and faith in Christ. And when the word "Gospel" is used in its   5 broad sense and apart from the strict distinction of law and Gospel, it is correct to define the word as the proclamation of both repentance and the forgiveness of sins. For John, Christ, and the apostles began in their preaching with repentance and expounded and urged not only the gracious promise of the forgiveness of sins but also the divine law. In addition, however, the word "Gospel" is also used in another   6 (that is, in a strict) sense. Here it does not include the proclamation of repentance but solely the preaching of God's grace. So it appears shortly afterward in the first chapter of St. Mark, where Christ said, "Repent and believe in the Gospel" (Mark 1:15).

Again, the little word "repentance" is not used in a single sense   7 in Holy Scripture. In some passages of Holy Writ the word is used and understood as the entire conversion of man, as in Luke 13:5, "Unless you repent you will all likewise perish," and in Luke 15:7, "Even so, there will be joy in heaven over one sinner who repents." But in   8 the cited passage in Mark 1:15, and in other places where repentance and faith in Christ (Acts 20:21) or repentance and forgiveness of sins (Luke 24:46) are distinguished from one another, the phrase "to repent" means nothing more than truly to recognize one's sins, to feel heartily sorry for them, and to desist from them. This knowledge   9 comes from the law, but it is not sufficient for a salutary conversion to God unless there is added faith in Christ, whose merit the comforting proclamation of the holy Gospel offers to all penitent sinners who have been terrified by the proclamation of the law. For the Gospel does not preach the forgiveness of sin to indifferent and secure hearts, but to the "oppressed" or penitent (Luke 4:18). And in order that contrition or the terrors of the law may not end in despair, the proclamation of the Gospel must be added so that it becomes a "contrition that leads to salvation" (II Cor. 7:10).

The mere preaching of the law without Christ either produces   10 presumptuous people, who believe that they can fulfill the law by external works, or drives man utterly to despair. Therefore Christ takes the law into his hands and explains it spiritually (Matt. 5:21ff.; Rom.

7:6, 14); thus he reveals his wrath from heaven over all sinners and shows how great this wrath is. This directs the sinner to the law, and there he really learns to know his sin, an insight that Moses could never have wrung out of him. For Paul testifies that although "Moses is read," the veil which "he put over his face" remains unremoved, so that they do not see the law spiritually, or how much it requires of us, or how severely it curses and condemns us because we could not fulfill or keep it. "When a man turns to the Lord, the veil is removed" (II Cor. 3:13-15).

Therefore the Spirit of Christ must not only comfort but, 11 through the office of the law, must also convince the world of sin. Thus, even in the New Testament, he must perform what the prophet calls "a strange deed"[6] (that is, to rebuke) until he comes to his own work (that is, to comfort and to preach about grace). To this end Christ has obtained and sent us the Spirit, and for this reason the latter is called the Paraclete,[7] as Luther explains it in his exposition of the Gospel for the Fifth Sunday after Trinity. He states: "Every- 12 thing that preaches about our sin and the wrath of God, no matter how or when it happens, is the proclamation of the law. On the other hand, the Gospel is a proclamation that shows and gives nothing but grace and forgiveness in Christ. At the same time it is true and right that the apostles and the preachers of the Gospel, just as Christ himself did, confirm the proclamation of the law and begin with the law in the case of those who as yet neither know their sins nor are terrified by the wrath of God, as he says in John 16:8, 'The Holy Spirit will convince the world of sin because they do not believe in me.' In fact, where is there a more earnest and terrible revelation and preaching of God's wrath over sin than the passion and death of Christ, his own Son? But as long as all this proclaims the wrath of God and terrifies man, it is not yet the Gospel nor Christ's own proclamation, but it is Moses and the law pronounced upon the unconverted. For the Gospel and Christ are not ordained and given us to terrify or to condemn us, but to comfort and lift upright those who are terrified and disconsolate." And again: "Christ says, 'The Holy Spirit will convince the world 13 of sin' (John 16:8), which cannot be done without the explanation of the law."[8]

In the same vein, the Smalcald Articles state: "The New Testa- 14 ment retains and performs the office of the law, which reveals sin and God's wrath, but to this office it immediately adds the promise of God's grace through the Gospel."[9]

[6] Isa. 28:21.
[7] John 16:7.
[8] *EA*, 13:153, 154; *WA*, 15:228.
[9] Smalcald Articles, Pt. III, Art. I, 4.

And the Apology says: "The preaching of the law is not 15 sufficient for genuine and salutary repentance; the Gospel must also be added to it."[1] Thus both doctrines are always together, and both of them have to be urged side by side, but in proper order and with the correct distinction. Therefore we justly condemn the Antinomians or nomoclasts[2] who cast the preaching of the law out of the churches and would have us criticize sin and teach contrition and sorrow not from the law but solely from the Gospel.

But in order that everyone may see that we are concealing 16 nothing in this present controversy but are presenting the entire matter nicely and clearly for the Christian reader, we submit the following:

We unanimously believe, teach, and confess on the basis of what 17 we have said that, strictly speaking, the law is a divine doctrine which reveals the righteousness and immutable will of God, shows how man ought to be disposed in his nature, thoughts, words, and deeds in order to be pleasing and acceptable to God, and threatens the transgressors of the law with God's wrath and temporal and eternal punishment. For, as Luther says against the nomoclasts, "Everything that rebukes sin is and belongs to the law, the proper function of which is to condemn sin and to lead to a knowledge of sin" (Rom. 3:20; 7:7). Since unbelief is a root and fountainhead of all culpable sin, the law reproves unbelief also. But it is also true that the Gospel illustrates 18 and explains the law and its doctrine; nevertheless the true function of the law remains, to rebuke sin and to give instruction about good works.

This is the way in which the law rebukes unbelief, when a 19 person does not believe the Word of God. Since the Gospel (which alone, strictly speaking, teaches and commands faith in Christ) is the Word of God, the Holy Spirit through the office of the law rebukes the unbelief involved in men's failure to believe in Christ. Nevertheless, this Gospel alone, strictly speaking, teaches about saving faith in Christ.

The Gospel, however, is that doctrine which teaches what a man 20 should believe in order to obtain the forgiveness of sins from God, since man has failed to keep the law of God and has transgressed it, his corrupted nature, thoughts, words, and deeds war against the law, and he is therefore subject to the wrath of God, to death, to temporal miseries, and to the punishment of hell-fire. The content of the Gospel is this, that the Son of God, Christ our Lord, himself assumed and bore the curse of the law and expiated and paid for all our sins, that through him alone we re-enter the good graces of God, obtain forgiveness of sins through faith, are freed from death and all the punishments of sin, and are saved eternally. For everything which 21

---

[1] Apology, IV, 257.
[2] German, *Gesetzstürmer*, formed on the analogy of *Bilderstürmer*, "iconoclasts."

comforts and which offers the mercy and grace of God to transgressors
of the law strictly speaking is, and is called, the Gospel, a good and
joyful message that God wills not to punish sins but to forgive them
for Christ's sake.

Accordingly every penitent sinner must believe—that is, he must   22
put his confidence solely on the Lord Jesus Christ, "who was put to
death for our trespasses and raised for our justification," [3] who "was
made sin though he knew no sin, so that in him we might become the
righteousness of God," [4] who was "made our righteousness," [5] and
whose obedience is reckoned to us as righteousness in the strict
judgment of God. Thus the law, as previously explained, is an office
which kills through the letter and is a "dispensation of condemnation," [6]
but the Gospel is "the power of God for salvation to everyone who has
faith," [7] "a dispensation of righteousness" [8] and "of the Spirit." [9]
Dr. Luther very diligently urged this distinction in nearly all his
writings and showed in detail that there is a vast difference between
the knowledge of God which comes from the Gospel and that which is
taught by and learned from the law, since from the natural law even
the heathen had to some extent a knowledge of God, although they
neither understood nor honored him rightly (Rom. 1:21).

Since the beginning of the world these two proclamations have   23
continually been set forth side by side in the church of God with the
proper distinction. The descendants of the holy patriarchs, like the
patriarchs themselves, constantly reminded themselves not only how
man in the beginning was created righteous and holy by God and
through the deceit of the serpent transgressed God's laws, became a
sinner, corrupted himself and all his descendants, and plunged them
into death and eternal damnation, but also revived their courage and
comforted themselves with the proclamation of the woman's seed, who
would bruise the serpent's head;[1] likewise, of the seed of Abraham, by
whom all nations should be blessed;[2] likewise, of David's son, who
should restore the kingdom of Israel and be a light to the nations,[3]
"who was wounded for our transgressions and bruised for our iniquities
and with whose stripes we are healed." [4]

We believe and confess that these two doctrines must be urged   24
constantly and diligently in the church of God until the end of the
world, but with the due distinction, so that in the ministry of the New
Testament the proclamation of the law and its threats will terrify the
hearts of the unrepentant and bring them to a knowledge of their sin

[*] Rom. 4:25.   [9] II Cor. 3:8.
[4] II Cor. 5:21.   [1] Gen. 3:15.
[5] I Cor. 1:30.   [2] Gen. 22:18; 28:14.
[6] II Cor. 3:6, 9.   [8] Ps. 110:1; Isa. 40:10; 49:6.
[7] Rom. 1:16.   [4] Isa. 53:5.
[8] II Cor. 3:9.

and to repentance, but not in such a way that they become despondent and despair therein. Rather, since "the law was our custodian until Christ came, that we might be justified by faith" (Gal. 3:24), and hence points and leads not away from but toward the Christ who is the end of the law (Rom. 10:4), the proclamation of the Gospel of 25 our Lord Christ will once more comfort and strengthen them with the assurance that if they believe the Gospel God forgives them all their sins through Christ, accepts them for his sake as God's children, and out of pure grace, without any merit of their own, justifies and saves them. But this does not mean that men may abuse the grace of God and sin against grace. This distinction between the law and the Gospel 26 is thoroughly and mightily set forth by St. Paul in II Cor. 3:7-9.

For this reason and in order that both doctrines, law and Gospel, 27 may not be mingled together and confused so that what belongs to one doctrine is ascribed to the other, it is necessary to urge and to maintain with all diligence the true and proper distinction between law and Gospel, and diligently to avoid anything that might give occasion for a confusion between them by which the two doctrines would be tangled together and made into one doctrine. Such a confusion would easily darken the merits and benefits of Christ, once more make the Gospel a teaching of law, as happened in the papacy, and thus rob Christians of the true comfort which they have in the Gospel against the terrors of the law and reopen the door to the papacy in the church of God. It is therefore dangerous and wrong to make of the Gospel, strictly so called in distinction from the law, a proclamation of repentance and punishment. Elsewhere, however, when it is generally understood as referring to the entire teaching, a usage that we find occasionally in the Apology too,[5] the Gospel is a proclamation both of repentance and of forgiveness of sins. But the Apology also indicates[6] that, strictly speaking, the Gospel is the promise of forgiveness of sins and justification through Christ, whereas the law is a message that rebukes and condemns sin.

VI. THE THIRD FUNCTION OF THE LAW

The law of God serves (1) not only to maintain external 1 discipline and decency against dissolute and disobedient people, (2) and to bring people to a knowledge of their sin through the law, (3) but those who have been born anew through the Holy Spirit, who have been converted to the Lord and from whom the veil of Moses has been

---

[5] For example, Apology IV, 62, 257; XII, 31, 45.
[6] For example, Apology IV, 40, 57; XII, 45, 52, 73, 76.

taken away, learn from the law to[7] live and walk in the law. A controversy has arisen among a few theologians concerning this third and last function of the law.

The one party taught and held that the regenerated do not learn   2 the new obedience (that is, in what good works they should walk) from the law; nor should this doctrine in any way be urged on the basis of the law, since they have been liberated by the Son of God, have become his Spirit's temple, and hence are free, so that just as the sun spontaneously completes its regular course without any outside impulse, they, too, through the inspiration and impulse of the Holy Spirit spontaneously do what God requires of them. The other party   3 taught that although true believers are indeed motivated by the Holy Spirit and hence according to the inner man do the will of God from a free spirit, nevertheless the Holy Spirit uses the written law on them to instruct them, and thereby even true believers learn to serve God not according to their own notions but according to his written law and Word, which is a certain rule and norm for achieving a godly life and behavior in accord with God's eternal and immutable will.

In order to explain and definitively to settle this controversy, we   4 unanimously believe, teach, and confess that, although truly believing Christians, having been genuinely converted to God and justified, have been freed and liberated from the curse of the law, they should daily exercise themselves in the law of the Lord, as it is written, "Blessed is the man whose delight is in the law of the Lord, and on his law he meditates day and night" (Ps. 1:1, 2; 119:1, 35, 47, 70, 97). For the law is a mirror in which the will of God and what is pleasing to him is correctly portrayed. It is necessary to hold this constantly before believers' eyes and continually to urge it upon them with diligence.

It is true that the law is not laid down for the just, as St. Paul   5 says (I Tim. 1:9), but for the ungodly. But this dare not be understood without qualification, as though the righteous should live without the law. For the law of God is written on their hearts, just as the first man immediately after his creation received a law according to which he should conduct himself. On the contrary, it is St. Paul's intention that the law cannot impose its curse upon those who through Christ have been reconciled with God, nor may it torture the regenerated with its coercion, for according to the inner man they delight in the law of God.

If believers and the elect children of God were perfectly renewed   6 in this life through the indwelling Spirit in such a way that in their nature and all its powers they would be totally free from sins, they would require no law, no driver. Of themselves and altogether

---

[7] The German original has no words corresponding to "learn from the law to." The Latin version translates at this place: *lege docentur ut in ~era pietate vivant et ambulant.*

spontaneously, without any instruction, admonition, exhortation, or driving by the law they would do what they are obligated to do according to the will of God, just as the sun, the moon, and all the stars of heaven regularly run their courses according to the order which God instituted for them once and for all, spontaneously and unhindered, without any admonition, exhortation, compulsion, coercion, or necessity, and as the holy angels render God a completely spontaneous obedience.

But in this life Christians are not renewed perfectly and completely. For although their sins are covered up through the perfect obedience of Christ, so that they are not reckoned to believers for damnation, and although the Holy Spirit has begun the mortification of the Old Adam and their renewal in the spirit of their minds, nevertheless the Old Adam still clings to their nature and to all its internal and external powers. Concerning this the apostle writes, 8 "I know that nothing good dwells within me." And again, "I do not do the good I want, but the evil I do not want is what I do." Likewise, "I see in my members another law at war with the law of my mind and making me captive to the law of sin." 8 Likewise, "The desires of the flesh are against the spirit and the desires of the spirit are against the flesh, for these are opposed to each other, to prevent you from doing what you would." 9

Hence, because of the desires of the flesh the truly believing, 9 elect, and reborn children of God require in this life not only the daily teaching and admonition, warning and threatening of the law, but frequently the punishment of the law as well, to egg them on so that they follow the Spirit of God, as it is written, "It is good for me that I was afflicted that I might learn thy statutes" (Ps. 119:71). And again, "I pommel my body and subdue it, lest after preaching to others I myself should be disqualified" (I Cor. 9:27), and again, "If you are left without discipline in which all have participated, then you are illegitimate children and not sons" (Heb. 12:8). Dr. Luther thoroughly explains this at greater length in the summer portion of the Church Postil, on the Epistle for the Nineteenth Sunday after Trinity.[1]

It is also necessary to set forth distinctly what the Gospel does, 10 creates, and works in connection with the new obedience of believers and what function the law performs in this matter, as far as the good works of believers are concerned. The law indeed tells us that it is 11 God's will and command that we should walk in the new life, but it does not give the power and ability to begin it or to do it. It is the Holy Spirit, who is not given and received through the law but through

[8] Rom. 7:18, 19, 23.
[9] Gal. 5:17.
[1] *WA*, 45:161-164.

the preaching of the Gospel (Gal. 3:2, 14), who renews the heart. Then he employs the law to instruct the regenerate out of it and |2 to show and indicate to them in the Ten Commandments what the acceptable will of God is (Rom. 12:2) and in what good works, which God has prepared beforehand, they should walk (Eph. 2:10). He also admonishes them to do these, and when because of the flesh they are lazy, negligent, and recalcitrant, the Holy Spirit reproves them through the law. In this way the Holy Spirit simultaneously performs both offices, "he kills and brings to life, he brings down into Sheol, and raises up." [2] His office is not alone to comfort but also to rebuke, as it is written, "When the Holy Spirit shall come, he will convince the world (to which the Old Adam belongs) of sin and of righteousness and of judgment." [3] Sin is everything that is contrary to the law |3 of God, and St. Paul says, "All Scripture is inspired by God and |4 profitable for teaching, for reproof." [4] But to reprove is the real function of the law. As often, therefore, as Christians trip, they are rebuked through the Spirit of God out of the law. But the same Spirit raises them up again and comforts them with the preaching of the holy Gospel.

In order as far as possible to avoid all misunderstandings, to |5 teach and to maintain the strict distinction between the works of the law and those of the Spirit, we must observe with special diligence that in speaking of good works that are in accord with the law of God —for otherwise they are not good works—the word "law" here has but one meaning, namely, the immutable will of God according to which man is to conduct himself in this life. The distinction between |6 works is due to the difference in the individuals who are concerned about living according to the law and the will of God. For as long as a person is not reborn, lives according to the law, and does its works merely because they are commanded, from fear of punishment or in hope of reward, he is still under the law. St. Paul calls the works of such a man "works of the law" [5] in the strict sense, because his good works are extorted by the law, just as in the case of bondservants. Such people are saints after the order of Cain.[6]

But when a person is born anew by the Spirit of God and is |7 liberated from the law (that is, when he is free from this driver and is driven by the Spirit of Christ), he lives according to the immutable will of God as it is comprehended in the law and, in so far as he is born anew, he does everything from a free and merry spirit. These works are, strictly speaking, not works of the law but works and fruits of

---

[2] I Sam. 2:6.
[3] John 16:8.
[4] II Tim. 3:16.
[5] Rom. 2:15; 3:20; Gal. 2:16; 3:2, 10.
[6] Latin adds: that is, hypocrites.

the Spirit, or, as St. Paul calls them, the law of the mind and the law of Christ. According to St. Paul, such people are no longer under law but under grace (Rom. 6:14; 8:2). Since, however, believers are 18 not fully renewed in this life but the Old Adam clings to them down to the grave, the conflict between spirit and flesh continues in them. According to the inmost self they delight in the law of God; but the law in their members is at war against the law of their mind.[7] Thus though they are never without law, they are not under but in the law, they live and walk in the law of the Lord, and yet do nothing by the compulsion of the law. As far as the Old Adam who still adheres 19 to them is concerned, he must be coerced not only with the law but also with miseries, for he does everything against his will and by coercion, just as the unconverted are driven and coerced into obedience by the threats of the law (I Cor. 9:27; Rom. 7:18, 19).

Believers, furthermore, require the teaching of the law so that 20 they will not be thrown back on their own holiness and piety and under the pretext of the Holy Spirit's guidance set up a self-elected service of God without his Word and command, as it is written, "You shall not do every man whatever is right in his own eyes, but heed all these words which I command you. You shall not add to it nor take from it" (Deut. 12:8, 28, 32).

Believers, furthermore, require the teaching of the law in 21 connection with their good works, because otherwise they can easily imagine that their works and life are perfectly pure and holy. But the law of God prescribes good works for faith in such a way that, as in a mirror, it shows and indicates to them that in this life our good works are imperfect and impure, so that we must say with St. Paul, "I am not aware of anything against myself, but I am not thereby acquitted" (I Cor. 4:4). Thus, when Paul admonishes those who have been born anew to do good works, he holds up before them precisely the Ten Commandments (Rom. 13:9), and he himself learns from the law that his works are still imperfect and impure (Rom. 7:18, 19). David says, "I will run in the way of thy commandments" (Ps. 119:32), but also, "Enter not into judgment with thy servant; for no man living is righteous before thee" (Ps. 143:2).

The law demands a perfect and pure obedience if it is to please 22 God. It does not teach us how and why the good works of believers are pleasing to God, even though in this life they are still imperfect and impure because of the sin in our flesh. But the Gospel teaches us that our spiritual sacrifices are acceptable to God through faith for Christ's sake (I Pet. 2:5; Heb. 11:4; 13:15). In this respect 23 Christians are not under the law but under grace because their persons have been freed from the curse and condemnation of the law through

---

[7] Cf. Rom. 7:23.

faith in Christ. Though their good works are still imperfect and impure, they are acceptable to God through Christ because according to their inmost self they do what is pleasing to God not by coercion of the law but willingly and spontaneously from the heart by the renewal of the Holy Spirit. Nevertheless, they continue in a constant conflict against the Old Adam. For the Old Adam, like an unmanageable 24 and recalcitrant donkey, is still a part of them and must be coerced into the obedience of Christ, not only with the instruction, admonition, urging, and threatening of the law, but frequently also with the club of punishments and miseries, until the flesh of sin is put off entirely and man is completely renewed in the resurrection. There he will no longer require either the preaching of the law or its threats and punishments, just as he will no longer require the Gospel. They belong to this imperfect life. But just as they will see God face to face, so 25 through God's indwelling Spirit they will do his will spontaneously, without coercion, unhindered, perfectly, completely, and with sheer joy, and will rejoice therein forever.

Hence we reject and condemn, as pernicious and contrary to Christian discipline and true godliness, the erroneous doctrine that the law in the manner and measure indicated above is not to be urged upon Christians and true believers but only upon unbelievers, non-Christians, and the unrepentant.

VII. THE HOLY SUPPER

It may be that in the opinion of some an explanation of this 1 article should not be included in this document in which we intend to deal only with those articles that were in controversy among the theologians of the Augsburg Confession. As early as 1530, when the Augsburg Confession was drafted and submitted to the emperor, the Sacramentarians completely disavowed the Augsburg Confession, withdrew from it, and submitted their own confession [8] Unfortunately, however, in later years a number of theologians and others[9] who professed adherence to the Augsburg Confession no longer secretly but in part openly approved the Sacramentarians' position and against their own consciences sought forcibly to adduce and pervert the

---

[8] The *Confessio Tetrapolitana* and Zwingli's *Fidei ratio*. The term "Sacramentarian" was applied by Lutherans to all left-wing opponents of their interpretation of the Lord's Supper.

[9] Chiefly the "Crypto-Calvinist" professors of theology, medicine, and law at the universities in Wittenberg and Leipzig who were responsible for the *Catechesis Wittebergica* (1571), the *"Grundfest"* and *Dresdner Abschied* (1571), and the *Exegesis perspicua* (1574), among them Wolfgang Crell, Caspar Cruciger, Jr., Joachim Eger, Christopher Pezel, Caspar Peucer, Erasmus Rüdinger, Jerome Schaller, and Christian Schütz (Sagittarius). (Calvin himself had signed the Unaltered Augsburg Confession in 1539-40.)

Augsburg Confession so as to make it appear to be in full agreement with the teaching of the Sacramentarians in this article. Hence we neither could nor should refrain from giving testimony to the divine truth by means of our confession in this document and from repeating the true intention and the right understanding of the words of Christ and of the Augsburg Confession in this article. With the help of God we shall do everything we can to preserve it for our descendants also, and faithfully to warn our hearers and other pious Christians against this pernicious error which is altogether contrary to the holy Word of God and to the Augsburg Confession and which has repeatedly been condemned.

THE CHIEF ISSUE BETWEEN OUR DOCTRINE AND THAT OF THE SACRAMENTARIANS IN THIS ARTICLE

Some Sacramentarians diligently endeavor to employ terminology 2 which is as close as possible to the formulas and speech-patterns of the Augsburg Confession and of our churches and confess that in the Holy Supper the body of Christ is truly received by believers. Yet when we press them to set forth their meaning clearly, honestly, and explicitly, they all declare unanimously that the true, essential body and blood of Christ are as far distant from the blessed bread and wine in the Supper as the highest heaven is distant from the earth. For their own words assert, "We say that the body and blood of Christ are distant from the signs by as great an interval as the earth is distant from the highest heavens." [1] Therefore they understand this 3 presence of the body of Christ not as taking place here on earth but only in respect to faith (that is, our faith, reminded and quickened by the visible signs in the same way as by the preached Word, lifts itself up and ascends above all heavens and receives and partakes truly and essentially, but still only spiritually, of the body of Christ which is there in heaven, yes, of Christ himself and all his benefits). For just as the bread and wine are here on earth and not in heaven, so also the body of Christ is now in heaven and not on earth, and consequently nothing but bread and wine are orally received in the Supper.

In the beginning they alleged that the Lord's Supper was only an 4 external sign whereby one can identify Christians,[2] and that nothing more than mere bread and wine, which are only signs of the absent body of Christ, are therein distributed. When this did not hold water, they confessed that the Lord Christ is truly present in the Supper, namely, according to the exchange of properties[3] (that is, only according to his divine nature, but not with his body and blood).[4] Later, 5

[1] *Consensus Tigurinus*, XXV.
[2] So Zwingli in his *Fidei Ratio*.
[3] Latin, *per communicationem idiomatum*.
[4] So the *"Grundfest"* (1571), 175b; *Catechesis Wittebergica* (1571), **83,** 128.

when they were constrained by the words of Christ to confess that the body of Christ is present in the Supper, they still did not understand and explain it except as something to be received spiritually (that is, according to its power, operation, and benefits, by faith). They say that through the Spirit of Christ, which is everywhere, our bodies, in which the Spirit of Christ dwells here upon earth, are united with the body of Christ, which is in heaven.

As a result many important people were deceived by the noble 6 and plausible words of the Sacramentarians when they alleged and boasted that they hold no other opinion than that the Lord Christ is present in his Supper truly, essentially, and alive. However, they understand that this is so only according to his divine nature and is not true of his body and blood, which is now in heaven and nowhere else, and that with the bread and wine Christ gives us his true body and blood to eat spiritually by faith but not to receive it orally with the mouth.[5]

They understand the words of the Supper, "This is my body," [6] 7 not strictly, the way the letters sound, but as figurative speech. They interpret "to eat Christ's body" as no more than "to believe." For them "body" is the same as a "symbol" (that is, a sign or figure of the body of Christ which is not in the Communion on earth but only in heaven). They interpret the word "is" sacramentally or in a figurative manner, so that nobody will imagine that the reality is joined to the symbols in such a way that Christ's body is even now present on earth in some invisible and impalpable manner. That is, the body of Christ is 8 sacramentally or symbolically united with the bread in such a way that as certainly as believing and pious Christians eat the bread with their mouths, just so certainly do they partake spiritually by faith also of the body of Christ which is up in heaven. But the teaching that the body of Christ is essentially present here on earth in the Lord's Supper, although invisibly and impalpably, and is orally received with the blessed bread even by hypocrites or counterfeit Christians, is something that they are accustomed to anathematize and condemn as a horrendous blasphemy.[7]

The Augsburg Confession, on the other hand, teaches on the basis 9 of God's Word "that the true body and blood of Christ are really present in the Holy Supper under the forms of bread and wine and that they are distributed and received," [8] and it condemns the contrary doctrine (that is, the doctrine of the Sacramentarians, who at the same time submitted their own confession at Augsburg to the effect

[5] So the *Exegesis perspicua* (1574), 17ff.
[6] I Cor. 11:24.
[7] Cf. John Calvin, *Institutes,* IV, 17, 26. *Consensus Tigurinus,* XXVI.
[8] See above, Augsburg Confession, X.

that since the body of Christ has ascended into heaven it is not truly and essentially present here on earth in the sacrament). Dr. Luther 10 clearly presents the same view in the Small Catechism in the following words: "The Sacrament of the Altar, instituted by Christ himself, is the true body and blood of our Lord Jesus Christ, under the bread and wine, given to us Christians to eat and to drink." [9] And it is not 11 only set forth still more clearly in the Apology, but it is also supported there with the words of Paul in I Cor. 10:16 and with a quotation from Cyril as follows: "Article X has been accepted, in which we confess that in the Lord's Supper the body and blood of Christ are truly and essentially present and are truly offered with the visible elements, the bread and the wine, to those who receive the sacrament. If the body of Christ were not truly present, but only the Holy Spirit, then when Paul says that the bread which we break is a participation in the body of Christ, etc., it would follow that the bread is a participation not in the body but in the spirit of Christ. And we know that not only the Roman but also the Greek Church has taught the bodily presence of Christ in the Holy Communion." Cyril is quoted to the effect that Christ dwells bodily in the Supper through the communication of his flesh in us.

Later on, those who at Augsburg had submitted their own 12 confession concerning this article adopted the confession of our churches. In 1536 the theologians of Saxony and Upper Germany drafted the following articles of Christian agreement in Wittenberg,[1] and Dr. Martin Luther and other theologians of both parties signed them:

"We have heard how Master Martin Bucer has explained his 13 opinion, and that of the other preachers who came with him from the cities, concerning the holy sacrament of the body and blood of Christ, namely thus: They confess, in accordance with the words of 14 Irenaeus,[2] that there are two things in this sacrament, one heavenly and the other earthly. Therefore they maintain and teach that with the bread and wine the body and blood of Christ are truly and essentially present, distributed, and received. And although they deny a transubstantiation (that is, an essential change of the bread and wine into the body and blood of Christ) and do not believe that the body and blood of Christ are locally enclosed in the bread, or are in some other way permanently united with it apart from the use[3] of the sacrament,

---

[9] See above, Small Catechism, VI, 2.
[1] The Wittenberg Concord (1536).
[2] Irenaeus, *Elenchos*, IV, 18, 5.
[3] Here and below, the German translation of the Wittenberg Concord incorporated in the German Book of Concord of 1580 has *Niessung*, but the Latin original has *usum*, reflecting the "rule" set forth in section 85 below, *Nihil habet rationem sacramenti extra usum a Christo institutum*.

they grant that through sacramental union the bread is the body of Christ, etc. For they do not maintain that the body of Christ is 15 present apart from the use, as when the bread is laid aside or reserved in the tabernacle or carried about and exposed in procession, as happens in the papacy.

"Secondly, they hold that it is the institution of this sacrament, 16 performed by Christ, that makes it valid in Christendom, and that it does not depend on the worthiness or unworthiness of the minister who distributes the sacrament or of him who receives it, since, as St. Paul says, the unworthy receive the sacrament too. Therefore they hold that, where Christ's institution and command are observed, the body and blood of Christ are truly distributed to the unworthy, too, and that they truly receive it. But they receive it for judgment, as St. Paul says, for they misuse the holy sacrament since they receive it without true repentance and without faith. For it was instituted to testify that those who truly repent and comfort themselves through faith in Christ there receive the grace and merits of Christ, are incorporated into Christ, and are washed by the blood of Christ."

In the following year the leading theologians who were com- 17 mitted to the Augsburg Confession assembled from all parts of Germany in Smalcald to consider what kind of doctrinal statement they should submit to the council.[4] By common consent Dr. Luther drafted the Smalcald Articles, which all the theologians collectively and individually subscribed. In these the correct and true meaning is set forth briefly and precisely in words which agree in the most exact way with the words of Christ. In this way was stopped up every 18 subterfuge and loop-hole which the Sacramentarians had employed to interpret the aforementioned articles of agreement,[5] adopted in the previous year, to their own advantage, namely, that the body of Christ, together with all his benefits, is distributed with the bread in precisely the same way as with the Word of the Gospel, and that the sacramental union is intended to mean nothing more than the spiritual presence of the body of the Lord Christ through faith.

The Smalcald Articles state that "the bread and the wine in the 19 Supper are the true body and blood of Jesus Christ which are given and received not only by godly but also by wicked Christians."[6]

Dr. Luther explains and confirms this position at greater length 20 from the Word of God in the Large Catechism, where he writes as

---

[4] Meant is the proposed Council of Mantua, called in 1537 but repeatedly postponed and finally replaced by the Council of Trent (1545-63). The account of the origin of the Smalcald Articles here given represents a rather hazy recollection of the facts (cf. the Introduction to the Smalcald Articles, above).

[5] Latin, *formula concordiae,* the Wittenberg Concord of 1536.

[6] See above, Smalcald Articles, Pt. III, VI.

follows: "What is the Sacrament of the Altar? Answer: It is the true body and blood of Christ in and under the bread and wine which Christ's word commands us Christians to eat and drink." And 21 shortly thereafter: "The Word, I say, is what makes this sacrament and so distinguishes it that it is not mere bread and wine but is and is called Christ's body and blood." And shortly thereafter: "You 22 can strengthen your conscience from the Word of God and declare, 'Let a hundred thousand devils and all the enthusiasts come along and ask, How can bread and wine be the body and blood of Christ?' I know that all the enthusiasts and scholars put together have less wisdom than the divine Majesty has in his little finger. Here we have Christ's word, 'Take eat, this is my body. Drink of it, all of you, this is the new covenant in my blood,' etc. We shall abide by these words and look anyone in the eye who thinks that he can correct Christ and change what he has spoken. It is true indeed 23 that if you take the Word away or look upon the elements without the Word, you then have nothing but ordinary bread and wine. But if the words remain with the elements, as they should and must, then in accordance with the words it is truly the body and blood of Christ. For it must be as Christ's lips speak and declare, since he cannot lie or deceive.

"Hence it is easy to answer all kinds of questions which now 24 trouble people—for example, whether even a wicked priest can administer and give the sacrament, and like questions. Our conclusion is that even though a rascal receives or gives the sacrament, it is the true sacrament (that is, Christ's body and blood) just as much as when one does so in the most worthy manner, for the sacrament is not based on the holiness of men but on the Word of God. As little as a saint on earth, or even an angel in heaven, can change bread and wine into the body and blood of Christ, so little can anyone alter or change the sacrament, even though it is misused. The Word by 25 which it has been instituted and has become a sacrament is not rendered false because of an individual's person or unbelief. Christ 26 does not say, 'If you believe and are worthy, you have my body and blood,' but, 'Take, eat and drink, this is my body and blood.' Likewise he says, 'Do this,' namely, what I am now doing, instituting, giving you, and commanding you to take. This is as much as to say, 'Whether you are worthy or unworthy, you here have his body and blood by virtue of these words which are added to the bread and wine.' Mark this and remember it well, for on these words rest our whole argument, protection, and defense against all errors and deceptions that have so far arisen or may yet arise." [7]

So far the quotation from the Large Catechism, which estab- 27

---

[7] See above, Large Catechism, V, 12-19.

lishes the true presence of the body and blood of Christ in the holy Supper from God's Word and confirms that it is to be understood not only with reference to believers and worthy communicants but also to the unbelieving and unworthy.

Since this highly enlightened man foresaw in the Spirit that after   28 his death some would try to make him suspect by giving the impression that he had departed from this doctrine and other Christian articles,[8] he appended the following protestation to his *Great Confession:* "I   29 see that schisms and errors are increasing proportionately with the passage of time, and that there is no end to the rage and fury of Satan. Hence lest any persons during my lifetime or after my death appeal to me or misuse my writings to confirm their error, as the Sacramentarians and Anabaptists are already beginning to do, I desire with this treatise to confess my faith before God and all the world, point by point. I am determined to abide by it until my death and (so help me God!) in this faith to depart from this world and to appear before the judgment seat of our Lord Jesus Christ. Hence if any one shall say after my death, 'If Dr. Luther were living now, he would teach and hold this or that article differently, for he did not consider it sufficiently,' etc., let me say now as then, and then as now, that by   30 the grace of God I have most diligently traced all these articles through the Scriptures, have examined them again and again in the light thereof, and have wanted to defend all of them as certainly as I have now defended the Sacrament of the Altar. I am not drunk or irrespon-   31 sible. I know what I am saying, and I well realize what this will mean for me before the Last Judgment at the coming of the Lord Christ. Let no one make this out to be a joke or idle talk; I am in dead earnest, since by the grace of God I have learned to know a great deal about Satan. If he can twist and pervert the Word of God, what will he not be able to do with my or someone else's words?"[9]

Following this protestation Luther, of blessed memory, listed   32 among other articles the following: "In the same way I also say and confess that in the Sacrament of the Altar the body and blood of Christ are truly eaten and drunk in the bread and wine, though the priests who distribute them or those who receive them do not believe or otherwise misuse the sacrament. It does not rest on man's faith or unbelief but on the Word and ordinance of God—unless they first change God's Word and ordinance and misinterpret them, as the enemies of the sacrament do at the present time. They, indeed, have

---

[8] The rumor had been spread that shortly before his death Luther instructed some of his intimate friends to make amends for his extreme views on the sacrament by gradually introducing a modified form of teaching. This became known among Lutherans as the "Heidelberg Roorback" (*Heidelberger Landlüge*).

[9] *WA*, 26:499, 500.

only bread and wine, for they do not also have the Word and instituted ordinance of God but have perverted and changed it according to their own imagination." [1]

Dr. Luther, who understood the true intention of the Augsburg   33 Confession better than any one else, remained by it steadfastly and defended it constantly until he died. Shortly before his death, in his last confession, he repeated his faith in this article with great fervor and wrote as follows: "I reckon them all as belonging together (that is, as Sacramentarians and enthusiasts), for that is what they are who will not believe that the Lord's bread in the Supper is his true, natural body, which the godless or Judas receive orally as well as St. Peter and all the saints. Whoever, I say, will not believe this, will please let me alone and expect no fellowship from me. This is final." [2]

From these statements and especially from the exposition of   34 Dr. Luther, as the chief teacher of the Augsburg Confession, every intelligent person who loves truth and peace can understand beyond all doubt what the Augsburg Confession's real meaning and intention in this article have always been.

In addition to the words of Christ and of St. Paul (the bread in   35 the Lord's Supper "is true body of Christ" or "a participation in the body of Christ"),[3] we at times also use the formulas "*under* the bread, *with* the bread, *in* the bread." We do this to reject the papistic transubstantiation and to indicate the sacramental union between the untransformed substance of the bread and the body of Christ. The   36 Scriptures do the same thing when they reproduce and explain the statement, "The Word became flesh," [4] with such equivalent phrases as, "The Word dwelt in us," [5] or "In Christ the whole fullness of the deity dwells bodily," [6] or "God was with him," [7] or "God was in Christ," [8] and similar expressions. Thus the Scriptures explain that the divine essence has not been transformed into the human nature but that both untransformed natures are personally united. Many prominent   37 ancient teachers, like Justin, Cyprian, Augustine, Leo, Gelasius, Chrysostom, and others, have cited the personal union as an analogy to the words of Christ's testament, "This is my body." For as in Christ two distinct and untransformed natures are indivisibly united, so in the Holy Supper the two essences, the natural bread and the true, natural body of Christ, are present together here on earth in the

---

[1] *WA*, 26:506.
[2] *WA*, 54:155, 156.
[3] Matt. 26:26; Luke 22:19; Mark 14:22; I Cor. 11:24; 10:16.
[4] John 1:14.
[5] John 1:14 (Vulgate).
[6] Col. 2:9.
[7] Acts 10:38.
[8] II Cor. 5:19.

ordered action of the sacrament, though the union of the body 38
and blood of Christ with the bread and wine is not a personal union,
like that of the two natures in Christ, but a sacramental union, as
Dr. Luther and our theologians call it in the above-mentioned articles
of agreement of 1536[9] and elsewhere. Thereby they wished to indicate
that, even though they also use these different formulas, "in the
bread, under the bread, with the bread," they still accept the words of
Christ in their strict sense and as they read, and they do not consider
that in the proposition (that is, the words of Christ's testament), "This
is my body," we have to do with a figurative predication, but with an
unusual[1] one (that is, it is not to be understood as a figurative, flowery
formula or quibble about words). As Justin says, "We receive this 39
not as ordinary bread or an ordinary beverage, but we believe that just
as Jesus Christ, our Saviour, was incarnate through the Word of God
and for the sake of our salvation had flesh and blood, so the food
blessed by him through the Word and prayer is the true flesh and blood
of the Lord Jesus Christ." In both his *Great Confession* and espe- 40
cially his *Last Confession Concerning the Communion*[2] Dr. Luther
defended with great zeal and earnestness the formula which Christ
employed in the Last Supper.

Since Dr. Luther is rightly to be regarded as the most eminent 41
teacher of the churches which adhere to the Augsburg Confession and
as the person whose entire doctrine in sum and content was comprehended in the articles of the aforementioned Augsburg Confession and
delivered to Emperor Charles V, therefore the true meaning and
intention of the Augsburg Confession cannot be derived more correctly
or better from any other source than from Dr. Luther's doctrinal and
polemical writings. Thus the position set forth above rests on a 42
unique, firm, immovable, and indubitable rock of truth in the words
of institution recorded in the holy Word of God and so understood,
taught, and transmitted by the holy evangelists and apostles, and by
their disciples and hearers in turn.

It is our Lord and Saviour Jesus Christ concerning whom, as our 43
unique teacher, the earnest command has been given from heaven to
all men, "Listen to him."[3] He is not a mere man or an angel; he is not
only truthful, wise, and mighty, but himself the eternal truth and
wisdom and the almighty God. He knows very well what and how he

[9] Above, section 12.

[1] The "Apology of the Formula of Concord" (f. 154a) explains that the
term "unusual" was chosen "because in the usual expressions no instance was
found that was exactly parallel to Christ's formula." As synonyms the
same source (f. 152b) lists *sacramentalis, singularis,* and Luther's *synec-
dochica* (though not in the sense of *continens pro absente contento*).

[2] *WA,* 26:271ff., 379ff.; 54:149ff.

[3] Matt. 17:5; Luke 3:22.

must speak, and he is able mightily to accomplish and achieve what he speaks and promises, as he says, "Heaven and earth shall pass away, but my words will not pass away," [4] and again, "All authority in heaven and on earth has been given to me." [5] After the Last   44 Supper, as he was about to begin his bitter passion and death for our sin, in this sad, last hour of his life, this truthful and almighty Lord, our Creator and Redeemer Jesus Christ, selected his words with great deliberation and care in ordaining and instituting this most venerable sacrament, which was to be observed with great reverence and obedience until the end of the world and which was to be an abiding memorial of his bitter passion and death and of all his blessings, a seal of the new covenant, a comfort for all sorrowing hearts, and a true bond and union of Christians with Christ their head and with one another. Under these circumstances Christ said of the blessed and proffered bread, "Take, eat, this is my body which is given for you," [6] and concerning the cup or the wine, "This is my blood of the new covenant which is shed for you for the remission of sins." [7]

We are therefore bound to interpret and explain these words of   45 the eternal, truthful, and almighty Son of God, Jesus Christ, our Lord, Creator, and Redeemer, not as flowery, figurative, or metaphorical expressions, as they appear to our reason, but we must accept them in simple faith and due obedience in their strict and clear sense, just as they read. Nor dare we permit any objection or human contradiction, spun out of human reason, to turn us away from these words, no matter how appealing our reason may find it. Abraham certainly   46 had sufficient ground for a disputation when he heard God's words about offering up his son, because these words were patently contrary not only to reason and to divine and natural law but also to the eminent article of faith concerning the promised seed, Christ, who was to be born of Isaac. He could have asked if this command was to be understood literally or if it was to receive a tolerable and loose interpretation. But as on the previous occasion when Abraham received the promise of the blessed seed of Isaac, although this seemed impossible to his reason, he gave God the honor of truthfulness and concluded and believed most certainly in his heart that what God promised he was also able to do. So Abraham understood and believed the words and command of God plainly and simply, as the words read, and committed the entire matter to God's omnipotence and wisdom, knowing that God had many more ways and means of fulfilling the promises concerning the seed of Isaac than he could comprehend with

[4] Luke 21:33.
[5] Matt. 28:18.
[6] Matt. 26:26; Luke 22:19.
[7] Mark 14:24; Luke 22:20; Matt. 26:28.

his blind reason. In the same way we are to believe in all humility 47
and obedience the explicit, certain, clear, and earnest words and
commands of our Creator and Redeemer, without any doubts or
arguments as to how it is to be reconciled with our reason or how it is
possible. The Lord who has spoken these words is himself infinite
Wisdom and Truth and can certainly accomplish and bring to pass
whatever he promises.

All circumstances of the institution of this Supper testify that 48
these words of our Lord and Saviour Jesus Christ, which in themselves
are simple, clear, manifest, certain, and indubitable, can and should be
understood only in their usual, strict, and commonly accepted meaning.
For since Christ gave this command at table and during supper, there
can be no doubt that he was speaking of true, natural bread and
natural wine as well as of oral eating and drinking. Hence there can
be no metaphor (that is, a change in meaning) in the word "bread," as
though the body of Christ were spiritual bread or a spiritual food for
the soul. Christ himself likewise precluded a metonymy (that is, a 49
change in meaning) in the word "body." He was not speaking of a
symbol of his body, or of a representation or of his body in a figurative
sense, or of the virtue of his body and the benefits which he had won
for us by the sacrifice of his body. He was speaking of his true,
essential body, which he gave into death for us, and of his true, essential
blood, which was shed for us on the tree of the cross for the forgiveness
of sins. There is, of course, no more faithful or trustworthy 50
interpreter of the words of Jesus Christ than the Lord Christ himself,
who best understands his words and heart and intention and is best
qualified from the standpoint of wisdom and intelligence to explain
them. In the institution of his last will and testament and of his
abiding covenant and union, he uses no flowery language but the most
appropriate, simple, indubitable, and clear words, just as he does in
all the articles of faith and in the institution of other covenant-signs
and signs of grace or sacraments, such as circumcision, the many kinds
of sacrifice in the Old Testament, and holy Baptism. And so that no
misunderstanding could creep in, he explained things more clearly by
adding the words, "given for you, shed for you." He let his 51
disciples keep this simple and strict understanding and commanded
them to teach all nations to observe all that he had commanded them
(that is, the apostles).

Therefore also all three evangelists, Matthew (26:26), Mark 52
(14:22), and Luke (22:19), as well as St. Paul who received the same
information after Christ's ascension (I Cor. 11:25), unanimously and
with the same words and syllables repeat these simple, clear, certain,
and truthful words of Christ, "This is my body," and apply them in one
and the same manner to the blessed and proffered bread without any
interpretation and change. There is therefore no doubt that in the 53

other part of the sacrament the words of Luke and Paul, "This cup is the new covenant in my blood" (Luke 22:20; I Cor. 11:25), have no other meaning than what the words of St. Matthew and St. Mark give us, "This (namely, what you are drinking with your mouth from the cup) is my blood of the new covenant, whereby I establish, seal, and confirm with you people this my testament and new covenant, namely, the forgiveness of sins." [8]

Thus, too, the repetition, confirmation, and exposition of the 54 words of Christ which St. Paul gives us in I Cor. 10:16 ("The cup of blessing which we bless, is it not a participation in the blood of Christ? The bread which we break, is it not a participation in the body of Christ?") are to be regarded diligently and earnestly as a special and manifest testimony to the true and essential presence and distribution of the body and blood of Christ in the Communion. From these words we learn clearly that not only the cup which Christ blessed in the Last Supper and not only the bread which Christ himself broke and distributed, but also that which we break and bless is participation in the body and blood of Christ, so that all who eat this bread and drink the cup truly receive and partake of the true body and blood of Christ. For if the body of Christ were not truly and essentially present 55 and were received only according to its virtue and operation, then the bread could not be called participation in the body but in the spirit, the virtue, and the benefits of Christ, as the Apology argues and concludes.[9] If Paul were speaking only of a spiritual participation 56 in the body of Christ through faith, as the Sacramentarians pervert this passage, he would not say that the bread but that the spirit or faith is participation in the body of Christ. But he says that the bread is participation in the body of Christ, and that means that all who receive the blessed bread also partake of the body of Christ. Therefore he certainly cannot be speaking of a spiritual eating but of a sacramental or oral eating of the body of Christ in which both the godly and the godless participate. As the purpose and context of St. Paul's entire 57 discourse[1] prove, he had in mind those who were eating idol-sacrifices and participating in pagan devil-worship and who likewise were going to the table of the Lord and partaking of the body and blood of Christ. He was discouraging them and warning them against receiving the body and blood of Christ to their own judgment and condemnation. Since he said that all who partake of the blessed and broken bread in the Supper participate in the body of Christ, St. Paul certainly could not be speaking of a spiritual fellowship with Christ, which no one could misuse and against which no one should be warned. There- 58

[8] Cf. Matt. 26:28; Mark 14:24.
[9] Above, Apology, X, 1.
[1] I Cor. 10:18-33.

fore our revered fathers and forebears, like Luther and other pure teachers of the Augsburg Confession, explained this passage of Paul in words which agree in the best possible way with the words of Christ by saying, "The bread which we break is the distributed body of Christ, or the common body of Christ distributed among those who receive the broken bread."

We shall abide unanimously by this simple and well-founded 59 explanation of the noble testimony in I Cor. 10:16. We are justly astonished that some are so rash that they now cite this passage, which they formerly advanced against the Sacramentarians, as a basis for their error that in the Lord's Supper the body of Christ is received only spiritually. They write as follows: "The bread is participation in the body of Christ (that is, it is that whereby we have participation in the body of Christ, which is the church), or it is the means whereby believers are united with Christ, just as the Word of the Gospel, when it is laid hold on by faith, is a means whereby we are spiritually united with Christ and are incorporated into the body of Christ, which is the church."

But St. Paul teaches expressly that not only godly, pious, and 60 believing Christians receive the true body and blood of Christ orally in the sacrament, but also the unworthy and godless hypocrites, like Judas and his ilk who have no fellowship with Christ, who come to the Lord's table without true repentance and conversion to God, and who by their unworthy eating and drinking sin grievously against the body and blood of Christ. St. Paul says, "Who eats the bread or drinks the cup of the Lord in an unworthy manner" (I Cor. 11:27) sins not only against bread and wine, not only against signs and symbols and figures of the body and blood, but becomes guilty of profaning the body and blood of the Lord Jesus Christ. Such a person dishonors, abuses, and desecrates him who is there present as certainly as did the Jews when they actually and in deed laid violent hands upon the body of Christ and murdered him. The ancient Christian fathers and teachers of the church have unanimously understood and explained this passage in this way.[2]

There is therefore a twofold eating of the flesh of Christ. The 61 one is spiritual, of which Christ speaks chiefly in John 6:48-58. This occurs, in no other way than with the spirit and faith, in the preaching and contemplation of the Gospel as well as in the Lord's Supper. It is intrinsically useful, salutary, and necessary to salvation for all Christians at all times. Without this spiritual participation, even the

[2] At this point the Torgau Book introduced quotations from Basil, *De baptismo*, I, 3, 3; II, 3; John Chrysostom, *In epistola I. ad Corinthios homilia XXVII*, 5; Pseudo-Augustine *Contra Fulgentium Donatistam*, IV; Augustine, *De baptismo contra Donatistas*, V, 8; *Epistola 43 (162)*, 8, 23; *Contra Donatistas post collationem*, VII, 9; XX, 27; *Sermo 71 (11) de verbis Domini, Quisquis blasphemaverit*, 11, 17.

sacramental or oral eating in the Supper is not only not salutary but actually pernicious and damning. This spiritual eating, however, is 62 precisely faith—namely, that we hear, accept with faith, and appropriate to ourselves the Word of God, in which Christ, true God and man, together with all the benefits that he has acquired for us by giving his body for us into death and by shedding his blood for us (that is to say, the grace of God, forgiveness of sins, righteousness, and everlasting life), is presented—and that we rest indomitably, with certain trust and confidence, on this comforting assurance that we have a gracious God and eternal salvation for the sake of Jesus Christ, and hold to it in all difficulty and temptation.

The other eating of the body of Christ is oral or sacramental, 63 when all who eat and drink the blessed bread and wine in the Lord's Supper receive and partake of the true, essential body and blood of Christ orally. Believers receive it as a certain pledge and assurance that their sins are truly forgiven, that Christ dwells and is efficacious in them; unbelievers receive it orally, too, but to their judgment and damnation. This is what Christ's words of institution say, when at table and 64 during supper he handed his disciples natural bread and natural wine, which he called his true body and blood, and said therewith, "Eat and drink." Under the circumstances this command can only be understood as referring precisely to oral eating and drinking—not, however, in a coarse, carnal, Capernaitic[3] manner, but in a supernatural, incomprehensible manner. But Christ adds another command, and in 65 addition to the oral eating he ordains the spiritual eating, when he said, "Do this in remembrance of me." In these words he required faith.

Hence, in harmony with these words of Christ's institution and 66 St. Paul's exposition of them, all the ancient Christian teachers and the entire holy Christian church teach unanimously that the body of Christ is received not only spiritually through faith, which occurs outside of the sacrament too, but also orally, and this by unworthy, unbelieving, false, and wicked Christians as well as by the godly and pious.[4] Since these testimonies are too long to list here, in the interest of desirable brevity we direct the Christian reader to our more extensive writings. From these it is evident how unjustly and poisonously the Sacra- 67

---

[3] At Capernaum (John 6:52-65) the Jews interpreted Christ's words as a purely natural and physical eating of his body. In sixteenth century controversial language "Capernaitic" was a "growl-word" that implied belief in transubstantiation.

[4] At this point the Torgau Book introduced quotations from Theodoret, *Interpretatio epistolae I. ad Corinthios, ad* 11, 27; John Chrysostom, *Sermo 3 in Ephesos 1; Homilia 59 in Matthaeum; In epistola I. ad Corinthios homilia XXVII, 5; Homilia 11 ad populum; Homilia 21;* Cyprian, *De lapsis* XVI, XXII; Leo, *Sermo 91 (6) de ieiunio;* Gregory the Great, *Dialogi, IV, 58; Homilia in evangelia XXII, 7;* Ambrose (unidentified); Augustine, *Epistola 54 (118), 4, 8.*

mentarian enthusiasts[5] ridicule the Lord Christ, St. Paul, and the entire church when they call oral eating and eating on the part of the unworthy "two hairs of a horse's tail and an invention of which even Satan himself would be ashamed," just as they describe the majesty of Christ as "Satan's dung, by which the devil amuses himself and deceives men." [6] These expressions are so terrible that a pious Christian should be ashamed to translate them.

It is essential to explain with great diligence who the unworthy 68 guests at this Supper are,[7] namely, those who go to this sacrament without true contrition and sorrow for their sins, without true faith, and without a good intention to improve their life and who by their unworthy oral eating of the body of Christ burden themselves with judgment (that is, temporal and eternal punishments) and profane the body and blood of Christ.

True and worthy communicants, on the other hand, are those 69 timid, perturbed Christians, weak in faith, who are heartily terrified because of their many and great sins, who consider themselves unworthy of this noble treasure and the benefits of Christ because of their great impurity, and who perceive their weakness in faith, deplore it, and heartily wish that they might serve God with a stronger and more cheerful faith and a purer obedience. This most venerable 70 sacrament was instituted and ordained primarily for communicants like this, as Christ says, "Come unto me, all who labor and are heavy laden, and I will give you rest" (Matt. 11:28). Likewise, "Those who are well have no need of a physician, but those who are sick." [8] Likewise, "The power of God is made perfect in weakness." [9] Likewise, "As for a man who is weak in faith, welcome him, for God has welcomed him" (Rom. 14:1, 3). For whoever believes on the Son of God, be his faith strong or weak, has eternal life (John 3:16). And 71 worthiness does not consist in the weakness or certainty of faith, be it greater or smaller, but solely in the merits of Christ, of which the distressed father of weak faith (Mark 9:24) partook no less than Abraham, Paul, and others who had a cheerful and strong faith.

Let this suffice concerning the true presence and the twofold 72 participation in the body and blood of Christ, the one through faith spiritually, the other orally, which happens in the case of both the worthy and the unworthy.

There has also arisen a misunderstanding and dissension among 73

---

[5] German, *Sakramentschwärmer.*

[6] These phrases were used by Theodore Beza and Peter Martyr Vermigli.

[7] Calvinists distinguished three types of communicants, (1) the worthy (*digni*), who have strong faith, (2) the unworthy (*indigni*), whose faith is weak, and (3) the godless (*impii*), who have no faith at all.

[8] Matt. 9:12.

[9] II Cor. 12:9.

some teachers of the Augsburg Confession concerning the consecration and the common rule that there is no sacrament apart from the instituted use. In this question we have reached the following 74 fraternal and unanimous agreement among ourselves: No man's word or work, be it the merit or the speaking of the minister, be it the eating and drinking or the faith of the communicants, can effect the true presence of the body and blood of Christ in the Supper. This is to be ascribed only to the almighty power of God and the Word, institution, and ordinance of our Lord Jesus Christ. For the 75 truthful and almighty words of Jesus Christ which he spoke in the first institution were not only efficacious in the first Supper but they still retain their validity and efficacious power in all places where the Supper is observed according to Christ's institution and where his words are used, and the body and blood of Christ are truly present, distributed, and received by the virtue and potency of the same words which Christ spoke in the first Supper. For wherever we observe his institution and speak his words over the bread and cup and distribute the blessed bread and cup, Christ himself is still active through the spoken words by the virtue of the first institution, which he wants to be repeated. Chrysostom says in his *Sermon on the Passion:* "Christ himself 76 prepares this table and blesses it. No human being, but only Christ himself who was crucified for us, can make of the bread and wine set before us the body and blood of Christ. The words are spoken by the mouth of the priest, but by God's power and grace through the words that he speaks, 'This is my body,' the elements set before us in the Supper are blessed. Just as the words, 'Be fruitful and multiply and fill the earth,' [1] were spoken only once but are ever efficacious in nature and make things grow and multiply, so this word was indeed spoken only once, but it is efficacious until this day, and until his return it brings it about that his true body and blood are present in the church's Supper." [2] And Luther states: "This his command and 77 institution can and does bring it about that we do not distribute and receive ordinary bread and wine but his body and blood, as his words read, 'This is my body,' etc., 'This is my blood,' etc. Thus it is not our work or speaking but the command and ordinance of Christ that, from the beginning of the first Communion until the end of the world, make the bread the body and the wine the blood that are daily distributed through our ministry and office." [3] Again, "Here, too, if I were to 78 say over all the bread there is, 'This is the body of Christ,' nothing would happen, but when we follow his institution and command in the Lord's Supper and say, 'This is my body,' then it is his body, not because of

---

[1] Gen. 1:28.
[2] John Chrysostom, *De proditione Iudae,* 1, 6.
[3] *WA*, 38:240.

our speaking or of our efficacious word, but because of his command in which he has told us so to speak and to do and has attached his own command and deed to our speaking." [4]

In the administration of Communion the words of institution 79 are to be spoken or sung distinctly and clearly before the congregation and are under no circumstances to be omitted. Thereby we render 80 obedience to the command of Christ, 'This do.' Thereby the faith 81 of the hearers in the essence and benefits of this sacrament (the presence of the body and blood of Christ, the forgiveness of sins, and all the benefits which Christ has won for us by his death and the shedding of his blood and which he gives to us in his testament) is awakened, strengthened, and confirmed through his Word. And 82 thereby the elements of bread and wine are hallowed or blessed in this holy use, so that therewith the body and blood of Christ are distributed to us to eat and to drink, as Paul says, "The cup of blessing which we bless," [5] which happens precisely through the repetition and recitation of the words of institution.

But this blessing or recitation of Christ's words of institution by 83 itself, if the entire action of the Lord's Supper as Christ ordained it is not observed (if, for instance, the blessed bread is not distributed, received, and eaten but is locked up, offered up, or carried about), does not make a sacrament. But the command of Christ, "Do 84 this," which comprehends the whole action or administration of this sacrament (namely, that in a Christian assembly we take bread and wine, consecrate it, distribute it, receive it, eat and drink it, and therewith proclaim the Lord's death), must be kept integrally and inviolately, just as St. Paul sets the whole action of the breaking of bread, or of the distribution and reception, before our eyes in I Cor. 10:16.

To maintain this true Christian doctrine concerning the Holy 85 Supper and to obviate and eliminate many kinds of idolatrous misuse and perversion of this testament, the following useful rule and norm has been derived from the words of institution: Nothing has the character of a sacrament apart from the use instituted by Christ, or apart from the divinely instituted action (that is, if one does not observe Christ's institution as he ordained it, it is no sacrament). This rule dare not in any way be rejected, but it can and should be profitably urged and retained in the church of God.

In this context "use" or "action" does not primarily mean faith, 86 or the oral eating alone, but the entire external and visible action of the Supper as ordained by Christ: the consecration or words of institution, the distribution and reception, or the oral eating of the blessed bread

---

[4] *WA*, 26:282ff.
[5] I Cor. 10:16.

and wine, the body and blood of Christ. Apart from this use it is   87
not to be deemed a sacrament, as when in the papistic Mass the bread
is not distributed but is offered up, or locked up, or carried about, or
exposed for adoration, just as the baptismal water is no sacrament or
Baptism if it should be used to consecrate bells, or to cure leprosy,
or is otherwise exposed for adoration. It was against such papistic
abuses that this rule was first formulated and explained by Dr. Luther.[6]

We must, however, also point out that the Sacramentarians   88
dishonestly and maliciously pervert this useful and necessary rule and
interpret it as referring only to the spiritual and internal use of faith
in order to deny the true, essential presence and the oral eating of the
body of Christ, in which here on earth both the worthy and the unworthy alike participate. This implies that for the unworthy it is no
sacrament, and that the reception of the body of Christ takes place only
spiritually through faith, or that faith effects the presence of Christ's
body in the Holy Supper and that therefore the unworthy and unbelieving hypocrites do not receive the body of Christ because it is not
present to them. It is not our faith which makes the sacrament,   89
but solely the Word and institution of our almighty God and Saviour,
Jesus Christ, which always remain efficacious in Christendom and which
are neither abrogated nor rendered impotent by either the worthiness
or unworthiness of the minister or the unbelief of him who receives
the sacrament. Just as the Gospel is and remains the true Gospel
even when godless hearers do not believe it (except that in them it does
not effect salvation), so whether those who receive the sacrament
believe or do not believe, Christ nonetheless remains truthful in his
words when he says, "Take eat, this is my body." This he effects not
through our faith, but solely through his omnipotence.

It is therefore a pernicious, impudent error when some by a   90
subtle perversion of this common rule ascribe to our faith the power
to achieve the presence of the body of Christ and to receive it, rather
than ascribe it to the omnipotence of our Lord and Saviour, Jesus
Christ.

All the imaginary reasons and futile counter-arguments of the   91
Sacramentarians concerning the essential and natural properties of the
human body, concerning the ascension of Christ, concerning his withdrawal from this world, and the like have been thoroughly, extensively,
and definitively refuted on the basis of God's Word by Dr. Luther in
his polemical writings, *Against the Heavenly Prophets, That These
Words "This Is My Body" Still Stand Firm,* his *Great* and *Small
Confessions concerning the Holy Supper,* and other writings of his.[7]
The spiritualists have advanced no new arguments since his death. We

---

[6] *WA,* 30[II]: 254, 255; cf. Smalcald Articles, Pt. III, Art. XV, 4.
[7] *WA,* 18:62-214; 23:64-320; 26:261-509; 54:141-167.

shall therefore, for the sake of desirable brevity, merely refer the Christian reader to these writings and desire to have them considered as appealed to herewith.

We shall not, can not, and should not permit any clever human   92 opinions, no matter what appearance or prestige they may have, to lead us away from the simple, explicit, and clear understanding of Christ's word and testament to a strange meaning different from the way the letters read, but, as stated above, we shall understand and believe them in the simple sense. Our basic arguments, on which we have stood   93 consistently from the outbreak of this controversy, are these (the same ones that Dr. Luther advanced against the Sacramentarians at the very beginning in the following words): "My grounds, on which I rest in this matter, are as follows:

"1. The first is this article of our faith: That Jesus Christ is   94 essential, natural, true, complete God and man in one person, undivided and inseparable.

"2. The second is that the right hand of God is everywhere.   95

"3. The third is that the Word of God is not false or deceitful.   96

"4. The fourth is that God has and knows various ways to be   97 present at a certain place, not only, as the enthusiasts vainly imagine, the one which the philosophers call local or spatial.

"Furthermore, the one body of Christ has three different modes,   98 or all three modes, of being at any given place.

"1. The comprehensible, corporeal mode of presence, as when   99 he walked bodily on earth and vacated or occupied space according to his size. He can still employ this mode of presence when he wills to do so, as he did after his resurrection and as he will do on the Last Day, as St. Paul says, "This will be made manifest at the proper time by the blessed God" (I Tim. 6:15), and, "When Christ who is our life appears" (Col. 3:4). He is not in God or with the Father or in heaven according to this mode, as the fanatic spirit dreams, for God is not a corporeal space or place. The passages which the enthusiasts adduce concerning Christ's leaving the world and going to the Father speak of this mode of presence.

"2. There is, secondly, the incomprehensible, spiritual mode of   100 presence according to which he neither occupies nor vacates space but penetrates every creature, wherever he wills. To use some imperfect illustrations, my vision penetrates air, light, or water and does not occupy or vacate any space; a musical sound or tone passes through air or water or a board and a wall and neither occupies nor vacates space; likewise light and heat go through air, water, glass, or crystal and exist without occupying or vacating space, and many more like these. He employed this mode of presence when he left the closed grave and came through locked doors, in the bread and wine in the

Lord's Supper, and, as people believe, when he was born of his mother,[8] etc.

"3. Thirdly, since he is one person with God, the divine, |01 heavenly mode, according to which all creatures are indeed much more penetrable and present to him than they are according to the second mode. For if according to the second mode he can be present in and with creatures in such a way that they do not feel, touch, measure, or comprehend him, how much more marvelously will he be present in all creatures according to this exalted third mode, where they cannot measure or comprehend him but where he has them present to himself, measures and comprehends them. You must posit this essence of Christ since he is one person with God, very far beyond creatures, as far as God transcends them, and you must posit it again as deep and as near in all creatures as God is immanent in them. For he is one indivisible person with God, and wherever God is, he must be also, otherwise our faith is false. But who can explain or even conceive |02 how this occurs? We know indeed that he is in God beyond all creatures and is one person with God. But how this happens, we do not know; it transcends nature and reason, even the comprehension of all the angels in heaven, and is known only to God. Since this is true, even though unknown to us, we should not give the lie to his words until we know how to prove certainly that the body of Christ cannot in any circumstances be where God is and that this mode of being is a fiction. Let the enthusiasts prove it! They will give it up.

"I do not wish to have denied by the foregoing that God may |03 have and know more modes whereby Christ's body can be anywhere. My only purpose was to show what crass fools our enthusiasts are, because they concede only the first, comprehensible mode of presence to the body of Christ although they are unable to prove that even this mode is contrary to our view. For I do not want to deny in any way that God's power is able to make a body be simultaneously in many places, even in a corporeal and comprehensible manner. For who wants to try to prove that God is unable to do that? Who has seen the limits of his power? The enthusiasts may indeed think that God is unable to do it, but who will believe their speculations? How will they establish that kind of speculation?" So far Luther.[9]

These words of Dr. Luther also show clearly in what sense our |04 churches use the word "spiritual" in this context. To the Sacramentarians this word "spiritual" means precisely that spiritual communion which is established when in spirit through faith the true believers are incorporated into Christ and become true, spiritual members of his body.[1]

[8] Cf. below, VIII, 24.
[9] *WA*, 26:335ff.
[1] Cf. *Consensus Tigurinus*, VI, IX.

But when Dr. Luther or we use the word "spiritual" in this 105
discussion, we have in mind the spiritual, supernatural, heavenly mode
according to which Christ is present in the Holy Supper, not only to
work comfort and life in believers but also to wreak judgment on
unbelievers. Thus we reject the Capernaitic conception of a gross,
carnal presence which the Sacramentarians ascribe to and force upon
our churches in spite of our public and oft-repeated testimony to the
contrary. In this sense, too, we use the word "spiritual'" when we say
that the body and blood of Christ in the Holy Supper are received,
eaten, and drunk spiritually, for although such eating occurs with the
mouth, the mode is spiritual.

Thus our faith in this article concerning the true presence of 106
the body and blood of Christ in the Holy Supper is built upon the
truth and omnipotence of the true and eternal God, our Lord and
Saviour Jesus Christ. These arguments are so strong and solid that
they will confirm and fortify our faith in all tensions concerning this
article. On the other hand, they will overthrow and refute all the
counter-arguments and objections of the Sacramentarians, no matter
how appealing and attractive they may appear to reason, and will
enable a Christian heart to rely on and trust in them with absolute
certainty.

Accordingly we reject and condemn with heart and mouth as 107
false, erroneous, and deceiving every error which is inconsistent with
or opposed and contrary to the aforementioned doctrine, based as it is
on the Word of God:

First, papistic transubstantiation, when they teach that the 108
consecrated or blessed bread and wine in the Holy Supper completely
lose their substance and essence and are converted into the substance
of the body and blood of Christ, so that only the mere species of
bread and wine, or their accidents without a subject, remain. Accordingly they assert that under the species of the bread, which they allege
has lost its natural substance and is no longer bread, the body of Christ
is present even apart from the action of the sacrament (when, for
instance, the bread is locked up in the tabernacle or is carried about
as a spectacle and for adoration). For nothing can be a sacrament
apart from God's command and the ordained use for which it is
instituted in the Word of God, as was shown above.

Secondly, we also reject and condemn all other papistic abuses 109
of this sacrament, such as the abomination of the sacrifice of the Mass
for the living and for the dead.

Furthermore, that only one species is administered to the laity 110
contrary to the explicit command and institution of Christ, etc. These
papistic abuses have been refuted at length in the common Confession[2]

---

[2] Augsburg Confession.

of our churches, the Apology, the Smalcald Articles, and other writings of ours on the basis of the Word of God and the testimony of the ancient church.

In this document we have intended to set forth primarily our | | | confession and explanation concerning the true presence of the body and blood of Christ against the Sacramentarians, some of whom have had the effrontery to penetrate our churches as adherents of the Augsburg Confession. We shall therefore set forth and recite the errors preeminently of the Sacramentarians and thereby forewarn our readers so they can avoid and shun these. Therefore we reject and | |2 condemn with heart and mouth as false, erroneous, and deceiving all Sacramentarian opinions and doctrines which are inconsistent with, opposed to, or contrary to the doctrine set forth above, based as it is on the Word of God.

1. The assertion that the words of institution are not to be | |3 simply understood in their strict sense, as they read, concerning the true essential presence of the body and blood of Christ in the Supper, but through tropes or a figurative interpretation are to be given a different, new, and strange sense. We reject all such Sacramentarian opinions and mutually contradictory views, no matter how manifold and various they may be.

2. Likewise, the denial of an oral eating of the body and blood | |4 of Christ in the Supper, and the contrary teaching that in the Supper the body of Christ is partaken of only spiritually through faith and that in the Supper our mouth receives only bread and wine.

3. Likewise, the teaching that bread and wine in the Supper | |5 are no more than badges whereby Christians recognize one another, or

4. that they are only figures, parables, and types of the far-distant body of Christ (for example, just as bread and wine are external food for our body, so the absent body of Christ with its merit is spiritual food for our souls).

5. Or that they are nothing more than symbols and reminders | |6 of the absent body of Christ, and that through these signs, as through an external pledge, we are assured that our faith, when it turns away from the Supper and rises above all heavens, partakes up there of the body and blood of Christ as truly as in the Supper we receive the external sign with our mouth. Thus the assurance and confirmation of our faith in the Supper allegedly take place not through the true, present body and blood of Christ, distributed to us, but through the external signs.

6. Or that in the Supper there is distributed to faith only the | |7 virtue, operation, and merit of the far-distant body of Christ, and that in this way we partake of his absent body. Accordingly the term "sacramental union" is to be understood in terms of the relation

between the sign and that which is signified—in other words, only as bread and wine have a similarity with the body and blood of Christ.

7. Or that the body and blood of Christ are only received and   118 partaken of through faith, spiritually.

8. Likewise, the teaching that because of his bodily ascension   119 to heaven Christ is so confined and circumscribed by a certain space in heaven that he is neither able nor willing to be truly and essentially present with us in the Supper, which is celebrated according to Christ's institution on earth, but that he is as far or as distant from it as heaven and earth are separated from each other. In support of their error, some Sacramentarians have deliberately and maliciously falsified the words in Acts 3:21, "Christ must take possession of heaven," to read "Christ must be received by heaven"—that is, Christ must be so taken in or circumscribed or comprehended by or in heaven that he in no way can or wills to be with us on earth with his human nature.

9. Likewise, the assertion that Christ could not or would not   120 have promised or have been able to achieve the true, essential presence of his body and blood in his Supper because the nature and properties of his assumed human nature neither permit nor allow this.

10. Likewise, the doctrine that it is not the words and the   121 omnipotence of Christ but faith that achieves the presence of the body of Christ in the Holy Supper, whence some omit the words of institution in the administration of the Supper. For while we justly criticize and condemn the papistic consecration which ascribes to the word and work of the priest the power allegedly to effect a sacrament, the words of institution cannot and should not in any case be omitted in the administration of the Supper, as shown above in a previous exposition.[3]

11. Likewise, that according to the words of Christ's institution   122 believers are not directed to seek the body of Christ in the bread and wine of the Supper, but to look away from the bread of the Supper and by their faith to look to that place in heaven where Christ is present with his body and there to partake of him.

12. We also reject the doctrine that unbelieving, unrepentant,   123 and wicked Christians, who only bear the name of Christ but do not have a right, truthful, living, and saving faith, receive only bread and wine in the Supper and not the body and blood of Christ. There are only two kinds of guests at this heavenly meal, the worthy and the unworthy. Therefore we reject the making of such a distinction among the unworthy which alleges that godless Epicureans and scoffers at the Word of God who are in the external community of the church receive only bread and wine in the use of the Holy Supper and not the body and the blood of Christ for their judgment.

³ Above, VII, 79-82.

13. We also reject the doctrine that worthiness does not 124 consist in true faith alone but also in man's own preparation.

14. Likewise, the teaching that even true believers who have 125 and retain a true, genuine, living faith, but who fail to meet their own self-devised standard of preparation, may receive this sacrament for judgment, just like unworthy guests.

15. Likewise, the teaching that the elements (the visible forms 126 of the blessed bread and wine) are to be adored. Of course, no one except an Arian heretic can or will deny that Christ himself, true God and man, who is truly and essentially present in the Supper when it is rightly used, should be adored in spirit and in truth in all places but especially where his community is assembled.

16. We also reject and condemn all presumptuous, scoffing, 127 and blasphemous questions and expressions which are advanced in a coarse, fleshly, Capernaitic way about the supernatural and heavenly mysteries of this Supper.[4]

Additional antitheses and rejected erroneous views have been 128 criticized and rejected in the foregoing exposition; for the sake of desirable brevity we have not wanted to repeat them at this point. Whatever additional condemnable opinions or erroneous views there may be can easily be discovered and identified by name from the foregoing exposition, for we reject and condemn everything that is inconsistent with, contrary to, or opposed to the doctrine set forth above, well founded as it is in God's Word.

VIII. THE PERSON OF CHRIST

A controversy has likewise arisen among theologians of the 1 Augsburg Confession concerning the person of Christ. It did not at first begin among them, however, but proceeded originally from the Sacramentarians.

For when Dr. Luther maintained with solid arguments the true, 2 essential presence of the body and blood of Jesus Christ in the Lord's Supper on the basis of the words of institution, the Zwinglians countered by saying that the body of Christ could not be a true and genuine human body if it were present at the same time in heaven and in the

---

[4] Paul Crell's "Kurtz Bekentnis" of 1571 lists some of these questions: "1. When and how does the body of Christ come to the bread or into the bread? 2. How near to or how far away from the bread is it? 3. How is it hidden under the bread? 4. How long does the sacramental union last? 5. When does the body of Christ leave the bread again? 6. Does the body of Christ which we receive orally enter our bodies and stomachs and is it digested there? 7. Is it crushed and chewed with the teeth? 8. Is it a living body or a dead corpse, since we receive the body under the bread separately from the blood under the wine?"

Holy Supper on earth since such majesty belongs to God alone and the body of Christ is incapable of it.[5]

Dr. Luther contradicted and mightily refuted this, as his doc- 3 trinal and polemical writings concerning the Holy Supper, to which we herewith publicly profess our adherence,[6] clearly demonstrate. But after his death a few theologians of the Augsburg Con- 4 fession, not quite ready to commit themselves publicly and explicitly to the Sacramentarians in the doctrine of the Supper of the Lord, did operate with and use the same basic arguments about the person of Christ with which the Sacramentarians ventured to eliminate from his Supper the true, essential presence of the body and blood of Christ. That is, they said that nothing is to be attributed to the human nature in the person of Christ that transcends or contravenes its natural, essential properties, and they went so far as to load down Dr. Luther's teaching, as well as that of those who follow it as being in harmony with the Word of God, with accusations of almost all the monstrous old heresies.[7]

In order to explain this controversy in a Christian way accord- 5 ing to the Word of God and in accordance with our plain Christian creed, and to settle it definitely by God's grace, our unanimous teaching, belief, and confession are as follows:

1. We believe, teach, and confess that although the Son of 6 God is a separate, distinct, and complete divine person and therefore has been from all eternity true, essential, and perfect God with the Father and the Holy Spirit, yet, when the time had fully come, he took the human nature into the unity of his person, not in such a manner that there are now two persons or two Christs, but in such a way that Christ Jesus is henceforth in *one* person simultaneously true eternal God, born of the Father from eternity, and also a true man, born of the most blessed virgin Mary, as it is written, "Of their race, according to the flesh, is the Christ, who is God over all, blessed for ever" (Rom. 9:5).

2. We believe, teach, and confess that henceforth in this single 7 undivided person there are two distinct natures: the divine, which is from all eternity, and the human, which was assumed in time into the unity of the person of the Son of God. These two natures in the person of Christ will henceforth never be separated, blended with each other, or the one changed into the other, but in the person of Christ each remains in its nature and essence through all eternity.

---

[5] Ulrich Zwingli, *Opera,* II/1, 64-320.

[6] See above, VII, 91.

[7] The subtitle of the *Grundfest* of 1571, one of the chief Crypto-Calvinist broadsides, reads: "Against the new Marcionites, Samosatenes, Sabellians, Arians, Nestorians, Eutychians, and Monothelites among the Flacians."

3. We furthermore believe, teach, and confess that in their   8
nature and essence the two natures referred to remain unmingled
and unabolished, so that each retains its natural properties and
throughout all eternity does not lay them aside, nor do the essential
properties of the one nature ever become the essential properties of
the other.

4. We also believe, teach, and confess that to be almighty, to be   9
eternal, to be infinite, to be everywhere at the same time naturally
(that is, according to the property of the nature and of its natural
essence), to be intrinsically present,[8] and to know everything are
essential properties of the divine nature, which throughout eternity
will never become the essential properties of the human nature.

5. On the other hand, to be a corporeal being or a creature,   10
to be flesh and blood, to be finite and circumscribed, to suffer and die,
to ascend and descend, to move from one place to another, to suffer
hunger, thirst, frost, heat, and similar things are properties of the
human nature, which never will become properties of the divine nature.

6. We also believe, teach, and confess that after the incarnation   11
neither nature in Christ henceforth subsists for itself so as to be or
constitute a distinct person, but that the two natures are united in
such a way that they constitute a single person in which there are
and subsist at the same time both the divine and the assumed human
nature, so that after the incarnation not only his divine nature but
also his assumed human nature belong to the total person of Christ;
and that without his humanity no less than without his deity the
person of Christ, or the Son of God who has assumed flesh and has
become man, is not complete. Therefore Christ is not two different
persons, but one single person, in spite of the fact that two distinct
natures, each with its natural essence and properties, are found unblended in him.

7. We furthermore believe, teach, and confess that the assumed   12
human nature in Christ not only possesses and retains its natural,
essential properties but that in addition thereto, through the personal
union with the deity and afterward through the exaltation or glorification, it has been elevated to the right hand of majesty, power, and
might over every name that is named not only in this age but also
in that which is to come.[9]

8. But Christ did not receive this majesty, to which he was   13
exalted according to his humanity, only after his resurrection from
the dead and his ascension, but when he was conceived in his mother's

---

[8] German, *für sich selbst gegenwärtig sein;* Latin, *per se ubique praesentem
esse.*

[9] Cf. Eph. 1:21.

womb and became man and when the divine and human nature were personally united.

9. But this personal union is not to be understood, as some 14 have incorrectly explained it, as if both natures, the divine and the human, are united with each other like two boards glued together, so that in deed and truth the two natures allegedly have no communion at all with each other. This was the error and heresy of Nestorius[1] 15 and the Samosatenes,[2] who on the witness of Suidas[3] and Theodore, the presbyter of Rhaitu,[4] taught that the two natures have no communion whatsoever with each other. This would separate the two natures from each other and thus make two Christs, so that Christ is one person and God the Word who dwells in Christ is another. Theodore the Presbyter wrote: "A contemporary of the heretic 16 Manes by the name of Paul, a native of Samosata who had become a bishop at Antioch in Syria, taught godlessly that the Lord Christ was a mere man in whom the Word of God dwelled just as in each of the prophets. Hence he also held that the divine and human natures are separated and distinct from each other and that in Christ they have no communion at all, just as if Christ were one individual and God the Word who dwells in him another."

In opposition to this condemned heresy the Christian church 17 has always held in simple faith that the divine and human natures in the person of Christ are united in such a way that they have true communion with each other, by which the natures are not blended into one essence but, as Dr. Luther writes, into one person. On 18 account of this personal union and communion, the ancient teachers of the church, both before and after the Council of Chalcedon, have often used the term "mixture" in a good sense and with the right distinction. We could adduce many testimonies on this point from the Fathers, if it were necessary, and have frequently quoted them in our writings. The Fathers further illustrated the personal union and communion by analogies of the soul and the body and of glowing iron.[5] For the body and soul, as well as fire and iron, have a com- 19 munion with each other, not only after a manner of speaking and in a strictly verbal fashion, but in deed and in truth. Yet there is not introduced thereby any sort of blending or equalization of the natures, as mead is made out of honey and water and ceases to be distinguish-

---

[1] Nestorius, who lived in the fifth century, was charged with teaching that the two natures of Christ were independent of each other.

[2] Followers of Paul of Samosata, a dynamistic monarchian of the third century.

[3] Suidas was a Greek lexicographer of the tenth century whose lexicon was first printed in the sixteenth century.

[4] A monk of the ninth century, author of a work entitled *De incarnatione*.

[5] The first of these comparisons is attributed to Justin Martyr by Augustine, and the second is used by Origen.

ably either water or honey but is a blended beverage. But the union of the divine and human natures in the person of Christ is far different from this. For the communion and union between the divine and the human nature in the person of Christ is far different, much higher, and more ineffable, since on account of this union and communion God is man and man is God but without thereby blending the natures or their properties; on the contrary, each nature retains its essence and properties.

On account of this personal union, without which such a true 20 communion of the natures is unthinkable and impossible, it is not only the bare human nature (whose property it is to suffer and to die) that has suffered for the sin of the world, but the Son of God himself has truly suffered (although according to the assumed human nature) and, in the words of our plain Christian Creed, has truly died, although the divine nature can neither suffer nor die. Dr. 21 Luther has explained this thoroughly in his *Great Confession concerning the Holy Supper* against the blasphemous *alloeosis*[6] of Zwingli, who taught that one nature must be taken and understood for the other. Luther called this the devil's mask and damned it to the depths of hell.[7]

For this reason the ancient teachers of the church have com- 22 bined both words, "communion" and "union," in expounding this mystery and have explained the one through the other (Irenaeus, Book IV, chap. 3; Anthanasius in his *Letter to Epictetus;* Hilary, *On the Trinity,* Book IX; Basil and Gregory of Nyssa, in Theodoret; John Damascene, Book III, chap. 19).

Because of this personal union and communion of the divine 23 and human natures in Christ, according to our plain Christian Creed we believe, teach, and confess everything that is said about the majesty of Christ according to his human nature at the right hand of the almighty power of God, and everything that follows from it. If the personal union and communion of the natures in the person of Christ did not exist in deed and truth, all of this would be nothing, nor could it even be.

On account of this personal union and communion of the 24 natures, Mary, the most blessed virgin, did not conceive a mere, ordinary human being, but a human being who is truly the Son of the most high God, as the angel testifies. He demonstrated his divine majesty even in his mother's womb in that he was born of a virgin without violating her virginity. Therefore she is truly the mother of God and yet remained a virgin.

[6] Rhetorical, not real, exchange of one part for another. See below, sections 39-43.
[7] *WA.* 26:317ff. See below, section 39.

On this basis, likewise, Christ performed all his miracles and 25 manifested his divine majesty according to his good pleasure, when and how he wanted to. He did so not only after his resurrection and ascension but also in the state of his humiliation—for example, at the wedding in Cana of Galilee,[8] again when he was twelve years old, among the teachers,[9] again in the garden when with one word he struck his enemies to the ground,[1] and again in death, when he died not just like another man but in such a way that by and in his death he conquered sin, death, the devil, hell, and eternal damnation. The human nature could not have accomplished this if it had not been personally united with the divine nature and had communion with it. Hence also the human nature has, after the resurrection from 26 the dead, its exaltation above all creatures in heaven and on earth. This is precisely that he has laid aside completely and entirely the form of a servant (without, however, laying aside the human nature, which he retains throughout eternity) and has been installed in the complete exercise and use of the divine majesty according to the assumed human nature. He had this majesty immediately at his conception even in his mother's womb, but, as the apostle testifies,[2] he laid it aside, and as Dr. Luther explains it,[3] he kept it hidden during the state of his humiliation and did not use it at all times, but only when he wanted to. But now since he ascended into heaven, 27 not just like some other saint but, in the words of the apostle (Eph. 4:10), far above all heavens that he might truly fill all things, he is everywhere present to rule, not only as God but also as man, from sea to sea and to the ends of the earth, as the prophets foretell (Ps. 8:6; 93:1; Zech. 9:10) and as the apostles testify that he worked with them everywhere and confirmed the message by the signs that attended it (Mark 16:20).

Yet, this does not take place in a mundane way, but as Dr. 28 Luther explains, after the manner of the right hand of God, which is not a specific place in heaven, as the Sacramentarians maintain without proof from the Holy Scriptures. The right hand of God is precisely the almighty power of God which fills heaven and earth, in which Christ has been installed according to his humanity in deed and in truth without any blending or equalization of the two natures in their essence and essential properties. Because of this communi- 29 cated power he can be and is truly present with his body and blood in the Holy Supper according to the words of his covenant, to which

[8] John 2:1-11.
[9] Luke 2:41-52.
[1] John 18:6.
[2] Phil. 2:7.
[3] *WA*, 54:50.

he has directed us through his Word. No other human being can do this, since no human being is united in this manner with the divine nature and installed in the exercise of the divine, omnipotent majesty and power through and in the personal union of both natures in Christ, the way Jesus, the son of Mary, is.

In him the divine and human natures are personally united in 30 such a way that in Christ the whole fullness of deity dwells bodily (Col. 2:9), and in this personal union they have such an exalted, intimate, and ineffable communion that even the angels marvel at it and find their delight and joy in looking into it, as St. Peter testifies (I Pet. 1:12). This we shall discuss in greater detail below.

The doctrine of an exchange of properties[4] (that is, of a true 31 communication of the properties of the natures) likewise flows from this same foundation, as we have indicated above and as we have explained the personal union (that is, the fact that the divine and human natures of Christ are united with each other in such a way that they not only have names in common but also in deed and truth have communion between each other without any blending or equalization of the natures in their essence). Of this, too, we shall say more below.

Since it is true that each nature retains its essential properties 32 and that these are not separated from one nature and poured into the other nature, the way water is poured from one container into another, an exchange of properties could not take place or continue if the personal union or communion of natures in the person of Christ did not truly exist. Next to the article of the holy Trinity, the greatest 33 mystery in heaven and on earth is the personal union, as Paul says, "Great indeed is the mystery of our religion: God was manifested in the flesh" (I Tim. 3:16). Since St. Peter testifies with clear words 34 that even we, in whom Christ dwells only by grace, have in Christ, because of this exalted mystery, "become partakers of the divine nature" (II Pet. 1:4), what kind of participation in the divine nature must that be of which the apostle says that "in Christ the whole fullness of deity dwells bodily" (Col. 2:9) in such a way that God and man are a single person!

It is highly important that this doctrine of the exchange of 35 properties[5] between the two natures be treated and explained with due discrimination because the statements that we make about the person of Christ, its natures, and their properties are not all of the same kind and mode, and if one talks about them without due discrimination, the doctrine becomes tangled up and the simple reader is easily misled. The following presentation should be noted diligently. For the sake of

---

[4] Latin, *communicatio idiomatum.*

[5] Latin, *communicatio idiomatum.*

a better and simpler presentation it can be comprehended under three main points.[6]

In the first place, since in Christ two distinct natures are and 36 remain unchanged and unblended in their natural essence and properties, and since both natures constitute only one person, therefore any property, though it belongs only to one of the natures, is ascribed not only to the respective nature as something separate but to the entire person who is simultaneously God and man (whether he is called God or whether he is called man).

But in this mode of speaking it does not follow that whatever 37 is ascribed to the person is simultaneously the property of both natures. On the contrary, it is distinctly explained according to which nature the property in question is being ascribed to the person. Thus, for example, "the Son was descended from David according to the flesh" (Rom. 1:3), and "Christ was put to death in the flesh" and "suffered for us in the flesh" (I Pet. 3:18; 4:1). But since secret as well 38 as open Sacramentarians hide their pernicious error under the words of the formula which says that we are *to ascribe to the entire person what is the property of one nature* (for while they mention the entire person, they nevertheless understand by that only the one nature and wholly eliminate the other nature, as if, for instance, only the human nature had suffered for us) and since Dr. Luther in his *Great Confession concerning the Holy Supper* has written about Zwingli's *alloeosis*,[7] we shall here quote Dr. Luther's own words, so that the church of God may be forearmed in the best possible way against this error. His words read:

"Zwingli calls that an *alloeosis* when something is said about 39 the deity of Christ which after all belongs to the humanity, or vice versa—for example, 'Was it not necessary that the Christ should suffer these things and enter into his glory?' (Luke 24:26). Here Zwingli performs a sleight-of-hand trick and substitutes the human nature for Christ. Beware, beware, I say, of this *alloeosis*, for it is the devil's 40 mask since it will finally construct a kind of Christ after whom I would not want to be called a Christian, that is, a Christ who is and does no more in his passion and death than any other ordinary saint. But if I believe that only the human nature suffered for me, then

---

[6] The division into three *genera* goes back to Martin Chemnitz. The designations *genus idiomaticum, genus maiestaticum* (or *auchematicum*), and *genus apotelesmaticum* came later. The first *genus* covers the ascription of the attributes of both natures to the whole person; the second (the real point at issue in the controversy) involves the ascription of divine majesty to Christ according to his human nature; the third considers that in the performance of his saving acts Christ used the properties of either nature or of both natures appropriate to the act in question.

[7] See above, section 21.

Christ would be a poor Saviour for me, in fact, he himself would need a Saviour. In short, it is indescribable what the devil attempts with this *alloeosis.*" [8] And shortly thereafter he states: "If the 41 old witch,[9] Dame Reason, the grandmother of the *alloeosis,* would say that the deity surely cannot suffer and die, then you must answer and say: That is true, but since the divinity and humanity are one person in Christ, the Scriptures ascribe to the deity, because of this personal union, all that happens to the humanity, and vice versa. And 42 this is likewise within the bounds of truth, for you must say that the person (pointing to Christ) suffers, dies. But this person is truly God, and therefore it is correct to say: the Son of God suffers. Although, so to speak, the one part (namely, the deity) does not suffer, nevertheless the person who is true God suffers in the other part (namely, in the humanity). For the Son of God truly is crucified for us—that is, this person who is God, for that is what he is—this person, I say, is crucified according to the humanity. If Zwingli's 43 *alloeosis* stands, then Christ will have to be two persons, one a divine and the other a human person, since Zwingli applies all the texts concerning the passion only to the human nature and completely excludes them from the divine nature. But if the works are divided and separated, the person will also have to be separated, since all the doing and suffering are not ascribed to the natures but to the person. It is the person who does and suffers everything, the one thing according to this nature and the other thing according to the other nature, all of which scholars know right well. Therefore we regard our Lord Christ as God and man in one person, neither confounding the natures nor dividing the person." [1]

Likewise, Dr. Luther states in his treatise *Concerning the* 44 *Councils and the Church:* "We Christians must know that unless God is in the balance and throws in weight as a counterbalance, we shall sink to the bottom with our scale. I mean that this way: If it is not true that God died for us, but only a man died, we are lost. But if God's death and God dead lie in the opposite scale, then his side goes down and we go upward like a light and empty pan. Of course, he can also go up again or jump out of his pan. But he could never have sat in the pan unless he had become a man like us, so that it could be said: God dead, God's passion, God's blood, God's death. According to his nature God cannot die, but since God and man are united in one person, it is correct to talk about God's death when that man dies who is one thing or one person with God." [2]

---

[8] *WA,* 26:319.
[9] German, *Wettermacherin.*
[1] *WA,* 26:321, 322.
[2] *WA,* 50:590.

So far Luther. From this it is evident that it is wrongly put to   45
say or to write that the cited locutions, "God suffered," "God died,"
are merely empty words which do not correspond to reality. For our
plain Christian Creed teaches us that the Son of God, who was made
man, suffered for us, died, and redeemed us with his blood.

In the second place, as far as the discharge of Christ's office   46
is concerned, the person does not act *in, with, through,* or *according to*
one nature only, but *in, according to, with,* and *through* both natures,
or as the Council of Chalcedon declares,[3] each nature according to
its own properties acts in communion with the other. Thus Christ   47
is our mediator, redeemer, king, high priest, head, shepherd, and so
forth, not only according to one nature only, either the divine or the
human, but according to both natures, as we presented this matter
previously.[4]

But it is an entirely different matter when, in the third place,   48
the question being treated in the discussion is this: Do the natures
in the personal union have nothing else and nothing more than their
own natural and essential properties (which, as has been indicated
above, they have and retain)?

Since there is no variation with God (James 1:17), nothing was   49
added to or detracted from the essence and properties of the divine
nature in Christ through the incarnation, nor was the divine nature
intrinsically diminished or augmented thereby. As far as the   50
assumed human nature in the person of Christ is concerned, some[5]
wanted to contend that even in the personal union with the deity the
human nature has nothing else and nothing more than its own natural
essential properties alone, according to which it is in every respect
made like its brethren, and that for this reason nothing should or can
be ascribed to the human nature in Christ which transcends or contravenes its natural properties, even though the testimony of the
Scripture points in that direction. But it is so clear on the basis   51
of God's Word that this opinion is erroneous and false, that even
their own co-religionists now criticize and reject this error. The
Holy Scriptures, and the ancient Fathers on the basis of the Scriptures,
testify mightily that, because the human nature in Christ is personally
united with the divine nature in Christ, the former (when it was glorified and exalted to the right hand of the majesty and power of God,
after the form of the servant had been laid aside and after the humiliation) received, in addition to its natural, essential, and abiding properties, special, high, great, supernatural, unsearchable, ineffable, heavenly

---

[3] Not the definition of the Council of Chalcedon, but the statement in the
Tome of Leo which the council approved.

[4] Above, III, 56.

[5] Crypto-Calvinists of Wittenberg, in the *Grundfest* of 1573.

prerogatives and privileges in majesty, glory, power, and might above every name that is named, not only in this age but also in that which is to come.[6] Accordingly, for the exercise of Christ's office, the human nature in Christ is employed after its own measure and fashion along with the other, and has its power and efficacy not only from and according to its natural and essential properties, or only as far as their capacity extends, but primarily from and according to the majesty, glory, power, and might which the human nature has received through the personal union, glorification, and exaltation. This even the adversaries cannot and dare not any longer deny. However, they argue 52 and contend that the gifts with which the human nature in Christ is endowed and adorned are created gifts or finite qualities, as in the saints, and on the basis of their own calculations and from their own arguments and demonstrations they attempt to determine and to fix the limit of what the human nature in Christ could or should be capable or incapable without being destroyed.

But the best, safest, and most certain way in this controversy 53 is to realize that no one can know better and more thoroughly than the Lord Christ himself what Christ has received through the personal union, glorification, or exaltation according to his assumed human nature and of what his assumed human nature is capable over and above its natural properties without being destroyed. In his Word he has revealed to us as much as we need to know in this life, and wherever the Scriptures in this case give us clear, certain testimony, we shall simply believe it and not argue that the human nature in Christ is not capable of it.

The statement is, of course, correct and true that Christ's human 54 nature in and by itself possesses all the created gifts which have been given to it. But these do not measure up to the majesty which the Scriptures, and the ancient Fathers on the basis of Scriptures, ascribe to the assumed human nature in Christ. For to give life, to execute 55 all judgment, to have all authority in heaven and on earth, to have all things given into his hands, to have all things under his feet, to cleanse from sin, and so forth are not created gifts but divine and infinite qualities. Yet according to the statement of the Scriptures these properties have been given and communicated to the man Christ (John 5:21, 27; 6:39, 40; Matt. 28:18; Dan. 7:14; John 3:31, 35; 13:3; Matt. 11:27; Eph. 1:22; Heb. 2:8; I Cor. 15:27; John 1:3, 10).

There are three strong and irrefutable arguments which show 56 that this communication is not merely a matter of words but is to be understood of the person not only according to the divine nature but also according to the assumed human nature. These reasons are the following:

[6] Cf. Eph. 1:21.

1. In the first place, it is a unanimously accepted rule of the   57
entire ancient orthodox church that whatever the Scriptures testify
that Christ received in time he received not according to his divine
nature (according to which he has everything from all eternity) but
that the person received this in time according to the assumed human
nature.

2. In the second place, Scripture testifies clearly (John 5:21,   58
27; 6:39, 40) that the power to make the dead alive and to execute
judgment has been given to Christ because he is the Son of Man and
inasmuch as he has flesh and blood.

3. In the third place, Scripture not only speaks in general terms   59
of the person of the Son of Man, but expressly points to his assumed
human nature when it states, "The blood of Jesus his Son cleanses us
from all sin" (I John 1:7). This does not refer only to the merit
that was once achieved on the cross. John is saying in this passage
that in the work or matter of our justification not only the divine
nature in Christ but also his blood actually cleanses us from all sins.
Likewise, John 6:48-58 says that Christ's flesh is a life-giving food,
and accordingly the Council of Ephesus decreed that the flesh of
Christ has the power to give life. Many other noble testimonies of
the ancient orthodox church[7] concerning this article are recorded
elsewhere.

According to the Scriptures we should and must believe that   60
Christ received all this according to his human nature and that it was
all given and communicated to the assumed human nature in Christ.
But, as we said above, since both natures in Christ are united in such
a way that they are not blended together or the one is changed into
the other, and since each retains its natural and essential properties in
such a way that the properties of the one nature never become the
properties of the other nature, we must correctly explain this doctrine
and defend it against all heresies. In this matter we have not   61
developed a new doctrine of our own, but we accept and repeat the
statements which the ancient orthodox church made herein on the
basis of sound passages of the Holy Scriptures, namely, that such
divine power, life, might, majesty, and glory were not given to Christ's
assumed human nature in the same way in which the Father communicated his own essence and all the divine properties from eternity
to the Son according to the divine nature so that he is of one essence
with the Father and equal with God. For only according to the divine
nature is Christ equal with the Father, but according to the assumed
human nature he is below God. From this it is evident that we do

---

[7] For instance, in the "Catalog of Testimonies," a catena of quotations
from the Church Fathers appended to but never officially a part of the
Formula of Concord.

not confuse, equalize, or abolish the natures in Christ. Thus also the power to give life is not in the flesh of Christ the way it is in his divine nature, that is, as an essential property.

This exchange or communication did not take place through an 62 essential or natural outpouring of the properties of the divine nature into the human nature in such a way that the humanity of Christ has them of itself and apart from the divine essence, nor in such a way that the human nature in Christ has completely laid aside its natural and essential properties and is now either transformed into the Godhead or by means of these communicated properties has become intrinsically equal with the Godhead, nor in such a way that the natural, essential properties and acts of both natures are henceforth of the same kind or even identical. These and similar erroneous doctrines have been justly rejected and condemned in the ancient approved councils on the basis of the Scriptures.[8] For in no way should any conversion, blending, or equalization of the natures in Christ or of their essential properties be taught or conceded.

We have never understood the term "real exchange"—a com- 63 munication or exchange that takes place in deed and in truth—to describe any essential, natural exchange or transfusion which would blend the natures in their essence and in their essential properties. Some of our opponents, against their own conscience, have maliciously and wickedly twisted our words and terminology in this direction in order to cast suspicion on the pure doctrine. We have used this term merely in opposition to a "verbal exchange," the doctrine which these people advance, namely, that it is all only a mode of speech, mere words, titles, and names. They have insisted so strongly on this that they will hear of no other exchange. To set forth correctly the majesty of Christ by way of contrast, we have spoken of a "real exchange" in order to indicate thereby that such an exchange has occurred in deed and in truth but without any blending of the natures and of their essential properties.

We therefore hold and teach with the ancient orthodox church, 64 as it explained this doctrine on the basis of Scripture, that the human nature in Christ has received this majesty according to the manner of the personal union, that is, because the fullness of deity dwells in Christ (Col. 2:9), not as in other godly human beings or in the angels, but "bodily," as in its own body. This fullness shines forth with all its majesty, power, glory, and efficacy in the assumed nature, spontaneously and when and where he wills. *In, with, and through* the same he manifests and exercises his divine power, glory, and efficacy, as the soul does in the body and fire in glowing iron, analogies which

[8] For example, the Second Council of Constantinople, canon 7 against Origen.

the entire ancient church used in explaining this doctrine, as we stated above.[9] During the time of the humiliation the divine majesty 65 was concealed and restrained, but now, since the form of a slave has been laid aside, it takes place fully, mightily, and publicly before all the saints in heaven and on earth, and in yonder life we shall behold his glory face to face (John 17:24). Thus there is and remains 66 in Christ only a single divine omnipotence, power, majesty, and glory, which is the property of the divine nature alone. But it shines forth and manifests itself fully, though always spontaneously, *in, with, and through* the assumed exalted human nature of Christ. Just as in glowing iron there are not two powers of illumination and combustion— the power of illumination and combustion is the property of fire— but since the fire is united with the iron, it demonstrates and manifests its power of illumination and combustion in and through the iron in such a way that on that account and through this union the glowing iron has the power of illumination and combustion without any transformation of the natural properties of either the fire or the iron.

Hence we do not understand the testimonies of the Scriptures 67 which speak of the majesty to which the human nature of Christ has been exalted either as if this divine majesty, which is the property of the divine nature of the Son of God, is to be ascribed in the person of the Son of Man only according to his divine nature, or as if this majesty is in Christ's human nature only in such a way that it merely shares the bare titles and the names in words alone, while in deed and in truth the human nature has no share in the divine majesty. If that were so, since God is a spiritual and indivisible essence 68 and is therefore everywhere present in all creatures, and since in whomever he is (especially believers and saints), he dwells, and since he there has his majesty with and about him at all times, it could be said with equal truth that in all creatures in whom God is, but especially in believers in whom God dwells, there likewise the fullness of deity dwells bodily, there likewise are hid all treasures of wisdom and knowledge, and to them all authority in heaven and on earth is given, for the Spirit, who has all power, has been given to them. In 69 this way no distinction would be made between Christ according to his human nature and other holy people, and thus Christ would be robbed of his majesty, which as a human being and according to his human nature he has received above all creatures. For no 70 other creature, whether man or angel, can or should say, "All authority in heaven and on earth has been given to me" (Matt. 28:18). For while it is true that God, together with the whole fullness of deity which he always has with him, dwells in believers, he does not do so bodily nor is he personally united with them as is the case in Christ.

[9] See above, VIII, 18.

It is because of the personal union that Christ says, also according to the human nature, "All authority in heaven and on earth has been given to me" (Matt. 28:18); likewise, when Jesus knew that "the Father had given all things into his hands" (John 13:3); likewise, "In him dwells the whole fullness of deity bodily" (Col. 2:9); likewise, "Thou hast crowned him with glory and honor and didst set him over the works of thy hands, putting everything in subjection under his feet. Now in putting everything in subjection to him, he left nothing outside his control" (Heb. 2:7, 8), and "he is excepted who put all things under him" (I Cor. 15:27).

We do not in any way believe, teach, and confess an outpouring 71 of the majesty of God and all its properties into the human nature of Christ of such a kind that thereby the divine nature is weakened or surrenders to another something that belongs to it without keeping it for itself. Nor do we believe that in its substance and essence the human nature allegedly received equal majesty, separated or divided from the nature and essence of the Son of God, as when water, wine, or oil is poured from one container into another. For the human nature, like every other creature in heaven or on earth, is not capable of the omnipotence of God in such a way that it would become an omnipotent essence intrinsically or have omnipotent properties intrinsically. Thereby Christ's human nature would be denied and completely transformed into the Godhead. This is contrary to our Christian Creed and to the entire prophetic and apostolic doctrine.

But we believe, teach, and confess that God the Father gave 72 his Spirit to Christ, his beloved Son, according to the assumed human nature (whence he is called Messiah, or the Anointed) in such a way that he received the Spirit's gifts not by measure, like other saints. The "Spirit of wisdom and understanding, of counsel and might and knowledge" (Isa. 11:2; 61:1) does not rest upon Christ the Lord according to his assumed human nature (according to the deity he is of one essence with the Holy Spirit) in such a manner that as 73 a man he therefore knows and can do only certain things in the way in which other saints know and can do things through the Holy Spirit who endows them only with created gifts. Rather, since Christ according to the Godhead is the second person in the holy Trinity and the Holy Spirit proceeds from him as well as from the Father (and therefore he is and remains to all eternity his and the Father's own Spirit, who is never separated from the Son), it follows that through personal union the entire fullness of the Spirit (as the ancient Fathers say)[1] is communicated to Christ according to the flesh that is personally united with the Son of God. This fullness demonstrates 74

---

[1] Cyril of Alexandria's "hypostatic union," defined by the Council of Chalcedon in 451.

and manifests itself spontaneously and with all power in, with, and through the human nature. The result is not that he knows only certain things and does not know certain other things, or that he can do certain things and cannot do certain other things, but that he knows and can do everything. The Father poured out upon him without measure the Spirit of wisdom and power, so that as a man, through the personal union, he really and truly has received all knowledge and all power. In this way all the treasures of wisdom are hid in him,[2] all authority is given to him,[3] and he is exalted to the right hand of the majesty and power of God.[4] The histories tell us that during   75 the time of Emperor Valens there was a peculiar sect among the Arians, called the Agnoetes, who taught that the Son, the Father's Word, indeed knows all things, but that according to his assumed human nature many things are unknown to him. Against this sect Gregory the Great also wrote.[5]

Because of this personal union and the resultant communion   76 that the divine and human natures have with each other in deed and truth in the person of Christ, things are attributed to Christ according to the flesh that the flesh, according to its nature and essence outside of this union, cannot intrinsically be or have—for example, that his flesh is truly a life-giving food and his blood truly a quickening beverage, as the two hundred fathers of the Council of Ephesus attested when they stated that Christ's flesh is a life-giving flesh,[6] whence only this man and no other human being in heaven and on earth can say truthfully, "Where two or three are gathered in my name, there am I in the midst of them," [7] likewise, "I am with you always even to the close of the age." [8] We do not understand these testimonies   77 to mean that only the deity of Christ is present with us in the Christian church and community and that this presence of Christ in no way involves his humanity. If that were true, Peter, Paul, and all the saints in heaven would also be with us on earth because the Godhead which is everywhere dwells in them. The Scriptures ascribe such presence only to Christ, and to no other human being. We   78 believe that the cited passages illustrate the majesty of the man Christ, which Christ received according to his humanity at the right hand of the majesty and power of God, so that, also according to and with this same assumed human nature of his, Christ can be and is present

²Col. 2:3.
⁸Matt. 28:18.
⁴Heb. 1:3.
⁶Gregory the Great, *Epistles*, X, 35, 39.
⁶The so-called canon 11 of the Council of Ephesus.
⁷Matt. 18:20.
⁸Matt. 28:20.

wherever he wills, and in particular that he is present with his church and community on earth as mediator, head, king, and high priest. Not part or only one-half of the person of Christ, but the entire person to which both natures, the divine and the human, belong is present. He is present not only according to his deity, but also according to and with his assumed human nature, according to which he is our brother and we flesh of his flesh and bone of his bone (Eph. 5:30). To make certainty and assurance doubly sure on this point, he 79 instituted his Holy Supper that he might be present with us, dwell in us, work and be mighty in us according to that nature, too, according to which he has flesh and blood.

On the basis of this solid foundation, Dr. Luther, of blessed 80 memory, has written about the majesty of Christ according to the human nature. In the *Great Confession concerning the Holy* 81 *Supper* he writes about the person of Christ: "Since he is a man like this—and apart from this man there is no God—it must follow that according to the third supernatural manner,[9] he is and can be everywhere that God is and that everything is full of Christ through and through, also according to the humanity—not, of course, according to the first, corporeal, comprehensible manner, but according to the supernatural, divine manner. Here you must take your stand 82 and say that wherever Christ is according to the deity, he is there as a natural, divine person and is also naturally and personally there, as his conception in his mother's womb proves conclusively. For if he was the Son of God, he had to be in his mother's womb naturally and personally and become man. But if he is present naturally and personally wherever he is, then he must be man there, too, since he is not two separate persons but a single person. Wherever this person is, it is the single, indivisible person, and if you can say, 'Here is God,' then you must also say, 'Christ the man is present too.' And if you could show me one place where God is and not the man, then the person is already divided and I could at once say truthfully, 'Here is God who is not man and has never become man.' But no God like 83 that for me! For it would follow from this that space and place had separated the two natures from one another and thus had divided the person, even though death and all the devils had been unable to separate and tear them apart. And he would remain a poor 84 Christ for me if he were present only at one single place as a divine and human person, and if at all other places he would have to be nothing more than a mere isolated God and a divine person without the humanity. No, comrade, wherever you put God down for me, you must also put the humanity down for me. They simply will not let themselves be separated and divided from each other. He has

[9] Cf. above, VII, 98-102.

become one person and never separates the assumed humanity from himself." [1]

In his tract *Concerning the Last Words of David*, which he   85 wrote shortly before his death, Dr. Luther states: "According to the second, temporal, human birth, the eternal power of God is also given to him—in a temporal way, however, and not from eternity. For the humanity of Christ has not, like the deity, existed from eternity, but according to our calendar Jesus the son of Mary is 1543 years old this year. But from the moment that the deity and the humanity were united in one person this man, Mary's son, is and is called the almighty and everlasting God, who by virtue of the exchange of qualities[2] has eternal power and has created and preserved everything because he is one person with the deity and is true God. This is what he means when he says, 'All things have been delivered to me by my Father' (Matt. 11:27), and 'All authority in heaven and on earth has been given to me' (Matt. 28:18). What 'me'? To me, Jesus of Nazareth, Mary's son, born a human being. From eternity I have this authority from the Father before I became man, but when I became man I received it in time according to the humanity and concealed it until my resurrection and ascension, when it was to have been revealed and demonstrated, as St. Paul says, 'He is designated the Son of God in power' (Rom. 1:4), and John calls it 'glorified' (John 7:39; 17:10)." [3]

There are many similar testimonies in Dr. Luther's writings,   86 especially in the book *That These Words Still Stand Firm* and in his *Great Confession concerning the Holy Supper*. For the sake of brevity we here merely go on record as having appealed to these as being clear expositions of the majesty of Christ at the right hand of God in connection with this article, as well as of his covenant in the Holy Supper in connection with the previous article.

Hence we consider it a pernicious error to deprive Christ   87 according to his humanity of this majesty. To do so robs Christians of their highest comfort, afforded them in the cited promises of the presence and indwelling of their head, king, and high priest, who has promised that not only his unveiled deity, which to us poor sinners is like a consuming fire on dry stubble, will be with them, but that he, he, the man who has spoken with them, who has tasted every tribulation in his assumed human nature, and who can therefore sympathize with us as with men and his brethren, he wills to be with us in all our troubles also according to that nature by which he is our brother and we are flesh of his flesh.

---

[1] *WA*, 26:332, 333.
[2] Latin, *communicatio idiomatum.*
[3] *WA*, 54:49, 50.

Therefore we unanimously reject and condemn with mouth   88
and heart all errors which are inconsistent with the doctrine here set
forth as contrary to the prophetic and apostolic writings, the orthodox
Creeds, and our Christian Augsburg Confession:

1. If anyone were to believe or teach that because of the per-   89
sonal union the human nature has allegedly been blended with the
divine or has been transformed into it.

2. Likewise, that the human nature in Christ is everywhere   90
present in the same way as the Deity, as an infinite essence, through
an essential power or property of its nature.

3. Likewise, that the human nature in Christ has been equalized   91
with and has become equal to the divine nature in its substance and
essence or in its essential properties.

4. Likewise, that the humanity of Christ is locally extended   92
into every place in heaven and earth, something which ought not be
attributed to the deity. Without transforming or destroying his true
human nature, Christ's omnipotence and wisdom can readily provide
that through his divine omnipotence Christ can be present with his
body, which he has placed at the right hand of the majesty and power
of God, wherever he desires and especially where he has promised his
presence in his Word, as in the Holy Communion.[4]

5. Likewise, that the mere human nature of Christ alone, with   93
which the Son of God had no communion whatever in the passion,
suffered for us and redeemed us.

6. Likewise, that in the preached Word and in the right use   94
of the holy sacraments Christ is present with us on earth only according to his deity, and that this presence does not involve his assumed
human nature in any way whatever.

7. Likewise, that the assumed human nature in Christ does   95
not share in deed and truth in the divine power, might, wisdom,
majesty, and glory, but has only the bare title and name in common
with it.

8. We reject and condemn these errors and all others that   96
contradict and contravene the above doctrine as being contrary to
the pure Word of God, the writings of the holy prophets and apostles,
and our Christian Creed and Confession. Since the Holy Scriptures
call Christ a mystery[5] over which all heretics break their heads, we
admonish all Christians not to pry presumptuously into this mystery
with their reason, but with the holy apostles simply to believe, close
the eyes of reason, take their intellect captive to obey Christ, comfort

---

[4] The antitheses listed in items 1-4 contemplate the charges which the
Sacramentarians made against the Lutherans.
[5] Col. 1:27.

themselves therewith, and rejoice constantly that our flesh and blood have in Christ been made to sit so high at the right hand of the majesty and almighty power of God. In this way they will be certain to find abiding comfort in all adversities and will be well protected against pernicious errors.

IX. CHRIST'S DESCENT INTO HELL

Different explanations of the article on Christ's descent into   1 hell have been discovered among some of our theologians just as among the ancient teachers of the Christian church. Hence we let matters rest on the simple statement of our Christian Creed, to which Dr. Luther directs us in the sermon that he held in the castle at Torgau in the year 1533,[6] "I believe in the Lord Christ, God's Son, who died, was buried, and descended into hell." Herein the burial and the descent into hell are differentiated as distinct articles, and   2 we simply believe that after the burial the entire person, God and man, descended into hell, conquered the devil, destroyed hell's power, and took from the devil all his might.

We are not to concern ourselves with exalted and acute specula-   3 tions about how this occurred. With our reason and five senses this article cannot be comprehended any more than the preceding one, how Christ has been made to sit at the right hand of the almighty power and majesty of God. We must only believe and cling to the Word. Then we shall retain the heart of this article and derive from it the comfort that neither hell nor the devil can take us or any believer in Christ captive or harm us.

X. THE ECCLESIASTICAL RITES THAT ARE CALLED ADIAPHORA OR THINGS INDIFFERENT

There has also been a controversy among some theologians   1 of the Augsburg Confession concerning ceremonies and church rites which are neither commanded nor forbidden in the Word of God but which have been introduced into the church with good intentions for the sake of good order and decorum[7] or else to preserve Christian discipline. The one party[8] held that even in a period of   2

---

[6] *WA,* 37:62-67. What follows is taken almost verbatim from Luther's sermon.

[7] German (here and afterward), *Wohlstand* (in the sense of *Wohlanständigkeit*)

[8] Chiefly Philip Melanchthon, John Bugenhagen, George Major, and Caspar Cruciger.

persecution and a case of confession,[9] when enemies of the holy Gospel have not come to an agreement with us in doctrine, one may still with a clear conscience, at the enemies' insistent demand, restore once more certain abrogated ceremonies that are in themselves matters of indifference and that are neither commanded nor forbidden by God, and that one may justifiably conform oneself to them in such adiaphora or matters of indifference. The other party,[1] how-   3 ever, contended that under no circumstances can this be done with a clear conscience and without prejudice to the divine truth, even as far as things indifferent are concerned, in a period of persecution and a case of confession, especially when the adversaries are attempting either by force and coercion or by surreptitious methods to suppress the pure doctrine and gradually to insinuate their false doctrines into our churches again. To explain this controversy and to settle   4 it definitively by the grace of God, we offer the Christian reader the following exposition:

We should not consider as matters of indifference, and we   5 should avoid as forbidden by God, ceremonies which are basically contrary to the Word of God, even though they go under the name and guise of external adiaphora and are given a different color from their true one. Nor do we include among truly free adiaphora or things indifferent those ceremonies which give or (to avoid persecution) are designed to give the impression that our religion does not differ greatly from that of the papists, or that we are not seriously opposed to it. Nor are such rites matters of indifference when these ceremonies are intended to create the illusion (or are demanded or agreed to with that intention) that these two opposing religions have been brought into agreement and become one body, or that a return to the papacy and an apostasy from the pure doctrine of the Gospel and from true religion has taken place or will allegedly result little by little from these ceremonies.

In this case the words of Paul must be heeded: "Do not be   6 mismated with unbelievers. For what partnership have righteousness and iniquity, or what fellowship has light with darkness? Therefore come out from them and be separate from them, says the Lord" (II Cor. 6:14, 17).

Neither are useless and foolish spectacles, which serve neither   7 good order, Christian discipline, nor evangelical decorum in the church, true adiaphora or things indifferent.

We believe, teach, and confess that true adiaphora or things   8

---

[9] German, *Fall der Bekenntnus*, i.e., when a confession of faith is called for.

[1] Notably Matthias Flacius, John Wigand, Nicholas Gallus, and Anthony Corvinus.

indifferent, as defined above,[2] are in and of themselves no worship of God or even a part of it, but that we should duly distinguish between the two, as it is written, "In vain do they worship me, teaching for doctrines the precepts of men" (Matt. 15:9).

We further believe, teach, and confess that the community of God in every place and at every time has the right, authority, and power to change, to reduce, or to increase ceremonies according to its circumstances, as long as it does so without frivolity and offense but in an orderly and appropriate way, as at any time may seem to be most profitable, beneficial, and salutary for good order, Christian discipline, evangelical decorum, and the edification of the church. Paul instructs us how we can with a good conscience give in and yield to the weak in faith in such external matters of indifference (Rom. 14) and demonstrates it by his own example (Acts 16:3; 21:26; I Cor. 9:10). 9

We believe, teach, and confess that at a time of confession, as when enemies of the Word of God desire to suppress the pure doctrine of the holy Gospel, the entire community of God, yes, every individual Christian, and especially the ministers of the Word as the leaders[3] of the community of God, are obligated to confess openly, not only by words but also through their deeds and actions, the true doctrine and all that pertains to it, according to the Word of God. In such a case we should not yield to adversaries even in matters of indifference, nor should we tolerate the imposition of such ceremonies on us by adversaries in order to undermine the genuine worship of God and to introduce and confirm their idolatry by force or chicanery. It is written, "For freedom Christ has set us free; stand fast therefore, and do not submit again to a yoke of slavery" (Gal. 5:1). And again, "But because of false brethren secretly brought in, who slipped in to spy out our freedom which we have in Christ Jesus, that they might bring us into bondage: to whom we did not yield submission even for a moment, that the truth of the gospel might be preserved for you" (Gal. 2:4, 5). Paul is here speaking of circumcision, which at that time was a matter of indifference[4] and which in his Christian liberty he employed in other instances (Acts 16:3). But when false prophets demanded circumcision and abused 10 11 12

---

[2] Matthias Flacius had included among "public" adiaphora hymns, chants, lessons, the hour and location of the service, the person participating, vestments, and the ringing of bells. Among "private" adiaphora he had included fasting, fixed times of prayer, temporary abstention from conjugal intercourse or from delicacies, reduction in one's food intake for the sake of prayer or spiritual exercises, etc.

[3] German, *Vorsteher,* translated in the Latin version with *ii quos Dominus ecclesiae suae regendae praefecit.*

[4] Gal. 2:3; I Cor. 7:18, 19.

it to confirm their false doctrine that the works of the law are necessary for righteousness and salvation, Paul said that he would not yield, not even for a moment, so that the truth of the Gospel might be preserved.[5] Thus Paul yielded and gave in to the weak as far | 3 as foods, times, and days were concerned (Rom. 14:6). But he would not yield to false apostles who wanted to impose such things on consciences as necessary, even in matters that were in themselves indifferent. "Therefore let no one pass judgment on you in questions of food and drink, or with regard to a festival or a new moon or a sabbath" (Col. 2:16). When Peter and Barnabas in a similar situation yielded to a certain extent, Paul criticized them publicly because they had not been straightforward about the truth of the Gospel (Gal. 2:14).

For here we are no longer dealing with the external adiaphora | 4 which in their nature and essence are and remain of themselves free and which accordingly are not subject either to a command or a prohibition, requiring us to use them or to discontinue them. Here we are dealing primarily with the chief article of our Christian faith, so that, as the apostle testifies, the truth of the Gospel might be preserved (Gal. 2:5). Any coercion or commandment darkens and perverts this article because the adversaries will forthwith publicly demand such matters of indifference to confirm false doctrines, superstition, and idolatry and to suppress the pure doctrine and Christian liberty, or they will misuse them and misinterpret them in this direction.

At the same time this concerns the article of Christian liberty | 5 as well, an article which the Holy Spirit through the mouth of the holy apostle so seriously commanded the church to preserve, as we have just heard. As soon as this article is weakened and human commandments are forcibly imposed on the church as necessary and as though their omission were wrong and sinful, the door has been opened to idolatry, and ultimately the commandments of men will be increased and be put as divine worship not only on a par with God's commandments, but even above them.

Hence yielding or conforming in external things, where Chris- | 6 tian agreement in doctrine has not previously been achieved, will support the idolaters in their idolatry, and on the other hand, it will sadden and scandalize true believers and weaken them in their faith. As he values his soul's welfare and salvation, every Christian is obligated to avoid both, as it is written, "Woe to the world for temptations to sin," [6] and again, "Whoever causes one of these little ones who believe in me to sin, it were better for him to have a great millstone fastened around his neck and to be drowned in the depth of

[5] Gal. 2:5.
[6] Matt. 18:7.

the sea." [7] We are to be particularly mindful that Christ says, 17 "So everyone who acknowledges me before men, I also will acknowledge before my Father who is in heaven" (Matt. 10:32).

The following testimonies drawn from the Smalcald Articles, 18 which were drafted and adopted in 1537, show that this has consistently been the conviction and the confession of the chief teachers of the Augsburg Confession concerning such matters of indifference, and we who are walking in their footsteps intend by the grace of God to abide by this their confession.

The Smalcald Articles of 1537 declare on this: "We do not 19 concede to the papists (the papist bishops) that they are the church, for they are not. Nor shall we pay any attention to what they command or forbid in the name of the church, for, thank God, a seven-year-old child knows what the church is, namely, holy believers and sheep who hear the voice of their Shepherd," etc.[8] Just before this the Smalcald Articles declare: "If the bishops were true bishops and were concerned about the church and the Gospel, they might be permitted (for the sake of love and unity, but not of necessity) to ordain and confirm us and our preachers, provided this could be done without pretense, humbug, and un-Christian ostentation. However, they neither are nor wish to be true bishops. They are temporal lords and princes who are unwilling to preach or teach or baptize or administer Communion or discharge any office or work in the church. More than that, they expel, persecute, and condemn those who have been called to do these things. Yet the church must not be deprived of ministers on their account." [9]

Under the article on the primacy or lordship of the pope, the 20 Smalcald Articles state: "Just as we cannot adore the devil himself as our lord or God, so we cannot suffer his apostle, the pope or Antichrist, to govern us as our head or lord, for deception, murder, and the eternal destruction of body and soul are characteristic of his papal government." [1]

In the Treatise on the Power and Primacy of the Pope, which 21 constitutes an appendix to the Smalcald Articles and which all the theologians assembled in Smalcald subscribed with their own hands,[2] we find the following statement: "No one should assume lordship or authority over the church, nor burden the church with traditions, nor let anybody's authority count for more than the Word of God." [3]

---

[7] Matt. 18:6.
[8] See above, Smalcald Articles, Pt. III, Art. XII, 1, 2.
[9] Pt. III, Art. X, 1, 2.
[1] Pt. II, Art. IV, 14.
[2] See above, Introductions to Smalcald Articles and Treatise on the Power and Primacy of the Pope.
[3] Above, Treatise, 11.

Shortly after: "Since this is the situation, all Christians ought to   22
beware of becoming participants in the impious doctrines, blasphemies,
and unjust cruelties of the pope. They ought rather abandon and
execrate the pope and his adherents as the kingdom of Antichrist.
Christ commanded, 'Beware of false prophets' (Matt. 7:15). Paul
also commanded that ungodly teachers should be shunned and ex-
ecrated as accursed, and he wrote in II Cor. 6:14, 'Do not be mismated with unbelievers, for what fellowship has light with darkness?' To dissent from the consensus of so many nations and   23
to be called schismatics is a serious matter. But divine authority
commands us all not to be associated with and not to support impiety
and unjust cruelty." [4]

In a special opinion Dr. Luther exhaustively instructs the   24
church of God on how we are to treat ceremonies in general and
matters of indifference in particular.[5] He did the same again in 1530.[6]

From this exposition everyone can learn what a Christian   25
community, each individual Christian, and particularly the preachers
may or may not do with a clear conscience in matters of indifference,
especially in a period of confession, so that they do not provoke the
wrath of God, violate love, confirm the enemies of God's Word, and
scandalize the weak in faith.

1. Therefore we reject and condemn as wrongful the view   26
that the commandments of men are to be considered as of themselves
worship of God or a part thereof.

2. We also reject and condemn as wrongful the procedure   27
whereby such commandments are imposed by force on the community
of God as necessary.

3. We reject and condemn as wrongful the opinion of those   28
who hold that in a period of persecution we may yield to enemies of
the holy Gospel or conform to their practices, since this serves to
imperil the truth.

4. Likewise we hold it to be a culpable sin when in a period   29
of persecution anything is done in deed or action to please enemies
of the Gospel contrary and in opposition to the Christian confession,
whether in things indifferent, in doctrine, or in whatever else pertains
to religion.

5. We also reject and condemn the procedure whereby mat-   30
ters of indifference are abolished in such a way as to give the impression that the community of God does not have the liberty to use one

---

[4] Treatise, 41, 42.

[5] *A Report to a Good Friend concerning Both Kinds* (1528), in *WA*,
26:560-618.

[6] Letters written by Luther to Augsburg between June and September,
1530, in *WA, Briefwechsel*, Vol. 5.

or more ceremonies at any time and place, according to its circumstances, as may in Christian liberty be most beneficial to the church.

6. In line with the above, churches will not condemn each   31 other because of a difference in ceremonies, when in Christian liberty one uses fewer or more of them, as long as they are otherwise agreed in doctrine and in all its articles and are also agreed concerning the right use of the holy sacraments, according to the well-known axiom, "Disagreement in fasting should not destroy agreement in faith." [7]

XI. ETERNAL FOREKNOWLEDGE AND DIVINE ELECTION

There has been no public, scandalous, and widespread dis-   1 sension among theologians of the Augsburg Confession concerning the eternal election of the children of God. Nevertheless, this article has become the occasion of very serious controversies at other places and has involved our people[8] also. Nor have our theologians always used the same terms. Therefore, in order by God's grace to prevent, as far as we can, disunity and schism in this article among our posterity, we have determined to set forth our explanation of this article in this document so that all men may know what we teach, believe, and confess in this article. If the teaching of this article is set   2 forth out of the divine Word and according to the example it provides, it neither can nor should be considered useless and unnecessary, still less offensive and detrimental, because the Holy Scriptures mention this article not only once, and as it were in passing, but discuss and present it in detail in many places. In the same way,   3 one must not by-pass or reject a teaching of the divine Word because some people misuse and misunderstand it; on the contrary, precisely in order to avert such misuse and misunderstanding, we must set forth the correct meaning on the basis of Scripture. Accordingly, the net total and content of the teaching on this article consists of the following points:

At the very outset we must carefully note the difference between   4 God's eternal foreknowledge[9] and the eternal election of his children to eternal salvation. For the fact that God sees and knows everything before it happens—what we call God's foreknowledge—extends to all creatures, good and evil. He sees and knows in advance all that

---

[7] Irenaeus against Victor of Rome, in Eusebius, *Church History*, V, 24, 13.

[8] The reference is to the attack of Heshusius on Calvin and Beza, the controversy between the Lutherans and Calvinists at Strasbourg prior to 1563, and the intensive discussions of the issue in Lower Saxony.

[9] Although the terms are used in both a narrow and a pregnant sense (represented in the Latin translation respectively by *praescientia* and *praedestinatio*), *Vorsehung* (or *Versehung*) and *vorsehen* (or *versehen*) are consistently rendered "foreknowledge" and "foreknow" in this translation.

is or shall be, all that happens or will happen, both good or evil, since all things, present or future, are manifest and present to God, as it is written, "Are not two sparrows sold for a penny? And not one of them will fall to the ground without your Father's will" (Matt. 10:29). Again, "Thine eyes beheld my unformed substance, in thy book were written every one of them, the days that were formed for me, when as yet there was none of them" (Ps. 139:16). And again, "I know your sitting down and your going out and coming in, and your raging against me" (Isa. 37:28).

On the other hand, the eternal election of God or God's pre- 5
destination to salvation does not extend over both the godly and the ungodly, but only over the children of God, who have been elected and predestined to eternal life "before the foundation of the world was laid," as St. Paul says, "Even as he chose us in him, he destined us in love to be his sons through Jesus Christ" (Eph. 1:4, 5).

God's foreknowledge (*praescientia*) sees and knows in advance 6
the evil as well, but not in such a way as though it were God's gracious will that it should happen. To be sure, he sees and knows beforehand whatever the perverse and wicked will of the devil and of men will attempt and do. But even in wicked acts and works God's fore-knowledge operates in such a way that God sets a limit and measure for the evil which he does not will—how far it is to go, how long it is to endure, and when and how he will interfere with it and punish it. For the Lord God governs everything in such a way that it must redound to the glory of his divine name and the salvation of his elect, and thereby the ungodly are confounded.

The source and cause of evil is not God's foreknowledge (since 7
God neither creates nor works evil, nor does he help it along and promote it), but rather the wicked and perverse will of the devil and of men, as it is written, "Israel, thou hast plunged thyself into misfortune, but in me alone is thy salvation" (Hos. 13:9). Likewise, "Thou art not a God who delights in wickedness" (Ps. 5:4).

God's eternal election, however, not only foresees and fore- 8
knows the salvation of the elect, but by God's gracious will and pleasure in Christ Jesus it is also a cause which creates, effects, helps, and furthers our salvation and whatever pertains to it. Our salvation is based on it in such a way that "the gates of Hades" are not able to do anything against it (Matt. 16:18), as it is written, "No one shall snatch my sheep out of my hand" (John 10:28), and again, "As many as were ordained to eternal life believed" (Acts 13:48).

Furthermore, we are not to view this eternal election or divine 9
ordering to eternal life only in the secret and inscrutable counsel of God, as though it comprised no more and that nothing more is in-volved in it, or that nothing more is to be considered in connection

with it, than that God has foreseen who and how many are to be saved, who and how many are to be damned, or that he merely held a sort of military muster: This one shall be saved, that one shall be damned, this one shall persevere, that one shall not persevere.

Such a view, however, leads many to draw and formulate 10 strange, dangerous, and pernicious opinions and causes and fortifies in people's minds either false security and impenitence or anxiety and despair. As a result they trouble themselves with burdensome doubts and say: "Since God has foreordained his elect to salvation 'before the foundations of the world were laid' (Eph. 1:4) and since God's foreknowledge can never fail and no one can ever change or hinder it (Isa. 14:27; Rom. 9:19, 11), therefore if I have been foreknown to salvation, it will do me no harm if I live in all kinds of sin and vice without repentance, despise Word and sacraments, and do not concern myself with repentance, faith, prayer, and godliness. On the contrary, I shall and must be saved since God's foreknowledge must be carried out. But if I am not foreknown, then everything is in vain, even though I were to hold to the Word, repent, believe, etc., since I cannot hinder or alter God's foreknowledge."

And such thoughts may well come to pious hearts, too, even 11 though by the grace of God they have repentance, faith, and the good resolve to lead a godly life. Especially when they see their own weakness and the example of such as did not persevere but fell away again, they may think, "If you are not foreknown to salvation from eternity everything is in vain." We must oppose such false 12 imagining and thoughts with the following clear, certain, and unfailing foundation: All Scripture, inspired by God, should minister not to security and impenitence but "to reproof, correction, and improvement" (II Tim. 3:16). Furthermore, everything in the Word of God is written down for us, not for the purpose of thereby driving us to despair but in order that "by steadfastness, by the encouragement of the Scriptures we might have hope" (Rom. 15:4). From this it is beyond all doubt that the true understanding or the right use of the teaching of God's eternal foreknowledge will in no way cause or support either impenitence or despair. So, too, Scripture presents this doctrine in no other way than to direct us thereby to the Word (Eph. 1:13, 14; I Cor. 1:21, 30, 31), to admonish us to repent (II Tim. 3:16), to urge us to godliness (Eph. 1:15ff.; John 15:16, 17, 3, 4, 10, 12), to strengthen our faith and to assure us of our salvation (Eph. 1:9, 13, 14; John 10:27-30; II Thess. 2:13-15). Hence if we wish to think or speak correctly and profitably about 13 eternal election or about the predestination and ordering of the children of God to eternal life, we should accustom ourselves not to speculate concerning the absolute, secret, hidden, and inscrutable foreknowledge of God. On the contrary, we should consider the counsel, purpose, and ordinance of God in Christ Jesus, who is the genuine and true "book of life" [1] as it is revealed to us through the Word. This means that we must always take as one unit the   14 entire doctrine of God's purpose, counsel, will, and ordinance concerning our redemption, call, justification, and salvation, as Paul treats and explains this article (Rom. 8:28ff.; Eph. 1:4ff.) and as Christ likewise does in the parable (Matt. 20:2-14), namely, that in his purpose and counsel God has ordained the following:

1. That through Christ the human race has truly been redeemed   15 and reconciled with God and that by his innocent obedience, suffering, and death Christ has earned for us "the righteousness which avails before God" [2] and eternal life.

2. That this merit and these benefits of Christ are to be offered,   16 given, and distributed to us through his Word and sacraments.

3. That he would be effective and active in us by his Holy   17 Spirit through the Word when it is preached, heard, and meditated on, would convert hearts to true repentance, and would enlighten them in the true faith.

4. That he would justify and graciously accept into the adop-   18 tion of children and into the inheritance of eternal life all who in sincere repentance and true faith accept Christ.

5. That he also would sanctify in love all who are thus justified,   19 as St. Paul says (Eph. 1:4).

6. That he also would protect them in their great weakness   20 against the devil, the world, and the flesh, guide and lead them in his ways, raise them up again when they stumble, and comfort and preserve them in tribulation and temptation.

7. That he would also strengthen and increase in them the good   21 work which he has begun, and preserve them unto the end, if they cling to God's Word, pray diligently, persevere in the grace of God, and use faithfully the gifts that they have received.

8. That, finally, he would eternally save and glorify in eternal   22 life those whom he has elected, called, and justified.

In this his eternal counsel, purpose, and ordinance God has   23 not only prepared salvation in general, but he has also graciously considered and elected to salvation each and every individual among the elect who are to be saved through Christ, and also ordained that in the manner just recounted he wills by his grace, gifts, and effective working to bring them to salvation and to help, further, strengthen, and preserve them to this end.

According to the Scriptures all this is included in the teaching   24

---

[1] Phil. 4:3; Rev. 3:5; 20:15.
[2] Rom. 1:17; II Cor. 5:21.

of the eternal election of God to adoption and to eternal salvation. It should be understood as included therein and never be excluded or omitted when we speak of the purpose, foreknowledge, election, and ordinance of God to eternal salvation. When we follow the Scriptures and organize our thinking about this article in this light, we can by the grace of God easily orient ourselves in it.

An answer to the following question is necessary for the further 25 exposition and the salutary use of the teaching of God's foreknowledge to salvation: Since only the elect "whose names are written in the book of life" [3] will be saved, how can and should one know, and wherefrom and whereby can and should one discover, who the elect are who can and should comfort themselves with this teaching? We should not pass judgment on the basis of our reason, or 26 on the basis of the law, or on the basis of some outward appearance. Neither should we permit ourselves to try to explore the secret and hidden abyss of divine foreknowledge. Instead we must heed the revealed will of God. For he has revealed and "made known to us the mystery of his will" and has brought it forth through Christ so that it should be preached (Eph. 1:9, 10; II Tim. 1:9-11).

This is revealed to us, however, as Paul says, "Those whom 27 God has foreknown, elected, and decreed, he has also called" (Rom. 8:29, 30). Now, God does not call without means but through the Word, as indeed he has commanded the preaching of repentance and forgiveness of sin.[4] St. Paul testified to the same effect when he wrote, "We are ambassadors in Christ's stead, and God is admonishing you through us, 'Be reconciled to God' " (II Cor. 5:20). And the guests whom the king invites to his son's wedding he calls through the messengers whom he sent out, some at the first, some at the second, at the third, at the sixth, at the ninth, and even at the eleventh hour (Matt. 20:1-16; 22:2-14).

Hence if we want to consider our eternal election to salvation 28 profitably, we must by all means cling rigidly and firmly to the fact that as the proclamation of repentance extends over all men (Luke 24:47), so also does the promise of the Gospel. Therefore Christ has commanded to preach "repentance and forgiveness of sins in his name among all nations." For God "loved the world" and gave to it his only begotten Son (John 3:16). Christ has taken away the sin of the world (John 1:29); he has given his flesh "for the life of the world" (John 6:51); his blood is "the propitiation for the whole world's" sin (I John 1:7; 2:2). Christ declares, "Come unto me, all who are heavy-laden, and I will give you rest" (Matt. 11:28). "God has included all men under disobedience so that he might have mercy on

---

[3] Phil. 4:3; Rev. 20:15.
[4] Luke 24:47.

all" (Rom. 11:32). "The Lord is not wishing that any should perish, but that all should turn to repentance" (II Pet. 3:9). "He is simultaneously one Lord of all, rich toward all who call upon him" (Rom. 10:12). Righteousness "comes through faith in Christ to all and on all who believe" (Rom. 3:22). "This is the will of the Father, that all who believe on Christ should have eternal life" (John 6:40). It is Christ's command that all in common to whom repentance is preached should also have this promise of the Gospel proclaimed to them (Luke 24:47; Mark 16:15). And we should not regard this call 29 of God which takes place through the preaching of the Word as a deception, but should know certainly that God reveals his will in this way, and that in those whom he thus calls he will be efficaciously active through the Word so that they may be illuminated, converted, and saved. For the Word through which we are called is a ministry of the Spirit—"which gives the Spirit" (II Cor. 3:8) and a "power of God" to save (Rom. 1:16). And because the Holy Spirit wills to be efficacious through the Word, to strengthen us, and to give us power and ability, it is God's will that we should accept the Word, believe and obey it. The elect are therefore described as follows: "My 30 sheep hear my voice, and I know them, and they follow me; and I give them eternal life" (John 10:27, 28), and they who are decreed "according to God's purpose" to "the inheritance" hear the Gospel, believe on Christ, pray and give thanks, are sanctified in love, have hope, patience, and comfort in afflictions (Eph. 1:11, 13; Rom. 8:25). Though this is still very weak in them, they nevertheless hunger and thirst after righteousness (Matt. 5:6). Thus the Spirit of God 31 gives "witness" to the elect "that they are the children of God," and when they "do not know how to pray as we ought," he intercedes for them "with inexpressible groanings" (Rom. 8:16-26). In the 32 same vein Holy Scripture also assures us that God who has called us will be so faithful that after "he has begun the good work in us" he will also continue it to the end and complete it, if we ourselves do not turn away from him but "hold fast until the end the substance which has been begun" in us. For such constancy he has promised his grace (I Cor. 1:8; Phil. 1:6ff.; II Pet. 3:9; Heb. 3.14).

We should concern ourselves with this revealed will of God, 33 follow it, and be diligent about it because the Holy Spirit gives grace, power, and ability through the Word by which he has called us. We should not explore the abyss of the hidden foreknowledge of God, even as Christ answered the question, "Lord, will those who are saved be few?" by saying, "Strive to enter by the narrow door" (Luke 13:23, 24). Luther puts it this way: "Follow the order in the Epistle to the Romans. Concern yourself first with Christ and his Gospel so that you learn to know your sins and his grace. Then take up the warfare against sin as Paul teaches from the first to the eighth chapter. Afterward, when in the eighth chapter you are tested under the cross and in tribulation, the ninth, tenth, and eleventh chapters will show you how comforting God's foreknowledge is." [5]

The reason why "many are called and few are chosen" [6] is   34 not that in his call, which takes place through the Word, God intended to say: "Externally I do indeed through the Word call all of you, to whom I give my Word, into my kingdom, but down in my heart I am not thinking of all, but only of a certain few. For it is my will that the majority of those whom I call through the Word are not to be illuminated or converted, but are to be and remain under condemnation, although I speak differently in my call to them." In   35 this way it would be taught that God, who is the eternal Truth, contradicts himself. Yet God himself punishes men for such wickedness when they say one thing and think and intend something different in their hearts (Ps. 5:10, 11; 12:3, 4). This would also   36 completely undermine and totally destroy for us the necessary and comforting foundation, which daily reminds and admonishes us to learn and to determine God's will toward us and what assures and promises it to us solely from his Word, through which he deals with us and calls us, so that we should believe it with absolute certainty and not doubt it in the least.

For this reason Christ has the promises of the Gospel offered   37 not only in general but also through the sacraments, which he has attached as a seal of the promise and by which he confirms it to every believer individually. For that reason also, as the Augsburg Con-   38 fession states in Article XI, we retain individual absolution and teach that it is God's command that we "believe this absolution and firmly hold that when we believe the word of absolution we are as truly reconciled with God as if we had heard a voice from heaven," as the Apology explains this article.[7] We would be deprived of this comfort completely if we could not determine God's will toward us from the call which comes to us through the Word and through the sacraments. This would also overturn and destroy for us the founda-   39 tion, namely, that the Holy Spirit wills to be certainly present with and efficacious and active through the Word when it is proclaimed, heard, and meditated upon. Hence, as was mentioned before, there is no basis for the assumption that those might be the elect who despise God's Word and who reject, blaspheme, and persecute it (Matt. 22:5, 6; Acts 13:40f., 46),[8] or who harden their hearts when they

[5] Preface to Romans, *EA*, 63:135.
[6] Matt. 20:16; 22:14.
[7] German version of the Apology of the Augsburg Confession, XI, 2, slightly condensed and adapted.
[8] The original refers erroneously to Acts 15.

hear it (Heb. 4:2, 7), resist the Holy Spirit (Acts 7:51), remain in sin without repentance (Luke 14:18, 24), do not truly believe in Christ (Mark 16:16), make only an outward pretense (Matt. 7:15; 22:12), or seek other ways to righteousness and salvation outside of Christ (Rom. 9:31). On the contrary, as God has ordained in his   40 counsel that the Holy Spirit would call, enlighten, and convert the elect through the Word and that he would justify and save all who accept Christ through true faith, so he has also ordained in his counsel that he would harden, reject, and condemn all who, when they are called through the Word, spurn the Word and persistently resist the Holy Spirit who wants to work efficaciously in them through the Word. In this sense "many are called, but few are chosen,"[9] for   41 few accept the Word and obey it; the majority despise the Word and refuse to come to the wedding.[1] The reason for such contempt of the Word is not God's foreknowledge but man's own perverse will, which rejects or perverts the means and instrument of the Holy Spirit which God offers to him through the call and resists the Holy Spirit who wills to be efficaciously active through the Word, as Christ says, "How often would I have gathered you together and you would not!" (Matt. 23:37).

In the same way many "receive the Word with joy," but after   42 that "they fall away again" (Luke 8:13). But the reason for this is not that God does not want to impart the grace of perseverance to those in whom he has "begun the good work." This would contradict St. Paul in Phil. 1:6. The reason is that they willfully turn away from the holy commandment, grieve and embitter the Holy Spirit, become entangled again in the filth of the world, and decorate their hearts as a tabernacle for the devil so that their last state will be worse than the first (II Pet. 2:10; Luke 11:24, 25; Heb. 10:26; Eph. 5:3-11, 18).

Thus far God has revealed the mystery of foreknowledge to   43 us in his Word. If we stay with this and hold ourselves thereto, it is indeed a useful, salutary, and comforting doctrine, for it mightily substantiates the article that we are justified and saved without our works and merit, purely by grace and solely for Christ's sake. Before the creation of time, "before the foundation of the world was laid" (Eph. 1:4), before we even existed, before we were able to have done any good, God elected us to salvation "according to his purpose" by grace in Christ (Rom. 9:11; II Tim. 1:9). This also   44 completely refutes all false opinions and erroneous doctrines about the powers of our natural will,[2] for in his counsel God has determined

[9] Matt. 20:16; 22:14.

[1] Matt. 22:5; Luke 14:18-20.

[2] See above, Solid Declaration, II, 7, 90.

and decreed before the world began that by the power of his Holy Spirit through the Word he would create and effect in us everything that belongs to our conversion.

This doctrine also affords the beautiful and glorious comfort 45 that God was so deeply concerned about every individual Christian's conversion, righteousness, and salvation and so faithfully minded about it that "even before the foundation of the world was laid" he held counsel and ordained "according to his purpose" [3] how he would bring me thereto and keep me therein. Furthermore, God 46 wanted to insure my salvation so firmly and certainly—for due to the weakness and wickedness of our flesh it could easily slip from our fingers, and through the deceit and power of the devil and the world it could easily be snatched and taken from our hands—that he ordained my salvation in his eternal purpose, which cannot fail or be overthrown, and put it for safekeeping into the almighty hand of our Saviour, Jesus Christ, out of which no one can pluck us (John 10:28). For this reason, too, Paul asks, Since we are called 47 according to the purpose of God, "who will separate us from the love of God in Christ?" (Rom. 8:35).

This doctrine will also give us the glorious comfort, in times 48 of trial and affliction, that in his counsel before the foundation of the world God has determined and decreed that he will assist us in all our necessities, grant us patience, give us comfort, create hope, and bring everything to such an issue that we shall be saved. Again, 49 Paul presents this in a most comforting manner when he points out that before the world began God ordained in his counsel through which specific cross and affliction he would conform each of his elect to "the image of his Son," and that in each case the afflictions should and must "work together for good" since they are "called according to his purpose." From this Paul draws the certain and indubitable conclusion that neither "tribulation nor anguish, neither death nor life, etc. can separate us from the love of God in Christ Jesus" (Rom. 8:28, 29, 35, 38, 39).

This article also gives a glorious testimony that the church of 50 God shall exist and remain against all the "gates of Hades." [4] At the same time it teaches us what the true church is, lest we be offended by the outward prestige of the false church (Rom. 9:8ff.).

This article also contains mighty admonitions and warnings, 51 among others: They "despise the counsel of God against themselves" (Luke 7:30); "I tell you, none of those men who were invited shall taste my banquet" (Luke 14:24); likewise, "Many are called, but few are chosen" (Matt. 22:14); likewise, "He who has ears to hear, let

[3] Eph. 1:4; II Tim. 1:9.
[4] Matt. 16:18.

him hear";[5] and "Take heed how ye hear." [6] Thus it is possible to use the teaching in this article in a profitable, comforting, and salutary way.

We must, however, carefully distinguish between what God has 52 expressly revealed in his Word and what he has not revealed. Beyond the matters which have been revealed in Christ and of which we have spoken thus far, there are many points in this mystery about which God has remained silent and which he has not revealed but has kept reserved solely to his own wisdom and knowledge. We are not to pry into these, nor are we to follow our own thoughts in this matter and draw our own conclusions and brood, but we are to adhere exclusively to the revealed Word. This admonition is eminently necessary. In our presumption we take much greater delight in con- 53 cerning ourselves with matters which we cannot harmonize—in fact, we have no command to do so—than with those aspects of the question which God has revealed to us in his Word.

Thus there is no doubt that before the world began God fore- 54 saw right well and with utter certainty, and that he still knows, who of those who are called will believe and who will not; likewise, who of the converted will persevere and who will not persevere; and who after falling away will return and who will become obdurate. God is also aware and knows exactly how many there will be 55 on either side. But because God has reserved this mystery to his own wisdom and not revealed anything concerning it in the Word, still less has commanded us to explore it through our speculations but has earnestly warned against it (Rom. 11:33), therefore we are not, on the basis of our speculations, to make our own deductions, draw conclusions, or brood over it, but cling solely to his revealed Word, to which he directs us.

Without doubt God also knows and has determined for each 56 person the time and hour of his call and conversion. But since he has not revealed this to us, we must obey his command and operate constantly with the Word, while we leave the time and hour to God (Acts 1:7).

The same applies when we observe that God gives his Word 57 at one place and not at another; that he removes it from one place but lets it remain at another; or that one becomes hardened, blinded, and is given over to a perverse mind while another in equal guilt is again converted. Paul sets a definite limit for us as to how far 58 we should go in these and similar questions (Rom. 9:14ff.; 11:22ff.). In the case of the one group we are to see God's judgment. It is indeed a well deserved punishment for sin when God so severely

[5] Luke 8:8.
[6] Luke 8:18.

punishes a land or a people for contempt of his Word that the punishment extends also to their posterity, as with the Jews. Thus 59 in the history of some nations and some persons God shows his own people what all of us would rightfully have deserved, earned, and merited because we misbehave over against God's Word and often sorely grieve the Holy Spirit. This will lead us to live in the fear of God and to recognize and glorify God's goodness to us without and contrary to our deserving, to whom he gives and preserves his Word and whom he does not harden and reject.

Since our nature is corrupted by sin and is worthy and deserving 60 of God's wrath and damnation, God owes us neither his Word, nor his Spirit, nor his grace; in fact, when he does graciously give us these we frequently cast them from us and make ourselves unworthy of eternal life (Acts 13:46). But God permits us to behold his righteous and well deserved judgment over certain lands, nations, and people so that, as we compare ourselves with them and find ourselves in the same condemnation, we may learn the more diligently to recognize and praise God's pure and unmerited grace toward the "vessels of mercy." [7] No injustice is done to those who are punished and 61 receive their "wages of sin." In the case of the others, however, to whom God gives and preserves his Word, whereby he enlightens, converts, and keeps them, God commends his pure and unmerited grace and mercy.

If we go thus far in this article we will remain on the right path, 62 as it is written, "O Israel, it is your own fault that you are destroyed, but that there is help for you is pure grace on my part" (Hos. 13:9).[8] But whenever something in the discussion of this subject 63 soars too high and goes beyond these limits, we must with Paul place our finger on our lips and say, "Who are you, a man, to answer back to God?" [9] The great apostle Paul shows us that we cannot and 64 should not try to explore and explain everything in this article. After a lengthy discussion of this article on the basis of the revealed Word of God, as soon as he comes to the point where he shows how much of this mystery God has reserved for his own hidden wisdom, Paul immediately commands silence and cuts off further discussion with the following words: "O the depth of the riches and wisdom and knowledge of God! How unsearchable are his judgments and how inscrutable his ways! For who has known the mind of the Lord?" [1]— that is, outside and beyond what he has revealed to us in his Word.

We should accordingly consider God's eternal election in Christ, 65

[7] Rom. 9:23; 11:5.
[8] The German text here is different from that in section 7, above.
[9] Rom. 9:20.
[1] Rom. 11:33, 34.

and not outside of or apart from Christ. For according to St. Paul's testimony we have been elected in Christ "before the foundation of the world was laid" (Eph. 1:4), as it is written, "He has loved us in the Beloved" (Eph. 1:6). This election is revealed from heaven through the proclaimed Word when the Father says, "This is my beloved Son with whom I am well pleased; listen to him" (Luke 3:22). And Christ says, "Come to me, all who are heavy-laden, and I will give you rest" (Matt. 11:28). And of the Holy Spirit Christ says, "He will glorify me" (John 16:14) and recall everything to you that I have told you. Thus the entire holy Trinity, God the Father, 66 Son, and Holy Spirit, directs all men to Christ as to the book of life in whom they are to seek the Father's eternal election. For the Father has decreed from eternity that whomever he would save he would save through Christ, as Christ himself says, "No one comes to the Father but by me" (John 14:6), and again, "I am the door; if anyone enters by me, he will be saved" (John 10:9). Christ, 67 "the only begotten Son, who is in the bosom of the Father" (John 1:18), has proclaimed the Father's will and thereby our eternal election to eternal life when he says, "The kingdom of God is at hand; repent and believe in the Gospel" (Mark 1:15); and again when he says, "This is the will of my Father, that everyone who sees the Son and believes in him should have eternal life" (John 6:40); and again, "God so loved the world," etc. (John 3:16).

The Father wills that all men should hear this proclamation 68 and come to Christ, and according to his own word Christ will not turn them away, "Him who comes to me I will not cast out" (John 6:37). In order that we may come to Christ, the Holy Spirit 69 creates true faith through the hearing of God's Word, as the apostle testifies, "Faith comes from the hearing of God's Word" (Rom. 10:17) when it is preached in sincerity and purity. Therefore no one 70 who wants to be saved should burden and torture himself with thoughts concerning the secret counsel of God, if he has been elected and ordained to eternal life. With such thoughts the troublesome adversary is accustomed to tempt and vex pious hearts. On the contrary, they should listen to Christ, who is the "book of life" and of the eternal election of all God's children to eternal life, and who testifies to all men without distinction that God wants all men who are laden and burdened with sin to come to him and find refreshment and be saved [a]

According to Christ's teaching they are to desist from sin, 71 repent, believe his promise, and trust in him completely and entirely And since we are unable to do this by our own powers, the Holy Spirit wills to work such repentance and faith in us through the Word and the sacraments. And in order that we may see it through 72

[a] Cf. Matt. 11:28.

and abide and persevere in it, we should implore God to give us his grace, of which he has assured us in holy Baptism, and not doubt that according to his promise he will give it to us. We have his word, "What father among you, if his son asks for a fish, will instead of a fish give him a serpent; or if he asks for an egg, will give him a scorpion? If you then, who are evil, know how to give good gifts to your children, how much more will the heavenly Father give the Holy Spirit to those who ask him?" (Luke 11:11-13).

Next, since the Holy Spirit dwells in the elect who have come to   73 faith as he dwells in his temple, and is not idle in them but urges them to obey the commandments of God, believers likewise should not be idle, still less oppose the urgings of the Spirit of God, but should exercise themselves in all Christian virtues, in all godliness, modesty, temperance, patience, and brotherly love, and should diligently seek to "confirm their call and election" [3] so that the more they experience the power and might of the Spirit within themselves, the less they will doubt their election. For the Spirit testifies to the elect that they are "children of God" (Rom. 8:16). And if per-   74 chance they should fall into such grave temptation that they feel that they are no longer experiencing any power whatever of the indwelling Spirit of God and say with David, "I had said in my alarm, I am driven far from thy sight" (Ps. 31:22), then, regardless of what they experience within themselves, they should nevertheless join David in the next words, "But thou didst hear my supplications when I cried to thee for help" (Ps. 31:23).

Our election to eternal life does not rest on our piety or virtue   75 but solely on the merit of Christ and the gracious will of the Father, who cannot deny himself because he is changeless in his will and essence. Hence when his children become disobedient and stumble, he arranges to recall them to repentance through the Word, and through it the Holy Spirit wills to effect their conversion in them. If they return to him in true repentance through a right faith, he will always show the same old fatherly heart to all who tremble at his Word and cordially return to him, as it is written, "If a man divorces his wife and she goes from him and becomes another man's wife, may he receive her again? Would not that land be greatly polluted? You have played the harlot with many lovers; yet return again to me, says the Lord" (Jer. 3:1).

It is indeed correct and true what Scripture states, that no one   76 comes to Christ unless the Father draw him.[4] But the Father will not do this without means, and he has ordained Word and sacraments as the ordinary means or instruments to accomplish this end. It is

---

[3] II Pet. 2:10. Cf. above, Solid Declaration, II, 65.
[4] John 6:44.

not the will of either the Father or the Son that any one should refuse to hear or should despise the preaching of his Word and should wait for the Father to draw him without Word and sacraments.[5] The Father indeed draws by the power of the Holy Spirit, but according to his common ordinance he does this through the hearing of his holy, divine Word, as with a net by which he snatches the elect from the maw of the devil. Every poor sinner must therefore attend on it, hear 77 it with diligence, and in no way doubt the drawing of the Father because the Holy Spirit wills to be present in the Word and to be efficacious with his power through it. And this is the drawing of the Father.

The reason why all who hear the Word do not come to faith 78 and therefore receive the greater damnation is not that God did not want them to be saved. It is their own fault because they heard the Word of God not to learn but only to despise, blaspheme, and ridicule it, and they resisted the Holy Spirit who wanted to work within them, as was the case with the Pharisees and their party at the time of Christ.[6]

Hence Paul very carefully distinguishes between the work of 79 God, who alone prepares vessels of honor, and the work of the devil and of man, who, through the instigation of the devil and not of God, has made himself a vessel of dishonor. It is written, "God endured with much patience the vessels of wrath fitted for damnation in order to make known the riches of his glory in the vessels of mercy, which he has prepared beforehand for salvation" (Rom. 9:22, 23). The apostle says in unmistakable terms that God "endured the 80 vessels of wrath with much patience." He does not say that God made them vessels of wrath. If that had been his will, he would not have needed any long-suffering. The devil and man himself, and not God, are the cause of their being fitted for damnation. Every- 81 thing which prepares and fits man for damnation emanates from the devil and man through sin, and in no way from God. Since God does not want any man to be damned, how could he prepare man for damnation? God is not the cause of sin, nor is he the cause of the punishment, the damnation. The only cause of man's damnation is sin, for the "wages of sin is death" (Rom. 6:23).[7] And as God does not will sin and has no pleasure in sin, so he also does not will the death of a sinner and has no pleasure in his damnation. He does not will that "any should perish, but that all should reach repentance" (II Pet 3:9). It is written in Ezekiel, "As I live, says the Lord God, I have no pleasure in the death of the wicked, but that the wicked

---

[5] See above, Solid Declaration, II, 4, 80.

[6] Matt. 23:26ff.; Luke 11:39ff.; John 7:48; 8:13; 9:16, 41; 12:42.

[7] This is directed against John Calvin's doctrine of a double election, and particularly against Theodore Beza's supralapsarianism.

turn from his way and live" (Ezek. 18:23; 33:11). And St.   82
Paul testifies with clear words that God's power and operation can
transform the vessels of dishonor into vessels of honor when he
writes, "If any one purifies himself from what is ignoble, then he will
be a vessel for noble use, consecrated and useful to the master of
the house, ready for any good work" (II Tim. 2:21). He who is to
purify himself must beforehand have been impure and therefore a
vessel of dishonor. Concerning "the vessels of mercy" he says specifically that the Lord himself "has prepared them unto glory." [8] He
does not say this of the damned, whom God has not prepared but who
have prepared themselves to be vessels of damnation.

It is to be considered diligently that God punishes sin with   83
sin, that is, because of their subsequent impurity, impenitence, and
deliberate sins God punishes with obduracy and blindness those who
have been converted. This must not be misconstrued as if it had
never been God's gracious will that such people should come to the
knowledge of the truth and be saved. God's revealed will involves
both items: First, that he would receive into grace all who repent and
believe in Christ; second, that he would punish those who deliberately
turn away from the holy commandment[9] and involve themselves again
in the filth of this world (II Pet. 2:20), prepare their hearts for Satan
(Luke 11:24, 25), and outrage the Holy Spirit (Heb. 10:29), and that
he would harden, blind, and for ever damn them if they continue
therein. Hence Pharoah (of whom we read, "For this purpose   84
have I let you live to show you my power, so that my name may be
declared throughout all the earth")[1] did not perish because God did
not want to grant him salvation or because it was God's good pleasure
that he should be damned and lost. For God "is not wishing that
any should perish," nor has he any "pleasure in the death of the
wicked, but that the wicked turn from his way and live." [2]

But that God hardened Pharaoh's heart so that Pharoah con-   85
tinued to sin and became the more obdurate the more he was admonished was a punishment for his preceding sin and his horrible tyranny
with which he oppressed the children of Israel by many, various, and
most inhuman devices contrary to the voice of his conscience. But
after God arranged to have his Word proclaimed and his will revealed to Pharaoh, and he deliberately rebelled against all the admonitions and warnings, God withdrew his hand from him, and so his
heart became hardened and calloused and God executed his judgment

[8] Rom. 9:23.
[9] Most manuscript copies and the German printed text of 1580 read
Gebet (prayer), but this is an obvious slip for *Gebot* (commandment), the
reading of the Latin version (*mandato*).
[1] Ex. 9:16; Rom. 9:17.
[2] II Pet. 3:9; Ezek. 33:11.

on him, for he was indeed guilty of "hell-fire." [3] The holy apostle 86 adduces Pharaoh's example for the sole purpose of thereby setting forth the righteousness of God which God manifests toward the impenitent and despisers of his Word, and in no way does he want us to infer that God had not wanted to grant Pharoah or any other person eternal life, or that in his secret counsel God had ordained him to eternal damnation so that he could not and might not be saved.

This teaching and explanation of the eternal and saving elec- 87 tion of the elect children of God gives God his due honor fully and completely. It sets forth that he saves us "according to the purpose" of his will through sheer mercy in Christ without our merit and good works, as it is written, "He destined us in love to be his son through Jesus Christ, according to the purpose of his will, and to the praise of his glorious grace which he freely bestowed on us in the Beloved" (Eph. 1:5, 6). It is therefore false and wrong when men teach 88 that the cause of our election is not only the mercy of God and the most holy merit of Christ, but that there is also within us a cause of God's election on account of which God has elected us unto eternal life. For not only before we had done any good, but even before we were born[4] (in fact, "before the foundation of the world was laid")[5] God elected us in Christ—"in order that God's purpose of election might continue, not because of works but because of his call, she was told, 'The elder will serve the younger.' As it is written, 'Jacob I loved, but Esau I hated' " (Rom. 9:11-13; Gen. 25:23; Mal. 1:2, 3).

Moreover, when people are taught to seek their eternal election 89 in Christ and in his holy Gospel as the "book of life," this doctrine never occasions either despondency or a riotous and dissolute life. This does not exclude any repentant sinner but invites and calls all poor, burdened, and heavy-laden sinners to repentance, to a knowledge of their sins, and to faith in Christ and promises them the Holy Spirit to cleanse and renew them. This doctrine gives sorrowing 90 and tempted people the permanently abiding comfort of knowing that their salvation does not rest in their own hands. If this were the case, they would lose it more readily than Adam and Eve did in paradise— yes, would be losing it every moment and hour. Their salvation rests in the gracious election of God, which he has revealed to us in Christ, out of whose hand "no one can pluck" us (John 10:28; II Tim. 2:19). Hence if anyone so sets forth this teaching concerning 91 God's gracious election that sorrowing Christians can find no comfort in it but are driven to despair, or when impenitent sinners are strengthened in their malice, then it is clearly evident that this teaching is

[3] Cf. Matt. 5:22.
[4] Rom. 9:11.
[5] Eph. 1:4.

not being set forth according to the Word and will of God but according to reason and the suggestion of the wicked devil. For the   92
apostle testifies that "Whatever was written in former days was written
for our instruction, that by steadfastness and by encouragement of
the Scriptures we might have hope" (Rom. 15:4). But it is certain
that any interpretation of the Scriptures which weakens or even removes this comfort and hope is contrary to the Holy Spirit's will and
intent. We shall abide by this simple, direct, and useful exposition   93
which is permanently and well grounded in God's revealed will, we
shall avoid and flee all abstruse and specious questions and disputations, and we reject and condemn all those things which are contrary
to these true, simple, and useful expositions.

This will suffice concerning the controverted articles which   94
have been disputed among theologians of the Augsburg Confession
for many years and in which some have erred and serious religious
contentions have arisen. From our exposition friends and foes   95
may clearly understand that we have no intention (since we have
no authority to do so) to yield anything of the eternal and unchangeable truth of God for the sake of temporal peace, tranquillity, and
outward harmony. Nor would such peace and harmony last, because
it would be contrary to the truth and actually intended for its sup-
pression. Still less by far are we minded to whitewash or cover up
any falsification of true doctrine or any publicly condemned errors.
We have a sincere delight in and deep love for true harmony and are
cordially inclined and determined on our part to do everything in our
power to further the same. We desire such harmony as will not   96
violate God's honor, that will not detract anything from the divine
truth of the holy Gospel, that will not give place to the smallest error
but will lead the poor sinner to true and sincere repentance, raise
him up through faith, strengthen him in his new obedience, and thus
justify and save him for ever through the sole merit of Christ, and
so forth.

XII. OTHER FACTIONS AND SECTS WHICH NEVER
ACCEPTED THE AUGSBURG CONFESSION

As far as the sects and factions are concerned which never   1
accepted the Augsburg Confession and to which we have not explicitly
adverted in this statement of ours (such as the Anabaptists, the
Schwenkfelders, and the New Arians and Anti-Trinitarians whose   2
errors all the churches of the Augsburg Confession have unanimously
condemned), we had not for that reason intended to make special
and detailed mention of them, although it now appears to be desirable.
Our adversaries have had the effrontery to pretend and pro-   3

claim to the whole world that among our churches and their teachers there are not two preachers who are agreed in each and every article of the Augsburg Confession, but are so disunited that they themselves no longer know what the Augsburg Confession really is and what it really means. Therefore it was our purpose not only to declare 4 our unanimous opinion with a few bare words or our signatures, but to present a clear, lucid, and unmistakable exposition of all the articles which were in controversy among theologians of the Augsburg Confession.

We wanted everyone to be able to see that we were not pro- 5 posing or hiding anything with intent to deceive and that our agreement was not a mere pretense but that we wanted to help matters fundamentally. We wanted to set forth our position so clearly 6 that our very adversaries would have to confess that in all these questions we abide by the true, simple, natural, and proper meaning of the Augsburg Confession. And we desire by God's grace to remain steadfastly in our commitment to this Confession until we die. As far as our ministry is concerned, we do not propose to look on idly or stand by silently while something contrary to the Augsburg Confession is imported into our churches and schools in which the almighty God and Father of our Lord Jesus Christ has appointed us teachers and shepherds.

Let no one as a result of our silence attribute to us the condemned 7 errors of the aforementioned factions and sects. For the most 8 part they insinuated themselves secretly, after the fashion of these spirits, into those places and especially at those times where the pure Word of the holy Gospel was allowed neither room nor scope, where the true teachers and confessors of the Gospel were being persecuted, where the profound darkness of the papacy still reigned, and where the poor, simple people, who were forced into contact with the open idolatry and false beliefs of the papacy, unfortunately accepted in their innocence what called itself evangelical and was not papistic. We have not been able to refrain from witnessing publicly before all Christendom that we have no part or share in their errors, be they few or many, and that on the contrary we reject and condemn all these errors as wrong, heretical, and contrary to our Christian and biblically-based Augsburg Confession.

Erroneous Articles of the Anabaptists

We reject and condemn the erroneous and heretical teaching 9 of the Anabaptists which cannot be suffered or tolerated in the churches or in the body politic or in domestic society. They teach:

1. That our righteousness before God does not depend alone 10 on the sole obedience and merit of Christ but in renewal and in our

own piety, in which we walk before God. But this piety rests for the greater part on their own peculiar precepts and self-chosen spirituality as on a kind of new monkery.

2. That unbaptized children are not sinners before God but 11 righteous and innocent, and hence in their innocence they will be saved without Baptism, which they do not need. Thus they deny and reject the entire teaching of original sin and all that pertains thereto.

3. That children should not be baptized until they have achieved 12 the use of reason and are able to make their own confession of faith.

4. That the children of Christians, because they are born of 13 Christian and believing parents, are holy and children of God even without and prior to Baptism. Therefore they do not esteem infant Baptism very highly and do not advocate it, contrary to the express words of the promise which extends only to those who keep the covenant and do not despise it (Gen. 17:4-8, 19-21).

5. That that is no truly Christian assembly or congregation in 14 the midst of which sinners are still found.

6. That one may not hear or attend on a sermon in those 15 temples in which the papistic Mass had formerly been read.

7. That one is to have nothing to do with those ministers of 16 the church who preach the Gospel according to the Augsburg Confession and censure the errors of the Anabaptists; neither may one serve them or work for them at all, but one is to flee and avoid them as people who pervert the Word of God.

8. That in the New Testament era government service is not 17 a godly estate.

9. That no Christian can hold an office in the government with 18 an inviolate conscience.

10. That no Christian may with an inviolate conscience use 19 an office of the government against wicked persons as occasion may arise, nor may a subject call upon the government for help.

11. That a Christian cannot with a good conscience swear an 20 oath before a court or pay oath-bound feudal homage to his prince or liege lord.

12. That the government cannot with an inviolate conscience 21 impose the death penalty on evil-doers.

13. That no Christian can with a good conscience hold or 22 possess private property but is obliged to give his property to the community.

14. That no Christian can with a good conscience be an inn- 23 keeper, a merchant, or a cutler.

15. That difference in faith is sufficient ground for married 24 people to divorce each other, to go their separate ways, and to enter into a new marriage with another person of the same faith.

16. That Christ did not assume his flesh and blood from the   25
virgin Mary but brought it along from heaven.

17. That Christ is not truly and essentially God but only pos-   26
sesses more and greater gifts and glory than other people.

They hold other similar articles. But they are divided into   27
many parties among themselves, with one party holding more and
another party holding fewer errors. The entire sect, however, can be
characterized as basically nothing else than a new kind of monkery.

ERRONEOUS ARTICLES OF THE SCHWENKFELDERS

We reject and condemn these errors of the Schwenkfelders: 28

1. In the first place, that no one has a true knowledge of   29
Christ, the reigning king of heaven, who believes that according to
the flesh or according to his assumed human nature Christ is a creature.
They also teach that through the exaltation Christ's flesh assumed
all the divine properties in such a way that in might, in power, in
majesty, and in glory he is in every way equal in grade and rank of
essence to the Father and the eternal Word, so that the two natures
of Christ have but one kind of essence, property, will, and glory and
so that Christ's flesh belongs to the essence of the holy Trinity.

2. That the ministry of the church, the Word proclaimed and   30
heard, is not a means whereby God the Holy Spirit teaches men the
saving knowledge of Christ, conversion, repentance, and faith or works
new obedience in them.

3. That the water of Baptism is not a means whereby the Lord   31
God seals the adoption of sons and works regeneration.

4. That the bread and wine in the Holy Supper are not means   32
through which Christ distributes his body and blood.

5. That a Christian who is truly born again through the Spirit   33
of God is able to keep and fulfill the law of God perfectly in this life.

6. That a congregation in which public expulsion or orderly   34
process of excommunication does not take place is not a true Christian
congregation.

7. That a minister of the church who is himself not truly re-   35
newed, righteous, and pious cannot teach profitably nor administer
genuine and true sacraments.

ERRONEOUS ARTICLES OF THE NEW ARIANS[6]

We reject and condemn the error of the New Arians who teach   36
that Christ is not a true, essential, and natural God, of one eternal,
divine essence with God the Father, but only adorned with divine
majesty inferior to and alongside the Father.

[6] Unitarians of the sixteenth century.

Erroneous Articles of the New Anti-Trinitarians

1. Some Anti-Trinitarians reject and condemn the old, approved 37 symbols, the Nicene and Athanasian Creeds, both as to content and terminology, and instead teach that there is not one eternal, divine essence of the Father, Son, and Holy Spirit but that, as there are three distinct persons, Father, Son, and Holy Spirit, so also each person has a distinct essence separate from the other two. Some teach that all three persons in the Trinity, like any three distinct and essentially separate human persons, have the same power, wisdom, majesty, and glory, while others teach that the three persons in the Trinity are unequal in their essence and properties.

2. That only the Father is genuinely and truly God. 38

All these and similar articles, and whatever attaches to them 39 or follows from them, we reject and condemn as false, erroneous, heretical, contrary to the Word of God, to the three Creeds, to the Augsburg Confession and the Apology, to the Smalcald Articles, to Luther's Catechisms. All pious Christians will and should avoid these as dearly as they love their soul's welfare and salvation.

Therefore, in the presence of God and of all Christendom 40 among both our contemporaries and our posterity, we wish to have testified that the present explanation of all the foregoing controverted articles here explained, and none other, is our teaching, belief, and confession in which by God's grace we shall appear with intrepid hearts before the judgment seat of Jesus Christ and for which we shall give an account. Nor shall we speak or write anything, privately or publicly, contrary to this confession, but we intend through God's grace to abide by it. In view of this we have advisedly, in the fear and invocation of God, subscribed our signatures with our own hands.

Dr. James Andreae, subscribed
Dr. Nicholas Selnecker, subscribed
Dr. Andrew Musculus, subscribed
Dr. Christopher Koerner, subscribed
David Chytraeus
Dr. Martin Chemnitz

BIBLICAL REFERENCES

13:1ff. — 223.7
13:1-4 — 355.4
13:5 — 223.5
13:5, 6 — 553.14
13:5-7 — 355.5
13:9 — 356.14;
  553.14; 567.21
14 — 612.9
14:1 — 582.70
14:3 — 582.70
14:6 — 613.13
14:13ff. — 493.5
14:17 — 175.36;
  273.27; 282.7
14:23 — 112.35;
  195.89; 217.17;
  273.23; 552.8
15:4 — 618.12; 632.92
15:16 — 256.34

I Corinthians
1:2 — 417.48
1:8 — 621.32
1:9 — 417.52
1:21 — 522.10;
  531.51; 618.12
1:30 — 119.86;
  154.306; 472.1;
  562.22
1:30, 31 — 618.12
1:31 — 315.3
2:4-12 — 535.71
2:8 — 488.14
2:11 — 415.36
2:14 — 39.3; 104.30;
  226.7; 470.2;
  522.10; 523.12
3:4-8 — 321.11
3:7 — 470.6
3:8 — 133.194;
  163.366; 233.29
3:9 — 521.8; 534.66
3:12 — 171.20
3:16 — 534.66
3:21, 22 — 321.11
3:23 — 139.230
4:1 — 264.80
4:4 — 129.163; 312.3;
  567.21
4:7 — 526.26
4:13 — 253.23;
  387.160
4:15 — 387.159
5:6 — 540.7
6:9 — 556.32

7:2 — 73.19; 241.14;
  248.63; 278.51
7:3 — 51.4
7:5 — 245.43
7:9 — 51.4; 241.16
7:10, 11 — 406.306
7:14 — 243.31
7:18, 19 — 612.12
7:32 — 245.40
8:8 — 273.26
8:9-13 — 493.5
9:9 — 553.14
9:10 — 612.9
9:14 — 354.3
9:16 — 470.6
9:27 — 69.37; 221.46;
  480.4; 554.19;
  565.9; 567.19
10:16 — 179.1; 311.5;
  483.9; 483.15;
  571.11; 575.35;
  579.54; 580.59;
  584.82; 584.84
10:17 — 179.3
10:18-33 — 579.57
11:5 — 90.54
11:12ff. — 60.35
11:20ff. — 49.3
11:23, 24 — 236.3
11:23-25 — 351.4;
  364.23; 447.3; 483.9
11:24 — 262.71;
  570.7; 575.35
11:25 — 59.30;
  213.20; 341.22;
  578.52; 579.53
11:26 — 136.210;
  256.35
11:27 — 57.13;
  266.91; 484.18;
  580.60
11:28 — 311.5
11:29 — 181.5; 484.18
11:31 — 147.268;
  208.163
11:33 — 60.39
12:3 — 526.26
12:4 — 300.9
12:8-10 — 300.9
12:22, 23 — 403.287
13:2 — 124.123;
  137.218
13:13 — 138.225
14:2 — 56.4
14:9 — 56.4

14:19 — 249.2
14:30 — 90.54
14:40 — 218.20
15:12 — 502.7
15:20 — 534.66
15:27 — 601.55;
  605.70
15:56 — 206.153
15:56, 57 — 118.79
15:57 — 205.146
16:1 — 133.192

II Corinthians
1:9 — 206.151
1:23 — 373.65
1:24 — 325.31
2:14ff. — 532.56
3:4-12 — 535.71
3:5 — 470.3; 522.12
3:6 — 260.59; 526.26;
  562.22
3:7-9 — 563.26
3:8 — 621.29
3:8, 9 — 562.22
3:12 — 139.229
3:13 — 110.21;
  193.78; 478.8
3:13-15 — 560.10
3:14-16 — 478.8
3:15 — 521.7
3:15-17 — 125.133
3:18 — 161.351;
  273.27
5:2, 3 — 161.352
5:17 — 526.26
5:19 — 575.36
5:20 — 264.80; 620.27
5:21 — 154.306;
  472.1; 478.5;
  549.54; 562.22;
  619.15
6:1 — 534.66
6:14 — 328.41; 493.6;
  611.6; 615.22
6:17 — 611.6
7:10 — 559.9
9:6 — 163.367
9:7 — 554.17
9:12 — 264.82
10:4 — 325.31
10:4, 5 — 83.17
10:8 — 88.42; 210.177
12:9 — 207.160;
  582.70
13:8 — 84.25; 84.26

GENERAL INDEX

has nothing to do with Christ's perfection, 273.27; the community may use its freedom in Christ, 612.9; 615.30; may alter adiaphora at any time, 612.9; one may give in here to the weak in faith, 612.9; Evangelicals in Augsburg were prepared to retain some adiaphora for the sake of peace, 222.52; in time of persecution one may not compromise, 612.10; 615.28. *See also* Ceremonies

Aerius, 267.96

Aeschines, 251.10

Affliction, every Christian must bear a cross, 434.105f.; afflictions are not signs of wrath, but of grace, 207.158; to be without afflictions drives one to doctrines of works and merits, 108.9; 110.20; 117.79. Afflictions should teach us to recognize our weaknesses and to seek God's help, 206.151; in afflictions only the certainty of God's justifying grace comforts us, 115.-60; 119.85; 166.387; 194.84; 195.-88; we are comforted by the sacrament as the seal of election, 187.42; through afflictions faith is destined to permeate all of life, 186.37; afflictions are good works, 133.193; 221.45; in afflictions the flesh murmurs against God, 130.-170; the Christian is to remain obedient to God when afflicted, 108.8; 221.45; without God it is impossible to overcome even the least affliction (temptation), 434.-105; without the Holy Spirit, 152.293. *See also* Temptation

Agnoetes, 606.75

Alexander the Great, 220.34

Alexandria, 61.41

Allegories prove nothing, 256.35

Alloeosis (Zwingli's), what it is, 595.21; repudiated by Luther, 598.38; it is a mask of the devil, 595.21; 598.40

Alms, their relationship to the righteousness of faith, 143.254; can be regarded as a sacrament, 213.-17; misuse by bishops and monks, 269.5; 333.80

Ambrose, 103.19; 121.103; 159.340;

166.389; 196.96; 242.20; 263.75; 483.15; 518.54

Anabaptists, 31.4; 33.3; 35.7; 37.3; 38.4; 178.2f.; 212.13; 498.2; 555.-27; 574.29; 632.1; 633.9; 634.19; 635.27; are new monastics, 498.5; 634.10; 635.27

Angelic spirituality of the monks, 78.48

Angels, pray for us, 230.8; 297.26; but are not to be invoked, 297.26; cannot establish articles of faith, 295.15

Anne, St., 233.32

Anthony, 136.211; 275.38

Antichrist, the papacy is, *see* Papacy. Kingdom of Antichrist is an invention of one's own service of God, 217.18; 259.51; 268.98; prohibition of the marriage of priests, 314.1; invocation of saints, 297.25; false teachers are antichrists, 177.-48; Antichrist is destined according to prophecy to have rule and office in the church, 169.4; Antichrist remains until Christ comes, 268.98

Antinomians, 561.15, 17

Anti-Trinitarians, New, 500.29; 632.-1; 636.37

Apollonia, St., 366.11

Apology of the Augsburg Confession, 97; acknowledged as a doctrinal norm, 465.4; 504.6; 506.11

Apostles, should preach in the stead of Christ, 284.18; 620.27; and administer the sacraments, 173.28; apostles are gifts of God, 324.26; Christ entrusted to them the preaching of the Gospel, not the sword or earthly rule, 223.7; 325.-31; do not have a command with unlimited authority but, rather, the command to preach God's Word, 284.18; God did not entrust to them judgeship but, rather, the proclamation of grace, 197.104; all apostles have the duty in common to preach the Gospel, 320.8; they govern the church in common, 300.9

Apostles' Creed, 18; 30.6; 107.1; 114.51; 292; 344; 363; 411; 465.3; 504.4. *See also* Articles of Faith

"Apple-God," 367.23

chisms, 338; 358; a teaching and
sermon for children, 362.1; 414.32;
a short summary of the Scriptures,
358; 361.18; 363.18; "the layman's Bible," 465.5; teaches what
is right and wrong, 497.22; pastors
should pray it (Lord's Prayer),
358.3; one should zealously
emphasize it, 338.6; 358; especially among the youth, see
Youth; the father of the house
among his children and servants,
362.4; 363.17; how one ought to
teach it, 338.7; 364.24; whoever
does not want to learn it is no
Christian, should not be admitted
to the sacrament, should not become a sponsor, 339.11; 362.2;
should be driven out of the country, 339.12; many scorn it as bad,
cheap doctrine, 359.5; 361.16;
God cannot finish teaching it,
361.16; Luther himself wants to
remain its student, 359.7; opponents do not have it, 221.43;
cohesiveness of the main parts,
411.1; 419.67; 420.1
Catholic, as designation of the
church, see Church. Meaning of
this name, 170.10; catholic faith,
see Faith, 5
Cause, of sin, see Sin; Original Sin;
of election, see Predestination;
third cause in conversion, see
Conversion
Celibacy, see Marriage of Priests
Celsus, 223.6
Ceremonies, 36; 63.1ff.; 86.36; 215;
316; 492; 610;
a) Meaning: they are adiaphora,
279.68; see Adiaphora; they are
not necessary, divine service, 89.-
53; 219.32; 493.3; 494.9; 611.8;
they are the work of children and
fools, 278.55; not necessary for
salvation, 199.113; 218.20; do not
serve unto justification, 69.41;
174.31; 219.30; 315.3; the justification of the law was bound to
them, 174.31; the kingdom of
Christ does not exist in them,
170.13; it is Jewish folly to seek
justification in them, 91.61; 199.-
114; 213.18; 216.10; 254.28; 259.-
52; the veil of Moses, 125.133;

see also Moses; thereby Christ is
obscured, 216.10; 218.20; 278.54;
ceremonies serve the edification of
the people, 56.3; 250.3; 278.55;
order in the church, 69.40; 89.53;
174.33; 215.1; 492.1; 493.3; 610.1;
indeed, uniformity of ceremonies
is not necessary, 32.3; 70.44; 170.-
10; 173.30; 217.18; 493.7; 616.31;
universal ceremonies, 173.30.
b) Value: they are not of divine
right, 176.40; in the Old Testament some ceremonies had to be
retained, 219.32; in the New Testament they were abolished, 91.-
59; 216.10; 245.41; 248.64; in
regard to them the church is free,
69.41; 199.113; 494.10; it can
change them at any time, 493.4;
612.9; Christ did not command
the establishment of ceremonies,
91.61; the apostles championed
freedom, 245.42; 612.11; the
bishops do not have the power to
establish necessary ceremonies,
85.30; see also Bishops; however,
they ought to be retained as long
as they do not lead to sin, 215.1;
see also Church Orders; ceremonies under the papacy, 278.55;
301.14; among Evangelicals, 56.2;
69.40; 221.44; 249.1. See Human
Traditions; Adiaphora
Certainty, of salvation, 124.122ff.;
see also Conscience; must be in
the church, 123.119; we are to be
certain of God's grace, 474.9; to
have a certain hope, 158.331; such
certainty is faith, 127.148; 160.-
346; 553.12; how to attain certainty is the most important question, 195.88; it does not come
from works, 129.164; 156.319ff.;
but from justification, 544.30; one
must trust the promise, not only
the nature, 159.340f.; the opponents leave the conscience in
doubt, 195.88. See also Doubt
Chalcedon, Council of, 323.19;
594.18; 600.46
Chalice, in the Lord's Supper, see
Lord's Supper
Chance, the natural man sets chance
in the place of foreknowledge,
125.135; 130.167

no authority over the church, 321.11; even unworthy servants stand in Christ's stead, 173.28; 177.47; false teachers excluded, however, being antichrists, 177.48; false doctrine of the Schwenckfelders: they must be born again, 500.27; 635.35. See also Pastors; Preachers; Bishops

Church Service, is a means of the Spirit (against the Schwenckfelders), 499.22; 635.30. See also Office of Preaching; Bishops

Church Usages, see Human Traditions; Ceremonies

Circumcision, not given for justification, 134.201; 213.19; is not adiaphorous, 612.12; spiritual circumcision, 188.46

Clay, image of man in conversion, 525.24

Cleansing, bodily cleansings of the Pharisees, 149.282

Clement (pseudo-Clement), 332.71

Clergy, misuse the Mass, 220.40ff.; their prayers are not proper prayers, 423.25; their divine services are called priceless works, 407.314; they want to overcome sin by their own strength, 305.14; the station of clergyman is supposed to be holier than the station of the layman, 237.9; their life leads to passionate lust, 245.44

Cloister, see Monastery

Comfort, see Consolation

Commands of God, see Sacrament; Office of Preaching; Worship; Works; Human Traditions

Commandments of God
a) God placed them as a boundary between good and evil, 389.183; are not optional 202.134; a man cannot abolish them, 74.24; 210.175; they remain real and valid, even when we do not keep them, 447.5; are to be observed more highly than all customs, 49; cannot be changed by any human vow or law, 52.8; 55.24; 73.18; whoever does not keep God's commandment is a sinner, 276.41; commandments of God have been obscured by tradition, human institutions (monasticism),

65.8; 205.145; 218.25; 281.4; through monastic life, 78.49; the pope teaches nothing of them, 301.14; he wants to set his own power over against them, 320.6. See also Divine Service; Human Traditions; Monks; Vows; Works
b) They do not justify, 119.87; 271.17; do not let themselves be fulfilled, 273.25; no man can keep them, 320.6; 411.3; the natural will is contrary to them, 111.27; 510.11; 529.43; they accuse us all, 121.103; 407.310; the Holy Spirit must help us fulfill them, 225.2; 628.73; we need a new heart, 409.324; 526.26; faith fulfills them, 202.131; 411.2; commandments and faith, 419.67
c) Ten Commandments, 41.2; 342; 365; a summary of divine doctrine, 407.311; no doctrine or state equal to them, 408.317; 410.333; written in the hearts of all men, 419.67; they teach us God's will, 566.12; the proper good works, 567.21; the proper spring and channel of good works, 407.311; a simple life for the common man, 408.315; one should have them continually before one's eyes, 360.14; 410.331; in all states one must observe them, 408.317; they are to be specially interpreted for each state in life, 340.18; one has one's hands full to keep them, 407.313; 408.317f.; whoever knows them fully and completely must know the entire Scriptures, 361.17; no man can keep one of the Ten Commandments, 408.316; they demand that we fear and love God from the heart, 124.124; concerning the arrangement of the commandments, 371.50; 379.103; 389.180; 392.200; 395.223; 399.255; 409.324.
d) First Commandment, 365; 409.324; the criterion of righteousness, 102.16; instructs the heart and teaches faith, 371.50; faith a response of the Christian to the First Commandment, 412.10; all others should flow out of it, 409.324; the chief source and foun-

work is emphasized, 459.16; public and private confession, 458.8; public confession must take place continually; the Lord's Prayer is such a confession, 458.9; the enumeration of sins is impossible and unnecessary, 34; 62.7; 180.1; 185.23; 197.102; 306.19; 311.1; 328.45; one should not seek sins and make a torture out of confession, 350.24; we should merely acknowledge to the confessor those sins we know and feel in our hearts, 350.18; however, it is good to acknowledge specific sins, 181.6; the confession which is made to God is the repentance in one's heart, 197.107; it refers to the whole man, 309.37; one receives forgiveness not because one has confessed, 196.95; not *ex opere operato*, 184.12; confession is not commanded, 458.14; not by the Scriptures, but rather by the church, 63.12; it should be free of coercion, 181.5; 457.1; 459.21; under the papacy it is a torture of hell, its comfort is not taught, 457.3; 460.25; we know it is blessed to practice, 457.4; coercion is not necessary, 459.23; 460.32; its great value, 458.13; 460.26; under the papacy it was uncertain, 309.37; one should not allow confession to be abandoned, 61.1; 312.1; freedom regarding confession is misused, 457.5; who does not confess is no Christian, 460.-29ff.; instruction for confession; formulae of confession for various conditions, 350.20; confession among the Fathers, 198.112; interference by the monks in the practice of confession, 95.2; 181.-8. *See also* Absolution

Confession of faith, belongs to the outer form of Christ's kingdom, 133.193; confession of saints sets Christ over against the kingdom of the devil, 133.189; it demonstrates the strength of our faith, 166.384; our works are to be our confession, 133.189; invocation of God is our confession, 374.70; Peter's confession as the founda-

tion of the church, 324.25. *See also* Symbols

Confidence, demanded by the First Commandment, 365.4; necessary to prayer, 432.92. *See also* Faith; Trust

Confirmation, not a sacrament, 212.-6; bishops have reserved it, 332.73; confirmation of bishops, 322.15.

Confutation, Roman, 98; its authors are godless sophists, 200.123ff.; 226.2; know nothing of Christ, 167.398; condemn the clear Word of Christ, 182.2; the chief article on forgiveness of sins by faith through Christ, 167.398; 191.67; 226.1

Congregation, *see* Communion of Saints

Congruity, Merit of, *see* Merit

Conscience, accused and shocked by the law, *see* Law; Repentance; Penitence; finds peace only through faith, not works, 43.15; 121.100; 124; 184.10; 195.88; 227.6; through the correct doctrine of repentance, 185.28ff.; not through the law, but the Gospel, 110.20; 144.257; 478.-7; through absolution, 187.39; 197.105; works leave it always in uncertainty, *see* Certainty; 150.-285; 153.301; 156.321; 216.14; thus it always seeks new works, 110.20; 135.208; 136.212; 151.288; 156.321; in terror of conscience, man forgets all merit, 110.20; *see also* Temptation; he recognizes the uselessness of works, 191.64; 196.95; the futility of philosophical thoughts of righteousness 112.37; feels God's wrath, 126.-142; 186.32; flees judgment, 147.-270; flees God, 112.38; seeks grace, 126.142; terrors of conscience do not earn grace, 205.-149; make one fit for the sacrament, 262.73; in them faith proves itself and grows, 126.142f.; a doubting conscience cannot pray, 195.89; 432.92; sin against conscience and faith cannot co-exist, 474.11; *see also,* Faith, 3,c; should not be burdened by traditions, *see* Human Traditions; one can work in an earthly vocation with a clear

665

conscience, 219.25f.; also in governmental offices, 222.1; conscience means nothing to the papists, 302
Consecration, in the Lord's Supper, *see* Lord's Supper, c; of priests, *see* Ordination
Consolation, to console or comfort is the Spirit's own work, 560.11; Christ's work, the Gospel's work, 478.7; 559.9; 560.12; smug hearts spurn consolation, 189.52; reason seeks it in works, 306.18; the flesh seeks human consolation, 130.170; troubles teach one to seek consosolation from God, 206.151; the consolation of forgiveness is new birth and new life, 115.62; consolation of the doctrine of predestination, *see* Predestination, a
Constance, Council of, 299.7; 311.2
Controversies concerning religion: in these the church is to judge, not the pope, 329.56; there were already controversies in apostolic times, 502.7; in the ancient church these were decided by the creeds, 502.4; controversy concerning the Reformation, *see* Church, c; unity of the church should be maintained, 24; no separation should take place because of the priests' holiness, 178.49; bishops are responsible for the schism, 94.78; 140.233; 214.2; 332.72; the pope, 329.56; the devil, the improper doctrine of the papacy, 328.42; the denial of truth, 247.59; mostly to do with traditions and abuses, 48.2; but faith is obscured through the misunderstanding of tradition, 65.12ff.; a serious matter to separate oneself, 328.42; divisions among Evangelicals, 502.6; 503.2; 507.19; not merely a quarrel of words, 502.9; controversy necessary if it concerns an article of faith, 506.15; even adiaphora can be occasion for necessary strife, 493.6; 494.11; 611.5; 612.10; 615.-28; but in regard to this, one can give in to the weak in faith, 612.9; 616.31; the disputed points should be decided in the light of God's Word and the Augsburg Confes-

sion (the Confessions), 465.4; 503.10; 506.12; decided in the Formula of Concord, 497.22; 507.-16; 632.3; without evasion, 561.16
Convent, *see* Monasteries
Conversion
a) Nature: conversion is a transformation of the whole man, 534.-70; 537.83; conversion is penance, 185.28; 202.131; two parts: repentance and faith, 185.28; 188.46; 189.56; 559.7; (as a third part, one could cite the fruits, 185.28)); conversion means mortifying and quickening, 188.46; the awakening from spiritual death, 538.87; however, not an extirpation and recreation of the substance, 471.14; 536.81; conversion and faith, 115.-61ff.; conversion is more inclusive than justification, 543.24; order of conversion, 546.41; it is repeatable, 534.69
b) Realization of, 530.48ff.; God alone effects conversion, 526.25; conversion and grace, 525.22; the Spirit effects conversion through the Word, 470.4; 520.5; 535.71; 627.71; has two, not three, causes, Spirit and Word, 472.19; 538.90; the will does not co-operate, 471.-9; not as two horses draw one wagon, 534.66; "God lays hold of the willing" is false, 537.86; start of conversion from natural power repudiated, 536.76; preparing one's own faculties for grace is repudiated, 536.78; God has enkindled even the longing after grace, 523.14; the co-operation of men after the inception of the Spirit repudiated, 536.77; purely passive, 472.18; 538.89; like a stone or a block, 532.59; 533.62; even worse than these, 524.19; still he has the passive capacity, 525.23; God does not coerce man, 532.60; he makes the unwilling willing, 472.17; 533.60; 538.88; conversion changes man so that he can accept grace, 537.83; after conversion the will co-operates, 472.17; 534.65; doctrines of the inability of man and of con-

to the scorning of the spiritual kingdom of Christ under the papacy, 325.32

Curia, etymology of the word "church," 416.48; the Roman curia fears a free Christian council, flees the light, 289.3

Curse of the law, *see* Law

Cusanus, Nicholas, 50.4

Custom, *see* Human Traditions; Usage.

Cyprian, 50.5; 55.25; 157.322; 229.2; 234.36; 236.4; 298.1; 322.14f.; 324.27; 483.15; 575.37; 581.66

Cyril of Alexandria, 179.3; 571.11; 518.54

Damnation, *see* Judgment; Punishment; guilt of damnation, *see* Predestination

Daniel, knew and preached the promise of Christ, 145.262; taught to trust God's compassion, not works, 158.331; 159.337; held high offices and wealth without sin, 224.9; his description of the Antichrist, 172.24; 217.19; 243.25; his word concerning the abomination of desolation applies not to the Evangelicals but to the papacy, 258.44

Darts, flaming, of the devil, 434.- 104; 435.109; 496.13

David, occupied the position of king without sin, 224.9; his making of war, etc., were holy works, 133.- 191; therein is an example for the emperor, 46.1; an example of proper evangelical poverty, 277.46; did not rely upon his merits but upon God's grace, 115.58; his contrition, 186.36; 189.56

Day, the last, 38; 224; 345.6; 417.53; *see also* Judgment; special days, *see* Holy Days; distinction of days, *see* Human Traditions; Ceremonies

Dead, nothing has been enjoined upon us concerning the dead, 295.12; we do not forbid prayers for the dead, 267.94,96; Masses and indulgences for the dead are to be repudiated, 58.22; 184.15; 251.11; 261.64; 265.89; 278.53; 294.12; monks put monastic hoods on the dead, 162.361

Death, afflictions of death, 112.36; 205.146; suffering and feeling of death, 304.2; not always punishment, it serves to the putting off of the sinful flesh, 206.151ff.; 207.- 159f.; spiritual death, *see* Nature; Christ's death, its salvatory significance, *see* Christ, B,2,c

Decretals, teach worldly business and ceremonies, but nothing of Christ, 301.14

Defect of original righteousness, *see* Original Sin

Demosthenes, 264.81

Descent into hell, of Christ, 18; 20.- 36; 29; 291; 345.3; 363.12; 413.25; 488.13; 492.610

Desire, of sexes, is God's creation and order, 240.7; after Fall intensified by concupiscence, 241.13,16; evil desire, *see* Lust; Original Sin

Desolation, of the church (Daniel), *see* Antichrist; in the papacy, not among Evangelicals, 258.44

Despair, the fruit of original sin, 302.2; comes from servile fear, 187.38; from the seduction of the devil, 347.18; from ignorance and doubt of God's grace, 66.13; 195.- 89; from the doctrine of works, *see* Works; doctrine of despair, 153.301; 157.321; 195.89; from the preaching of the law without the Gospel, 559.10; from the doctrine of enumeration of sins, 182.- 10; 328.45; from a false understanding of predestination, 485.9; 497.16; 618.10; *see also* Predestination; God's consolation rescues us, 162.364

Devil, believes the history, but not in forgiveness, 44.23,25; 113.48; 154.303; 159.337; 187.45; the devil is a liar and murderer, 40; 55.23; 226.1; 247.58; 435.115; 456.81; God's enemy, 44.25; receives eternal punishment, 38.3; the cause of sin, 40; 226; 414.28; 494.4; 509.2; 510.7; 512.27; 515.41; 519.61; 617.7; 629.81; creates no substance, merely corrupts it, 469.25; 512.27; his work is to be separated from God's work, 469.25; 509.3; 515.42; 629.79; hinders God's Word and work, 434.104;

428.62; prayer, 424.29; makes
people enthusiasts, 106.47; 312.5;
hinders spiritual and earthly government, 431.80; is after our lives,
435.115; history shows his power,
106.49; all men are subjected to
him, 106.46; 126.138; 302.1; 378.-
100; 417.52; 528.37; see also Nature; the punishment for original
sin, see Original Sin; but God's
foreknowledge sets his limit and
measure, 617.6; his kingdom and
will are to be destroyed, 427.54;
429.70; God's Word routs him,
359.10; 379.100; 629.76; as does
God's name, 374.71; and prayer,
see Prayer; pastors should teach
him to death, 361.19; Baptism
snatches us from him, 348.6; 441.-
41; 446.83; pact with the devil,
366.12; doctrines of the devil,
204.141; 247.58; 313.10. See also
under I Tim. 4:1
Diana, 367.18
Dietrich of Bern, 360.11
Dionysius, 332.71
Disciple, see Apostle
Discipline, outward discipline of the
law, see Law, 3,b; good, but to
be distinguished from inner piety,
226.9; see Righteousness, Civil;
Evangelicals do not forbid it, 68.-
30; church discipline, see Jurisdiction; Excommunication
Disease, original sin is an inborn
sickness, 29.2
Dispensation, the pope dispenses
where he should stand firm but
is strict in regard to human laws,
247.56; dispensation of vows shows
they are not of divine law, 74.24
Dissension, in the church, see Controversies
Distinction, between law and Gospel, see Law, 3,a; between foods,
see Foods; of days, see Holy Days,
of reward, see Reward
Divine Service, see Worship
Division, of the church, see Controversies
Doctrine, the church needs a consistent form of doctrine, 503.1; 505.9;
506.14; the right doctrine of the
Gospel; its signs, see Church 2, c;
in this the bishops should be

united, 300.9; the norm of doctrine is Scripture alone, 464.1:
465.7; 503.3; true doctrine sanctifies God's name, false doctrine
profanes it, 346.5; 373.64; 425.39,
41; 426.47; the devil does not want
to suffer true doctrine, 428.62;
doctrine of the Evangelicals is
grounded in Scripture and is not
contrary to the Christian church,
48.1; 95.5; the most important
parts of doctrine, see Articles of
Faith
Dominic, 136.211
Dominicans, have occasioned idolatry with the rosary, 278.53; their
false doctrine of Baptism, 310.2
Donatists, 33.3; 173.29; 178.49
Doubt, we should not doubt God's
grace, 156.320; 474.9; nor election, 627.70; 628.73; whoever
doubts reviles Christ, 127.149;
cannot pray, 135.204; 195.89;
423.22; 432.92; 436.123; is not
prepared for Lord's Supper, 349.-
16; doubt leads to despair, 157.-
321; 195.89; opponents make consciences doubt, 123.119; 328.44;
doubt in God's foreknowledge,
125.135; 130.167; see also Faith;
Certainty; Conscience
Dragon's Tail, the Mass, 294.11
Duns Scotus, John, 192.68; 204.143;
205.148; 310.3

Easter, was not celebrated simul-
taneously everywhere before the
Council of Nicaea, 70.43; 174.32;
176.42
Ecclesiastical Power, power of juris-
diction, power of order, see
Church Power; power of the sword
(earthly power) is mixed with
ecclesiastical power by the papists,
81. See also Church
Eck, John, 238.11
Elect, Election, see Predestination;
election of bishops, ministers, see
Bishops; Ordination
Element, see Sacraments ; Lord's
Supper
Elijah and Elisha, did not receive
the Spirit without the Ten Com-
mandments, 313.11
Emperor, should follow the example

of David and wage war against the Turks, 46.1; his position in relation to the pope, *see* Pope

Encratites, 245.45; 246.50

Enthusiasm, Enthusiasts, 212.13; 235.43; 312.3,6; 426.47; 444.61,63; 448.12; 471.13; 520.4; 530.46; 536.80; 573.22; 587.102,103; those who, without the Word of a mediator, await the immediate illumination of the Holy Spirit, 471.13; 520.4; 536.80; boast that they possess the Spirit without the Word, 312.3; through their own preparation, 212.13; scorn the spoken Word and the office of preaching, 212.13; condemn the spoken Word but do not keep quiet themselves, 312.6; misuse the doctrine of the impotence of man, 530.46; enthusiasm is of the devil, 312.5; 313.9; is implanted in Adam and Eve and all their descendants, 312.5; 313.9; is the source of all heresy, 313.9; papacy is enthusiasm, 312.4; *see also* Sacramentarians; Anabaptists

Enumeration of sins, 181.6; 184.11; 185.23; 197.102. *See also* Confession

Ephesus, Council of, 602.59; 606.76

Epicureans, 166.390; 246.50; 530.46; 590.123; Epicurean life, 239.2; 246.50; 495.9; 557.39

Epicurus, 112.35

Epiphanius, 176.42; 245.45; 246.49; 250.8; 267.96

Erasmus, 529.44.

Essence, in the doctrine of original sin, *see* Original Sin; Nature; in the doctrine of the Trinity: God in three persons is a unified (spiritual) inseparable essence, 27.2; 100.1; 291; 604.68; error of the Anti-Trinitarians, 500.29; 636.-37; in Christology, *see* Christ, A; Christ according to his divinity is of one essence with the Father and the Spirit, 18ff.; 605.72; error of the Arians, 500.28; 635.36; according to his humanity of one essence with us, 515.43; the natures in their essence are not mixed, 487.6; 489.18; 490.2,27; 605.71; error of the Schwenckfelders, 499.21; 635.29

Essential Properties, of the two natures in Christ, 603.62; properties do not leave their subject, 597.32

Estates (in life): a good and perfect estate is that which has God's command for it, 80.58; that proceeds from God's Word, 377.93; the spiritual (clerical) estate, especially monasticism, has been elevated above all others, 72.13; 224.13; could be the state of perfection, *see* Monks, a; other stations are explained as worldly, ungodly, damned, 224.9ff.; but the common estate of being a Christian is worth more than the spiritual (clerical) state, 391.197; all estates should seek Christian perfection, 275.37; earthly stations have God's Word and command, 72.13; we should use them in this life, 222.2; they serve God in their vocation according to his commandments, 72.13; demanded by the Gospel, 38.5; to fear, trust God in one's station is perfection, 79.50; *see also* Perfection; God has exalted the estate of fatherhood and motherhood, 379.105; 382.126; parenthood and government are divine estates, 389.182; *see also* Parents; Father; Authority; Marriage; spiritual estates (monasticism) are unholy, 377.93; because they are chosen without God's Word, 224.13; 395.221; have arisen through scorn of his commandments, 380.112; table of duties for all estates, 354; in confession, each person should view his station according to the commandments, 350.20; whoever knows the Ten Commandments can judge all estates, 361.17; grievances in the civil estates, 290.-12; *see also* Vocation; the four states of the human will, 469.1; 520.2

Eucharist, 261.66; 263.76

Eunomians, 28.5

Euripides, 132.185

Eusebius of Caesarea, 518.54

Eutyches, 489.18; 490.21

Evangelicals, not heretics, 47.1; teach nothing new, 104.32; 106.50; 157.-

lack of love, 137.219; still, works
are not to support faith, 556.34
4. Doctrine of faith should be
emphasized in the church, 67.20;
78.48; is the chief part of Christian life, 42.8; 89.52; the most true,
certain, and necessary article, 16; -
398; for it gives knowledge of
Christ and consolation to the
conscience, 123.118; it is the
Gospel's own Word, 182.2; reason
does not understand it, 146.265;
scorned by untried people, 43.15;
completely neglected under the
papacy, 416.43; obscured through
the doctrine of works, see Works;
through the doctrine of penance
(enumeration of sins), 181.9; 305.-
14; 306.20; through the Mass,
184.16; 260.60; human traditions,
64.4; monastic works, 136.211;
papacy, 326.37
5. Content, see Articles of Faith;
the true Christian faith, 19.1;
21.40; whoever does not hold this
completely and purely is eternally lost, 19.1; faith equals Apostles'
Creed, 338.3,5,7; 339.8; 344; 352.-
2; 353.5; 363; 411; grasped most
concisely: Trinitarian faith, 411.-
7; separates Christians from
heathen, Turks, etc., 419.66; must
be taught by the Spirit, 420.67;
faith and commandments (first and
second chief parts), 408.316; 411.-
2; 419.67ff.
Fall, corruption of nature through
the Fall, 29.1 103.24; 302.4; 467.-
8; 510.8ff.; 512.23,26; 520.5; man's
nature remains God's creation
even since the Fall, 466.2; 508.2;
514.38; he retains a certain degree
of free will, 531.53; the natural
inclination of the species is
strengthened by evil lust, 241.13,-
16; penalties of the Fall, 106.46;
511.13; before the Fall men did
not live without the law, 480.2
Fanatics, see Enthusiasts; Factions
Fasting, works to tame the Old
Adam, 218.24; 221.47; true fasting has God's command, 203.139;
204.143; should take place all the
time, 221.47; good as preparation
for the Lord's Supper, 352.10;

450.37; however, the doctrine that
it is a necessary divine service is
repudiated, 41.3; 65.12; 69.39;
221.47; that it has salvatory significance, 63.1; 64.6; 87.41; 204.143;
218.24; 306.21; that it makes holy,
308.28; see also Mortification;
Human Traditions
Father: God places fathers and
mothers next to himself, 379.105;
382.126; their estate rests on
God's command, 439.20; 441.38;
that is the crown on the head of
the father, 439.20; governing the
household belongs to the office of
fatherhood, 384.142; God's command is to honor him, 343; 362;
379; 409.327; fatherhood has the
promise of reward, 134.197; 163.-
367; different kinds of father:
fathers in blood, in office, spiritual
fathers, 387.158. See also Parents.
Father's vocation, 65.10; 356.11;
he should keep his wife, children,
servants in Christian discipline,
218.25; emphasize the catechism
with them, 342; 362.4; 363.17;
456.87; teach them to pray morning and evening, 352f.; his vocation scorned under the papacy,
65.10; is a proper good work, 218.-
215
God the Father, see God, 1,a;
through Christ and the Spirit he
showers us with eternal blessings,
413.24; in Christ's name we can
ask of him, 158.333; see Fatherly
Heart
Father of the country, 384.142
Fatherly Heart, of God, revealed in
the three articles, 419.64; in Christ,
419.65; God shows it to those who
are converted, 628.75
Fathers, Church Fathers: their
faith and works, 136.211; their
authority: can be mistaken, 267.-
95; occasionally built stubble on
the foundation of the church, 172.-
21; one is not to make articles of
faith out of their words, 295.15;
their writings are to be subordinated to the Scriptures, 464.2;
evangelical doctrine agrees with
them, 47.1; 166.389; fathers of

the evangelical church, 579.58. *See also* Patriarchs

Fear, of God: filial fear and servile fear, 187.38; 477.12; 566.16; true fear of God belongs to the divine image, 102.17f.; to Christian perfection, 273.27; is lacking in natural man, *see* Original Sin; Nature; is a working of the Spirit, *see* Holy Spirit; grows under the terrors and comfort of the conscience, 161.351; God wills to attain this in us by examples of punishment, 626.59

Febris, 233.32

Financial practices, 396.227; 405.302

Flesh, human

a) In broad sense, equals human nature; resurrection of the flesh, 18; 345.5; 415.34; 418.57; 467.10; 469.1; 538.87; the same flesh, only without sin, will rise, 516.46; more properly, resurrection of the body, 418.60; Christ took on our flesh, 576.39; 593.11; however, without original sin, 466.5; we are flesh of his flesh, 607.78; Christ has redeemed our flesh and sanctified it, 466.6

b) In narrow sense: the flesh is sinful, 206.153; vile in itself and inclined toward evil, 428.63; 432.-89; 566.12; there is nothing good in it, 468.16; 523.17; it does not trust God, 130.167; 432.89; but grumbles in afflictions, 130.170; in carnal people there can be no faith, 126.143f.; 160.348; it wars against the Spirit, 130.169; 523.-17; 533.64; 537.84; 554.19; 565.-84; is enmity against God, 111.32; 470.3; 523.13,17; its righteousness cannot endure God's judgment, 158.329; *see also* Righteousness, Civil. It remains after Baptism, 449.23; after the rebirth, 479.1; 537.84; still wars against the Spirit, 133.189; 534.68; makes the faithful lazy and obstinate, 566.12; makes their renewal imperfect, 544.28; *see also* Renewal; Sanctification; its works impure, 552.8; 567.21; never lets man be without sin, 417.54; 543.23; is fought through the Spirit, 126.143; 480.4;

567.18; through repentance, 309.-40; 527.34

Flood, the, 246.54

Foods: distinction of foods, *see* Human Traditions; 63; 87.39; 219.-30; distinction of foods is a human tradition, 150.283; 175.35; hence not divine service, 273.26; adiaphoron, 613.13; as meritorious, contrary to the Gospel, 37.4; the food of the soul is the Lord's Supper, 449.23

Foreknowledge 494f.; 616.1ff.; difference from predestination, 494.2; 616.4; it extends over good and evil, 494.4; 616.4; its relation to evil, 494.4; 617.6; God's foreknowledge is not the cause of scorning of the Word, 623.41; foreknowledge unto blessedness, 619.-24; *see also* Predestination

Forgive, to, *see* Office of the Keys

Formula of Concord, 463; not intended to be a new confession, 502.5; a repetition of the original evangelical doctrines, 507.20; intended to make clear the unanimous opinion of the church on controversial articles, 507.16

Forsake, to, wife and child, etc., 276.-41; 296.18. *See also* Vocation; Monks; Perfection

Fountain: God an eternal, inexhaustible fountain, 427.56

Francis of Assisi, 136.211; 250.7; 272.21

Franciscans: the story of John Hilten, 268.1

Fraternities, 41.3; 296.21

Freedom, Christian: must be retained in the church, 89.51; 613.15; may not be destroyed through human rules and ceremonies, 70.42; 283.-15; 493.6; 494.10,12; *see also* Human Traditions; Ceremonies; Holy Days; the apostles kept it, 177.44; an example of Christian freedom is the abolition of the Sabbath, 91.60; must be used so that no offense arises, 222.51; misuse of freedom by the people, 338.3; by the pastors, 358.3; freedom of the will, *see* Will; freedom, immunities of the clergy, 281.1

Fruits of repentance, *see* Repentance, c; of faith, *see* Faith, 3,c; illustration of the tree and its fruits, 527.-32. *See also* Cross; Original Sin, Spirit
Function, *see* Office

Gabriel (angel), 313.12
Gelasius I (Pope), 50.7; 575.37
George, St., 233.32
Gerson, John, 66.13,16; 80.60; 219.-28; 242.20; 271.16; 275.36; 289.-6; 443.50
Glory, of God, *see* God; of Christ, *see* Christ, B,4; of the saints, *see* Saints
God, 18ff.; 27; 100; 291; 344; 363; 365; 411
1. God's nature
a) Trinity, 548.54; 592.6; the Trinity is the greatest mystery, 489.18; 597.33; in the three articles God reveals the depths of his fatherly heart, 419.64; the whole divine nature, will, and work are portrayed therein, 419.63; the entire Trinity directs us to Christ, 627.66; Anti-Trinitarian false doctrines, 500.29ff.; 636.37ff.
b) Attributes: God is unchangeable in will and essence, 628.75; is everywhere in all creatures, 604.-68; there are many modes of his presence, 483.14; 586.97; his right hand is everywhere, 483.12; 586.-95; it is the omnipotence of God which fills heaven and earth, 596.-28; God himself, not just his gifts, dwells in the faithful, 475.18; 550.65; God, Father, Son, and Holy Spirit, 548.54; with all the fullness of the Godhead, but yet not physically or personally united, 604.70; all learned men are not as wise as the divine majesty in his little finger, 448.12
c) God is only eternal good, 366.-15; his name derived from "good," 368.25; an eternal, imperishable fountain, 427.56; God means him to whom one should look for all good, 365.2; 366.10; does not let himself be grasped except in his Word, 116.67; we should concern ourselves with his revealed will,

not search into the hidden things, 621.33; *see also* Predestination; the Gospel teaches us to know him otherwise than the law, 562.-22; he can only be known in Christ, 44.24; 126.141; 419.65; grasped by the heart, 366.13f.; in that we accept his grace, 115.60; he who doubts never experiences what God is, 195.89; both belong together, faith and God, 365.3; faith makes God and idols, 365.2; to have God is to trust and believe in him from the heart, 365.2; 366.10; 367.18; 368.28; it means to devote oneself to God, 126.142
2. God's activities:
a) Creator: what that means, 412.-13; God's foreknowledge, *see* Foreknowledge; God is not the creator or cause of sin, 40; 226; 494.4; 510.7; 514.38; 515.40; 617.-7; does not will evil, 617.6; created man righteous and holy, 562.23; work in regard to man is to be distinguished from the devil's work, 469.25; 509.3; 515.-42; 629.79; *see also* Original Sin; Nature
b) Lord: *see* Law; Commandments; God wills that we fear, love, trust, serve him, etc., 78.49; 108.8; 124.124; 125.130; 342.2; 365.4; 412.19; wills to be feared, not despised, 369.34; wills to be honored through accepting his promise in faith, 114.49; 115.60; *see also* Worship; through calling on him in need, 108.8; 420.2; no man can do that by nature, *see* Nature; God is a devouring fire, 158.329. *See also* Judgment
c) Redeemer: God wills no one's damnation, but that all become blessed, *see* Predestination; he punishes only in order to reform, 208.164ff.; does an alien work in order to come to his proper work, 189.51,53; 207.158; is gracious to those who trust him wholeheartedly, 369.32; gives himself to us completely and fully, 420.69; his glory is that he makes us blessed out of sheer mercy, 631.87; that he gives much more than anyone

can grasp, 427.56; glory is given to him through a right doctrine of original sin, 509.3; works-righteousness makes God into an idol, 367.22; some make mammon into their god, 365.6; the saints into gods, 230.11; the pope wants to be an earthly god, 172.23; 298.-4; 300.13; see also Pope

Godless, see Wicked

Godly, see Pious

God-parents, see Sponsors

Good: anything which is or is called good flows out of God, 368.25; outside of the Ten Commandments no work is good, 407.311; only he who is good can do the good, 122.106; the difference between good and evil does not depend on the doctrine of merits, 158.332f.; to do the good, see Works

Goods, temporal, the Christian may possess them, see Property; the flesh trusts in them, 130.170; the world misuses them, 412.21; we should use them to God's glory and praise, 413.23; only for temporal necessities, 371.47; stolen goods do not bring prosperity, 397.243

Gospel, 108.5; 310; 477; 558
1. Nature of the Gospel, 561.20; various concepts of the Gospel: (a) in the general sense: the whole doctrine of Christ; (b) in the specialized sense: in contrast to the law, 478.6; 558.3
a) As the whole doctrine of Christ, embraces repentance and forgiveness of sins, 115.62; 185.29; 278.-54; 478.6; 559.5; teaches first proper repentance, 278.54; 309.41; is necessary to repentance, see Repentance; however, that is its alien office through which it comes to its own office, 479.10; 560.12; 563.27; see also Christ, B, 2,d
b) In the narrow sense, it is solely the consoling proclamation of grace (forgiveness of sins), 310; 478.7; 479.10; 559.9; 560.12; 561.-21; the promise, 108.5; 124.121; 129.159; 132.186; 166.388; of grace, forgiveness of sins, justifica

tion through faith alone for Christ's sake, 32.2; 113.43; 115.-62; 123.110; 148.274; 182.2; 270.-11; 272.23; 474.9; 546.39; its summation is: forgiveness of sins through faith in Christ, 271.13; absolution is the voice of the Gospel; 147.271; 182.2; 187.39; 190.61; 197.105; 271.13; the Gospel should be set forth to the terrified conscience, 86.35; it offers Christ and pure grace, 193.76; it drives one to need Christ, 152.-291; the entire Gospel stands on the second article, 415.33; without the Gospel we would know nothing of Christ, 415.38; it forces one to assert the doctrine of faith, 67.20; fosters faith, since we have no merit, 159.337; is God's command to believe in his free grace, 139.-228; 160.345; 193.76; 195.88; 561.-19; gives in many ways comfort and aid against sin, 304.8; 310; is valid for all with its promise, see Predestination (universality of grace); 620.28; 622.37; its promise belongs immediately to the entire church, 324.24; was already given to Adam, 189.53; was the comfort of all the patriarchs, 192.-73; see also Patriarchs; law and Gospel, see Law; may not be made into a preaching of repentance or of the law, 479.11; 563.27; teaches another righteousness than the law, 113.43; than reason, 139.230; is to be distinguished from philosophy, 109.16; under the papacy it was made into a doctrine of law, 563.27; thus the Gospel was abrogated, 193.77; 195.89; the opponents beat it to the ground through a doctrine of works, 123.-110; through the disregarding of faith, 124.121; through the Mass, 266.91
2. Relationships: (a) Gospel and church, see Church; it is the right foundation of the church, 171.20; outward mark of the church, 32; 168.400; 170.10; 171.20. (b) Gospel and Holy Spirit, see Holy Spirit, B,2,a; it is an outward spoken proclamation, 440.30; but

wants a pure heart, 407.310; we should direct our whole heart to him, 125.130f.; 365.2; 369.32; 370.40; God is grasped with the heart, 366.14; 368.28; faith is in the heart, see Faith, 1; when one's heart is not in them, works are hypocrisy, 126.137; where one's heart is at peace with God, everything else follows after, 371.48; when the Scriptures speak of works, they include the righteousness of the heart, 163.365; 164.-371; Christ's kingdom exists in the righteousness of the heart, 170.13; what the creating of a new heart means, 532.60; 535.81.

Heathen: the church is separated from them not through civil ordinances but through the Spirit, 170.-14; they have a knowledge of God from the natural law, 562.22; origin of their idolatry, 367.18; they want to obtain grace through sacrifices, 135.207; through human sacrifices, 151.288; 253.23; through expiations, 199.114; their divine services wrong because they are not commanded by God, 217.15f.; Christ is also promised to them, 145.262

Hell: Christ has destroyed it for us, 414.30; 492.4; 596.25; 610.2; the Holy Spirit leads us in and back out of hell, 566.12; parents can earn hell for their poor upbringing of children, 389.176; its portals are powerless against our election, 495.5; 617.8; against the church of God, 624.50

Helpers in Need (the saints), 297.-26; 366.11

Hercules, 262.72; 367.18

Heretic, Heresy: arise out of disunity in the church, 139.232; 141.-242; enthusiasm is the source of all heresies, 313.9; against them the Confessions are put forward, 504.4; Evangelicals are unjustly rebuked as heretics, 47.1; 309.41; pious preachers are regarded by the world as heretics, 400.262; ordination by heretics is valid, 314.3

High Priest, see Christ, B,2,b

Hilary, 233.30; 324.27; 325.29; 595.-22

Hilten, John, Franciscan in Eisenach, 268.1; 269.3

History, teaches how powerful the devil's kingdom is, 106.49; the history of Christ's life: its purpose is forgiveness, 114.51; Christian festivals serve to remind us of it, 176.40; knowledge of Christ's history is not the same as faith, see Faith, 1

Holy, God calls us holy for Christ's sake, 315.1; God's Word makes us saints, 377.92; 378.94; faith makes us holy, 385.147; the church is holy, 169.7.

Holy Days, are good for church order, 36; 91.60; 218.20; 220.38; they should serve the knowledge of Christ, 176.40; 218.20; but they are not necessary for salvation, 36; 41.3; 87.39; 91.58; 220.38; do not have God's command, 176.-41; one should not make a law out of them and thereby burden consciences, 174.33; 175.35; 613.-13; to keep a holy day means to do holy works, 376.87; thus Christians should keep every day a holy day, 377.89. See also Sunday; Human Traditions

Holy Spirit, Spirit of God, Spirit of Christ; God's Spirit alone is called a Holy Spirit, 415.36

A. Third person of the Trinity, 18ff.; 27; 291; 345; 363.13; 415; formula for Baptism, 348.4; 364.-21; 437.4; formula for absolution, 351.28; proceeding from the Father and the Son, 19; 20.22; 291; 605.73; is not a created movement in creatures, 28.6; Spirit of God as the mediator of the exchange of properties in Christ, 605.72

B. Activity:

1. Operations, 345.6; 415.35ff.; in the saints he works only created gifts, 605.73; his office and work, 415.35; 418.59; his alien work is to punish, his own work is to comfort, 560.11; his office militates against opus operatum, 565.-11; 566.14; to the scholastics he is an empty thing, 115.63; he

militates against original sin, 105.-
35; 130.170; fights the remaining
sin, 106.45; 127.146; 309.40; 527.-
34; restrains sin, 310.44; wars
against the flesh, 126.143; 480.4;
567.18; gives forgiveness of sins,
345.6; 418.55; leads to Christ,
125.132; 345.6; 415.38; 419.65;
leads to the kingdom of God,
273.27; 427.52; alone effects right
fulfillment of the law, see Law;
116.70; 125.130; a right relation
to God, 39.2f.; 102.10; 111.31;
125.130; love to God and one's
neighbor, 543.23; fruits of the
Spirit, 566.17; he is not idle in the
elect, 628.73; because man is impelled by him, he does good, 533.-
63; works are an evidence of his
presence, 477.15
2. Conditions of activity: (a)
Spirit and Word: he is given
through the Word, see Enthusiasts; 39.3; 125.135; 312.3; 531.-
54; through the external, spoken
Word, 31.4; 312.3; through proclamation and sacrament, 31.2;
82.9; through Baptism, 105.35;
441.41; even the prophets did not
receive him apart from the Ten
Commandments, 313.11; the Spirit
without Word and sacrament is
the devil, 313.10; the Word is
the office of the Spirit, 621.29;
office and work of the Spirit, 531.-
55f.; the Spirit is the endorsement
of the sermon, 192.71; where the
Word is, he works, 187.44; 312.3;
415.38; 418.58; 470.4; 520.5; 528.-
37f.; 629.77; through Word and
sacrament, 262.70; 469.1; 534.65;
541.16; the Spirit knows what he
says, 122.108; Word (and sacrament) his means, instruments,
470.4; 471.13; 472.19; 520.4; 530.-
48; 535.72. (b) Spirit and church,
168; 415; see also Church; the
Spirit works through the congregation, 415.37; 419.61; remains
with it until the last day, 417.53.
(c) The Spirit is received through
faith, 45.29; 113.45; 119.86; 123.-
116; 124.125; 125.127,132; 152.-
293; 229.15; out of grace, not by
works, 228.13; the regenerate re-

ceive him, 131.175; 194.82; the
promise of the Spirit is valid also
for children, 178.2f. (d) The impulse of the Spirit is not force,
533.64; but spontaneity, 553.12;
564.3,6; 566.17; 568.25; the converted will is his instrument, 472.-
18; we have only the first fruits of
the Spirit, 534.68; the flesh remains in opposition to him, see
Flesh; he can be lost, 35.7;
through deliberate sin (against
conscience), 228.13; 477.19; 534.-
69; through lack of love, 137.-
219; he is not where sin has its
way, 310.44; false appearance of
the Spirit, 567.20; we should retain his gifts, 535.72. (e) He carries on his work without ceasing
until the last day, 417.53; 419.61f.
C. Spirit of Christ: present in the
Lord's Supper (doctrine of the Sacramentarians), 571.11; as mediator
of the union with Christ's body in
the Lord's Supper, 482.5; 569.5;
he rules the church as the body
of Christ, 169.5; 170.16; 171.18

Holy Water, 149.282; true holy
water is God's Word and commandments, 360.10

Hope: its difference from faith, 155.-
312; it directs itself to the future,
155.312; becomes certain through
Christ, promise, faith, 160.346;
not uncertain through the offering up of merits, 160.344; vacil-
lates in every Christian, 534.68;
grows under experiences of conscience, 161.351; is a proper sacrifice, 255.29

Horace, 140.236

Hours, Canonical, 87.41; 358.3

Household, 384.142; see also Commandment, Fourth

Hugo of St. Victor, 104.29

Human, see Man

Human Commandments, see Human
Traditions

Human Sacrifices, 135.209; 151.288;
253.23

Human Traditions, 36.3; 63; 86.36;
215; 281; 316; 492; 610; the controversy: whether they are divine
services necessary to salvation,
175.34,37; in the papacy they are

367.21; idolatry with the saints, 231.16; 278.53; 297.26; 328.47; with angels, 297.26; the greatest idolatry is works-righteousness, 367.22; grows out of human and ecclesiastical laws, 217.14; 613.-15; is the work of Antichrist in the church, 268.98; the Mass is idolatry, 268.98; 294.11; the greatest idolatry in the papacy, 293.1; idolatry of the rosary, 278.53; the world practices idolatry, 366.17; idolatry of the papacy, 293.1; 465.4; of monasticism, 278.54,56. *See also* God; Faith; Worship

Illumination, God's Spirit effects it, 621.29; 623.40; whoever despises the instruments of the Spirit is not illumined, 532.58; false doctrine of Anabaptists, 212.13; 471.13; 536.80; of Schwenckfelders, 635.30

Image of God, in Adam, 102.18; 480.2; lost through the Fall, 510.-10; in us, 161.351; image hewn out of stone, as an illustration of man in conversion, repudiated, 538.89; God wills to make the elect into the image of Christ through the cross, 624.49

Images of the saints, *see* Saints

Impenitents: the law should be preached to them, 560.12; 562.24; *see also* Law; God's judgment upon them, 630.83

Impulse, new, spiritual, 124.125; 143.250; 160.349; the flesh hinders it, 133.289; the impulse of the Spirit is not coercion, 533.64; 564.2; 566.17

Imputation, *see* Righteousness of Christ

Incense, the best is God's Word and command, 360.10

Indulgences: distribution of merits of saints as satisfactions for sins, 232.23; they are said to remit satisfactions, 203.135; 307.24; can only apply to the public penance of the church, 210.175; but are applied by the church to purgatory, 184.15; 185.26; indulgences for the dead, 184.15; 296.24; in the practice of confession, 62.5; the uncertainty of salvation resulting from indulgences, 307.27;

a great fraud, 328.46; devised only for the sake of money, 307.25; misunderstanding of the name, 210.175

Indwelling, of God in the faithful, 604.68; God himself dwells in them, not merely his gifts, 475.18; 550.65; the Holy Spirit, 477.15,19; 628.73; the triune God, 548.54; indwelling of Christ or of essential righteousness is not our justification but follows it, 475.16; 539.2; 548.54

Infant Baptism, 33; 178.1; 311.4; 442.47ff.; necessary and proper (against the Anabaptists), 33; 178; 311.4; 498.6; 634.11; God has endorsed it through the giving of his Spirit, 442.49; problem of infants' faith, 443.52. *See also* Baptism

Instruments, *see* Means

Intention: faith cannot be combined with evil intention, 474.11; 543.-26; 546.41; good and evil intentions in the Lord's Supper, 302.9. *See also* Obstacle

Intercession, of angels, *see* Angels; of the saints, *see* Saints; of Mary, *see* Mary; of Christians for one another, 424.28; of members of a congregation for their pastor, 424.28; of the pastor for the congregation, 358.3

Interim, 509.19; 540.5; 555.29

Intermediaries, *see* Adiaphora

Interpretation: the most certain interpreter of his Word is Christ himself, 578.50; interpretations of Scriptures are useful, 506.10

Invocation, of saints, *see* Saints

Irenaeus, 70.44; 103.19; 494.7; 571.-14; 595.22; 616.31

Iron, glowing: illustration of the union of natures, 488.9; 594.18; 603.64; 604.66

Israel (Jews) does not know God rightly, 419.66; sees only the veiled countenance of Moses, 110.21; 193.78; multiplication of divine services in Israel, 167.395; 218.23; false divine services, 135.-207; 268.97; 268.98; human sacrifice, 151.288; significance of sin-offering, 252.21; Sabbath observ-

ance, 375.80; human commandments, 216.10; 254.27; idolatry,
218.23; Israel an example of divine judgment, 625.58; nevertheless God sustained his church in
Israel, 268.98; the true church
should be separated from the people, 170.14; 171.19; promise of
physical and spiritual goods, 170.-
14; the pure fountain of Israel is
Scripture, 503.3

Januarius, 66.17
Jerome,   50.6;   131.173;   146.264;
229.2; 236.4; 300.9; 308.28; 314.3;
323.18; 330.62; 332.73; 448.81
Jews, see Israel
John Damascene, 595.22
Jovinian, 68.30; 244.37; 248.67ff.
Joy, only faith gives joy, 121.100;
553.12; it alternates with terrors
of conscience among Christians,
534.68
Jubilee Year, 307.25
Judaizing, 215.4
Judas, despaired under the law,
304.7; Judas' and Peter's contrition, 183.8; 186.36; he received
the body of Christ in the Lord's
Supper, 575.33; 580.60
Judge: God is the judge of all
hearts, and apart from Christ an
angry judge, 419.65; Christ is the
judge of us all, 290.9; or the living
and the dead, see second article
of the Creed; the opponents make
him into a severe judge, 231.15;
232.28; ministers are not to be
judges, 197.103; see also Office
of Keys; Absolution; to judge
one's neighbor is to usurp God's
office, 401.268; the authorities are
to judge, see Government; Punishment; Christians can serve as civil
judges, 37.2; how judges are to
act, 400.259; God's Word is the
only judge in matters of faith,
465.7; whoever knows the Scriptures entirely can be a judge of
doctrine, 361.17
Judgment of God, no man can bear
it, 157.326; 158.329; human nature flees from it, is angry at it,
13...176; 153.301; we can only
place Christ over against it, 136.-

214; not our works, merits, or
love, 137.221; 198.108; the opponents do not feel God's judgment, 108.9; God exercises his
judgment when he withholds his
Word from a people, 625.57;
God's judgment on unworthy reception of the Lord's Supper, see
Lord's Supper; in human judgment, justice is certain, not grace
as in God's judgment, grace is
certain, 160.345; see also Day;
Last Times; Wrath of God; Punishment; Afflictions
——— of Christ, at his second coming, 18f.; 20.37; 30.6; 38; 224;
291; 345; 363.12; 413.25
———, human: (a) Spiritual judgment, see Bishops; Ecclesiastical
Power; in the power of the keys
Christ has entrusted the highest
judgment to the church, 324.24;
see also Office of Keys; Absolution. (b) Civil judgment, 399.258;
misuse of the divine name before
a court, 371.53; oaths before a
court, see Oath
Julian the Apostate, 223.6
Juno, 233.32
Jupiter, 367.18
Jurisdiction, of bishops, see Bishops;
common jurisdiction consists of
excommunication, 330.60; 332.74;
see also Excommunication; every
pastor should have jurisdiction,
332.74; matrimonial cases belong
before civil authorities, 333.77
Jurists, 309.41; 400.261; 405.299
Justification, 30; 107-168; 292; 315;
472; 539; chief article of Christian doctrine, 107.2; 540.6; it is
like leaven, 540.7; it may not be
surrendered, 292–95
a) Concept and nature: justification has a double sense, 117.72;
to obtain forgiveness, and from a
sinner to become pious and born
anew, 117.76ff.; to reconcile and
to regenerate and to make acceptable, 132.181; that we, through
faith, receive a new, pure heart
and that God, for Christ's sake,
regards us as righteous, 315.1;
from unrighteous men we are
made and regenerated into right-

eous men, 123.117; forensic sense, 143.252; 154.305; reconciliation for Christ's sake, 121.97; 129.158; 152.292; first forgiveness of sins is necessary, 117.75; forgiveness of sins and acceptance as a child of God, 473.7; 540.9; 541.17ff.; 544.30ff.; 550.62; acceptance of the whole person, not specific works, 137.222; through it we become God's children, 134.196; 161.354; with justification we also receive salvation, 548.52f.; relationship with repentance, see Repentance

b) Justification and conversion do not coincide, 543.24; 546.41; not the same as regeneration, 474.8; 542.18; to be differentiated from its subsequent renewal and sanctification, 542.18; 546.39; neither the prior penitence nor the subsequent works belong to justification, 474.11; 543.24,27; justification for Christ's sake through faith also remains the principle of the new life, 131.177; 152.293; 156.317; 216.12; 477.14; 543.22; 544.32; initial keeping of the law pleases God only through faith, 131.177; see also Works

c) Conditions of justification: a gift of God, 162.362; the promised grace for Christ's sake, 137.217; in justification we are dealing with God, hence the works of the second table do not justify, 138.224; not our merit, but God's act, 198.108; the Gospel emphasizes that Christ is necessary to justification, 152.291; Christ, our Righteousness, see Righteousness; that it is part Christ's, part our own justification, repudiated, 475.71; 548.51; justification takes place through faith in Christ, not through works, 41.6; 43.13; 59.28; 115.61; 117.75ff.; 131.176; 32.-183f.; 212.8; 231.19; 232.22; 270.-11; 272.23; 275.38; 292.3; 315; 472; 539; not through confession of faith, 166.384; not through love, 122.109; 127.145; 129.159; 132.181; 137.218; 151.289; 195.87; not by reason or law, 150.287;

see also Law; through faith alone (*sola fide*, the exclusive particle), 117.73; 474.10; 540.7; 545.36; 547.43; 548.53; 551.2; faith is not only preparation for justification, 116.71; love and renewal do not first make justification through faith complete, 475.20; 547.45; indeed, not faith as knowledge but as certain trust, 113.48; a living faith that has works, 143.250; works must follow, see Works; they are the goal of justification, 160.348f.; the justified not in mortal sin, 113.48; but they can still lose the Spirit, 35.8; opponents' doctrine of justification taken in part from reason, in part from the law, 150.287; they eliminate Christ, 151.290

Justinian, 333.77

Justin Martyr, 575.37; 576.39

Kingdom of God, of Christ: must be distinguished from the kingdom of the worla as a spiritual kingdom, 210.176; 222.2; 325.31; see also Government; opponents have confused them, 200.120; 223.4; not a temporal possession but an eternal treasure, 427.55; redemption through Christ, 426.-51; righteousness of the heart and the gift of the Spirit, 170.13; daily activity of the Spirit in the heart, 171.18; 273.27; daily taking away of the old Adam, 444.65; good works of the saints, 133.189f.; does not consist of rites and ceremonies, 170.13; 273.27; it is only where God's Word and sacrament are, 178.2; see also Church; still concealed under the cross, 171.18; 325.32; indeed, the godless and false teachers do not belong to it, 170.11; 171.18; 172.22; it comes temporally through Word and faith, eternally through revelation, 427.53; an earthly kingdom of Christ before the resurrection (Chiliasm) repudiated, 38.5
—— of Antichrist (of the pope), 172.23f.; 217.18; 243.25
—— of heaven, Christ, 499.20

Kings, see Princes

Knowledge: relation to faith, *see* Faith, 1

—— of God, belongs to original righteousness, 102.18; the heathen also have a certain knowledge of God from natural law, 562.22; the proper knowledge of God is to receive grace from him, 115.60; we receive knowledge of him under the terrors and the consolations of the conscience, 161.351; *see also* God

—— of Christ: true knowledge of Christ and faith in him is the foundation of the church, 171.20; not so in the papacy, 416.43 *see also* Christ, B,2,a

—— of Sin, *see* Sin; Original Sin

Laity: can pronounce absolution, 331.67; chalice for the laity, 236; 484.24; 588.110; the catechism, "the layman's Bible," 465.5; 505.8

Lamb of God, 122.103; 292.2; 293.1; 294.7; 309.38

Lapsed, they must be accepted again if they repent, 35.9; the custom of the ancient church, 199.113

Last Times, 53.14; they are now, 201.126; 246.53

Latin, language in the Mass, 249.2

Law, 303; 477; 479; 558; 562

1. Concept of the law: (a) Natural and revealed law; the law is written in the hearts of men, 419.67; 480.2; 564.5; the sentence of the law, 188.48; natural law agrees with the Ten Commandments, 108.7; the divine, eternal law, 530.50. (b) Ceremonial law, civil law, and moral law, 108.6. Ceremonial law, 219.32; 279.58; with its sacrifices a foreshadowing of Christ, 252.21; 256.34,36; had to cease when the real sacrifice was offered, 253.23; 255.30; Christians are free from it, 87.39f.; 91.59; 245.41; 259.52; 271.15f.; 279.58. Civil law: faith brings no new law into earthly government, 222.3; Christians are to obey the existing laws (against Carlstadt), 222.3; Moral law, *see* the following:

2. Content and fulfillment, *see*

also Righteousness; the two tables, 102.14; 112.34; 125.131; 138.224; 139.231; 225.7; demands more than outward respectability, 108.8; 112.35; works do not fulfill it, 162.362ff.; demands a good heart inwardly and works outwardly, 126.136; completely perfect, pure obedience, 567.22; true fear and love of God, 111.27; 193.75; 204.142; love of God and neighbor, 151.289; love is the fulfillment of the law, 127.147; 129.159; 132.181; 152.294; reason can grasp it to a certain extent, 108.7; *see also* Righteousness, Civil; reason thinks it can be fulfilled, 303.3; through it to become righteous, 108.7; 146.265; but it relates only to external works, 109.18; 112.35; 125.134; 146.265; it exceeds all capabilities of reason, 108.8; 111.27; no one can keep it, 109.18; 112.40; 125.128; 195.88; 204.142; 536.75; fulfilling it only possible through Christ, 124.126; 125.135; 129.159; 132.184; 146.266ff.; 151.290; 153.299; 154.305; 186.37; 194.86; attained its fulfillment first at the hand of Christ, 559.10; through the Spirit, 113.45; 116.70; 124.126; 152.293; 194.82; fulfilled through faith, 113.46; 124.126f.; 129.159; 144.256; 147.270; 152.295; 165.377; 194.82; after redemption (forgiveness), 163.368; 194.80ff.; after justification, 163.366; 368; by the reborn, 113.46; 124.126; 131.175; 137.219; 144.256; 156.315; even after rebirth it is unfulfillable, 127.146; 471.12; 536.79; we never satisfy it in the flesh, 152.296; it instantly accuses the reborn, 130.167; even the beginnings of fulfillment please God only through faith, 129.161; 155.308; 163.368; 471.12; 500.25; 536.79; 635.33

False doctrines: works of supererogation, *see* Works; Counsels, Evangelical; fulfillment of the law with respect to the essence of the acts, 225.2; without Christ, 151.290; meritorious righteousness of the reborn, 471.12; 536.79

3. Nature and office of the law,
561.17; revelation of the righteous
will of God, 478.3; 565.11; 566.-
15; a mirror of the same, 564.4
a) Law and Gospel, 108.5; 477;
558; doctrine of law and Gospel
is a particularly beautiful light,
478.2; 558.1; all Scripture has
these two parts, 108.5; 121.102;
132.186; 189.53; since the world's
beginning, 114.57; 562.23; see also
Patriarchs; to be differentiated
carefully, 562.24; their contrast,
108.5; 129.159; 132.186; 14.257;
148.274; 189.53; teach a different
knowledge of God, 562.22; a
different righteousness, 113.43f.;
139.230; see also Righteousness;
the law agrees with reason, 108.7;
146.265; therefore opponents tie
themselves to the law, 108.7; teach
only law, not Gospel, 139.229;
150.287; 186.34; law or works the
foundation of their doctrine, 309.-
39; law does not justify, does not
earn grace, 107ff.; 124ff.; 193.79;
216.8; 271.14; 292.4; God himself
does not so honor the law, 274.30;
slavery of the law is not necessary
for justification, 89.51; its office
is to punish sin and to teach works,
561.18; to reveal and punish sin,
121.103; 122.106; 144.256f.; 188.-
48; 189.53; 303.4; 478.4; 560.11;
561.17; to accuse, condemn, and
terrify, 112.37ff.; 124; 131.179;
186.34; 195.88; it punishes unbelief, 561.17,19; it condemns our
nature or person, 509.6; 513.32; it
is God's thunderbolt, 304.2; a
proclamation of his wrath, 560.12;
shows God's wrath, 118.79; 125.-
128; 152.295; 560.14; brings wrath,
112.38; 135.204; 144.257; 145.260;
147.270; 157.326ff.; 195.88; brings
death and hell, 304.7; excites enmity against God, 303.2,4; effects
wrath, 303.5; drives to presumption or despair, 153.301; 195.89;
304.7; 559.10; effects contrition,
531.54; the Gospel must come in,
effect the proper repentance, 144.-
257; repentance and faith, 189.-
56ff.; 530.50; 531.54; thus both
must be emphasized until the very

end, 562.24; Christ places both
together, 558.4; God lets both be
preached, 530.50; the New Testament retains the office of the law,
303.1; the law is not abolished
by faith, but is upheld, 124.123;
131.175; 229.15; Christ and the
law, see Christ, B,2,d
b) twofold use of the law, 303.1;
threefold use, 479.1; 563.1; first
use: see Righteousness, civil; to
restrain gross sins by outward discipline, 303.1; the law as custodian, 110.22; makes some people
worse, 303.2; makes false saints,
303.3; third use: 133.188; 479;
563; given to the unrighteous, not
to the righteous, 110.22; 564.5; the
reborn do not stand under the law,
566.17; they live in the law, 481.6;
delight in the law according to the
inner man, 537.85; 554.19; 564.4;
567.18; but are not without the
law, 564.5; are to keep it, 124.124;
126.136; redemption has in view
that they should exercise themselves in the law, 480.2; 564.4;
they require this, that they might
follow the Spirit, 565.9; a mirror
for the faithful, 564.4; 567.21;
punishes and teaches them. 566.12;
a rule for the reborn, 479.1; 564.-
3; to guard them from self-chosen
divine service, 567.20. See also
Commandments; Works; Righteousness

Law, Civil, 27; 83.13; 222
Lawrence, St., 366.11
Laying on of hands, 212.12
Laymen, see Laity
Leaders, ministers of the Word,
612.10
Leo I, 482.15; 575.37
Leo X, 104.35; 167.397; 185.26;
191.67
Leprosy: original sin as spiritual
leprosy, 509.6; 514.33
Levitical worship and priesthood do
not concern the Christian church,
87.39; 91.61; 212.7; 243.27; 245.-
41; 254.26; were forerunners of
Christ, 256.34; 259.53. See also
Worship; Priest
Liar: unbelief makes God a liar,
153.297; 190.62; 195.88; 196.94;

under bread and wine, 351.2; 570.9; "in, with, under," 575.35; united with them through a sacramental union, 482.7; 483.15; 571.-14; 572.18; 575.35; 589.117; not merely spiritual manducation, 589.114; 590.118; rather also sacramental and oral manducation, 579.56; see Oral Reception; according to the words of institution, 578.48; indeed, in a spiritual way, not in a Capernaitic way, 483.15; 486.41; 489.17; 581.64; 588.105; 591.127
b) Effect, 449.20; 577.44: not merely a sign of profession but rather a sign of the divine will, 262.69; the testament of Christ, 236.2; 482.7; 578.53; 596.29; gives God's grace through Christ, 258.-49; contains the whole Gospel, 450.32; united with Christ, 237.-10; 607.79; bestows forgiveness of sins, 136.210; 258.49; 266.90; 449.22; 578.53; and God's grace and Spirit, 454.70; a life-engendering food, 449.23; 602.59; 606.76; for daily nourishment and feeding, 449.24; a healing, comforting medicine, 454.68; should awaken faith and comfort the conscience, 56.7; 59.30; 136.210; 187.43; 237.-10; twofold benefit: comfort and thanksgiving, 262.74; 263.75
c) Validity: Christ's body and blood as the treasure in the Lord's Supper must be comprehended in the Word, 449.28f.; the most important part in the Supper is God's Word and command, 447.4; without that, only bread and wine, 448.14; the "consecration" does not beget Christ's presence, 482.8; 582.73; 590.121; but rather God's power and Christ's institution, 583.74; not faith, but Christ, 590.-121; the sacrament rests on God's Word, not on faith, 573.25; 574.-32; not on human "holiness," 448.15; not on worthiness, 453.61; remains efficacious despite misuse, 447.5; 448.15; even unworthy men administer and receive it, 173.28; 177.47; 311.1; 570.8; 572.16, 19; 573.24, 27; 574.32; 579.57; 580.-

60; 581.63; 590.123
d) Proper reception: the Supper demands faith, 60.33; 450.33; you must take it to yourself, 450.35; see also Memorial of Christ; worthiness consists only in faith, 262.73; 352.10; 450.33; 484.20; 582.69; 591.124; our unworthiness may not hinder us, 453.55; unworthiness in regard to the Supper, 453.61; 454.69; 484.18; 580.60; 582.68; to receive unworthily is to invite damnation, 181.5; 454.-69; 483.16; 572.16; 579.57; 590.-123
e) Place in the Christian life: one should be urged and attracted to it, not forced, 340.21; as under the papacy, 452.51; coercion kills the soul, 451.42; should not be bound to special times, 452.47; all are not ready at the same time, 181.5; one should esteem it and receive it often, 451.39; to this end Christ's command urges us, 451.45; and also his promise, 454.64; our need, 341.23; 455.73; the Supper should be administered only after examination and absolution, 56.1; 61.1; 249.1; not to those who do not understand it, 447.2; who do not learn the catechism, 339.11; 362.5; who do not go to confession, 460.-29; who live in public scandal, 180.4; 453.58
f) Place in public worship: a divine ordinance, 177.46; must be completely kept, otherwise no sacrament, 583.75; 584.83; must be administered in both kinds, 49; 236; 311.2; 484.24; 588.110; not a matter of indifference, 238.15; the whole sacrament instituted for the whole church, 236.1f.; not obeyed under the papacy so the clergy might seem holier, 237.9; words of institution should be spoken distinctly, 584.79; adoration rejected, 486.40; 591.126; to communicate oneself is forbidden, 294.8; lay communion, 237.8. See also Sacrament; Mass

Love, 124; is the fulfillment of the law, 127.147; 129.159; 142.245; 151.289; righteousness of the law,

132.181; 141.238; its highest work and virtue, 138.226; yet does not make righteous, 123.111; 124; 127.149; 129.159; 132.181; 142.-245; 193.78; 195.87; 474.15; 543.-27; 546.38; see also Justification; no one loves God as he ought, 123.110; 160.342; impossible without faith in forgiveness through Christ, 109.18; 112.36; 123.110; even difficult for the saints, 226.8; love of neighbor also goes against nature, 405.297; opponents talk about love, but have no love, 140.236; love follows faith, justification, as a necessary fruit, 117.-74; 123.111; 124; 186.37; 194.82; 229.15; 474.11; 543.27; should always grow, 126.136; 275.37; whoever loses it, loses the Spirit and faith, 137.219; 138.224; 475.17; 550.64; without it faith is dead, 551.1. See also Faith

Lucian, 234.37

Lucina, 367.18

Lust, Evil (concupiscence): its nature, 103.24; no adiaphoron, 105.-42; sin, not only penalty, 105.38; not a created, essential attribute of nature, 467.12; remains after Baptism, 104.35; see also Flesh; seeks the sensual pleasure of the body, 103.26; since the Fall it has strengthened sexual drive, 241.13, 16; its over powering strength, 225.5; the Spirit drives it out of the heart, 39.3; the reborn hate it, 160.349. See also Original Sin; Desire

Luther, 270.10; 483.10; 489.17f.; 492.3; 505.9; 519.61,62; 524.20; 529.44; 540.6; 542.21; 544.29; 546.41; 552.10; 555.28; 560.11f., 14; 561.17; 565.9; 574.28ff.; 575.-33,34; 576.40ff.; 583.77,78; 585.-87,91; 586.93; 594.17; 598.38; 599.41,44; 607.81; 608.85,86; 610.-1; 615.24; 621.33; "this highly enlightened man," 574.28; before him the doctrine of repentance was obscure, hazy, 183.4f.; through him God brought the truth of his Word (the light of the Gospel) to light, 501.1; 503.-2; the foremost teacher of the

Augsburg Confession, 575.34; 576.41; "I must remain a child and a pupil of the catechism," 359.7f.

Magicians, 366.12

Magnet, repudiated as an analogy for original sin, 468.15; 512.22

Maid, the works of her calling are right, holy, good, 385.145. See also Servants

Making Alive, like renewal, rebirth, 474.8; 542.20; the second part of repentance, 188.46; see also Repentance; takes place through faith, 186.36; see also Faith, 3; not to be understood platonically, 188.46; God's own work, 189.-51,53; the flesh of Christ is a life-giving meal, 602.59,61; 606.76

Mammon, the most common idol on earth, 365.6; those who serve it have power in the eyes of the world, 370.42

Man: natural man, see Nature; Will; Original Sin; the old man, see Adam; the new man, 349.12; 533.-63; 536.81; see also Life, New; Regeneration; the inner man in the faithful, 564.3; see also under Rom. 7:22; man cannot do away with God's command and order, see Commandments; Order; God is more to be obeyed than man, see under Acts 5:29; human nature, humanity of Christ, see Christ, A,2

Manes, 594.16

Manichaeans, 28.5; 225.1; 468.17, 19; 469.22; 470.8; 509.3; 511.16; 512.26,27; 513.30; 518.55; 535.74

Mantua, Council of, 287; 288.1; 505.7

Marcion, 490.23

Marks, see also Signs; of the church, see Church; of Christians, see Sacraments; Lord's Supper, a; of the elect, see Predestination; of faith, see Faith

Marriage, 51; 239; 392.199; a natural right, a divine order of nature, 240.9; already established with creation, 213.14; its purpose: God created man for procreation, 51.5; 241.13; for the fostering of chastity, 51.2ff.; 54.15; 242.19; 393.-212; doubly necessary since the Fall, 241.13; to be esteemed as a divinely blessed estate, 393.206; between believers it is a holy, pure estate, 243.28; not impure, as the monks teach, 243.26; 246.47; patriarchs were purer than many celibates, 248.64; higher than all other estates, 393.209; indeed, it has God's command, God blessed it before all other estates, 393.208; virginity is a higher gift, but neither virginity nor marriage justifies before God, 244.38; 249.-69; who does not have the gift of maintaining virginity should marry, 74.20; to forbid marriage is a doctrine of the devil, 55.22; 68.29; 248.63; scorning of marriage is anti-Christian, 243.25; should not be broken, 242.23; 248.63; 249.71; divorce permitted in the Old Testament, 404.295; 406.305; forbidden in the New Testament, 406.306; even not for the sake of faith (contrary to the Anabaptists), 499.19; 634.24; duties of married people, 218.25; 343.11; 355.6ff.; 392.199; see also Father; Parents; their vocation is a just and good work, 218.25; misuse of the divine name in marital affairs, 371.53; 373.68; not a sacrament, 213.14; marital matters lie under the jurisdiction of bishops, but the princes must also enter the picture, 85.29; belong to the sphere of civil authority, 333.77; ecclesiastical statutes are unjust, 333.78; remarriage and secret marriages, 333.78

—— of Priests, and celibacy, 51; 239; 314; prohibition of sacerdotal marriage merely a human law, 247.56; a real papal law, 243.25; unjust, 314.1; 333.78; contrary to God's Word and command, 54.18; 394.213,216; contrary to divine and natural law, 240.6; 247.60; especially the rending apart of marriage, 53.13; 239.3; 242.23; also contrary to councils and canons, 53.13; 239.3; 240.6; 242.23; celibacy is a doctrine of the devil, 247.58; 248.63; anti-Christian, 243.25; 314.1; priests were married in the ancient church, 52.10; 248.67; even Pius II was in favor of it, 51.2; 53.13; celibacy introduced by force, 52.12; many innocent priests were put to death, 55.23; 239.3; 247.57; 249.70f.; one does not become holier through celibacy than by being married, 243.26; 244.36; not right purity, 244.35; see also Chastity; has only the false appearance of spirituality, of chastity, 239.1,5; 243.26; 394.213; leads to scandals, disgrace, lust, 54.18; 240.6; 246.-51; 285.26; 314.1; 328.48; 394.-213f.; lust of the priests, 239.1; 246.50; see also Monks; thus God avenges the scorning of his gifts and his commandments, 246.53; celibacy is vanity, dangerous to conscience, 240.6; 243.26; 246.50; motive is a thirst for power, 239.5; 247.60; marriage of priests serves the avoidance of scandal, 51.2; impure, unmarried priests should become pure, married priests, 248.66. See also Marriage; Chastity

Mary, the pure virgin, 29.1; 292; 595.24; see also Christ, B,1; mother of God, 488.12; 595.24; as intercessor, 232.25; has displaced Christ, 232.28; fraud with images of Mary, 234.34

Mass, 56; 249; 293; explanation of the name, 264.84; its names in the Greek church, 263.79
a) Nature; should be Communion, 60.34; Mass as sacrifice, 58.22; 250.9; 215.14; as daily sacrifice, 256.35; 258.49; 260.62f.; may be called a sacrifice of praise, 255.-33; 263.74; or sacrifice of thanks, 262.74; as by the Fathers, 261.65; 263.75; (in the Greek church), 267.93; still it is not a sin-offering, 58.22; 59.30; 252.19; not meritorious, justifying, etc. 136.-210; 203.137; 249.2; 250.9; 257.-42; 293.1,7; ex opere operato, 58.-22; 136.210; 151.288; 249.2; 250.9; 254.27; 265.87f.; without faith it does not make blessed, 263.77;

was instituted for the sake of proclamation, 256.35; proclamation, confession, etc. are the chief things therein, 257.40

b) Abuses: the Mass in the papacy is simply a human invention, 293.-2,5; sheer idolatry, 268.97; 293.1; 328.43; the greatest abomination, 392.1; 588.109; a dragon's tail, 294.11; Masses for the dead, 184.-15; 260.59; 265.89; 278.53; 294.-12; 484.23; 588.109; made into a business, 58.20; 184.16; 251.13; 285.26; 293.6; 328.43; private Masses, 60.35; 250.6; 294.8; misuses stem from the *opus operatum*, 214.23; from mimicking the Old Testament, 259.52; consequences, 294.11ff.; if the Mass falls, the papacy lies in ruins, 294.10

c) Mass among Evangelicals: not done away with, 56.1; 60.40; 174.-33; 249.1; only the unnecessary Masses, the private Masses, 60.40; 250.6; German hymns in, 56; also Latin Masses, 250.3

Material element of original sin is concupiscence, 101.4; *see also* Original Sin

Means: God does not work without means, 313.10; 471.13; 499.22; 520.4; 530.46; 628.76; 635.30,31; means of the Spirit, *see* Holy Spirit; human traditions are not God's means, 175.36; the means of God to grasp grace, Christ, the promise, is faith, 473.5; 541.10; 544.31; 546.38; *see also* Faith

Mediator: concept of the mediator, 231.17; Christ is the Mediator, *see* Christ, B,2,b; according to both natures, 549.56; 600.47; also for the regenerate, 129.162,165; 156.317; knowledge of Christ disappears if one seeks other mediators, 233.34; under the papacy, saints have been made into mediators, *see* Saints; priests and celebrants of the Mass, 260.57; human traditions (and works), 215.-5; 216.7

Members of Christ, of the church, 139.232; 168; 417.51; 528.36; 587.104; *see also* Church; kings and princes the chief members of the church, 329.54

Mendicancy, *see* Begging

Mendicant Orders, abuses of the Mass have arisen in them, 250.7

Merchants, Christians may be merchants, 499.18; 634.23

Mercury, 367.18

Mercy of God, in God's judgment compassion is assured, 160.345; mercy and faith are correlative, 157.324; 160.346; 165.381; we need mercy even in good works, 157.323; vessels of mercy, 626.60; 629.79,82; *see also* Grace; Promise; God

Merit: repudiation of the scholastic doctrine of merit, 41; 107; 124; 226; *see also* Works; Human Traditions; Vows; Monasticism; of attrition, 192.68; 211.178; merit of condignity and of congruity, 162.360; 270.9; 273.24; 275.34; 296.24; 308.28; merits of saints, 229-36; 296.24; thinking of merit takes Christ's glory from him, 128.156; 271.17; 275.34; 276.40; merit and justification, *see* Justification; merit and election, *see* Predestination; man trusts easily in merits, 108.10; confronted by God's wrath, conscience forgets about merits, 110.20; faith does not hold out merits before God, 113.44,46; Christ's merit, *see* Christ, B,2,c; the treasure which pays for sin, 114.53; the foundation of our righteousness, etc., 31.3; 138.227; 141:238; 231.19; 251.12; 271.17; 274.32; 474.10; 509.6; 547.43; of our election, 497.20; 628.75; *see also* Predestination; error of the Anabaptists: that Christ's merit alone does not suffice, 498.5; 633.10; in him is our worthiness to receive Lord's Supper, 484.20; 582.72; on it must our prayer be based, 231.-20; it is not obtained through works or money, but through faith, 152.296; 231.19; 296.24; it must be completely distinguished from our works, 474.10; we should not tack on our merits, 207.157; exalted through the

Monks' Hoods, put on the dead, 162.361; honored more than Christ, 275.34

Morning Prayer, 352.1ff.

Mortal Sin (against scholasticism): mortal sin and love of God, 112.-37; mortal sin and faith are irreconcilable, 113.48; 116.64; 123.-109,115; 127.144; 310.43; in scholastic doctrine of penance: penance for mortal sin, 306.22; satisfactions supposed to be valid in spite of mortal sin, 199.118; 202.132; 204.143; 208.162, 165; to break human precepts regarded as mortal sin, 316.2

Mortification, a good physical discipline, but still not righteousness, 68.30; 221.45; cross of the Christian is true mortification, 68.32; 221.45. See also Cross

Moses, see Law; and Christ, 152.296; 194.86; 271.15; 478.7; 559.10; 560.12; the veiled countenance of Moses, 110.21; 139.229; 193.78; 478.8; 479.9; 560.10; 563.1

Mother, of God, see Mary; church as mother of the Christian, 416.-42; see also Father; Parents

Münzer, Thomas, 312.3

Mystery, the highest is the Trinity, 489.18; 597.33; then the person of Christ, 609.96; Christ's presence in the Lord's Supper, 486.42; 591.127

Name, of God, 371; 425; our highest treasure, 425.38; where it is, life and salvation must also be, 440.-27; its misuse the highest outward sin, 372.56; how God's name is misused, 371.51; 425.40; through the Mass, 265.89; through monks, 277.44; its proper use, 342.4; 373.-63; the proper honor of the name of God is to trust and call upon him, 374.70; 421.8; to be baptized in the name of God means to be baptized by God himself, 427.10; his name is therein, 439.26; given to us, 425.37; the name of Christ given to us (Acts 4:12) means: he is the cause of our salvation, 121.98; in the name of Christ we must pray, 158.333; and we re-

ceive forgiveness of sin, 148.273; 191.65

Nature: its course is God's ordinance, 223.6; no vow or human command can change it, 240.8; 241.16; 314.2; human nature, see Will; Reason; Original Sin; Flesh; 100; 466; 469; 508; 519; sense of the word "nature," 469.22; 517.-51; human nature originally created good, 512.27; but corrupted through the Fall, 302.3; 467.8; 509.5; 513.30; the nature itself (the person) is sinful, 509.6; 510.-11ff.; 517.53; see also "Nature-sin"; but not transformed into another substance, 513.30; see also Substance; Accident; one must differentiate between the nature and its corruption, 466.2,5; 468.19; 508.2; 514.33; 515.41; thus Christ took on human nature without sin, 466.5; 515.43; human nature still God's creation even after the Fall, 466.2; 508.2; 513.32; 514.34; God's creation in it distinguished from the work of the devil, 469.-25; 509.3; 515.42; 629.79; it is in the devil's power who goads it into all sins, 45.32; 106.47; 225.5; 511.13; 527.29; 529.44; incapable of good, 45.31; 302.5; plunged so deeply in sin that it cannot see the same, 62.9; the law condemns it, 509.6; 513.32; by nature we are children of wrath, 509.6; human nature indeed has power in external matters, 510.11f.; see also Will; but not a particle of spiritual power, 521.7; 522.12; spiritually dead, 522.10; 536.77; cannot begin, effect, or co-operate with anything, 468.16; 512.23; see also Conversion; cannot heartily love, fear, believe, trust God, 39.2; 101.7ff.; 108.8; 11.27; 125.128; 130.167; 159.342; 225.6; rather set against him, 510.11; 529.44; always flees before God, 421.10; no thought can turn itself to the Gospel, 529.44; but natural man can outwardly hear God's Word, 531.-53; possesses passive capacity for conversion, 525.23; God works in man differently than in irrational creatures, 533.62; Christ the saviour of corrupted nature, 111.30; redeems and sanctifies it, 466.6; 516.45; through the Holy Spirit it is born again and renewed, 511.-14; sin remains in the nature even after rebirth, 543.22; will be taken away finally in the resurrection, 516.46; false doctrines of scholastics, 302.4; 467.11; 511.17; see also Original Sin; the nature cannot be evil, 106.43; of the Pelagians, 467.13; 511.17,20; of the Manichaeans, 468.19; 512.26

Natures, two natures in Christ, see Christ, A,2

"Nature-sin," 468.20; 517.53

Nazianzus, 223.6

Necessity, of good works, 475.3; 476.9; 551.14; 554.16; see also Works; of unchanging order in scholastic doctrine of merits, 108.-11; of all happenings (Stoics, Manichaeans), 470.8; 535.74

Nestorius, 489.18; 490.20; 594.15

Net, an illustration of the church, 168.1; 171.19; of the Word of God, 629.76

New Birth, see Regeneration

Nicaea, Council of, 27.1; 176.42; 321.12; 322.13; 323.17

Nicholas, 374.74

Nicholas of Lyra, 172.22

Nicholas of Tudeschi, 181.8

Norm, only true norm of doctrine is God's Word, 1; 465.7; 503.3. See also Doctrine

Novatians, 35.9

Oath, 371; permissible for Christians, 37.2; 222.1; 499.15; 634.20; Christ himself swore an oath, 373.65; to take oath for the good of our neighbor is a just and good work, 373.66; should not be a bond to sin, 77.40; complaint about false oaths, especially in marital affairs, 71.53; 373.68; God punishes false oaths, 373.68

Obduracy, as divine punishment, 625.57; 630.83; to harden one's heart, 496.12. See also Predestination

Obedience, (a) To God: all men obligated, 551.4; should prove it-self in the sacrifice of the body, 207.160; in afflictions it means to commit oneself to God's will, 108.8; see also Cross; proper obedience is to accept the promise, 139.228; obedience of the Gospel: faith, obedience of the law: works, 155.308; new obedience of reborn, 31; 124; see also Law (third use); Life, New; the reborn are bound to it, 475.3; 476.10; results through Gospel and law, 565.10; pleases God for Christ's sake, 155.308. (b) To parents, see Commandment, Fourth; to the government, see Government; in their obedience to heathen government, Christians show their love, 222.3; to bishops, see Bishops; to the pope, see Pope; to monastic vows, 271.16; 272.21; see also Vows; obedience of Christ, 549.-56; 550.58; see also Christ, B,2,c

Object: God first becomes an object of love when we recognize his mercy, 125.129

Obligation: no man can annul an obligation (of a vow) by divine right, 74.24

Obstacle, in scholastic doctrine of sacraments, 213.18; 260.63; 267.-96; 302.9

Office, see also Estate; Calling; 37; 222; false doctrines of Anabaptists (forbidden to Christians), 499.-13f.; 634.18f.; all offices in Christianity directed toward forgiveness, 417.54; devotion to one's office is Christian perfection, 273.-27; true fulfillment of office is only possible through Christ, 46.-36; office of emperor, of princes, requires preservation of Christian doctrine, 235.44; offices of the church: of bishops, see Bishops; of priests, see Priests; of preaching, 31; 81.5ff.; 283.13; 284.18; God instituted office of preaching, 31.1; 212.11; thus ordination could be called a sacrament, 212.11; through it God wants to preach and work, 212.12; 284.18f.; has promised it efficacy, 532.56; not bound to specific persons and places, the person has nothing

15; it is both kinds in the Lord's Supper, 50.12; 236.2; ecclesiastical order, *see* Church Order; earthly order (authority, property, etc.) is God's order, 37.1; 178.50; 223.-5; should be retained, 281.2; order of salvation, 546.40; 619.15

Orders: for the sake of merits, new ones are invented daily, 64.2; monks sell their merits, 233.29; have won no brother with their works, 402.278. *See also* Monks

Ordinance, of God unto salvation, *see* Predestination; *see also* Order

Ordination, 212.11; 314; 331.64; as a sacrament, 212.11; originally only the endorsement by a congregation of chosen servants, 331.-70; the church has the right of ordination, 324.24; 331.66f.; it goes back to its office of preaching, 212.11; to its power of keys, 324.24; the pastors' right to ordain, 331.65; the bishops' right of ordination, 330.62; 332.73; could be left to them, 314.1; 614.19; the pope's right of ordination, 320.5; ordination by heretics valid, 314.3. *See also* Bishops

Origen, 223.6; 324.27

Original Righteousness, 510.10; 512.-27; *see also* Righteousness

Original Sin, 29; 100; 302; 466; 508
a) Names: chief sin, 509.5; root sin, 302.1; disease of sin, 29; 101.-6; 519.62; "nature-sin" or "person-sin" (Luther), 468.20; 508.1; 509.6; 517.53; a spiritual leprosy, 509.6; 514.33
b) Nature: Augustine's definition, 103.24; scholastic definition, 103.27; original sin is not merely blameworthy acts but rather a continual inclination of the nature, 101.3; root and fountain of all actual sins, 509.5; its fruits are evil works, unbelief, etc., 302.-2; not only guilt on account of distant sins but a corruption of the nature, 467.11; 511.17; innate evil disposition, 101.5; 510.11; consists in lack of faith and of fear of God, 100.2; 101.7; evil lust (concupiscence) and lack of original righteousness, 102.14;

103.26f.; evil lust, 29.1; 100.2; 101.4; 103.24,27; 510.11f.; concupiscence strengthens natural sensuality, 241.13; lack of original righteousness, 102.15; 510.10; truly sin, 29.2; 509.5; as concupiscence, 105.38; 467.12; 511.18; as well as defect, 511.19; not only an outward blemish, 467.14; 511.21; not only an impediment of good powers (analogy of the magnet), 468.15; 512.22; the entire man together with his whole nature, 101.6; corrupted especially in his highest faculties, 103.25; 510.11; an incapacity for the things of God, 510.10; man is spiritually dead, 519.60; whether original sin is substance or accident, 469.23; 517.54; whether the soul itself be original sin, 466.-1; 508.1; not only a corruption of accidents or qualities, 467.14; 511.21; yet not man's substance, nature, and essence, 468.19; 518.-55; not as some sort of essence poured into the nature (like poison into wine), 468.17; 512.26; differentiated from human nature, 466.2; 508.2; 514.33 (comparison with leprosy); one must distinguish between the work of God and the work of the devil, 469.25; 515.41; however, only God can separate the nature from the corruption of the nature, 467.10; children also are sinful, 634.11
c) Transmission of original sin: on account of Adam's disobedience, we are by nature children of wrath, 510.9; original sin planted in the nature through physical conception, 510.7; 512.-27; we were conceived of sinful seed, 513.28; made out of a corrupt mass, 514.38
d) Penalty of original sin: death, damnation, earthly penalties, dominion by the devil, 106.46; 511.13,19
e) Abrogation of original sin: can only be forgiven for Christ's sake, 511.13f.; is forgiven in Baptism, not that it might not be, but that it might not be imputed

(after Augustine), 105.36; the remaining original sin is in need of Christ and the Holy Spirit, 106.45; is to be killed through afflictions, 206.152f.; is separated from the nature in the resurrection, 516.46

f) Knowledge of original sin: cannot be grasped by reason but must be learned from revelation, 320.3; 467.9; 510.8; proper knowledge of it leads to knowledge of Christ's grace, 104.33; 106.50; 509.3; without such knowledge, human righteousness is a sham, 104.33

g) False doctrines of original sin: of the Anabaptists, 498.6; 634.11; of the new Pelagians and Manichaeans, 467.11; 511.17; 512.26; 516.45; of scholastics, 302.4; of Zwingli, 101.5. *See also* Sin; Lust; Nature; Righteousness

Ovid, 245.44

Pain, *see* Punishment
Panormitanus, 181.8
Papacy, *see* Pope
Paradise, 510.10
Parents, are in God's stead and in a divine position, 379.108; 389.-182; out of their authority flows all other authority, 384.141; obedience to them is the highest work after obedience to God, 381.116; the greatest treasure on earth, 380.109; their duties, 339.12; 340.-19; 356.8; 388.167ff.; bad parents earn hell for their own children, 389.176. *See also* Father
Pastors, were originally chosen by the congregation, 331.70; ordination was only endorsement, 331.-70; pastors and bishops equal according to divine right, 330.61; each pastor has right to ordain in the church, 331.65; should have the common jurisdiction, 332.74; should not meddle with earthly punishments, 314; interference of monks in the pastoral office, 95.2; 181.8; marriage of pastors, *see* Marriage; table of duties, 354.2; should exercise themselves in the catechism, 220.41; 338.6; 358.3; 361.19; pray for their parishioners,

358.3; complaints about inefficiency and negligence, 338.2; 358.1; 360.13; pastors are a gift of God, 324.26; 331.67; congregations should obey them, 90.55; honor and concern for them, 387.161; some think that one does not need them, 359.6. *See also* Preachers; Office
Patriarchs, had the law and the Gospel, 562.23; became righteous through faith in the promise of Christ, 114.57; 189.54; 192.72f.; their sacrifices made in faith, 135.-206
Paul, the Apostle, champion of Evangelicals, 222.50; his afflictions, 206.151ff.; his dangers, works, and sermons are holy works, 133.190; speaks differently of faith than sophists do, 280.68; was not ordained or endorsed by Peter, 321.10; James not opposed to him, 143.252f.; calls himself the father of his congregations, 387.159; also took oaths, 373.65
Paul III, Pope, 288.1
Paul of Samosata, 594.15f.; Samosatenes, 28.6
Peace, with God, means a happy and quiet conscience, 120.91; we receive it through the righteousness of God, 137.216; through Christ, 150.285; not through works but faith, *see* Works; Faith; peace in the church may not be purchased by sacrificing the truth, 632.95
Peasants' War (1525), 309.42
Pelagians, 29.3; 40.8; 109.19; 111.29; 122.106; 224.1ff.; 228.14; 467.13; 471.9; 509.3; 511.16,17,20; 536.75
Penalty, of God, for original sin: death, evil, tyranny of the devil, 106.47; 511.13,19; loss of original righteousness, 513.27; penalties for sin are a concern of God, not of the power of keys, 207.156; 208.162; 210.176; temporal and eternal penalties, 125.128; 561.17,-20; punishment of the ungodly and of the devil, 38.3; real eternal punishments are terrors of conscience, 205.148f.; tribulations, 206.151; *see also* Cross; but they are not always punishments, 206.-

48; grow in faith and in devotion
to one's vocaticn, 78.49; 273.27;
the shoemaker of Alexandria,
275.38; perfection consists in faith
and fear of God, 37.4; 78.49; 224.-
9; in the growing of repentance
and of faith, 161.353; we never
attain perfection, 147.270; 152.-
293; 204.142; 471.12; *see also*
Law, 2; false doctrine of Anabaptists, 35.8; of Schwenckfelders,
500.25; 635.33. *See also* Estates;
Law
Permission, of God, 469.25; 494.4;
617.6
Persecution: in time of persecution,
one may not compromise in matters of adiaphora, 493.6; 494.11;
611.3; 615.28f.; a clear confession
is especially necessary, 555.29;
persecution of the divine Word in
the world, 400.262
Person, in the doctrine of the Trinity, *see* God, 1,a; Christ, A,1; in
Christology, *see* Christ, A,2; person of Christ: our righteousness
is based on the person of Christ,
549.55; faith sees him, 550.58;
human person: the whole person
corrupted through original sin,
468.20; 509.6; 510.11; 517.53; *see
also* Nature; person must first be
righteous before he is able to do
good works, 543.27; 552.8; *see
also* Justification; Faith; Works;
God does not regard the person
when he listens to prayer, 422.16
Personal Union, of the natures in
Christ, *see* Christ, A,2,b; by Sacramentarians, 487.3; 490.24; personal union of Christ with God,
587.101
Pertinax, 264.81
Peter: his penitence and that of
Judas, 183.8; 186.36; he received
forgiveness, 299.5; 234.36; he too
is a sinner, 273.25; Peter and
Cornelius, *see under* Acts 10:1ff.;
his word concerning the royal
priesthood (I Pet. 2:9), 331.69;
warning about false prophets,
239.5; wicked bishops, 334.82; his
authority more valid than that of
all the Sententiarists, 192.70;
called himself a presbyter, a priest,

330.62; the assertion of his primacy not scriptural, 321.10; had no
authority over the church, 321.11;
see also under Matt. 16:18; Peter
stands for all apostles, 323.23f.;
the "rock" is not his person but
the office of proclamation, 324.25;
his faith (according to Chrysostom, Hilary), 325.28f.
Phalaris, 168.399
Pharisees: Christ rebukes them because they teach precepts contrary
to God's commandment, 278.52;
do not acknowledge him as
Christ, 128.154; saw only the
veiled countenance of Moses,
139.229; thus they became presumptuous hypocrites, 478.8; they
intended to be holy as the monks
do, 308.29; pharisaic righteousness, 109.16; pharisaic prayer,
158.332
Philosophy, philosophers: the influence of philosophy on the scholastics corrupted Christian doctrine, 101.4; 102.12; 108.9; 164.-
376; 166.390; 192.68; 521.8; the
difference between philosophy and
Christianity is abolished by the
doctrine of works, 108.12; philosophy knows nothing of the corruption of human nature, 302.4; 519.-
60; teaches the outward righteousness of works, 154.306; 226.9; sees
only the veiled face of Moses,
139.229; its thoughts about love
are the dreams of idle men, 112.-
37; not blameless, 45.33; 225.5
Phocas, Emperor, 323.21
Piety, outward, philosophical, *see*
Righteousness, Civil; 110.22; 226.-
9; inner: effected only by the
Holy Spirit, 226.9; does not come
from self-chosen divine service but
from faith and trust, 77.37
Pilgrimages, 41.3; 62.5; 95.2; 184.-
14; 204.144; 295.16; 296.18
Pillar, of truth is the church, not
the pope, 171.20; 173.27; of salt
(illustration of man prior to conversion), 524.20
Pious, 130.167; 495.5; 617.5
Pius II, Pope, 51.2; 53.2
Platina, 51.2; 53.2
Plato, 252.16; 269.5; Platonic re-

public is not the true church, 171.20; monasticism, 224.13; Platonic understanding of mortification, quickening, repudiated, 188.-46

Pledge: the elements in the Lord's Supper not merely a pledge, 485.-29; 589.116

Pollux, 233.32

Polyphemus, 234.35

Pompey, 141.241

Poor: the poor are greatly oppressed, 397.240; 399.257f.; 481.-84; princes should protect them, 145.262; they should be cared for from the church treasury, 333.80

Pope, papacy, 298; 319

a) Pretensions: the pope wants to be called most gracious lord, 298.2; the head of Christendom, 172.23; 300.13; vicar of Christ, 172.23; 320.3; has set himself over Christ, wants to be an earthly god, 172.23; 299.4; 300.13; 327.40; wants to be infallible, 173.27; to have power of forgiveness in the next life, 327.40; even to command angels, 330.17; has interpreted the power of the keys to apply to earthly power, 326.-36; "Two-Sword Theory," 81.1ff.; 172.23; 320.2; 325.31; wants to stand over the emperor, 172.23; 298.2; 329.50; to bestow and transfer kingdoms to emperors and kings, 81.2; 172.23; 320.2; has vexed them with excommunications and wars, 325.35; demands primacy in the church, *see* Peter; and by divine right at that, 320.5; his power is to extend over the councils, 242.24; 327.40; 328.-49; no one may criticize him, 327.40; 329.50; he wants to be able to change Christian doctrine and divine services, 172.23; 320.6; 327.40; belief in his primacy and obedience are supposed to be necessary to salvation, 298.4; 300.-12; 320.3,6; 326.36

b) Activity in the church: the pope is more concerned about his dominion than about the Gospel of Christ, 166.390; 173.27f.; 325.-34; under the papacy, right doctrine and the church have been suppressed, 169.9; 416.43; the pope teaches nothing of Christ, faith, and God's commandments, 301.14; takes Christ's glory from him, 328.44; does not want Christ, 291.15; some popes have ridiculed Christ and his Gospel, 173.27; are openly Epicureans, 166.390; invent false doctrines and divine services, 172.23; 301.14; 326.38; 330.57; idolatry, 326.38; 328.44; *see also* Mass; Saints; the pope's teachings extend to puerilities, 301.14; 316.4; where best, they have been taken from civil law, 301.14; for the sake of money pope instituted indulgences and jubilee year, 307.-25; *see also* Jubilee Year; Indulgences; sells the merits of Christ and of the saints, 296.24; is the head of all thieves, 396.230; the more money he swallows, the larger his gullet gets, 307.25; a jailer, the devil, and hangman of God, 457.6; pays little heed to God's judgment, 202.129; does not want to reform, 289.3; does not let religious matters be judged in orderly way, 328.49; binds his people with oaths contrary to God's Word, 329.55; defends his error with force and murder, 327.-40; 328.49; 329.51

c) Criticism: evidence against the earthly power of the pope, 325.31; the emperor used to confirm his election, 323.20; documentary evidence against the primacy of the pope, 320.7; evidence from history, 321.12ff.; under the apostles no one had a special power, 320.8; 324.24; the church existed for centuries without a pope, 299.4; the pope originally had neither ordination nor confirmation, 322.15; in the ancient councils he did not preside, 323.17; Council of Constance deposed popes, 299.7; Council of Nicaea placed only a part of the church under the bishop of Rome, 321.12; Jerome and Gregory were against the primacy, 323.18f.; the authority of the pope not by divine right, 298.1;

children to be preachers, 340.20; 388.174; monasteries should again be used for that purpose, 297; ministers have no authority over the church, 321.11; they should emphasize the catechism, 220.41; 338.6; preach in the stead of Christ, 173.28; God wills to proclaim and to work through them, 212.12; they should not doubt the operation of the Spirit, 531.55; even the preaching of godless men is not without power, 171.19; 173.-28; see also Office of Preaching; no one should preach without an orderly call, 36; 214.1; ordination, 314; see also Ordination; preachers who preach falsely misuse and profane God's name, 372.52; 425.-41; sin against the Eighth Commandment, 400.263; do not stand in Christ's stead, 177.48; Evangelical preachers teach diligently the most necessary parts of Christian doctrine and life, 221.43; table of duties for preachers, 354.2; should have patience with the people, 140.234; not mingle earthly punishments, 314; the people should honor them and care for them, 387.161; pray for them, 424.28; have patience with them, 140.234; some think they are not needed, 359.6; let preachers go hungry, 387.162; want to govern them, 140.233; 404.289; the world regards godly preachers as heretics, 400.262. See also Pastors; Teachers; Church Servants

Predestination, 494; 616
a) Differentiated from foreknowledge, 494.2; 616.4; is not a matter for reason but faith, 495.9; 620.26; not a hidden counsel of God, but rather to be sought in the revealed Word, 495.6; 617.9; 620.26; 622.36; 623.43; 625.52; in Christ, 496.13; 617.9; 618.13; 626.65; its meaning, 623.43; 631.-89; a healing, comforting doctrine, 494.1; 495.11; 496.13; 623.43; a comfort in the most intense afflictions, 496.13; 624.28; wants to assure us of our salvation, 618.-12; but also to admonish to re-

pentance, 618.12; 624.51; 627.71; confirms the article of justification by grace, 623.43
b) Embraces the entire saving work of God for mankind and for the individual, 619.15; is the cause of our salvation, 495.5; 617.8; does not originate in us, but in God's gracious will and Christ's merit, 628.75; 631.88; God has sealed it through oath and sacrament, 496.13; grace (promise) is universal, 620.28; the call always meant seriously, 622.34; God has resolved to make no one blessed outside of Christ, 496.13; the cause of nonelection, damnation, is not God but sin, 629.80; man himself, 496.12; 629.78; through scorning God's Word, 622.35; 623.40; election is God's free grace, impenitence his righteous judgment, 626.61; God's election covers only the children of God, 495.5; 617.5; marks of election, 620.25f.

Preparation, for grace impossible for men, 536.78; Enthusiasts aspire to enlightenment through their own preparations, 212.13; preparation for the Lord's Supper, 352.10; 450.36; 486.38; 591.124

Presence, of God, see God, 1,b; of Christ in the Lord's Supper, see Lord's Supper; of Christ in us, see Christ, A,2,c

Price: there must be a price for sin, 114.53; works are not the price, 128.155; 135.204; 136.212; 205.-144; nor vows, 275.35; Christ has paid it, 114.53; 415.38; 441.37; 454.66; he is the price (or treasure), 128.155; 135.204; 142.245; 205.144; Christ on the cross, a treasure offered through the Word and grasped by faith, 441.37; there is no lack of treasure, just a lack of obtaining and holding it, 441.40

Priest, Priesthood: Jesus Christ, the only high priest, 47.2; 260.58; Levitical priesthood only a prototype of his priesthood, 259.53; there is no such priesthood in the New Testament, 212.7ff.; priesthood of the New Testament a ministry of the Spirit, 260.59; ministry not sacrifice but proclamation, 212.7; Romanists have again made the priest into a mediator through the sacrifice of the Mass, 260.57; 266.89; the true church has the priesthood, 331.69; all pastors are priests and bishops, 330.61f.; marriage and nonmarriage of priests, *see* Marriage of Priests; priests may own property, 178.50; 224.11; priest and sacrament, *see* Sacraments; Lord's Supper; cup for the laity, *see* Lord's Supper, f; station of the Roman priest supposed to be holier than that of the laity, 237.9; among Evangelicals, priests attend their proper ministry, 258.48

Primacy, of the pope, *see* Pope

Princes, office of prince, *see* Government; earthly office of princes scorned under papacy, 65.10f.; 219.26; Christians can be princes without sin, 37.2; like Abraham, David, 224.9; the foremost concern of princes should be to foster the glory of God, 329.54; to maintain the Gospel, 235.44; as the leading members of the church they should abolish grievances, 329.54; in place of the bishops dispense justice, 85.29; should banish people who do not want to learn the catechism, 339.11; their office is the protection of their subjects, 46.1; should place a loaf of bread on their coat-of-arms, 430.75; sins of princes against the Seventh Commandment, 396.230

Privileges, of the clergy, 281.1

Private Confession, *see* Confession; Absolution

Private Mass, *see* Mass

Procession, with the sacrament, is wrong, 51.12; 588.108

Proclamation: God gathers the church through the proclamation, 530.50; Christ rules his kingdom, 222.2; no Spirit, no church without proclamation of Christ, 324.-25; 416.45; the sermon is the means of the Spirit, 470.4; 499.22; 531.52; 535.71f.; 635.30; through it God works faith, 255.32; 531.-

54; 535.71; opens up the book of life (Christ) for us, 496.13; through it Christ's work becomes ours, 296.24; 450.31; 531.52; whoever wants to be saved must hear it, 531.52; whoever scorns it is lost, 532.57; everyone should hear it, 627.68; God is present with his grace at the pure proclamation of his Word, 532.55; there must be proclamation in the church which gives certain hope, 123.119; its proper content: the Gospel, Christ, forgiveness of sins, 258.48; *see also* Word of God; Gospel; pure proclamation of the Gospel is the mark of the church, 32; 171.20; proclamation belongs to the sacrifice of the New Testament, 255.30; 257.38; through it the name of the Lord is magnified, 255.32; the chief worship, 220.42; the main part in the Lord's Supper, 256.35; the right adornment in the church, 259.51; lack of proclamation and false proclamation in the papists' church, 220.-41ff.; 258.44ff.; 278.54; among Evangelicals preaching is zealous and right, 221.43; 258.48; to attend the sermon only out of habit is to sin against the Third Commandment, 378.96; preaching on the catechism, 364.26; 414.32

Promise,
a) Nature: promise and law are the two parts of Scripture, 108.5; 121.102; 132.183; 145.261; 189.-53; 193.79; 304.4; 560.14; *see also* Law, 3,a; the promise is the Gospel, *q.v.;* its content is forgiveness of sin, 113.43; 121.102; 150.-287; 152.292; 262.69; 474.9; 546.-39; makes God for the first time a lovable object for us, 125.129; we must commit ourselves to it, 129.-165; given already to Adam and the patriarchs, 114.57; 189.53; 259.55; 577.46; universal, 620.28; *see also* Universality
b) Appropriation: promise excludes merit, 199.84; if bound to works, it would be useless, 113.-42; uncertain, 150.285; 228.10; however, works are its outward

sign, 148.275; it does away with him who would be righteous through love, works, etc., without Christ, 123.110; 137.221; 138.223; 271.17; 275.34; can only be grasped through faith, 113.43; 116.70; 119.84; 125.127; 194.80; 216.11; 262.70; 475.22; 544.30; 548.51; promise and faith go hand in hand, 114.50; 145.261f.; 160.346; 216.10; they are correlative, 157.324; to accept promise is to have faith, 114.50; 123.113; 138.227; 145.263; 154.304; see also Faith, 3,a; not to believe it dishonors God, 423.21
c) In the broad sense: promise of the First Commandment (Conclusion), 147.270; 368.29; 370.39; 410.333; of the Fourth Commandment, 134.197; 163.367; 383.131; 387.164; purpose of the promise, 303.1; promises of marriage, 213.-14; of prayer, 213.16; 231.20; 423.19; of the office of preaching, 212.11; 284.18; 532.56. See also Assurance
Property, the Christian may own property, 37.2; 79.53; 222.1; (against Anabaptists), 499.17; 634.22; also the priest, 178.50; (against Wycliffe), 224.11; property is an earthly order, therefore also a divine order, 178.50; to own no property is not Christian perfection, 224.9; this is pagan, not Christian, holiness, 277.45f.
Prophets, gifts of God, 324.26; highly regarded by God and a treasure for the world, 191.66; 226.2; did not receive the Spirit apart from the Ten Commandments, 313.11; their teaching came from the First Commandment, 273.25; they witness to Christ, see under Acts 10:43; Christ was their treasure and comfort, 192.73; teach justification through faith, 167.395; value faith as the highest divine service, 114.57; condemn self-chosen divine services, 216.14; 298.2; sacrifice ex opere operato, 254.28; because these come out of godless hearts, 135.207; separated themselves from the priests,

326.38; false prophets in the church, 177.48; 239.5
Propitiator, see Mediator; Reconciler
Protection: our protection consists only in prayer, 424.30
Providence, see Foreknowledge
Psalms, value faith as the highest worship, 114.57; should be learned alongside the catechism, 364.25
Psalter, is simply contemplation on and exercise of the First Commandment, 361.18
Pseudo-Ambrose, 32.3; 43.14; 45.30; 60.33; 140.235
Pseudo-Augustine, 39.4; 45.26; 205.-148; 209.168
Pseudo-Basil, 472.16; 537.86
Pseudo-Clement, 332.71
Pseudo-Dionysius the Areopagite, 332.71
Pseudo-Jerome, 170.11
Punishment, see Penalty
Purgatory, 184.13; 185.26; 199.118; 202.132; 205.147; 207.156; 209.-167; 261.64; 266.90; 294.12; 306.-22; 307.26
Purity: does not come from outward purifications, 149.282; does not consist in celibacy, 244.33; Gospel demands purity of heart, 248.64; 407.310; where evil lust has been killed, 244.35; God demands inward and outward purity (faith and works), 149.283; patriarchs were purer than many virgins, 244.35; 248.64; "to the pure, all things are pure" (Titus 1:15), 244.34; 245.41; 248.64; always imperfect, 129.160f.; 407.310; does not make us righteous before God, 119.86; 129.160. See also Chastity

Qualities, in the doctrine of original sin, 519.62; see also Original Sin; finite qualities (created gifts): the human nature of Christ has not only finite qualities like the saints, 601.52

Ratisbon, Diet of, 26.18
Real, sharing of the natures in Christ, 487.2; 488.11,15; 603.63; see also Christ, A,2; its significance for Christology, 595.23

132; repentance should continue throughout the whole life, 309.40; 527.34; 538.88; wars against the remaining sin (in the flesh) throughout life, 309.40; faith and repentance should increase together, 161.353

d) As the third sacrament, 187.-41; 211.4; 445.74; repentance and absolution, see Absolution; repentance of the baptized possible, 34.1; 35.9

Reservation of cases, see Cases

Resist, to: those who continually resist are not converted, 532.60; 537.83, see also Conversion; resistance remains even in the reborn, 537.84; the Christian who resists the Spirit loses faith and grace, 556.31

Resurrection of the dead, 206.153; 224.1; 418.59ff.; 467.10; 516.46f.; 568.24; daily resurrection means the new man through Baptism, 444.65; takes place through faith, 143.250; 188.46

Revenge, the prohibition of revenge applies only to private revenge, not to government, 79.55; 223.7; see also Punishment

Reward: God rewards good works (virtue) with physical gifts, 110.-24; with physical and spiritual gifts, 161.335; 210.174; in this and the future life, 133.194; 163.367; different rewards in glory, 161.-355; 163.368; but the reward is not forgiveness, etc., 133.194; 163.365f.; how eternal life is called reward, 161.357; 162.362; 163.365f.; in the proclamation of rewards, grace is shown, 163.365; reward is not to be an incentive, 134.198; 162.364; 210.174. See also Merit

Right, human and divine, 160.345; divine right or law cannot be abrogated by human authority, laws, or vows, 74.24; 176.41; 210.175; 277.51; divine or human right of the papacy, 298.1; 299.7; 300.13; 316.5; 319; see also Pope; right of episcopal power, 331.65; see also Bishops; the office of high priest was by divine right, 326.38; cere-

monies, festival days are not by divine right, 176.41; also the enumeration of sins, see Sin; celibacy, see Marriage of Priests; natural right (or law) arises out of God's creation and order, 240.9; thus it is unchangeable, 277.51; marriage rests on natural right (law), see Marriage; Marriage of Priests

Righteous, see Righteousness; Justification

Righteousness of God: Christ the essential righteousness of God, see Christ; difference between the essential righteousness and the justifying righteousness of God, 548.-54; the righteousness of God proves itself in the impenitence of sinners, 625.57; 629.78; 631.86; see also Predestination

—— of Christ: is imparted to us, 154.305; 251.12; reckoned to us, 473.4; 475.21; 541.17; 543.23,25; this righteousness is not the essential righteousness of God, q.v.; but rather the obedience of Christ, see Christ, B,2,c

—— of Man: (a) Original righteousness: its nature, 102.9,15ff.; 510.10; 512.27. (b) Outward righteousness (civil) and inner righteousness must be distinquished, 226.9; righteousness of reason and of the Gospel, 139.230; 154.306; of the law and of the Gospel, of faith, 114.49; 167.394 Civil righteousness, 102.12; 110.-21; 132.181; 140.238; 225.4; to a certain extent within our power, 102.12; 151.288; 225.4; however, it seldom exists, 225.5; God demands it, 110.24,26; rewards it with material gifts, 110.24; but it does not suffice before God, 226.9; see also Law; Works; Justification; opponents teach it only according to the example of philosophy, 108.9ff.; see also Law; Gospel True righteousness: in it we deal with God, 138.224; its nature, 102.15ff.; we are not righteous as long as we flee God and are angry with him, 131.176; it is obedience which God accepts,

c) Proper use, 213.18; 261.68; faith, not *opus operatum,* 35; 59.-30; 184.12; 185.25; *see also* Mass; faith, not the sacrament, makes us righteous (Augustine), 214.23; through the Mass the use of the sacrament is shamefully perverted, 266.91

d) Validity, *see* Lord's Supper; efficacious on account of its institution and command by Christ, 33.2; the sacrament is nothing outside the use for which it was instituted, 582.73; 584.85; 588.108; the sacrament does not regard our worthiness or holiness but God's Word, 448.16; 453.61f.; not faith or unbelief, but God's Word and order, 573.25; 574.32; 585.89; not dependent on the person of the priest, 33.2; 168.3; 171.19; 448.16; even godless men act in the stead of Christ, 173.28; 177.-47; even unbelievers receive the real sacrament, 443.54; no one without a public call should administer the sacraments, 36; that belongs to the New Testament office of priest, 212.7,9; to the office of keys, 81.5; to the office of bishop, 283.13; 330.60

e) Number of sacraments, 211; repentance as a sacrament, *see* Repentance, d; Absolution; the pope wants to have the power to change sacraments, 320.6; monks have instituted a new sacrament, 162.361; *see also* Baptism; Lord's Supper

Sacrifice: the concept of sacrifice, 250.9; 251.14; difference between sacrifice and sacrament, 252.16ff.; sacrifice is a work which we give to God, 252.18; two types: propitiatory sacrifice and eucharistic sacrifice, 252.19; there is only one true propitiatory sacrifice: Christ's death, 58.25; 253.22; 259.53; *see also* Christ, B,2,c; we need none other, 212.8; 259.52ff.; daily sacrifice, 256.35; 258.49; 266.91; means the daily sacrifice of the heart, 257.38; Levitical sacrifices in the law were prototypes of Christ's sacrifice, 253.22; 256.34;

259.54; they had to cease when the real sacrifice was made, 212.8; 253.23; slaying of victims signified the killing of the old Adam, 256.-34; sacrifice *ex opere operato* does not occur in the New Testament, 254.27; 260.59; the prophets (and psalms) were already against it, 135.207; 167.395; the Mass is not a sacrifice, *see* Mass, a; sacrifices of the New Testament are faith, thanksgiving, proclamation, cross, etc., 255.30; good works, the dangers and troubles of the preacher, are sacrifices, 133.189ff.; pleasing to God through faith, 133.189; 567.22; sacrifice of Israel, *see* Israel; of the patriarchs, 135.-200; of Abraham, 135.209; 577.-46; of the heathen, 135.206; of praise, 255.33; human sacrifice, *q.v.*

Saints,

a) In the general sense: communion of saints, *see* Church; works do not make saints, but God's Word does, 377.92; they can produce no work like the Ten Commandments, 407.312; 408.315; 410.333; cannot perfectly keep the law, *see* Law; faith is hard for them, 226.8; they do not honor and fear God as they should, 273.-25; also have sins, 158.328; are not in mortal sin, 113.48; remain halfway holy, 418.58; do not become righteous through works, 134.203; but through faith in the Gospel, 192.72; God exercises them in many ways, 134.198; through cross and affliction, 206.-151; their sufferings, proclamations, works are eucharistic sacrifices, 253.25; through them God works great things, 234.36; their witness sets Christ against the kingdom of the devil, 133.189; saints after the order of Cain (hypocrites), 566.16

b) In the specialized sense: invocation of the saints, 41.3; 46; 229; 297; papists make gods out of their saints, 230.11; make them into mediators and Christ into a judge, 230.14; 232.27f.; to media-

69; repentance fights against the remaining sin, 309.40; 527.34; see also Repentance; as does the Spirit, see Holy Spirit, B,1; and tribulation, see Cross
d) Punishment of sin, see Punishment; acknowledgment (confession) of sin, see Law; Gospel; saints are also sinners, 273.25; God's special punishments for individual sinners, 207.156; sinners should come to the Lord's Supper, but not brazen sinners, 453.58; obstinate sinners are to be excluded, 314; see also Excommunication; sinners are not true members of the church, 170.11; penance in ancient church, 200.120f.

Smalcald Articles, acknowledged as a confession of faith, 465.4; 505.7; give correct doctrine concerning the Lord's Supper as opposed to the Sacramentarians, 572.17

Smalcald, Assembly of (1537), 334; 505.7; 572.17

Socrates, 109.15; 252.16

Sodom, and Rome, 246.54

Sola Fide, see Justification, c

Son, of God, see Christ; Son of God and Son of man are one Christ, 487.5; 490.20; see also Christ, A,2,b

Sophists, have falsified doctrine, 220.123; understand nothing of original sin, 104.32; 519.60; of faith, 159.335; 280.68

Soul, not healthy but corrupted by original sin, 303.11; 508.1; see also Nature; not destroyed and recreated in rebirth, 471.14; 536.-81; Lord's Supper is food of the soul, 449.23; body and soul as illustration of personal union, see Christ, A,2,b; souls in purgatory, see Purgatory; whether Christ descended into hell only with the soul, 492; All Souls' Day, 294.12

Spengler, Lazarus, 467.3; 508.1; 512.23

Spires, Diet of (1526), 26.15; (1529), 26.17

Spirits, evil, as spirits of the departed, 295.16

Spirituality, false, of the monks, 72.11ff.; 77.38; 277.93; of the

Anabaptists, 498.5; 633.10; of the celibates, see Marriage of Priests

Sponsors, 316.4; 333.78; 339.11

Spontaneity, of spirit in the faithful, 476.10; 533.64; 553.12; 554.18; 564.2,6; of works, 551.3,4; see also Works; not perfect, 477.13; 567.18

Station in life, see Estates

Stoics, 570.8; 535.74

Strife, in the church, see Controversies

Substance: in the doctrine of original sin, 466; 468.17; 469.25; 508; 513.30; 516.46,48; 517.54; see also Original Sin; in the doctrine of conversion, 471.14; 536.81; in Christology, see Christ, A,2,c; substance of human nature not changed, 490.28; 605.71; 609.91; in the doctrine of the Lord's Supper, see Lord's Supper, a; Transubstantiation; keeping the law according to the substance of the acts, 40.8; 101.8; 225.2

Suffering, of Christ: proclaims God's wrath (law) and grace, 479.9; 560.12; its salvatory significance, see Christ, B,2,c; Cross

Suidas, 594.15

Sum, Summary, of doctrine, 47.1; 505.9; of doctrine and life, 363.19; of faith, 142.245; of the Gospel, 185.29; of the second article, 413.26

Summists, 66.14; 174.32; torture consciences, 181.9

Sunday, 375.78; transformation of the Sabbath into Sunday, 86.33; 91.58; Sunday not a necessary institution, 91.58; Scripture has abrogated the Sabbath, 91.59; yet it should be retained for the sake of order, 376.85; its proper hallowing, 376.87; necessary work is not forbidden, 376.86; its desecration, 378.96. See also Holy Days

Swearing: sense of the prohibition in the Gospel, 373.65. See also Oath

Sword: the "Two Swords Theory," see Pope, a; power of the sword to be distinguished from ecclesiastical power, 81; sword not entrusted to the disciples, 325.31;

Law; Commandment, First; Christ demands it, 159.339; we are to trust only in him, 233.31; 562.22; is proper obedience, 155ff.; and worship, 114.57; see also Worship; Faith, 3,a; trust in works, see Works, 3,a; Christ, B,4; trust in saints, see Saints. See also Faith

Truth: eternal truth is Christ himself, 576.43; 578.47; is God's Word, 506.13; 531.51; church cannot exist without it, 99.16; 227.6; church is the pillar of truth, 171.-20; consciences long for it, 202.-129; may not be disavowed, 195.-90; truth was brought to light through Luther, 504.5; Evangelicals teach it, 182.3; their Confessions are witnesses to it, 506.13; must acknowledge it under persecution, 227.9; opponents condemn and persecute it, 195.90; 278.56

Turks, also have monks, 273.27; tolerate faith in Christ, 300.11; emperor should make war against them, 46.1; 431.77

Type, see Shadow

Tyrant, Tyranny: even through tyrants God permits blessings to take place in earthly government, 298.3; tyranny over consciences, 181.9; tyranny of bishops, 214.2; of the pope, 243.25; 266.91; 281.-3f.; 289.3; 328.49; 459.21; Christ viewed as tyrant by the papacy, 231.15

Ulpian, 264.81
Ulysses, 262.72
Unbelief, the greatest sin, 558.2; deeply imbedded in us, 125.135; does not like to pray, 428.58; the law rebukes it, 558.2; 561.17,19; works of unbelievers are sins, 552.8; see also Sin; they also receive the body and blood of Christ in the Lord's Supper, 485.37; 573.27; see Lord's Supper, c. See also Faith

Unchastity, see Chastity; Marriage of Priests; Monks

Unction, Extreme, no sacrament, 212.6

Ungodly, see Wicked

Union, ecclesiastical, see Church,

2,c; personal, see Personal Union; sacramental, see Sacramental Union

Universality, of grace, 494.4; 495.-10; 497.17; 530.49; 620.28; 629.-81. See also Predestination

Unrepentant, see Impenitents

Unworthy, people administer and receive the Lord's Supper, see Lord's Supper, c,d

Usages, in the church, see Human Traditions; Ceremonies

Use, of the sacraments, see Sacraments; third use of the law, see Law

Usury, 290.12

Valens, Emperor, 606.75
Valentine, St., 233.32
Valentinians, 27.5
Veil of Moses, see Moses
Vengeance, see Revenge
Venus, 367.18
Vergil, 227.9
Vessels, of honor and of dishonor, 629.79
Vicar, of Christ, 172.23; 320.3. See also Pope
Vigilantius, 229.2
Vigils, 294.12; 307.26
Virginity, a special gift of God, 242.19; higher one than marriage, but does not make one righteous, 244.36,38; 249.69; is not Christian perfection, 273.27; in the ungodly it is impure, 244.34; praised by Scripture but only as a means to service, 244.40; one can recommend it, but not command it, 242.20; those who do not have the gift should marry, 74.20; 241.16; inordinate praise of it has done much harm, 246.47. See also Chastity
Virtue: its praise and reward, 110.-24; see also Righteousness (civil righteousness); love the highest virtue of the law, 138.226; our virtues do not make us righteous, see Justification; the faithful should exercise themselves in all Christian virtues, 628.73
Visitations, 338.1
Vivification, Vivifying, see Making Alive

Vocation,
a) Earthly: scorned under the papacy as unspiritual, 65.10; 72.-13; 219.26; 275.37; 328.48; yet it has God's command, 218.25; one should not reject it for the sake of pilgrimages and the like, 37.4; 276.41; 296.18; but rather seek Christian perfection in one's vocation, 78.49; 273.27; 275.37; 277.46; works of one's vocation that stem from faith are pleasing to God, 244.32; these are the just, good, and holy works, 218.-25; through works of the Christian's vocation Christ triumphs over the devil, 133.192
b) As calling: call of God, see Predestination; issued to all men, 495.8; 621.29; meant earnestly, 622.34; does not take place without means, through the Word, 495.8; 620.27; we should confirm our call, 496.14; 628.73; through works of faith, 228.12f.; 556.33; call to the office of preaching, 314; without a proper call no one should preach, 36; 214.1. See also Estates; Works; Perfection

Vows (monastic), 70; 268; 315; the controversy, 269.9; should be voluntary and uncoerced in possible matters, 75.27; adiaphora and bodily exercise, 272.21; cannot abrogate God's order and command, 52.8; 55.24; 73.18; 277.51; no vow can change human nature, 240.8; 241.16; vows contrary to God's command are null and void, 77.40; they are false divine service, 77.39; 280.65; are alleged to earn forgiveness of sins, 270.11; 280.65; contrary to the Gospel, 37.4; 328.48; blasphemy of Christ, 77.43; 270.11; 274.30; monastic vows equated with Baptism, 72.11; 272.20; that is blasphemy of God, 316; they are not binding, 76.36; 279.57; 280.-66; a prison, 71.2; there are many godless opinions about them, 80.-61; the vow of chastity (see Marriage) has occasioned much scandal, 54.18; un-Christian for those who do not have the gift

of continence, 277.51; forbidden by the Sixth Commandment, 76.-36; 394.216; useless vows of canons and popes repudiated, 270.10; vows made in youth, 55.-26; 71.8; 270.9; age limit, 75.31; vows in the law of Moses, 279.58. See also Monks; Monastery

Vulgarius, 179.2

War, caused by the devil, 431.80; to wage just wars allowed to Christian government, 37.2; 222.1; 223.7; wars of David were holy works, 133.191; thus the emperor should wage war against Turks, 46.1

Water, in Baptism, see Baptism

Wax, as a simile of conversion, repudiated, 538.89

Weak in faith, not unworthy to come to the Lord's Supper, 484.-19; 582.69

Wedding, see Marriage

Wicked believe the history, but not the forgiveness of sins, 44.23; 154.303; 159.337; see also Faith, 1; their relation to the church, 168.1ff.; see also Church; to the sacraments, see Sacraments; Lord's Supper, c; they are not members of Christ but of the devil, 171.19; 173.29; will not be destroyed before the resurrection, but will be condemned to eternal punishment, 38.3; 224.1

Widows, 280.64; table of duties for, 356.13

Will, of God, see God; Predestination; of man (freedom of will), see Nature; 39; 224; 469; 519
a) Natural will: error of scholasticism: it is good and free by nature, 102.12; 109.17; 302.4; 304.10; then Christ has died in vain, 111.-29; 303.11; Stoic-Manichaean doctrine of no freedom repudiated, 470.8; 535.74; in external things the will has a certain freedom, 39; 225.4; 510.12; 526.26; 527.31; but not in spiritual things, 225.7; 521.7; 522.12; 527.32; it is God's enemy, wills evil, 470.3; 510.11; 520.5; 523.17; by disposition and nature completely evil, corrupt,

523.17; only capable of evil, 521.-
7; spiritually dead, 470.3; 522.11;
533.61; flees God's judgment,
154.304; the will in conversion,
see Conversion; cannot of its own
power accept grace or co-operate,
471.9; 521.7; purely passive in
conversion, 472.18; 538.89; like a
stone or a block, 524.19; even
worse, 526.24; 532.59; it strives
against conversion, 524.18
b) Will after conversion: wills the
good, 533.63; the baptized have
a liberated will, 534.67; will cooperates as an instrument of the
Spirit, 472.18; not like two
horses pulling one wagon, 534.66;
even then it still strives against
the law of God, 524.18; doctrine
of the inability of the will ought
not lead to indolence, 530.46
William Peraldus (of Paris), 226.10
Wine: the Rechabites did not drink
it, 279.59; neither did the Encratites, 245.45; wine in the
Lord's Supper, see Lord's Supper
Wisdom: God's concealed wisdom,
626.64; Christ is wisdom, 576.43;
578.47; divine wisdom belongs to
the image of God in man, 102.18;
lacks it since the Fall, 111.32;
wisdom of the world (I Cor.
1:21), 522.10; 531.51
Witness, of the Holy Spirit in the
heart, 621.31; 628.73f.; works are
witnesses of faith, of righteousness, of the Spirit, 132.184; 164.-
374; 477.15; see also Works;
sacraments as witnesses of grace,
see Sacraments; symbols are witnesses of faith, of the truth, 465.8;
506.13; 507.16
Wittenberg Concord (1536), 571.12;
576.38
Wolves in the church (false teachers), 172.22
Word of God, in the doctrine of
God (logos), 28.6; 575.36; 594.-
16; as revelation, Scripture,
see Scriptures; Gospel
a) Certainty and power: contrary
to reason, 521.8; does not lie, cannot fail, 213.20; 444.57; 483.13;
the Spirit knows what he says,
122.108; the eternal truth, 506.13;

alone establishes articles of faith,
295.15; norm and rule of all
doctrine, 505.9; see also Scriptures; the power of God, 212.11;
360.11; the living and creating
Word, 379.101; never departs
without fruit, 212.11; more than
a hundred masters of a thousand
arts, 360.12; conquers the devil,
359.10; 379.102; 629.76
b) Effect: God does not work
without the Word, 471.13; likewise the Spirit, see Holy Spirit,
B,2,a; only through the Word
does God let himself (his will)
be known and grasped, 116.67;
217.17; and we come to Christ,
415.38; 417.52; (third article)
through the Word God's kingdom
comes to us, 427.53; God calls
and converts us through it, 530.50;
621.33; 623.44; through it faith
is given, see Faith, 2; the Word
gives forgiveness of sins, 450.31;
458.14; consoles the conscience,
131.180; 186.35; 188.49; 192.72;
gives new life and comfort in the
heart, 187.40; makes us saints,
377.92
c) Relations: Word and church,
see Church, 1,b; and sacrament,
211.5; 265.89; 310.1; 348.2; 352.-
6; 359.10; 438.18; 442.45; 447.4;
448.10; 573.21; only God's Word
shows proper worship, see Worship; through the Word all things
are sanctified, 377.91
d) Spoken Word, see Proclamation; Office of Preaching; the primary office of the Gospel, 310;
remains efficacious even when
proclaimed by godless, 33; 171.-
19. See also Preachers
e) Claim: Word is a treasure and
a jewel, 377.91; 381.117; God
wills us to hear it, 378.95; 470.5;
532.57; and learn it, 378.98; to
have it always in heart, lips, and
ears, 379.100; 523.16; unconverted can also hear it outwardly,
531.53; the devil drives us to
scorn the Word, 378.99; 434.104;
as does our natural disposition
(original sin), 112.35; 302.2; 623.-
41; it must undergo persecution

and blasphemy, 400.262; 404.289;
God punishes such scorning in
that he takes the Word away, 625.-
57; through obduracy and damnation, 532.57f.; 623.40
f) Interpretation: Christ himself
is the most certain interpreter of
his Word, 578.50; to apply it according to one's own whims is the
work of sophists, 200.123
Works, of God, of Christ, of the
Holy Spirit, see God; Christ; Holy
Spirit; works, good: 31; 41; 107;
124; 226; 315; 475; **551**
1. Content: Evangelicals teach
proper good works, 41.2; 126.136;
258.48; the Gospel teaches them,
278.54; the Ten Commandments,
the law, God's Word, 203.139;
210.174; 377.93; 552.7; 566.15;
568.25; apart from these, no work
is good, 407.311; these are better
than pilgrimages, monastic life,
etc., 379.102; 381.116; 385.143;
410.333; proper works are those
of one's vocation, 65.10; 218.25;
243.32; highest and noblest are
those of the first table, 225.7; to
believe in God, in Christ, 64.4;
108.8; 210.174; these works are
of no consequence in the eyes of
the world, 407.313; under the
papacy only self-invented works
were emphasized, see Human
Traditions; Monastery; Monks;
these are childish, unnecessary
works, 41.3; hyprocites' works,
379.102; works of the devil, 382.-
120f.
2. Possibility: according to scholastic doctrine, the Spirit and
grace are not necessary for them,
225.2,6; 303.10; and works within
and without grace are equal, 109.-
17; 225.6; man can do them
meritoriously by his own power,
302.8; can even do superfluous
works, 80.61; 162.360; 204.142;
308.28; see also Merit; Counsels,
Evangelical; monks sold such
works, 78.44; 276.39; 308.28; outward works man can fulfill by
himself, 39; 108.8; 109.18; 125.130;
144.256; 204.142; 225.4; see also
Righteousness, Civil; but they do

not suffice, 204.142; see also Law,
2; one's heart must be in them,
164.371; one must regard works
according to the person, 438.12;
552.8; our works do not stand
up before God's judgment, 141.-
239; 198.108; before him they are
hypocrisy, 104.33; sins because
they proceed from wicked hearts,
111.33; 112.35; because they are
not of faith, 552.8; Evangelicals
show how good works can take
place, 46.35; 126.136; only he
can do them, who is justified,
122.106; see also Justification;
only those who are redeemed,
born again, 143.252; 538.90; 552.-
7; they proceed from faith, follow
it with necessity, see Faith, 3,b;
from penitence, see Repentance,
c; 34; 148.275; 185.28; 189.58;
202.131; 210.174; the Spirit works
them, 45.29; 160.349; 225.7; 527.-
29; 528.38f.; 538.90; thus they
are not works of the law, but
fruits of the Spirit, 480.5; 552.9;
566.15; so long as man is impelled by the Spirit, he does good
works, 533.63; they are signs of
the Spirit's presence, 477.15
3. Worth:
a) Salvatory significance: works
are the foundation of the Catholic
system, 309.39; doctrine of works
suppressed doctrines of faith and
of Christ, 42.8; 64.4; see also
Christ, B,4; contrary to the
Gospel, 42.10; separates one from
Christianity, 418.56; a doctrine of
the devil, 204.141; 382.120; 385.-
144; salvatory significance of
works repudiated, 30; 31; 41; 59.-
28; 107ff.; 124; 192.72; 194.84;
204.142; 215.6; 216.10; 226; 292.-
4; 440.34; 459.21; 472; 475; 539;
551; see also Justification; threefold reason: glory of Christ, see
Christ, B,4; peace of conscience,
see Conscience; knowledge of
God, 135.205; works exclude
grace, 120.89; make rebirth superfluous, 109.12; forgiveness (promise) uncertain, 133.187; 196.95;
228.10; trusting in works is vain,
110.21; 204.142; 309.39; and

wicked, 204.142; idolatry and blasphemy of Christ, 367.22; makes prayer impossible, 436.122; but in themselves they are not detrimental to salvation, 475.2; 477.17; 551.3; 557.37
b) True worth: works are praiseworthy, 110.24; 134.200; 552.8; meritorious in relation to other temporal and eternal gifts, 163.-366; see also Reward; holy among believers for the sake of faith, 133.189; are signs of the promise, of forgiveness, 148.275; an indication of salvation, 557.38; but even the works of the faithful are impure, 133.189; 552.8; 567.22; the law shows that, 567.21; in all works we need mercy, forgiveness, 157.323; for the sake of Christ their deficiency is not reckoned to us, 315.2; they are pleasing to God only for the sake of Christ and of faith, 130.172; 143.252; 147.269; 155.308; 164.372; 166.-385; 244.32; 527.32; 552.8; 567.-22; when Scriptures praise them, Christ, the righteousness of the heart, and faith are included, 163.365; 164.372; so the works of the saints were works of their faith, 134.203
4. Necessity, 475; 551; not necessary for salvation, 477.16; 554.22; see also 3, above; contrary to Anabaptists, 555.27; foundation of their necessity, 133.189; God's will, command, order, 31; 210.-174; 476.8; 552.7; 553.14; to God's praise and glory, 210.174; necessity of order, not of coercion, 476.10; 554.16; necessary as fruits of the Spirit, of faith, of repentance, see 2, above; the goal of justification, 160.348; to confirm our heavenly calling, 228.-13; 556.33; but they do not preserve faith and salvation, 160.348; 477.15; 556.33; thus the people are to be admonished to do good works, 477.18; in them they are not to seek reward but God's will and glory, 134.198; 162.364
World, does not know God, 419.63; does not believe, 370.42; does not

acknowledge God as creator and lord, 413.21; condemns truth and God's children, 400.262; is full of idolatry, 366.17; full of blasphemy, error, factions, false teachers, 106.49; 426.47; the error of the doctrine of works sticks fast to it, 135.206; 136.212; does not know the right works, 404.290; 407.313; misuses God's gifts, 413.21; regards some things as just which are unjust, 406.304; a stable full of thieves, 396.228; becomes worse and worse, 53.14; drives us to evil, 347.18; 434.103; the flesh trusts in it, 130.170; to flee from it is not to go into a monastery, 80.57
Worship, 376.84; see also Commandment, Third; Sacrifice
a) Inward worship: God wants to be worshiped in spirit and in truth, 254.27; highest worship goes inward to the heart, 262.74; it is a spiritual worship (against the opus operatum), 265.88; First Commandment points it up, 125.-133; all divine service must be directed to the First Commandment, 273.25; worship of the Gospel (faith) is to accept what God offers; of the law, to offer works to God, 114.49; 155.310; the proper, highest worship is to acknowledge one's sins and to seek forgiveness, 128.154; 155.-310; to want to accept the promise, 139.228; faith, see Faith, 3,a, with its fruits, 128.155; to know no other comfort and confidence but in him, 366.16; to call upon him from the heart, 47.3; 255.29; fear, faith, invocation, thanksgiving, 265.88; killing of the old Adam and rebirth, 262.71f.
b) Outward worship: see Ceremonies; Human Traditions; Holy Days; there is no people without divine services, 367.17; outward divine services do not make one pious and righteous before God, 69.41; 217.17; 220.36; they serve for bodily exercises and discipline, 218.20; in this the church should be free, 220.32; 492; 610; God